THE VITAMIN FACT FILE

DR H. WINTER GRIFFITH

THE
Vitamin
FACT FILE

**A VITAL, AUTHORITATIVE GUIDE TO VITAMINS,
MINERALS, SUPPLEMENTS AND MEDICINAL HERBS**

DIAMOND BOOKS

This edition published 1995 by
Diamond Books
77–85 Fulham Palace Road
Hammersmith, London W6 8JB

First published in the UK as *The Vital Vitamin Fact File*
by Thorsons Publishers, 1988

Original American edition published by
Fisher Books, 3499 N Campbell Avenue, Suite 909,
Tucson, Arizona 85712, USA

© 1988 Fisher Books

ISBN 0 261 66729 7

Contents

About the Author

H. Winter Griffith, M.D., received his medical degree from Emory University in 1953 and spent more than 20 years in private practice. At Florida State University, he established a basic medical-science program and also directed the family-practice residency program at Tallahassee Memorial Hospital. After moving to the southwest, he became associate professor of Family and Community Medicine at the University of Arizona College of Medicine, where he is currently an adjunct professor. At present, he devotes most of his time to writing medical-information books for non-medical readers. He has published several popular books and continues to pursue this avenue of interest.

Technical Consultants

Gail Harrison, Ph.D., Professor
Department of Family Community Medicine
University of Arizona College of Medicine

Dan Levinson, M.D.,
Adjunct Associate Professor
Department of Family Community Medicine
University of Arizona College of Medicine

Dedication

To each of you who wishes to be informed enough to become the most important member of your own health-care team.

Vitamins, Minerals and Supplements

Everyone consumes vitamins, minerals or supplements in some form. Most people rely on diet to supply all they need. Many take pills, tonics, capsules or injections to meet their needs. Of those who supplement their diet with products from non-food sources, most take the amounts recommended by knowledgeable professionals. The vitamins, minerals and supplements they take may help them feel better. Without vitamins and minerals from some source, life cannot endure.

The American Institute of Nutrition and The American Society for Clinical Nutrition recently issued an official statement on vitamin and mineral supplements. This statement was developed jointly with the American Dietetic Association and the National Council Against Health Fraud. The American Medical Association's Council on Scientific Affairs reviewed this statement and found it to be consistent with its official statement on dietary supplements. The statement reads:

"Healthy children and adults should obtain adequate nutrient intakes from dietary sources. Meeting nutrient needs by choosing a variety of foods in moderation, rather than by supplementation, reduces the potential risk for both nutrient deficiencies and nutrient excesses. Individual recommendations regarding supplements and diets should come from physicians and registered dietitians."

This is similar to the recommendations of British authorities.

Supplement usage may be indicated in various circumstances. Some of these situations are listed below.

- Women with excessive menstrual bleeding may need iron supplements.
- Pregnant or breast-feeding women have an increased need of certain nutrients, especially iron, folic acid and calcium.
- People with very low calorie intakes frequently consume diets that do not meet their needs for all nutrients.
- Some vegetarians may not receive adequate calcium, iron, zinc and vitamin B-12.
- Newborns are commonly given a single dose of vitamin K to prevent abnormal bleeding. (This is done under the direction of a doctor.)
- Certain disorders or diseases and some medications interfere with nutrient intake, digestion, absorption, metabolism or excretion. This changes vitamin and mineral requirements.

Nutrients are potentially toxic when ingested in sufficiently large amounts. Safe intake levels vary widely from nutrient to nutrient and may vary with the age and health of the individual. In addition, high-dosage vitamin and mineral supplements can interfere with the normal metabolism of other nutrients and with the therapeutic effects of certain drugs.

The *Recommended Dietary Allowance* (RDA) represents the best currently available assessment of safe and adequate intakes. It serves as the basis for the recommended daily allowances shown on many product labels. There are no demonstrated benefits of self-supplementation beyond these allowances. When no RDA has been established, a daily Estimated Safe Intake may be listed.

Every health professional wants consumers to take proper nutrients and supplements if they need them. But some people abuse these essential substances by taking megadoses—doses 10 to 20 times the recommended amount or more.

Some people believe if one pill is good, 20 pills must be better. They also believe vitamins, minerals and supplements aren't medicine. They are wrong!

Vitamins, minerals and supplements *are* medicine because with some doses in some people, they can cause a change in the body's physiology or internal anatomy. Many of these substances are not regulated but that doesn't mean they can't cause harmful as well as beneficial effects. As the information in this book points out, these substances cause side effects, adverse reactions, interactions with other drugs and unexpected problems. Some people should *not* take certain things because of a unique situation, such as pregnancy or age. Others need to be aware that medical conditions, such as heart problems or various disease conditions, can be an indication not to take certain substances.

When you make the decision about whether to supplement your diet with vitamins and minerals, there are important things to remember. Too much can be harmful—don't overdose or take megadoses! For example, megadoses of vitamin A can cause bone pain and hypertension. It can also cause birth defects in babies if a pregnant woman takes megadoses. Long-term excess vitamin E can cause a low sperm count, degeneration of testicles and sterility. Vitamin C can also have toxic effects, including gout and perhaps kidney stones. Megadoses of this vitamin can interfere with the white blood cells' ability to kill bacteria. This can make infections worse, rather than clearing them up.

Many conditions may also rule out taking some substances. Always be alert to any side effects or interactions you may experience that could put your health in jeopardy.

It's up to you to be a "smart" consumer of the vitamins, minerals and supplements your body may need. Get them from the food you eat when you can—supplement with available products when you must.

Vitamins

Vitamins are chemical compounds necessary for growth, health, normal metabolism and physical well-being. Some vitamins are essential parts of *enzymes*—the chemical molecules that catalyze or facilitate the completion of chemical reactions. Other vitamins form essential parts of *hormones*—the chemical substances that promote and protect body health and reproduction. If you're in good health, you need vitamins only in small amounts. They can be found in sufficient quantities in the foods you eat. This assumes you eat a normal, well-balanced diet of foods grown in a nutritionally adequate soil. Traditionally, vitamins have been divided into two categories: *fat soluble* and *water soluble*.

Fat-soluble vitamins can be stored in the body. If you take excessive amounts of fat-soluble vitamins, they accumulate to provide needed amounts at a later time. That's the good news. The bad news is, if you take *excessive* amounts of fat-soluble vitamins, toxic levels can accumulate in storage areas such as the liver. Too much of any fat-soluble vitamin can lead to potentially dangerous, long-term physical problems.

Water-soluble vitamins cannot be stored in the body to any great extent. The daily amount you need must be provided by what you eat or drink each day or two.

Under some circumstances, it may be difficult or impossible for you to obtain and assimilate enough vitamins simply by eating your customary diet. The amount of vitamins you need, such as during illness or following surgery, may be increased. A vitamin supplement may be necessary. People with special needs for supplements or others at risk of vitamin deficiency are identified and discussed in detail later in this section. See page 9.

Taking vitamin supplements cannot

take the place of good nutrition. Vitamins do not provide energy. Your body needs other substances besides vitamins for adequate nutrition, including carbohydrates, fats, proteins and minerals. Vitamins cannot help maintain a healthy body except in the presence of other nutrients, mainly from food and minerals.

Detailed charts are provided for many important, necessary vitamins including:

- Vitamin A
- Vitamin C
- Vitamin D
- Vitamin E
- All the B vitamins

Minerals

Minerals are inorganic chemical elements not attached to a carbon atom. They participate in many biochemical and physiological processes necessary for optimum growth, development and health. There is a clear and important distinction between the terms *mineral* and *trace element*. If the body requires more than 100 milligrams of a mineral each day, the substance is labeled *mineral*. If the body requires less than 100 milligrams of a mineral each day, the substance is labeled *trace element*.

Many minerals are essential parts of enzymes. They also participate actively in regulating many physiological functions, including transporting oxygen to each of the body's 60-trillion cells, providing the stimulus for muscles to contract and in many ways guaranteeing normal function of the central nervous system. Minerals are required for growth, maintenance, repair and health of tissues and bones.

Most minerals are widely distributed in foods. *Severe* mineral deficiency is unusual in the Western world. Of all essential minerals, only a few may be deficient in a typical diet. Even so, there are exceptions. Iron deficiency is common in infants, children and pregnant women. Zinc and copper deficiencies occur fairly frequently.

Detailed charts are provided for many minerals, including:

- Calcium
- Chloride
- Magnesium
- Phosphorous
- Potassium
- Sodium
- Sulphur

In addition, detailed charts are provided for trace elements, including:

- Chromium
- Fluorine
- Iodine
- Iron
- Manganese
- Molybdenum
- Selenium
- Vanadium
- Zinc

Nickel, tin, silicon and arsenic are also considered essential. Charts are *not* included because all available information about these trace elements comes from studies done on animals, not human experiments or experience.

Multivitamin/Mineral Preparations

Some foods contain all the nutrients you need. For healthy people who are past the growing stage and not over 55, food is the best, most-reliable source of nutrients—if you eat a well-balanced, nutritious diet every day. Not many people fit all these parameters.

If you or your children need supplementation, it is probably better to take one of the commercially available multivitamin/mineral preparations rather than attempt to augment your food intake with separate products containing only one or two substances. Commercial over-the-counter products usually have a good balance of nutrients. Taking separate products may lead to an imbalance of nutrients, which can lead to an overabundance of one substance at the expense of decreased absorption or effectiveness of another. The cost is also much less if you take a combination

3

product rather than separate products.

There are exceptions to this rule. For example, iron and folic-acid needs during pregnancy should be met with a single product.

Most major pharmacentical manufacturers supply widely advertised combination products. The brand names are too numerous to list and change constantly. Your chemist or doctor should be able to recommend a good source for a superior multivitamin/mineral preparation.

If you study vitamins and minerals, you may find you need supplements for one reason or another. I hope this book provides you with enough information to choose wisely or be able to ask the right questions to find out what is best for you.

Supplements

Supplements are chemical substances that are neither vitamins nor minerals, but they have received notice as nutritional supplements. Many supplements have proven effects in the body but may not yet have proved safe and effective when taken in pill or capsule form to supplement normal food intake. Speculated benefits and claims frequently go beyond what can be proved at present. These include anti-aging properties and claims that substances create and preserve health.

People separate into two distinct groups almost immediately when talk turns to supplementation. On one hand, the traditional medical establishment (of which I am part—partially renegade—but still a part) usually cries, "Eat a well-balanced diet, and you'll get all the carbohydrates, fat, fibre, protein, vitamins, minerals and micronutrients you need."

But hard data now available about our "normal, well-balanced" diet shows we are overfed and undernourished. The majority of experts in the medical field and in nutrition now agree. We consume too many calories, too much fat, too little fibre, too much refined sugar, too much sodium and not enough unrefined carbohydrates. So insisting a normal, well-balanced diet is all we need is a concept that is in deep trouble.

On the other hand, some view every new supplement or every new promising piece of information about the existing supplements as a miracle that will cure our ills if the overly conservative medical establishment will get out of the way. Advertisers are quite successful with this group because many people are easily persuaded if they take a product, they will be healthier, live longer and look and feel sexier, slimmer and smarter.

Not much is written that takes a middle ground. I believe this position represents the true status of human nutrition at present. But this book *does* take a middle ground! No personal opinions are expressed, only the consensus of the majority of experts, presented as impartially as possible.

Selected supplements discussed in this book include amino acids, nucleic acids and other supplements. Detailed charts are provided for many supplements. Amino acids detailed in charts include:

- Arginine
- L-cysteine
- L-lysine
- Methionine
- Phenylalanine

Nucleic acids detailed in charts include:

- Adenosine
- DNA/RNA
- Inosine
- Orotate
- Taurine
- Tryptophan
- Tyrosine

Other supplements detailed in charts include:

- Coenzyme Q
- Dietary fibre
- Gamma-linolenic acid (evening primrose oil)
- Inositol
- L-carnitine
- Lecithin
- Omega-3 fatty acids (EPA/Max EPA)
- Superoxide dismutase
- Wheatgrass

How to Use the Vitamin-Minerals-Supplements Section of This Book

Information in this book is organized in condensed, easy-to-read charts. Each vitamin or mineral is described in a multipage format as shown in the sample charts on the following pages. Vitamins and minerals are arranged alphabetically by the most frequently recognized name—usually a generic name instead of a brand name.

Each name appears at the top of the chart. For example, vitamin B-12 is frequently called *cyanocobalamin*. Both names are given when there are two or more names. In addition, many substances are sold by brand names rather than generic names.

To learn more about any vitamin, mineral or supplement, you need only one name. Look in the Index for any name you have, page 487. The Index provides a page number for the information you seek about that vitamin, mineral, supplement or herb.

The book is divided into five main section—vitamins, minerals, nucleic acids and amino acids, other supplements and medicinal herbs. Information on the medicinal-herbs section and charts begins on page 255. Names of substances are listed alphabetically within each section. Chart design is the same for every substance in the first three sections. When you become familiar with the chart, you can quickly find the information you seek.

On the next few pages, each numbered section is explained. This information will help you read and understand the charts that begin on page 22.

1-Generic name

Each chart is titled by the *generic name*. Sometimes there are two or more generic names. Each entry is titled by the most common one. Each name is listed on the top line or under the *Basic Information* section. If a substance has two or more generic names, the Index includes a reference for each name.

A product container may show a generic name. Any name listed on the label should be listed in the Index. If the container has no name, ask the chemist or health-shop attendant for the name.

2-Available from natural sources?
3-Available from synthetic sources?

Many vitamins, minerals and supplements are advertised as "natural," implying the product is derived from natural sources as opposed to synthetic sources. By definition, minerals are basic chemical substances that can't be manufactured (or synthesized) from other substances. However, many vitamins and supplements are derived from both sources.

This is confusing to many consumers. Many manufacturers have done everything possible to take financial advantage of that confusion. Advertisers claim natural sources are good and synthetic sources are bad. The truth is, natural and synthetic versions of the same chemical are identical!

Don't pay extra money for *natural* vitamins or supplements. They all have the same effect on your body. The *synthetic* version may even be purer or less contaminated with extraneous materials such as insecticides and fertilizers.

Guide to Vitamins, Minerals, Supplements Charts

To find information about a specific vitamin, mineral, amino acid, nucleic acid or supplement, look in the easy-to-read charts starting on page 22. Charts like the samples shown below and on the opposite page appear alphabetically by generic name.

A *generic* name is the official chemical name. A substance listed by generic name may

1—Riboflavin (Vitamin B-2)

Basic Information

2 — Available from natural sources? Yes
3 — Available from synthetic sources? Yes
4 — Prescription required? No
5 — Fat-soluble or water-soluble: Water-soluble

6 — **Natural Sources**

Almonds
Brewer's yeast
Cheese
Chicken
Organ meats (beef, kidney)
Wheat germ

7 — **Reasons to Use**

- Aids in release of energy from food.
- Maintains healthy mucous membranes lining respiratory, digestive, circulatory and excretory tracts when used in conjunction with vitamin A.
- Preserves integrity of nervous system, skin, eyes.
- Promotes normal growth and development.
- Aids in treating infections, stomach problems, burns, alcoholism, liver disease.

8 — **Unproved Speculated Benefits**

- Cures various eye diseases.
- Treats skin disorders.
- Prevents cancer.
- Increases body growth during normal developmental stages.
- Helps overcome infertility.
- Prevents stress.
- Stimulates hair growth in bald men.
- Improves vision.

9 — **Who Needs Additional Amounts?**

- Anyone with inadequate caloric or nutritional dietary intake or increased nutritional requirements.
- Pregnant or breast-feeding women.
- Those who abuse alcohol or other drugs.
- People with a chronic wasting illness, excess stress for long periods or who have recently undergone surgery.
- Athletes and workers who participate in vigorous physical activities.

- Those with a portion of the gastrointestinal tract surgically removed.
- People with recent severe burns or injuries.
- Those who rely almost exclusively on processed foods for their daily diet.
- Women taking oral contraceptives or oestrogen.

Deficiency Symptoms — 10

- Cracks and sores in corners of mouth
- Inflammation of tongue and lips
- Eyes overly sensitive to light and easily tired
- Itching and scaling of skin around nose, mouth, scrotum, forehead, ears, scalp
- Trembling
- Dizziness
- Insomnia
- Slow learning
- Itching, burning and reddening of eyes
- Damage to cornea of eye.

Unproved Speculated — 11
Symptoms

- Mild anaemia
- Mild lethargy
- Acne
- Migraine headaches
- Muscle cramps

Lab Tests to Detect — 12
Deficiency

- Serum riboflavin
- Erythrocyte riboflavin
- Glutathione reductase

Dosage and Usage Information

Recommended Dietary Allowance (RDA):
Estimate of adequate daily intake by the Food — 13
and Nutrition Board of the National Research
Council, 1980. See Glossary.

have many brand names.

Chart design and information presentation is similar for vitamins, minerals, amino acids, nucleic acids and supplements. On the next few pages I explain each of the sections, using the numbers on the charts as a reference. All charts are organized similarly, making it easy to make comparisons.

Riboflavin (Vitamin B-2)

Age	RDA
0–6 months	0.4mg
6–12 months	0.6mg
1–3 years	0.8mg
4–6 years	1.0mg
7–10 years	1.4mg
Males	
11–14 years	1.6mg
15–22 years	1.7mg
23–50 years	1.6mg
51+ years	1.4mg
Females	
11–22 years	1.3mg
23+ years	1.2mg
Pregnant	+0.3mg
Lactating	+0.5mg

23 Storage:
- Store in cool, dry place away from direct light, but don't freeze.
- Store safely out of reach of children.
- Don't store in bathroom medicine cabinet. Heat and moisture may change action of vitamin.

24 Others:
- Unlikely to cause toxic symptoms in healthy people with normal kidney function.

Overdose/Toxicity

25 Signs and symptoms:
Dark urine, nausea, vomiting.

What to do:
For symptoms of overdosage: Discontinue vitamin, and consult doctor. Also see *Adverse Reactions or Side Effects* section below.
26 For accidental overdosage (such as child taking entire bottle): Dial 999 (emergency).

14 — What this vitamin does:
- Acts as component in two co-enzymes (flavin mononucleotide and flavin adenine dinucleotide) needed for normal tissue respiration.
- Activates pyridoxine.

15 — Miscellaneous information:
- A balanced diet prevents deficiency without supplements.
- Large doses may produce dark-yellow urine.
- Processing food may decrease quantity of vitamin B-2.
- Mixing with baking powder destroys riboflavin.

16 — Available as:
- Tablets: Swallow whole with full glass of liquid. Don't chew or crush. Take with or immediately after food to decrease stomach irritation.
- A constituent of many multivitamin/mineral preparations.

27 Adverse Reactions or Side Effects

Reaction or effect	What to do
Yellow urine, with large doses	No action necessary

28 Interaction with Medicine, Vitamins or Minerals

Interacts with	Combined effect
Anti-depressants (tricyclic)	Decreases B-2 effect.
Phenothiazines	Decreases B-2 effect.
Probenecid	Decreases B-2 effect.

Warnings and Precautions

17 — Don't take if you:
- Are allergic to any B vitamin.
- Have chronic kidney failure.

18 — Consult your doctor if you are:
- Pregnant or planning a pregnancy.

19 — Over age 55:
- Need for vitamin B-2 is greater.

20 — Pregnancy:
- Don't take megadoses.

21 — Breast-feeding:
- Don't take megadoses.

22 — Effect on lab tests:
- Urinary catecholamine concentration may show false elevation.
- Urobilongen determinations (Ehrlich's) may produce false-positive results.

29 Interaction with Other Substances

Tobacco decreases absorption. Smokers may require supplementary vitamin B-2.

Alcohol prevents uptake and absorption of vitamin B-2.

pharmacist or retail merchant to suggest another form.

4 -Prescription required?

Most vitamins, minerals and supplements are available without prescription. Some formulas with higher dosages to treat specific diseases require a prescription from your doctor. "Yes" means your doctor must prescribe. "No" means you can buy this product without prescription. The information about a generic product is the same, whether it requires a prescription or not. If generic ingredients are the same, non-prescription products have the same uses, dangers, warnings, precautions, side effects and interactions with other substances that prescription products do.

5 -Fat soluble or water soluble?

This section applies *only* to vitamins. Fat-soluble vitamins can accumulate in the body and might cause toxic effects in excessive doses, either in a single day or in small, periodic excesses over a long time. Water-soluble vitamins do not accumulate to any great extent in the body. Except under unusual circumstances, the body readily eliminates excess water-soluble accumulation in the body. The dangers of water-soluble vitamins generally depend on the effects of excessive dosages taken over a relatively short period.

6 -Natural sources

This is a list of the food and beverage sources from which vitamins, minerals and supplements may be obtained. No attempt has been made to rank them according to the richest sources. They are listed alphabetically. If you want more information about natural sources, many reference works are available at your local library.

7 -Reasons to use

This section consists of *proved benefits*, including body functions the substance maintains or improves. It also lists disease processes and malfunctions the substance cures or improves. These proved benefits have withstood the scrutiny of scientifically controlled studies with results published in medical literature. This medical literature is subjected to review by top authorities in many fields before the material can be published in respected scientific journals.

8-Unproved speculated benefits

Some authors and many newspaper, magazine and television advertisers make unjustified, sometimes outrageous, claims for products.

This list contains claims that have *not* withstood the same scientific scrutiny the *Reasons to use* section has passed. These claims may be as accurate and as effective as the proved claims. But they haven't been proved with well-controlled studies. Such studies can take years to complete and may be very expensive. Until such studies have been completed, the claims must be listed as unproved.

9 -Who needs additional amounts?

People listed in this category are most likely to need significant care to regain or maintain normal health or who are less likely to meet their requirements through diet alone. A summary of groups follows, with a list of reasons why the risk is greater.
Anyone with inadequate dietary intake or increased nutritional needs—Included in this group are people whose energy needs are less than 1,200 calories a day. Fewer than 1,200 calories a day for energy requirements

almost never provides enough vitamins and minerals, so supplements are needed. Those most likely to have inadequate dietary intake include:

🙠 People of small stature or body build who eat only minimal nutrients per day to maintain current weight.

🙠 Elderly people with greatly decreased daily activities. This applies particularly to aging women.

🙠 People who have had limbs amputated.

🙠 People with reduced physical activity because of activity-limiting disease, such as coronary-artery disease, intermittent lameness, angina pectoris.

🙠 Fad dieters with a dietary imbalance and inadequacy.

🙠 People with eating disorders such as anorexia nervosa and bulimia.

🙠 Vegetarians.

Older people (55 and over)—People in this age group may have inadequate dietary intake because of difficulty obtaining an adequate diet, or because of disability and depression.

Pregnancy—Pregnant women uniformly need supplementation of folic acid and iron. Sometimes they need other supplements as well. Pregnant women need to increase dietary intake so total body weight increases from 12 to 30 pounds during pregnancy. Many women do not consume enough calories to allow this weight gain and therefore develop a nutritional deficiency. This causes a need for supplementation with a well-rounded, well-balanced preparation containing vitamins and minerals as well as the need for separate folic-acid and iron supplementation.

Ask your doctor for recommendations on specific brand names of acceptable multivitamin/mineral preparations. Also seek advice about folic acid and iron.

Breast-feeding women—Breast-feeding women who are healthy and active need to continue supplementation. Make sure you get enough iron. Talk to

your doctor about your concerns.

Most authorities suggest iron and folic-acid supplements for pregnant and breast-feeding women should be taken as separate products. Iron occasionally causes gastrointestinal side effects that are so uncomfortable to some women that they discontinue the supplements.

Another important nutritional factor with breast-feeding is the need for extra fluids. Fluid deficiency can be as disabling as a nutritional deficiency. Drink at least eight 8-ounces glasses of water a day.

People who abuse alcohol and other drugs—People who consume too much alcohol are likely to develop nutritional deficiencies. Much of the daily caloric intake of these people is the alcohol they consume; it is deficient in nutritional substances. In addition, there is also poor absorption of food and increased excretion of nutrients because of diarrhoea and fluid loss. When the excessive alcohol consumption stops, the nutritional deficiency can be treated with good food and supplements for a while, if liver disease has not already occurred.

Abuse of other drugs frequently leads to decreased appetite and decreased interest in food. Addicts need supplements of both vitamins and minerals.

People with a chronic wasting illness—This group includes people with malignant disease, chronic malabsorption, hyperthyroidism, chronic obstructive airways disease, congestive heart failure, cystic fibrosis and other illnesses. Nutritional risk is increased because these prople have greatly increased caloric and nutritional requirements that are difficult to satisfy with food.

People who have recently undergone surgery—Surgery can cause a relative deficiency, even if a person is well nourished before surgery. People who have undergone surgery on the gastrointestinal tract are particularly likely to develop deficiencies during the post-operative period. Supplementation is very helpful. Vitamins and minerals are frequently administered intravenously until the patient can eat. After that, most people benefit from vitamin and mineral supplements for several weeks post-operatively.

People with a portion of the gastrointestinal tract removed— These people are likely to develop deficiencies because important nutrient-absorbing parts of the gastrointestinal tract may be absent from the body. A good multivitamin/mineral preparation usually prevents signs and symptoms of deficiencies. Vitamin B-12 must be supplemented for life (usually by injection) for *all* people with a significant portion of the stomach removed.

People who must take medicines— Many medications can cause a deficiency of vitamins and minerals. Specific drugs are listed in the separate profiles for each substance in this book. In general, laxatives, antacids, medicines to treat epilepsy, oral contraceptives and several other medications can cause a special need for supplementation for adequate vitamin and mineral absorption.

People who have recently sustained severe injuries or severe burns— The nutritional requirement for these people is greatly increased. Faster healing and recovery can be aided by adequate supplementation. Ask your doctor for specific advice.

10-Deficiency symptoms

Contains a list of *proved symptoms*. These symptoms of deficiency have withstood the scrutiny of scientifically controlled studies with results published in medical literature.

11-Unproved speculated symptoms

Contains deficiency symptoms that have *not* withstood the scrutiny of scientifically controlled studies. Results have not been published in medical literature.

12-Lab tests to detect deficiency

Sometimes clinical features—medical history, signs and symptoms as interpreted by a competent professional—are all that are required to make an accurate diagnosis of deficiency. At other times, although clinical features may suggest a specific diagnosis, objective proof by a specific laboratory test adds confidence. As much data as can be collected is desirable before committing to a prolonged, sometimes expensive, sometimes hazardous, course of treatment. When lab tests are readily available and reasonable in cost, doctors can treat their patients with greater confidence than is possible without laboratory confirmation of the diagnosis. This section lists many of those studies.

Note: Analysis of hair samples to detect deficiencies of minerals and trace elements, while easily available commercially, cannot be regarded as a valid test. Minerals and trace elements appear in shampoos, hair-care products and generally in the environment. In addition, when nutrition is poor for any reason, hair growth actually slows—causing greater concentration of minerals in the hair. This greater concentration gives falsely high values. Hair tests are entirely without value except for experimental purposes.

13-Recommended dietary allowance (RDA)

RDA is an estimate of amounts of a nutrient required daily by people with the highest requirements in the general healthy population. Estimates are made by the American Food and Nutrition Board of the National Academy of Sciences, which began publishing recommendations in the 1940s. Recommendations are updated periodically to reflect changing opinions of the majority of experts. Because knowledge of human requirements is always changing, there is continuing controversy over the optimal levels of intake.

Many dieticians and nutrition experts believe the RDAs do not ensure optimum health. The RDAs represent the only official guide to safety. They have been carefully calculated and, at the very least, are a good reference point.

It is probably impossible to get all the recommended nutrients from today's diet because the foods it includes are highly processed and refined.

For some nutrients, no RDA has been established. An Estimated Safe Intake (per day) may be included.

14-What this substance does

Includes a brief discussion of the part each substance plays in chemical reactions or combinations that affect growth, development and health maintenance.

15-Miscellaneous information

Information in this section doesn't fit readily into other information blocks on the charts. Some information includes:

ᐁ Cooking tips to preserve the substance during food preparation.

ᐁ Time lapse before changes can be expected.

ᐁ Information of special interest.

16-Available as

Different available forms of the vitamin, mineral or supplement are discussed. These include tablets, powders, capsules, injections and oral forms.

17-Don't take if you have

Lists circumstances when use of this vitamin, mineral or supplement may not be safe. In formal medical literature, these circumstances are called *absolute contraindications.*

18-Consult your doctor if you have

Lists conditions under which a vitamin, mineral or supplement should be used with caution. In formal medical literature, these circumstances are frequently listed as *relative contraindications.* Using this product under these circumstances may require special consideration on your part and your doctor's. The rule is—*the potential benefit must outweigh the possible risk!*

19-Over age 55

As a person ages, physical changes occur that require special consideration when using vitamins, minerals and supplements. Liver and kidney function usually decreases, metabolism slows and other changes take place. These are expected and must be considered.

Most chemical substances introduced into the body are metabolized or excreted at a rate that depends on kidney and liver functions. In the aging population, smaller doses or longer intervals between doses may be necessary to prevent an unhealthy concentration of vitamins, minerals or supplements. These principles are exactly the same for therapeutic medicines and drugs. Toxic effects, severe side effects and adverse reactions occur more frequently and may cause more serious problems in this age group.

20-Pregnancy

Pregnancy creates an increased need for optimal nutrition, which may be difficult to maintain without using some supplementary vitamins and minerals.

11

What you take depends on your age, your present state of nutrition, your state of health and other factors. Work with your doctor to determine what supplements you will need and how much. Don't take *any* substance without consulting your doctor first!

21-Breast-feeding

Lactating mothers require sound nutrition. Follow your doctor's recommendations about diet, vitamins, minerals and supplements during this time. Don't be reluctant to ask questions and challenge your doctor regarding these important topics. But don't take *any* substance without consulting your doctor first!

22-Effect on lab tests

This section lists lab studies that may be affected when you take vitamins, minerals or supplements. Possible effects include causing a false-positive or false-negative test, resulting in a low result or high result when your actual physical state is the opposite. In general, some tests can be performed accurately only after discontinuing vitamins, minerals or supplements for a few days before the test is scheduled.

23-Storage

This serves as a reminder to keep these substances safely away from children. It also discusses how and where to store vitamins, minerals and supplements.

24-Others

Special warnings and precautions appear here if they don't fit any other specific information block. This section may contain information about the best time to take the substance, instructions about mixing or diluting or anything else that is important about this substance.

25-Overdose signs and symptoms

Symptoms listed are the ones most likely to develop with accidental or deliberate overdose. An overdosed person may not show all symptoms listed and may experience other symptoms not listed. Sometimes signs and symptoms are identical with ones listed as side effects or adverse reactions. The difference is intensity and severity. You must be the judge. Consult a doctor if you are in doubt.

26-What to do

If you suspect an overdose, whether symptoms are apparent or not, follow instructions in this section. Expanded instructions for overdose or *anaphylaxis*—severe, life-threatening allergic reaction—appear in the Glossary. See page 485.

27-Adverse reactions or side effects

Adverse reactions or side effects are symptoms that may occur when you ingest any substance, whether it is food, medicine, vitamin, mineral, herb or supplement. These are effects on the body other than the desired effect for which you take them.

The term *side effect* may include an expected, perhaps unavoidable, effect of a vitamin, mineral or supplement. For example, various forms of niacin may cause dramatic dizziness and flushing of the face and neck in the blush zone in almost everyone who takes a high enough dose. These symptoms are harmless, although sometimes uncomfortable, and have nothing to do with the intended use or therapeutic effect of niacin.

The term *adverse effect* is more significant. These effects can cause hazards that outweigh benefits.

28 - Interaction with medicine, vitamins or minerals

Vitamins, minerals, supplements, herbs and various medicines may interact in your body with other vitamins, minerals, supplements, herbs and medicines. It doesn't matter if they are prescription or non-prescription, natural or synthetic.

Interactions affect absorption, elimination or distribution of the substances that interact with each other. Sometimes they are beneficial, but at other times they are deadly. You may not be able to determine from the chart whether an interaction is good or bad. Don't guess! Ask your doctor or chemist—some interactions can kill!

29 - Interaction with other substances

This list includes possible interactions with food, beverages, tobacco, cocaine, alcohol and other substances you may ingest.

Medicinal Herbs

You may be wondering why a conservative, traditional doctor would write about medicinal herbs. Many medical professionals ignore their existence. There are several reasons why these substances are included in this book.

A popular backlash currently exists against traditional medicine as it is practiced today. The medical profession has brought some negative feelings upon itself. Part of this backlash takes the form of returning to "natural" medicine—specifically to any of the 2,500 herbs that have been used throughout history for medicinal purposes. People self-prescribe these plant materials and believe they are saving time and money by not consulting a traditional doctor. Because medicinal herbs are natural and unregulated, many people believe they are without hazards. This is not true!

For centuries, people have collected herbs to use for medicinal purposes. Very little of the experience has been written down. It has been passed down verbally instead. Most uses for herbs in the past and most of the reasons people use them today are probably without scientific foundation. Yet some of mankind's most useful medicines, such as digitalis, rauwolfia (used for mental illness and hypertension), cromlyn (used for preventing asthma attacks) and curare (a muscle relaxant), have all come from herbal "folk remedies."

Many medicinal herbs have pharmacological properties that we know are useful. But at the same time they may be harmful or toxic. Medicinal herbs are available in many forms. Most have *not* been scrutinized for safety and effectiveness by the medical establishment.

People have turned to medicinal herbs, believing they are "natural," safe, effective and wonderful. However, experience has taught us *any* effective medicine can also have uncomfortable side effects, adverse reactions and dangerous possible toxicity, just as many pharmaceuticals do.

Active ingredients of medicinal herbs vary greatly, whether you personally collect plant drugs or buy them. Variable factors include:

- Conditions under which the plant was grown (soil conditions, temperature, season).
- Degree of maturity of the plant when it was collected.
- Type of drying process.
- Type and duration of storage.

In conventional medicine, these variables are controlled by manufacturing procedures or government tests or assays to standardize the amount of the active principal and therefore the predictable safety and efficacy of the material. None of these safeguards exist for medicinal herbs.

The Placebo

The *placebo effect* has long been held as an advantage of using medicinal herbs. Many scientists and researchers claim most herbs do not really help people— it's the placebo effect of using these herbs that really heals. The word *placebo* comes from a Latin predecessor meaning "to please" or "to serve." Under a strict interpretation of the term as it is now used, a placebo medication has no pharmacologically or biologically active ingredients. Another interpretation asserts amounts *commonly* used could not affect the body, but *large amounts* of the same substance may.

For centuries, healers have helped people who were ill, no matter what the illness. Many ancient healers used remedies that have no pharmacological effects in the body. But these remedies were not always useless. They frequently proved to be very effective.

Modern studies conclusively prove *all* remedies help relieve symptoms in *some* people. In the early 1900s, many patients and doctors believed placebo therapy was quackery. Today, we know this to be untrue. Placebos *can* mimic the effect of almost any active drug. Placebo effects are real, although we cannot scientifically determine why.

How does the placebo effect work? We don't know for certain, but there are different theories.

Endorphins—chemicals normally present in the brain—can be activated by exercise, stress, mental exercises and imaging. Once endorphins have been activated, they kill pain the same way narcotics kill pain. Placebo treatment can trigger the production of hormones in the body, such as cortisone and adrenalin. This can affect the way we behave, the way we feel, the way we think. If the placebo can cause production of these chemicals, this may relieve symptoms of many disorders.

Harder to explain is the part that "power of suggestion" may play in the effectiveness of any remedy, whether it is a powerful drug, a supplement, an herb or a placebo. The gentle touch of the healer, the taste and smell of the product, the packaging, the cost—all are factors that have been studied and found to play a part in the placebo effect.

Understanding Common Terms

When you read about medicinal herbs, some of the following terms are used repeatedly. They refer to ways in which medicinal herbs can be useful.

Compress—Cloth is soaked in a cool liquid form of an herb, wrung out and applied directly to skin.

Decoction—Herb is boiled 10 to 15 minutes, then allowed to steep.

Extract—Solution resulting from soaking herb in cold water for 24 hours.

Fomentation—Cloth is soaked in a hot liquid form of an herb, wrung out and applied directly to skin.

Infusions—Tea is prepared by steeping herb in hot water. Infusions can be made from any part of a plant.

Ointment—Powdered form of an herb is mixed with any soft-based salve, such as lanolin, wax or lard.

Poultice—Herb applied to a moistened cloth, then applied directly to skin.

Powder—Useful part of herb is ground into a powder.

Syrup—Herb is added to brown sugar dissolved in boiling water, then boiled and strained.

Tincture—Powdered herb is added to a 50-50 solution of alcohol and water.

Points to Remember

Precautions apply to herbal medications. Read the checklist on page 19. Also keep in mind:

❧ Children under age 2 should *not* be given herbal medications.

❧ Pregnant and lactating women should avoid herbal medicines because of potential damage to the fetus or breast-feeding child.

❧ Collecting medicinal herbs for yourself is unwise, unless you have received a great deal of training. Correctly identifying plants and knowing how to select, preserve and use them properly requires a great deal of knowledge and judgment.

The medicinal-herb section of the book, page 255, contains profiles of the herbs most generally available. An extensive toxicity list, beginning on page 458, follows the charts. This list contains the names and possible toxic effects of over 350 medicinal herbs. Some herbs in this list do not have charts in this book. They are included for your reference.

Guide to Medicinal-Herbs Charts

The medicinal-herb information in this book is organized into condensed, easy-to-read charts. Each medicinal herb is described on a 1-page chart, as shown in the sample chart below. Charts are arranged alphabetically by the most-common herbal name. If you cannot find a name, look for alternative names in the Index or ask your herbal-medication retailer.

Boneset (Richweed, White Snakeroot, Ague Weed) —A

B— **Basic Information**
Biological name (genus and species):
Eupatorium perfoliatum, E. rugosum
C— Parts used for medicinal purposes:
Leaves
Petals/flower
D— Chemicals this herb contains:
Eupatroin
Resin (See Glossary)
Sugar
Tremetrol
Volatile oils (See Glossary)
Wax (See Glossary)

E— 👍 **Known Effects**

• Irritates gastrointestinal tract.
• Can produce "milk sickness" in humans, an acute disease characterized by trembling, vomiting and severe abdominal pain. It is caused by eating dairy products or beef from cattle poisoned by eating boneset.
• Increases perspiration.
• Causes vomiting.

F— **Miscellaneous information:**
• Tremetrol can accumulate slowly in animal bodies and cause toxic symptoms. It may do the same in humans.

G— 😀 **Unproved Speculated Benefits**

• Decreases blood sugar.
• Treats malaria.
• Treats fever.

🌳 **Warnings and Precautions**

H— **Don't take if you:**
• Are pregnant, think you may be pregnant or plan pregnancy in the near future.
• Have any chronic disease of the gastrointestinal tract, such as stomach or duodenal ulcers, oesophageal reflux (reflux oesophagitis), ulcerative colitis, spastic colitis, diverticulosis, diverticulitis.

I— **Consult your doctor if you:**
• Take this herb for any medical problem that doesn't improve in 2 weeks. There may be safer, more effective treatments.

• Take any medicinal drugs or herbs including aspirin, laxatives, cold and cough remedies, antacids, vitamins, minerals, amino acids, supplements, other prescription or non-prescription drugs.

Pregnancy: —J
• Dangers outweigh any possible benefits. Don't use.

Breast-feeding: —K
• Dangers outweigh any possible benefits. Don't use.

Infants and children: —L
• Treating infants and children under 2 with any herbal preparation is hazardous.

Others: —M
• Dangers outweigh any possible benefits. Don't use.

Storage: —N
• Keep cool and dry, but don't freeze. Store safely away from children.

Safe dosage: —O
• At present no "safe" dosage has been established.

💀 **Toxicity** —P

Comparative-toxicity rating not available from standard references.

For symptoms of toxicity: See below.

🌀 **Adverse Reactions, Side Effects or Overdose Symptoms** —Q

Signs and symptoms:	What to do:
Breathing difficulties	Seek emergency treatment.
Coma	Seek emergency treatment.
Drooling	Discontinue. Call doctor when convenient.
Muscle trembling	Discontinue. Call doctor immediately.
Nausea	Discontinue. Call doctor immediately.
Stiffness	Discontinue. Call doctor when convenient.
Vomiting	Discontinue. Call doctor immediately.
Weakness	Discontinue. Call doctor when convenient.

A-Popular name

Each chart is titled by the most popular name. Sometimes there may be two or more names. Alternative names are shown in parentheses. The Index contains a reference to each name listed. Popular names may vary in different parts of the world.

B-Biological name (genus and species)

Identifies the medicinal herb by genus and species. These Latin names are commonly used by biologists and plant scientists. They are included to help you make a positive identification.

C-Parts used for medicinal purposes

Describes what parts of the herb are used to supply the expected effects. Roots, leaves, bark and flowers are commonly used portions of the plant. Sometimes the entire plant is used.

D-Chemicals this herb contains

Chemicals and family names of chemically related groups are listed. Chemically related groups include saponins, tannins, volatile oils and others.

E-Known effects

Expected effects of these chemicals are the identified chemical actions of the medicinal herb being discussed. These effects have been identified and validated by scientists and researchers through various studies. Some effects may be beneficial; others are harmful.

F-Miscellaneous information

Contains information that doesn't fit into other information blocks on the chart.

G-Unproved speculated benefits

List of symptoms or medical problems

this drug has been reported to treat or improve. These claims may be accurate, but they haven't been proved with well-controlled studies.

H-Don't take if you

Lists circumstances under which the use of this herb may not be safe. In formal medical literature, these circumstances are listed as *absolute contraindications*.

I-Consult your doctor if you

Lists conditions in which this herb should be used with caution. In formal medical literature, these circumstances are called *relative contraindications*. Using an herb under these circumstances may require special consideration by you and your doctor. The rule to follow is— *the potential benefit must outweigh the possible risk*.

J-Pregnancy

As more is learned about effective medications, including herbal medications, the more health-care workers fear the possible effects of any medicinal product on an unborn child. This fear holds for *all* chemicals that cause changes in the body. The fact herbal medicines occur naturally does not free them from possibly causing harm. *The best rule to follow is don't take anything during pregnancy if you can avoid it!*

K-Breast-feeding

Although a breast-feeding newborn infant is not as likely to be harmed as an unborn fetus, caution should be observed. If you take a medicine or an herb during the time you breast-feed, do so *only* under professional supervision.

L-Infants and children

Treating infants and children under 2 years old with any herbal medication or preparation is hazardous. Dosages, uses and effects of an herb cannot be gauged easily with a young child. Do not use medicinal herbs to treat a problem your child may have without first discussing it thoroughly with your doctor.

M-Others

Warnings and precautions appear here if they don't fit into other categories.

N-Storage

This serves as a reminder to keep these substances safely away from children. It also discusses how and where to store medicinal herbs.

O-Safe dosage

Safe dosages have *not* been documented by the medical establishment. It is impossible to list a "safe" dosage and have it carry any significance. People who have had experience with herbs are usually qualified to predict safe doses if they know the person's age, past medical history and some important facts about his or her current health.

Many reputable distributors of herb products have recommendations for ranges of safety, but these may vary a great deal from manufacturer to manufacturer, according to age and purity of the product. The most important fact to understand is the more you ingest of a medicinal herb over a long period of time, the more likely a toxic reaction will occur. Most available herbs are safe when taken in small doses for short periods of time. Never fall into the trap of thinking "if a little is good, more is better."

P-Toxicity

Includes a general, average toxicity rating for each medicinal herb.

Q-Adverse reactions, side effects or overdose symptoms

Adverse reactions or side effects are symptoms that may occur when you ingest any substance, whether it is food, medicine, vitamin, mineral, herb or supplement. These are effects on the body other than the desired effect for which you take them.

The term *adverse effect* means the effects can cause hazards that outweigh benefits.

The term *side effect* may include an expected, perhaps unavoidable, effect of a vitamin, mineral, supplement or medicinal herb. For example, a side effect of horseradish may be nausea. This symptom is harmless although sometimes uncomfortable and has nothing to do with the intended use.

If you suspect an overdose, whether symptoms are present or not, follow instructions in this section.

Warning

Whether you use medicinal herbs or not is your decision. If you choose to use them, be sure you take them with knowledge and understanding of what they are. Know the supplier, and be sure you know the possible dangers. And consider that self-medication with medicinal herbs may prevent you from receiving better help from more effective medications that have withstood critical scientific investigations.

Checklist for Safer Use of Vitamins, Minerals, Supplements & Medicinal Herbs

The most important caution regarding all vitamins, minerals, supplements and medicinal herbs deals with the amount you take. Despite many popular articles in magazines and newspapers and reports on television, large doses of some of these substances can be hazardous to your health. Don't believe sensational advertisements and take large doses or megadoses. The belief "if a little does good, a lot will do much more" has no place in rational thinking regarding products to protect your health. Stay within safe-dose ranges!

1. Learn all you can about the vitamins, minerals, supplements and medicinal herbs *before* you take them. Information sources include this book, books from your public library, your doctor or your chemist.

2. Don't take vitamins, minerals, supplements or medicinal herbs prescribed for someone else, even if your symptoms are the same. At the same time, keep prescription items to yourself. They may be harmful to someone else.

3. Tell your doctor or health-care professional about any symptoms you experience that you suspect may be caused by anything you take.

4. Take vitamins, minerals, supplements and medicinal herbs in good light after you have identified the contents of the container. If you wear glasses, put them on to check and recheck labels.

5. Don't keep medicine by your bedside. You may unknowingly repeat a dose when you are half-asleep or confused.

6. Know the names of all the substances you take.

7. Read labels on medications you take.

If information in incomplete, ask your chemist for more details.

8. If they are in liquid form, shake vitamins, minerals, supplements and medicinal herbs before you take them.

9. Store all vitamins, minerals, supplements and medicinal herbs in cool places away from sunlight and moisture. Bathroom medicine cabinets are usually unacceptable because it's too warm and too humid there.

10. If a vitamin, mineral, supplement or medicinal herb requires refrigeration, don't freeze!

11. Obtain a standard measuring spoon from your pharmacy for liquid vitamins and a graduated dropper to use for liquid preparations for infants and children.

12. Follow manufacturer's or doctor's suggestions regarding diet instructions. Some products work better on a full stomach. Others work best on an empty stomach. Some products work best when you follow a special diet. For example, a low-salt diet enhances effectiveness of any product expected to lower blood pressure.

13. Avoid any substance you know you are allergic to.

14. If you become pregnant while taking any vitamin, mineral, supplement or medicinal herb, tell your doctor and discontinue taking it until you have discussed it with him or her. Try to remember the exact dose and the length of time you have taken the substance.

15. Tell your health-care worker about vitamins, minerals, supplements, medicinal herbs and other substances you take, even if you

bought them without a prescription. During an illness or prior to surgery, this information is *crucial*. Even mention antacids, laxatives, tonics and over-the-counter preparations. Many people believe these products are completely safe and forget to inform doctors, nurses or chemists they are using them.

16. Regard all vitamins, minerals, supplements and medicinal herbs as potentially harmful to children. Store them safely away from their reach.

Store any substances that may be harmful out of the reach of children.

17. Alcohol, marijuana, cocaine, other mood-altering drugs and tobacco can cause life-threatening interactions when mixed with some vitamins, minerals, supplements and medicinal herbs. They can also prevent treatment from being effective or delay your return to good health. Common sense dictates you avoid them, particularly during an illness.

Vitamins

Vitamins are chemical compounds necessary for normal growth, health, metabolism and physical well-being. They provide essential parts of enzymes—the chemical molecules that catalyze or facilitate the completion of chemical reactions. Vitamins also form an essential part of many hormones—the chemical substances that promote and protect body health and reproduction.

If you're in good health, vitamins are needed only in small amounts. They are usually found in sufficient quantities in the foods you eat.

Vitamin A (Beta-carotene, Retinol)

Basic Information

Beta-carotene is a previtamin-A compound found in plants. The body converts beta-carotene to vitamin A.
Available from natural sources? Yes
Available from synthetic sources? Yes
Prescription required? No
Fat-soluble or water-soluble: Fat-soluble

Natural Sources

Apricots, fresh	Liver
Asparagus	Mustard greens
Broccoli	Pumpkin
Cantaloupe	Spinach
Carrots, sliced	Squash, winter
Endive, raw	Sweet potatoes
Kale	Watermelon
Leaf lettuce	

Reasons to Use

- Aids in treatment of many eye disorders, including prevention of night blindness and formation of visual purple in the eye.
- Promotes bone growth, teeth development, reproduction.
- Helps form and maintain healthy skin, hair, mucous membranes.
- Builds body's resistance to respiratory infections.
- Helps treat acne, impetigo, boils, carbuncles, open ulcers when applied externally.

Unproved Speculated Benefits

- Helps control glaucoma.
- Buffers against cancer.
- Guards against effects of pollution and smog.
- Cushions against stress.
- Speeds healing.
- Helps in removal of age spots.
- Fights infections.
- Fights skin diseases.
- Shortens duration of some illnesses.

Who Needs Additional Amounts?

- Anyone with inadequate caloric or nutritional dietary intake or increased nutritional requirements.
- Pregnant or breast-feeding women.
- Those who abuse alcohol or other drugs.
- People with a chronic wasting illness, excess stress for long periods or who have recently undergone surgery.
- Those with a portion of the gastrointestinal tract surgically removed.
- People with recent severe burns or injuries.

Deficiency Symptoms

- Night blindness
- Lack of tear secretion
- Changes in eyes with eventual blindness if deficiency is severe and untreated
- Susceptibility to respiratory infection
- Dry, rough skin
- Changes in mucous membranes
- Weight loss
- Poor bone growth
- Weak tooth enamel
- Diarrhoea
- Slow growth

Unproved Speculated Symptoms

- Bone thickening
- Kidney stones
- Diarrhoea
- Birth defects
- Reduced production of steroid hormones

Lab Tests to Detect Deficiency

Many months of deficiency required before lab studies reflect deficiency.
- Plasma vitamin A and plasma carotene
- Dark-adaptation test
- Electronystagmogram
- Electroretinogram

Vitamin A (Beta-carotene, Retinol)

Dosage and Usage Information

Recommended Dietary Allowance (RDA):
Estimate of adequate daily intake by the Food and Nutrition Board of the National Research Council, 1980. See Glossary.
RDA for vitamin A is expressed in retinol equivalents (RE). One RE = 1mcg retinol or 6mcg beta-carotene. IU = International units.

Age	Retinol Equivalents	International Units
0–6 months	420RE	2,100IU
6–12 months	400RE	2,100IU
1–3 years	400RE	2,000IU
4–6 years	500RE	2,500IU
7–10 years	700RE	3,300IU
Males		
11+ years	1,000RE	5,000IU
Females		
11+ years	800RE	4,000IU
Pregnant	+200RE	+1,000IU
Lactating	+400RE	+2,000IU

What this vitamin does:
- Essential for normal function of retina. Combines with red pigment of retina (opsin) to form rhodopsin, which is necessary for sight in partial darkness.
- May act as co-factor in enzyme systems.
- Necessary for growth of bone, testicular function, ovarian function, embryonic development, regulation of growth, differentiation of tissues.

Miscellaneous information:
- Many months of a vitamin-A-deficient diet are required before symptoms develop. Average person has a 2-year supply of vitamin A stored in the liver.
- Steroids are produced by the adrenal gland and are part of the natural response to stress and immune function. Failure to make these important hormones leaves immune system in a less-than-ideal state.

Available as:
- Extended-release capsules or tablets: Swallow whole with full glass of liquid. Don't chew or crush. Take with or immediately after food to decrease stomach irritation.
- Oral solution: Dilute in at least 1/2 glass water or other liquid. Take with meals or 1 to 1-1/2 hours after meals unless otherwise directed by your doctor.
- A constituent of many multivitamin/mineral preparations.
- Some forms available by generic name.

Warnings and Precautions

Don't take if you:
- Are allergic to any preparation containing vitamin A.

Consult your doctor if you have:
- Cystic fibrosis
- Diabetes
- Intestinal disease with diarrhoea
- Kidney disease
- Liver disease
- Overactive thyroid function
- Disease of the pancreas

Over age 55:
- More likely to be malnourished and need supplement.
- Dosage must be taken carefully to avoid possible toxicity.

Pregnancy:
- Daily doses exceeding 6,000IU can produce growth retardation and urinary-tract malformations of fetus.
- Don't take megadoses.

Breast-feeding:
- Don't take megadoses.

Effect on lab tests:
- With chronic vitamin-A toxicity, lab tests show *increased* blood glucose, blood-urea nitrogen, serum calcium, serum cholesterol, serum triglycerides.
- Poor results on dark-adaptation test (See Glossary)
- Poor results on electronystagmogram (See Glossary)
- Poor results on electroretinogram (See Glossary)

Storage:
- Store in cool, dry place away from direct light, but don't freeze.
- Store safely out of reach of children.
- Don't store in bathroom medicine cabinet. Heat and moisture may change action of vitamin.

Others:
- Children are more sensitive to vitamin A and are more likely to develop toxicity with dosages exceeding the RDA.
- Toxicity is slowly reversible on withdrawal of vitamin A but may persist for several weeks.

»▸

Vitamin A (Beta-carotene, Retinol), Continued

 ## Overdose/Toxicity

Signs and symptoms:
Bleeding from gums or sore mouth, bulging soft spot on head in babies, sometimes hydrocephaly ("water on brain"), confusion or unusual excitement, diarrhoea, dizziness, double vision, headache, irritability, dry skin, hair loss, peeling skin on lips, palms and in other areas, seizures, vomiting, enlarged spleen and liver.

Note: Toxicity symptoms usually appear about 6 hours after ingestion of overdoses of vitamin A. Symptoms may also develop gradually if overdose is milder and over a long period of time.

What to do:
For symptoms of overdosage: Discontinue vitamin, and consult doctor. Also see *Adverse Reactions or Side Effects* section below.
For accidental overdosage (such as child taking entire bottle): Dial 999 (emergency).

 ## Adverse Reactions or Side Effects

Reaction or effect	What to do
Abdominal pain	Discontinue. Call doctor immediately.
Appetite loss	Discontinue. Call doctor when convenient.
Bone or joint pain	Discontinue. Call doctor immediately.
Discomfort, tiredness or weakness	Discontinue. Call doctor when convenient.
Drying or cracking of skin or lips	Discontinue. Call doctor immediately.
Fever	Discontinue. Call doctor immediately.
Hair loss	Discontinue. Call doctor immediately.
Headache	Discontinue. Call doctor when convenient.
In children, premature closure of epiphyses (the end parts of bones where growth occurs from birth through adolescence)	Discontinue. Call doctor immediately.
Increase in frequency of urination	Discontinue. Call doctor when convenient.
Increased sensitivity of skin to sunlight	Discontinue. Call doctor when convenient.
Irritability	Discontinue. Call doctor immediately.
Vomiting	Seek emergency treatment.
Yellow-orange patches on soles of feet, palms of hands or skin around nose and lips	Seek emergency treatment.

 ## Interaction with Medicine, Vitamins or Minerals

Interacts with	Combined effect
Antacids	Decreases absorption of vitamin A and fat-soluble vitamins D, E, K.
Anti-coagulants	Increases likelihood of spontaneous or hidden bleeding.
Cholestyramine, colestipol	Decreases absorption of vitamin A.
Mineral oil, neomycin, sucralfate, isioretinoin	Increases likelihood of vitamin-A toxicity.
Oral contraceptives	Increases vitamin-A concentrations.
Vitamin E	Normal amount facilitates absorption, storage in liver and utilization of vitamin A. Excessive dosage may deplete vitamin-A stores in liver.

 ## Interaction with Other Substances

Tobacco decreases absorption. Smokers may need supplementary vitamin A.

Chronic alcoholism interferes with the body's ability to transport and use vitamin A.

Basic Information

Available from natural sources? Yes
Available from synthetic sources? Yes
Prescription required? No
Fat-soluble or water-soluble: Water-soluble

Natural Sources

Black currants	Orange juice
Broccoli	Oranges
Brussels sprouts	Papayas
Cabbage	Potatoes
Collards	Rose hips
Grapefruit	Spinach
Green peppers	Strawberries
Guava	Sweet and hot peppers
Kale	Tangerines
Lemons	Tomatoes
Mangos	Watercress

Reasons to Use

- Promotes healthy capillaries, gums, teeth.
- Aids iron absorption.
- Helps heal wounds and broken bones.
- Prevents and treats scurvy.
- Treats anaemia, especially for iron-deficiency anaemia.
- Treats urinary-tract infections.
- Helps form collagen in connective tissue.
- Increases iron absorption from intestines.
- Contributes to haemoglobin and red-blood-cell production in bone marrow.
- Blocks production of nitrosamines.

Unproved Speculated Benefits

- Prevents or cures the common cold and other infections.
- Cures some forms of cancer.
- Reduces cholesterol.
- Protects against heart disease.
- Prevents blood clots.
- Prevents allergies.
- Prevents or cures poisoning from various substances.
- Cures arthritis, skin ulcers, hay fever.
- Reduces rectal polyps.
- Alleviates mental illness.
- Relieves herpes infections of eyes and genitals.
- Prevents periodontal disease.

- Detoxifies those who abuse alcohol and drugs.
- Heals bed sores.
- Retards aging.

Who Needs Additional Amounts?

- Anyone with inadequate caloric or nutritional dietary intake or increased nutritional requirements.
- Older people (over 55 years).
- Pregnant or breast-feeding women.
- Those who abuse alcohol or other drugs.
- People with a chronic wasting illness, acute illness with fever, hyperthyroidism, tuberculosis, cold exposure.
- Anyone who experiences excess stress for long periods or who has recently undergone surgery.
- Athletes and workers who participate in vigorous physical activities.
- Those with a portion of the gastrointestinal tract surgically removed.
- People with recent severe burns or injuries.
- Those receiving kidney dialysis.
- Infants on unfortified formulas.

Deficiency Symptoms

- Scurvy: muscle weakness, swollen gums, loss of teeth, tiredness, depression, bleeding under skin, bleeding gums
- Shortness of breath
- Digestive difficulties
- Easy bruising
- Swollen or painful joints
- Nosebleeds
- Anaemia, weakness, tiredness, paleness
- Frequent infections
- Slow healing of wounds

Unproved Speculated Symptoms

- Blood-vessel weakness

Lab Tests to Detect Deficiency

- Vitamin-C levels in blood plasma.
- Measurement of ascorbic-acid level in white-blood cells. (Expensive and used mostly for experimental purposes.)

➤➤

Ascorbic Acid (Vitamin C), Continued

Dosage and Usage Information

Recommended Dietary Allowance (RDA):
Estimate of adequate daily intake by the Food and Nutrition Board of the National Research Council, 1980. See Glossary.

Age	RDA
0–12 months	35mg
1–10 years	45mg
11–14 years	50mg
15+ years	60mg
Pregnant	+20mg
Lactating	+40mg

What this vitamin does:
- Necessary for collagen formation and tissue repair.
- Participates in oxidation-reduction reactions.
- Needed for metabolism of phenylalanine, tyrosine, folic acid, iron.
- Helps utilization of carbohydrates, synthesis of fats and proteins, preservation of integrity of blood-vessel walls.
- Strengthens blood vessels.

Miscellaneous information:
Food preparation tips to conserve vitamin C:
- Eat food raw or minimally cooked.
- Shorten cooking time by putting vegetables in very small amounts of water.
- Avoid prolonged standing of food at room temperature.
- Avoid overexposure of food to air and light.
- Avoid soaking vegetables.

Available as:
- Tablets: Swallow whole with full glass of liquid. Don't chew or crush. Take with meals or 1 to 1-1/2 hours after meals unless otherwise directed by your doctor.
- Extended-release capsules or tablets: Swallow whole with full glass of liquid. Don't chew or crush. Take with or immediately after food to decrease stomach irritation.
- Oral solution: Dilute in at least 1/2 glass water or other liquid. Take with meals or 1 to 1-1/2 hours after meals unless otherwise directed by your doctor.
- Injectable forms are administered by doctor or nurse.
- Chewable tablets: Chew well before swallowing.
- Effervescent tablets: Allow to dissolve completely in liquid before swallowing.
- A constituent of many multivitamin/mineral preparations.

Warnings and Precautions

Don't take if you:
- Are allergic to vitamin C.

Consult your doctor if you have:
- Gout.
- Kidney stones.
- Sickle-cell anaemia.

Over age 55:
- Needs are greater.
- Side effects are more likely.
- If you take 1,000mg a day or more, drink *at least* 3 pints of water.

Pregnancy:
- Requires vitamin-C supplements because of demands made by bone development, teeth and connective-tissue formation of fetus. Consult doctor to ensure correct dose.
- If mother takes megadoses, newborn may develop deficiency symptoms after birth.
- Don't take megadoses.

Breast-feeding:
- Requires vitamin-C supplementation to support rapid growth of child. Consult doctor to ensure correct dose.
- Don't take megadoses.

Effect on lab tests:
With megadoses (10 times recommended RDA):
- Blood in stool. Large doses may cause false-negative test results.
- LDH and SGOT (See Glossary)
- Glucose in urine. Depends on method used.
- Serum bilirubin. False low level.
- Urinary pH. False low level.

Storage:
- Store in cool, dry place away from direct light, but don't freeze.
- Store safely out of reach of children.
- Don't store in bathroom medicine cabinet. Heat and moisture may change action of vitamin.

Others:
- Very high doses may cause kidney stones, although reported studies do not confirm this.

Overdose/Toxicity

Signs and symptoms:
Flushed face, headache, increased urination, lower-abdominal cramps, mild diarrhoea, nausea, vomiting for oral forms. Dizziness and faintness (if given by injection).

What to do:
For symptoms of overdosage: Discontinue vitamin and consult doctor. Also see *Adverse Reactions or Side Effects* section below.
For accidental overdosage (such as child taking entire bottle): Dial 999 (emergency).

Adverse Reactions or Side Effects

Reaction or effect	What to do
Anaemia	Discontinue. Call doctor immediately.
Flushed face	Discontinue. Call doctor when convenient.
Headache	Discontinue. Call doctor when convenient.
Increased urination	Discontinue. Call doctor when convenient.
Lower abdominal cramps	Seek emergency treatment.
Mild diarrhoea	Discontinue. Call doctor when convenient.
Nausea	Seek emergency treatment.
Vomiting	Seek emergency treatment.

Interaction with Medicine, Vitamins or Minerals

Interacts with	Combined effect
Aminosalicylic acid (PAS for tuberculosis)	Increases chance of formation of drug crystals in urine. Large doses of vitamin C must be taken to produce this effect.
Anti-cholinergics	Decreases anti-cholinergic effect.
Anti-coagulants (oral)	Decreases anti-coagulant effect.
Aspirin	Decreases vitamin-C effect.
Barbiturates	Decreases vitamin-C effect. Increases barbiturate effect.
Calcium	Assists in absorption of calcium.
Copper	Decreases absorption of copper. Large doses of vitamin C must be taken to produce this effect.
Iron supplements	Increases iron effect.
Mineral oil	Decreases vitamin-C effect.
Oral contraceptives	Decreases vitamin-C effect.
Quinidine	Decreases quinidine effect.
Salicylates	Decreases vitamin-C effect.
Sulpha drugs	Decreases vitamin-C effect. May cause kidney stones.
Tetracyclines	Decreases vitamin-C effect.

Interaction with Other Substances

Tobacco decreases absorption. Smokers may require supplementary vitamin C.

Alcohol can be more rapidly broken down in body with large doses of vitamin C.

Vitamin B-12

Basic Information

Vitamin B-12 is also called cyanocobalamin.
Available from natural sources? Yes
Available from synthetic sources? Yes
Prescription required? Yes, for high doses and injectable forms
Fat-soluble or water-soluble: Water-soluble

Natural Sources

Beef	Liverwurst
Beef liver	Mackerel
Blue cheese	Milk
Clams	Milk products
Eggs	Sardines
Flounder	Snapper
Herring	Swiss cheese

Note: Vitamin B-12 is not found in vegetables.

Reasons to Use

- Promotes normal growth and development.
- Treats some types of nerve damage.
- Treats pernicious anaemia.
- Treats and prevents vitamin B-12 deficiencies in people who have had a portion of the gastrointestinal tract surgically removed.
- Prevents vitamin-B12 deficiency in vegan vegetarians and persons with absorption diseases.

Unproved Speculated Benefits

- Helps mental and nervous disorders.
- Improves resistance to infection and disease.
- Increases appetite.
- Promotes growth of someone who has smaller-than-average stature.
- Improves memory and the ability to learn.
- Increases energy.

Who Needs Additional Amounts?

- Strict vegetarians.
- Anyone with inadequate caloric or nutritional dietary intake or increased nutritional requirements.
- Those who abuse alcohol or other drugs.
- People with a chronic wasting illness, excess stress for long periods or who have recently undergone surgery.

- Those with a portion of the gastrointestinal tract surgically removed.
- People with recent severe burns or injuries.

Deficiency Symptoms

- Pernicious anaemia, with the following symptoms:
  Fatigue, profound
  Weakness, especially in arms and legs
  Sore tongue
  Nausea, appetite loss, weight loss
  Bleeding gums
  Numbness and tingling in hands and feet
  Difficulty maintaining balance
  Pale lips, pale tongue, pale gums
  Yellow eyes and skin
  Shortness of breath
  Depression
  Confusion and dementia
  Headache
  Poor memory

Unproved Speculated Symptoms

- Aging
- Allergies
- Eye problems
- Slow growth
- Skin problems
- Easy fatigue
- Mental symptoms
- Sterility
- Thyroid disorders
- Menstrual disorders
- Delusions and hallucinations

Lab Tests to Detect Deficiency

- Serum vitamin B-12, a radioactive study usually performed with serum-folic-acid test, called the *Schilling Test*
- Reticulocyte count

Dosage and Usage Information

Recommended Dietary Allowance (RDA):
Estimate of adequate daily intake by the Food and Nutrition Board of the National Research Council, 1980. See Glossary.

➤➤

Age	RDA
0–6 months	0.5mcg
6–12 months	1.5mcg
1–3 years	2mcg
4–6 years	2.5mcg
7–10 years	3mcg
11+ years	3mcg
Pregnant	+1mcg
Lactating	+1mcg

What this vitamin does:
- Acts as co-enzyme for normal DNA synthesis.
- Promotes normal fat and carbohydrate metabolism and protein syntheses.
- Promotes growth, cell development, blood-cell development, manufacture of covering to nerve cells, maintenance of normal function of nervous system.

Miscellaneous information:
- There is a very low incidence of toxicity of vitamin B-12, even with large amounts up to 1,000mcg/day.

Available as:
- Oral and injectable forms. Oral forms are used only as diet supplement. Only people with portions of the gastrointestinal tract removed surgically or those with pernicious anaemia require injections.
- Tablets: Swallow whole with full glass of liquid. Don't chew or crush. Take with meals or 1 to 1-1/2 hours after meals unless otherwise directed by your doctor.
- Extended-release capsules or tablets: Swallow whole with full glass of liquid. Don't chew or crush. Take with or immediately after food to decrease stomach irritation.
- Injectable forms are administered by doctor or nurse.
- A constituent of many multivitamin/mineral preparations.

Warnings and Precautions

Don't take if you:
- Are allergic to B-12 given by injection. Allergy to injections produces itching, redness, swelling and rarely blood-pressure drop with loss of consciousness.
- Have Leber's disease.

Consult your doctor if you have:
- Gout.

Over age 55:
- No problems expected.

Pregnancy:
- No problems expected.
- Don't take megadoses.

Breast-feeding:
- No problems expected.
- Don't take megadoses.

Effect on lab tests:
- Tests for serum potassium may show precipitous drop (hypokalaemia) during 48 hours after beginning treatment for anaemia.

Storage:
- Store in cool, dry place away from direct light, but don't freeze. Liquid forms should be refrigerated.
- Store safely out of reach of children.
- Don't store in bathroom medicine cabinet. Heat and moisture may change action of vitamin.

Others:
- The injectable form is the only effective form to treat pernicious anaemia or people with portions of the gastrointestinal tract surgically removed. These individuals do not absorb oral forms.

Overdose/Toxicity

Signs and symptoms:
- If taken with large doses of vitamin C, vitamin B-12 may cause nosebleed, ear bleeding, dry mouth.

What to do:
For symptoms of overdosage: Discontinue vitamin, and consult doctor. Also see *Adverse Reactions or Side Effects* section below.
For accidental overdosage (such as child taking entire bottle): Dial 999 (emergency). operator or your nearest Poison Control Center. »→

Vitamin B-12, Continued

Adverse Reactions or Side Effects

Reaction or effect	What to do
Diarrhoea (rare)	Discontinue. Call doctor immediately.
Itching skin after injections (rare)	Seek emergency treatment.

Interaction with Medicine, Vitamins or Minerals

Interacts with	Combined effect
Aminosalicylates	Reduces absorption of vitamin B-12.
Antibiotics	May cause false-low test results for vitamin B-12.
Ascorbic acid (vitamin C)	Large doses may destroy vitamin B-12. Separate doses by at least 1 hour.
Chloramphenicol	May prevent therapeutic response when vitamin B-12 is used to treat anaemia.
Cholestyramine	Reduces absorption of vitamin B-12.
Colchicine	Reduces absorption of vitamin B-12.
Folic acid	Large doses decrease vitamin B-12 concentrations in blood.
Neomycin (oral forms only)	Reduces absorption of vitamin B-12.
Potassium in extended-release forms	Reduces absorption of vitamin B-12. May increase need for vitamin B-12.

Interaction with Other Substances

Tobacco decreases absorption. Smokers may require supplementary vitamin B-12.

Alcohol in excessive amounts for long periods may lead to vitamin B-12 deficiency.

Basic Information

Biotin is also called vitamin H.
Available from natural sources? Yes
Available from synthetic sources? No
Prescription required? No
Fat-soluble or water-soluble: Water-soluble

Natural Sources

Brewer's yeast	Mackerel
Brown rice	Meats
Bulgur wheat	Milk
Butter	Oats
Calves' liver	Peanuts
Cashew nuts	Soybeans
Cheese	Split peas
Chicken	Sunflower seeds
Eggs	Tuna
Green peas	Walnuts
Lentils	

Reasons to Use

• Helps formation of fatty acids.
• Facilitates metabolism of amino acids and carbohydrates.
• Promotes normal health of sweat glands, nerve tissue, bone marrow, male sex glands, blood cells, skin, hair.

Unproved Speculated Benefits

• Cures baldness.
• Alleviates muscle pain.
• Cures dermatitis.
• Alleviates depression.

Who Needs Additional Amounts?

• Anyone with inadequate caloric or nutritional dietary intake or increased nutritional requirements.
• People who consume huge quantities of raw eggs, which contain a compound that inhibits biotin. Cooking eggs destroys this compound and eliminates the problem.

Deficiency Symptoms

Babies:
• Dry scaling on scalp and face
Adults:
• Fatigue
• Depression
• Sleepiness
• Nausea
• Loss of appetite
• Muscular pains
• Loss of muscular reflexes
• Tongue becomes smooth and pale
• Hair loss
• Blood-cholesterol levels increase
• Anaemia
• Skin disorders

Unproved Speculated Symptoms

• Sudden infant death syndrome (SIDS)

Lab Tests to Detect Deficiency

• None available, except for experimental purposes.

Dosage and Usage Information

Recommended Dietary Allowance (RDA):
No RDA has been established. Estimated safe intake given below:

Age	Estimated Safe Intake
0–6 months	35mg/day
6–12 months	50mg/day
1–3 years	65mg/day
4–6 years	85mg/day
7–10 years	120mg/day
11+ years	100–200mg/day

What this vitamin does:
• Biotin is necessary for normal growth, development and health.

Miscellaneous information:
• Intestinal bacteria produce all the biotin the body needs, so there is no substantial evidence that normal, healthy adults need dietary supplements of biotin.

≫➤

Biotin (Vitamin H), Continued

Available as:
- Tablets or capsules: Swallow whole with full glass of liquid. Don't chew or crush. Take with or immediately after food to decrease stomach irritation.
- A constituent of many multivitamin/mineral preparations.

 ## Warnings and Precautions

Don't take if you:
- No specific precautions.

Consult your doctor if you have:
- No specific precautions.

Over age 55:
- No specific precautions.

Pregnancy:
- No specific precautions.
- Don't take megadoses.

Breast-feeding:
- No specific precautions.
- Don't take megadoses.

Effect on lab tests:
- None expected.

Storage:
- Store in cool, dry place away from direct light, but don't freeze.
- Store safely out of reach of children.
- Don't store in bathroom medicine cabinet. Heat and moisture may change action of vitamin.

 ## Overdose/Toxicity

Signs and symptoms:
Supplements in amounts suggested by manufacturers on the label are non-toxic.

What to do:
For symptoms of overdosage: Discontinue vitamin, and consult doctor.
For accidental overdosage (such as child taking entire bottle): Dial 999 (emergency).

 ## Adverse Reactions or Side Effects

None expected.

 ## Interaction with Medicine, Vitamins or Minerals

Interacts with	Combined effect
Antibiotics (broad spectrum)	Destroys "friendly" bacteria in intestines that produce biotin. This can lead to significant biotin deficiency.
Sulphonamides	Destroys "friendly" bacteria in intestines that produce biotin. This can lead to significant biotin deficiency.

 ## Interaction with Other Substances

Tobacco decreases absorption. Smokers may require supplementary biotin.

Foods
- Eating large quantities of *raw egg whites* may cause biotin deficiency. Egg whites contain *avidin*, which prevents biotin from being absorbed into the body.

Basic Information

Calcifidiol is a form of vitamin D. *It is also called* ergocalciferol.
Available from natural sources? Yes
Available from synthetic sources? Yes
Prescription required? Yes
Fat-soluble or water-soluble: Fat-soluble

Natural Sources

Cod-liver oil	Salmon
Halibut-liver oil	Sardines
Herring	Sunlight
Mackerel	Vitamin-D-fortified milk

Reasons to Use

- Calcifidiol is a form of vitamin D primarily used as an additional medicine to treat hypocalaemia (not enough calcium in blood). It is also frequently prescribed to treat bone disease in people undergoing renal dialysis and those with hypoparathyroidism.
- Regulates growth, hardening and repair of bone by controlling absorption of calcium and phosphorus from small intestine.
- Prevents rickets.
- Treats post-operative muscle contractions.
- Works with calcium to control bone formation.
- Promotes normal growth and development of infants and children, particularly bones and teeth.

Unproved Speculated Benefits

- Cures arthritis.
- Prevents colon cancer.
- Treats aging symptoms.
- Treats acne.
- Treats alcoholism.
- Treats herpes simplex and herpes zoster.
- Treats cystic fibrosis.

Who Needs Additional Amounts?

- Children who live in sunshine-deficient areas.
- Anyone with inadequate caloric or nutritional dietary intake or increased nutritional requirements.
- Older people (over 55 years), especially women after menopause.
- Pregnant or breast-feeding women.
- Those who abuse alcohol or other drugs.

- People with a chronic wasting illness, excess stress for long periods or those who have recently undergone surgery.
- Those with a portion of the gastrointestinal tract surgically removed.
- People with recent severe burns or injuries.

Deficiency Symptoms

- Rickets (a childhood deficiency disease): bent, bowed legs, malformations of joints or bones, late tooth development, weak muscles, listlessness.
- Osteomalacia (adult rickets): muscle weakness and spasm, brittle, easily broken bones, pain in ribs, lower spine, pelvis and legs.

Unproved Speculated Symptoms

- Muscle diseases (myopathies)

Lab Tests to Detect Deficiency

- Reduced levels of vitamin D forms in blood.
- Decreased serum phosphate, decreased calcium, increased alkaline phosphatase, urinary hydroxyproline, PTH levels.
- Bone X-ray.

Dosage and Usage Information

Recommended Dietary Allowance (RDA):
Estimate of adequate daily intake by the Food and Nutrition Board of the National Research Council, 1980. See Glossary.

Age	RDA
0–6 months	10mcg
6–12 months	10mcg
1–10 years	10mcg
Males	
11–18 years	10mcg
19–22 years	7.5mcg
23+ years	5mcg
Females	
11–18 years	10mcg
19–22 years	7.5mcg
23+ years	5mcg
Pregnant	+5mcg
Lactating	+5mcg

>>➤

Calcifidiol, Continued

What this vitamin does:
- Absorbs and uses calcium and phosphorous to make bone.
- Essential for normal growth and development.

Miscellaneous information:
- Take at the same time every day.
- Put liquid vitamin D directly into mouth or mix with cereal, fruit juice or food.

Available as:
- Extended-release capsules or tablets: Swallow whole with full glass of liquid. Don't chew or crush. Take with or immediately after food to decrease stomach irritation.
- Oral solution: Dilute in at least 1/2 glass water or other liquid. Take with meals or 1 to 1-1/2 hours after meals unless otherwise directed by your doctor.
- Some forms available by generic name.

 Warnings and Precautions

Don't take if you:
- Are allergic to vitamin D, ergocalciferol or any vitamin-D derivative.

Consult your doctor if you have:
- Any plans to become pregnant while taking vitamin D.
- Epilepsy.
- Heart or blood-vessel disease.
- Kidney, liver, pancreatic disease.
- Chronic diarrhoea.
- Intestinal problems.
- Sarcoidosis.

Over age 55:
- Adverse reactions and side effects are more likely. Supplements are often necessary.

Pregnancy:
- Taking too much during pregnancy may cause abnormalities in fetus. Consult doctor before taking supplement to ensure correct dosage.
- Don't take megadoses.

Breast-feeding:
- Important for you to receive correct amount so enough vitamin D is available for normal growth and development of baby. Consult doctor about supplements.
- Don't take megadoses.

Effect on lab tests:
- May decrease serum alkaline phosphatase.
- May increase levels of calcium, cholesterol and phosphate in test results.
- May increase level of magnesium in test results.
- May increase amounts of calcium and phosphorous in urine.

Storage:
- Store in cool, dry place away from direct light, but don't freeze. Avoid overexposure to air.
- Store safely out of reach of children.
- Don't store in bathroom medicine cabinet. Heat and moisture may change action of vitamin.

Others:
- Absence of sunlight prevents natural formation of vitamin D by skin. Sunshine provides sufficient amounts of vitamin D for people who live in sunny climates. Those who live in northern areas with fewer days of sunshine and extended periods of cloud cover and darkness must depend on dietary sources for vitamin D.
- Avoid megadoses.

 Overdose/Toxicity

Signs and symptoms:
High blood pressure, irregular heartbeat, nausea, weight loss, seizures, abdominal pain, appetite loss, mental and physical-growth retardation, premature hardening of arteries, kidney damage.

What to do:
For symptoms of overdosage: Discontinue vitamin, and consult doctor. Also see *Adverse Reactions or Side Effects* section below.
For accidental overdosage (such as child taking entire bottle): Dial 999 (emergency).
For toxic symptoms: Discontinue vitamin, and seek immediate medical help. Hospitalization may be necessary.

VITAMIN

Adverse Reactions or Side Effects

Reaction or effect	What to do
Appetite loss	Discontinue. Call doctor when convenient.
Constipation	Discontinue. Call doctor when convenient.
Diarrhoea	Discontinue. Call doctor immediately.
Dry mouth	Discontinue. Call doctor when convenient.
Headache	Discontinue. Call doctor immediately.
Increased thirst	Discontinue. Call doctor when convenient.
Mental confusion	Discontinue. Call doctor immediately.
Metallic taste	Discontinue. Call doctor when convenient.
Nausea	Discontinue. Call doctor immediately.
Unusual tiredness	Discontinue. Call doctor when convenient.
Vomiting	Discontinue. Call doctor immediately.

Interaction with Medicine, Vitamins or Minerals

Interacts with	Combined effect
Antacids with aluminium	Decreases absorption of vitamin D and fat-soluble vitamins A, D, E, K.
Antacids with magnesium	May cause too much magnesium in blood, especially for people with kidney failure.
Anti-convulsants	May reduce effect of vitamin D from natural sources and require supplements to prevent loss of strength in bones.
Barbiturates	May reduce effect of vitamin D from natural sources and require supplements to prevent loss of strength in bones.
Calcitonin	Reduces effect of calcitonin when treating hypercalcaemia
Calcium (high doses)	Increases risk of hypercalcaemia
Cholestyramine	Impairs absorption of vitamin D. May need supplements.
Colestipol	Impairs absorption of vitamin D. May need supplements.
Digitalis preparations	Increases risk of heartbeat irregularities.
Diuretics, thiazide	Increases risk of hypercalcaemia
Hydantoin	May reduce effect of vitamin D from natural sources and require supplements to prevent loss of strength in bones.
Mineral oil	Increases absorption of vitamin D. May need supplements.
Phosphorous-containing medicines	Increases risk of too much phosphorous in blood.
Primidone	May reduce effect of vitamin D from natural sources and require supplements to prevent loss of strength in bones.
Vitamin-D derivatives, such as calciferol, calcitrol, dihydrotachysterol, ergocalciferol	Additive effects may increase potential for toxicity.

Interaction with Other Substances

Chronic alcoholism depletes liver stores of vitamin D.

Calcitrol

Basic Information

Calcitrol is a form of vitamin D. *It is also called* ergocalciferol.
Available from natural sources? Yes
Available from synthetic sources? Yes
Prescription required? Yes
Fat-soluble or water-soluble: Fat-soluble

Natural Sources

Cod-liver oil	Salmon
Halibut-liver oil	Sardines
Herring	Sunlight
Mackerel	Vitamin-D-fortified milk

Reasons to Use

- Calcitrol is a form of vitamin D primarily used to treat hypocalcaemia (not enough calcium in blood). It is also frequently prescribed to treat bone disease in people undergoing renal dialysis, and patients with hypoparathyroidism.
  bone by controlling absorption of calcium and phosphorus from small intestine.
- Prevents rickets.
- Treats post-operative muscle contractions.
- Works with calcium to control bone formation.
- Promotes normal growth and development of infants and children, particularly bones and teeth.

Unproved Speculated Benefits

- Cures arthritis.
- Prevents colon cancer.
- Treats aging symptoms.
- Treats acne.
- Treats alcoholism.
- Treats herpes simplex and herpes zoster.
- Treats cystic fibrosis.

Who Needs Additional Amounts?

- Children who live in sunshine-deficient areas.
- Anyone with inadequate caloric or nutritional dietary intake or increased nutritional requirements.
- Older people (over 55 years), especially women after menopause.
- Pregnant or breast-feeding women.
- Those who abuse alcohol or other drugs.
- People with a chronic wasting illness, excess stress for long periods or those who have recently undergone surgery.
- Those with a portion of the gastrointestinal tract surgically removed.
- People with recent severe burns or injuries.

Deficiency Symptoms

- Rickets (a childhood deficiency disase): bent, bowed legs, malformations of joints or bones, late tooth development, weak muscles, listlessness.
- Osteomalacia (adult rickets): muscle weakness and spasm, brittle, easily broken bones, pain in ribs, lower spine, pelvis and legs,

Unproved Speculated Symptoms

- Muscle diseases (myopathies)

Lab Tests to Detect Deficiency

- Reduced levels of vitamin D forms in blood.
- Decreased serum phosphate, decreased calcium, increased alkaline phosphatase, urinary hydroxyproline, PTH levels.
- Bone X-ray.

Dosage and Usage Information

Recommended Dietary Allowance (RDA):
Estimate of adequate daily intake by the Food and Nutrition Board of the National Research Council, 1980. See Glossary.

Age	RDA
0–6 months	10mcg
6–12 months	10mcg
1–10 years	10mcg
Males	
11–18 years	10mcg
19–22 years	7.5mcg
23+ years	5mcg
Females	
11–18 years	10mcg
19–22 years	7.5mcg
23+ years	5mcg
Pregnant	+5mcg
Lactating	+5mcg

➤➤

What this vitamin does:
- Absorbs and uses calcium and phosphorous to make bone.
- Essential for normal growth and development.

Miscellaneous information:
- Take at the same time every day.
- Put liquid vitamin D directly into mouth or mix with cereal, fruit juice or food.

Available as:
- Extended-release capsules or tablets: Swallow whole with full glass of liquid. Don't chew or crush. Take with or immediately after food to decrease stomach irritation.
- Oral solution: Dilute in at least 1/2 glass water or other liquid. Take with meals or 1 to 1-1/2 hours after meals unless otherwise directed by your doctor.
- Some forms available by generic name.

Warnings and Precautions

Don't take if you:
- Are allergic to vitamin D, ergocalciferol or any vitamin-D derivative.

Consult your doctor if you have:
- Any plans to become pregnant while taking vitamin D.
- Epilepsy.
- Heart or blood-vessel disease.
- Kidney, liver, pancreatic disease.
- Chronic diarrhoea.
- Intestinal problems.
- Sarcoidosis.

Over age 55:
- Adverse reactions and side effects are more likely. Supplements are often necessary.

Pregnancy:
- Taking too much during pregnancy may cause abnormalities in fetus. Consult doctor before taking supplement to ensure correct dosage.
- Don't take megadoses.

Breast-feeding:
- Important for you to receive correct amount so enough vitamin D is available for normal growth and development of baby. Consult doctor about supplements.
- Don't take megadoses.

Effect on lab tests:
- May decrease serum alkaline phosphatase.
- May increase levels of calcium, cholesterol and phosphate in test results.
- May increase level of magnesium in test results.
- May increase amounts of calcium and phosphorous in urine.

Storage:
- Store in cool, dry place away from direct light, but don't freeze. Avoid overexposure to air.
- Store safely out of reach of children.
- Don't store in bathroom medicine cabinet. Heat and moisture may change action of vitamin.

Others:
- Absence of sunlight prevents natural formation of vitamin D by skin. Sunshine provides sufficient amounts of vitamin D for people who live in sunny climates. Those who live in northern areas with fewer days of sunshine and extended periods of cloud cover and darkness must depend on dietary sources for vitamin D.
- Avoid megadoses.

Overdose/Toxicity

Signs and symptoms:
High blood pressure, irregular heartbeat, nausea, weight loss, seizures, abdominal pain, appetite loss, mental and physical-growth retardation, premature hardening of arteries, kidney damage.

What to do:
For symptoms of overdosage: Discontinue vitamin, and consult doctor. Also see *Adverse Reactions or Side Effects* section below.

For accidental overdosage (such as child taking entire bottle): Dial 999 (emergency).

For toxic symptoms: Discontinue vitamin, and seek immediate medical help. Hospitalization may be necessary.

≫▶

Calcitrol, Continued

Adverse Reactions or Side Effects

Reaction or effect	What to do
Appetite loss	Discontinue. Call doctor when convenient.
Constipation	Discontinue. Call doctor when convenient.
Diarrhoea	Discontinue. Call doctor immediately.
Dry mouth	Discontinue. Call doctor when convenient.
Headache	Discontinue. Call doctor immediately.
Increased thirst	Discontinue. Call doctor when convenient.
Mental confusion	Discontinue. Call doctor immediately.
Metallic taste	Discontinue. Call doctor when convenient.
Nausea	Discontinue. Call doctor immediately.
Unusual tiredness	Discontinue. Call doctor when convenient.
Vomiting	Discontinue. Call doctor immediately.

Interaction with Medicine, Vitamins or Minerals

Interacts with	Combined effect
Antacids with aluminium	Decreases absorption of vitamin D and fat-soluble vitamins A, D, E, K.
Antacids with magnesium	May cause too much magnesium in blood, especially for people with kidney failure.
Anti-convulsants	May reduce effect of vitamin D from natural sources and require supplements to prevent loss of strength in bones.
Barbiturates	May reduce effect of vitamin D from natural sources and require supplements to prevent loss of strength in bones.
Calcitonin	Reduces effect of calcitonin when treating hypercalcaemia
Calcium (high doses)	Increases risk of hypercalcaemia
Cholestyramine	Impairs absorption of vitamin D. May need supplements.
Colestipol	Impairs absorption of vitamin D. May need supplements.
Digitalis preparations	Increases risk of heartbeat irregularities.
Diuretics, thiazide	Increases risk of hypercalcaemia
Hydantoin	May reduce effect of vitamin D from natural sources and require supplements to prevent loss of strength in bones.
Mineral oil	Increases absorption of vitamin D. May need supplements.
Phosphorous-containing medicines	Increases risk of too much phosphorous in blood.
Primidone	May reduce effect of vitamin D from natural sources and require supplements to prevent loss of strength in bones.
Vitamin-D derivatives, such as calciferol, calcitrol, dihydrotachysterol, ergocalciferol	Additive effects may increase potential for toxicity.

Interaction with Other Substances

Chronic alcoholism depletes liver stores of vitamin D.

Children's Multivitamin With Fluoride

Basic Information

Available from natural sources? No
Available from synthetic sources? Yes
Prescription required? Yes
Fat-soluble or water-soluble: Fat-soluble and water-soluble

 ## Natural Sources

These are all manufactured products.

 ## Reasons to Use

• Prevents vitamin deficiency of essential fat-soluble and water-soluble vitamins when the daily diet doesn't include enough of these vitamins needed for good health.
• Prevents dental caries in children who live in areas where naturally occurring fluoride in drinking water is inadequate.

 ## Unproved Speculated Benefits

• Prevents dental caries in adults.
• Prevents dental plaque bacteria from causing damage to normal teeth.

 ## Who Needs Additional Amounts?

• Anyone with inadequate caloric or nutritional dietary intake or increased nutritional requirements.

 ## Deficiency Symptoms

• Frequent dental caries (cavities in teeth)
• Failure to grow and develop normally

 ## Unproved Speculated Symptoms

• Dental plaque in adolescents and adults

 ## Lab Tests to Detect Deficiency

• None readily available to test for multiple-vitamin deficiency.
• Dental X-rays detect dental caries and suggest fluoride deficiency.

 ## Dosage and Usage Information

Recommended Dietary Allowance (RDA):
No RDA has been established for multiple vitamins. See individual vitamin charts for recommendations for vitamins A, D, C.

What this vitamin does:
• Fluoride becomes incorporated into bone and teeth, promotes remineralization of decalcified enamel and *may* interfere with growth and development of bacteria that cause dental plaque.

Miscellaneous information:
• Fluorides dissolve easily and can be absorbed easily from the stomach and intestines.
• Fluoride applications to teeth and fluoride toothpaste and mouthwash also help prevent caries.

Available as:
• Oral solution: Dilute in at least 1/2 glass water or other liquid. Take after brushing teeth, immediately before bedtime.
• Chewable tablets: Chew well before swallowing. Take after brushing teeth, immediately before bedtime.

 ## Warnings and Precautions

Don't take if you:
• Are allergic to vitamins A, D, C or fluoride.
• Have evidence of dental fluorosis (dark-brown stains on teeth).

Consult your doctor if you have:
• Ever lived in an area where fluoride in drinking water is excessive.
• Hypothyroidism.

Over age 55:
• Probably not useful.

Pregnancy:
• Take only under medical supervision.

Breast-feeding:
• Take only under medical supervision.

»»▶

Children's Multivitamin With Fluoride, Continued

Effect on lab tests:
- Falsely decreases serum acid phosphatase
- Falsely increases SGOT (serum aspartate aminotransferase)
- Falsely decreases PBI (protein-bound iodine)
- Decreases serum calcium

Storage:
- Store in cool, dry place away from direct light, but don't freeze.
- Store safely out of reach of children.
- Don't store in bathroom medicine cabinet. Heat and moisture may change action of combination.

 ## Overdose/Toxicity

Signs and symptoms:
Black, tarry stools, bloody vomit, diarrhoea, drowsiness, shallow breathing, abdominal cramping, pain, increased salivation.

What to do:
For symptoms of overdosage: Discontinue vitamin, and consult doctor. Also see *Adverse Reactions or Side Effects* section below.
For accidental overdosage (such as child taking entire bottle): Dial 999 (emergency).

 ## Adverse Reactions or Side Effects

Reaction or effect	What to do
Aching pain in bones	Discontinue. Call doctor immediately.
Appetite loss	Discontinue. Call doctor when convenient.
Joint stiffness	Discontinue. Call doctor when convenient.
Mouth sores	Discontinue. Call doctor immediately.
Skin rash	Discontinue. Call doctor immediately.
Weight loss, large	Discontinue. Call doctor immediately.
White, brown or black mottled discolouration of teeth	Discontinue. Call doctor when convenient.

 ## Interaction with Medicine, Vitamins or Minerals

Interacts with	Combined effect
Anti-coagulants	Increases bleeding
Aluminum hydroxide	Decreases absorption of vitamins and fluoride
Iron supplements	Decreases effect of iron
Vitamin-D preparations	Increases possibility of toxic effects of vitamin D

 ## Interaction with Other Substances

Milk and **milk products** may decrease absorption of fluoride. Take fluoride at least 2 hours before or after drinking milk.

Vitamin D

Basic Information

Vitamin D is also called cholecalciferol.
Available from natural sources? Yes
Available from synthetic sources? Yes
Prescription required? No
Fat-soluble or water-soluble: Fat-soluble

Natural Sources

Cod-liver oil	Salmon
Halibut-liver oil	Sardines
Herring	Sunlight
Mackerel	Vitamin-D-fortified milk

Reasons to Use

- Regulates growth, hardening and repair of bone by controlling absorption of calcium and phosphorus from small intestine.
- Prevents rickets.
- Treats hypocalcaemia (low blood calcium) in kidney disease.
- Treats post-operative muscle contractions.
- Works with calcium to control bone formation.
- Promotes normal growth and development of infants and children, particularly bones and teeth.

Unproved Speculated Benefits

- Cures arthritis.
- Prevents colon cancer.
- Treats aging symptoms.
- Treats acne.
- Treats alcoholism.
- Treats herpes simplex and herpes zoster.
- Treats cystic fibrosis.

Who Needs Additional Amounts?

- Children who live in sunshine-deficient areas.
- Anyone with inadequate caloric or nutritional dietary intake or increased nutritional requirements.
- Older people (over 55 years), especially women after menopause.
- Pregnant or breast-feeding women.
- Those who abuse alcohol or other drugs.
- People with a chronic wasting illness, excess stress for long periods or who have recently undergone surgery.

- Those with a portion of the gastrointestinal tract surgically removed.
- People with recent severe burns or injuries.

Deficiency Symptoms

- Rickets (a childhood deficiency disease): bent, bowed legs, malformations of joints or bones, late tooth development, weak muscles, listlessness.
- Osteomalacia (adult rickets): pain in ribs, lower spine, pelvis and legs, muscle weakness and spasm, brittle, easily broken bones.

Unproved Speculated Symptoms

- Muscle diseases (myopathies)

Lab Tests to Detect Deficiency

- Reduced levels of vitamin D forms in blood.
- Decreased serum phosphate, decreased calcium, increased alkaline phosphatase, urinary hydroxyproline, PTH levels.
- Bone X-ray.

Dosage and Usage Information

Recommended Dietary Allowance (RDA):
Estimate of adequate daily intake by the Food and Nutrition Board of the National Research Council, 1980. See Glossary.

Age	RDA
0–6 months	10mcg
6–12 months	10mcg
1–10 years	10mcg
Males	
11–18 years	10mcg
19–22 years	7.5mcg
23+ years	5mcg
Females	
11–18 years	10mcg
19–22 years	7.5mcg
23+ years	5mcg
Pregnant	+5mcg
Lactating	+5mcg

What this vitamin does:
- Absorbs and uses calcium and phosphorous to make bone.
- Essential for normal growth and development.

⟫→

Vitamin D, Continued

Miscellaneous Information:
- Take at the same time every day.
- Put liquid vitamin D directly into mouth or mix with cereal, fruit juice or food.

Available as:
- Extended-release capsules or tablets: Swallow whole with full glass of liquid. Don't chew or crush. Take with or immediately after food to decrease stomach irritation.
- Oral solution: Dilute in at least 1/2 glass water or other liquid. Take with meals or 1 to 1-1/2 hours after meals unless otherwise directed by your doctor.
- A constituent of many multivitamin/mineral preparations.
- Some forms available by generic name.

Warnings and Precautions

Don't take if you:
- Are allergic to vitamin D, ergocalciferol or any vitamin-D derivative.

Consult your doctor if you have:
- Any plans to become pregnant while taking vitamin D.
- Epilepsy.
- Heart or blood-vessel disease.
- Kidney, liver, pancreatic disease.
- Chronic diarrhoea.
- Intestinal problems.
- Sarcoidosis.

Over age 55:
- Adverse reactions and side effects are more likely. Supplements are often necessary.

Pregnancy:
- Taking too much during pregnancy may cause abnormalities in fetus. Consult doctor before taking supplement to ensure correct dosage.
- Don't take megadoses.

Breast-feeding:
- Important for you to receive correct amount so enough vitamin D is available for normal growth and development of baby. Consult doctor about supplements.
- Don't take megadoses.

Effect on lab tests:
- May decrease serum alkaline phosphatase.
- May increase levels of calcium, cholesterol and phosphate in test results.
- May increase level of magnesium in test results.
- May increase amounts of calcium and phosphorous in urine.

Storage:
- Store in cool, dry place away from direct light, but don't freeze. Avoid overexposure to air.
- Store safely out of reach of children.
- Don't store in bathroom medicine cabinet. Heat and moisture may change action of vitamin.

Others:
- Absence of sunlight prevents natural formation of vitamin D by skin. Sunshine provides sufficient amounts of vitamin D for people who live in sunny climates. Those who live in northern areas with fewer days of sunshine and extended periods of cloud cover and darkness must depend on dietary sources for vitamin D.
- Avoid megadoses.

Overdose/Toxicity

Signs and symptoms:
High blood pressure, irregular heartbeat, nausea, weight loss, seizures, abdominal pain, appetite loss, mental and physical-growth retardation, premature hardening of arteries, kidney damage.

What to do:
For symptoms of overdosage: Discontinue vitamin, and consult doctor. Also see *Adverse Reactions or Side Effects* section below.
For accidental overdosage (such as child taking entire bottle): Dial 999 (emergency).
For toxic symptoms: Discontinue vitamin and seek immediate medical help. Hospitalization may be necessary.

»▸

Adverse Reactions or Side Effects

Reaction or effect	What to do
Appetite loss	Discontinue. Call doctor when convenient.
Constipation	Discontinue. Call doctor when convenient.
Diarrhoea	Discontinue. Call doctor immediately.
Dry mouth	Discontinue. Call doctor when convenient.
Headache	Discontinue. Call doctor immediately.
Increased thirst	Discontinue. Call doctor when convenient.
Mental confusion	Discontinue. Call doctor immediately.
Metallic taste	Discontinue. Call doctor when convenient.
Nausea	Discontinue. Call doctor immediately.
Unusual tiredness	Discontinue. Call doctor when convenient.
Vomiting	Discontinue. Call doctor immediately.

Interaction with Medicine, Vitamins or Minerals

Interacts with	Combined effect
Antacids with aluminium	Decreases absorption of vitamin D and fat-soluble vitamins A, D, E, K.
Antacids with magnesium	May cause too much magnesium in blood, especially for people with kidney failure.
Anti-convulsants	May reduce effect of vitamin D from natural sources and require supplements to prevent loss of strength in bones.
Barbiturates	May reduce effect of vitamin D from natural sources and require supplements to prevent loss of strength in bones.

Calcitonin	Reduces effect of calcitonin when treating hypercalcaemia
Calcium (high doses)	Increases risk of hypercalcaemia
Cholestyramine	Impairs absorption of vitamin D. May need supplements.
Colestipol	Impairs absorption of vitamin D. May need supplements.
Digitalis preparations	Increases risk of heartbeat irregularities.
Diuretics, thiazide	Increases risk of hypercalcaemia
Hydantoin	May reduce effect of vitamin D from natural sources and require supplements to prevent loss of strength in bones.
Mineral oil	Increases absorption of vitamin D. May need supplements.
Phosphorous-containing medicines	Increases risk of too much phosphorous in blood.
Primidone	May reduce effect of vitamin D from natural sources and require supplements to prevent loss of strength in bones.
Vitamin-D derivatives, such as calciferol, calcitrol, dihydrotachysterol, ergocalciferol	Additive effects may increase potential for toxicity.

Interaction with Other Substances

Chronic alcoholism depletes liver stores of vitamin D.

Dihydrotachysterol

Basic Information

Dihydrotachysterol is a form of vitamin D. *It is also called* ergocalciferol.
Available from natural sources? Yes
Available from synthetic sources? Yes
Prescription required? Yes
Fat-soluble or water-soluble: Fat-soluble

Natural Sources

Cod-liver oil	Salmon
Halibut-liver oil	Sardines
Herring	Sunlight
Mackerel	Vitamin-D-fortified milk

Reasons to Use

- Dihydrotachysterol is primarily used to treat hypocalcaemia (not enough calcium in blood) in people with chronic kidney failure or hypoparathyroidism.
- Regulates growth, hardening and repair of bone by controlling absorption of calcium and phosphorus from small intestine.
- Prevents rickets.
- Treats post-operative muscle contractions.
- Works with calcium to control bone formation.
- Promotes normal growth and development of infants and children, particularly bones and teeth.

Unproved Speculated Benefits

- Cures arthritis.
- Prevents colon cancer.
- Treats aging symptoms.
- Treats acne.
- Treats alcoholism.
- Treats herpes simplex and herpes zoster.
- Treats cystic fibrosis.

Who Needs Additional Amounts?

- Children who live in sunshine-deficient areas.
- Anyone with inadequate caloric or nutritional dietary intake or increased nutritional requirements.
- Older people (over 55 years), especially women after menopause.
- Pregnant or breast-feeding women.
- Those who abuse alcohol or other drugs.

- People with a chronic wasting illness, excess stress for long periods or those who have recently undergone surgery.
- Those with a portion of the gastrointestinal tract surgically removed.
- People with recent severe burns or injuries.

Deficiency Symptoms

- Rickets (a childhood deficiency disease): bent, bowed legs, malformations of joints or bones, late tooth development, weak muscles, listlessness.
- Osteomalacia (adult rickets): muscle weakness and spasm, brittle, easily broken bones, pain in ribs, lower spine, pelvis, legs.

Unproved Speculated Symptoms

- Muscle diseases (myopathies)

Lab Tests to Detect Deficiency

- Reduced levels of vitamin D forms in blood.
- Decreased serum phosphate, decreased calcium, increased alkaline phosphatase, urinary hydroxyproline, PTH levels.
- Bone X-ray.

Dosage and Usage Information

Recommended Dietary Allowance (RDA):
Estimate of adequate daily intake by the Food and Nutrition Board of the National Research Council, 1980. See Glossary.

Age	RDA
0–6 months	10mcg
6–12 months	10mcg
1–10 years	10mcg
Males	
11–18 years	10mcg
19–22 years	7.5mcg
23+ years	5mcg
Females	
11–18 years	10mcg
19–22 years	7.5mcg
23+ years	5mcg
Pregnant	+5mcg
Lactating	+5mcg

⟫▸

Dihydrotachysterol

VITAMIN

What this vitamin does:
- Absorbs and uses calcium and phosphorous to make bone.
- Essential for normal growth and development.

Miscellaneous information:
- Take at the same time every day.
- Put liquid vitamin D directly into mouth or mix with cereal, fruit juice or food.

Available as:
- Extended-release capsules or tablets: Swallow whole with full glass of liquid. Don't chew or crush. Take with or immediately after food to decrease stomach irritation.
- Oral solution: Dilute in at least 1/2 glass water or other liquid. Take with meals or 1 to 1-1/2 hours after meals unless otherwise directed by your doctor.
- A constituent of many multivitamin/mineral preparations.
- Some forms available by generic name.

Warnings and Precautions

Don't take if you:
- Are allergic to vitamin D, ergocalciferol or any vitamin-D derivative.

Consult your doctor if you have:
- Any plans to become pregnant while taking vitamin D.
- Epilepsy.
- Heart or blood-vessel disease.
- Kidney, liver, pancreatic disease.
- Chronic diarrhoea.
- Intestinal problems.
- Sarcoidosis.

Over age 55:
- Adverse reactions and side effects are more likely. Supplements are often necessary.

Pregnancy:
- Taking too much during pregnancy may cause abnormalities in fetus. Consult doctor before taking supplement to ensure correct dosage.
- Don't take megadoses.

Breast-feeding:
- Important for you to receive correct amount so enough vitamin D is available for normal growth and development of baby. Consult doctor about supplements.
- Don't take megadoses.

Effect on lab tests:
- May decrease serum alkaline phosphatase.
- May increase levels of calcium, cholesterol and phosphate in test results.
- May increase level of magnesium in test results.
- May increase amounts of calcium and phosphorous in urine.

Storage:
- Store in cool, dry place away from direct light, but don't freeze. Avoid overexposure to air.
- Store safely out of reach of children.
- Don't store in bathroom medicine cabinet. Heat and moisture may change action of vitamin.

Others:
- Absence of sunlight prevents natural formation of vitamin D by skin. Sunshine provides sufficient amounts of vitamin D for people who live in sunny climates. Those who live in northern areas with fewer days of sunshine and extended periods of cloud cover and darkness must depend on dietary sources for vitamin D.
- Avoid megadoses.

Overdose/Toxicity

Signs and symptoms:
High blood pressure, irregular heartbeat, nausea, weight loss, seizures, abdominal pain, appetite loss, mental and physical-growth retardation, premature hardening of arteries, kidney damage.

What to do:
For symptoms of overdosage: Discontinue vitamin, and consult doctor. Also see *Adverse Reactions or Side Effects* section below.
For accidental overdosage (such as child taking entire bottle): Dial 999 (emergency).
For toxic symptoms: Discontinue vitamin, and seek immediate medical help. Hospitalization may be necessary.

45

Dihydrotachysterol, Continued

Adverse Reactions or Side Effects

Reaction or effect	What to do
Appetite loss	Discontinue. Call doctor when convenient.
Constipation	Discontinue. Call doctor when convenient.
Diarrhoea	Discontinue. Call doctor immediately.
Dry mouth	Discontinue. Call doctor when convenient.
Headache	Discontinue. Call doctor immediately.
Increased thirst	Discontinue. Call doctor when convenient.
Mental confusion	Discontinue. Call doctor immediately.
Metallic taste	Discontinue. Call doctor when convenient.
Nausea	Discontinue. Call doctor immediately.
Unusual tiredness	Discontinue. Call doctor when convenient.
Vomiting	Discontinue. Call doctor immediately.

Interaction with Medicine, Vitamins or Minerals

Interacts with	Combined effect
Antacids with aluminium	Decreases absorption of vitamin D and fat-soluble vitamins A, D, E, K.
Antacids with magnesium	May cause too much magnesium in blood, especially for people with kidney failure.
Anti-convulsants	May reduce effect of vitamin D from natural sources and require supplements to prevent loss of strength in bones.
Barbiturates	May reduce effect of vitamin D from natural sources and require supplements to prevent loss of strength in bones.
Calcitonin	Reduces effect of calcitonin when treating hypercalcaemia.
Calcium (high doses)	Increases risk of hypercalcaemia.
Cholestyramine	Impairs absorption of vitamin D. May need supplements.
Colestipol	Impairs absorption of vitamin D. May need supplements.
Digitalis preparations	Increases risk of heartbeat irregularities.
Diuretics, thiazide	Increases risk of hypercalcaemia.
Hydantoin	May reduce effect of vitamin D from natural sources and require supplements to prevent loss of strength in bones.
Mineral oil	Increases absorption of vitamin D. May need supplements.
Phosphorous-containing medicines	Increases risk of too much phosphorous in blood.
Primidone	May reduce effect of vitamin D from natural sources and require supplements to prevent loss of strength in bones.
Vitamin-D derivatives, such as calciferol, calcitrol, dihydrotachysterol, ergocalciferol	Additive effects may increase potential for toxicity.

Interaction with Other Substances

Chronic alcoholism depletes liver stores of vitamin D.

VITAMIN

Basic Information

Vitamin E is also called alpha-tocopherol.
Available from natural sources? Yes
Available from synthetic sources? Yes
Prescription required? Yes, for injectable forms
Fat-soluble or water-soluble: Fat-soluble

Natural Sources

Almonds	Peanut oil
Apricot oil	Safflower nuts
Corn oil	Sunflower seeds
Cottonseed oil	Walnuts
Hazelnuts (filberts)	Wheat germ
Margarine	Whole-wheat flour

Reasons to Use

- Promotes normal growth and development.
- Treats and prevents vitamin-E deficiency in premature or low-birth-weight infants.
- Prevents oxidation of free radicals in body.
- Acts as anti-blood clotting agent.
- Protects tissue against oxidation.
- Promotes normal red-blood-cell formation.

Unproved Speculated Benefits

- Treats fibrocystic disease of breast.
- Treats circulatory problems of lower extremities.
- Treats sickle-cell anaemia.
- Treats lung toxicity from air pollution.
- Prevents or alleviates coronary-artery heart disease.
- Enhances sexual performance.
- Improves muscle strength and stamina.
- Heals burns and wounds.
- Retards aging.
- Prevents hair loss.
- Prevents abortion.
- Treats menopause.
- Helps overcome infertility.
- Treats bee stings, liver spots on hands, bursitis, nappy rash.
- Prevents and treats cancer.
- Decreases scarring.
- Improves athletic performance.
- Treats muscular dystrophy, heart degeneration, anaemia.
- Treats acne.
- Prevents eye problems and lung problems in low-birth-weight or premature infants.

Who Needs Additional Amounts?

- Anyone with inadequate caloric or nutritional dietary intake or increased nutritional requirements.
- Older people (over 55 years).
- Those who abuse alcohol or other drugs.
- People who have a chronic wasting illness, excess stress for long periods or those who have recently undergone surgery.
- Those with part of the gastrointestinal tract surgically removed.
- People with recent severe burns or injuries.
- People with hyperthyroidism.

Deficiency Symptoms

Premature infants and children:
- Irritability
- Oedema
- Haemolytic anaemia

Adults:
- Lack of vitality
- Lethargy
- Apathy
- Inability to concentrate
- Irritability
- Disinterest in physical activity
- Decreased sexual performance
- Muscle weakness

Unproved Speculated Symptoms

- Indigestion
- Low libido and impotence
- Premature aging
- Chest pain

Lab Tests to Detect Deficiency

- Blood tocopherol level
- Excess creatine in urine to indicate muscle breakdown
- Red-blood-cell fragility test

»➤

Dosage and Usage Information

Estimate of adequate daily intake by the Food and Nutrition Board of the National Research Council, 1980. See Glossary.

Age	RDA
0–12 months	3–4mg
1–7 years	5–7mg
11–18 years	8mg
Males	
18+ years	10mg
Females	
18+ years	8mg
Pregnant	+ 2mg
Lactating	+ 3mg

Note: 1mg vitamin E equals 1IU. Labels may list as mg or IU.

What this vitamin does:
* Prevents a chemical reaction called *oxidation.* Excessive oxidation can sometimes cause harmful effects.
* Acts as a co-factor in several enzyme systems.

Miscellaneous information:
* Take at same time every day.
* Vitamin E is a constituent of many skin ointments, salves and creams. Claims for beneficial effects have not been confirmed, but topical application probably does not cause harm.
* May require several weeks of treatment before symptoms caused by deficiency will improve.
* Freezing may destroy vitamin E.
* Extreme heat causes vitamin E to break down. Avoid deep-fat frying foods that are natural sources of vitamin E.
* Vitamin E functions as an anti-oxidant, prevents enzyme action of peroxidase on unsaturated bonds of cell membranes and protects red blood cells from disintegrating.

Available as:
* Tablets or capsules: Swallow whole with full glass of liquid. Don't chew or crush. Take with or immediately after food to decrease stomach irritation.
* Drops: Dilute dose in beverage before swallowing, or squirt directly into mouth.
* A constituent of many multivitamin/mineral preparations.

Warnings and Precautions

Don't take if you:
* Are allergic to vitamin E.

Consult your doctor if you have:
* Iron-deficiency anaemia.
* Bleeding or clotting problems.
* Cystic fibrosis.
* Intestinal problems.
* Liver disease.
* Overactive thyroid.

Over age 55:
* No problems expected.

Pregnancy:
* No problems expected, except with megadoses.

Breast-feeding:
* No problems expected.
* Don't take megadoses.

Effect on lab tests:
* Serum cholesterol and serum triglycerides may register *high* if you take large doses of vitamin E.

Storage:
* Store in cool, dry area away from direct light, but don't freeze.
* Store safely out of reach of children.
* Don't store in bathroom medicine cabinet. Heat and moisture may change action of the vitamin.

Others:
* Beware of megadoses.

Overdose/Toxicity

Signs and symptoms:
High doses deplete vitamin-A stores in body. Very high doses (over 800 mg/day) causes tendency to bleed, altered immunity, impaired sex functions, increased risk of blood clots, altered metabolism of thyroid, pituitary and adrenal hormones.

What to do:
For other symptoms of toxicity: Discontinue vitamin, and consult doctor. Also see *Adverse Reactions or Side Effects* section below.
For accidental overdosage (such as child taking entire bottle): Dial 999 (emergency).

➥➤

Adverse Reactions or Side Effects

Reaction or Effect	What to do
Abdominal pain	Discontinue. Call doctor immediately.
Breast enlargement	Discontinue. Call doctor when convenient.
Diarrhoea	Discontinue. Call doctor immediately.
Dizziness	Discontinue. Call doctor when convenient.
Flu-like symptoms	Discontinue. Call doctor immediately.
Headache	Discontinue. Call doctor when convenient.
Nausea	Discontinue. Call doctor immediately.
Tiredness or weakness	Discontinue. Call doctor when convenient.
Vision blurred	Discontinue. Call doctor immediately.

 ## Interaction with Medicine, Vitamins or Minerals

Interacts with	Combined effect
Antacids	Decreases vitamin-E absorption.
Anti-coagulants, coumarin- or indandione-type	May increase spontaneous or hidden bleeding.
Cholestyramine	May decrease absorption of vitamin E.
Colestipol	May decrease absorption of vitamin E.
Iron supplements	Decreases effect of iron supplement in people with iron-deficiency anaemia. Decreases vitamin-E effect in healthy people.
Mineral oil	May decrease absorption of vitamin E.
Sucralfate	May decrease absorption of vitamin E.
Vitamin A	Facilitates absorption, storage and utilization of vitamin A. Reduces potential toxicity of vitamin A. Excessive doses of vitamin E causes vitamin-A depletion.

 ## Interaction with Other substances

Tobacco decreases absorption. Smokers may require supplementary vitamin E.

Chronic alcoholism depletes vitamin-E stores in liver.

Folic Acid (Vitamin B-9)

Basic Information

Folic acid is also called folate, pteroyglutamic acid, folacin.
Available from natural sources? Yes
Available from synthetic sources? Yes
Prescription required? Yes, for injectable forms
Fat-soluble or water-soluble? Water-soluble

Natural Sources

Barley	Lentils
Beans	Orange juice
Brewer's yeast	Oranges
Calves' liver	Peas
Endive	Rice
Fruits	Soybeans
Garbanzo beans	Split peas
(chickpeas)	Sprouts
Green, leafy	Wheat
vegetables	Wheat germ

Reasons to Use

- Promotes normal red-blood-cell formation.
- Maintains nervous system, intestinal tract, sex organs, white blood cells, normal patterns of growth.
- Regulates embryonic and fetal development of nerve cells.
- Promotes normal growth and development.
- Treats anaemias due to folic-acid deficiency occurring from alcoholism, liver disease, haemolytic anaemia, sprue, pregnancy, breast-feeding, oral-contraceptive use.

Unproved Speculated Benefits

- Prevents mental problems.
- Acts as a natural analgesic or pain killer.

Who Needs Additional Amounts?

- Anyone with inadequate caloric or nutritional dietary intake or increased nutritional requirements.
- Older people (over 55 years).
- Pregnant or breast-feeding women.
- Women who use oral contraceptives.
- Those who abuse alcohol or other drugs.

- People with a chronic wasting illness, excess stress for long periods or those who have recently undergone surgery.
- Those with a portion of the gastrointestinal tract surgically removed.
- People with recent severe burns or injuries.
- Young infants not receiving breast milk or fortified commercial formula.
- Extremely ill people who must be fed intravenously or by naso-gastric tube.

Deficiency Symptoms

- Haemolytic and megaloblastic anaemia in which red blood cells are large and uneven in size, have a shorter life span or are likely to have cell membranes rupture
- Irritability
- Weakness
- Lack of energy
- Sleeping difficulties
- Paleness
- Sore red tongue
- Mild mental symptoms, such as forgetfulness and confusion
- Diarrhoea

Unproved Speculated Symptoms

- Depression
- Cervical dysplasia
- Psychosis

Lab Tests to Detect Deficiency

- Serum folic acid
- Blood cells showing macrocytic anaemia coupled with normal levels of B-12 in blood.

Dosage and Usage Information

Recommended Dietary Allowance (RDA):
Estimate of adequate daily intake by the Food and Nutrition Board of the National Research Council, 1980. See Glossary.

➤➤

Age	RDA
0–6 months	30mcg
6–12 months	45mcg
1–3 years	100mcg
4–6 years	200mcg
7–10 years	300mcg
11+ years	400mcg
Pregnant	+400mcg
Lactating	+100mcg

What this vitamin does:
• Acts as co-enzyme for normal DNA synthesis.
• Functions as part of co-enzyme in amino acid and nucleoprotein synthesis.
• Promotes normal red-blood-cell formation.

Miscellaneous information:
• Cooking vegetables causes loss of some folic-acid content.

Available as:
• Tablets: Swallow whole with full glass of liquid. Don't chew or crush. Take with meals or 1 to 1-1/2 hours after meals unless otherwise directed by your doctor.
Note: Folic acid is sometimes omitted from multivitamin/mineral preparations. Check labels.

 Warnings and Precautions

Don't take if you:
• Have pernicious anaemia. Folic acid will make the blood appear normal, but neurological problems may progress and be irreversible.

Consult your doctor if you have:
• Anaemia

Over age 55:
• No problems expected.

Pregnancy:
• No problems expected.
• Don't take megadoses.

Breast-feeding:
• No problems expected.
• Don't take megadoses.

Effect on lab tests:
• May cause false-low results in tests for vitamin B-12.

Storage:
• Store in cool, dry place away from direct light, but don't freeze.
• Store safely out of reach of children.
• Don't store in bathroom medicine cabinet. Heat and moisture may change action of vitamin.

Others:
• Renal dialysis reduces blood folic acid. Patients on dialysis should increase RDA by 300%.

 Overdose/Toxicity

Signs and symptoms:
Prolonged use of high doses can produce damaging folacin crystals in the kidney. Doses over 1,500mcg/day can cause appetite loss, nausea, flatulence, abdominal distension, may obscure existence of pernicious anaemia.

What to do:
For symptoms of overdosage: Discontinue vitamin, and consult doctor. Also see *Adverse Reactions or Side Effects* section below.
For accidental overdosage (such as child taking entire bottle): Dial 999 (emergency).

Folic Acid (Vitamin B-9), Continued

 Adverse Reactions or Side Effects

Reaction or effect	What to do
Bright-yellow urine (always)	Nothing.
Diarrhoea	Discontinue. Call doctor immediately.
Fever	Discontinue. Call doctor immediately.
Skin rash	Discontinue. Call doctor when convenient.

 Interaction with Medicine, Vitamins or Minerals

Interacts with	Combined effect
Analgesics	Decreases effect of folic acid.
Antibiotics	May cause false-low results in tests for serum-folic acid.
Anti-convulsants	Decreases effect of folic acid and anti-convulsant.
Chloramphenicol	Produces folic-acid deficiency.
Cortisone drugs	Decreases effect of folic acid.
Methotrexate	Decreases effect of folic acid.
Oral contraceptives	Decreases effect of folic acid. Those who take oral contraceptives require additional folic acid.
Phenytoin	Decrease phenytoin effect. Patients taking phenytoin should avoid taking folic acid.
Pyrimethamine	Decreases effect of folic acid and interferes with effectiveness of pyrimethamine. Avoid this combintation.
Quinine	Decreases effect of folic acid.
Sulphasalazine and other sulpha drugs	Decreases effect of folic acid.
Trimethoprim	Decreases effect of folic acid.
Trimterene	Decreases effect of folic acid.

 Interaction with Other Substances

Tobacco decreases absorption. Smokers may require supplementary folic acid.

Alcohol abuse makes deficiency more likely. Alcoholism is the principal cause of folic-acid deficiency.

VITAMIN

Basic Information

Menadiol is one form of Vitamin K.
Available from natural sources? Yes
Available from synthetic sources? Yes
Prescription required? Yes
Fat-soluble or water-soluble: Fat-soluble.
Menadiol sodium diphosphate is water-soluble.

Natural Sources

Alfalfa	Green tea
Brussels sprouts	Oats
Cabbage	Soybeans
Camembert cheese	Spinach
Cauliflower	Turnip greens
Cheddar cheese	

Reasons to Use

- Promotes normal growth and development.
- Prevents haemorrhagic disease of the newborn.
- Prevents abnormal bleeding, particularly in those with chronic intestinal disease or those taking anti-coagulant medicines. Vitamin K is normally manufactured in the intestinal tract by "friendly" bacteria. If bacteria are destroyed or damaged by disease or antibiotics, vitamin-K deficiency may develop.
- Treats bleeding disorders due to vitamin-K deficiency.

Unproved Speculated Benefits

- None.

Who Needs Additional Amounts?

- Anyone with inadequate caloric or nutritional dietary intake or increased nutritional requirements.
- Those with a portion of the gastrointestinal tract surgically removed.
- People with recent severe burns or injuries.
- Premature newborns.
- Those with recent severe burns or injuries.
- Anyone taking antibiotics that may destroy normal "friendly" bacteria in the intestinal tract.
- People who do not have enough bile to absorb fats. Replacement must be given by injection.

Deficiency Symptoms

Infants:
- Failure to grow and develop normally.
- Haemorrhagic disease of the newborn characterized by vomiting blood and bleeding from intestine, imbilical cord, circumcision site. Symptoms begin 2 or 3 days after birth.

Adults:
- Abnormal blood clotting that can lead to nosebleeds, blood in urine, stomach bleeding, bleeding from capillaries or skin causing spontaneous black-and-blue marks, prolonged clotting time (a laboratory test).

Unproved Speculated Symptoms

- Excessive diarrhoea.

Lab Tests to Detect Deficiency

- Prothrombin time.
- Serum prothrombin.
- Serum vitamin K.

Dosage and Usage Information

Recommended Dietary Allowance (RDA):
No RDA has been established. Adequate and safe range is 2mcg/kg body weight per day. Estimated Safe Intake/day is given below.

Age	Estimated Safe Intake
0–6 months	12mcg
6–12 months	10–20mcg
1–3 years	15–30mcg
4–6 years	20–40mcg
7–10 years	30–60mcg
11–17 years	50–100mcg
18+ years	70–140mcg

What this vitamin does:
- Promotes production of active prothrombin (factor II), proconvertin (factor VII) and other clotting factors. These are all necessary for normal blood clotting.

Miscellaneous information:
- Very little vitamin K is lost from processing or cooking foods.
- When a severe bleeding disorder exists due to a vitamin-K deficiency, fresh whole blood may be needed during severe bleeding episodes.
- There is a significant delay before vitamin K becomes effective when given by injection.

Menadiol (Vitamin K), Continued

Available as:
- Tablets: Swallow whole with full glass of liquid. Don't chew or crush. Take with meals or 1 to 1-1/2 hours after meals unless otherwise directed by your doctor.
- Injectable forms are administered by doctor or nurse.

Note: Vitamin K is not usually included in most multivitamin/mineral preparations.

Warnings and Precautions

Don't take if you:
- Are allergic to vitamin K.
- Have a G6PD deficiency. See Glossary.
- Have liver disease.

Consult your doctor if you have:
- Cystic fibrosis.
- Had prolonged diarrhoea.
- Had prolonged intestinal problems.
- Taken any other medicines.
- Plans for surgery (including dental surgery) in the near future.

Over age 55:
- No problems expected.

Pregnancy:
- No studies available in humans. Avoid if possible.
- Don't take megadoses.

Breast-feeding:
- Don't take megadoses.

Effect on lab tests:
- Changes prothrombin times.

Storage:
- Store in cool, dry place away from direct light, but don't freeze.
- Store safely out of reach of children.
- Don't store in bathroom medicine cabinet. Heat and moisture may change action of vitamin.

Others:
- Avoid overdosage. Vitamin K is a fat-soluble vitamin. Excess intake can lead to impaired liver function.
- Tell any dentist or doctor who plans surgery that you take vitamin K.

Overdose/Toxicity

Signs and symptoms:
In Infants: Brain damage.
In All: Large doses may impair liver function.

What to do:
For symptoms of overdosage: Discontinue vitamin, and consult doctor. Also see *Adverse Reactions or Side Effects* section below.
For accidental overdosage (such as child taking entire bottle): Dial 999 (emergency).

Adverse Reactions or Side Effects

Reaction or effect	What to do
Haemolytic anaemia in infants	Seek emergency treatment.
Hyperbilirubinemia (too much bilirubin in the blood) in newborns or infants given too much vitamin K	Seek emergency treatment.
Jaundice (yellow skin and eyes) resulting from hyperbilirubinaemia	Seek emergency treatment.
Allergic reactions, including:	
Face flushing	Discontinue. Call doctor immediately.
Gastrointestinal upset	Discontinue. Call doctor immediately.
Rash	Discontinue. Call doctor immediately.
Redness, pain or swelling at injection site	Discontinue. Call doctor immediately.
Skin itching	Seek emergency treatment.

≫➤

VITAMIN

Interaction with Medicine, Vitamins or Minerals

Interacts with	Combined effect
Anti-coagulants (oral)	Decreases anti-coagulant effect.
Antibiotics, broad spectrum	Causes vitamin-K deficiency.
Cholestyramine	Decreases vitamin-K effect.
Colestipol	Decreases vitamin-K effect.
Coumarin (isolated from sweet clover)	Decreases vitamin-K effect.
Mineral oil (long term)	Causes vitamin-K deficiency.
Primaquine	Increases potential for toxic side effects.
Quinidine	Causes vitamin-K deficiency.
Salicylates	Increases need for vitamin K when administered over long time.
Sucralfate	Decreases vitamin-K effect.
Sulpha drugs	Causes vitamin-K deficiency.

Interaction with Other Substances

None known

Niacin (Vitamin B-3)

Basic Information
Niacin is also called Vitamin B-3.
Available from natural sources? Yes
Available from synthetic sources? Yes
Prescription required? Yes, for high doses used
  for cholesterol reduction
Fat-soluble or water-soluble: Water-soluble

Natural Sources

Beef liver	Salmon
Brewer's yeast	Sunflower seeds
Chicken, white meat	Swordfish
Halibut	Tuna
Peanuts	Turkey
Pork	Veal

Reasons to Use

- Maintains normal function of skin, nerves, digestive system.
- Reduces cholesterol and triglycerides in blood.
- Corrects niacin deficiency.
- Dilates blood vessels.
- Treats vertigo (dizziness) and ringing in ears.
- Prevents premenstrual headache.
- Treats pellagra.

Unproved Speculated Benefits

- Prevents heart attacks.
- Treats or prevents motion sickness.
- Alleviates mental illness, notably schizophrenia.
- Cures depression.
- Prevents migraine headaches.
- Improves poor digestion.
- Protects against pollutants and toxins.
- Treats leprosy.
- Stimulates sex drive.

Who Needs Additional Amounts?

- Anyone with inadequate caloric or nutritional dietary intake or increased nutritional requirements.
- Older people (over 55 years).
- Pregnant or breast-feeding women.
- Those who abuse alcohol or other drugs.

- People with a chronic wasting illness including malignancies, pancreatic insufficiency, cirrhosis of the liver, sprue.
- Anyone who experiences excess stress for long periods or who has recently undergone surgery.
- Athletes and workers who participate in vigorous physical activities.
- Those with a portion of the gastrointestinal tract surgically removed.
- People with recent severe burns or injuries.
- Those with diabetes.
- Infants born with errors of metabolism (congenital disorders due to chromosome abnormalities).
- Anyone with hyperthyroidism.

Deficiency Symptoms

Early Symptoms
- Muscle weakness
- General fatigue
- Loss of appetite
- Headaches
- Swollen, red tongue
- Skin lesions, including rashes, dry scaly skin, wrinkles, coarse skin texture
- Nausea and vomiting
- Dermatitis
- Diarrhoea
- Irritability
- Dizziness

Late Symptoms of severe deficiency called pellagra:
- Dementia
- Death

Unproved Speculated Symptoms

- Acne
- Poor circulation
- Mental problems

Lab Tests to Detect Deficiency

- Urinary N-1 methylnicotinamide
- Urinary 2—pyrindone/N-1 methylnicotinamide. Test results not always conclusive.
- Abnormal-liver-function studies

‒>>

Niacin (Vitamin B-3)

Dosage and Usage Information

Recommended Dietary Allowance (RDA):
Estimate of adequate daily intake by the Food and Nutrition Board of the National Research Council, 1980. See Glossary.

Age	RDA
0–6 months	6mg
6–12 months	8mg
1–3 years	9mg
4–6 years	11mg
7–10 years	16mg
Males	
11–18 years	18mg
19–22 years	19mg
23–50 years	18mg
50+ years	16mg
Females	
11–14 years	15mg
15–22 years	14mg
23+ years	13mg
Pregnant	+2mg
Lactating	+4mg

What this vitamin does:
- Aids in release of energy from foods.
- Helps synthesize DNA.
- Becomes component of two co-enzymes (NAD and NADP), which are both necessary for utilization of fats, tissue respiration and production of sugars.

Miscellaneous information:
- The body manufactures niacin from tryptophan, an amino acid.

Available as:
- Tablets or capsules: Swallow whole with full glass of liquid. Don't chew or crush. Take with meals or 1 to 1-1/2 hours after meals unless otherwise directed by your doctor.
- Extended-release capsules or tablets: Swallow whole with full glass of liquid. Don't chew or crush. Take with or immediately after food to decrease stomach irritation.
- Oral solution: Dilute in at least 1/2 glass water or other liquid. Take with meals or 1 to 1-1/2 hours after meals unless otherwise directed by your doctor.
- Injectable forms are administered by doctor or nurse.
- A constituent of many multivitamin/mineral preparations.
- Some forms available by generic name.

Warnings and Precautions

Don't take if you:
- Are allergic to niacin or any niacin-containing vitamin mixtures.
- Have impaired liver function.
- Have an active peptic ulcer.

Consult your doctor if you have:
- Diabetes.
- Gout.
- Gallbladder or liver disease.

Over age 55:
- Response to drug cannot be predicted. Dose must be individualized.

Pregnancy:
- Risk to fetus with high doses outweighs benefits. Do not use.

Breast-feeding:
- Studies are inconclusive. Consult doctor about supplements.
- Don't take megadoses.

Effect on lab tests:
- Urinary catecholamine concentration may falsely elevate results.
- Urine glucose (using Benedict's reagent) may produce false-positive reactions.
- Falsely elevates blood sugar.
- Falsely increases growth-hormone level in blood.
- Falsely elevates blood uric acid with large daily doses.

Storage:
- Store in cool, dry place away from direct light, but don't freeze.
- Store safely out of reach of children.
- Don't store in bathroom medicine cabinet. Heat and moisture may change action of vitamin.

Others:
- High dosages over long periods may cause liver damage or aggravate a stomach ulcer.

Overdose/Toxicity

Signs and symptoms:
Body flush, nausea, vomiting, abdominal cramps, diarrhoea, weakness, lightheadedness, headache, fainting, sweating, high blood sugar, high uric acid, heart-rhythm disturbances, jaundice.

Niacin (Vitamin B-3), Continued

What to do:
For symptoms of overdosage: Discontinue vitamin, and consult doctor. Also see *Adverse Reactions or Side Effects* section below.
For accidental overdosage (such as child taking entire bottle): Dial 999 (emergency).

 ## Adverse Reactions or Side Effects

Reaction or effect	What to do
Abdominal pain	Discontinue. Call doctor immediately.
Diarrhoea	Discontinue. Call doctor when convenient.
Faintness	Discontinue. Call doctor immediately.
Headache	Discontinue. Call doctor when convenient.
"Hot" feeling, with skin flushed in blush zone (always)	Nothing.
Jaundice (yellow skin and eyes)	Discontinue. Call doctor immediately.
Nausea or vomiting	Discontinue. Call doctor immediately.
Skin dryness	Discontinue. Call doctor when convenient.
Vomiting	Discontinue. Call doctor immediately.

 ## Interaction with Medicine, Vitamins or Minerals

Interacts with	Combined effect
Anti-diabetics	Decreases anti-diabetic effect.
Beta-adrenergic blockers	Lowers blood pressure to extremely low level.
Chenodiol	Decreases chenodiol effect.
Guanethidine	Increases guanethidine effect.
Isoniazid	Decreases niacin effect.
Mecamylamine	Lowers blood pressure to extremely low level.
Pargyline	Lowers blood pressure to extremely low level.

 ## Interaction with Other Substances

Tobacco decreases absorption. Smokers may require supplementary niacin.

Alcohol may cause extremely low blood pressure. Use caution.

Niacinamide

Basic Information

Niacinamide is a form of vitamin B-3 and sometimes called nicotinamide.
Available from natural sources? Yes
Available from synthetic sources? Yes
Prescription required? Yes, for high doses used for cholesterol reduction
Fat-soluble or water-soluble: Water-soluble

Natural Sources

Beef liver	Salmon
Brewer's yeast	Sunflower seeds
Chicken	Swordfish
Halibut	Tuna
Peanuts	Turkey
Pork	Veal

Reasons to Use

- Maintains normal function of skin, nerves, digestive system.
- Corrects niacin deficiency.
- Dilates blood vessels.
- Treats dizziness and ringing in ears.
- Prevents premenstrual headache.
- Treats pellagra.

Unproved Speculated Benefits

- Prevents heart attacks.
- Treats or prevents motion sickness.
- Alleviates mental illness, notably schizophrenia.
- Cures depression.
- Prevents migraine or headaches.
- Improves digestion.
- Protects against pollutants and toxins.
- Treats leprosy.
- Stimulates sex drive.

Who Needs Additional Amounts?

- Anyone with inadequate caloric or dietary intake or increased nutritional requirements.
- Those who abuse alcohol or other drugs.
- People with a chronic wasting illness, including malignancies, pancreatic insufficiency, cirrhosis of the liver, sprue.
- Anyone who experiences excess stress for long periods, or who has recently undergone surgery.
- Athletes and workers who participate in vigorous physical activities.
- Those with a portion of the gastrointestinal tract surgically removed.
- People with recent severe burns or injuries.
- Those with diabetes.
- Anyone with hyperthyroidism.

Deficiency Symptoms

Early symptoms:
- Muscular weakness
- General fatigue
- Irritability
- Dizziness
- Loss of appetite
- Headaches
- Swollen, red tongue
- Skin lesions, including rashes, dry scaly skin in areas exposed to sunlight, wrinkles, coarse skin texture
- Nausea and vomiting

Late symptoms of severe deficiency called pellagra:
- Dementia
- Death

Unproved Speculated Symptoms

- Acne
- Poor circulation
- Mental problems

Lab Tests to Detect Deficiency

- Urinary N-1 methylnicotinamide
- Urinary 2—pyrindone/N-1 methylnicotinamide; test results not always conclusive
- Liver-function studies

>>>►

VITAMIN

Niacinamide, Continued

Dosage and Usage Information

Recommended Dietary Allowance (RDA):
Estimate of adequate daily intake by the Food and Nutrition Board of the National Research Council, 1980. See Glossary.

Age	RDA
0–6 months	6mg
6–12 months	8mg
1–3 years	9mg
4–6 years	11mg
7–10 years	16mg
Males	
11–18 years	18mg
19–22 years	19mg
23–50 years	18mg
50+ years	16mg
Females	
11–14 years	15mg
15–22 years	14mg
23+ years	13mg
Pregnant	+2mg
Lactating	+4mg

What this vitamin does:
• Aids in release of energy from foods.
• Helps synthesis of DNA.
• Becomes a component of two co-enzymes (NAD and NADP), which are necessary for utilization of fats, tissue respiration, production of sugars.

Miscellaneous information:
• The body manufactures niacinamide from tryptophan, an amino acid.

Available as:
• Tablets or capsules: Swallow whole with full glass of liquid. Don't chew or crush. Take with meals or 1 to 1-1/2 hours after meals unless otherwise directed by your doctor.
• Extended-release capsules or tablets: Swallow whole with full glass of liquid. Don't chew or crush. Take with or immediately after food to decrease stomach irritation.
• Oral solution: Dilute in at least 1/2 glass water or other liquid. Take with meals or 1 to 1-1/2 hours after meals unless otherwise directed by your doctor.
• Injectable forms are administered by doctor or nurse.
• Some forms available by generic name.

Warnings and Precautions

Don't take if you:
• Are allergic to niacin or any niacin-containing vitamin mixtures.

• Have impaired liver function.
• Have an active peptic ulcer.

Consult your doctor if you have:
• Diabetes.
• Gout.
• Gallbladder or liver disease.

Over age 55:
• Response to drug cannot be predicted. Dose must be individualized.

Pregnancy:
• Risk with high doses to unborn child outweighs benefits. Don't use.

Breast-feeding:
• Studies inconclusive. Consult doctor about supplements.
• Don't take megadoses.

Effect on lab tests:
• Urinary catecholamine concentration may show falsely elevate results.
• Urine glucose (using Benedict's reagent) may produce false-positive reactions.
• Falsely elevates blood sugar.
• Falsely increases growth-hormone level in blood.
• Falsely elevates blood-uric acid with large daily doses.

Storage:
• Store in cool, dry place away from direct light, but don't freeze.
• Store safely out of reach of children.
• Don't store in bathroom medicine cabinet. Heat and moisture may change action of vitamin.

Others:
• High doses over long periods may cause liver damage or aggravate a stomach ulcer.

Overdose/Toxicity

Signs and symptoms:
Body flush, nausea, vomiting, abdominal cramps, diarrhoea, weakness, lightheadedness, fainting, sweathing, headache, high blood sugar, high uric acid, heart-rhythm disturbances, jaundice.

What to do:
For symptoms of overdosage: Discontinue vitamin, and consult doctor. Also see *Adverse Reactions or Side Effects* section below.
For accidental overdosage (such as child taking entire bottle): Dial 999 (emergency).

》➔

Adverse Reactions or Side Effects

Reaction or effect	What to do
Abdominal pain	Discontinue. Call doctor immediately.
Diarrhoea	Discontinue. Call doctor immediately.
Faintness	Discontinue. Call doctor immediately.
Headache	Discontinue. Call doctor when convenient.
"Hot" feeling, with skin flushed in blush zone (always)	Nothing.
Jaundice (yellow skin and eyes)	Seek emergency treatment.
Nausea	Discontinue. Call doctor immediately.
Skin dryness	Discontinue. Call doctor immediately.
Vomiting	Discontinue. Call doctor immediately.

 Interaction with Medicine, Vitamins or Minerals

Interacts with	Combined effect
Anti-diabetics	Decreases anti-diabetic effect.
Beta-adrenergic blockers	Lowers blood pressure to extremely low level.
Chenodiol	Decreases chenodiol effect.
Guanethidine	Increases guanethidine effect.
Isoniazid	Decreases niacin effect.
Mecamylamine	Lowers blood pressure to extremely low level.
Pargyline	Lowers blood pressure to extremely low level.

 Interaction with Other Substances

Tobacco decreases absorption. Smokers may require supplementary niacin.

Alcohol may cause excessively low blood pressure. Use caution.

Pantothenic Acid (Vitamin B-5)

Basic Information
Available from natural sources? Yes
Available from synthetic sources? Yes
Prescription required? Yes, for injectable forms
Fat-soluble-or water-soluble: Water-soluble

Natural Sources

Blue cheese	Meats, all kinds
Brewer's yeast	Peanuts
Corn	Peas
Eggs	Soya beans
Lentils	Sunflower seeds
Liver	Wheat germ
Lobster	Whole-grain products

Reasons to Use

• Promotes normal growth and development.
• Aids in release of energy from foods.
• Helps synthesis of numerous body materials.

Unproved Speculated Benefits

• Stimulates wound healing.
• Alleviates stress.
• Restores grey hair to normal colour.
• Prevents hair from turning grey.
• Cures allergies.
• Treats alcoholism, liver cirrhosis.
• Treats constipation.
• Treats fatigue.
• Treats stomach ulcers.
• Retards aging.

Who Needs Additional Amounts?

• Anyone with inadequate caloric or nutritional dietary intake or increased nutritional requirements.
• Older people (over 55 years).
• Pregnant or breast-feeding women.
• Those who abuse alcohol or other drugs.
• People with a chronic wasting illness, excess stress for long periods or who have recently undergone surgery.
• Athletes and workers who participate in vigorous physical activities.

• People with a portion of the gastrointestinal tract surgically removed.
• People with recent severe burns or injuries.

Deficiency Symptoms

None proved for pantothenic acid alone. However, lack of one B vitamin usually means lack of other B nutrients. Pantothenic acid is usually given with other B vitamins if there are symptoms of *any* vitamin-B deficiency, including excessive fatigue, sleep disturbances, loss of appetite, nausea.

Unproved Speculated Symptoms

• Nerve damage
• Breathing problems
• Skin problems
• Grey hair.
• Arthritis
• Allergies
• Birth defects
• Mental fatigue
• Headaches
• Sleep disturbances
• Muscle spasms, cramps

Lab Tests to Detect Deficiency

• Methods are limited and expensive. Tests are used only for research at present. Methods are available to measure blood levels and levels in 24-hour urine collections.

Dosage and Usage Information

Recommended Dietary Allowance (RDA):
No RDA has been established. Estimated safe intake given below.

Age	Estimated Safe Intake
0–6 months	2mg/day
6 months–3 years	3mg/day
4–6 years	3–4mg/day
7–9 years	4–5mg/day
10+ years	4–7mg/day

Pregnancy and lactation may increase the need by one-third.

What this vitamin does:
• Acts as co-enzyme in energy metabolism of carbohydrates, protein and fat.

⟫▸

Available as:
- Tablets: Swallow whole with full glass of liquid. Don't chew or crush. Take with meals or 1 to 1-1/2 hours after meals unless otherwise directed by your doctor.
- A constituent of many multivitamin/mineral preparations.
- Pantothenic acid is also sold as dexpanthenol (panthoderm), a lotion or cream applied to burns, cuts or abrasions. It relieves itching and soothes the wound.

 ## Warnings and Precautions

Don't take if you:
- Are allergic to pantothenic acid.
- Are taking levodopa for Parkinson's disease.

Consult your doctor if you have:
- Haemophilia

Over age 55:
- No problems expected.

Pregnancy:
- Don't exceed recommended dose.

Breast-feeding:
- Don't exceed recommended dose.

Effect on lab tests:
- None expected.

Storage:
- Store in cool, dry place away from direct light, but don't freeze.
- Store safely out of reach of children.
- Don't store in bathroom medicine cabinet. Heat and moisture may change action of vitamin.

Others:
- Avoid megadoses.
- Don't exceed recommended doses if you take pantothenic acid without medical supervision.

 ## Overdose/Toxicity

Signs and symptoms:
Diarrhoea and water retention with ingestion of megadoses—over 10 to 20 grams/day (10,000mg–20,000mg). This dose is not life-threatening.

What to do:
For symptoms of overdosage: Discontinue vitamin, and consult doctor.
For accidental overdosage (such as child taking entire bottle): Dial 999 (emergency).

 ## Adverse Reactions or Side Effects

Reaction or effect	What to do
None expected with normal intake	Call doctor if you suspect new symptoms are caused by taking pantothenic acid.

 ## Interaction with Medicine, Vitamins or Minerals

Interacts with	Combined effect
Levodopa	Small amounts of pantothenic acid nullify levodopa's effect. Carbidopa-levodopa combination is not affected by this interaction.

 ## Interaction with Other Substances

Tobacco decreases absorption. Smokers may require supplementary vitamin B-5.

Phytonadione (Vitamin K)

Basic Information

Phytonadione is one form of vitamin K.
Available from natural sources? Yes
Available from synthetic sources? Yes
Prescription required? Yes
Fat-soluble or water-soluble: Fat-soluble

Natural Sources

Alfalfa	Green tea
Brussels sprouts	Oats
Cabbage	Soya beans
Camembert cheese	Spinach
Cauliflower	Turnip greens
Cheddar cheese	

Reasons to Use

- Promotes normal growth and development.
- Prevents haemhorrhagic disease of the newborn.
- Prevents abnormal bleeding, particularly in those with chronic intestinal disease or those taking anti-coagulant medicines. Vitamin K is normally manufactured in the intestinal tract by "friendly" bacteria. If bacteria are destroyed or damaged by disease or antibiotics, vitamin-K deficiency may develop.
- Treats bleeding disorders due to vitamin K deficiency.

Unproved Speculated Benefits

- None.

Who Needs Additional Amounts?

- Anyone with inadequate caloric or nutritional dietary intake or increased nutritional requirements.
- Those with a portion of the gastrointestinal tract surgically removed.
- Premature newborns.
- People with recent severe burns or injuries.
- Anyone taking antibiotics that may destroy normal "friendly" bacteria in the intestinal tract.
- People who do not have enough bile to absorb fats. Replacement must be given by injection.

Deficiency Symptoms

Infants:
- Failure to grow and develop normally.
- Haemhorrhagic disease of the newborn characterized by vomiting blood and bleeding from the intestine, umbilical cord, circumcision site. Symptoms begin 2 or 3 days after birth.

Adults:
- Abnormal blood clotting that can lead to nosebleeds, blood in urine, stomach bleeding, bleeding from capillaries or skin causing spontaneous black-and-blue marks, prolonged clotting time (a laboratory test).

Unproved Speculated Symptoms

- Excessive diarrhoea.

Lab Tests to Detect Deficiency

- Prothrombin time
- Serum prothrombin
- Serum vitamin K

Dosage and Usage Information

Recommended Dietary Allowance (RDA):
No RDA has been established. Adequate and safe range is 2mcg/kg body weight per day. Estimated safe intake per day given below.

Age	Estimated Safe Intake
0–6 months	12mcg/day
6 months–12 months	10–20mcg/day
1–3 years	15–30mcg/day
4–6 years	20–40mcg/day
7–10 years	30–60mcg/day
11–17 years	50–100mcg/day
18+ years	70–140mcg/day

What this vitamin does:
- Promotes production of active prothrombin (factor II), proconvertin (factor VII) and other clotting factors. All are necessary for normal blood clotting.

Miscellaneous Information:
- Very little vitamin K is lost from processing or cooking foods.
- When a severe bleeding disorder exists due to a vitamin-K deficiency, fresh whole blood may be needed during severe bleeding episodes.
- There is a significant delay before vitamin K becomes effective when given by injection.

VITAMIN

Available as:
- Tablets: Swallow whole with full glass of liquid. Don't chew or crush. Take with meals or 1 to 1-1/2 hours after meals unless otherwise directed by your doctor.
- Injectable forms are administered by doctor or nurse.

Note: Vitamin K is not usually included in most multivitamin/mineral preparations.

Warnings and Precautions

Don't take if you:
- Are allergic to vitamin K.
- Have a G6PD deficiency. See Glossary.
- Have liver disease.

Consult your doctor if you have:
- Cystic fibrosis.
- Had prolonged diarrhoea.
- Prolonged intestinal problems.
- Taken any other medicines.
- Plans for surgery (including dental surgery) in the near future.

Over age 55:
- No problems expected.

Pregnancy:
- No studies available in humans. Avoid if possible.
- Don't take megadoses.

Breast-feeding:
- Don't take megadoses.

Effect on lab tests:
- Changes prothrombin times.

Storage:
- Store in cool, dry place away from direct light, but don't freeze.
- Store safely out of reach of children.
- Don't store in bathroom medicine cabinet. Heat and moisture may change action of vitamin.

Others:
- Avoid overdosage. Vitamin K is a fat-soluble vitamin. Excess intake can lead to impaired liver function.
- Tell any dentist or doctor who plans surgery that you take vitamin K.

Overdose/Toxicity

Signs and symptoms:
In Infants: Brain damage
In All: Large doses may impair liver function.

What to do:
For symptoms of overdosage: Discontinue vitamin, and consult doctor. Also see *Adverse Reactions or Side Effects* section below.
For accidental overdosage (such as child taking entire bottle): Dial 999 (emergency).

Adverse Reactions or Side Effects

Reaction or effect	What to do
Haemolytic anaemia in infants	Seek emergency treatment.
Hyperbilirubinaemia (too much bilirubin in the blood) in newborns or infants given too much vitamin K	Seek emergency treatment.
Jaundice (yellow skin and eyes) resulting from hyperbilirubinaemia	Seek emergency treatment.
Allergic reactions, including:	
Face flushing	Discontinue. Call doctor immediately.
Gastrointestinal upset	Discontinue. Call doctor immediately.
Rash	Discontinue. Call doctor immediately.
Redness, pain or swelling at injection site	Discontinue. Call doctor immediately.
Skin itching	Seek emergency treatment.

Phytonadione (Vitamin K), Continued

 Interaction with Medicine, Vitamins or Minerals

Interacts with	Combined effect
Anti-coagulants (oral)	Decreases anti-coagulant effect.
Antibiotics, broad spectrum	Causes vitamin-K deficiency.
Cholestyramine	Decreases vitamin-K effect.
Colestipol	Decreases vitamin-K effect.
Coumarin (isolated from sweet clover)	Decreases vitamin-K effect.
Mineral oil (long term)	Causes vitamin-K deficiency.
Primaquine	Increases potential for toxic side effects.
Quinidine	Causes vitamin-K deficiency.
Salicylates	Increases need for vitamin K when administered over long time.
Sucralfate	Decreases vitamin-K effect.
Sulpha drugs	Causes vitamin-K deficiency.

 Interaction with Other Substances

None known

Basic Information

Pyridoxine is also called pyridoxal phosphate.
Available from natural sources? Yes
Available from synthetic sources? Yes
Prescription required? No
Fat-soluble-or water-soluble: Water-soluble

Natural Sources

Avocados	Rice
Bananas	Salmon
Bran	Shrimp
Brewer's yeast	Soyabeans
Carrots	Sunflower seeds
Flour, whole-wheat	Tuna
Hazelnuts (filberts)	Wheat germ
Lentils	

Reasons to Use

- Participates actively in many chemical reactions of proteins and amino acids.
- Helps normal function of brain.
- Promotes normal red-blood-cell formation.
- Maintains chemical balance among body fluids.
- Regulates excretion of water.
- Helps in energy production and resistance to stress.
- Acts as co-enzyme in carbohydrate, protein and fat metabolism.
- Treats some forms of anaemia.
- Treats cycloserine and isoniazid poisoning.

Unproved Speculated Benefits

- Treats or prevents depression when used with oral contraceptives.
- Treats premenstrual syndrome.
- Reduces breast milk in nursing mothers with congested breasts.
- Relieves morning sickness.
- Helps arthritis.
- Cures migraines.
- Relieves nausea.
- Acts as a tranquilizer.
- Relieves nervous and muscle disorders.
- Prevents tooth decay.
- Lowers blood cholesterol.
- Retards aging.
- Treats diabetes.
- Treats mental retardation.
- Improves vision.

- Helps weight-reduction efforts.
- Helps infertility.
- Cures carpal-tunnel syndrome.

Who Needs Additional Amounts?

- Anyone with inadequate caloric or nutritional dietary intake or increased nutritional requirements.
- Older people (over 55 years)
- Pregnant or breast-feeding women.
- Those who abuse alcohol or other drugs.
- People with a chronic wasting illness, excess stress for long periods or who have recently undergone surgery.
- Those with a portion of the gastrointestinal tract surgically removed.
- People with recent severe burns or injuries.
- Women taking oral contraceptives or oestrogen.

Deficiency Symptoms

Symptoms of vitamin B-6 deficiency are non-specific and hard to reproduce experimentally.
- Weakness
- Mental confusion
- Irritability
- Nervousness
- Insomnia
- Poor coordination walking
- Hyperactivity
- Abnormal electroencephalogram
- Anaemia
- Skin lesions
- Discolouration of tongue
- Muscle twitching
- Kidney stones

Unproved Speculated Symptoms

- Depression
- Diabetes

Lab Tests to Detect Deficiency

- Pyridoxine level in blood
- Xanthurenic-acid level in urine

Dosage and Usage Information

Recommended Dietary Allowance (RDA):
Estimate of adequate daily intake by the Food and Nutrition Board of the National Research Council, 1980. See Glossary.

Age	RDA
0–6 months	0.3mg
6–12 months	0.6mg
1–3 years	0.9mg
4–6 years	1.3mg
7–10 years	1.8mg
Males	
11+ years	2.2mg
Females	
11+ years	2.0mg
Pregnant	+0.6mg
Lactating	+0.5mg

What this vitamin does:
- Acts as co-enzyme for metabolic functions affecting protein, carbohydrates and fat utilization.
- Promotes conversion of tryptophan to niacin or serotonin.

Miscellaneous information:
- Avoid cooking foods that contain vitamin B-6 in large amounts of water.
- Freezing vegetables results in a 30 to 56% reduction of vitamin B-6.
- Canning vegetables results in a 57 to 77% reduction of vitamin B-6.

Available as:
- Tablets: Swallow whole with full glass of liquid. Don't chew or crush. Take with meals or 1 to 1-1/2 hours after meals unless otherwise directed by your doctor.
- Extended-release capsules or tablets: Swallow whole with full glass of liquid. Don't chew or crush. Take with or immediately after food to decrease stomach irritation.
- A constituent of many multivitamin/mineral preparations.

Warnings and Precautions

Don't take if you:
- You are allergic to vitamin B-6.

Consult your doctor if you have:
- Been under severe stress with illness, burns, an accident, recent surgery.
- Intestinal problems.
- Liver disease.
- Overactive thyroid.
- Parkinson's disease.

Over age 55:
- More likely to have marginal deficiency.

Pregnancy:
- Don't take megadoses.

Breast-feeding:
- Megadoses can cause dangerous side effects in the infant.

Effect on lab tests:
- May produce false-positive results in urobilinogen determinations using Ehrlich's reagent.

Storage:
- Store in cool, dry place away from direct light, but don't freeze.
- Store safely out of reach of children.
- Don't store in bathroom medicine cabinet. Heat and moisture may change action of vitamin.

Others:
- Regular B-6 supplements are recommended if you take chloramphenicol, cycloserine, ethionamide, hydralazine, immunosuppressants, isoniazid or penicillamine. These decrease pyridoxine absorption and can cause anaemia or tingling and numbness in hands and feet.
- Don't crush, break or chew tablets before swallowing.

Overdose/Toxicity

Signs and symptoms:
Clumsiness, numbness in hands and feet.

What to do:
For symptoms of overdosage: Discontinue vitamin, and consult doctor. Also see *Adverse Reactions or Side Effects* section below.
For accidental overdosage (such as child taking entire bottle): Dial 999 (emergency).

»→

Adverse Reactions or Side Effects

Reaction or effect	What to do
Doses of 200mg/day can produce dependency, requiring need to continue to take high doses (undesirable).	Discontinue megadoses gradually.
Large doses (2 to 6 grams of pyridoxine/ day) taken for several months are reported to cause severe sensory neuropathy (see Glossary) with unsteady gait, numb feet and hands, clumsiness.	Discontinue megadoses. Call doctor immediately.
Causes depression when taken with oral contraceptive pills.	Discontinue pyridoxine. Call doctor when convenient.

 ## Interaction with Medicine, Vitamins or Minerals

Interacts with	Combined effect
Chloramphenicol, cycloserine, ethionamide, hydralazine, isoniazid, penicillamine, immuno-suppressants, such as adrenocorticoids, azathioprine, chlorambucil, ACTH, cyclophosphamide, cyclosporine, mercaptopurine	May increase excretion of pyridoxine and cause anaemia or peripheral neuritis, which includes pain, numbness and coldness in feet and fingertips. If you take these medicines, you may need increased pyridoxine. Consult your doctor.
Oestrogen or oral contraceptives	Increases requirements of pyridoxine. Also causes depression.
Levodopa	Prevents levodopa from controlling symptoms of Parkinson's disease. This problem does not occur with carbidopa-levodopa combination.
Phenytoin	Large doses of B-6 hasten break-down of phenytoin.

 ## Interaction with Other Substances

Tobacco decreases absorption. Smokers may require supplementary vitamin B-6.

VITAMIN

Riboflavin (Vitamin B-2)

Basic Information

Available from natural sources? Yes
Available from synthetic sources? Yes
Prescription required? No
Fat-soluble or water-soluble: Water-soluble

 ## Natural Sources

Almonds
Brewer's yeast
Cheese
Chicken
Organ meats (beef, kidney)
Wheat germ

 ## Reasons to Use

- Aids in release of energy from food.
- Maintains healthy mucous membranes lining respiratory, digestive, circulatory and excretory tracts when used in conjunction with vitamin A.
- Preserves integrity of nervous system, skin, eyes.
- Promotes normal growth and development.
- Aids in treating infections, stomach problems, burns, alcoholism, liver disease.

 ## Unproved Speculated Benefits

- Cures various eye diseases.
- Treats skin disorders.
- Prevents cancer.
- Increases body growth during normal developmental stages.
- Helps overcome infertility.
- Prevents stress.
- Stimulates hair growth in bald men.
- Improves vision.

 ## Who Needs Additional Amounts?

- Anyone with inadequate caloric or nutritional dietary intake or increased nutritional requirements.
- Pregnant or breast-feeding women.
- Those who abuse alcohol or other drugs.
- People with a chronic wasting illness, excess stress for long periods or who have recently undergone surgery.
- Athletes and workers who participate in vigorous physical activities.

- Those with a portion of the gastrointestinal tract surgically removed.
- People with recent severe burns or injuries.
- Those who rely almost exclusively on processed foods for their daily diet.
- Women taking oral contraceptives or oestrogen.

 ## Deficiency Symptoms

- Cracks and sores in corners of mouth
- Inflammation of tongue and lips
- Eyes overly sensitive to light and easily tired
- Itching and scaling of skin around nose, mouth, scrotum, forehead, ears, scalp
- Trembling
- Dizziness
- Insomnia
- Slow learning
- Itching, burning and reddening of eyes
- Damage to cornea of eye.

 ## Unproved Speculated Symptoms

- Mild anaemia
- Mild lethargy
- Acne
- Migraine headaches
- Muscle cramps

 ## Lab Tests to Detect Deficiency

- Serum riboflavin
- Erythrocyte riboflavin
- Glutathione reductase

 ## Dosage and Usage Information

Recommended Dietary Allowance (RDA):
Estimate of adequate daily intake by the Food and Nutrition Board of the National Research Council, 1980. See Glossary ➤➤

VITAMIN

Age	RDA
0–6 months	0.4mg
6–12 months	0.6mg
1–3 years	0.8mg
4–6 years	1.0mg
7–10 years	1.4mg
Males	
11–14 years	1.6mg
15–22 years	1.7mg
23–50 years	1.6mg
51+ years	1.4mg
Females	
11–22 years	1.3mg
23+ years	1.2mg
Pregnant	+0.3mg
Lactating	+0.5mg

What this vitamin does:
- Acts as component in two co-enzymes (flavin mononucleotide and flavin adenine dinucleotide) needed for normal tissue respiration.
- Activates pyridoxine.

Miscellaneous information:
- A balanced diet prevents deficiency without supplements.
- Large doses may produce dark-yellow urine.
- Processing food may decrease quantity of vitamin B-2.
- Mixing with baking powder destroys riboflavin.

Available as:
- Tablets: Swallow whole with full glass of liquid. Don't chew or crush. Take with or immediately after food to decrease stomach irritation.
- A constituent of many multivitamin/mineral preparations.

 ## Warnings and Precautions

Don't take if you:
- Are allergic to any B vitamin.
- Have chronic kidney failure.

Consult your doctor if you are:
- Pregnant or planning a pregnancy.

Over age 55:
- Need for vitamin B-2 is greater.

Pregnancy:
- Don't take megadoses.

Breast-feeding:
- Don't take megadoses.

Effect on lab tests:
- Urinary catecholamine concentration may show false elevation.
- Urobilongen determinations (Ehrlich's) may produce false-positive results.

Storage:
- Store in cool, dry place away from direct light, but don't freeze.
- Store safely out of reach of children.
- Don't store in bathroom medicine cabinet. Heat and moisture may change action of vitamin.

Others:
- Unlikely to cause toxic symptoms in healthy people with normal kidney function.

 ## Overdose/Toxicity

Signs and symptoms:
Dark urine, nausea, vomiting.

What to do:
For symptoms of overdosage: Discontinue vitamin, and consult doctor. Also see *Adverse Reactions or Side Effects* section below.
For accidental overdosage (such as child taking entire bottle): Dial 999 (emergency).

 ## Adverse Reactions or Side Effects

Reaction or effect	What to do
Yellow urine, with large doses	No action necessary

 ## Interaction with Medicine, Vitamins or Minerals

Interacts with	Combined effect
Anti-depressants (tricyclic)	Decreases B-2 effect.
Phenothiazines	Decreases B-2 effect.
Probenecid	Decreases B-2 effect.

 ## Interaction with Other Substances

Tobacco decreases absorption. Smokers may require supplementary vitamin B-2.

Alcohol prevents uptake and absorption of vitamin B-2.

Thiamine (Vitamin B-1)

Basic Information
Available from natural sources? Yes
Available from synthetic sources? Yes
Prescription required? Yes, for injectable forms
Fat-soluble or water-soluble: Water-soluble

Natural Sources

Beef kidney	Navy beans, dried
Beef liver	Pork
Brewer's yeast	Rice bran
Flour,	Rice, brown, raw
rye and whole-wheat	Salmon steak
Garbanzo beans	Soyabeans, dried
(chickpeas), dried	Sunflower seeds, dried
Kidney beans, dried	Wheat germ
	Whole-grain products

Reasons to Use

- Keeps mucous membranes healthy.
- Maintains normal function of nervous system, muscles, heart.
- Aids in treatment of herpes zoster.
- Promotes normal growth and development.
- Treats beriberi (thiamine-deficiency disease).
- Replaces deficiency caused by alcoholism, cirrhosis, overactive thyroid, infection, breast-feeding, absorption diseases, pregnancy, prolonged diarrhoea, burns.

Unproved Speculated Benefits

- Cures depression.
- Prevents fatigue.
- Is used as an insect repellent. If you take large amounts of thiamine by mouth, insects are repelled by unpleasant taste and odour of thiamine in perspiration.
- Treats motion sickness.
- Decreases pain.
- Improves appetite, digestion, mental alertness.

Who Needs Additional Amounts?

- People who abuse alcohol or other drugs. Alcoholics need more thiamine. Thiamine accelerates metabolism, using extra carbohydrates and calories from alcohol.
- Anyone with inadequate caloric or nutritional dietary intake or increased nutritional requirements.

- Older people (over 55 years).
- Pregnant or breast-feeding women.
- People with a chronic wasting illness, especially diabetes, excess stress for long periods or who have recently undergone surgery.
- People with a portion of the gastrointestinal tract surgically removed.
- Those with recent severe burns or injuries.
- People with liver disease, overactive thyroid, prolonged diarrhoea.

Deficiency Symptoms

Normal deficiency:
- Loss of appetite
- Fatigue
- Nausea
- Vomiting
- Mental problems, such as rolling of eyeballs, depression, memory loss, difficulty concentrating and dealing with details, personality changes, rapid heartbeat
- Gastrointestinal disorders
- Muscles become tender and atrophied

Gross deficiency:
- Leads eventually to beriberi, which is rare, except in severely ill alcoholics.
- Pain or tingling in arms or legs
- Decreased reflex activity
- Fluid accumulation in arms and legs
- Heart enlargement
- Constipation
- Nausea
- Vomiting

Unproved Speculated Symptoms

- Gastric hydrochloric acid lower than normal
- Nerve problems
- Skin problems
- Ulcerative colitis

Lab Tests to Detect Deficiency

- Transketolase function study on red blood cells
- Pyruvic-acid blood level
- 24-hour urine collection

Dosage and Usage Information

Recommended Dietary Allowance (RDA):
Estimate of adequate daily intake by the Food and Nutrition Board of the National Research Council, 1980. See Glossary.

Age	RDA
0–6 months	0.3mg
6–12 months	0.5mg
1–3 years	0.7mg
4–6 years	0.9mg
7–10 years	1.2mg
Males	
11–18 years	1.4mg
19–22 years	1.5mg
23–50 years	1.4mg
51+ years	1.2mg
Females	
11–22 years	1.1mg
23+ years	1.0mg
Pregnant	+0.4mg
Lactating	+0.5mg

What this vitamin does:
• Functions in combination with adenosine triphosphate to form co-enzyme necessary for converting carbohydrate into energy in muscles and nervous system.

Miscellaneous information:
• Cook foods in minimum amount of water or steam.
• Avoid high cooking temperatures and long heat exposure.
• Avoid using baking powder when you take thiamine unless it is used as a leavening agent in baked products.
• Thiamine is stable when frozen and stored.
• A balanced diet should provide enough thiamine for healthy people to make supplementation unnecessary. Best dietary sources of thiamine are whole-grain cereals and meat.
• Take at same time every day.
• If you forget a dose, take it when you remember it. Return to regular schedule.

Available as:
• Tablets: Swallow whole with full glass of liquid. Don't chew or crush. Take with meals or 1 to 1-1/2 hours after meals unless otherwise directed by your doctor.
• Liquid: Dilute in at least 1/2 glass of water or other liquid. Take with meals or 1 to 1-1/2 hours after meals unless otherwise directed by your doctor.
• Injectable forms are administered by doctor or nurse.

Warnings and Precautions

Don't take if you:
• Are allergic to any B vitamin.

Consult your doctor if you have:
• Liver or kidney disease.

Over age 55:
• No problems expected.

Pregnancy:
• Consult doctor about supplements.
• Don't take megadoses.

Breast-feeding:
• No problems expected. Consult doctor about supplements.
• Don't take megadoses.

Effect on lab tests:
• Interferes with results of serum theophylline.
• May produce false-positive results in tests for uric acid or urobilinogen.

Storage:
• Store in cool, dry place away from direct light, but don't freeze.
• Store safely out of reach of children.
• Don't store in bathroom medicine cabinet. Heat and moisture may change action of vitamin.

Others:
• Most excess thiamine is excreted in urine if kidney function is normal.

Overdose/Toxicity

Signs and symptoms:
Occasionally large doses of vitamin B-1 have caused hypersensitive reactions resembling anaphylactic shock. Several-hundred milligrams may cause drowsiness in some people.

What to do:
For symptoms of overdosage: Discontinue vitamin, and consult doctor. Also see *Adverse Reactions or Side Effects* section below.

For accidental overdosage (such as child taking entire bottle): Dial 999 (emergency).

>>➤

Thiamine (Vitamin B-1), Continued

 ## Adverse Reactions or Side Effects

Reaction or effect	What to do
Skin rash or itching (rare)	Discontinue. Call doctor immediately.
Wheezing (more likely after intravenous dose)	Seek emergency treatment.

 ## Interaction with Medicine, Vitamins or Minerals

Interacts with	Combined effect
Drugs used to relax muscles during surgery	Produces excessive muscle relaxation. Tell your doctor before surgery if you are taking supplements.

 ## Interaction with Other Substances

Tobacco decreases absorption. Smokers may require supplementary vitamin B-1.

Alcohol reduces intestinal absorption of vitamin B-1, which is necessary to metabolize alcohol.

Beverages
• Carbonates and citrates (additives listed on many beverage labels) decrease thiamine effect.

Foods
• Carbonates and citrates (additives listed on many food labels) decrease thiamine effect.

Minerals

Many minerals are essential parts of enzymes. They also actively participate in regulating many physiological functions. These include transporting oxygen to each of the body's cells, providing sparks to make muscles contract and participating in many ways to guarantee normal function of the central nervous system. Minerals are required for growth, maintenance, repair and health of tissues and bones.

Most minerals (zinc is an exception) are widely distributed in foods. *Severe* mineral deficiency is unusual in Britain. A typical diet will only be deficient in a few essential minerals. Even so, there are exceptions. Iron deficiency is common in infants, children and pregnant women. Zinc and copper deficiencies occur frequently.

Alumina/Magnesia/Calcium Carbonate

Basic Information

Provides additional magnesium. Other substances in title are not supplied in large enough amounts for use by your body.
Available from natural sources? Yes
Available from synthetic sources? No
Prescription required? Yes, for some forms

Natural Sources

Almonds	Leafy, green	Snails
Bluefish	vegetables	Soya beans
Carp	Mackerel	Sunflower
Cod	Molasses	seeds
Flounder	Nuts	Swordfish
Halibut	Ocean perch	Wheat germ
Herring	Shrimp	

Reasons to Use

- Aids bone growth.
- Aids function of nerves and muscles, including regulation of normal heart rhythm.
- Keeps metabolism steady.
- Conducts nerve impulses.
- Works as laxative in large doses.
- Acts as antacid in small doses.
- Strengthens tooth enamel.

Unproved Speculated Benefits

- Cures alcoholism.
- Cures kidney stones.
- Alleviates heart disease.
- Helps control bad breath and body odour.
- Helps contain lead poisoning.

Who Needs Additional Amounts?

- Anyone with inadequate caloric or dietary intake or increased nutritional requirements.
- Those who abuse alcohol or other drugs.
- People with a chronic wasting illness or who have recently undergone surgery.
- Those with recent severe burns or injuries.

Deficiency Symptoms

Following symptoms occur rarely:
- Muscle contractions
- Convulsions
- Confusion and delirium
- Irritability
- Nervousness
- Skin problems
- Hardening of soft tissues

Unproved Speculated Symptoms

- Sudden heart failure

Lab Tests to Detect Deficiency

- Serum magnesium

Dosage and Usage Information

Recommended Dietary Allowance (RDA):
Estimate of adequate daily intake by the Food and Nutrition Board of the National Research Council, 1980 (See Glossary).

Age	RDA
0–6 months	50mg
6–12 months	70mg
1–3 years	150mg
4–6 years	200mg
7–10 years	250mg
Males	
11–14 years	350mg
15–18 years	400mg
18+ years	350mg
Females	
11+ years	300mg
Pregnant	+150mg
Lactating	+150mg

What this mineral does:
- Activates essential enzymes.
- Affects metabolism of proteins and nucleic acids.
- Helps transport sodium and potassium across cell membranes.
- Influences calcium levels inside cells.

Available as:
- Oral suspension: Dilute in at least 1/2 glass of water or other liquid. Take with meals or 1 to 1-1/2 hours after meals unless otherwise directed by your doctor.
- Chewable tablets: Chew well before swallowing.

Alumina/Magnesia/Calcium Carbonate

 Warnings and Precautions

Don't take if you have:
- Kidney failure.
- Heart block (unless you have a pacemaker).
- An ileostomy.

Consult your doctor if you have:
- Chronic constipation, colitis, diarrhoea.
- Symptoms of appendicitis.
- Stomach or intestinal bleeding.

Over age 55:
- Adverse reactions/side effects more likely.

Pregnancy:
- Risk to fetus outweighs benefits. Don't use.

Breast-feeding:
- Avoid magnesium in large quantities.
- If you must take temporarily, discontinue breast-feeding. Consult doctor for advice on maintaining milk supply.
- Don't take megadoses.

Effect on lab tests:
- Makes test for stomach-acid secretion inaccurate.
- May increase or decrease serum-phosphate concentrations.
- May decrease serum and urine pH.

Storage:
- Store in cool, dry place away from direct light, but don't freeze.
- Store safely out of reach of children.
- Don't store in bathroom medicine cabinet. Heat and moisture may change action of mineral.

Others:
- Chronic kidney disease frequently causes body to retain excess magnesium.
- Adverse reactions, side effects and interactions with medicines, vitamins or minerals occur *only rarely* when too much magnesium is taken for too long or if you have kidney disease.

 Overdose/Toxicity

Signs and symptoms:
Severe nausea and vomiting, extremely low blood pressure, extreme muscle weakness, difficulty breathing, heartbeat irregularity.

What to do:
For symptoms of overdosage: Discontinue mineral, and consult doctor immediately. Also see *Adverse Reactions or Side Effects* section below.
For accidental overdosage (such as child taking entire bottle): Dial 999 (emergency).

 Adverse Reactions or Side Effects

Reaction or effect	What to do
Abdominal pain	Discontinue. Call doctor immediately.
Appetite loss	Discontinue. Call doctor when convenient.
Diarrhoea	Discontinue. Call doctor immediately.
Irregular heartbeat	Seek emergency treatment.
Mood changes or mental changes	Discontinue. Call doctor when convenient.
Nausea	Discontinue. Call doctor immediately.
Tiredness or weakness	Discontinue. Call doctor when convenient.
Urination discomfort	Discontinue. Call doctor when convenient.
Vomiting	Discontinue. Call doctor immediately.

 Interaction with Medicine, Vitamins or Minerals

Interacts with	Combined effect
Cellulose sodium phosphate	Decreases magnesium effect. Take 1 or more hours apart.
Fat-soluble vitamins (A, E, K)	Decreases absorption of mineral.
Ketoconazole	Reduces absorption of ketoconazole. Take 2 hours apart.
Mecamylamine	May slow urinary excretion of mecamylamine. Avoid combination.
Tetracycline	Decreases absorption of tetracycline.
Vitamin D	May raise magnesium level too high.

 Interaction with Other Substances

None known

MINERAL

Alumina/Magnesia/Simethicone

Basic Information

Provides additional magnesium. Other substances in title are not supplied in large enough amounts for use by your body.
Available from natural sources? Yes
Available from synthetic sources? No
Prescription required? Yes, for some forms

Natural Sources

Almonds	Leafy, green	Snails
Bluefish	vegetables	Soya beans
Carp	Mackerel	Sunflower
Cod	Molasses	seeds
Flounder	Nuts	Swordfish
Halibut	Ocean perch	Wheat germ
Herring	Shrimp	

Reasons to Use

- Aids bone growth.
- Aids function of nerves and muscles, including regulation of normal heart rhythm.
- Keeps metabolism steady.
- Conducts nerve impulses.
- Works as laxative in large doses.
- Acts as antacid in small doses.
- Strengthens tooth enamel.

Unproved Speculated Benefits

- Cures alcoholism.
- Cures kidney stones.
- Alleviates heart disease.
- Helps control bad breath and body odour.
- Helps contain lead poisoning.

Who Needs Additional Amounts?

- Anyone with inadequate caloric or dietary intake or increased nutritional requirements.
- Those who abuse alcohol or other drugs.
- People with a chronic wasting illness or who have recently undergone surgery.
- Those with recent severe burns or injuries.

Deficiency Symptoms

Following symptoms occur rarely:
- Muscle contractions
- Convulsions
- Confusion and delirium
- Irritability
- Nervousness
- Skin problems
- Hardening of soft tissues

Unproved Speculated Symptoms

- Sudden heart failure

Lab Tests to Detect Deficiency

- Serum magnesium

Dosage and Usage Information

Recommended Dietary Allowance (RDA):
Estimate of adequate daily intake by the Food and Nutrition Board of the National Research Council, 1980 (See Glossary).

Age	RDA
0–6 months	50mg
6–12 months	70mg
1–3 years	150mg
4–6 years	200mg
7–10 years	250mg
Males	
11–14 years	350mg
15–18 years	400mg
18+ years	350mg
Females	
11+ years	300mg
Pregnant	+150mg
Lactating	+150mg

What this mineral does:
- Activates essential enzymes.
- Affects metabolism of proteins and nucleic acids.
- Helps transport sodium and potassium across cell membranes.
- Influences calcium levels inside cells.

Available as:
- Oral suspension: Dilute in at least 1/2 glass of water or other liquid. Take with meals or 1 to 1-1/2 hours after meals unless otherwise directed by your doctor.
- Chewable tablets: Chew well before swallowing.

Warnings and Precautions

Don't take if you have:
- Kidney failure.
- Heart block (unless you have a pacemaker).
- An ileostomy.

Consult your doctor if you have:
- Chronic constipation, colitis, diarrhoea.
- Symptoms of appendicitis.
- Stomach or intestinal bleeding.

Over age 55:
- Adverse reactions/side effects more likely.

Pregnancy:
- Risk to fetus outweighs benefits. Don't use.

Breast-feeding:
- Avoid magnesium in large quantities.
- If you must take temporarily, discontinue breast-feeding. Consult doctor for advice on maintaining milk supply.
- Don't take megadoses.

Effect on lab tests:
- Makes test for stomach-acid secretion inaccurate.
- May increase or decrease serum-phosphate concentrations.
- May decrease serum and urine pH.

Storage:
- Store in cool, dry place away from direct light, but don't freeze.
- Store safely out of reach of children.
- Don't store in bathroom medicine cabinet. Heat and moisture may change action of mineral.

Others:
- Chronic kidney disease frequently causes body to retain excess magnesium.
- Adverse reactions, side effects and interactions with medicines, vitamins or minerals occur *only rarely* when too much magnesium is taken for too long or if you have kidney disease.

Overdose/Toxicity

Signs and symptoms:
Severe nausea and vomiting, extremely low blood pressure, extreme muscle weakness, difficulty breathing, heartbeat irregularity.

What to do:
For symptoms of overdosage: Discontinue mineral, and consult doctor immediately. Also see *Adverse Reactions or Side Effects* section below.
For accidental overdosage (such as child taking entire bottle): Dial 999 (emergency).

Adverse Reactions or Side Effects

Reaction or effect	What to do
Abdominal pain	Discontinue. Call doctor immediately.
Appetite loss	Discontinue. Call doctor when convenient.
Diarrhoea	Discontinue. Call doctor immediately.
Irregular heartbeat	Seek emergency treatment.
Mood changes or mental changes	Discontinue. Call doctor when convenient.
Nausea	Discontinue. Call doctor immediately.
Tiredness or weakness	Discontinue. Call doctor when convenient.
Urination discomfort	Discontinue. Call doctor when convenient.
Vomiting	Discontinue. Call doctor immediately.

Interaction with Medicine, Vitamins or Minerals

Interacts with	Combined effect
Cellulose sodium phosphate	Decreases magnesium effect. Take 1 or more hours apart.
Fat-soluble vitamins (A, E, K)	Decreases absorption of mineral.
Ketoconazole	Reduces absorption of ketoconazole. Take 2 hours apart.
Mecamylamine	May slow urinary excretion of mecamylamine. Avoid combination.
Tetracycline	Decreases absorption of tetracycline.
Vitamin D	May raise magnesium level too high.

Interaction with Other Substances

None known

Alumina/Magnesium Carbonate

Basic Information

Provides additional magnesium. Other substances in title are not supplied in large enough amounts for use by your body.
Available from natural sources? Yes
Available from synthetic sources? No
Prescription required? Yes, for some forms

Natural Sources

Almonds	Leafy, green	Snails
Bluefish	vegetables	Soya beans
Carp	Mackerel	Sunflower
Cod	Molasses	seeds
Flounder	Nuts	Swordfish
Halibut	Ocean perch	Wheat germ
Herring	Shrimp	

Reasons to Use

- Aids bone growth.
- Aids function of nerves and muscles, including regulation of normal heart rhythm.
- Keeps metabolism steady.
- Conducts nerve impulses.
- Works as laxative in large doses.
- Acts as antacid in small doses.
- Strengthens tooth enamel.

Unproved Speculated Benefits

- Cures alcoholism.
- Cures kidney stones.
- Alleviates heart disease.
- Helps control bad breath and body odour.
- Helps contain lead poisoning.

Who Needs Additional Amounts?

- Anyone with inadequate caloric or dietary intake or increased nutritional requirements.
- Those who abuse alcohol or other drugs.
- People with a chronic wasting illness or who have recently undergone surgery.
- Those with recent severe burns or injuries.

Deficiency Symptoms

Following symptoms occur rarely:
- Muscle contractions
- Convulsions
- Confusion and delirium
- Irritability
- Nervousness
- Skin problems
- Hardening of soft tissues

Unproved Speculated Symptoms

- Sudden heart failure

Lab Tests to Detect Deficiency

- Serum magnesium

Dosage and Usage Information

Recommended Dietary Allowance (RDA):
Estimate of adequate daily intake by the Food and Nutrition Board of the National Research Council, 1980 (See Glossary).

Age	RDA
0–6 months	50mg
6–12 months	70mg
1–3 years	150mg
4–6 years	200mg
7–10 years	250mg
Males	
11–14 years	350mg
15–18 years	400mg
18+ years	350mg
Females	
11+ years	300mg
Pregnant	+150mg
Lactating	+150mg

What this mineral does:
- Activates essential enzymes.
- Affects metabolism of proteins and nucleic acids.
- Helps transport sodium and potassium across cell membranes.
- Influences calcium levels inside cells.

Available as:
- Oral suspension: Dilute in at least 1/2 glass of water or other liquid. Take with meals or 1 to 1-1/2 hours after meals unless otherwise directed by your doctor.
- Chewable tablets: Chew well before swallowing.

Warnings and Precautions

Don't take if you have:
- Kidney failure.
- Heart block (unless you have a pacemaker).
- An ileostomy.

Consult your doctor if you have:
- Chronic constipation, colitis, diarrhoea.
- Symptoms of appendicitis.
- Stomach or intestinal bleeding.

Over age 55:
- Adverse reactions/side effects more likely.

Pregnancy:
- Risk to fetus outweighs benefits. Don't use.

Breast-feeding:
- Avoid magnesium in large quantities.
- If you must take temporarily, discontinue breast-feeding. Consult doctor for advice on maintaining milk supply.
- Don't take megadoses.

Effect on lab tests:
- Makes test for stomach-acid secretion inaccurate.
- May increase or decrease serum-phosphate concentrations.
- May decrease serum and urine pH.

Storage:
- Store in cool, dry place away from direct light, but don't freeze.
- Store safely out of reach of children.
- Don't store in bathroom medicine cabinet. Heat and moisture may change action of mineral.

Others:
- Chronic kidney disease frequently causes body to retain excess magnesium.
- Adverse reactions, side effects and interactions with medicines, vitamins or minerals occur *only rarely* when too much magnesium is taken for too long or if you have kidney disease.

Overdose/Toxicity

Signs and symptoms:
Severe nausea and vomiting, extremely low blood pressure, extreme muscle weakness, difficulty breathing, heartbeat irregularity.

What to do:
For symptoms of overdosage: Discontinue mineral, and consult doctor immediately. Also see *Adverse Reactions or Side Effects* section below.
For accidental overdosage (such as child taking entire bottle): Dial 999 (emergency).

Adverse Reactions or Side Effects

Reaction or effect	What to do
Abdominal pain	Discontinue. Call doctor immediately.
Appetite loss	Discontinue. Call doctor when convenient.
Diarrhoea	Discontinue. Call doctor immediately.
Irregular heartbeat	Seek emergency treatment.
Mood changes or mental changes	Discontinue. Call doctor when convenient.
Nausea	Discontinue. Call doctor immediately.
Tiredness or weakness	Discontinue. Call doctor when convenient.
Urination discomfort	Discontinue. Call doctor when convenient.
Vomiting	Discontinue. Call doctor immediately.

Interaction with Medicine, Vitamins or Minerals

Interacts with	Combined effect
Cellulose sodium phosphate	Decreases magnesium effect. Take 1 or more hours apart.
Fat-soluble vitamins (A, E, K)	Decreases absorption of mineral.
Ketoconazole	Reduces absorption of ketoconazole. Take 2 hours apart.
Mecamylamine	May slow urinary excretion of mecamylamine. Avoid combination.
Tetracycline	Decreases absorption of tetracycline.
Vitamin D	May raise magnesium level too high.

Interaction with Other Substances

None known

Alumina/Magnesium Trisilicate

Basic Information
Provides additional magnesium. Other substances in title are not supplied in large enough amounts for use by your body. Available from natural sources? Yes Available from synthetic sources? No Prescription required? Yes, for some forms

Natural Sources

Almonds	Leafy, green	Snails
Bluefish	vegetables	Soya beans
Carp	Mackerel	Sunflower
Cod	Molasses	seeds
Flounder	Nuts	Swordfish
Halibut	Ocean perch	Wheat germ
Herring	Shrimp	

Reasons to Use

- Aids bone growth.
- Aids function of nerves and muscles, including regulation of normal heart rhythm.
- Keeps metabolism steady.
- Conducts nerve impulses.
- Works as laxative in large doses.
- Acts as antacid in small doses.
- Strengthens tooth enamel.

Unproved Speculated Benefits

- Cures alcoholism.
- Cures kidney stones.
- Alleviates heart disease.
- Helps control bad breath and body odour.
- Helps contain lead poisoning.

Who Needs Additional Amounts?

- Anyone with inadequate caloric or dietary intake or increased nutritional requirements.
- Those who abuse alcohol or other drugs.
- People with a chronic wasting illness or who have recently undergone surgery.
- Those with recent severe burns or injuries.

Deficiency Symptoms

Following symptoms occur rarely:
- Muscle contractions
- Convulsions
- Confusion and delirium
- Irritability
- Nervousness
- Skin problems
- Hardening of soft tissues

Unproved Speculated Symptoms

- Sudden heart failure

Lab Tests to Detect Deficiency

- Serum magnesium

Dosage and Usage Information

Recommended Dietary Allowance (RDA):
Estimate of adequate daily intake by the Food and Nutrition Board of the National Research Council, 1980 (See Glossary).

Age	RDA
0–6 months	50mg
6–12 months	70mg
1–3 years	150mg
4–6 years	200mg
7–10 years	250mg
Males	
11–14 years	350mg
15–18 years	400mg
18+ years	350mg
Females	
11+ years	300mg
Pregnant	+150mg
Lactating	+150mg

What this mineral does:
- Activates essential enzymes.
- Affects metabolism of proteins and nucleic acids.
- Helps transport sodium and potassium across cell membranes.
- Influences calcium levels inside cells.

Available as:
- Chewable tablets: Chew well before swallowing.

➤➤➤

Alumina/Magnesium Trisilicate

Warnings and Precautions

Don't take if you have:
- Kidney failure.
- Heart block (unless you have a pacemaker).
- An ileostomy.

Consult your doctor if you have:
- Chronic constipation, colitis, diarrhoea.
- Symptoms of appendicitis.
- Stomach or intestinal bleeding.

Over age 55:
- Adverse reactions/side effects more likely.

Pregnancy:
- Risk to fetus outweighs benefits. Don't use.

Breast-feeding:
- Avoid magnesium in large quantities.
- If you must take temporarily, discontinue breast-feeding. Consult doctor for advice on maintaining milk supply.
- Don't take megadoses.

Effect on lab tests:
- Makes test for stomach-acid secretion inaccurate.
- May increase or decrease serum-phosphate concentrations.
- May decrease serum and urine pH.

Storage:
- Store in cool, dry place away from direct light, but don't freeze.
- Store safely out of reach of children.
- Don't store in bathroom medicine cabinet. Heat and moisture may change action of mineral.

Others:
- Chronic kidney disease frequently causes body to retain excess magnesium.
- Adverse reactions, side effects and interactions with medicines, vitamins or minerals occur *only rarely* when too much magnesium is taken for too long or if you have kidney disease.

Overdose/Toxicity

Signs and symptoms:
Severe nausea and vomiting, extremely low blood pressure, extreme muscle weakness, difficulty breathing, heartbeat irregularity.

What to do:
For symptoms of overdosage: Discontinue mineral, and consult doctor immediately. Also see *Adverse Reactions or Side Effects* section below.

For accidental overdosage (such as child taking entire bottle): Dial 999 (emergency).

Adverse Reactions or Side Effects

Reaction or effect	What to do
Abdominal pain	Discontinue. Call doctor immediately.
Appetite loss	Discontinue. Call doctor when convenient.
Diarrhoea	Discontinue. Call doctor immediately.
Irregular heartbeat	Seek emergency treatment.
Mood changes or mental changes	Discontinue. Call doctor when convenient.
Nausea	Discontinue. Call doctor immediately.
Tiredness or weakness	Discontinue. Call doctor when convenient.
Urination discomfort	Discontinue. Call doctor when convenient.
Vomiting	Discontinue. Call doctor immediately.

Interaction with Medicine, Vitamins or Minerals

Interacts with	Combined effect
Cellulose sodium phosphate	Decreases magnesium effect. Take 1 or more hours apart.
Fat-soluble vitamins (A, E, K)	Decreases absorption of mineral.
Ketoconazole	Reduces absorption of ketoconazole. Take 2 hours apart.
Mecamylamine	May slow urinary excretion of mecamylamine. Avoid combination.
Tetracycline	Decreases absorption of tetracycline.
Vitamin D	May raise magnesium level too high.

Interaction with Other Substances

None known

MINERAL

83

Alumina/Magnesium Trisilicate/Sodium Bicarbonate

Basic Information

Provides additional magnesium. Other substances in title are not supplied in large enough amounts for use by your body.
Available from natural sources? Yes
Available from synthetic sources? No
Prescription required? Yes, for some forms

Natural Sources

Almonds	Leafy, green	Snails
Bluefish	vegetables	Soya beans
Carp	Mackerel	Sunflower
Cod	Molasses	seeds
Flounder	Nuts	Swordfish
Halibut	Ocean perch	Wheat germ
Herring	Shrimp	

Reasons to Use

- Aids bone growth.
- Aids function of nerves and muscles, including regulation of normal heart rhythm.
- Keeps metabolism steady.
- Conducts nerve impulses.
- Works as laxative in large doses.
- Acts as antacid in small doses.
- Strengthens tooth enamel.

Unproved Speculated Benefits

- Cures alcoholism.
- Cures kidney stones.
- Alleviates heart disease.
- Helps control bad breath and body odour.
- Helps contain lead poisoning.

Who Needs Additional Amounts?

- Anyone with inadequate caloric or dietary intake or increased nutritional requirements.
- Those who abuse alcohol or other drugs.
- People with a chronic wasting illness or who have recently undergone surgery.
- Those with recent severe burns or injuries.

Deficiency Symptoms

Following symptoms occur rarely:
- Muscle contractions
- Convulsions
- Confusion and delirium
- Irritability
- Nervousness
- Skin problems
- Hardening of soft tissues

Unproved Speculated Symptoms

- Sudden heart failure

Lab Tests to Detect Deficiency

- Serum magnesium

Dosage and Usage Information

Recommended Dietary Allowance (RDA):
Estimate of adequate daily intake by the Food and Nutrition Board of the National Research Council, 1980 (See Glossary).

Age	RDA
0–6 months	50mg
6–12 months	70mg
1–3 years	150mg
4–6 years	200mg
7–10 years	250mg
Males	
11–14 years	350mg
15–18 years	400mg
18+ years	350mg
Females	
11+ years	300mg
Pregnant	+150mg
Lactating	+150mg

What this mineral does:
- Activates essential enzymes.
- Affects metabolism of proteins and nucleic acids.
- Helps transport sodium and potassium across cell membranes.
- Influences calcium levels inside cells.

Available as:
- Chewable tablets: Chew well before swallowing.

➤➤

Alumina/Magnesium Trisilicate/Sodium Bicarbonate

 Warnings and Precautions

Don't take if you have:
- Kidney failure.
- Heart block (unless you have a pacemaker).
- An ileostomy.

Consult your doctor if you have:
- Chronic constipation, colitis, diarrhoea.
- Symptoms of appendicitis.
- Stomach or intestinal bleeding.

Over age 55:
- Adverse reactions/side effects more likely.

Pregnancy:
- Risk to fetus outweighs benefits. Don't use.

Breast-feeding:
- Avoid magnesium in large quantities.
- If you must take temporarily, discontinue breast-feeding. Consult doctor for advice on maintaining milk supply.
- Don't take megadoses.

Effect on lab tests:
- Makes test for stomach-acid secretion inaccurate.
- May increase or decrease serum-phosphate concentrations.
- May decrease serum and urine pH.

Storage:
- Store in cool, dry place away from direct light, but don't freeze.
- Store safely out of reach of children.
- Don't store in bathroom medicine cabinet. Heat and moisture may change action of mineral.

Others:
- Chronic kidney disease frequently causes body to retain excess magnesium.
- Adverse reactions, side effects and interactions with medicines, vitamins or minerals occur *only rarely* when too much magnesium is taken for too long or if you have kidney disease.

 Overdose/Toxicity

Signs and symptoms:
Severe nausea and vomiting, extremely low blood pressure, extreme muscle weakness, difficulty breathing, heartbeat irregularity.

What to do:
For symptoms of overdosage: Discontinue mineral, and consult doctor immediately. Also see *Adverse Reactions or Side Effects* section below.

For accidental overdosage (such as child taking entire bottle): Dial 999 (emergency).

 Adverse Reactions or Side Effects

Reaction or effect	What to do
Abdominal pain	Discontinue. Call doctor immediately.
Appetite loss	Discontinue. Call doctor when convenient.
Diarrhoea	Discontinue. Call doctor immediately.
Irregular heartbeat	Seek emergency treatment.
Mood changes or mental changes	Discontinue. Call doctor when convenient.
Nausea	Discontinue. Call doctor immediately.
Tiredness or weakness	Discontinue. Call doctor when convenient.
Urination discomfort	Discontinue. Call doctor when convenient.
Vomiting	Discontinue. Call doctor immediately.

 Interaction with Medicine, Vitamins or Minerals

Interacts with	Combined effect
Cellulose sodium phosphate	Decreases magnesium effect. Take 1 or more hours apart.
Fat-soluble vitamins (A, E, K)	Decreases absorption of mineral.
Ketoconazole	Reduces absorption of ketoconazole. Take 2 hours apart.
Mecamylamine	May slow urinary excretion of mecamylamine. Avoid combination.
Tetracycline	Decreases absorption of tetracycline.
Vitamin D	May raise magnesium level too high.

 Interaction with Other Substances

None known

Calcium Carbonate

Basic Information
Available from natural sources? Yes
Available from synthetic sources? Yes
*Prescription required? Some forms, yes;
  others, no*

Natural Sources

Almonds	Salmon, canned
Brazil nuts	Sardines, canned
Caviar	Shrimp
Cheese	Soya beans
Kelp	Tofu
Milk	Turnip greens
Milk products	Yogurt
Molasses	

Reasons to Use

- Helps prevent osteoporosis in older people.
- Treats calcium depletion in people with hypoparathyroidism, osteomalacia, rickets.
- Treats low-calcium levels in people taking anti-convulsant medication.
- Treats tetany (severe muscle spasms) caused by insect bites, sensitivity reactions, cardiac arrest, lead poisoning.
- Is used as an antidote to magnesium poisoning.
- Prevents muscle cramps in some people.
- Promotes normal growth and development.
- Builds bones and teeth
- Maintains bone density and strength.
- Buffers acid in stomach and acts as antacid.
- Helps regulate heartbeat, blood clotting, muscle contraction.
- Treats neonatal hypocalcaemia.
- Promotes storage and release of some body hormones.
- Promotes use of amino acids.
- Lowers phosphate concentrations in people with chronic kidney disease.

Unproved Speculated Benefits

- Helps prevent insomnia and anxiety (acts as a natural tranquilizer).
- Helps prevent hypertension.
- Treats allergies.
- Decreases likelihood of hardening of arteries.
- Treats leg cramps.
- Treats diabetes.
- Treats throat spasms.

Who Needs Additional Amounts?

- Anyone with inadequate caloric or dietary intake or increased nutritional requirements or who does not like or consume milk products.
- People allergic to milk and milk products or who don't tolerate them well.
- Older people (over 55 years), particularly women.
- Women throughout adult life, especially during pregnancy and lactation, but not limited to these times.
- Those who abuse alcohol or other drugs.
- People with a chronic wasting illness, excess stress for long periods or who have recently undergone surgery.
- Those with a portion of the gastrointestinal tract surgically removed.
- People with recent severe burns or injuries.

Deficiency Symptoms

- Osteoporosis (late symptoms): frequent fractures in spine and other bones, deformed spinal column with humps, loss of height
- Osteomalacia: frequent fractures
- Muscle contractions
- Convulsive seizures
- Muscle cramps
- Low backache

Unproved Speculated Symptoms

- Uncontrollable temper outbursts

Lab Tests to Detect Deficiency

- 24-hour urine collection to measure calcium levels (Sulkowitch)
- Serum-calcium levels
- Imaging procedures to scan for bone density (more reliable than above tests)

Dosage and Usage Information

Recommended Dietary Allowance (RDA):
Estimate of adequate daily intake by the Food and Nutrition Board of the National Research Council, 1980 (See Glossary).
Many doctors and nutritionists recommend women take more calcium than quoted by the ⟩⟩▸

RDA. They recommend 1,000 milligrams per day for premenopausal women and 1,500 milligrams per day for post-menopausal women and elderly men.

Age	RDA
0–6 months	360mg
6–12 months	540mg
1–10 years	800mg
11–18 years	1,000mg
18+ years	800mg
Pregnant	+400mg
Lactating	+400mg

Different types of calcium supplements contain more available calcium (also called *elemental calcium*) than others. To provide 1,000mg of available calcium, you must take:

4 tablets/day of 625mg calcium carbonate
4 tablets/day of 650mg calcium carbonate
4 tablets/day of 750mg calcium carbonate
3 tablets/day of 835mg calcium carbonate
2 tablets/day of 1,250mg calcium carbonate
2 tablets/day of 1,500mg calcium carbonate

Check contents of product you choose to determine how many tablets are needed to provide the amount of calcium you require.

What this mineral does:
• Participates in metabolic functions necessary for normal activity of nervous, muscular, skeletal systems.
• Plays important role in normal heart function, kidney function, blood clotting, blood-vessel integrity.
• Helps utilization of vitamin B-12.

Miscellaneous information:
• Bones serve as storage site for calcium in the body. There is a constant interchange between calcium in bone and the bloodstream.
• Foods rich in calcium (or supplements) help maintain the balance between bone needs and blood needs.
• Don't discard outer parts of vegetables during food preparation.
• Exercise, a balanced diet, calcium from natural sources or supplements and oestrogens are important in treating and preventing osteoporosis.

Available as:
• Tablets: Swallow whole with full glass of liquid. Don't chew or crush. Take with meals or 1 to 1-1/2 hours after meals unless otherwise directed by your doctor.
• Chewable tablets: Chew well before swallowing.

Warnings and Precautions

Don't take if you:
• Are allergic to calcium or antacids.
• Have kidney stones.
• Have a high blood-calcium level.
• Have sarcoidosis.

Consult your doctor if you have:
• Kidney disease.
• Chronic constipation, colitis, diarrhoea.
• Stomach or intestinal bleeding.
• Irregular heartbeat.

Over age 55:
• Adverse reactions and side effects are more likely.
• Diarrhoea, or constipation are particularly likely.

Pregnancy:
• May need extra calcium. Consult doctor about supplements.
• Don't take megadoses.

Breast-feeding:
• Drug passes into milk. Consult doctor about supplements.
• Don't take megadoses.

Effect on lab tests:
• Serum-amylase and serum 11-hydroxycorticosteroid concentrations can be increased.
• Decreases serum-phosphate concentration with excessive, prolonged use.

Storage:
• Store in cool, dry area away from direct light, but don't freeze.
• Store safely out of reach of children.
• Don't store in bathroom medicine cabinet. Heat and moisture may change action of mineral.

Others:
• Dolomite or bone meal are probably *unsafe* sources of calcium because they contain lead.
• Avoid taking calcium within 1 or 2 hours of meals or ingestion of other medicines, if possible.
• Some calcium carbonate is derived from oyster shells. Calcium carbonate derived from this source is *not* recommended!

➤➤➤

MINERAL

Calcium Carbonate, Continued

☠ Overdose/Toxicity

Signs and symptoms:
Confusion, high blood pressure, increased sensitivity of eyes and skin to light, increased thirst, slow or irregular heartbeat, depression, bone or muscle pain, nausea, vomiting, skin itching, skin rash, increased urination.

What to do:
For symptoms of overdosage: Discontinue mineral, and consult doctor immediately. Also see *Adverse Reactions or Side Effects* section below.
For accidental overdosage (such as child taking entire bottle): Dial 999 (emergency).

Adverse Reactions or Side Effects

Reaction or effect	What to do
Early signs of too much calcium in blood:	
Appetite loss	Discontinue. Call doctor when convenient.
Constipation	Discontinue. Call doctor when convenient.
Drowsiness	Discontinue. Call doctor immediately.
Dry mouth	Discontinue. Call doctor when convenient.
Headache	Discontinue. Call doctor when convenient.
Metallic taste	Discontinue. Call doctor when convenient.
Tiredness or weakness	Discontinue. Call doctor immediately.
Late signs of too much calcium in blood:	
Confusion	Discontinue. Call doctor immediately.
Depression	Discontinue. Call doctor when convenient.
High blood pressure	Discontinue. Call doctor immediately.
Increased thirst	Discontinue. Call doctor when convenient.
Increased urination	Discontinue. Call doctor when convenient.
Muscle or bone pain	Discontinue. Call doctor immediately.
Nausea	Discontinue. Call doctor immediately.
Skin rash	Discontinue. Call doctor immediately.
Slow or irregular heartbeat	Seek emergency treatment.
Vomiting	Discontinue. Call doctor immediately.

Interaction with Medicine, Vitamins or Minerals

Interacts with	Combined effect
Digitalis preparations	Heartbeat irregularities.
Iron supplements	Decreases absorption of iron unless vitamin C is taken at same time.
Magnesium-containing medications or supplements	Increases blood level of both.
Oral contraceptives and oestrogens	May increase calcium absorption.
Potassium supplements	Increases chance of heartbeat irregularities.
Tetracyclines (oral)	Decreases absorption of tetracycline.
Vitamin A (megadoses)	Stimulates bone loss.
Vitamin D (megadoses)	Excessively increases absorption of calcium supplements.

Interaction with Other Substances

Tobacco decreases absorption.

Alcohol decreases absorption.

Beverages
• Tea decreases absorption.
• Coffee decreases absorption.
• Don't take calcium with milk or other dairy products so your body can absorb the most calcium from food *and* calcium supplement.

Foods
• Avoid eating spinach, rhubarb, bran, whole-grain cereals, fresh fruits or fresh vegetables at same time you take calcium. They may prevent efficient absorption.

Calcium Carbonate/Magnesia

Basic Information

Provides additional magnesium. Other substances in title are not supplied in large enough amounts for use by your body. Available from natural sources? Yes Available from synthetic sources? No Prescription required? Yes, for some forms

Natural Sources

Almonds	Leafy, green	Snails
Bluefish	vegetables	Soya beans
Carp	Mackerel	Sunflower
Cod	Molasses	seeds
Flounder	Nuts	Swordfish
Halibut	Ocean perch	Wheat germ
Herring	Shrimp	

Reasons to Use

- Aids bone growth.
- Aids function of nerves and muscles, including regulation of normal heart rhythm.
- Keeps metabolism steady.
- Conducts nerve impulses.
- Works as laxative in large doses.
- Acts as antacid in small doses.
- Strengthens tooth enamel.

Unproved Speculated Benefits

- Cures alcoholism.
- Cures kidney stones.
- Alleviates heart disease.
- Helps control bad breath and body odour.
- Helps contain lead poisoning.

Who Needs Additional Amounts?

- Anyone with inadequate caloric or dietary intake or increased nutritional requirements.
- Those who abuse alcohol or other drugs.
- People with a chronic wasting illness or who have recently undergone surgery.
- Those with recent severe burns or injuries.

Deficiency Symptoms

Following symptoms occur rarely:
- Muscle contractions
- Convulsions
- Confusion and delirium
- Irritability
- Nervousness
- Skin problems
- Hardening of soft tissues

Unproved Speculated Symptoms

- Sudden heart failure

Lab Tests to Detect Deficiency

- Serum magnesium

Dosage and Usage Information

Recommended Dietary Allowance (RDA):
Estimate of adequate daily intake by the Food and Nutrition Board of the National Research Council, 1980 (See Glossary).

Age	RDA
0–6 months	50mg
6–12 months	70mg
1–3 years	150mg
4–6 years	200mg
7–10 years	250mg
Males	
11–14 years	350mg
15–18 years	400mg
18+ years	350mg
Females	
11+ years	300mg
Pregnant	+150mg
Lactating	+150mg

What this mineral does:
- Activates essential enzymes.
- Affects metabolism of proteins and nucleic acids.
- Helps transport sodium and potassium across cell membranes.
- Influences calcium levels inside cells.

Available as:
- Chewable tablets: Chew well before swallowing.

Calcium Carbonate/Magnesia, Continued

Warnings and Precautions

Don't take if you have:
- Kidney failure.
- Heart block (unless you have a pacemaker).
- An ileostomy.

Consult your doctor if you have:
- Chronic constipation, colitis, diarrhoea.
- Symptoms of appendicitis.
- Stomach or intestinal bleeding.

Over age 55:
- Adverse reactions/side effects more likely.

Pregnancy:
- Risk to fetus outweighs benefits. Don't use.

Breast-feeding:
- Avoid magnesium in large quantities.
- If you must take temporarily, discontinue breast-feeding. Consult doctor for advice on maintaining milk supply.
- Don't take megadoses.

Effect on lab tests:
- Makes test for stomach-acid secretion inaccurate.
- May increase or decrease serum-phosphate concentrations.
- May decrease serum and urine pH.

Storage:
- Store in cool, dry place away from direct light, but don't freeze.
- Store safely out of reach of children.
- Don't store in bathroom medicine cabinet. Heat and moisture may change action of mineral.

Others:
- Chronic kidney disease frequently causes body to retain excess magnesium.
- Adverse reactions, side effects and interactions with medicines, vitamins or minerals occur *only rarely* when too much magnesium is taken for too long or if you have kidney disease.

Overdose/Toxicity

Signs and symptoms:
Severe nausea and vomiting, extremely low blood pressure, extreme muscle weakness, difficulty breathing, heartbeat irregularity.

What to do:
For symptoms of overdosage: Discontinue mineral, and consult doctor immediately. Also see *Adverse Reactions or Side Effects* section below.
For accidental overdosage (such as child taking entire bottle): Dial 999 (emergency).

Adverse Reactions or Side Effects

Reaction or effect	What to do
Abdominal pain	Discontinue. Call doctor immediately.
Appetite loss	Discontinue. Call doctor when convenient.
Diarrhoea	Discontinue. Call doctor immediately.
Irregular heartbeat	Seek emergency treatment.
Mood changes or mental changes	Discontinue. Call doctor when convenient.
Nausea	Discontinue. Call doctor immediately.
Tiredness or weakness	Discontinue. Call doctor when convenient.
Urination discomfort	Discontinue. Call doctor when convenient.
Vomiting	Discontinue. Call doctor immediately.

Interaction with Medicine, Vitamins or Minerals

Interacts with	Combined effect
Cellulose sodium phosphate	Decreases magnesium effect. Take 1 or more hours apart.
Fat-soluble vitamins (A, E, K)	Decreases absorption of mineral.
Ketoconazole	Reduces absorption of ketoconazole. Take 2 hours apart.
Mecamylamine	May slow urinary excretion of mecamylamine. Avoid combination.
Tetracycline	Decreases absorption of tetracycline.
Vitamin D	May raise magnesium level too high.

Interaction with Other Substances

None known

Calcium Carbonate/Magnesia/Simethicone

Basic Information

Provides additional magnesium. Other substances in title are not supplied in large enough amounts for use by your body.
Available from natural sources? Yes
Available from synthetic sources? No
Prescription required? Yes, for some forms

Natural Sources

Almonds	Leafy, green	Snails
Bluefish	vegetables	Soya beans
Carp	Mackerel	Sunflower
Cod	Molasses	seeds
Flounder	Nuts	Swordfish
Halibut	Ocean perch	Wheat germ
Herring	Shrimp	

Reasons to Use

- Aids bone growth.
- Aids function of nerves and muscles, including regulation of normal heart rhythm.
- Keeps metabolism steady.
- Conducts nerve impulses.
- Works as laxative in large doses.
- Acts as antacid in small doses.
- Strengthens tooth enamel.

Unproved Speculated Benefits

- Cures alcoholism.
- Cures kidney stones.
- Alleviates heart disease.
- Helps control bad breath and body odour.
- Helps contain lead poisoning.

Who Needs Additional Amounts?

- Anyone with inadequate caloric or dietary intake or increased nutritional requirements.
- Those who abuse alcohol or other drugs.
- People with a chronic wasting illness or who have recently undergone surgery.
- Those with recent severe burns or injuries.

Deficiency Symptoms

Following symptoms occur rarely:
- Muscle contractions
- Convulsions
- Confusion and delirium
- Irritability
- Nervousness
- Skin problems
- Hardening of soft tissues

Unproved Speculated Symptoms

- Sudden heart failure

Lab Tests to Detect Deficiency

- Serum magnesium

Dosage and Usage Information

Recommended Dietary Allowance (RDA):
Estimate of adequate daily intake by the Food and Nutrition Board of the National Research Council, 1980 (See Glossary).

Age	RDA
0–6 months	50mg
6–12 months	70mg
1–3 years	150mg
4–6 years	200mg
7–10 years	250mg
Males	
11–14 years	350mg
15–18 years	400mg
18+ years	350mg
Females	
11+ years	300mg
Pregnant	+150mg
Lactating	+150mg

What this mineral does:
- Activates essential enzymes.
- Affects metabolism of proteins and nucleic acids.
- Helps transport sodium and potassium across cell membranes.
- Influences calcium levels inside cells.

Available as:
- Tablets: Swallow whole with full glass of liquid. Don't chew or crush. Take with meals or 1 to 1-1/2 hours after meals unless otherwise directed by your doctor.

➤➤➤

Calcium Carbonate/Magnesia/Simethicone, Continued

 Warnings and Precautions

Don't take if you have:
- Kidney failure.
- Heart block (unless you have a pacemaker).
- An ileostomy.

Consult your doctor if you have:
- Chronic constipation, colitis, diarrhoea.
- Symptoms of appendicitis.
- Stomach or intestinal bleeding.

Over age 55:
- Adverse reactions/side effects more likely.

Pregnancy:
- Risk to fetus outweighs benefits. Don't use.

Breast-feeding:
- Avoid magnesium in large quantities.
- If you must take temporarily, discontinue breast-feeding. Consult doctor for advice on maintaining milk supply.
- Don't take megadoses.

Effect on lab tests:
- Makes test for stomach-acid secretion inaccurate.
- May increase or decrease serum-phosphate concentrations.
- May decrease serum and urine pH.

Storage:
- Store in cool, dry place away from direct light, but don't freeze.
- Store safely out of reach of children.
- Don't store in bathroom medicine cabinet. Heat and moisture may change action of mineral.

Others:
- Chronic kidney disease frequently causes body to retain excess magnesium.
- Adverse reactions, side effects and interactions with medicines, vitamins or minerals occur *only rarely* when too much magnesium is taken for too long or if you have kidney disease.

 Overdose/Toxicity

Signs and symptoms:
Severe nausea and vomiting, extremely low blood pressure, extreme muscle weakness, difficulty breathing, heartbeat irregularity.

What to do:
For symptoms of overdosage: Discontinue mineral, and consult doctor immediately. Also see *Adverse Reactions or Side Effects* section below.
For accidental overdosage (such as child taking entire bottle): Dial 999 (emergency).

 Adverse Reactions or Side Effects

Reaction or effect	What to do
Abdominal pain	Discontinue. Call doctor immediately.
Appetite loss	Discontinue. Call doctor when convenient.
Diarrhoea	Discontinue. Call doctor immediately.
Irregular heartbeat	Seek emergency treatment.
Mood changes or mental changes	Discontinue. Call doctor when convenient.
Nausea	Discontinue. Call doctor immediately.
Tiredness or weakness	Discontinue. Call doctor when convenient.
Urination discomfort	Discontinue. Call doctor when convenient.
Vomiting	Discontinue. Call doctor immediately.

 Interaction with Medicine, Vitamins or Minerals

Interacts with	Combined effect
Cellulose sodium phosphate	Decreases magnesium effect. Take 1 or more hours apart.
Fat-soluble vitamins (A, E, K)	Decreases absorption of mineral.
Ketoconazole	Reduces absorption of ketoconazole. Take 2 hours apart.
Mecamylamine	May slow urinary excretion of mecamylamine. Avoid combination.
Tetracycline	Decreases absorption of tetracycline.
Vitamin D	May raise magnesium level too high.

 Interaction with Other Substances

None known

Basic Information

Available from natural sources? Yes
Available from synthetic sources? Yes
Prescription required? Some forms, yes;
  others, no

Natural Sources

Almonds	Salmon, canned
Brazil nuts	Sardines, canned
Caviar	Shrimp
Cheese	Soya beans
Kelp	Tofu
Milk	Turnip greens
Milk products	Yogurt
Molasses	

Reasons to Use

- Helps prevent osteoporosis in older people.
- Treats calcium depletion in people with hypoparathyroidism, osteomalacia, rickets.
- Treats low-calcium levels in people taking anti-convulsant medication.
- Treats tetany (severe muscle spasms) caused by insect bites, sensitivity reactions, cardiac arrest, lead poisoning.
- Is used as an antidote to magnesium poisoning.
- Prevents muscle cramps in some people.
- Promotes normal growth and development.
- Builds bones and teeth.
- Maintains bone density and strength.
- Buffers acid in stomach and acts as antacid.
- Helps regulate heartbeat, blood clotting, muscle contraction.
- Treats neonatal hypocalcaemia
- Promotes storage and release of some body hormones.
- Promotes use of amino acids.
- Lowers phosphate concentrations in people with chronic kidney disease.

Unproved Speculated Benefits

- Helps prevent insomnia and anxiety (acts as a natural tranquilizer).
- Helps prevent hypertension.
- Treats allergies.
- Decreases likelihood of hardening of arteries.
- Treats leg cramps.
- Treats diabetes.
- Treats throat spasms.

Who Needs Additional Amounts?

- Anyone with inadequate caloric or nutritional dietary intake or increased nutritional requirements or who does not like or consume milk products.
- People allergic to milk and milk products or who don't tolerate them well.
- Older people (over 55 years), particularly women.
- Women throughout adult life, especially during pregnancy and lactation, but not limited to these times.
- Those who abuse alcohol or other drugs.
- People who have a chronic wasting illness, excess stress for long periods or who have recently undergone surgery.
- Those with a portion of the gastrointestinal tract surgically removed.
- People with recent severe burns or injuries.

MINERAL

Deficiency Symptoms

- Osteoporosis (late symptoms): frequent fractures in spine and other bones, deformed spinal column with humps, loss of height
- Osteomalacia: frequent fractures
- Muscle contractions
- Convulsive seizures
- Muscle cramps
- Low backache

Unproved Speculated Symptoms

- Uncontrollable temper outbursts

Lab Tests to Detect Deficiency

- 24-hour urine collection to measure calcium levels (Sulkowitch)
- Serum-calcium levels
- Imaging procedures to scan for bone density (more reliable than above tests)

Calcium Citrate, Continued

Dosage and Usage Information

Recommended Dietary Allowance (RDA):
Estimate of adequate daily intake by the Food and Nutrition Board of the National Research Council, 1980 (See Glossary).
Many doctors and nutritionists recommend women take more calcium than quoted by the RDA. They recommend 1,000 milligrams per day for premenopausal women and 1,500 milligrams per day for post-menopausal women and elderly men.

Age	RDA
0–6 months	360mg
6–12 months	540mg
1–10 years	800mg
11–18 years	1,000mg
18+ years	800mg
Pregnant	+400mg
Lactating	+400mg

Different types of calcium supplements contain more available calcium (also called *elemental calcium*) than others. To provide 1,000mg of available calcium, you must take 5 tablets/day of 950mg calcium citrate. Take in divided doses after meals. Check contents of product to determine how many tablets are needed to provide the amount of calcium you require.

What this mineral does:
• Participates in metabolic functions necessary for normal activity of nervous, muscular, skeletal systems.
• Plays important role in normal heart function, kidney function, blood clotting, blood-vessel integrity.
• Helps utilization of vitamin B-12.

Miscellaneous information:
• Bones serve as storage site for calcium in the body. There is a constant interchange between calcium in bone and the bloodstream.
• Foods rich in calcium (or supplements) help maintain the balance between bone needs and blood needs.

Available as:
• Tablets: Swallow whole with full glass of liquid. Don't chew or crush. Take with meals or 1 to 1-1/2 hours after meals unless otherwise directed by your doctor.

Warnings and Precautions

Don't take if you:
• Are allergic to calcium or antacids.
• Have kidney stones.
• Have a high blood-calcium level.
• Have sarcoidosis.

Consult your doctor if you have:
• Kidney disease.
• Chronic constipation, colitis, diarrhoea.
• Stomach or intestinal bleeding.
• Irregular heartbeat.

Over age 55:
• Adverse reactions and side effects are more likely.
• Diarrhoea or constipation are particularly likely.

Pregnancy:
• May need extra calcium. Consult doctor about supplements.
• Don't take megadoses.

Breast-feeding:
• Drug passes into milk. Consult doctor about supplements.
• Don't take megadoses.

Effect on lab tests:
• Serum-amylase and serum 11-hydroxycorticosteroid concentrations can be increased.
• Decreases serum-phosphate concentration with excessive, prolonged use.

Storage:
• Store in cool, dry area away from direct light, but don't freeze.
• Store safely out of reach of children.
• Don't store in bathroom medicine cabinet. Heat and moisture may change action of mineral.

Others:
• Dolomite or bone meal are probably *unsafe* sources of calcium because they contain lead.
• Avoid taking calcium within 1 or 2 hours of meals or ingestion of other medicines, if possible.

Overdose/Toxicity

Signs and symptoms:
Confusion, high blood pressure, increased sensitivity of eyes and skin to light, increased thirst, slow or irregular heartbeat, depression, bone or muscle pain, nausea, vomiting, skin itching, skin rash, increased urination.

What to do:
For symptoms of overdosage: Discontinue mineral, and consult doctor immediately. Also see *Adverse Reactions or Side Effects* section below.

For accidental overdosage (such as child taking entire bottle): Dial 999 (emergency).

»→

Adverse Reactions or Side Effects

Reaction or effect	What to do
Early signs of too much calcium in blood:	
Appetite loss	Discontinue. Call doctor when convenient.
Constipation	Discontinue. Call doctor when convenient.
Drowsiness	Discontinue. Call doctor immediately.
Dry mouth	Discontinue. Call doctor when convenient.
Headache	Discontinue. Call doctor when convenient.
Metallic taste	Discontinue. Call doctor when convenient.
Tiredness or weakness	Discontinue. Call doctor immediately.
Late signs of too much calcium in blood:	
Confusion	Discontinue. Call doctor immediately.
Depression	Discontinue. Call doctor when convenient.
High blood pressure	Discontinue. Call doctor immediately.
Increased thirst	Discontinue. Call doctor when convenient.
Increased urination	Discontinue. Call doctor when convenient.
Muscle or bone pain	Discontinue. Call doctor immediately.
Nausea	Discontinue. Call doctor immediately.
Skin rash	Discontinue. Call doctor immediately.
Slow or irregular heartbeat	Seek emergency treatment.
Vomiting	Discontinue. Call doctor immediately.

Interaction with Medicine, Vitamins or Minerals

Interacts with	Combined effect
Digitalis preparations	Heartbeat irregularities.
Iron supplements	Decreases absorption of iron unless vitamin C is taken at same time.
Magnesium-containing medications or supplements	Increases blood level of both.
Oral contraceptives and oestrogens	May increase calcium absorption.
Potassium supplements	Increases chance of heartbeat irregularities.
Tetracyclines (oral)	Decreases absorption of tetracycline.
Vitamin A (megadoses)	Stimulates bone loss.
Vitamin D (megadoses)	Excessively increases absorption of calcium supplements.

Interaction with Other Substances

Tobacco decreases absorption.

Alcohol decreases absorption.

Beverages
• Tea decreases absorption.
• Coffee decreases absorption.
• Don't take calcium with milk or other dairy products so your body can absorb the most calcium from food *and* calcium supplement.

Foods
• Avoid eating spinach, rhubarb, bran, whole-grain cereals, fresh fruits or fresh vegetables at same time you take calcium. They may prevent efficient absorption.

MINERAL

Calcium Glubionate

Basic Information

Available from natural sources? Yes
Available from synthetic sources? Yes
Prescription required? Some forms, yes;
others, no

Natural Sources

Almonds	Salmon, tinned
Brazil nuts	Sardines, tinned
Caviar	Shrimp
Cheese	Soya beans
Kelp	Tofu
Milk	Turnip greens
Milk products	Yogurt
Molasses	

Reasons to Use

- Helps prevent osteoporosis in older people.
- Treats calcium depletion in people with hypoparathyroidism, osteomalacia, rickets.
- Treats low-calcium levels in people taking anticonvulsant medication.
- Treats tetany (severe muscle spasms) caused by insect bites, sensitivity reactions, cardiac arrest, lead poisoning.
- Is used as an antidote to magnesium poisoning.
- Prevents muscle cramps in some people.
- Promotes normal growth and development.
- Builds bones and teeth.
- Maintains bone density and strength.
- Buffers acid in stomach and acts as antacid.
- Helps regulate heartbeat, blood clotting, muscle contraction.
- Treats neonatal hypocalcaemia.
- Promotes storage and release of some body hormones.
- Promotes use of amino acids.
- Lowers phosphate concentrations in people with chronic kidney disease.

Unproved Speculated Benefits

- Helps prevent insomnia and anxiety (acts as a natural tranquilizer).
- Helps prevent hypertension.
- Treats allergies.
- Decreases likelihood of hardening of arteries.
- Treats leg cramps.
- Treats diabetes.
- Treats throat spasms.

Who Needs Additional Amounts?

- Anyone with inadequate caloric or nutritional dietary intake or increased nutritional requirements or who does not like or consume milk products.
- People allergic to milk and milk products or who don't tolerate them well.
- Older people (over 55 years), particularly women.
- Women throughout adult life, especially during pregnancy and lactation, but not limited to these times.
- Those who abuse alcohol or other drugs.
- People who have a chronic wasting illness, excess stress for long periods or who have recently undergone surgery.
- Those with a portion of the gastrointestinal tract surgically removed.
- People with recent severe burns or injuries.

Deficiency Symptoms

- Osteoporosis (late symptoms): frequent fractures in spine and other bones, deformed spinal column with humps, loss of height
- Osteomalacia: frequent fractures
- Muscle contractions
- Convulsive seizures
- Muscle cramps
- Low backache

Unproved Speculated Symptoms

- Uncontrollable temper outbursts

Lab Tests to Detect Deficiency

- 24-hour urine collection to measure calcium levels (Sulkowitch)
- Serum-calcium levels
- Imaging procedures to scan for bone density (more reliable than above tests)

Dosage and Usage Information

Recommended Dietary Allowance (RDA):
Estimate of adequate daily intake by the Food and Nutrition Board of the National Research Council, 1980 (See Glossary).
Many doctors and nutritionists recommend

▶▶

women take more calcium than quoted by the RDA. They recommend 1,000 milligrams per day for premenopausal women and 1,500 milligrams per day for post-menopausal women and elderly men.

Age	RDA
0–6 months	360mg
6–12 months	540mg
1–10 years	800mg
11–18 years	1,000mg
18+ years	800mg
Pregnant	+400mg
Lactating	+400mg

Different types of calcium supplements contain more available calcium (also called *elemental calcium*) than others. To provide 1,000mg of available calcium, you must take 12 teaspoons a day of calcium glubionate. Take in divided doses after meals.

What this mineral does:
• Participates in metabolic functions necessary for normal activity of nervous, muscular, skeletal systems.
• Plays important role in normal heart function, kidney function, blood clotting, blood-vessel integrity.
• Helps utilization of vitamin B-12.

Miscellaneous information:
• Bones serve as storage site for calcium in the body. There is a constant interchange between calcium in bone and the bloodstream.
• Foods rich in calcium (or supplements) help maintain the balance between bone needs and blood needs.
• Don't discard outer parts of vegetables during food preparation.
• Exercise, a balanced diet, calcium from natural sources or supplements and oestrogens are important in treating and preventing osteoporosis.

Available as:
• Syrup: Dilute in at least 1/2 glass of water or other liquid. Take with meals or 1 to 1-1/2 hours after meals unless otherwise directed by your doctor.

 ## Warnings and Precautions

Don't take if you:
• Are allergic to calcium or antacids.
• Have kidney stones.
• Have a high blood-calcium level.
• Have sarcoidosis.

Consult your doctor if you have:
• Kidney disease.
• Chronic constipation, colitis, diarrhoea.
• Stomach or intestinal bleeding.
• Irregular heartbeat.

Over age 55:
• Adverse reactions and side effects are more likely.
• Diarrhoea or constipation are particularly likely.

Pregnancy:
• May need extra calcium. Consult doctor about supplement.
• Don't take megadoses.

Breast-feeding:
• Drug passes into milk. Consult doctor about need for supplements.
• Don't take megadoses.

Effect on lab tests:
• Serum-amylase and serum 11-hydroxycorticosteroid concentrations can be increased.
• Decrease serum-phosphate concentration decreased by excessive, prolonged use.

Storage:
• Store in cool, dry area away from direct light, but don't freeze.
• Store safely out of reach of children.
• Don't store in bathroom medicine cabinet. Heat and moisture may change action of mineral.

Others:
• Dolomite or bone meal are probably *unsafe* sources of calcium because they contain lead.
• Avoid taking calcium within 1 or 2 hours of meals or ingestion of other medicines, if possible.

 ## Overdose/Toxicity

Signs and symptoms:
Confusion, high blood pressure, increased sensitivity of eyes and skin to light, increased thirst, slow or irregular heartbeat, depression, bone or muscle pain, nausea, vomiting, skin itching, skin rash, increased urination.

What to do:
For symptoms of overdosage: Discontinue mineral, and consult doctor immediately. Also see *Adverse Reactions or Side Effects* section below.
For accidental overdosage (such as child taking entire bottle): Dial 999 (emergency).

Calcium Glubionate, Continued

Adverse Reactions or Side Effects

Reaction or effect	What to do
Early signs of too much calcium in blood:	
Appetite loss	Discontinue. Call doctor when convenient.
Constipation	Discontinue. Call doctor when convenient.
Drowsiness	Discontinue. Call doctor immediately.
Dry mouth	Discontinue. Call doctor when convenient.
Headache	Discontinue. Call doctor when convenient.
Metallic taste	Discontinue. Call doctor when convenient.
Tiredness or weakness	Discontinue. Call doctor immediately.
Late signs of too much calcium in blood:	
Confusion	Discontinue. Call doctor immediately.
Depression	Discontinue. Call doctor when convenient.
High blood pressure	Discontinue. Call doctor immediately.
Increased thirst	Discontinue. Call doctor when convenient.
Increased urination	Discontinue. Call doctor when convenient.
Muscle or bone pain	Discontinue. Call doctor immediately.
Nausea	Discontinue. Call doctor immediately.
Skin rash	Discontinue. Call doctor immediately.
Slow or irregular heartbeat	Seek emergency treatment.
Vomiting	Discontinue. Call doctor immediately.

Interaction with Medicine, Vitamins or Minerals

Interacts with	Combined effect
Digitalis preparations	Heartbeat irregularities.
Iron supplements	Decreases absorption of iron unless vitamin C is taken at same time.
Magnesium-containing medications or supplements	Increases blood level of both.
Oral contraceptives and oestrogens	May increase calcium absorption.
Potassium supplements	Increases chance of heartbeat irregularities.
Tetracyclines (oral)	Decreases absorption of tetracycline.
Vitamin A (megadoses)	Stimulates bone loss.
Vitamin D (megadoses)	Excessively increases absorption of calcium supplements.

Interaction with Other Substances

Tobacco decreases absorption.

Alcohol decreases absorption.

Beverages
• Tea decreases absorption.
• Coffee decreases absorption.
• Don't take calcium with milk or other dairy products so your body can absorb the most calcium from food *and* calcium supplement.

Foods
• Avoid eating spinach, rhubarb, bran, whole-grain cereals, fresh fruits or fresh vegetables at same time you take calcium. They may prevent efficient absorption.

Basic Information

Available from natural sources? Yes
Available from synthetic sources? Yes
Prescription required? Some forms, yes;
 others, no

Natural Sources

Almonds	Salmon, tinned
Brazil nuts	Sardines, tinned
Caviar	Shrimp
Cheese	Soya beans
Kelp	Tofu
Milk	Turnip greens
Milk products	Yogurt
Molasses	

Reasons to Use

- Helps prevent osteoporosis in older people.
- Treats calcium depletion in people with hypoparathyroidism, osteomalacia, rickets.
- Treats low-calcium levels in people taking anti-convulsant medication.
- Treats tetany (severe muscle spasms) caused by insect bites, sensitivity reactions, cardiac arrest, lead poisoning.
- Is used as an antidote to magnesium poisoning.
- Prevents muscle cramps in some people.
- Promotes normal growth and development.
- Builds bones and teeth.
- Maintains bone density and strength.
- Buffers acid in stomach and acts as antacid.
- Helps regulate heartbeat, blood clotting, muscle contraction.
- Treats neonatal hypocalcaemia.
- Promotes storage and release of some body hormones.
- Promotes use of amino acids.
- Lowers phosphate concentrations in people with chronic kidney disease.

Unproved Speculated Benefits

- Helps prevent insomnia and anxiety (acts as a natural tranquilizer).
- Helps prevent hypertension.
- Treats allergies.
- Decreases likelihood of hardening of arteries.
- Treats leg cramps.
- Treats diabetes.
- Treats throat spasms.

Who Needs Additional Amounts?

- Anyone with inadequate caloric or nutritional dietary intake or increased nutritional requirements or who does not like or consume milk products.
- People allergic to milk and milk products or who don't tolerate them well.
- Older people (over 55 years), particularly women.
- Women throughout adult life, especially during pregnancy and lactation, but not limited to these times.
- Those who abuse alcohol or other drugs.
- People who have a chronic wasting illness, excess stress for long periods or who have recently undergone surgery.
- Those with a portion of the gastrointestinal tract surgically removed.
- People with recent severe burns or injuries.

Deficiency Symptoms

- Osteoporosis (late symptoms): frequent fractures in spine and other bones, deformed spinal column with humps, loss of height
- Osteomalacia: frequent fractures
- Muscle contractions
- Convulsive seizures
- Muscle cramps
- Low backache

Unproved Speculated Symptoms

- Uncontrollable temper outbursts

Lab Tests to Detect Deficiency

- 24-hour urine collection to measure calcium levels (Sulkowitch)
- Serum-calcium levels
- Imaging procedures to scan for bone density (more reliable than above tests)

Calcium Gluconate, Continued

Dosage and Usage Information

Recommended Dietary Allowance (RDA):
Estimate of adequate daily intake by the Food and Nutrition Board of the National Research Council, 1980 (See Glossary).
Many doctors and nutritionists recommend women need more calcium than quoted by the RDA. They recommend 1,000 milligrams per day for premenopausal women and 1,500 milligrams per day for post-menopausal women and elderly men.

Age	RDA
0–6 months	360mg
6–12 months	540mg
1–10 years	800mg
11–18 years	1,000mg
18+ years	800mg
Pregnant	+400mg
Lactating	+400mg

Different types of calcium supplements contain more available calcium (also called *elemental calcium*) than others. To provide 1,000mg of available calcium, you must take:
22 tablets/day of 500mg calcium gluconate
17 tablets/day of 650mg calcium gluconate
11 tablets/day of 1,000mg calcium gluconate
Take in divided doses after meals. Check contents of product you choose to determine how many tablets are needed to provide the amount of calcium you require.

What this mineral does:
• Participates in metabolic functions necessary for normal activity of nervous, muscular, skeletal systems.
• Plays important role in normal heart function, kidney function, blood clotting, blood-vessel integrity.
• Helps utilization of vitamin B-12.

Miscellaneous information:
• Bones serve as storage site for calcium in the body. There is a constant interchange between calcium in bone and the bloodstream.
• Foods rich in calcium (or supplements) help maintain the balance between bone needs and blood needs.
• Don't discard outer parts of vegetables during food preparations.
• Exercise, a balanced diet, calcium from natural sources or supplements and oestrogens are important in treating and preventing osteoporosis.

Available as:
• Chewable tablets: Chew well before swallowing.
• Injectable forms are administered by doctor or nurse.

Warnings and Precautions

Don't take if you:
• Are allergic to calcium or antacids.
• Have kidney stones.
• Have a high blood-calcium level.
• Have sarcoidosis.

Consult your doctor if you have:
• Kidney disease.
• Chronic constipation, colitis, diarrhoea.
• Stomach or intestinal bleeding.
• Irregular heartbeat.

Over age 55:
• Adverse reactions and side effects are more likely.
• Diarrhoea or constipation are particularly likely.

Pregnancy:
• May need extra calcium. Consult doctor about supplements.
• Don't take megadoses.

Breast-feeding:
• Drug passes into milk. Consult doctor about need for supplements.
• Don't take megadoses.

Effect on lab tests:
• Serum-amylase and serum 11-hydroxycorticosteroid concentrations can be increased.
• Decreases serum-phosphate concentration with excessive, prolonged use.

Storage:
• Store in cool, dry area away from direct light, but don't freeze.
• Store safely out of reach of children.
• Don't store in bathroom medicine cabinet. Heat and moisture may change action of mineral.

Others:
• Dolomite or bone meal are probably *unsafe* sources of calcium because they contain lead.
• Avoid taking calcium within 1 or 2 hours of meals or ingestion of other medicines, if possible.

Overdose/Toxicity

Signs and symptoms:
Confusion, high blood pressure, increased sensitivity of eyes and skin to light, increased thirst, slow or irregular heartbeat, depression, bone or muscle pain, nausea, vomiting, skin itching, skin rash, increased urination.

»→

What to do:
For symptoms of overdosage: Discontinue mineral, and consult doctor immediately. Also see *Adverse Reactions or Side Effects* section below.
For accidental overdosage (such as child taking entire bottle): Dial 999 (emergency).

Adverse Reactions or Side Effects

Reaction or effect	What to do
Early signs of too much calcium in blood:	
Appetite loss	Discontinue. Call doctor when convenient.
Constipation	Discontinue. Call doctor when convenient.
Drowsiness	Discontinue. Call doctor immediately.
Dry mouth	Discontinue. Call doctor when convenient.
Headache	Discontinue. Call doctor when convenient.
Metallic taste	Discontinue. Call doctor when convenient.
Tiredness or weakness	Discontinue. Call doctor immediately.
Late signs of too much calcium in blood:	
Confusion	Discontinue. Call doctor immediately.
Depression	Discontinue. Call doctor when convenient.
High blood pressure	Discontinue. Call doctor immediately.
Increased thirst	Discontinue. Call doctor when convenient.
Increased urination	Discontinue. Call doctor when convenient.
Muscle or bone pain	Discontinue. Call doctor immediately.
Nausea	Discontinue. Call doctor immediately.
Skin rash	Discontinue. Call doctor immediately.
Slow or irregular heartbeat	Seek emergency treatment.
Vomiting	Discontinue. Call doctor immediately.

Interaction with Medicine, Vitamins or Minerals

Interacts with	Combined effect
Digitalis preparations	Heartbeat irregularities.
Iron supplements	Decreases absorption of iron unless vitamin C is taken at same time.
Magnesium-containing medications or supplements	Increases blood level of both.
Oral contraceptives and oestrogen	May increase calcium absorption.
Potassium supplements	Increases chance of heartbeat irregularities.
Tetracyclines (oral)	Decreases absorption of tetracycline.
Vitamin A (megadoses)	Stimulates bone loss.
Vitamin D (megadoses)	Excessively increases absorption of calcium supplements

Interaction with Other Substances

Tobacco decreases absorption.

Alcohol decreases absorption.

Beverages
• Tea decreases absorption.
• Coffee decreases absorption.
• Don't take calcium with milk or other dairy products so your body can absorb the most calcium from food *and* calcium supplement.

Foods
• Avoid eating spinach, rhubarb, bran, whole-grain cereals, fresh fruits or fresh vegetables at same time you take calcium. They may prevent efficient absorption.

MINERAL

Calcium Lactate

Basic Information

Available from natural sources? Yes
Available from synthetic sources? Yes
Prescription required? Some forms, yes;
others, no

Natural Sources

Almonds	Salmon, tinned
Brazil nuts	Sardines, tinned
Caviar	Shrimp
Cheese	Soya beans
Kelp	Tofu
Milk	Turnip greens
Milk products	Yogurt
Molasses	

Reasons to Use

- Helps prevent osteoporosis in older people.
- Treats calcium depletion in people with hypoparathyroidism, osteomalacia, rickets.
- Treats low-calcium levels in people taking anti-convulsant medication.
- Treats tetany (severe muscle spasms) caused by insect bites, sensitivity reactions, cardiac arrest, lead poisoning.
- Is used as an antidote to magnesium poisoning.
- Prevents muscle cramps in some people.
- Promotes normal growth and development.
- Builds bones and teeth.
- Maintains bone density and strength.
- Buffers acid in stomach and acts as antacid.
- Helps regulate heartbeat, blood clotting, muscle contraction.
- Treats neonatal hypocalcaemia
- Promotes storage and release of some body hormones.
- Promotes use of amino acids.
- Lowers phosphate concentrations in people with chronic kidney disease.

Unproved Speculated Benefits

- Helps prevent insomnia and anxiety (acts as a natural tranquilizer).
- Helps prevent hypertension.
- Treats allergies.
- Decreases likelihood of hardening of arteries.
- Treats leg cramps.
- Treats diabetes.
- Treats throat spasms.

Who Needs Additional Amounts?

- Anyone with inadequate caloric or nutritional dietary intake or increased nutritional requirements or who does not like or consume milk products.
- People allergic to milk and milk products or who don't tolerate them well.
- Older people (over 55 years), particularly women.
- Women throughout adult life, especially during pregnancy and lactation, but not limited to these times.
- Those who abuse alcohol or other drugs.
- People who have a chronic wasting illness, excess stress for long periods or who have recently undergone surgery.
- Those with a portion of the gastrointestinal tract surgically removed.
- People with recent severe burns or injuries.

Deficiency Symptoms

- Osteoporosis (late symptoms): frequent fractures in spine and other bones, deformed spinal column with humps, loss of height
- Osteomalacia: frequent fractures
- Muscle contractions
- Convulsive seizures
- Muscle cramps
- Low backache

Unproved Speculated Symptoms

- Uncontrollable temper outbursts

Lab Tests to Detect Deficiency

- 24-hour urine collection to measure calcium levels (Sulkowitch)
- Serum-calcium levels
- Imaging procedures to scan for bone density (more reliable than above tests)

Dosage and Usage Information

Recommended Dietary Allowance (RDA):
Estimate of adequate daily intake by the Food and Nutrition Board of the National Research Council, 1980 (See Glossary).
Many doctors and nutritionists recommend ⟫→

women take more calcium than quoted by the RDA. They recommend 1,000 milligrams per day for premenopausal women and 1,500 milligrams per day for post-menopausal women and elderly men.

Age	RDA
0–6 months	360mg
6–12 months	540mg
1–10 years	800mg
11–18 years	1,000mg
18+ years	800mg
Pregnant	+400mg
Lactating	+400mg

Different types of calcium supplements contain more available calcium (also called *elemental calcium*) than others. To provide 1,000mg of available calcium, you must take:

  24 tablets/day of 325mg calcium lactate
  12 tablets/day of 650mg calcium lactate

Take in divided doses after meals. Check contents of product you choose to determine how many tablets are needed to provide the amount of calcium you require.

What this mineral does:
- Participates in metabolic functions necessary for normal activity of nervous, muscular, skeletal systems.
- Plays important role in normal heart function, kidney function, blood clotting, blood-vessel integrity.
- Helps utilization of vitamin B-12.

Miscellaneous information:
- Bones serve as storage site for calcium in the body. There is a constant interchange between calcium in bone and the bloodstream.
- Foods rich in calcium (or supplements) help maintain the balance between bone needs and blood needs.
- Don't discard outer parts of vegetables during food preparations.
- Exercise, a balanced diet, calcium from natural sources or supplements and oestrogens are important in treating and preventing osteoporosis.

Available as:
- Tablets: Swallow whole with full glass of liquid. Don't chew or crush. Take with meals or 1 to 1-1/2 hours after meals unless otherwise directed by your doctor.

Warnings and Precautions

Don't take if you:
- Are allergic to calcium or antacids.
- Have kidney stones.
- Have a high blood-calcium level.
- Have sarcoidosis.

Consult your doctor if you have:
- Kidney disease.
- Chronic constipation, colitis, diarrhoea
- Stomach or intestinal bleeding.
- Irregular heartbeat.

Over age 55:
- Adverse reactions and side effects are more likely.
- Diarrhoea or constipation are particularly likely.

Pregnancy:
- May need extra calcium. Consult doctor about supplements.
- Don't take megadoses.

Breast-feeding:
- Drug passes into milk. Consult doctor about need for supplements.
- Don't take megadoses.

Effect on lab tests:
- Serum-amylase and serum 11-hydroxycorticosteroid concentrations can be increased.
- Decreases serum-phosphate concentration with excessive, prolonged use.

Storage:
- Store in cool, dry area away from direct light, but don't freeze.
- Store safely out of reach of children.
- Don't store in bathroom medicine cabinet. Heat and moisture may change action of mineral.

Others:
- Dolomite or bone meal are probably *unsafe* sources of calcium because they contain lead.
- Avoid taking calcium within 1 or 2 hours of meals or ingestion of other medicines, if possible.

Overdose/Toxicity

Signs and symptoms:
Confusion, high blood pressure, increased sensitivity of eyes and skin to light, increased thirst, slow or irregular heartbeat, depression, bone or muscle pain, nausea, vomiting, skin itching, skin rash, increased urination.

What to do:
For symptoms of overdosage: Discontinue mineral, and consult doctor immediately. Also see *Adverse Reactions or Side Effects* section below.

For accidental overdosage (such as child taking entire bottle): Dial 999 (emergency).

                »→

Calcium Lactate, Continued

 Adverse Reactions or Side Effects

Reaction or effect	What to do
Early signs of too much calcium in blood:	
Appetite loss	Discontinue. Call doctor when convenient.
Constipation	Discontinue. Call doctor when convenient.
Drowsiness	Discontinue. Call doctor immediately.
Dry mouth	Discontinue. Call doctor when convenient.
Headache	Discontinue. Call doctor when convenient.
Metallic taste	Discontinue. Call doctor when convenient.
Tiredness or weakness	Discontinue. Call doctor immediately.
Late signs of too much calcium in blood:	
Confusion	Discontinue. Call doctor immediately.
Depression	Discontinue. Call doctor when convenient.
High blood pressure	Discontinue. Call doctor immediately.
Increased thirst	Discontinue. Call doctor when convenient.
Increased urination	Discontinue. Call doctor when convenient.
Muscle or bone pain	Discontinue. Call doctor immediately.
Nausea	Discontinue. Call doctor immediately.
Skin rash	Discontinue. Call doctor immediately.
Slow or irregular heartbeat	Seek emergency treatment.
Vomiting	Discontinue. Call doctor immediately.

 Interaction with Medicine, Vitamins or Minerals

Interacts with	Combined effect
Digitalis preparations	Heartbeat irregularities.
Iron supplements	Decreases absorption of iron unless vitamin C is taken at same time.
Magnesium-containing medications or supplements	Increases blood level of both.
Oral contraceptives and oestrogens	May increase calcium absorption.
Potassium supplements	Increases chance of heartbeat irregularities.
Tetracyclines (oral)	Decreases absorption of tetracycline.
Vitamin A (megadoses)	Stimulates bone loss.
Vitamin D (megadoses)	Excessively increases absorption of calcium supplements.

 Interaction with Other Substances

Tobacco decreases absorption.

Alcohol decreases absorption.

Beverages
- Tea decreases absorption.
- Coffee decreases absorption.
- Don't take calcium with milk or other dairy products so your body can absorb the most calcium from food *and* calcium supplement.

Foods
- Avoid eating spinach, rhubarb, bran, whole-grain cereals, fresh fruits or fresh vegetables at same time you take calcium. They may prevent efficient absorption.

Calcium/Magnesium Carbonate

Basic Information

Provides additional magnesium. Other substances in title are not supplied in large enough amounts for use by your body.
Available from natural sources? Yes
Available from synthetic sources? No
Prescription required? Yes, for some forms

Natural Sources

Almonds	Leafy, green	Snails
Bluefish	vegetables	Soya beans
Carp	Mackerel	Sunflower
Cod	Molasses	seeds
Flounder	Nuts	Swordfish
Halibut	Ocean perch	Wheat germ
Herring	Shrimp	

Reasons to Use

- Aids bone growth.
- Aids function of nerves and muscles, including regulation of normal heart rhythm.
- Keeps metabolism steady.
- Conducts nerve impulses.
- Works as laxative in large doses.
- Acts as antacid in small doses.
- Strengthens tooth enamel.

Unproved Speculated Benefits

- Cures alcoholism.
- Cures kidney stones.
- Alleviates heart disease.
- Helps control bad breath and body odour.
- Helps contain lead poisoning.

Who Needs Additional Amounts?

- Anyone with inadequate caloric or dietary intake or increased nutritional requirements.
- Those who abuse alcohol or other drugs.
- People with a chronic wasting illness or who have recently undergone surgery.
- Those with recent severe burns or injuries.

Deficiency Symptoms

Following symptoms occur rarely:
- Muscle contractions
- Convulsions
- Confusion and delirium
- Irritability
- Nervousness
- Skin problems
- Hardening of soft tissues

Unproved Speculated Symptoms

- Sudden heart failure

Lab Tests to Detect Deficiency

- Serum magnesium

Dosage and Usage Information

Recommended Dietary Allowance (RDA):
Estimate of adequate daily intake by the Food and Nutrition Board of the National Research Council, 1980 (See Glossary).

Age	RDA
0–6 months	50mg
6–12 months	70mg
1–3 years	150mg
4–6 years	200mg
7–10 years	250mg
Males	
11–14 years	350mg
15–18 years	400mg
18+ years	350mg
Females	
11+ years	300mg
Pregnant	+150mg
Lactating	+150mg

What this mineral does:
- Activates essential enzymes.
- Affects metabolism of proteins and nucleic acids.
- Helps transport sodium and potassium across cell membranes.
- Influences calcium levels inside cells.

Available as:
- Tablets: Swallow whole with full glass of liquid. Don't chew or crush. Take with meals or 1 to 1-1/2 hours after meals unless otherwise directed by your doctor.
- Liquid: Dilute in at least 1/2 glass of water or other liquid. Take with meals or 1 to 1-1/2 hours after meals unless otherwise directed by your doctor.
- Chewable tablets: Chew well before swallowing.

MINERAL

Calcium/Magnesium Carbonate

 Warnings and Precautions

Don't take if you have:
- Kidney failure.
- Heart block (unless you have a pacemaker).
- An ileostomy.

Consult your doctor if you have:
- Chronic constipation, colitis, diarrhoea.
- Symptoms of appendicitis.
- Stomach or intestinal bleeding.

Over age 55:
- Adverse reactions/side effects more likely.

Pregnancy:
- Risk to fetus outweighs benefits. Don't use.

Breast-feeding:
- Avoid magnesium in large quantities.
- If you must take temporarily, discontinue breast-feeding. Consult doctor for advice on maintaining milk supply.
- Don't take megadoses.

Effect on lab tests:
- Makes test for stomach-acid secretion inaccurate.
- May increase or decrease serum-phosphate concentrations.
- May decrease serum and urine pH.

Storage:
- Store in cool, dry place away from direct light, but don't freeze.
- Store safely out of reach of children.
- Don't store in bathroom medicine cabinet. Heat and moisture may change action of mineral.

Others:
- Chronic kidney disease frequently causes body to retain excess magnesium.
- Adverse reactions, side effects and interactions with medicines, vitamins or minerals occur *only rarely* when too much magnesium is taken for too long or if you have kidney disease.

 Overdose/Toxicity

Signs and symptoms:
Severe nausea and vomiting, extremely low blood pressure, extreme muscle weakness, difficulty breathing, heartbeat irregularity.

What to do:
For symptoms of overdosage: Discontinue mineral, and consult doctor immediately. Also see *Adverse Reactions or Side Effects*.
For accidental overdosage (such as child taking entire bottle): Dial 999 (emergency).

 Adverse Reactions or Side Effects

Reaction or effect	What to do
Abdominal pain	Discontinue. Call doctor immediately.
Appetite loss	Discontinue. Call doctor when convenient.
Diarrhoea	Discontinue. Call doctor immediately.
Irregular heartbeat	Seek emergency treatment.
Mood changes or mental changes	Discontinue. Call doctor when convenient.
Nausea	Discontinue. Call doctor immediately.
Tiredness or weakness	Discontinue. Call doctor when convenient.
Urination discomfort	Discontinue. Call doctor when convenient.
Vomiting	Discontinue. Call doctor immediately.

 Interaction with Medicine, Vitamins or Minerals

Interacts with	Combined effect
Cellulose sodium phosphate	Decreases magnesium effect. Take 1 or more hours apart.
Fat-soluble vitamins (A, E, K)	Decreases absorption of mineral.
Ketoconazole	Reduces absorption of ketoconazole. Take 2 hours apart.
Mecamylamine	May slow urinary excretion of mecamylamine. Avoid combination.
Tetracycline	Decreases absorption of tetracycline.
Vitamin D	May raise magnesium level too high.

 Interaction with Other Substances

None known

Calcium/Magnesium Carbonate/Magnesium Oxide

Basic Information

Provides additional magnesium. Other substances in title are not supplied in large enough amounts for use by your body.
Available from natural sources? Yes
Available from synthetic sources? No
Prescription required? Yes, for some forms

Natural Sources

Almonds	Leafy, green	Snails
Bluefish	vegetables	Soya beans
Carp	Mackerel	Sunflower
Cod	Molasses	seeds
Flounder	Nuts	Swordfish
Halibut	Ocean perch	Wheat germ
Herring	Shrimp	

Reasons to Use

- Aids bone growth.
- Aids function of nerves and muscles, including regulation of normal heart rhythm.
- Keeps metabolism steady.
- Conducts nerve impulses.
- Works as laxative in large doses.
- Acts as antacid in small doses.
- Strengthens tooth enamel.

Unproved Speculated Benefits

- Cures alcoholism.
- Cures kidney stones.
- Alleviates heart disease.
- Helps control bad breath and body odour.
- Helps contain lead poisoning.

Who Needs Additional Amounts?

- Anyone with inadequate caloric or dietary intake or increased nutritional requirements.
- Those who abuse alcohol or other drugs.
- People with a chronic wasting illness or who have recently undergone surgery.
- Those with recent severe burns or injuries.

Deficiency Symptoms

Following symptoms occur rarely:
- Muscle contractions
- Convulsions
- Confusion and delirium
- Irritability
- Nervousness
- Skin problems
- Hardening of soft tissues

Unproved Speculated Symptoms

- Sudden heart failure

Lab Tests to Detect Deficiency

- Serum magnesium

Dosage and Usage Information

Recommended Dietary Allowance (RDA):
Estimate of adequate daily intake by the Food and Nutrition Board of the National Research Council, 1980 (See Glossary).

Age	RDA
0–6 months	50mg
6–12 months	70mg
1–3 years	150mg
4–6 years	200mg
7–10 years	250mg
Males	
11–14 years	350mg
15–18 years	400mg
18+ years	350mg
Females	
11+ years	300mg
Pregnant	+150mg
Lactating	+150mg

What this mineral does:
- Activates essential enzymes.
- Affects metabolism of proteins and nucleic acids.
- Helps transport sodium and potassium across cell membranes.
- Influences calcium levels inside cells.

Available as:
- Tablets: Swallow whole with full glass of liquid. Don't chew or crush. Take with meals or 1 to 1-1/2 hours after meals unless otherwise directed by your doctor.

➤➤

Calcium/Magnesium Carbonate/Magnesium Oxide

Warnings and Precautions

Don't take if you have:
• Kidney failure.
• Heart block (unless you have a pacemaker).
• An ileostomy.

Consult your doctor if you have:
• Chronic constipation, colitis, diarrhea.
• Symptoms of appendicitis.
• Stomach or intestinal bleeding.

Over age 55:
• Adverse reactions/side effects more likely.

Pregnancy:
• Risk to fetus outweighs benefits. Don't use.

Breast-feeding:
• Avoid magnesium in large quantities.
• If you must take temporarily, discontinue breast-feeding. Consult doctor for advice on maintaining milk supply.
• Don't take megadoses.

Effect on lab tests:
• Makes test for stomach-acid secretion inaccurate.
• May increase or decrease serum-phosphate concentrations.
• May decrease serum and urine pH.

Storage:
• Store in cool, dry place away from direct light, but don't freeze.
• Store safely out of reach of children.
• Don't store in bathroom medicine cabinet. Heat and moisture may change action of mineral.

Others:
• Chronic kidney disease frequently causes body to retain excess magnesium.
• Adverse reactions, side effects and interactions with medicines, vitamins or minerals occur *only rarely* when too much magnesium is taken for too long or if you have kidney disease.

Overdose/Toxicity

Signs and symptoms:
Severe nausea and vomiting, extremely low blood pressure, extreme muscle weakness, difficulty breathing, heartbeat irregularity.

What to do:
For symptoms of overdosage: Discontinue mineral, and consult doctor immediately. Also see *Adverse Reactions or Side Effects*.
For accidental overdosage (such as child taking entire bottle): Dial 999 (emergency).

Adverse Reactions or Side Effects

Reaction or effect	What to do
Abdominal pain	Discontinue. Call doctor immediately.
Appetite loss	Discontinue. Call doctor when convenient.
Diarrhoea	Discontinue. Call doctor immediately.
Irregular heartbeat	Seek emergency treatment.
Mood changes or mental changes	Discontinue. Call doctor when convenient.
Nausea	Discontinue. Call doctor immediately.
Tiredness or weakness	Discontinue. Call doctor when convenient.
Urination discomfort	Discontinue. Call doctor when convenient.
Vomiting	Discontinue. Call doctor immediately.

Interaction with Medicine, Vitamins or Minerals

Interacts with	Combined effect
Cellulose sodium phosphate	Decreases magnesium effect. Take 1 or more hours apart.
Fat-soluble vitamins (A, E, K)	Decreases absorption of mineral.
Ketoconazole	Reduces absorption of ketoconazole. Take 2 hours apart.
Mecamylamine	May slow urinary excretion of mecamylamine. Avoid combination.
Tetracycline	Decreases absorption of tetracycline.
Vitamin D	May raise magnesium level too high.

Interaction with Other Substances

None known

Basic Information

This form of calcium is also called tribasic calcium phosphate *or* dibasic calcium phosphate.
Available from natural sources? Yes
Available from synthetic sources? Yes
Prescription required? Some forms, yes; others, no

Natural Sources

Almonds
Brazil nuts
Caviar
Cheese
Kelp
Milk
Milk products
Molasses

Salmon, tinned
Sardines, tinned
Shrimp
Soya beans
Tofu
Turnip greens
Yogurt

Reasons to Use

- Helps prevent osteoporosis in older people.
- Treats calcium depletion in people with hypoparathyroidism, osteomalacia, rickets.
- Treats low-calcium levels in people taking anti-convulsant medication.
- Treats tetany (severe muscle spasms) caused by insect bites, sensitivity reactions, cardiac arrest, lead poisoning.
- Is used as an antidote to magnesium poisoning.
- Prevents muscle cramps in some people.
- Promotes normal growth and development.
- Builds bones and teeth.
- Maintains bone density and strength.
- Buffers acid in stomach and acts as antacid.
- Helps regulate heartbeat, blood clotting, muscle contraction.
- Treats neonatal hypocalcaemia.
- Promotes storage and release of some body hormones.
- Promotes use of amino acids.
- Lowers phosphate concentrations in people with chronic kidney disease.

Unproved Speculated Benefits

- Helps prevent insomnia and anxiety (acts as a natural tranquilizer).
- Helps prevent hypertension.
- Treats allergies.
- Decreases likelihood of hardening of arteries.

- Treats leg cramps.
- Treats diabetes.
- Treats throat spasms.

Who Needs Additional Amounts?

- Anyone with inadequate caloric or nutritional dietary intake or increased nutritional requirements or who does not like or consume milk products.
- People allergic to milk and milk products or who don't tolerate them well.
- Older people (over 55 years), particularly women.
- Women throughout adult life, especially during pregnancy and lactation, but not limited to these times.
- Those who abuse alcohol or other drugs.
- People who have a chronic wasting illness, excess stress for long periods or who have recently undergone surgery.
- Those with a portion of the gastrointestinal tract surgically removed.
- People with recent severe burns or injuries.

Deficiency Symptoms

- Osteoporosis (late symptoms): frequent fractures in spine and other bones, deformed spinal column with humps, loss of height
- Osteomalacia: frequent fractures
- Muscle contractions
- Convulsive seizures
- Muscle cramps
- Low backache

Unproved Speculated Symptoms

- Uncontrollable temper outbursts

Lab Tests to Detect Deficiency

- 24-hour urine collection to measure calcium levels (Sulkowitch)
- Serum-calcium levels
- Imaging procedures to scan for bone density (more reliable than above tests)

»►

MINERAL

Calcium Phosphate, Continued

 ## Dosage and Usage Information

Recommended Dietary Allowance (RDA):
Estimate of adequate daily intake by the Food and Nutrition Board of the National Research Council, 1980 (See Glossary).

Many doctors and nutritionists recommend women take more calcium than quoted by the RDA. They recommend 1,000 milligrams per day for premenopausal women and 1,500 milligrams per day for post-menopausal women and elderly men.

Age	RDA
0–6 months	360mg
6–12 months	540mg
1–10 years	800mg
11–18 years	1,000mg
18+ years	800mg
Pregnant	+400mg
Lactating	+400mg

Different types of calcium supplements contain more available calcium (also called *elemental calcium*) than others. To provide 1,000mg of available calcium, you must take:

4 tablets/day of 800mg calcium phosphate
2 tablets/day of 1,600mg calcium phosphate

Take in divided doses after meals. Check contents of product you choose to determine how many tablets are needed to provide the amount of calcium you require.

What this mineral does:
• Participates in metabolic functions necessary for normal activity of nervous, muscular, skeletal systems.
• Plays important role in normal heart function, kidney function, blood clotting, blood-vessel integrity.
• Helps utilization of vitamin B-12.

Miscellaneous information:
• Bones serve as storage site for calcium in the body. There is a constant interchange between calcium in bone and the bloodstream.
• Foods rich in calcium (or supplements) help maintain the balance between bone needs and blood needs.
• Don't discard outer parts of vegetables during food preparation.
• Exercise, a balanced diet, calcium from natural sources or supplements and estrogens are important in treating and preventing osteoporosis.

Available as:
• Tablets: Swallow whole with full glass of liquid. Don't chew or crush. Take with meals or 1 to 1-1/2 hours after meals unless otherwise directed by your doctor.

 ## Warnings and Precautions

Don't take if you:
• Are allergic to calcium or antacids.
• Have kidney stones.
• Have a high blood-calcium level.
• Have sarcoidosis.

Consult your doctor if you have:
• Kidney disease.
• Chronic constipation, colitis, diarrhoea.
• Stomach or intestinal bleeding.
• Irregular heartbeat.

Over age 55:
• Adverse reactions and side effects are more likely.
• Diarrhoea or constipation are particularly likely.

Pregnancy:
• May need extra calcium. Consult doctor about supplements.
• Don't take megadoses.

Breast-feeding:
• Drug passes into milk. Consult doctor about need for supplements.
• Don't take megadoses.

Effect on lab tests:
• Serum-amylase and serum 11-hydroxycorticosteroid concentrations can be increased.
• Decreases serum-phosphate concentration with excessive, prolonged use.

Storage:
• Store in cool, dry area away from direct light, but don't freeze.
• Store safely out of reach of children.
• Don't store in bathroom medicine cabinet. Heat and moisture may change action of mineral.

Others:
• Dolomite or bone meal are probably *unsafe* sources of calcium because they contain lead.
• Avoid taking calcium within 1 or 2 hours of meals or ingestion of other medicines, if possible.

»→

Overdose/Toxicity

Signs and symptoms:
Confusion, high blood pressure, increased sensitivity of eyes and skin to light, increased thirst, slow or irregular heartbeat, depression, bone or muscle pain, nausea, vomiting, skin itching, skin rash, increased urination.

What to do:
For symptoms of overdosage: Discontinue mineral, and consult doctor immediately. Also see *Adverse Reactions or Side Effects* section below.

For accidental overdosage (such as child taking entire bottle): Dial 999 (emergency).

Adverse Reactions or Side Effects

Reaction or effect	What to do
Early signs of too much calcium in blood:	
Appetite loss	Discontinue. Call doctor when convenient.
Constipation	Discontinue. Call doctor when convenient.
Drowsiness	Discontinue. Call doctor immediately.
Dry mouth	Discontinue. Call doctor when convenient.
Headache	Discontinue. Call doctor when convenient.
Metallic taste	Discontinue. Call doctor when convenient.
Tiredness or weakness	Discontinue. Call doctor immediately.
Late signs of too much calcium in blood:	
Confusion	Discontinue. Call doctor immediately.
Depression	Discontinue. Call doctor when convenient.
High blood pressure	Discontinue. Call doctor immediately.
Increased thirst	Discontinue. Call doctor when convenient.
Increased urination	Discontinue. Call doctor when convenient.
Muscle or bone pain	Discontinue. Call doctor immediately.
Nausea	Discontinue. Call doctor immediately.
Skin rash	Discontinue. Call doctor immediately.
Slow or irregular heartbeat	Seek emergency treatment.
Vomiting	Discontinue. Call doctor immediately.

Interaction with Medicine, Vitamins or Minerals

Interacts with	Combined effect
Digitalis preparations	Heartbeat irregularities.
Iron supplements	Decreases absorption of iron unless vitamin C is taken at same time.
Magnesium-containing medications or supplements	Increases blood level of both.
Oral contraceptives and oestrogens	May increase calcium absorption.
Potassium supplements	Increases chance of heartbeat irregularities.
Tetracyclines (oral)	Decreases absorption of tetracycline.
Vitamin A (megadoses)	Stimulates bone loss.
Vitamin D (megadoses)	Excessively increases absorption of calcium supplements.

Interaction with Other Substances

Tobacco decreases absorption.

Alcohol decreases absorption.

Beverages
• Tea decreases absorption.
• Coffee decreases absorption.
• Don't take calcium with milk or other dairy products so your body can absorb the most calcium from food *and* calcium supplement.

Foods
• Avoid eating spinach, rhubarb, bran, whole-grain cereals, fresh fruits or fresh vegetables at same time you take calcium. They may prevent efficient absorption.

MINERAL

111

Charcoal, Activated

Basic Information
Available from natural sources? No
Available from synthetic sources? Yes
Prescription required? No

Natural Sources

Not available from natural sources

Reasons to Use

- Helps prevent poison from being absorbed from stomach and intestines.
- Treats poisonings from medication.
- Helps absorb gas in intestinal tract.

Unproved Speculated Benefits

- Removes bacteria and contaminants from food.
- Acts as a hangover cure.
- Treats infections.
- Treats hiccups.
- Treats diarrhoea.

Who Needs Additional Amounts?

- People who have ingested poisonous substances.

Deficiency Symptoms

- None

Unproved Speculated Symptoms

- None

Lab Tests to Detect Deficiency

- None available, except for experimental purposes.

Dosage and Usage Information

Recommended Dietary Allowance (RDA):
No RDA has been established.

What this mineral does:
- Charcoal can adsorb almost anything it contacts. An *adsorbent* is a substance that attaches things to its surface rather than absorbing them to itself. Activated charcoal is used for the treatment of ingested poison.

Miscellaneous information:
- Activated charcoal is used for treatment of potential toxicity from ingesting poisonous substances.
- Charcoal used for medicinal purposes is treated with steam under high pressure and high temperature.
- Charcoal will *not* help remove from the intestinal tract the following potential poisons—cyanide, caustic alkalis, ethyl alcohol (as in whiskey and beer), methyl alcohol, iron supplements, mineral acids.

Available as:
- Powder: Dissolve powder in cold water or juice. Take with meals or 1 to 1-1/2 hours after meals unless otherwise directed by your doctor.
- Tablets: Swallow whole with full glass of liquid. Don't chew or crush. Take with meals or 1 to 1-1/2 hours after meals unless otherwise directed by your doctor.
- Capsules: Swallow whole with full glass of liquid. Don't chew or crush. Take with meals or 1 to 1-1/2 hours after meals unless otherwise directed by your doctor.

Warnings and Precautions

Don't take if:
- Poison ingested is lye (or other strong alkali), strong acid (such as sulphuric acid), cyanide, iron, ethyl alchohol or methyl alcohol. Charcoal will *not* prevent these poisons from causing ill effects.

Consult your doctor if you have:
- Taken charcoal as an antidote for poison.

Over age 55:
- No problems expected.

Pregnancy:
- No problems expected.
- Don't take megadoses.

Breast-feeding:
- No problems expected.
- Don't take megadoses.

Effect on lab tests:
- None expected.

Storage:
- Store in cool, dry place away from direct light, but don't freeze.
- Store safely out of reach of children.
- Don't store in bathroom medicine cabinet. Heat and moisture may change action of mineral.

Others:
- If used with syrup of ipecac, wait until vomiting has stopped before giving charcoal.

 ## Overdose/Toxicity

Signs and symptoms:
None expected. Charcoal is not absorbed from intestines into bloodstream.

What to do:
Overdose unlikely to threaten life. If person takes much larger amount than prescribed, call doctor, or hospital emergency department for instructions.

 ## Adverse Reactions or Side Effects

Reaction or effect	What to do
Black bowel movements	Normal, expected side effect. No action necessary.

 ## Interaction with Medicine, Vitamins or Minerals

Interacts with	Combined effect
Acetylcysteine, oral (an antidote to paracetamol overdose)	Nullifies effectiveness of acetylcysteine.
Any medication taken at same time	May decrease absorption of medicine.

 ## Interaction with Other Substances

Foods
- **Ice cream** decreases charcoal effect.
- **Sherbet** decreases charcoal effect.

MINERAL

Chloride

Basic Information

Available from natural sources? Yes
Available from synthetic sources? Yes
Prescription required? No

Natural Sources

Salt substitutes (potassium chloride)
Sea salt
Table salt (sodium chloride)
Found in combination with other molecules

Reasons to Use

• Regulates body's electrolyte balance.
• Regulates body's acid-base balance.

Unproved Speculated Benefits

• None known

Who Needs Additional Amounts?

• Anyone with inadequate caloric or nutritional dietary intake or increased nutritional requirements.
• Older people (over 55 years).
• Those who abuse alcohol or other drugs.
• People with a chronic wasting illness, excess stress for long periods or who have recently undergone surgery.
• Athletes and workers who participate in vigorous physical activities.
• Those with a portion of the gastrointestinal tract surgically removed.
• People with recent severe burns or injuries.

Deficiency Symptoms

• Continuous vomiting
• When chloride is intentionally neglected in infant-formula preparations, infant develops metabolic alkalosis, hypovolaemia and significant urinary loss. Psychomotor defects, memory loss and growth retardation also occur.
• Upsets balance of acids and bases in body fluids (rare)

• Nausea
• Vomiting
• Confusion
• Weakness
• Coma

Unproved Speculated Symptoms

• None

Lab Tests to Detect Deficiency

• Serum chloride

Dosage and Usage Information

Recommended Dietary Allowance (RDA):
Estimate of adequate daily intake by the Food and Nutrition Board of the National Research Council, 1980 (See Glossary).

Age	RDA
0–6 months	0.275–0.7g
6–12 months	0.4–1.2g
1–3 years	0.5–1.5g
4–6 years	0.7–2.1g
7–10 years	0.925–2.775g
11–17 years	1.4–4.2g
18+ years	1.75–5.1g

What this mineral does:
• Chloride is a constituent of acid in the stomach (hydrochloric acid).
• Interacts with sodium, potassium and carbon dioxide to maintain acid-base balance in body cells and fluids. It is crucial to normal health.
• Concentrations of sodium, potassium, carbon dioxide and chlorine are controlled by mechanisms inside each body cell.

Miscellaneous information:
• Healthy people do not have to make any special efforts to maintain sufficient chloride.
• Eating a balanced diet supplies all daily needs.
• Extremely ill patients, with acid-base imbalance, require hospitalization, frequent laboratory studies and skillful professional care.

Available as:
• Sodium-chloride (salt) tablets. These may cause stomach distress and overload on kidneys.
• A constituent of many multivitamin/mineral preparations.

»▶

Warnings and Precautions

Don't take if you:
• No known contraindications.

Consult your doctor if you have:
• No known contraindications.

Over age 55:
• No special problems expected.

Pregnancy:
• No special problems expected.
• Don't take megadoses.

Breast-feeding:
• No special problems expected.
• Don't take megadoses.

Effect on lab tests:
• No special problems expected.

Storage:
• Store in cool, dry place away from direct light, but don't freeze.
• Store safely out of reach of children.
• Don't store in bathroom medicine cabinet. Heat and moisture may change action of mineral.

Overdose/Toxicity

Signs and symptoms:
Upset balance of acids and bases in body fluids can occur with "too-much-chloride" or with "too-little-chloride." Symptoms of either include weakness, confusion, coma.

What to do:
For symptoms of overdosage: Discontinue mineral, and consult doctor.
For accidental overdosage (such as child taking a large amount): Dial 999 (emergency).

Adverse Reactions or Side Effects

None expected

Interaction with Medicine, Vitamins or Minerals

Interacts with	Combined effect
Chlorine	Maintains normal acid-base balance in body.
Potassium	Maintains normal acid-base balance in body.
Sodium	Maintains normal acid-base balance in body.

Interaction with Other Substances

None known

MINERAL

Chromium

Basic Information

Available from natural sources? Yes
Available from synthetic sources? No
Prescription required? No

Natural Sources

Beef	Fish and seafood
Brewer's yeast	Fresh fruit
Calves' liver	Oysters
Chicken	Potatoes, with skin
Dairy products	Whole-grain products
Eggs	

Reasons to Use

- Promotes glucose metabolism.
- Helps insulin regulate blood sugar.
- Decreases insulin requirements and improves glucose tolerance of some people with maturity-onset diabetes.

Unproved Speculated Benefits

- Relieves atherosclerosis and diabetes.
- Facilitates binding of insulin to cell membrane.

Who Needs Additional Amounts?

- Anyone with inadequate caloric or dietary intake or increased nutritional requirements.
- Those who abuse alcohol or other drugs.
- People with a chronic wasting illness or who have recently undergone surgery.
- Those with a portion of the gastrointestinal tract surgically removed.
- People with recent severe burns or injuries.

Deficiency Symptoms

- Reduced tissue sensitivity to glucose, similar to diabetes
- Disturbances of glucose, fat and protein metabolism
- Symptoms exhibited by people with maturity-onset diabetes, such as overweight, fatigue, excess thirst, increased appetite, frequent urination, decreased resistance to infection, urinary-tract infections and yeast infections of the skin, mouth and vagina

Unproved Speculated Symptoms

- None

Lab Tests to Detect Deficiency

- Serum chromium
- Hair analysis is *not* a reliable test for deficiency or toxicity

Dosage and Usage Information

Recommended Dietary Allowance (RDA):
No RDA has been established. Estimated safe range of intake per day given below.

Age	Estimated Safe Intake
0–6 months	0.01–0.04mg
6–12 months	0.02–0.06mg
1–3 years	0.02–0.08mg
4–6 years	0.03–0.12mg
7+ years	0.05–0.20mg

What this mineral does:
- Aids transport of amino acids to liver and heart cells.
- Enhances effect of insulin in glucose utilization.

Miscellaneous information:
- Chromium toxicity can result from industrial overexposure, such as tanning, electroplating, steel making, abrasives manufacturing, cement manufacturing, diesel-locomotive repairs, furniture polishing, fur processing, glass making, jewelry making, metal cleaning, oil drilling, photography, textile dyeing, wood-preservative manufacturing.
- Nutritional science has yet to determine exact amounts of chromium in most foods. Less than 1% of dietary chromium is absorbed.

Available as:
- A constituent of many multivitamin/mineral preparations.

>>>

Warnings and Precautions

Don't take if you:
• Work in an environment that has high concentrations of chromium.

Consult your doctor if you have:
• Diabetes.
• Lung disease.
• Liver disease.
• Kidney disease.

Over age 55:
• No special needs if you eat a balanced diet.

Pregnancy:
• Avoid during pregnancy.

Breast-feeding:
• Avoid during breast-feeding.

Effect on lab tests:
• Diagnostic tests, such as red-blood-cell-survival studies, performed after radioactive hexavalent chromium is used for 3 months may cause falsely elevated levels in blood.

Storage:
• Store in cool, dry place away from direct light, but don't freeze.
• Store safely out of reach of children.
• Don't store in bathroom medicine cabinet. Heat and moisture may change action of mineral.

Overdose/Toxicity

Signs and symptoms:
Dietary form has very low toxicity. Long-term exposure to chromium may lead to skin problems, perforation of nasal septum, lung cancer, liver, impairment, kidney impairment.

What to do:
For symptoms of overdosage: Discontinue mineral, and consult doctor.
For accidental overdosage (such as child taking entire bottle): Dial 999 (emergency).

Adverse Reactions or Side Effects

None expected

Interaction with Medicine, Vitamins or Minerals

Interacts with	Combined effect
Insulin	May decrease amount of insulin needed to treat diabetes.

Interaction with Other Substances

Sugar is partially destroyed by chromium.

MINERAL

Cobalt

Basic Information
Available from natural sources? Yes
Available from synthetic sources? Yes
Prescription required? No

 ## Natural Sources

Beet greens	Lettuce
Buckwheat	Liver
Cabbage	Milk
Clams	Oysters
Figs	Spinach
Kidney	Watercress

Note: Small amounts in diet satisfy requirements, except under unusual circumstances.

 ## Reasons to Use

- Promotes normal red-blood-cell formation.
- Acts as substitute for manganese in activation of several enzymes.
- Replaces zinc in some enzymes.

 ## Unproved Speculated Benefits

- Treats anaemia that does not respond to other treatment.
- Prevents and treats pernicious anaemia.

 ## Who Needs Additional Amounts?

Supplements are difficult to locate, so adequate food sources become more important.
- People with recent severe burns or injuries.
- Those with anorexia nervosa or bulimia.
- Vegetarians.

 ## Deficiency Symptoms

- Pernicious anaemia, with the following symptoms:
  Weakness, especially in arms and legs
  Sore tongue
  Nausea, appetite loss, weight loss
  Bleeding gums
  Numbness and tingling in hands and feet
  Difficulty maintaining balance
  Pale lips, pale tongue, pale gums

Yellow eyes and skin
Shortness of breath
Depression
Confusion and dementia
Headache
Poor memory

 ## Unproved Speculated Symptoms

- None

 ## Lab Tests to Detect Deficiency

- Concentration in human plasma
- Measured in bioassay as part of vitamin B-12

 ## Dosage and Usage Information

Recommended Dietary Allowance (RDA):
No RDA has been established.

What this mineral does:
- Acts as a catalyst in complex reactions to form vitamin B-12.

Miscellaneous information:
- This is a trace element stored mainly in the liver.
- Deficiency is extremely rare.
- Cobalt is a necessary ingredient to manufacture vitamin B-12 in the body. A deficiency of cobalt may lead to a deficiency of vitamin B-12 and therefore to pernicious anaemia.

Available as:
- Capsules: Swallow whole with full glass of liquid. Don't chew or crush. Take with meals or 1 to 1-1/2 hours after meals unless otherwise directed by your doctor.
- A constituent of many multivitamin/mineral preparations.

 ## Warnings and Precautions

Don't take if you:
- Are healthy and eat a nutritious balanced diet.

Consult your doctor if you:
- No problems expected.

Over age 55:
- Eat a balanced diet to prevent deficiency.

»➤

Pregnancy:
- No problems expected, except with megadoses.
- Don't take megadoses.

Breast-feeding:
- No problems expected, except with megadoses.
- Don't take megadoses.

Effect on lab tests:
- None expected.

Storage:
- Store in cool, dry place away from direct light, but don't freeze.
- Store safely out of reach of children.
- Don't store in bathroom medicine cabinet. Heat and moisture may change action of mineral.

Overdose/Toxicity

Signs and symptoms:
- In megadoses, 20-30mg per day, cobalt can produce polycythaemia, enlargement of thyroid gland and enlargement of the heart leading to congestive heart failure (See Glossary). produce polycythaemia enlargement of thyroid gland and enlargement of the heart leading to congestive heart failure (See Glossary).
- Cobalt toxicity can cause thyroid overgrowth in infants.

What to do:
For symptoms of overdosage: Discontinue mineral, and consult doctor. Also see *Adverse Reactions or Side Effects* section below.
For accidental overdosage (such as child taking entire bottle): Dial 999 (emergency).

Adverse Reactions or Side Effects

Reaction or effect	What to do
With megadoses:	
Polycythaemia	Discontinue. Call doctor immediately.
Enlargement of thyroid gland	Discontinue. Call doctor immediately.
Enlargement of heart	Discontinue. Call doctor immediately.

Interaction with Medicine, Vitamins or Minerals

Interacts with	Combined effect
Colchicine	May cause inaccurate laboratory studies of cobalt or vitamin B-12.
Neomycin	May cause inaccurate laboratory studies of cobalt or vitamin B-12.
Para-aminosalicylic acid	May cause inaccurate laboratory studies of cobalt or vitamin B-12.
Phenytoin	May cause inaccurate laboratory studies of cobalt or vitamin B-12.

Interaction with Other Substances

Some beer contains cobalt as a stabilizer. People who consume large quantities of **cobalt-stabilized beer** over long periods may develop cobalt toxicity leading to cardiomyopathy and congestive heart failure.

MINERAL

119

Copper

Basic Information
Available from natural sources? Yes
Available from synthetic sources? No
Prescription required? No

Natural Sources

Barley	Mushrooms
Brazil nuts	Mussels
Cashew nuts	Oats
Hazelnuts (filberts)	Oysters
Honey	Peanuts
Lentils	Salmon
Molasses, black-strap	Walnuts
	Wheat germ

Reasons to Use

- Promotes normal red-blood-cell formation.
- Acts as a catalyst in storage and release of iron to form haemoglobin for red blood cells.
- Assists in production of several enzymes involved in respiration.
- Promotes connective-tissue formation and central-nervous-system function.
- Is used as a nutritional supplement for anyone receiving prolonged feedings through veins or tubes into the stomach.

Unproved Speculated Benefits

- Stimulates hair growth in bald men.
- Treats anaemia.
- Protects against cancer.
- Protects against cardiovascular disease.
- Reduces inflammation.
- Helps arthritis.

Who Needs Additional Amounts?

- Anyone with inadequate caloric or dietary intake or increased nutritional requirements.
- Older people (over 55 years).
- Pregnant or breast-feeding women.
- Those who abuse alcohol or other drugs.
- People with a chronic wasting illness, particularly those with chronic diarrhoea, malabsorption disorders, kidney disease.
- Anyone who experiences excess stress for long periods or who has recently undergone surgery.

- Those with a portion of the gastrointestinal tract surgically removed.
- People with recent severe burns or injuries.
- Malnourished children whose diet consists of milk without supplements.
- People who receive intravenous nourishment for long periods of time.

Deficiency Symptoms

- Anaemia
- Low white-blood-cell count associated with reduced resistance to infection
- Faulty collagen formation
- Bone demineralization

Unproved Speculated Symptoms

- Arthritis
- Cancer
- Heart disease
- Baldness
- Anaemia

Lab Tests to Detect Deficiency

- Plasma copper levels
- Urine copper levels in 24-hour collection

Dosage and Usage Information

Recommended Dietary Allowance (RDA):
No RDA has been established. Estimated safe intake given below.

Age	Estimated Safe Intake
0–6 months	0.5–0.7mg/day
6–12 months	0.7–1.0mg/day
1–3 years	1.0–1.5mg/day
4–6 years	1.5–2.0mg/day
7–10 years	2.0–2.5mg/day
11+ years	2.0–3.0mg/day

What this mineral does:
- Copper is an essential component of a number of proteins and enzymes, including lysyl, hydroxylase, dopamine beta-hydroxylase.

Miscellaneous information:
- Plasma-copper levels may *increase* in people with rheumatoid arthritis, pregnancy, cirrhosis of the liver, myocardial infarction (heart attack), schizophrenia, tumours, severe infections. **➤➤**

- Processed foods may reduce normal copper absorption.
- Plasma-copper levels *decrease* with hypothyroidism, dysproteinuria of infancy, kwashiorkor, sprue, nephrosis.
- Hair analysis may be used as a measure of copper nutrition. (An unreliable test.)
- Most dieticians recommend a balanced diet rather than extra supplementation that could upset the body's delicate mineral balance.

Available as:
- Tablets: Swallow whole with full glass of liquid. Don't chew or crush. Take with meals or 1 to 1-1/2 hours after meals unless otherwise directed by your doctor.
- A constituent of many multivitamin/mineral preparations.

 ## Warnings and Precautions

Don't take if you:
- Have hepatolenticular degeneration (Wilson's disease).

Consult your doctor if you:
- Are considering taking a copper supplement.

Over age 55:
- No special considerations.

Pregnancy:
- Increased plasma copper levels are noted during pregnancy. Significance of this to human health is unknown at present.
- Don't take megadoses.

Breast-feeding:
- No information available at present.
- Don't take megadoses.

Effect on lab tests:
- Cobalt, iron, nickel and oral contraceptives with oestrogens can cause false-positive or elevated copper values.

Storage:
- Store in cool, dry place away from direct light, but don't freeze.
- Store safely out of reach of children.
- Don't store in bathroom medicine cabinet. Heat and moisture may change action of mineral.

 ## Overdose/Toxicity

Signs and symptoms:
Nausea, vomiting, muscle aches, abdominal pain, anaemia.

What to do:
For symptoms of overdosage: Discontinue mineral, and consult doctor.
For accidental overdosage (such as child taking entire bottle): Dial 999 (emergency).

 ## Adverse Reactions or Side Effects

None expected

 ## Interaction with Medicine, Vitamins or Minerals

Interacts with	Combined effect
Cadmium	Can interfere with copper absorption and utilization.
Fibre	Can interfere with copper absorption and utilization.
Molybdenum	Maintains appropriate ratio of copper to molybdenum in body. If you have excessive amounts of copper, your molybdenum level drops. If you have excessive amounts of molybdenum, your copper level drops.
Oral contraceptives	Increases copper level. Significance unknown at present.
Phytates (cereals, vegetables)	Can interfere with copper absorption and utilization.
Vitamin C	Decreases absorption of copper. Large doses of vitamin C must be taken to produce this effect.
Zinc	Can interfere with copper absorption and utilization.

 ## Interaction with Other Substances

None known

Dihydroxyaluminium Aminoacetate/
Magnesia/Alumina

Basic Information

Provides additional magnesium. Other substances in title are not supplied in large enough amounts for use by your body.
Available from natural sources? Yes
Available from synthetic sources? No
Prescription required? Yes, for some forms

Natural Sources

Almonds	Leafy, green	Snails
Bluefish	vegetables	Soya beans
Carp	Mackerel	Sunflower
Cod	Molasses	seeds
Flounder	Nuts	Swordfish
Halibut	Ocean perch	Wheat germ
Herring	Shrimp	

Reasons to Use

- Aids bone growth.
- Aids function of nerves and muscles, including regulation of normal heart rhythm.
- Keeps metabolism steady.
- Conducts nerve impulses.
- Works as laxative in large doses.
- Acts as antacid in small doses.
- Strengthens tooth enamel.

Unproved Speculated Benefits

- Cures alcoholism.
- Cures kidney stones.
- Alleviates heart disease.
- Helps control bad breath and body odour.
- Helps contain lead poisoning.

Who Needs Additional Amounts?

- Anyone with inadequate caloric or dietary intake or increased nutritional requirements.
- Those who abuse alcohol or other drugs.
- People with a chronic wasting illness or who have recently undergone surgery.
- Those with recent severe burns or injuries.

Deficiency Symptoms

Following symptoms occur rarely:
- Muscle contractions
- Convulsions
- Confusion and delirium
- Irritability
- Nervousness
- Skin problems
- Hardening of soft tissues

Unproved Speculated Symptoms

- Sudden heart failure

Lab Tests to Detect Deficiency

- Serum magnesium

Dosage and Usage Information

Recommended Dietary Allowance (RDA):
Estimate of adequate daily intake by the Food and Nutrition Board of the National Research Council, 1980 (See Glossary).

Age	RDA
0–6 months	50mg
6–12 months	70mg
1–3 years	150mg
4–6 years	200mg
7–10 years	250mg
Males	
11–14 years	350mg
15–18 years	400mg
18+ years	350mg
Females	
11+ years	300mg
Pregnant	+150mg
Lactating	+150mg

What this mineral does:
- Activates essential enzymes.
- Affects metabolism of proteins and nucleic acids.
- Helps transport sodium and potassium across cell membranes.
- Influences calcium levels inside cells.

Available as:
- Oral suspension: Dilute in at least 1/2 glass of water or other liquid. Take with meals or 1 to 1-1/2 hours after meals unless otherwise directed by your doctor.

»»➔

Dihydroxyaluminium Aminoacetate/ Magnesia/Alumina

Warnings and Precautions

Don't take if you have:
• Kidney failure.
• Heart block (unless you have a pacemaker).
• An ileostomy.

Consult your doctor if you have:
• Chronic constipation, colitis, diarrhoea.
• Symptoms of appendicitis.
• Stomach or intestinal bleeding.

Over age 55:
• Adverse reactions/side effects more likely.

Pregnancy:
• Risk to fetus outweighs benefits. Don't use.

Breast-feeding:
• Avoid magnesium in large quantities.
• If you must take temporarily, discontinue breast-feeding. Consult doctor for advice on maintaining milk supply.
• Don't take megadoses.

Effect on lab tests:
• Makes test for stomach-acid secretion inaccurate.
• May increase or decrease serum-phosphate concentrations.
• May decrease serum and urine pH.

Storage:
• Store in cool, dry place away from direct light, but don't freeze.
• Store safely out of reach of children.
• Don't store in bathroom medicine cabinet. Heat and moisture may change action of mineral.

Others:
• Chronic kidney disease frequently causes body to retain excess magnesium.
• Adverse reactions, side effects and interactions with medicines, vitamins or minerals occur *only rarely* when too much magnesium is taken for too long or if you have kidney disease.

Overdose/Toxicity

Signs and symptoms:
Severe nausea and vomiting, extremely low blood pressure, extreme muscle weakness, difficulty breathing, heartbeat irregularity.

What to do:
For symptoms of overdosage: Discontinue mineral, and consult doctor immediately. Also see *Adverse Reactions or Side Effects* section below.

For accidental overdosage (such as child taking entire bottle): Dial 999 (emergency).

Possible Adverse Reactions or Side Effects

Reaction or effect	What to do
Abdominal pain	Seek emergency treatment.
Abnormal bleeding	Seek emergency treatment.
Gastric ulceration (burning pain in upper chest relieved by food or antacid)	Discontinue. Call doctor immediately.
Mild diarrhoea	Discontinue. Call doctor when convenient.
Nausea, vomiting	Discontinue. Call doctor immediately.

Interactions with Medicine, Vitamins or Minerals

Interacts With	Combined Effect
Calcium	Interferes with zinc absorption.
Copper	Decreases absorption of copper. Large doses of zinc must be taken to produce this effect.
Cortisone drugs	May interfere with lab tests measuring zinc.
Diuretics	Increases zinc excretion. Requires taking greater amounts.
Iron	Decreases absorption of iron. Large doses of zinc must be taken to produce this effect.
Oral contraceptives	Lowers zinc blood levels.
Tetracycline	Decreases amount of tetracycline absorbed into bloodstream.
Vitamin A	Assists in absorption of vitamin A.

Interaction with Other Substances

Alcohol can increase zinc excretion in urine and impair body's ability to combine zinc into its correct enzyme combinations in liver.
Coffee and zinc should not be consumed together because they may decrease zinc absorption.

Ferrous Fumarate

Basic Information
Ferrous fumarate is 33% elemental iron.
Available from natural sources? Yes
Available from synthetic sources? Yes
Prescription required? Yes

Natural Sources

Bread, enriched	Molasses, black-strap
Cashews	Mussels
Caviar	Pistachios
Cheddar cheese	Pumpkin seeds
Egg yolk	Seaweed
Garbanzo beans	Walnuts
(chickpeas)	Wheat germ
Lentils	Whole-grain products

Note: Even iron-rich foods are poorly absorbed by humans. Only about 10% of food iron is absorbed from food consumed by an individual with normal iron stores. However, an iron-deficient person may absorb 20 to 30%.

Reasons to Use

- Prevents and treats iron-deficiency anaemia due to dietary iron deficiency or other causes.
- Stimulates bone-marrow production of haemoglobin, the red-blood-cell pigment that carries oxygen to the body cells.
- Forms part of several enzymes and proteins in the body.

Unproved Speculated Benefits

- Controls alcoholism.
- Helps alleviate menstrual discomfort.
- Stimulates immunity.
- Boosts physical performance.
- Prevents learning disorders in children.

Who Needs Additional Amounts?

- Many women of child-bearing age are mildly iron-deficient even when they get all their nutritional requirements.
- Anyone with inadequate caloric or dietary intake or increased nutritional requirements.
- Older people (over 55 years).
- Pregnant or breast-feeding women.
- Women with heavy menstrual flow, long menstrual periods or short menstrual cycles.
- Those who abuse alcohol or other drugs.
- People with a chronic wasting illness, excess stress for long periods or who have recently undergone surgery.
- Athletes and workers who participate in vigorous physical activities.
- Those with a portion of the gastrointestinal tract surgically removed.
- People with recent severe burns or injuries.
- Anyone who has lost blood recently, such as from heavy menstrual periods or from an accident.
- Vegetarians.
- Infants from 2 to 24 months.

Deficiency Symptoms

- Listlessness
- Heart palpitations upon exertion
- Fatigue
- Irritability
- Pale appearance to skin
- Cracking of lips and tongue
- Difficulty swallowing
- General feeling of poor health

Unproved Speculated Symptoms

- None

Lab Tests to Detect Deficiency

- Red-blood-cell count
- Microscopic examination of red blood cells.
- Serum iron
- Haemoglobin determinations

Dosage and Usage Information

Recommended Dietary Allowance (RDA):
Estimate of adequate daily intake by the Food and Nutrition Board of the National Research Council, 1980 (See Glossary).

➤➤

Age	RDA
0–6 months	10mg
6–12 months	15mg
1–3 years	15mg
4–6 years	10mg
7–10 years	10mg
Males	
11–18 years	18mg
19+ years	10mg
Females	
11–50 years	18mg
51+ years	10mg
Pregnant	+30–60mg
Lactating	+30–60mg

What this mineral does:

- Iron is an essential component of haemoglobin, myoglobin and a co-factor of several essential enzymes. Of the total iron in the body, 60 to 70% is stored in haemoglobin (the red part of red blood cells).
- Haemoglobin is also a component of myoglobin, an iron-protein complex in muscles. This complex helps muscles get extra energy when they work hard.

Miscellaneous information:

- Iron-deficiency anaemia in older men is usually considered to be due to slow loss of blood from a malignancy in the gastrointestinal tract until proved otherwise.
- Iron content of foods, especially acidic foods, can be dramatically increased by preparation in iron cookware.
- May require 3 weeks of treatment before you receive maximum benefit.
- Works best with vitamin C (ascorbic acid).

Available as:

- Tablets and capsules: Swallow whole with full glass of liquid. Don't chew or crush. Take with or immediately after food to decrease stomach irritation.
- Oral solution: Dilute in at least 1/2 glass water or other liquid. Take with meals or 1 to 1-1/2 hours after meals unless otherwise directed by your doctor.
- Chewable tablets: Chew well before swallowing.
- Enteric-coated tablets: Swallow whole with full glass of liquid. Take with meals or 1 to 1-1/2 hours after meals unless otherwise directed by your doctor.

Warnings and Precautions

Don't take if you:
- Are allergic to any iron supplement.
- Have acute hepatitis.
- Have haemosiderosis or haemochromatosis (conditions involving excess iron in body).
- Have haemolytic anaemia.
- Have had repeated blood transfusions.

Consult your doctor if you have:
- Plans to become pregnant while taking medication.
- Had stomach surgery.
- Had peptic-ulcer disease, enteritis, colitis.
- Had pancreatitis or hepatitis.
- Alcoholism.
- Kidney disease.
- Rheumatoid arthritis.
- Intestinal disease.

Over age 55:
- Deficiency more likely. Check frequently with doctor for anaemia symptoms or slow blood loss in stool.

Pregnancy:
- Pregnancy increases need. Check with doctor. During first 3 months of pregnancy, take *only* if doctor prescribes it.
- Don't take megadoses.

Breast-feeding:
- Supplements probably not needed if you are healthy and eat a balanced diet.
- Baby may need supplementation. Ask your doctor.
- Don't take megadoses.

Effect on lab tests:
- May cause abnormal results in serum bilirubin, serum calcium, serum iron, special radioactive studies of bones using technetium (Tc 99m-labeled agents), stool studies for blood.

Storage:
- Store in cool, dry place away from direct light, but don't freeze.
- Store safely out of reach of children. Iron tablets look like sweets, and children love them.
- Don't store in bathroom medicine cabinet. Heat and moisture may change action of mineral.

Others:
- Iron can accumulate to harmful levels (haemosiderosis) in patients with chronic kidney failure, Hodgkins disease, rheumatoid arthritis.
- Prolonged use in high doses can cause haemochromatosis (iron-storage disease), leading to bronze skin, diabetes, liver damage, impotence, heart problems.

MINERAL

Ferrous Fumarate, Continued

 Overdose/Toxicity

Signs and symptoms:
Early signs: Diarrhoea with blood, severe nausea, abdominal pain, vomiting with blood.
Late signs: Weakness, collapse, pallor, blue lips, blue hands, blue fingernails, shallow breathing, convulsions, coma, weak, rapid heartbeat.

What to do:
For symptoms of overdosage: Discontinue mineral, and consult doctor. Also see *Adverse Reactions or Side Effects* section below.
For accidental overdosage (such as child taking entire bottle): Dial 999 (emergency).

 Adverse Reactions or Side Effects

Reaction or effect	What to do
Abdominal pain	Discontinue. Call doctor immediately.
Black or grey stools (always)	Nothing.
Blood in stools	Seek emergency treatment.
Chest pain	Seek emergency treatment.
Drowsiness	Discontinue. Call doctor when convenient.
Stained teeth (liquid forms)	Mix with water or juice to lessen effect. Brush teeth with baking powder or hydrogen peroxide to help remove stain.
Throat pain	Discontinue. Call doctor immediately.

 Interaction with Medicine, Vitamins or Minerals

Interacts with	Combined effect
Allopurinol	May cause excess iron storage in liver.
Antacids	Causes poor iron absorption.
Calcium	Combination necessary for efficient calcium absorption.
Cholestyramine	Decreases iron effect.
Copper	Assists in copper absorption.
Iron supplements (other)	May cause excess iron storage in liver.
Pancreatin	Decreases iron absorption.
Penicillamine	Decreases penicillamine effect.
Sulfasalazine	Decreases iron effect.
Tetracyclines	Decreases tetracycline effect. Take iron 3 hours before or 2 hours after taking tetracycline.
Vitamin C	Increases iron effect. Necessary for red-blood-cell and haemoglobin formation.
Vitamin E	Decreases iron absorption.
Zinc (large doses)	Decreases iron absorption.

 Interaction with Other Substances

Alcohol increases iron utilization. May cause organ damage. Avoid or use in moderation.

Beverages
• Milk decreases iron absorption.
• Tea decreases iron absorption.
• Coffee decreases iron absorption.

Basic Information

Ferrous gluconate is 11.6% elemental iron.
Available from natural sources? Yes
Available from synthetic sources? Yes
Prescription required? Yes

Natural Sources

Bread, enriched	Molasses, black-strap
Cashews	Mussels
Caviar	Pistachios
Cheddar cheese	Pumpkin seeds
Egg yolk	Seaweed
Garbanzo beans	Walnuts
(chickpeas)	Wheat germ
Lentils	Whole-grain products

Note: Even iron-rich foods are poorly absorbed by humans. Only about 10% of food iron is absorbed from food consumed by an individual with normal iron stores. However, an iron-deficient person may absorb 20 to 30%.

Reasons to Use

- Prevents and treats iron-deficiency anaemia due to dietary iron deficiency or other causes.
- Stimulates bone-marrow production of haemoglobin, the red-blood-cell pigment that carries oxygen to the body cells.
- Forms part of several enzymes and proteins in the body.

Unproved Speculated Benefits

- Controls alcoholism.
- Helps alleviate menstrual discomfort.
- Stimulates immunity.
- Boosts physical performance.
- Prevents learning disorders in children.

Who Needs Additional Amounts?

- Many women of child-bearing age are mildly iron-deficient even when they get all their nutritional requirements.
- Anyone with inadequate caloric or dietary intake or increased nutritional requirements.
- Older people (over 55 years).
- Pregnant or breast-feeding women.
- Women with heavy menstrual flow, long menstrual periods or short menstrual cycles.
- Those who abuse alcohol or other drugs.
- People with a chronic wasting illness, excess stress for long periods or who have recently undergone surgery.
- Athletes and workers who participate in vigorous physical activities.
- Those with a portion of the gastrointestinal tract surgically removed.
- People with recent severe burns or injuries.
- Anyone who has lost blood recently, such as from heavy menstrual periods or from an accident.
- Vegetarians.
- Infants from 2 to 24 months.

Deficiency Symptoms

- Listlessness
- Heart palpitations upon exertion
- Fatigue
- Irritability
- Pale appearance to skin
- Cracking of lips and tongue
- Difficulty swallowing
- General feeling of poor health

Unproved Speculated Symptoms

- None

Lab Tests to Detect Deficiency

- Red-blood-cell count
- Microscopic examination of red blood cells.
- Serum iron
- Heamoglobin deteminations

>>>

Ferrous Gluconate, Continued

Dosage and Usage Information

Recommended Dietary Allowance (RDA):
Estimate of adequate daily intake by the Food and Nutrition Board of the National Research Council, 1980 (See Glossary).

Age	RDA
0–6 months	10mg
6–12 months	15mg
1–3 years	15mg
4–6 years	10mg
7–10 years	10mg
Males	
11–18 years	18mg
19+ years	10mg
Females	
11–50 years	18mg
51+ years	10mg
Pregnant	+30–60mg
Lactating	+30–60mg

What this mineral does:
- Iron is an essential component of haemoglobin, myoglobin and a co-factor of several essential enzymes. Of the total iron in the body, 60 to 70% is stored in haemoglobin (the red part of red blood cells).
- Haemoglobin is also a component of myoglobin, an iron-protein complex in muscles. This complex helps muscles get extra energy when they work hard.

Miscellaneous information:
- Iron-deficiency anaemia in older men is usually considered to be due to slow loss of blood from a malignancy in the gastrointestinal tract until proved otherwise
- Iron content of foods, especially acidic foods, can be dramatically increased by preparation in iron cookware.
- May require 3 weeks of treatment before you receive maximum benefit.
- Works best with vitamin C (ascorbic acid).

Available as:
- Capsules: Swallow whole with full glass of liquid. Don't chew or crush. Take with or immediately after food to decrease stomach irritation.
- Oral solution: Dilute in at least 1/2 glass water or other liquid. Take with meals or 1 to 1-1/2 hours after meals unless otherwise directed by your doctor.
- Tablets: Swallow whole with full glass of liquid. Don't chew or crush. Take with meals or 1 to 1-1/2 hours after meals unless otherwise directed by your doctor.

Warnings and Precautions

Don't take if you:
- Are allergic to any iron supplement.
- Have acute hepatitis.
- Have haemosiderosis or haemochromatosis (conditions involving excess iron in body).
- Have haemolytic anaemia.
- Have had repeated blood transfusions.

Consult your doctor if you have:
- Plans to become pregnant while taking medication.
- Had stomach surgery.
- Had peptic-ulcer disease, enteritis, colitis.
- Had pancreatitis or hepatitis.
- Alcoholism.
- Kidney disease.
- Rheumatoid arthritis.
- Intestinal disease.

Over age 55:
- Deficiency more likely. Check frequently with doctor for anaemia symptoms or slow blood loss in stool.

Pregnancy:
- Pregnancy increases need. Check with doctor. During first 3 months of pregnancy, take *only* if doctor prescribes it.
- Don't take megadoses.

Breast-feeding:
- Supplements probably not needed if you are healthy and eat a balanced diet.
- Baby may need supplementation. Ask your doctor.
- Don't take megadoses.

Effect on lab tests:
- May cause abnormal results in serum bilirubin, serum calcium, serum iron, special radioactive studies of bones using technetium (Tc 99m-labeled agents), stool studies for blood.

Storage:
- Store in cool, dry place away from direct light, but don't freeze.
- Store safely out of reach of children. Iron tablets look like sweets, and children love them.
- Don't store in bathroom medicine cabinet. Heat and moisture may change action of mineral.

Others:
- Iron can accumulate to harmful levels (haemosiderosis) in patients with chronic kidney failure, Hodgkins disease, rheumatoid arthritis.
- Prolonged use in high doses can also cause haemochromatosis (iron-storage disease), leading to bronze skin, diabetes, liver damage, impotence, heart problems.

➤➤

Overdose/Toxicity

Signs and symptoms:
Early signs: Diarrhoea with blood, severe nausea, abdominal pain, vomiting with blood.
Late signs: Weakness, collapse, pallor, blue lips, blue hands, blue fingernails, shallow breathing, convulsions, coma, weak, rapid heartbeat.

What to do:
For symptoms of overdosage: Discontinue mineral, and consult doctor. Also see *Adverse Reactions or Side Effects* section below.
For accidental overdosage (such as child taking entire bottle): Dial 999 (emergency).

 Adverse Reactions or Side Effects

Reaction or effect	What to do
Abdominal pain	Discontinue. Call doctor immediately.
Black or grey stools (always)	Nothing.
Blood in stools	Seek emergency treatment.
Chest pain	Seek emergency treatment.
Drowsiness	Discontinue. Call doctor when convenient.
Stained teeth (liquid forms)	Mix with water or juice to lessen effect. Brush teeth with baking powder or hydrogen peroxide to help remove stain.
Throat pain	Discontinue. Call doctor immediately.

 Interaction with Medicine, Vitamins or Minerals

Interacts with	Combined effect
Allopurinol	May cause excess iron storage in liver.
Antacids	Causes poor iron absorption.
Calcium	Combination necessary for efficient calcium absorption.
Cholestyramine	Decreases iron effect.
Copper	Assists in copper absorption.
Iron supplements (other)	May cause excess iron storage in liver.
Pancreatin	Decreases iron absorption.
Penicillamine	Decreases penicillamine effect.
Sulfasalazine	Decreases iron effect.
Tetracyclines	Decreases tetracycline effect. Take iron 3 hours before or 2 hours after taking tetracycline.
Vitamin C	Increases iron effect. Necessary for red-blood-cell and haemoglobin formation
Vitamin E	Decreases iron effect.
Zinc (large doses)	Decreases iron absorption.

 Interaction with Other Substances

Alcohol increases iron utilization. May cause organ damage. Avoid or use in moderation.

Beverages
• Milk decreases iron absorption.
• Tea decreases iron absorption.
• Coffee decreases iron absorption.

MINERAL

Ferrous Sulphate

Basic Information
Ferrous sulfate is 20% elemental iron.
Available from natural sources? Yes
Available from synthetic sources? Yes
Prescription required? Yes

Natural Sources

Bread, enriched	Molasses, black-strap
Cashews	Mussels
Caviar	Pistachios
Cheddar cheese	Pumpkin seeds
Egg yolk	Seaweed
Garbanzo beans	Walnuts
(chickpeas)	Wheat germ
Lentils	Whole-grain products

Note: Even iron-rich foods are poorly absorbed by humans. Only about 10% of food iron is absorbed from food consumed by an individual with normal iron stores. However, an iron-deficient person may absorb 20-30%.

Reasons to Use

- Prevents and treats iron-deficiency anaemia due to dietary iron deficiency or other causes.
- Stimulates bone-marrow production of haemoglobin, the red-blood-cell pigment that carries oxygen to body cells.
- Forms part of several enzymes and proteins in the body.

Unproved Speculated Benefits

- Controls alcoholism.
- Helps alleviate menstrual discomfort.
- Stimulates immunity.
- Boosts physical performance.
- Prevents learning disorders in children.

Who Needs Additional Amounts?

- Many women of child-bearing age are mildly iron-deficient even when they get all their nutritional requirements.
- Anyone with inadequate caloric or dietary intake or increased nutritional requirements.
- Older people (over 55 years).
- Pregnant or breast-feeding women.
- Women with heavy menstrual flow, long menstrual periods or short menstrual cycles.

- Those who abuse alcohol or other drugs.
- People with a chronic wasting illness, excess stress for long periods or who have recently undergone surgery.
- Athletes and workers who participate in vigorous physical activities.
- Those with a portion of the gastrointestinal tract surgically removed.
- People with recent severe burns or injuries.
- Anyone who has lost blood recently, such as from heavy menstrual periods or from an accident.
- Vegetarians.
- Infants from 2 to 24 months.

Deficiency Symptoms

- Listlessness
- Heart palpitations upon exertion
- Fatigue
- Irritability
- Pale appearance to skin
- Cracking of lips and tongue
- Difficulty swallowing
- General feeling of poor health

Unproved Speculated Symptoms

- None

Lab Tests to Detect Deficiency

- Red-blood-cell count
- Microscopic examination of red blood cells
- Serum iron
- Haemoglobin determinations

Dosage and Usage Information

Recommended Dietary Allowance (RDA):
Estimate of adequate daily intake by the Food and Nutrition Board of the National Research Council, 1980 (See Glossary).

⋙➤

Ferrous Sulphate

Age	RDA
0–6 months	10mg
6–12 months	15mg
1–3 years	15mg
4–6 years	10mg
7–10 years	10mg
Males	
11–18 years	18mg
19+ years	10mg
Females	
11–50 years	18mg
51+ years	10mg
Pregnant	+30–60mg
Lactating	+30–60mg

What this mineral does:
- Iron is an essential component of haemoglobin, myoglobin and a co-factor of several essential enzymes. Of the total iron in the body, 60 to 70% is stored in haemoglobin (the red part of red blood cells).
- Haemoglobin is also a component of myoglobin, an iron-protein complex in muscles. This complex helps muscles get extra energy when they work hard.

Miscellaneous information:
- Iron-deficiency anaemia in older men is usually considered to be due to slow loss of blood from a malignancy in the gastrointestinal tract until proved otherwise.
- Iron content of foods, especially acidic foods, can be dramatically increased by preparation in iron cookware.
- May require 3 weeks of treatment before you receive maximum benefit.
- Works best with vitamin C (ascorbic acid).

Available as:
- Extended-release capsules or tablets: Swallow whole with full glass of liquid. Don't chew or crush. Take with or immediately after food to decrease stomach irritation.
- Oral solution: Dilute in at least 1/2 glass water or other liquid. Take with meals or 1 to 1-1/2 hours after meals unless otherwise directed by your doctor.
- Enteric-coated tablets: Swallow whole with full glass of liquid. Take with meals or 1 to 1-1/2 hours after meals unless otherwise directed by your doctor.
- Tablets: Swallow whole with full glass of liquid. Don't chew or crush. Take with meals or 1 to 1-1/2 hours after meals unless otherwise directed by your doctor.

Warnings and Precautions

Don't take if you:
- Are allergic to any iron supplement.
- Have acute hepatitis.
- Have haemosiderosis or haemochromatosis (conditions involving excess iron in body).
- Have haemolytic anaemia.
- Have had repeated blood transfusions.

Consult your doctor if you have:
- Plans to become pregnant while taking medication.
- Had stomach surgery.
- Had peptic-ulcer disease, enteritis, colitis.
- Had pancreatitis or hepatitis.
- Alcoholism.
- Kidney disease.
- Rheumatoid arthritis.
- Intestinal disease.

Over age 55:
- Deficiency more likely. Check frequently with doctor for anaemia symptons or slow blood loss in stool.

Pregnancy:
- Pregnancy increases need. Check with doctor. During first 3 months of pregnancy, take *only* if doctor prescribes it.
- Don't take megadoses.

Breast-feeding:
- Supplements probably not needed if you are healthy and eat a balanced diet.
- Baby may need supplementation. Ask your doctor.
- Don't take megadoses.

Effect on lab tests:
- May cause abnormal results in serum bilirubin, serum calcium, serum iron, special radioactive studies of bones using technetium (Tc 99m-labeled agents), stool studies for blood.

Storage:
- Store in cool, dry place away from direct light, but don't freeze.
- Store safely out of reach of children. Iron tablets look like sweets, and children love them.
- Don't store in bathroom medicine cabinet. Heat and moisture may change action of mineral.

Others:
- Iron can accumulate to harmful levels (haemosiderosis) in patients with chronic kidney failure, Hodgkins disease, rheumatoid arthritis.
- Prolonged use in high doses can cause haemochromatosis (iron-storage disease), leading to bronze skin, diabetes, liver damage, impotence, heart problems.

MINERAL

⟫➤

Overdose/Toxicity

Signs and symptoms:
Early signs: Diarrhoea with blood, severe nausea, abdominal pain, vomiting with blood.
Late signs: Weakness, collapse, pallor, blue lips, blue hands, blue fingernails, shallow breathing, convulsions, coma, weak, rapid heartbeat.

What to do:
For symptoms of overdosage: Discontinue mineral, and consult doctor. Also see *Adverse Reactions or Side Effects* section below.
For accidental overdosage (such as child taking entire bottle): Dial 999 (emergency).

Adverse Reactions or Side Effects

Reaction or effect	What to do
Abdominal pain	Discontinue. Call doctor immediately.
Black or grey stools (always)	Nothing.
Blood in stools	Seek emergency treatment.
Chest pain	Seek emergency treatment.
Drowsiness	Discontinue. Call doctor when convenient.
Stained teeth (liquid forms)	Mix with water or juice to lessen effect. Brush teeth with baking powder or hydrogen peroxide to help remove stain.
Throat pain	Discontinue. Call doctor immediately.

Interaction with Medicine, Vitamins or Minerals

Interacts with	Combined effect
Allopurinol	May cause excess iron storage in liver.
Antacids	Causes poor iron absorption.
Calcium	Combination necessary to efficient calcium absorption.
Cholestyramine	Decreases iron effect.
Copper	Assists in copper absorption.
Iron supplements (other)	May cause excess iron storage in liver.
Pancreatin	Decreases iron absorption.
Penicillamine	Decreases penicillamine effect.
Sulfasalazine	Decreases iron effect.
Tetracyclines	Decreases tetracycline effect. Take iron 3 hours before or 2 hours after taking tetracycline.
Vitamin C	Increases iron effect. Necessary for red-blood-cell and haemoglobin formation.
Vitamin E	Decreases iron effect.
Zinc (large doses)	Decreases iron absorption.

Interaction with Other Substances

Alcohol increases iron utilization. May cause organ damage. Avoid or use in moderation.

Beverages
• Milk decreases iron absorption.
• Tea decreases iron absorption.
• Coffee decreases iron absorption.

Basic Information

Fluoride is available commercially as sodium fluoride.
Available from natural sources? Yes
Available from synthetic sources? Yes
Prescription required? Yes

Natural Sources

Apples	Kidneys
Calves' liver	Salmon, canned
Cod	Sardines, canned
Eggs	Tea

Note: The fluoride content of foods varies tremendously. It is relatively high where soils are rich and water is fluoridated and low otherwise.

Reasons to Use

- Prevents dental caries (cavities) in children when level of fluoride in water is inadequate.
- Treats osteoporosis with calcium and vitamin D, but use must be carefully monitored by a doctor.

Unproved Speculated Benefits

- Prevents osteoporosis in older people.
- Prevents the most-common cause of hearing loss in the elderly by recalcifying ear's inner-bone structure.

Who Needs Additional Amounts?

- Anyone with inadequate caloric or dietary intake or increased nutritional requirements.
- People living in an area with low fluoride water content. Check with your doctor or dentist.

Deficiency Symptoms

- Significant increase in dental caries

Unproved Speculated Symptoms

- Softening of bones in post-menopausal women

Lab Tests to Detect Deficiency

- None available. Examinations of mouth for dental caries once or twice a year yields all necessary evidence.

Dosage and Usage Information

Recommended Dietary Allowance (RDA):
No RDA has been established. Estimated safe intake given below.

Age	Estimated Safe Intake
0–6 months	0.1–0.5mg/day
6–12 months	0.20–1.0mg/day
1–3 years	0.5–1.5mg/day
4–6 years	1.0–2.5mg/day
7–10 years	1.5–2.5mg/day
11+ years	1.5–4.0mg/day

What this mineral does:
- Contributes to solid bone and tooth formation by helping body retain calcium.
- Interferes with growth and development of bacteria that cause dental plaque.

Miscellaneous information:
- Taking fluoride does not remove need for good dental habits, including a good diet, brushing and flossing teeth and regular dental visits.
- If fluoride supplementation is needed in your area, continue until child is 16. Subsequent topical applications every year or two may be continued to prevent caries.
- Claims that persons residing in areas with fluoridated water supplies have a higher incidence of cancer have not been proven.

Available as:
- Tablets: Swallow whole with full glass of liquid. Don't chew or crush. Take with meals or 1 to 1-1/2 hours after meals unless otherwise directed by your doctor.
- Drops: Dilute in at least 1/2 glass of water or other liquid. Take with meals or 1 to 1-1/2 hours after meals unless otherwise directed by your doctor. Do not take with milk or dairy products.
- Rinses: Follow directions, and use just before bedtime, after proper brushing and flossing.
- Gels: Follow directions, and use just before bedtime, after proper brushing and flossing.
- Paste: Follow directions, and use just before bedtime, after proper brushing and flossing.

MINERAL

Fluoride, Continued

Warnings and Precautions

Don't take if:
- Sodium intake is restricted or fluoride intake from drinking water exceeds 0.7 parts fluoride/million. Too much fluoride stains teeth permanently.
- You have underactive thyroid function.

Consult your doctor if you have:
- Osteoporosis.

Over age 55:
- No problems expected.

Pregnancy:
- Reports do not agree regarding benefit and risk to unborn child. Follow doctor's instructions.
- Don't take megadoses.

Breast-feeding:
- No problems expected.
- Don't take megadoses.

Effect on lab tests:
- Serum acid phosphatase, serum calcium and protein-bound iodine may be falsely decreased.
- Serum aspartase aminotranfererase (SGOT) may be falsely increased. (See Glossary)

Storage:
- Store in cool, dry place away from direct light, but don't freeze. Keep in original plastic container. Fluoride decomposes glass.
- Store safely out of reach of children.
- Don't store in bathroom medicine cabinet. Heat and moisture may change action of mineral.

Others:
- High dosage needed to treat osteoporosis leads to likelihood of toxic effects, including increased number of bone fractures.

Overdose/Toxicity

Signs and symptoms:
- Stomach cramps or pain, faintness, vomiting (possibly bloody), diarrhoea, black stools, shallow breathing, tremors, increased saliva, unusual excitement.

What to do:
For symptoms of overdosage: Discontinue mineral, and consult doctor. Also see *Adverse Reactions or Side Effects* section below.
For accidental overdosage (such as child taking entire bottle): Dial 999 (emergency).

Adverse Reactions or Side Effects

Reaction or effect	What to do
Excessive amounts of fluoride can cause:	
Appetite loss	Discontinue. Call doctor when convenient.
Constipation	Discontinue. Call doctor when convenient.
Decreased calcium in body characterized by bone pain, leg cramps	Continue. Call doctor when convenient.
Mottling of teeth with brown, black or white discolouration	Continue. Call doctor when convenient.
Nausea	Discontinue. Call doctor when convenient.
Pain and aching in bones	Discontinue. Call doctor immediately.
Skin rash	Discontinue. Call doctor immediately.
Sores in mouth	Discontinue. Call doctor immediately.
Stiffness	Discontinue. Call doctor immediately.
Weight loss	Discontinue. Call doctor when convenient.

Interaction with Medicine, Vitamins or Minerals

Interacts with	Combined effect
Aluminium hydroxide	Decreases absorption of fluoride.
Calcium supplements	Decreases absorption of fluoride.

Interaction with Other Substances

Beverages
- Milk decreases absorption of fluoride. Take dose 2 hours before or after milk.

Iodine

Basic Information
Available from natural sources? Yes
Available from synthetic sources? No
Prescription required? Yes, for strengths
over 130mg

Natural Sources

Cod	Salmon, canned
Cod-liver oil	Salt, table (iodized)
Haddock	and sea
Herring	Seaweed
Lobster	Shrimp
Oysters	Sunflower seeds

Reasons to Use

- Promotes normal function of thyroid gland.
- Promotes normal cell function.
- Shrinks thyroid prior to thyroid surgery.
- Tests thyroid function before and after administration of a radioactive form of iodine.
- Keeps skin, hair, nails healthy.
- Protects thyroid gland after accidental exposure to radiation.
- Prevents goitre.

Unproved Speculated Benefits

- Cures anaemia.
- Treats angina pectoris.
- Treats arteriosclerosis.
- Treats arthritis.
- Treats erythema nodosum.
- Restores vigour.
- Solves hair problems.
- Treats sporotrichosis infection of skin.

Who Needs Additional Amounts?

- Anyone with inadequate caloric or nutritional dietary intake or increased nutritional requirements.
- Anyone who lives in a region where the soil is deficient in iodine. Deficiency is usually treated by using iodized table salt.
- People who eat large amounts of food that can cause thyroid goitre, such as spinach, lettuce, turnips, beets, rutabagas, kale.

Deficiency Symptoms

Childhood deficiencies:
- Depressed growth
- Delayed sexual development
- Mental retardation
- Deafness

Adult deficiencies:
- Goitre

Symptoms of low-thyroid-hormone level (children and adults):
- Listlessness
- Sluggish behaviour

Unproved Speculated Symptoms

- Baldness
- Tiredness
- Chest pain

Lab Tests to Detect Deficiency

- Tests may indicate lower-than-normal thyroid function, implying a deficiency of iodine in some cases

Dosage and Usage Information

Recommended Dietary Allowance (RDA):
Estimate of adequate daily intake by the Food and Nutrition Board of the National Research Council, 1980 (See Glossary).

Age	RDA
0–6 months	40mcg
6–12 months	50mcg
1–3 years	70mcg
4–6 years	90mcg
7–10 years	120mcg
11+ years	150mcg
Pregnant	+25mcg
Lactating	+50mcg

What this mineral does:
- Iodine is an integral part of the thyroid hormones tetraiodothyronine (thyroxin) and triiodothyronine.

Miscellaneous information:
- Iodated salt and use of iodophores as antiseptics by the dairy industry are the main source of iodine in most diets.
- It is safe to consume 100–300mcg/day.

———➤➤➤

MINERAL

Iodine, Continued

Available as:
- Tablets: Swallow whole with full glass of liquid. Don't chew or crush. Take with meals or 1 to 1-1/2 hours after meals unless otherwise directed by your doctor.
- Oral solution: Dilute in at least 1/2 glass water or other liquid. Take with meals or 1 to 1-1/2 hours after meals unless otherwise directed by your doctor.
- Enteric-coated tablets are *not recommended*. They may cause obstruction, bleeding, perforation of small bowel.

Warnings and Precautions

Don't take if you:
- Have elevated serum potassium (determined by laboratory study).
- Have myotonia congenita.

Consult your doctor if you have:
- Hyperthyroidism.
- Kidney disease.
- Taken or are taking amiloride, antithyroid medications, lithium, spironolactone, triamterene.

Over age 55:
- No special considerations.

Pregnancy:
- If too much iodine is consumed during pregnancy, the infant may have thyroid enlargement, hypothyroidism or cretinism (dwarfism and mental deficiency).

Breast-feeding:
- Avoid supplements while nursing.
- Iodine in milk can cause skin rash and suppression of normal thyroid function in infant.
- Don't take megadoses.

Effect on lab tests:
- May cause false elevation in all thyroid-function studies.
- Interferes with test for naturally occurring steroids in urine.

Storage:
- Store in cool, dry place away from direct light, but don't freeze.
- Store safely out of reach of children.
- Don't store in bathroom medicine cabinet. Heat and moisture may change action of mineral.

Overdose/Toxicity

Signs and symptoms:
Irregular heartbeat, confusion, swollen neck or throat, bloody or black, tarry stools.

What to do:
For symptoms of overdosage: Discontinue mineral, and consult doctor. Also see *Adverse Reactions or Side Effects* section below.

For accidental overdosage (such as child taking entire bottle): Dial 999 (emergency).

➤➤

Adverse Reactions or Side Effects

Reaction or effect	What to do
Abdominal pain	Discontinue. Call doctor immediately.
Burning in mouth or throat	Discontinue. Call doctor immediately.
Diarrhoea	Discontinue. Call doctor immediately.
Fever	Discontinue. Call doctor immediately.
Headache	Discontinue. Call doctor immediately.
Heavy legs	Discontinue. Call doctor when convenient.
Increased salivation	Discontinue. Call doctor immediately.
Metallic taste	Discontinue. Call doctor when convenient.
Nausea	Continue. Tell doctor at next visit.
Numbness, tingling or pain in hands or feet	Discontinue. Call doctor immediately.
Swelling of salivary gland	Seek emergency treatment.
Skin rash	Discontinue. Call doctor immediately.
Sore teeth or gums	Discontinue. Call doctor immediately.
Tiredness or weakness	Discontinue. Call doctor immediately.

 Interaction with Medicine, Vitamins or Minerals

Interacts with	Combined effect
Lithium carbonate for manic-depressive illness	Produces abnormally low thyroid activity. People taking lithium carbonate should avoid iodine, which suppresses the thyroid gland.

 Interaction with Other Substances

None known

MINERAL

Iron Dextran

Basic Information

Iron dextran contains 50mg elemental iron per millilitre. It is a special form or iron designed to be used as an injection deep into muscle, usually in the buttocks.
Available from natural sources? Yes
Available from synthetic sources? Yes
Prescription required? Yes

 ## Natural Sources

Bread, enriched	Molasses, black-strap
Cashews	Mussels
Caviar	Pistachios
Cheese, cheddar	Pumpkin seeds
Egg yolk	Seaweed
Garbanzo beans	Walnuts
(chickpeas)	Wheat germ
Lentils	Whole-grain products

Note: Even iron-rich foods are poorly absorbed by humans. Only about 10% of food iron is absorbed from food consumed by an individual with normal iron stores. However, an iron-deficient person, may absorb 20 to 30%.

 ## Reasons to Use

- Prevents and treats iron-deficiency anaemia due to dietary iron deficiency or other causes. Iron dextran is particularly useful for people who develop sever gastrointestinal symptoms when they take iron orally.
- Stimulates bone-marrow production of haemoglobin, the red-blood-cell pigment that carries oxygen to the body cells.
- Forms part of several enzymes and proteins in the body.

 ## Unproved Speculated Benefits

- Controls alcoholism.
- Helps alleviate menstrual discomfort.
- Stimulates immunity.
- Boosts physical performance.
- Prevents learning disorders in children.

 ## Who Needs Additional Amounts?

- Many women of child-bearing age are mildly iron-deficient even when they get all their nutritional requirements.
- Anyone with inadequate caloric or dietary intake or increased nutritional requirements.

- Older people (over 55 years).
- Pregnant or breast-feeding women.
- Women with heavy menstrual flow, long menstrual periods or short menstrual cycles.
- Those who abuse alcohol or other drugs.
- People with a chronic wasting illness, excess stress for long periods or those who have recently undergone surgery.
- Athletes and workers who participate in vigorous physical activities.
- Those with a portion of the gastrointestinal tract surgically removed.
- People with recent severe burns or injuries.
- Anyone who has lost blood recently, such as from heavy menstrual periods or from an accident.
- Vegetarians.
- Infants from 2 to 24 months.

 ## Deficiency Symptoms

- Listlessness
- Heart palpitations upon exertion
- Fatigue
- Irritability
- Paleness of skin
- Cracking of lips and tongue
- Difficulty swallowing
- General feeling of poor health

 ## Unproved Speculated Symptoms

- None

 ## Lab Tests to Detect Deficiency

- Red-blood-cell count
- Microscopic examination of red blood cells.
- Serum iron
- Haemoglobin determinations.

 ## Dosage and Usage Information

Recommended Dietary Allowance (RDA):
Estimate of adequate daily intake by the Food and Nutrition Board of the National Research Council, 1980 (See Glossary).

⟫▶

Iron Dextran

Age	RDA
0–6 months	10mg
6–12 months	15mg
1–3 years	15mg
4–6 years	10mg
7–10 years	10mg
Males	
11–18 years	18mg
19+ years	10mg
Females	
11–50 years	18mg
51+ years	10mg
Pregnant	+30–60mg
Lactating	+30–60mg

What this mineral does:

- Iron is an essential component of haemoglobin, myoglobin and a co-factor of several essential enzymes. Of the total iron in the body, 60 to 70% is stored in haemoglobin (the red part of red blood cells).
- Haemoglobin is also a component of myoglobin, an iron-protein complex in muscles. This complex helps muscles get extra energy when they work hard.

Miscellaneous information:

- Iron-deficiency anaemia in older men is usually considered to be due to slow loss of blood from a malignancy in the gastrointestinal tract until proved otherwise.
- Iron content of foods, especially acidic foods, can be dramatically increased by preparation in iron cookware.
- May require 3 weeks of treatment before you receive maximum benefit.
- Works best with vitamin C (ascorbic acid).

Available as:

- Injectable forms are administered by doctor or nurse.

 Warnings and Precautions

Don't take if you:

- Are allergic to any iron supplement.
- Have acute hepatitis.
- Have Haemosiderosis or Haemochromatosis. (conditions involving excess iron in body).
- Have haemolytic anaemia.
- Have had repeated blood transfusions.

Consult your doctor if you have:

- Plans to become pregnant while taking medication.
- Had stomach surgery.
- Had peptic-ulcer disease, enteritis, colitis.
- Had pancreatitis or hepatitis.
- Alcoholism.
- Kidney disease.
- Rheumatoid arthritis.
- Intestinal disease.

Over age 55:

- Deficiency more likely. Check frequently with doctor for anaemia symptoms or slow blood loss in stool.

Pregnancy:

- Pregnancy increases need. Check with doctor. During first 3 months of pregnancy, take *only* if doctor prescribes it.
- Don't take megadoses.

Breast-feeding:

- Supplements probably not needed if you are healthy and eat a balanced diet.
- Baby may need supplementation. Ask your doctor.
- Don't take megadoses.

Effect on lab tests:

- May cause abnormal results in serum bilirubin, serum calcium, serum iron, special radioactive studies of bones using technetium (Tc 99m-labeled agents), stool studies for blood.

Storage:

- Store in cool, dry place away from direct light, but don't freeze.
- Store safely out of reach of children. Iron tablets look like sweets, and children love them.
- Don't store in bathroom medicine cabinet. Heat and moisture may change action of mineral.

Others:

- Iron can accumulate to harmful levels (haemosiderosis) in patients with chronic kidney failure, Hodgkins disease, rheumatoid arthritis. haemochromatosis (iron-storage disease),
- Prolonged use in high doses can cause haemochromatosis (iron-storage disease), leading to bronze skin, diabetes, liver damage, impotence, heart problems.

➤➤

Iron Dextran, Continued

Overdose/Toxicity

Signs and symptoms:
Early signs: Diarrhoea with blood, severe nausea, abdominal pain, vomiting with blood. *Late signs:* Weakness, collapse, pallor, blue lips, blue hands, blue fingernails, shallow breathing, convulsions, coma, weak, rapid heartbeat.

What to do:
For symptoms of overdosage: Discontinue mineral, and consult doctor. Also see *Adverse Reactions or Side Effects* section below.
For accidental overdosage (such as child taking entire bottle): Dial 999 (emergency).

Adverse Reactions or Side Effects

Reaction or effect	What to do
Abdominal pain	Discontinue. Call doctor immediately.
Anaphylaxis (extremely rare)— symptoms include immediate severe itching, paleness, low blood pressure, loss of consciousness, coma	Yell for help. Don't leave victim. Begin CPR (cardiopulmonary resuscitation), mouth-to-mouth breathing and external cardiac massage. Have someone dial "999" (emergency)
Black or grey stools (always)	Nothing.
Blood in stools	Seek emergency treatment.
Chest pain	Seek emergency treatment.
Chills	Seek emergency treatment.
Drowsiness	Discontinue. Call doctor when convenient.
Hives	Seek emergency treatment.
Loss of consciousness	Seek emergency treatment.
Shortness of breath	Seek emergency treatment.
Skin rash	Seek emergency treatment.

| **Throat pain** | Discontinue. Call doctor immediately. |

Interaction with Medicine, Vitamins or Minerals

Interacts with	Combined effect
Allopurinol	May cause excess iron storage in liver.
Antacids	Causes poor iron absorption.
Calcium	Combination necessary for efficient calcium absorption.
Cholestyramine	Decreases iron effect.
Copper	Assists in copper absorption.
Iron supplements (other)	May cause excess iron storage in liver.
Pancreatin	Decreases iron absorption.
Penicillamine	Decreases penicillamine effect.
Sulfasalazine	Decreases iron effect.
Tetracyclines	Decreases tetracycline effect. Take iron 3 hours before or 2 hours after taking tetracycline.
Vitamin C	Increases iron effect. Necessary for red-blood-cell and haemoglobin formation
Vitamin E	Decreases iron effect.
Zinc (large doses)	Decreases iron absorption.

Interaction with Other Substances

Alcohol increases iron utilization. May cause organ damage. Avoid or use in moderation.

Beverages
• Milk decreases iron absorption.
• Tea decreases iron absorption.
• Coffee decreases iron absorption.

Iron-Polysaccharide

Basic Information
Available from natural sources? Yes
Available from synthetic sources? Yes
Prescription required? Yes

Natural Sources

Bread, enriched	Molasses, black-strap
Cashews	Mussels
Caviar	Pistachios
Cheddar cheese	Pumpkin seeds
Egg yolk	Seaweed
Garbanzo beans	Walnuts
(chickpeas)	Wheat germ
Lentils	Whole-grain products

Note: Even iron-rich foods are poorly absorbed by humans. Only about 10% of iron from food is absorbed from food consumed by an individual with normal iron stores. However, an iron-deficient person may absorb 20 to 30%.

Reasons to Use

- Prevents and treats iron-deficiency anaemia due to dietary iron deficiency or other causes.
- Stimulates bone-marrow production of haemoglobin, the red-blood-cell pigment that carries oxygen to body cells.
- Forms part of several enzymes and proteins in the body.

Unproved Speculated Benefits

- Controls alcoholism.
- Helps alleviate menstrual discomfort.
- Stimulates immunity.
- Boosts physical performance.
- Prevents learning disorders in children.

Who Needs Additional Amounts?

- Many women of child-bearing age are mildly iron-deficient even when they get all their nutritional requirements.
- Anyone with inadequate caloric or nutritional dietary intake or increased nutritional requirements.
- Older people (over 55 years).
- Pregnant or breast-feeding women.
- Those who abuse alcohol or other drugs.
- People with a chronic wasting illness, excess stress for long periods or who have recently undergone surgery.

- Athletes and workers who participate in vigorous physical activities.
- Those with a portion of the gastrointestinal tract surgically removed.
- People with recent severe burns or injuries.
- Anyone who has lost blood recently, such as from heavy menstrual periods or from an accident.
- Vegetarians.
- Infants from 2 to 24 months.

Deficiency Symptoms

- Listlessness
- Heart palpitations upon exertion
- Fatigue
- Irritability
- Pale appearance to skin
- Cracking of lips and tongue
- Difficulty swallowing
- General feeling of poor health

Unproved Speculated Symptoms

- None

Lab Tests to Detect Deficiency

- Red-blood-cell count
- Microscopic examination of red blood cells.
- Serum iron
- Haemoglobin determinations

»→

Iron-Polysaccharide, Continued

Dosage and Usage Information

Recommended Dietary Allowance (RDA):
Estimate of adequate daily intake by the Food and Nutrition Board of the National Research Council, 1980 (See Glossary).

Age	RDA
0–6 months	10mg
6–12 months	15mg
1–3 years	15mg
4–6 years	10mg
7–10 years	10mg
Males	
11–18 years	18mg
19+ years	10mg
Females	
11–50 years	18mg
51+ years	10mg
Pregnant	+30–60mg
Lactating	+30–60mg

What this mineral does:
- Iron is an essential component of haemoglobin, myoglobin and a co-factor of several essential enzymes. Of the total iron in the body, 60 to 70% is stored in haemoglobin (the red part of red blood cells).
- Haemoglobin is also a component of myoglobin, an iron-protein complex in muscles. This complex helps muscles get extra energy when they work hard.

Miscellaneous information:
- Iron-deficiency anaemia in older men is usually considered to be due to slow loss of blood from a malignancy in the gastrointestinal tract until proved otherwise.
- Iron content of foods, especially acidic foods, can be dramatically increased by preparation in iron cookware.
- May require 3 weeks of treatment before you receive maximum benefit.
- Works best with vitamin C (ascorbic acid).

Available as:
- Capsules: Swallow whole with full glass of liquid. Don't chew or crush. Take with or immediately after food to decrease stomach irritation.
- Oral solution: Dilute in at least 1/2 glass water or other liquid. Take with meals or 1 to 1-1/2 hours after meals unless otherwise directed by your doctor.
- Tablets: Swallow whole with full glass of liquid. Don't chew or crush. Take with meals or 1 to 1-1/2 hours after meals unless otherwise directed by your doctor.

Warnings and Precautions

Don't take if you:
- Are allergic to any iron supplement.
- Have acute hepatitis.
- Have haemosiderosis or haemochromatosis (conditions involving excess iron in body).
- Have haemolytic anaemia.
- Have had repeated blood transfusions.

Consult your doctor if you have:
- Plans to become pregnant while taking medication.
- Had stomach surgery.
- Had peptic-ulcer disease, enteritis or colitis.
- Had pancreatitis or hepatitis.
- Alcoholism.
- Kidney disease.
- Rheumatoid arthritis.
- Intestinal disease.

Over age 55:
- Deficiency more likely. Check frequently with doctor for anaemia symptoms or slow blood loss in stool.

Pregnancy:
- Pregnancy increases need. Check with your doctor. During first 3 months of pregnancy, take *only* if your doctor prescribes it.
- Don't take megadoses.

Breast-feeding:
- Supplements probably not needed if you are healthy and eat a balanced diet.
- Baby may need supplement. Ask your doctor.
- Don't take megadoses.

Effect on lab tests:
- May cause abnormal results in serum bilirubin, serum calcium, serum iron, special radioactive studies of bones using technetium (Tc 99m-labeled agents), stool studies for blood.

Storage:
- Store in cool, dry place away from direct light, but don't freeze.
- Store safely out of reach of children. Iron tablets look like sweets, and children love them.
- Don't store in bathroom medicine cabinet. Heat and moisture may change action of mineral.

Others:
- Iron can accumulate to harmful levels (haemosiderosis) in patients, with chronic kidney failure, Hodgkins disease, rhuematoid arthritis.
- Prolonged use in high doses can cause haemochromatosis (iron-storage disease), leading to bronze skin, diabetes, liver damage, impotence, heart problems.

➤➤

Overdose/Toxicity

Signs and symptoms:
Early signs: Diarrhoea with blood, severe nausea, abdominal pain, vomiting with blood.
Late signs: Weakness, collapse, pallor, blue lips, blue hands, blue fingernails, shallow breathing, convulsions, coma, weak, rapid heartbeat.

What to do:
For symptoms of overdosage: Discontinue mineral, and consult doctor. Also see *Adverse Reactions or Side Effects* section below.
For accidental overdosage (such as child taking entire bottle): Dial 999 (emergency).

 Adverse Reactions or Side Effects

Reaction or effect	What to do
Abdominal pain	Discontinue. Call doctor immediately.
Black stools or gray stools (always)	Nothing.
Blood in stools	Seek emergency treatment.
Chest pain	Seek emergency treatment.
Drowsiness	Discontinue. Call doctor when convenient.
Stained teeth (liquid forms)	Mix with water or juice to lessen effect. Brush teeth with baking powder or hydrogen peroxide to help remove stain.
Throat pain	Discontinue. Call doctor immediately.

 Interaction with Medicine, Vitamins or Minerals

Interacts with	Combined effect
Allopurinol	Possible excess iron storage in liver.
Antacids	Poor iron absorption.
Calcium	Combination necessary for efficient calcium absorption.
Cholestyramine	Decreases iron effect.
Copper	Assists in copper absorption.
Iron supplements (other)	Possible excess iron storage in liver.
Pancreatin	Decreases iron absorption.
Penicillamine	Decreases penicillamine effect.
Sulfasalazine	Decreases iron effect.
Tetracyclines	Decreases tetracycline effect. Take iron 3 hours before or 2 hours after taking tetracycline.
Vitamin C	Increases iron effect. Contribution necessary for red-blood-cell and haemoglobin formation.
Vitamin E	Decreases iron absorption.
Zinc (large doses)	Decreases iron absorption.

 Interaction with Other Substances

Alcohol increases iron utilization. May cause organ damage. Avoid or use in moderation.

Beverages
• Milk decreases iron absorption.
• Tea decreases iron absorption.
• Coffee decreases iron absorption.

MINERAL

Magnesium

Basic Information

Available from natural sources? Yes
Available from synthetic sources? No
Prescription required? Yes, for some forms

Natural Sources

Almonds	Leafy, green	Snails
Bluefish	vegetables	Soya beans
Carp	Mackerel	Sunflower
Cod	Molasses	seeds
Flounder	Nuts	Swordfish
Halibut	Ocean perch	Wheat germ
Herring	Shrimp	

Reasons to Use

- Aids bone growth.
- Aids function of nerves and muscles, including regulation of normal heart rhythm.
- Keeps metabolism steady.
- Conducts nerve impulses.
- Works as laxative in large doses.
- Acts as antacid in small doses.
- Strengthens tooth enamel.

Unproved Speculated Benefits

- Cures alcoholism.
- Cures kidney stones.
- Alleviates heart disease.
- Helps control bad breath and body odour.
- Helps contain lead poisoning.

Who Needs Additional Amounts?

- Anyone with inadequate caloric or dietary intake or increased nutritional requirements.
- Those who abuse alcohol or other drugs.
- People with a chronic wasting illness or who have recently undergone surgery.
- Those with recent severe burns or injuries.

Deficiency Symptoms

Following symptoms occur rarely:
- Muscle contractions
- Convulsions
- Confusion and delirium
- Irritability
- Nervousness
- Skin problems
- Hardening of soft tissues

Unproved Speculated Symptoms

- Sudden heart failure

Lab Tests to Detect Deficiency

- Serum magnesium

Dosage and Usage Information

Recommended Dietary Allowance (RDA):
Estimate of adequate daily intake by the Food and Nutrition Board of the National Research Council, 1980 (See Glossary).

Age	RDA
0–6 months	50mg
6–12 months	70mg
1–3 years	150mg
4–6 years	200mg
7–10 years	250mg
Males	
11–14 years	350mg
15–18 years	400mg
18+ years	350mg
Females	
11+ years	300mg
Pregnant	+150mg
Lactating	+150mg

What this mineral does:
- Activates essential enzymes.
- Affects metabolism of proteins and nucleic acids.
- Helps transport sodium and potassium across cell membranes.
- Influences calcium levels inside cells.

Available as:
- A constituent of many multivitamin/mineral preparations.

»▸

Warnings and Precautions

Don't take if you have:
- Kidney failure.
- Heart block (unless you have a pacemaker).
- An ileostomy.

Consult your doctor if you have:
- Chronic constipation, colitis, diarrhoea.
- Symptoms of appendicitis.
- Stomach or intestinal bleeding.

Over age 55:
- Adverse reactions/side effects more likely.

Pregnancy:
- Risk to fetus outweighs benefits. Don't use.

Breast-feeding:
- Avoid magnesium in large quantities.
- If you must take temporarily, discontinue breast-feeding. Consult doctor for advice on maintaining milk supply.
- Don't take megadoses.

Effect on lab tests:
- Makes test for stomach-acid secretion inaccurate.
- May increase or decrease serum-phosphate concentrations.
- May decrease serum and urine pH.

Storage:
- Store in cool, dry place away from direct light, but don't freeze.
- Store safely out of reach of children.
- Don't store in bathroom medicine cabinet. Heat and moisture may change action of mineral.

Others:
- Chronic kidney disease frequently causes body to retain excess magnesium.
- Adverse reactions, side effects and interactions with medicines, vitamins or minerals occur *only rarely* when too much magnesium is taken for too long or if you have kidney disease.

Overdose/Toxicity

Signs and symptoms:
Severe nausea and vomiting, extremely low blood pressure, extreme muscle weakness, difficulty breathing, heartbeat irregularity.

What to do:
For symptoms of overdosage: Discontinue mineral, and consult doctor immediately. Also see *Adverse Reactions or Side Effects* section below.
For accidental overdosage (such as child taking entire bottle): Dial 999 (emergency).

Adverse Reactions or Side Effects

Reaction or effect	What to do
Abdominal pain	Discontinue. Call doctor immediately.
Appetite loss	Discontinue. Call doctor when convenient.
Diarrhoea	Discontinue. Call doctor immediately.
Irregular heartbeat	Seek emergency treatment.
Mood changes or mental changes	Discontinue. Call doctor when convenient.
Nausea	Discontinue. Call doctor immediately.
Tiredness or weakness	Discontinue. Call doctor when convenient.
Urination discomfort	Discontinue. Call doctor when convenient.
Vomiting	Discontinue. Call doctor immediately.

Interaction with Medicine, Vitamins or Minerals

Interacts with	Combined effect
Cellulose sodium phosphate	Decreases magnesium effect. Take 1 or more hours apart.
Fat-soluble vitamins (A, E, K)	Decreases absorption of mineral.
Ketoconazole	Reduces absorption of ketoconazole. Take 2 hours apart.
Mecamylamine	May slow urinary excretion of mecamylamine. Avoid combination.
Tetracycline	Decreases absorption of tetracycline.
Vitamin D	May raise magnesium level too high.

Interaction with Other Substances

None known

Manganese

Basic Information
Available from natural sources? Yes
Available from synthetic sources? Yes
Prescription required? Yes

Natural Sources

Avocados	Ginger
Barley	Hazelnuts (filberts)
Beans, dried	Oatmeal
Blackberries	Peanuts
Bran	Peas
Buckwheat	Pecans
Chestnuts	Seaweed
Cloves	Spinach
Coffee	

Reasons to Use

- Promotes normal growth and development.
- Promotes cell function.
- Helps many body enzymes generate energy. Without manganese they could not function.
- Used as a supplement for those receiving long-term nutrition intravenously or through a naso-gastric tube.

Unproved Speculated Benefits

- Alleviates asthma.
- Helps overcome infertility.
- Alleviates diabetes.
- Helps relieve fatigue.
- Acts as an anti-aging substance.
- Helps treat schizophrenia.
- Provides part of molecules necessary for reproduction.

Who Needs Additional Amounts?

- Anyone with inadequate caloric or nutritional dietary intake or increased nutritional requirements.
- Extremely ill people who must be fed intravenously or by naso-gastric tube.

Deficiency Symptoms

- Abnormal growth and development of children
- No proven symptoms caused by manganese deficiency in adults

Unproved Speculated Symptoms

- Changes in beard and hair growth—usually a slowing of growth
- Occasional nausea and vomiting
- Hypocholesterolaemia
- Weight loss

Lab Tests to Detect Deficiency

- Serum manganese

Dosage and Usage Information

Recommended Dietary Allowance (RDA):
No RDA has been established. Estimated safe intake given below.

Age	Estimated Safe Intake
0–6 months	0.5–0.7mg/day
6–12 months	0.7–1.0mg/day
1–3 years	1.0–1.5mg/day
4–6 years	1.5–2.0mg/day
7–10 years	2.0–3.0mg/day
11+ years	2.5–5.0mg/day

What this mineral does:
- Manganese is concentrated in cells of pituitary gland, liver, pancreas, kidney and bone. It influences syntheses of muropolysaccharides, stimulates production of cholesterol by the liver and is a co-factor in many enzymes.

Miscellaneous information:
- Manganese is abundant in many foods.
- Miners and workers in some industries are at risk of toxicity from inhaling manganese. Chronic inhalation can lead to symptoms of Parkinson's disease, with the following signs and symptoms:
  Tremors, especially when not moving
  General muscle stiffness and soreness
  Awkward or shuffling walk
  Stooped posture
  Loss of facial expression
  Voice changes—voice becomes weak and high pitched

$\gg\blacktriangleright$

Difficulty swallowing
Intellectual ability unchanged until advanced stages, when it deteriorates slowly.
* *Manganese* and *magnesium* are *not* related to each other!

Available as:
* Capsules: Swallow whole with full glass of liquid. Don't chew or crush. Take with or immediately after food to decrease stomach irritation.
* A constituent of many multivitamin/mineral preparations.

Warnings and Precautions

Don't take if you:
* Are healthy and eat regular, balanced meals.

Consult your doctor if you have:
* Liver disease.

Over age 55:
* No special problems expected.

Pregnancy:
* Don't take supplements with manganese unless prescribed by your doctor.
* Don't take megadoses.

Breast-feeding:
* Don't take supplements with manganese unless prescribed by your doctor.
* Don't take megadoses.

Effect on lab tests:
* Excess manganese can reduce serum iron.

Storage:
* Store in cool, dry place away from direct light, but don't freeze.
* Store safely out of reach of children.
* Don't store in bathroom medicine cabinet. Heat and moisture may change action of mineral.

Others:
* Check with your industrial health office if you are a miner or industrial worker to make sure your work environment does not contain toxic amounts of manganese.

Overdose/Toxicity

Signs and symptoms:
Delusions, hallucinations, insomnia, depression, impotence.

What to do:
For symptoms of overdosage: Discontinue mineral, and consult doctor. Also see *Adverse Reactions or Side Effects* section below.
For accidental overdosage (such as child taking entire bottle): Dial 999 (emergency).

Adverse Reactions or Side Effects

Reaction or effect	What to do
Appetite loss	Discontinue. Call doctor when convenient.
Breathing problems	Seek emergency treatment.
Headaches	Discontinue. Call doctor when convenient.
Impotence	Discontinue. Call doctor when convenient.
Leg cramps	Discontinue. Call doctor immediately.
Unusual tiredness	Discontinue. Call doctor when convenient.

Interaction with Medicine, Vitamins or Minerals

Interacts with	Combined effect
Calcium (from food or supplements)	May decrease manganese absorption when taken in large doses.
Iron (from food or supplements)	Excess manganese interferes with iron absorption and can lead to iron-deficiency anaemia.
Magnesium (from food or supplements)	May decrease manganese absorption when taken in large doses.
Oral contraceptives	Decreases manganese in blood.
Phosphate (from food or supplements)	When taken in large doses, may decrease manganese absorption.

Interaction with Other Substances

None known

Molybdenum

Basic Information
Available from natural sources? Yes
Available from synthetic sources? No
Prescription required? Yes

Natural Sources

Beans
Cereal grains
Dark-green, leafy vegetables
Organ meats (liver, kidney, sweetbreads)
Peas and other legumes
Note: Dietary concentration of molybdenum may vary according to status of soil in which grains and vegetables are raised.

Reasons to Use

- Promotes normal growth and development.
- Promotes normal cell function.
- Is a component of xanthine oxidase, an enzyme involved in converting nucleic acid to uric acid, a waste product eliminated in the urine.

Unproved Speculated Benefits

- Protects against cancer.
- Protects teeth.
- Prevents anaemia by mobilizing iron.

Who Needs Additional Amounts?

- Anyone with inadequate caloric or nutritional dietary intake or increased nutritional requirements.
- People with recent severe burns or injuries.
- Extremely ill people who must be fed intravenously or by naso-gastric tube.

Deficiency Symptoms

- None

Unproved Speculated Symptoms

- Rapid heartbeat
- Rapid breathing
- Night blindness
- Irritability

Lab Tests to Detect Deficiency

- None available, except for experimental purposes.

Dosage and Usage Information

Recommended Dietary Allowance (RDA):
No RDA has been established. Estimated safe intake given below.

Age	Estimated Safe Intake
0–6 months	0.03–0.06mg/day
6–12 months	0.04–0.08mg/day
1–3 years	0.05–0.10mg/day
4–6 years	0.06–0.15mg/day
7–10 years	0.10–0.30mg/day
11+ years	0.15–0.50mg/day

What this mineral does:
- Becomes a part of bones, liver, kidney.
- Forms part of the enzyme system of xanthine oxidase.

Miscellaneous information:
- Balanced diet provides all the molybdenum that is necessary in a healthy child or adult.

Available as:
- Capsules: Swallow whole with full glass of liquid. Don't chew or crush. Take with meals or 1 to 1-1/2 hours after meals unless otherwise directed by your doctor.
- A constituent of many multivitamin/mineral preparations.

⟫➔

Warnings and Precautions

Don't take if you:
• No absolute contraindications to 0.15 to 0.5mg/day. Don't take higher doses without doctor's prescription.

Consult your doctor if you have:
• High levels of uric acid.
• Gout.

Over age 55:
• No problems expected.

Pregnancy:
• Don't take.

Breast-feeding:
• Don't take.

Effect on lab tests:
• Excess molybdenum causes serum copper to drop.

Storage:
• Store in cool, dry place away from direct light, but don't freeze.
• Store safely out of reach of children.
• Don't store in bathroom medicine cabinet. Heat and moisture may change action of mineral.

 ## Overdose/Toxicity

Signs and symptoms:
Gout can be produced by massive intake (10 to 15mg/daily). Moderate excess (up to 0.54mg/day) can cause excess loss of copper in urine.

Possible Consequences of Overdose:
Daily intake of 10 to 15mg of molybdenum has been associated with a gout-like syndrome. A moderate excess of 0.54mg/daily may be associated with significant urinary loss of copper.

What to do:
For symptoms of overdosage: Discontinue mineral, and consult doctor.
For accidental overdosage (such as child taking entire bottle): Dial 999 (emergency).

 ## Adverse Reactions or Side Effects

None expected

 ## Interaction with Medicine, Vitamins or Minerals

Interacts with	Combined effect
Copper	Maintains appropriate ratio of molybdenum and copper in body. With excess molybdenum, copper level drops. With excess copper, molybdenum level drops.
Sulphur	Increased sulphur intake causes decline in molybdenum concentration.

 ## Interaction with Other Substances

None known

MINERAL

Potassium Acetate/Bicarbonate/Citrate

Basic Information

This combination is also called trikates.
Available from natural sources? Yes
Available from synthetic sources? Yes
Prescription required? Some yes; others no

Natural Sources

Avocados
Bananas
Chard
Citrus fruits
Juices
  grapefruit, tomato,
  orange
Lentils, dried
Milk
Molasses

Nuts
  almonds, Brazil,
  cashews, peanuts,
  pecans, walnuts
Parsnips
Peaches, dried
Potatoes
Raisins
Sardines, canned
Spinach, fresh
Whole-grain cereals

Reasons to Use

- Promotes regular heartbeat.
- Promotes normal muscle contraction.
- Regulates transfer of nutrients to cells.
- Maintains water balance in body tissues and cells.
- Preserves or restores normal function of nerve cells, heart cells, skeletal-muscle cells, kidneys, stomach-juice secretion.
- Treats potassium deficiency from illness or taking diuretics (water pills), cortisone drugs or digitalis preparations.

Unproved Speculated Benefits

- Cures alcoholism.
- Cures acne.
- Cures allergies.
- Cures heart disease.
- Helps heal burns.
- Prevents high blood pressure.

Who Needs Additional Amounts?

- People who take diuretics, cortisone drugs or digitalis preparations.
- Anyone with inadequate caloric or nutritional dietary intake or increased nutritional requirements.
- Older people (over 55 years).

- Pregnant or breast-feeding women.
- Women taking oral contraceptives.
- People who abuse alcohol or other drugs.
- Tobacco smokers.
- People with a chronic wasting illness, excess stress for long periods or who have recently undergone surgery.
- Athletes and workers who participate in vigorous physical activities, especially when endurance is an important aspect of the activity.
- Those with part of the gastrointestinal tract surgically removed.
- People with malabsorption illnesses (See Glossary).
- Those with recent severe burns or injuries.
- Vegetarians.

Deficiency Symptoms

- Hypokalaemia
- Weakness, paralysis
- Low blood pressure
- Life-threatening, irregular or rapid heartbeat that can lead to cardiac arrest and death

Unproved Speculated Symptoms

- Acne
- Allergies
- High blood pressure

Lab Tests to Detect Deficiency

- Serum-potassium determinations
- Serum creatinine
- Electrocardiograms
- Serum-pH determinations

Dosage and Usage Information

Recommended Dietary Allowance (RDA):
No RDA has been established. Nutritionists recommend a *decrease* in sodium (table salt) intake and an *increase* in foods high in potassium for a total daily intake of 40 to 150 milliequivalents per day.

⋙➤

Potassium Acetate/Bicarbonate/Citrate

What this mineral does:
- Potassium is the predominant positive electrolyte in body cells. An enzyme (adenosinetriphosphatase) controls flow of potassium and sodium into and out of cells to maintain normal function of heart, brain, skeletal muscles, normal kidney function, acid-base balance.

Miscellaneous Information:
- Normal potassium content is reduced when foods are tinned or frozen.
- Avoid peeling food.
- Avoid cooking food in large amounts of water.
- Keep meat drippings and use as gravies.

Available as:
- Oral solution: Dilute in at least 1/2 glass water or other liquid. Take with meals or 1 to 1-1/2 hours after meals unless otherwise directed by your doctor.
- Potassium is not recommended for children.
- Some forms are available by generic name.

Warnings and Precautions

Don't take if you:
- Take potassium-sparing diuretics, such as spironolactone, triamterene or amiloride.
- Are allergic to any potassium supplement.
- Have kidney disease.

Consult your doctor if you have:
- Addison's disease.
- Heart disease.
- Intestinal blockage.
- A stomach ulcer.
- To use diuretics.
- To use heart medicine.
- To use laxatives or if you have chronic diarrhoea.
- To use salt substitutes or low-salt milk.

Over age 55:
- Observe dose schedule strictly. Potassium balance is critical. Deviation above or below normal can have serious results.

Pregnancy:
- No problems expected, except with megadoses.

Breast-feeding:
- Studies inconclusive on harm to infant. Consult doctor about supplements.
- Don't take megadoses.

Effect on lab tests:
- ECG and kidney function studies can be affected by too much or too little potassium.
- None expected on blood studies, except serum-potassium levels.

Storage:
- Store in cool, dry area away from direct light, but don't freeze.
- Store safely out of reach of children.
- Don't store in bathroom medicine cabinet. Heat and moisture may change action of the mineral

Others:
- Take with meals or with food.

Overdose/Toxicity

Signs and symptoms:
Irregular or fast heartbeat, paralysis of arms and legs, blood-pressure drop, convulsions, coma, cardiac arrest.

What to do:
For symptoms of overdosage: Discontinue mineral, and consult doctor. Also see *Adverse Reactions or Side Effects* section below.

For accidental overdosage (such as child taking entire bottle): Dial 999 (emergency). If a persons heart has stopped beating, render CPR until trained help arrives.

⟫➤

Adverse Reactions or Side Effects

Reaction or effect	What to do
Black, tarry stool	Seek emergency treatment.
Bloody stool	Seek emergency treatment.
Breathing difficulty	Seek emergency treatment.
Confusion	Discontinue. Call doctor immediately.
Diarrhoea	Discontinue. Call doctor immediately.
Extreme fatigue	Discontinue. Call doctor when convenient.
Heaviness in legs	Discontinue. Call doctor when convenient.
Irregular heartbeat	Seek emergency treatment.
Nausea	Discontinue. Call doctor when convenient.
Numbness in hands or feet	Discontinue. Call doctor when convenient.
Stomach discomfort	Discontinue. Call doctor when convenient.
Tingling in hands and feet	Discontinue. Call doctor when convenient.
Vomiting	Discontinue. Call doctor immediately.
Weakness	Discontinue. Call doctor immediately.

 Interaction with Medicine, Vitamins or Minerals

Interacts with	Combined effect
Amiloride	Causes dangerous rise in blood potassium.
Atropine	Increases possibility of intestinal ulcers, which may occur with oral potassium tablets.
Belladonna	Increases possibility of intestinal ulcers, which may occur with oral potassium.
Calcium	Increases possibility of heartbeat irregularities.
Captopril	Increases chance of excessive amounts of potassium.
Cortisone	Decreases effect of potassium.
Digitalis preparations	May cause irregular heartbeat.
Enalapril	Increases chance of excessive amounts of potassium.
Laxatives	May decrease potassium effect.
Spironolactone	Increases blood potassium.
Triamterene	Increases blood potassium.
Vitamin B-12	Extended-release tablets may decrease vitamin B-12 absorption and increase vitamin B-12 requirements.

 Interaction with Other Substances

Tobacco decreases absorption. Smokers may require supplementary potassium.

Alcohol intensifies gastrointestinal symptoms.

Cocaine may cause irregular heartbeat.

Marijuana may cause irregular heartbeat.

Beverages
- Salty drinks, such as tomato juice and commercial thirst quenchers, cause increased fluid retention.
- Coffee decreases potassium absorption and intensifies gastrointestinal symptoms.
- Low-salt milk increases fluid retention.

Foods
- Salty foods increase fluid retention.
- Sugar decreases potassium absorption.

Basic Information

Available from natural sources? Yes
Available from synthetic sources? Yes
Prescription required? Some yes; others no

Natural Sources

Avocados
Bananas·
Chard
Citrus fruit
Juices
  grapefruit, tomato,
  orange
Lentils, dried
Milk
Molasses

Nuts
  almonds, Brazil,
  cashews, peanuts,
  pecans, walnuts
Parsnips
Peaches, dried
Potatoes
Raisins
Sardines, canned
Spinach, fresh
Whole-grain cereals

Reasons to Use

• Promotes regular heartbeat.
• Promotes normal muscle contraction.
• Regulates transfer of nutrients to cells.
• Maintains water balance in body tissues and cells.
• Preserves or restores normal function of nerve cells, heart cells, skeletal-muscle cells, kidneys, stomach-juice secretion.
• Treats potassium deficiency from illness or taking diuretics (water pills), cortisone drugs or digitalis preparations.

Unproved Speculated Benefits

• Cures alcoholism.
• Cures acne.
• Cures allergies.
• Cures heart disease.
• Helps heal burns.
• Prevents high blood pressure.

Who Needs Additional Amounts?

• People who take diuretics, cortisone drugs or digitalis preparations.
• Anyone with inadequate caloric or nutritional dietary intake or increased nutritional requirements.
• Older people (over 55 years).
• Pregnant or breast-feeding women.
• Women taking oral contraceptives.
• People who abuse alcohol or other drugs.
• Tobacco smokers.
• People with a chronic wasting illness, excess stress for long periods or who have recently undergone surgery.
• Athletes and workers who participate in vigorous physical activities, especially when endurance is an important aspect of the activity.
• Those with part of the gastrointestinal tract surgically removed.
• People with malabsorption illnesses (See Glossary).
• Those with recent severe burns or injuries.
• Vegetarians.

Deficiency Symptoms

• Hypokalaemia
• Weakness, paralysis
• Low blood pressure
• Life-threatening, irregular or rapid heartbeat that can lead to cardiac arrest and death

Unproved Speculated Symptoms

• Acne
• Allergies
• High blood pressure

Lab Tests to Detect Deficiency

• Serum-potassium determinations
• Serum creatinine
• Electrocardiograms
• Serum-pH determinations

Dosage and Usage Information

Recommended Dietary Allowance (RDA):
No RDA has been established. Nutritionists recommend a *decrease* in sodium (table salt) intake and an *increase* in foods high in potassium for a total daily intake of 40 to 150 milliequivalents per day.

⟫▶

MINERAL

153

Potassium Bicarbonate, Continued

What this mineral does:
- Potassium is the predominant positive electrolyte in body cells. An enzyme (adenosinetriphosphatase) controls flow of potassium and sodium into and out of cells to maintain normal function of heart, brain, skeletal muscles, normal kidney function, acid-base balance.

Miscellaneous information:
- Normal potassium content is reduced when foods are tinned or frozen.
- Avoid peeling food.
- Avoid cooking food in large amounts of water.
- Keep meat drippings and use as gravies.

Available as:
- Effervescent tablets: Dilute in at least 1/2 glass water or other liquid. Take with meals or 1 to 1-1/2 hours after meals unless otherwise directed by your doctor.
- Potassium is not recommended for children.
- Some forms available by generic name.

Warnings and Precautions

Don't take if you:
- Take potassium-sparing diuretics, such as spironolactone, triamterene or amiloride.
- Are allergic to any potassium supplement.
- Have kidney disease.

Consult your doctor if you have:
- Addison's disease.
- Heart disease.
- Intestinal blockage.
- A stomach ulcer.
- To use diuretics.
- To use heart medicine.
- To use laxatives or if you have chronic diarrhoea.
- To use salt substitutes or low-salt milk.

Over age 55:
- Observe dose regime strictly. Potassium balance is critical. Deviation above or below normal can have serious results.

Pregnancy:
- No problems expected, except with megadoses.

Breast-feeding:
- Studies inconclusive on harm to infant. Consult doctor about supplement.
- Don't take megadoses.

Effect on lab tests:
- ECG and kidney function studies can be affected by too much or too little potassium.
- None expected on blood studies, except serum-potassium levels.

Storage:
- Store in cool, dry area away from direct light, but don't freeze.
- Store safely out of reach of children.
- Don't store in bathroom medicine cabinet. Heat and moisture may change action of the mineral.

Others:
- Take with meals or with food.

Overdose/Toxicity

Signs and symptoms:
Irregular or fast heartbeat, paralysis of arms and legs, blood-pressure drop, convulsions, coma, cardiac arrest.

What to do:
For symptoms of overdosage: Discontinue mineral, and consult doctor. Also see *Adverse Reactions or Side Effects* section below.
For accidental overdosage (such as child taking entire bottle): Dial 999 (emergency). If person's heart has stopped beating, render CPR until trained help arrives.

Adverse Reactions or Side Effects

Reaction or effect	What to do
Black, tarry stool	Seek emergency treatment.
Bloody stool	Seek emergency treatment.
Breathing difficulty	Seek emergency treatment.
Confusion	Discontinue. Call doctor immediately.
Diarrhoea	Discontinue. Call doctor immediately.
Extreme fatigue	Discontinue. Call doctor when convenient.
Heaviness in legs	Discontinue. Call doctor when convenient.
Irregular heartbeat	Seek emergency treatment.
Nausea	Discontinue. Call doctor when convenient.
Numbness in hands or feet	Discontinue. Call doctor when convenient.
Stomach discomfort	Discontinue. Call doctor when convenient.
Tingling in hands and feet	Discontinue. Call doctor when convenient.
Vomiting	Discontinue. Call doctor immediately.
Weakness	Discontinue. Call doctor immediately.

Interaction with Medicine, Vitamins or Minerals

Interacts with	Combined effect
Amiloride	Causes dangerous rise in blood potassium.
Atropine	Increases possibility of intestinal ulcers, which may occur with oral potassium.
Belladonna	Increases possibility of intestinal ulcers, which may occur with oral potassium.
Calcium	Increases possibility of heartbeat irregularities.
Captopril	Increases chance of excessive amounts of potassium.
Cortisone	Decreases effect of potassium.
Digitalis preparations	May cause irregular heartbeat.
Enalapril	Increases chance of excessive amounts of potassium.
Laxatives	May decrease potassium effect.
Spironolactone	Increases blood potassium.
Triamterene	Increases blood potassium.
Vitamin B-12	Extended-release tablets may decrease vitamin B-12 absorption and increase vitamin B-12 requirements.

Interaction with Other Substances

Tobacco decreases absorption. Smokers may require supplementary potassium.

Alcohol intensifies gastrointestinal symptoms.

Cocaine may cause irregular heartbeat.

Marijuana may cause irregular heartbeat.

Beverages
• Salty drinks, such as tomato juice and commercial thirst quenchers, cause increased fluid retention.
• Coffee decreases potassium absorption and intensifies gastrointestinal symptoms.
• Low-salt milk increases fluid retention.

Foods
• Salty foods increase fluid retention.
• Sugar decreases potassium absorption.

MINERAL

Potassium Bicarbonate/Chloride

Basic Information
Available from natural sources? Yes
Available from synthetic sources? Yes
Prescription required? Some yes; others no

 ## Natural Sources

Avocados
Bananas
Chard
Citrus fruit
Juices
  grapefruit, tomato,
  orange
Lentils, dried
Milk
Molasses

Nuts
  almonds, Brazil,
  cashews, peanuts,
  pecans, walnuts
Parsnips
Peaches, dried
Potatoes
Raisins
Sardines, canned
Spinach, fresh
Whole-grain cereals

 ## Reasons to Use

- Promotes regular heartbeat.
- Promotes normal muscle contraction.
- Regulates transfer of nutrients to cells.
- Maintains water balance in body tissues and cells.
- Preserves or restores normal function of nerve cells, heart cells, skeletal-muscle cells, kidneys, stomach-juice secretion.
- Treats potassium deficiency from illness or taking diuretics (water pills), cortisone drugs or digitalis preparations.

 ## Unproved Speculated Benefits

- Cures alcoholism.
- Cures acne.
- Cures allergies.
- Cures heart disease.
- Helps heal burns.
- Prevents high blood pressure.

 ## Who Needs Additional Amounts?

- People who take diuretics, cortisone drugs or digitalis preparations.
- Anyone with inadequate caloric or nutritional dietary intake or increased nutritional requirements.
- Older people (over 55 years).
- Pregnant or breast-feeding women.
- Women taking oral contraceptives.

- People who abuse alcohol or other drugs.
- Tobacco smokers.
- People with a chronic wasting illness, excess stress for long periods or who have recently undergone surgery.
- Athletes and workers who participate in vigorous physical activities, especially when endurance is an important aspect of the activity.
- Those with part of the gastrointestinal tract surgically removed.
- People with malabsorption illnesses (See Glossary).
- Those with recent severe burns or injuries.
- Vegetarians.

 ## Deficiency Symptoms

- Hypokalaemia
- Weakness, paralysis
- Low blood pressure
- Life-threatening, irregular or rapid heartbeat that can lead to cardiac arrest and death

 ## Unproved Speculated Symptoms

- Acne
- Allergies
- High blood pressure

 ## Lab Tests to Detect Deficiency

- Serum-potassium determinations
- Serum creatinine
- Electrocardiograms
- Serum-pH determinations

 ## Dosage and Usage Information

Recommended Dietary Allowance (RDA):
No RDA has been established. Nutritionists recommend a *decrease* in sodium (table salt) intake and an *increase* in foods high in potassium for a total daily intake of 40 to 150 milliequivalents per day.

Potassium Bicarbonate/Chloride

What this mineral does:
- Potassium is the predominant positive electrolyte in body cells. An enzyme (adenosinetriphosphatase) controls flow of potassium and sodium into and out of cells to maintain normal function of heart, brain, skeletal muscles, normal kidney function, acid-base balance.

Miscellaneous Information:
- Normal potassium content is reduced when foods are tinned or frozen.
- Avoid peeling food.
- Avoid cooking food in large amounts of water.
- Keep meat drippings and use as gravies.

Available as:
- Tablets: Swallow whole with full glass of liquid. Don't chew or crush. Take with or immediately after food to decrease stomach irritation.
- Powder for effervescent oral solution: Dissolve powder in cold water or juice. Take with meals or 1 to 1-1/2 hours after meals unless otherwise directed by your doctor.
- Potassium is not recommended for children.
- Not available by generic name.

Warnings and Precautions

Don't take if you:
- Take potassium-sparing diuretics, such as spironolactone, triamterene or amiloride.
- Are allergic to any potassium supplement.
- Have kidney disease.

Consult your doctor if you have:
- Addison's disease.
- Heart disease.
- Intestinal blockage.
- A stomach ulcer.
- To use diuretics.
- To use heart medicine.
- To use laxatives or if you have chronic diarrhoea.
- To use salt substitutes or low-salt milk.

Over age 55:
- Observe dose regime strictly. Potassium balance is critical. Deviation above or below normal can have serious results.

Pregnancy:
- No problems expected, except with megadoses

Breast-feeding:
- Studies inconclusive on harm to infant. Consult doctor about supplement.
- Don't take megadoses.

Effect on lab tests:
- ECG and kidney function studies can be affected by too much or too little potassium.
- None expected on blood studies, except serum-potassium levels.

Storage:
- Store in cool, dry area away from direct light, but don't freeze.
- Store safely out of reach of children.
- Don't store in bathroom medicine cabinet. Heat and moisture may change action of the mineral.

Others:
- Take with meals or with food.

Overdose

Signs and symptoms:
Irregular or fast heartbeat, paralysis of arms and legs, blood-pressure drop, convulsions, coma, cardiac arrest.

What to do:
For symptoms of overdosage: Discontinue mineral, and consult doctor. Also see *Adverse Reactions or Side Effects* section below.

For accidental overdosage (such as child taking entire bottle): Dial 999 (emergency). If person's heart has stopped beating, render CPR until trained help arrives.

Adverse Reactions or Side Effects

Reaction or effect	What to do
Black, tarry stool	Seek emergency treatment.
Bloody stool	Seek emergency treatment.
Breathing difficulty	Seek emergency treatment.
Confusion	Discontinue. Call doctor immediately.
Diarrhoea	Discontinue. Call doctor immediately.
Extreme fatigue	Discontinue. Call doctor when convenient.
Heaviness in legs	Discontinue. Call doctor when convenient.
Irregular heartbeat	Seek emergency treatment.
Nausea	Discontinue. Call doctor when convenient.
Numbness in hands or feet	Discontinue. Call doctor when convenient.
Stomach discomfort	Discontinue. Call doctor when convenient.
Tingling in hands and feet	Discontinue. Call doctor when convenient.
Vomiting	Discontinue. Call doctor immediately.
Weakness	Discontinue. Call doctor immediately.

Interaction with Medicine, Vitamins or Minerals

Interacts with	Combined effect
Amiloride	Causes dangerous rise in blood potassium.
Atropine	Increases possibility of intestinal ulcers, which may occur with oral potassium tablets.
Belladonna	Increases possibility of intestinal ulcers, which may occur with oral potassium.
Calcium	Increases possibility of heartbeat irregularities.
Captopril	Increases chance of excessive amounts of potassium.
Cortisone	Decreases effect of potassium.
Digitalis preparations	May cause irregular heartbeat.
Enalapril	Increases chance of excessive amounts of potassium.
Laxatives	May decrease potassium effect.
Spironolactone	Increases blood potassium.
Triamterene	Increases blood potassium.
Vitamin B-12	Extended-release tablets may decrease vitamin B-12 absorption and increase vitamin B-12 requirements.

Interaction with Other Substances

Tobacco decreases absorption. Smokers may require supplementary potassium.

Alcohol intensifies gastrointestinal symptoms.

Cocaine may cause irregular heartbeat.

Marijuana may cause irregular heartbeat.

Beverages
- Salty drinks, such as tomato juice and commercial thirst quenchers, cause increased fluid retention.
- Coffee decreases potassium absorption and intensifies gastrointestinal symptoms.
- Low-salt milk increases fluid retention.

Foods
- Salty foods increase fluid retention.
- Sugar decreases potassium absorption.

Potassium Bicarbonate/Citrate

Basic Information

Available from natural sources? Yes
Available from synthetic sources? Yes
Prescription required? Some yes; others no

Natural Sources

Avocados
Bananas
Chard
Citrus fruit
Juices
  grapefruit, tomato,
  orange
Lentils, dried
Milk
Molasses

Nuts
  almonds, Brazil,
  cashews, peanuts,
  pecans, walnuts
Parsnips
Peaches, dried
Potatoes
Raisins
Sardines, canned
Spinach, fresh
Whole-grain cereals

Reasons to Use

- Promotes regular heartbeat.
- Promotes normal muscle contraction.
- Regulates transfer of nutrients to cells.
- Maintains water balance in body tissues and cells.
- Preserves or restores normal function of nerve cells, heart cells, skeletal-muscle cells, kidneys, stomach-juice secretion.
- Treats potassium deficiency from illness or taking diuretics (water pills), cortisone drugs or digitalis preparations.

Unproved Speculated Benefits

- Cures alcoholism.
- Cures acne.
- Cures allergies.
- Cures heart disease.
- Helps heal burns.
- Prevents high blood pressure.

Who Needs Additional Amounts?

- People who take diuretics, cortisone drugs or digitalis preparations.
- Anyone with inadequate caloric or nutritional dietary intake or increased nutritional requirements.
- Older people (over 55 years).
- Pregnant or breast-feeding women.

- Women taking oral contraceptives.
- People who abuse alcohol or other drugs.
- Tobacco smokers.
- People with a chronic wasting illness, excess stress for long periods or who have recently undergone surgery.
- Athletes and workers who participate in vigorous physical activities, especially when endurance is an important aspect of the activity.
- Those with part of the gastrointestinal tract surgically removed.
- People with malabsorption illnesses (See Glossary).
- Those with recent severe burns or injuries.
- Vegetarians.

Deficiency Symptoms

- Hypokalaemia
- Weakness, paralysis
- Low blood pressure
- Life-threatening, irregular or rapid heartbeat that can lead to cardiac arrest and death

Unproved Speculated Symptoms

- Acne
- Allergies
- High blood pressure

Lab Tests to Detect Deficiency

- Serum-potassium determinations
- Serum creatinine
- Electrocardiograms
- Serum-pH determinations

Dosage and Usage Information

Recommended Dietary Allowance (RDA):
No RDA has been established. Nutritionists recommend a *decrease* in sodium (table salt) intake and an *increase* in foods high in potassium for a total daily intake of 40 to 150 milliequivalents per day.

⟫⟫➤

Potassium Bicarbonate/Citrate, Continued

What this mineral does:
• Potassium is the predominant positive electrolyte in body cells. An enzyme (adenosinetriphosphatase) controls flow of potassium and sodium into and out of cells to maintain normal function of heart, brain, skeletal muscles, normal kidney function, acid-base balance.

Miscellaneous Information:
• Normal potassium content is reduced when foods are tinned or frozen.
• Avoid peeling food.
• Avoid cooking food in large amounts of water.
• Keep meat drippings and use as gravies.

Available as:
• Effervescent tablets: Dissolve in cold water to make a palatable, bubbly solution. Take with or immediately after food to decrease stomach irritation.
• Potassium is not recommended for children.
• Not available by generic name.

Warnings and Precautions

Don't take if you:
• Take potassium-sparing diuretics, such as spironolactone, triamterene or amiloride.
• Are allergic to any potassium supplement.
• Have kidney disease.

Consult your doctor if you have:
• Addison's disease.
• Heart disease.
• Intestinal blockage.
• A stomach ulcer.
• To use diuretics.
• To use heart medicine.
• To use laxatives or if you have chronic diarrhoea.
• To use salt substitutes or low-salt milk.

Over age 55:
• Observe dose regime strictly. Potassium balance is critical. Deviation above or below normal can have serious results.

Pregnancy:
• No problems expected, except with megadoses.

Breast-feeding:
• Studies inconclusive on harm to infant. Consult doctor about supplement.
• Don't take megadoses.

Effect on lab tests:
• ECG and kidney function studies can be affected by too much or too little potassium.
• None expected on blood studies, except serum-potassium levels.

Storage:
• Store in cool, dry area away from direct light, but don't freeze.
• Store safely out of reach of children.
• Don't store in bathroom medicine cabinet. Heat and moisture may change action of the mineral.

Others:
• Take with meals or with food.

Overdose/Toxicity

Signs and symptoms:
Irregular or fast heartbeat, paralysis of arms and legs, blood-pressure drop, convulsions, coma, cardiac arrest.

What to do:
For symptoms of overdosage: Discontinue mineral, and consult doctor. Also see *Adverse Reactions or Side Effects* section below.
For accidental overdosage (such as child taking entire bottle): Dial 999 (emergency). If person's heart has stopped beating render CPR until trained help arrives.
➤➤➤

Adverse Reactions or Side Effects

Reaction or effect	What to do
Black, tarry stool	Seek emergency treatment.
Bloody stool	Seek emergency treatment.
Breathing difficulty	Seek emergency treatment.
Confusion	Discontinue. Call doctor immediately.
Diarrhoea	Discontinue. Call doctor immediately.
Extreme fatigue	Discontinue. Call doctor when convenient.
Heaviness in legs	Discontinue. Call doctor when convenient.
Irregular heartbeat	Seek emergency treatment.
Nausea	Discontinue. Call doctor when convenient.
Numbness in hands or feet	Discontinue. Call doctor when convenient.
Stomach discomfort	Discontinue. Call doctor when convenient.
Tingling in hands and feet	Discontinue. Call doctor when convenient.
Vomiting	Discontinue. Call doctor immediately.
Weakness	Discontinue. Call doctor immediately.

 Interaction with Medicine, Vitamins or Minerals

Interacts with	Combined effect
Amiloride	Causes dangerous rise in blood potassium.
Atropine	Increases possibility of intestinal ulcers, which may occur with oral potassium tablets.
Belladonna	Increases possibility of intestinal ulcers, which may occur with oral potassium.
Calcium	Increases possibility of heartbeat irregularities.
Captopril	Increases chance of excessive amounts of potassium.
Cortisone	Decreases effect of potassium.
Digitalis preparations	May cause irregular heartbeat.
Enalapril	Increases chance of excessive amounts of potassium.
Laxatives	May decrease potassium effect.
Spironolactone	Increases blood potassium.
Triamterene	Increases blood potassium.
Vitamin B-12	Extended-release tablets may decrease vitamin B-12 absorption and increase vitamin B-12 requirements.

 Interaction with Other Substances

Tobacco decreases absorption. Smokers may require supplemental potassium.

Alcohol intensifies gastrointestinal symptoms.

Cocaine may cause irregular heartbeat.

Marijuana may cause irregular heartbeat.

Beverages
- Salty drinks, such as tomato juice and commercial thirst quenchers, cause increased fluid retention.
- Coffee decreases potassium absorption and intensifies gastrointestinal symptoms.
- Low-salt milk increases fluid retention.

Foods
- Salty foods increase fluid retention.
- Sugar decreases potassium absorption.

MINERAL

Potassium Chloride

Basic Information

Available from natural sources? Yes
Available from synthetic sources? Yes
Prescription required? Some yes; others no

Natural Sources

Avocados
Bananas
Chard
Citrus fruit
Juices
  grapefruit, tomato,
  orange
Lentils, dried
Milk
Molasses

Nuts
  almonds, Brazil,
  cashews, peanuts,
  pecans, walnuts
Parsnips
Peaches, dried
Potatoes
Raisins
Sardines, canned
Spinach, fresh
Whole-grain cereals

Reasons to Use

- Promotes regular heartbeat.
- Promotes normal muscle contraction.
- Regulates transfer of nutrients to cells.
- Maintains water balance in body tissues and cells.
- Preserves or restores normal function of nerve cells, heart cells, skeletal-muscle cells, kidneys, stomach-juice secretion.
- Treats potassium deficiency from illness or taking diuretics (water pills), cortisone drugs or digitalis preparations.

Unproved Speculated Benefits

- Cures alcoholism.
- Cures acne.
- Cures allergies.
- Cures heart disease.
- Helps heal burns.
- Prevents high blood pressure.

Who Needs Additional Amounts?

- People who take diuretics, cortisone drugs or digitalis preparations.
- Anyone with inadequate caloric or nutritional dietary intake or increased nutritional requirements.
- Older people (over 55 years).
- Pregnant or breast-feeding women.
- Women taking oral contraceptives.
- People who abuse alcohol or other drugs.
- Tobacco smokers.
- People with a chronic wasting illness, excess stress for long periods or who have recently undergone surgery.
- Athletes and workers who participate in vigorous physical activities, especially when endurance is an important aspect of the activity.
- Those with part of the gastrointestinal tract surgically removed.
- People with malabsorption illnesses (See Glossary).
- People with recent severe burns or injuries.
- Vegetarians.

Deficiency Symptoms

- Hypokalaemia
- Weakness, paralysis
- Low blood pressure
- Life-threatening, irregular or rapid heartbeat that can lead to cardiac arrest and death

Unproved Speculated Symptoms

- Acne
- Allergies
- High blood pressure

Lab Tests to Detect Deficiency

- Serum-potassium determinations
- Serum creatinine
- Electrocardiograms
- Serum-pH determinations

Dosage and Usage Information

Recommended Dietary Allowance (RDA):
No RDA has been established. Nutritionists recommend a *decrease* in sodium (table salt) intake and an *increase* in foods high in potassium for a total daily intake of 40 to 150 milliequivalents per day.

⏵⏵

What this mineral does:
- Potassium is the predominant positive electrolyte in body cells. An enzyme (adenosinetriphosphatase) controls flow of potassium and sodium into and out of cells to maintain normal function of heart, brain, skeletal muscles, normal kidney function, acid-base balance.

Miscellaneous Information:
- Normal potassium content is reduced when foods are tinned or frozen.
- Avoid peeling food.
- Avoid cooking food in large amounts of water.
- Keep meat drippings and use as gravies.

Available as:
- Extended-release tablets or capsules: Swallow whole with full glass of liquid. Don't chew or crush. Take with meals or 1 to 1-1/2 hours after meals unless otherwise directed by your doctor.
- Oral solution: Dilute in 1/2 glass water or other liquid. Take with meals or 1 to 1-1/2 hours after meals unless otherwise directed by your doctor.
- Potassium chloride for oral solution: Dissolve powder in cold water or juice. Take with meals or 1 to 1-1/2 hours after meals unless otherwise directed by your doctor.
- Enteric-coated tablets are no longer recommended.
- Potassium is not recommended for children.
- Some forms available by generic name.

 Warnings and Precautions

Don't take if you:
- Take potassium-sparing diuretics, such as spironolactone, triamterene or amiloride.
- Are allergic to any potassium supplement.
- Have kidney disease.

Consult your doctor if you have:
- Addison's disease.
- Heart disease.
- Intestinal blockage.
- A stomach ulcer.
- To use diuretics.
- To use heart medicine.
- To use laxatives or if you have chronic diarrhoea.
- To use salt substitutes or low-salt milk.

Over age 55:
- Observe dose regime strictly. Potassium balance is critical. Deviation above or below normal can have serious results.

Pregnancy:
- No problems expected, except with megadoses.

Breast-feeding:
- Studies inconclusive on harm to infant. Consult doctor about supplement.
- Don't take megadoses.

Effect on lab tests:
- ECG and kidney function studies can be affected by too much or too little potassium.
- None expected on blood studies, except serum-potassium levels.

Storage:
- Store in cool, dry area away from direct light, but don't freeze.
- Store safely out of reach of children.
- Don't store in bathroom medicine cabinet. Heat and moisture may change action of the mineral.

Others:
- Take with meals or with food.

 Overdose/Toxicity

Signs and symptoms:
Irregular or fast heartbeat, paralysis of arms and legs, blood-pressure drop, convulsions, coma, cardiac arrest.

What to do:
For symptoms of overdosage: Discontinue mineral, and consult doctor. Also see *Adverse Reactions or Side Effects* section below.
For accidental overdosage (such as child taking entire bottle): Dial 999 (emergency). If person's heart has stopped beating, render CPR until trained help arrives.

⇉

MINERAL

Potassium Chloride, Continued

Adverse Reactions or Side Effects

Reaction or effect	What to do
Black, tarry stool	Seek emergency treatment.
Bloody stool	Seek emergency treatment.
Breathing difficulty	Seek emergency treatment.
Confusion	Discontinue. Call doctor immediately.
Diarrhoea	Discontinue. Call doctor immediately.
Extreme fatigue	Discontinue. Call doctor when convenient.
Heaviness in legs	Discontinue. Call doctor when convenient.
Irregular heartbeat	Seek emergency treatment.
Nausea	Discontinue. Call doctor when convenient.
Numbness in hands or feet	Discontinue. Call doctor when convenient.
Stomach discomfort	Discontinue. Call doctor when convenient.
Tingling in hands and feet	Discontinue. Call doctor when convenient.
Vomiting	Discontinue. Call doctor immediately.
Weakness	Discontinue. Call doctor immediately.

Interaction with Medicine, Vitamins or Minerals

Interacts with	Combined effect
Amiloride	Causes dangerous rise in blood potassium.
Atropine	Increases possibility of intestinal ulcers, which may occur with oral potassium tablets.
Belladonna	Increases possibility of intestinal ulcers, which may occur with oral potassium.
Calcium	Increases possibility of heartbeat irregularities.

Captopril	Increases chance of excessive amounts of potassium.
Cortisone	Decreases effect of potassium.
Digitalis preparations	May cause irregular heartbeat.
Enalapril	Increases chance of excessive amounts of potassium.
Laxatives	May decrease potassium effect.
Spironolactone	Increases blood potassium.
Triamterene	Increases blood potassium.
Vitamin B-12	Extended-release tablets may decrease vitamin B-12 absorption and increase vitamin B-12 requirements.

Interaction with Other Substances

Tobacco decreases absorption. Smokers may require supplementary potassium.

Alcohol intensifies gastrointestinal symptoms.

Cocaine may cause irregular heartbeat.

Marijuana may cause irregular heartbeat.

Beverages
- Salty drinks, such as tomato juice and commercial thirst quenchers, cause increased fluid retention.
- Coffee decreases potassium absorption and intensifies gastrointestinal symptoms.
- Low-salt milk increases fluid retention.

Foods
- Don't take dairy products within 2 hours of taking potassium chloride or potassium iodide.
- Salty foods increase fluid retention.
- Sugar decreases potassium absorption.

Potassium Chloride/Bicarbonate/Citrate

Basic Information
Available from natural sources? Yes
Available from synthetic sources? Yes
Prescription required? Some yes; others no

 Natural Sources

Avocados
Bananas
Chard
Citrus fruit
Juices
  grapefruit, tomato,
  orange
Lentils, dried
Milk
Molasses

Nuts
  almonds, Brazil,
  cashews, peanuts,
  pecans, walnuts
Parsnips
Peaches, dried
Potatoes
Raisins
Sardines, canned
Spinach, fresh
Whole-grain cereals

 Reasons to Use

- Promotes regular heartbeat.
- Promotes normal muscle contraction.
- Regulates transfer of nutrients to cells.
- Maintains water balance in body tissues and cells.
- Preserves or restores normal function of nerve cells, heart cells, skeletal-muscle cells, kidneys, stomach-juice secretion.
- Treats potassium deficiency from illness or taking diuretics (water pills), cortisone drugs or digitalis preparations.

 Unproved Speculated Benefits

- Cures alcoholism.
- Cures acne.
- Cures allergies.
- Cures heart disease.
- Helps heal burns.
- Prevents high blood pressure.

 Who Needs Additional Amounts?

- People who take diuretics, cortisone drugs or digitalis preparations.
- Anyone with inadequate caloric or nutritional dietary intake or increased nutritional requirements.
- Older people (over 55 years).
- Pregnant or breast-feeding women.

- Women taking oral contraceptives.
- People who abuse alcohol or other drugs.
- Tobacco smokers.
- People with a chronic wasting illness, excess stress for long periods or who have recently undergone surgery.
- Athletes and workers who participate in vigorous physical activities.
- Those with part of the gastrointestinal tract surgically removed.
- People with malabsorption illnesses (See Glossary).
- People with recent severe burns or injuries.
- Vegetarians.

 Deficiency Symptoms

- Hypokalemia
- Weakness, paralysis
- Low blood pressure
- Life-threatening, irregular or rapid heartbeat that can lead to cardiac arrest and death

 Unproved Speculated Symptoms

- Acne
- Allergies
- High blood pressure

 Lab Tests to Detect Deficiency

- Serum-potassium determinations
- Serum creatinine
- Electrocardiograms
- Serum-pH determinations

⟫▶

MINERAL

165

Dosage and Usage Information

Recommended Dietary Allowance (RDA):
No RDA has been established. Nutritionists recommend a *decrease* in sodium (table salt) intake and an *increase* in foods high in potassium for a total daily intake of 40 to 150 milliequivalents per day.

What this mineral does:
• Potassium is the predominant positive electrolyte in body cells. An enzyme (adenosinetriphosphatase) controls flow of potassium and sodium into and out of cells to maintain normal function of heart, brain, skeletal muscles, normal kidney function, acid-base balance.

Miscellaneous Information:
• Normal potassium content is reduced when foods are canned or frozen.
• Avoid peeling food.
• Avoid cooking food in large amounts of water.
• Keep meat drippings and use as gravies.

Available as:
• Effervescent tablets: Dissolve in cold water or other liquid. Take with meals or 1 to 1-1/2 hours after meals unless otherwise directed by your doctor.
• Potassium is not recommended for children.
• Not available by generic name.

Warnings and Precautions

Don't take if you:
• Take potassium-sparing diuretics, such as spironolactone, triamterene or amiloride.
• Are allergic to any potassium supplement.
• Have kidney disease.

Consult your doctor if you have:
• Addison's disease.
• Heart disease.
• Intestinal blockage.
• A stomach ulcer.
• To use diuretics.
• To use heart medicine.
• To use laxatives or if you have chronic diarrhoea.
• To use salt substitutes or low-salt milk.

Over age 55:
• Observe dose schedule strictly. Potassium balance is critical. Deviation above or below normal can have serious results.

Pregnancy:
• No problems expected, except with megadoses.

Breast-feeding:
• Studies inconclusive on harm to infant. Consult doctor about supplement.
• Don't take megadoses.

Effect on lab tests:
• ECG and kidney function studies can be affected by too much or too little potassium.
• None expected on blood studies, except serum-potassium levels.

Storage:
• Store in cool, dry area away from direct light, but don't freeze.
• Store safely out of reach of children.
• Don't store in bathroom medicine cabinet. Heat and moisture may change action of the mineral.

Others:
• Take with meals or with food.

Overdose/Toxicity

Signs and symptoms:
Irregular or fast heartbeat, paralysis of arms and legs, blood-pressure drop, convulsions, coma, cardiac arrest.

What to do:
For symptoms of overdosage: Discontinue mineral, and consult doctor. Also see *Adverse Reactions or Side Effects* section below.
For accidental overdosage (such as child taking entire bottle): Dial 999 (emergency). If person's heart has stopped beating, render CPR until trained help arrives.

Potassium Chloride/Bicarbonate/Citrate, Continued

Adverse Reactions or Side Effects

Reaction or effect	What to do
Black, tarry stool	Seek emergency treatment.
Bloody stool	Seek emergency treatment.
Breathing difficulty	Seek emergency treatment.
Confusion	Discontinue. Call doctor immediately.
Diarrhoea	Discontinue. Call doctor immediately.
Extreme fatigue	Discontinue. Call doctor when convenient.
Heaviness in legs	Discontinue. Call doctor when convenient.
Irregular heartbeat	Seek emergency treatment.
Nausea	Discontinue. Call doctor when convenient.
Numbness in hands or feet	Discontinue. Call doctor when convenient.
Stomach discomfort	Discontinue. Call doctor when convenient.
Tingling in hands and feet	Discontinue. Call doctor when convenient.
Vomiting	Discontinue. Call doctor immediately.
Weakness	Discontinue. Call doctor immediately.

Interaction with Medicine, Vitamins or Minerals

Interacts with	Combined effect
Amiloride	Causes dangerous rise in blood potassium.
Atropine	Increases possibility of intestinal ulcers, which may occur with oral potassium tablets.
Belladonna	Increases possibility of intestinal ulcers, which may occur with oral potassium.
Calcium	Increases possibility of heartbeat irregularities.
Captopril	Increases chance of excessive amounts of potassium.
Cortisone	Decreases effect of potassium.
Digitalis preparations	May cause irregular heartbeat.
Enalapril	Increases chance of excessive amounts of potassium.
Laxatives	May decrease potassium effect.
Spironolactone	Increases blood potassium.
Triamterene	Increases blood potassium.
Vitamin B-12	Extended-release tablets may decrease vitamin B-12 absorption and increase vitamin B-12 requirements.

Interaction with Other Substances

Tobacco decreases absorption. Smokers may require supplementary potassium.

Alcohol intensifies gastrointestinal symptoms.

Cocaine may cause irregular heartbeat.

Marijuana may cause irregular heartbeat.

Beverages
- Salty drinks, such as tomato juice and commercial thirst quenchers, cause increased fluid retention.
- Coffee decreases potassium absorption and intensifies gastrointestinal symptoms.
- Low-salt milk increases fluid retention.

Foods
- Don't take dairy products within 2 hours of taking potassium chloride.
- Salty foods increase fluid retention.
- Sugar decreases potassium absorption.

MINERAL

167

Potassium Gluconate

Basic Information

Available from natural sources? Yes
Available from synthetic sources? Yes
Prescription required? Some yes; others no

Natural Sources

Avocados
Bananas
Chard
Citrus fruit
Juices
  grapefruit, tomato,
  orange
Lentils, dried
Milk
Molasses

Nuts
  almonds, Brazil,
  cashews, peanuts,
  pecans, walnuts
Parsnips
Peaches, dried
Potatoes
Raisins
Sardines, canned
Spinach, fresh
Whole-grain cereals

Reasons to Use

- Promotes regular heartbeat.
- Promotes normal muscle contraction.
- Regulates transfer of nutrients to cells.
- Maintains water balance in body tissues and cells.
- Preserves or restores normal function of nerve cells, heart cells, skeletal-muscle cells, kidneys, stomach-juice secretion.
- Treats potassium deficiency from illness or taking diuretics (water pills), cortisone drugs or digitalis preparations.

Unproved Speculated Benefits

- Cures alcoholism.
- Cures acne.
- Cures allergies.
- Cures heart disease.
- Helps heal burns.
- Prevents high blood pressure.

Who Needs Additional Amounts?

- People who take diuretics, cortisone drugs or digitalis preparations.
- Anyone with inadequate caloric or nutritional dietary intake or increased nutritional requirements.
- Older people (over 55 years).
- Pregnant or breast-feeding women.

- Women taking oral contraceptives.
- People who abuse alcohol or other drugs.
- Tobacco smokers.
- People with a chronic wasting illness, excess stress for long periods or who have recently undergone surgery.
- Athletes and workers who participate in vigorous physical activities, especially when endurance is an important aspect of the activity.
- Those with part of the gastrointestinal tract surgically removed.
- People with malabsorption illnesses (See Glossary).
- People with recent severe burns or injuries.
- Vegetarians.

Deficiency Symptoms

- Hypokalaemia
- Weakness, paralysis
- Low blood pressure
- Life-threatening, irregular or rapid heartbeat that can lead to cardiac arrest and death

Unproved Speculated Symptoms

- Acne
- Allergies
- High blood pressure

Lab Tests to Detect Deficiency

- Serum-potassium determinations
- Serum creatinine
- Electrocardiograms
- Serum-pH determinations

Dosage and Usage Information

Recommended Dietary Allowance (RDA):
No RDA has been established. Nutritionists recommend a *decrease* in sodium (table salt) intake and an *increase* in foods high in potassium for a total daily intake of 40 to 150 milliequivalents per day.

What this mineral does:
- Potassium is the predominant positive electrolyte in body cells. An enzyme (adenosinetriphosphatase) controls flow of potassium and sodium into and out of cells

➤➤

Potassium Gluconate

to maintain normal function of heart, brain, skeletal muscles, normal kidney function, acid-base balance.

Miscellaneous Information:
• Normal potassium content is reduced when foods are tinned or frozen.
• Avoid peeling food.
• Avoid cooking food in large amounts of water.
• Keep meat drippings and use as gravies.

Available as:
• Extended-release capsules or tablets: Swallow whole with full glass of liquid. Don't chew or crush. Take with meals or 1 to 1-1/2 hours after meals unless otherwise directed by your doctor.
• Elixir for oral solution: Dilute in at least 1/2 glass water or other liquid. Take with meals or 1 to 1-1/2 hours after meals unless otherwise directed by your doctor.
• Potassium is not recommended for children.
• Some forms available by generic name.

Warnings and Precautions

Don't take if you:
• Take potassium-sparing diuretics, such as spironolactone, triamterene or amiloride.
• Are allergic to any potassium supplement.
• Have kidney disease.

Consult your doctor if you have:
• Addison's disease.
• Heart disease.
• Intestinal blockage.
• A stomach ulcer.
• To use diuretics.
• To use heart medicine.
• To use laxatives or if you have chronic diarrhoea.
• To use salt substitutes or low-salt milk.

Over age 55:
• Observe dose regime strictly. Potassium balance is critical. Deviation above or below normal can have serious results.

Pregnancy:
• No problems expected, except with megadoses.

Breast-feeding:
• Studies inconclusive on harm to infant. Consult doctor about supplement.
• Don't take megadoses.

Effect on lab tests:
• ECG and kidney function studies can be affected by too much or too little potassium.
• None expected on blood studies, except serum-potassium levels.

Storage:
• Store in cool, dry area away from direct light, but don't freeze.
• Store safely out of reach of children.
• Don't store in bathroom medicine cabinet. Heat and moisture may change action of the mineral

Others:
• Take with meals or with food.

Overdose/Toxicity

Signs and symptoms:
Irregular or fast heartbeat, paralysis of arms and legs, blood-pressure drop, convulsions, coma, cardiac arrest.

What to do:
For symptoms of overdosage: Discontinue mineral, and consult doctor. Also see *Adverse Reactions or Side Effects* section below.
For accidental overdosage (such as child taking entire bottle): Dial 999 (emergency). If person's heart has stopped beating, render CPR until trained help arrives.

MINERAL

169

Potassium Gluconate, Continued

 Adverse Reactions or Side Effects

Reaction or effect	What to do
Black, tarry stool	Seek emergency treatment.
Bloody stool	Seek emergency treatment.
Breathing difficulty	Seek emergency treatment.
Confusion	Discontinue. Call doctor immediately.
Diarrhoea	Discontinue. Call doctor immediately.
Extreme fatigue	Discontinue. Call doctor when convenient.
Heaviness in legs	Discontinue. Call doctor when convenient.
Irregular heartbeat	Seek emergency treatment.
Nausea	Discontinue. Call doctor when convenient.
Numbness in hands or feet	Discontinue. Call doctor when convenient.
Stomach discomfort	Discontinue. Call doctor when convenient.
Tingling in hands and feet	Discontinue. Call doctor when convenient.
Vomiting	Discontinue. Call doctor immediately.
Weakness	Discontinue. Call doctor immediately.

 Interaction with Medicine, Vitamins or Minerals

Interacts with	Combined effect
Amiloride	Causes dangerous rise in blood potassium.
Atropine	Increases possibility of intestinal ulcers, which may occur with oral potassium tablets.
Belladonna	Increases possibility of intestinal ulcers, which may occur with oral potassium.
Calcium	Increases possibility of heartbeat irregularities.
Captopril	Increases chance of excessive amounts of potassium.
Cortisone	Decreases effect of potassium.
Digitalis preparations	May cause irregular heartbeat.
Enalapril	Increases chance of excessive amounts of potassium.
Laxatives	May decrease potassium effect.
Spironolactone	Increases blood potassium.
Triamterene	Increases blood potassium.
Vitamin B-12	Extended-release tablets may decrease vitamin B-12 absorption and increase vitamin B-12 requirements.

 Interaction with Other Substances

Tobacco decreases absorption. Smokers may require supplementary potassium.

Alcohol intensifies gastrointestinal symptoms.

Cocaine may cause irregular heartbeat.

Marijuana may cause irregular heartbeat.

Beverages
- Salty drinks, such as tomato juice and commercial thirst quenchers, cause increased fluid retention.
- Coffee decreases potassium absorption and intensifies gastrointestinal symptoms.
- Low-salt milk increases fluid retention.

Foods
- Salty foods increase fluid retention.
- Sugar decreases potassium absorption.

Potassium Gluconate/Chloride

Basic Information

Available from natural sources? Yes
Available from synthetic sources? Yes
Prescription required? Some yes; others no

Natural Sources

Avocados
Bananas
Chard
Citrus fruit
Juices
  grapefruit, tomato,
  orange
Lentils, dried
Milk
Molasses

Nuts
  almonds, Brazil,
  cashews, peanuts,
  pecans, walnuts
Parsnips
Peaches, dried
Potatoes
Raisins
Sardines, canned
Spinach, fresh
Whole-grain cereals

Reasons to Use

- Promotes regular heartbeat.
- Promotes normal muscle contraction.
- Regulates transfer of nutrients to cells.
- Maintains water balance in body tissues and cells.
- Preserves or restores normal function of nerve cells, heart cells, skeletal-muscle cells, kidneys, stomach-juice secretion.
- Treats potassium deficiency from illness or taking diuretics (water pills), cortisone drugs or digitalis preparations.

Unproved Speculated Benefits

- Cures alcoholism.
- Cures acne.
- Cures allergies.
- Cures heart disease.
- Helps heal burns.
- Prevents high blood pressure.

Who Needs Additional Amounts?

- People who take diuretics, cortisone drugs or digitalis preparations.
- Anyone with inadequate caloric or nutritional dietary intake or increased nutritional requirements.
- Older people (over 55 years).
- Pregnant or breast-feeding women.
- Women taking oral contraceptives.

- People who abuse alcohol or other drugs.
- Tobacco smokers.
- People with a chronic wasting illness, excess stress for long periods or who have recently undergone surgery.
- Athletes and workers who participate in vigorous physical activities, especially when endurance is an important aspect of the activity.
- Those with part of the gastrointestinal tract surgically removed.
- People with malabsorption illnesses (See Glossary).
- People with recent severe burns or injuries.
- Vegetarians.

Deficiency Symptoms

- Hypokalaemia
- Weakness, paralysis
- Low blood pressure
- Life-threatening, irregular or rapid heartbeat that can lead to cardiac arrest and death

Unproved Speculated Symptoms

- Acne
- Allergies
- High blood pressure

Lab Tests to Detect Deficiency

- Serum-potassium determinations
- Serum creatinine
- Electrocardiograms
- Serum-pH determinations

≫➤

Potassium Gluconate/Chloride, Continued

Dosage and Usage Information

Recommended Dietary Allowance (RDA):
No RDA has been established. Nutritionists recommend a *decrease* in sodium (table salt) intake and an *increase* in foods high in potassium for a total daily intake of 40 to 150 milliequivalents per day.

What this mineral does:
• Potassium is the predominant positive electrolyte in body cells. An enzyme (adenosinetriphosphatase) controls flow of potassium and sodium into and out of cells to maintain normal function of heart, brain, skeletal muscles, normal kidney function, acid-base balance.

Miscellaneous Information:
• Normal potassium content is reduced when foods are canned or frozen.
• Avoid peeling food.
• Avoid cooking food in large amounts of water.
• Keep meat drippings and use as gravies.

Available as:
• Oral solution: Dilute in at least 1/2 glass water or other liquid. Take with meals or 1 to 1-1/2 hours after meals unless otherwise directed by your doctor.
• Powder for oral solution: Dissolve powder in cold water or juice. Take with meals or 1 to 1-1/2 hours after meals unless othewise directed by your doctor.
• Special instructions for children.
• Not available by generic name.

Warnings and Precautions

Don't take if you:
• Take potassium-sparing diuretics, such as spironolactone, triamterene or amiloride.
• Are allergic to any potassium supplement.
• Have kidney disease.

Consult your doctor if you have:
• Addison's disease.
• Heart disease.
• Intestinal blockage.
• A stomach ulcer.
• To use diuretics.
• To use heart medicine.
• To use laxatives or if you have chronic diarrhoea.
• To use salt substitutes or low-salt milk.

Over age 55:
• Observe dose schedule strictly. Potassium balance is critical. Deviation above or below normal can have serious results.

Pregnancy:
• No problems expected, except with megadoses.

Breast-feeding:
• Studies inconclusive on harm to infant. Consult doctor about supplement.
• Don't take megadoses.

Effect on lab tests
• ECG and kidney function studies can be affected by too much or too little potassium.
• None expected on blood studies, except serum-potassium levels.

Storage:
• Store in cool, dry area away from direct light, but don't freeze.
• Store safely out of reach of children.
• Don't store in bathroom medicine cabinet. Heat and moisture may change action of the mineral.

Others:
• Take with meals or with food.

Overdose/Toxicity

Signs and symptoms:
Irregular or fast heartbeat, paralysis of arms and legs, blood-pressure drop, convulsions, coma, cardiac arrest.

What to do:
For symptoms of overdosage: Discontinue mineral, and consult doctor. Also see *Adverse Reactions or Side Effects* section below.
For accidental overdosage (such as child taking entire bottle): Dial 999 (emergency). If person's heart has stopped beating, render CPR until trained help arrives.

⟫➤

Adverse Reactions or Side Effects

Reaction or effect	What to do
Black, tarry stool	Seek emergency treatment.
Bloody stool	Seek emergency treatment.
Breathing difficulty	Seek emergency treatment.
Confusion	Discontinue. Call doctor immediately.
Diarrhoea	Discontinue. Call doctor immediately.
Extreme fatigue	Discontinue. Call doctor when convenient.
Heaviness in legs	Discontinue. Call doctor when convenient.
Irregular heartbeat	Seek emergency treatment.
Nausea	Discontinue. Call doctor when convenient.
Numbness in hands or feet	Discontinue. Call doctor when convenient.
Stomach discomfort	Discontinue. Call doctor when convenient.
Tingling in hands and feet	Discontinue. Call doctor when convenient.
Vomiting	Discontinue. Call doctor immediately.
Weakness	Discontinue. Call doctor immediately.

Interaction with Medicine, Vitamins or Minerals

Interacts with	Combined effect
Amiloride	Causes dangerous rise in blood potassium.
Atropine	Increases possibility of intestinal ulcers, which may occur with oral potassium tablets.
Belladonna	Increases possibility of intestinal ulcers, which may occur with oral potassium.
Calcium	Increases possibility of heartbeat irregularities.

Captopril	Increases chance of excessive amounts of potassium.
Cortisone	Decreases effect of potassium.
Digitalis preparations	May cause irregular heartbeat.
Enalapril	Increases chance of excessive amounts of potassium.
Laxatives	May decrease potassium effect.
Spironolactone	Increases blood potassium.
Triamterene	Increases blood potassium.
Vitamin B-12	Extended-release tablets may decrease vitamin B-12 absorption and increase vitamin B-12 requirements.

Interaction with Other Substances

Tobacco decreases absorption. Smokers may require supplemental potassium.

Alcohol intensifies gastrointestinal symptoms.

Cocaine may cause irregular heartbeat.

Marijuana may cause irregular heartbeat.

Beverages
- Salty drinks, such as tomato juice and commercial thirst quenchers, cause increased fluid retention.
- Coffee decreases potassium absorption and intensifies gastrointestinal symptoms.
- Low-salt milk increases fluid retention.

Foods
- Don't take dairy products within 2 hours of taking potassium chloride.
- Salty foods increase fluid retention.
- Sugar decreases potassium absorption.

MINERAL

Potassium Gluconate/Citrate

Basic Information

Available from natural sources? Yes
Available from synthetic sources? Yes
Prescription required? Some yes; others no

Natural Sources

Avocados
Bananas
Chard
Citrus fruit
Juices
  grapefruit, tomato,
  orange
Lentils, dried
Milk
Molasses

Nuts
  almonds, Brazil,
  cashews, peanuts,
  pecans, walnuts
Parsnips
Peaches, dried
Potatoes
Raisins
Sardines, canned
Spinach, fresh
Whole-grain cereals

Reasons to Use

- Promotes regular heartbeat.
- Promotes normal muscle contraction.
- Regulates transfer of nutrients to cells.
- Maintains water balance in body tissues and cells.
- Preserves or restores normal function of nerve cells, heart cells, skeletal-muscle cells, kidneys, stomach-juice secretion.
- Treats potassium deficiency from illness or taking diuretics (water pills), cortisone drugs or digitalis preparations.

Unproved Speculated Benefits

- Cures alcoholism.
- Cures acne.
- Cures allergies.
- Cures heart disease.
- Helps heal burns.
- Prevents high blood pressure.

Who Needs Additional Amounts?

- People who take diuretics, cortisone drugs or digitalis preparations.
- Anyone with inadequate caloric or nutritional dietary intake or increased nutritional requirements.
- Older people (over 55 years).
- Pregnant or breast-feeding women.

- Women taking oral contraceptives.
- People who abuse alcohol or other drugs.
- Tobacco smokers.
- People with a chronic wasting illness, excess stress for long periods or who have recently undergone surgery.
- Athletes and workers who participate in vigorous physical activities, especially when endurance is an important aspect of the activity.
- Those with part of the gastrointestinal tract surgically removed.
- People with malabsorption illnesses (See Glossary).
- People with recent severe burns or injuries.
- Vegetarians.

Deficiency Symptoms

- Hypokalaemia
- Weakness, paralysis
- Low blood pressure
- Life-threatening, irregular or rapid heartbeat that can lead to cardiac arrest and death

Unproved Speculated Symptoms

- Acne
- Allergies
- High blood pressure

Lab Tests to Detect Deficiency

- Serum-potassium determinations
- Serum creatinine
- Electrocardiograms
- Serum-pH determinations

Dosage and Usage Information

Recommended Dietary Allowance (RDA):
No RDA has been established. Nutritionists recommend a *decrease* in sodium (table salt) intake and an *increase* in foods high in potassium for a total daily intake of 40 to 150 milliequivalents per day.

What this mineral does:
- Potassium is the predominant positive electrolyte in body cells. An enzyme (adenosinetriphosphatase) controls flow of potassium and sodium into and out of cells to maintain normal function of heart, brain,   ➤➤

skeletal muscles, normal kidney function, acid-base balance.

Miscellaneous Information:
• Normal potassium content is reduced when foods are tinned or frozen.
• Avoid peeling food.
• Avoid cooking food in large amounts of water.
• Keep meat drippings and use as gravies.

Available as:
• Oral solution: Dilute in at least 1/2 glass water or other liquid. Take with meals or 1 to 1-1/2 hours after meals unless otherwise directed by your doctor.
• Special instructions for children.
• Not available by generic name.

Warnings and Precautions

Don't take if you:
• Take potassium-sparing diuretics, such as spironolactone, triamterene or amiloride.
• Are allergic to any potassium supplement.
• Have kidney disease.

Consult your doctor if you have:
• Addison's disease.
• Heart disease.
• Intestinal blockage.
• A stomach ulcer.
• To use diuretics.
• To use heart medicine.
• To use laxatives or if you have chronic diarrhoea.
• To use salt substitutes or low-salt milk.

Over age 55:
• Observe dose regime strictly. Potassium balance is critical. Deviation above or below normal can have serious results.

Pregnancy:
• No problems expected, except with megadoses.

Breast-feeding:
• Studies inconclusive on harm to infant. Consult doctor about supplement.
• Don't take megadoses.

Effect on lab tests:
• ECG and kidney function studies can be affected by too much or too little potassium.
• None expected on blood studies, except serum-potassium levels.

Storage:
• Store in cool, dry area away from direct light, but don't freeze.
• Store safely out of reach of children.
• Don't store in bathroom medicine cabinet. Heat and moisture may change action of the mineral.

Others:
• Take with meals or with food.

Overdose/Toxicity

Signs and symptoms:
Irregular or fast heartbeat, paralysis of arms and legs, blood-pressure drop, convulsions, coma, cardiac arrest.

What to do:
For symptoms of overdosage: Discontinue mineral, and consult doctor. Also see *Adverse Reactions or Side Effects* section below.
For accidental overdosage (such as child taking entire bottle): Dial 999 (emergency). If person's heart has stopped beating, render CPR until trained help arrives.

MINERAL

Potassium Gluconate/Citrate, Continued

Adverse Reactions or Side Effects

Reaction or effect	What to do
Black, tarry stool	Seek emergency treatment.
Bloody stool	Seek emergency treatment.
Breathing difficulty	Seek emergency treatment.
Confusion	Discontinue. Call doctor immediately.
Diarrhoea	Discontinue. Call doctor immediately.
Extreme fatigue	Discontinue. Call doctor when convenient.
Heaviness in legs	Discontinue. Call doctor when convenient.
Irregular heartbeat	Seek emergency treatment.
Nausea	Discontinue. Call doctor when convenient.
Numbness in hands or feet	Discontinue. Call doctor when convenient.
Stomach discomfort	Discontinue. Call doctor when convenient.
Tingling in hands and feet	Discontinue. Call doctor when convenient.
Vomiting	Discontinue. Call doctor immediately.
Weakness	Discontinue. Call doctor immediately.

Interaction with Medicine, Vitamins or Minerals

Interacts with	Combined effect
Amiloride	Causes dangerous rise in blood potassium.
Atropine	Increases possibility of intestinal ulcers, which may occur with oral potassium tablets.
Belladonna	Increases possibility of intestinal ulcers, which may occur with oral potassium.
Calcium	Increases possibility of heartbeat irregularities.
Captopril	Increases chance of excessive amounts of potassium.
Cortisone	Decreases effect of potassium.
Digitalis preparations	May cause irregular heartbeat.
Enalapril	Increases chance of excessive amounts of potassium.
Laxatives	May decrease potassium effect.
Spironolactone	Increases blood potassium.
Triamterene	Increases blood potassium.
Vitamin B-12	Extended-release tablets may decrease vitamin B-12 absorption and increase vitamin B-12 requirements.

Interaction with Other Substances

Tobacco decreases absorption. Smokers may require supplemental potassium.

Alcohol intensifies gastrointestinal symptoms.

Cocaine may cause irregular heartbeat.

Marijuana may cause irregular heartbeat.

Beverages
- Salty drinks, such as tomato juice and commercial thirst quenchers, cause increased fluid retention.
- Coffee decreases potassium absorption and intensifies gastrointestinal symptoms.
- Low-salt milk increases fluid retention.

Foods
- Salty foods increase fluid retention.
- Sugar decreases potassium absorption.

Potassium Gluconate/Citrate/Ammonium Chloride

Basic Information

Available from natural sources? Yes
Available from synthetic sources? Yes
Prescription required? Some yes; others no

Natural Sources

Avocados
Bananas
Chard
Citrus fruit
Juices
  grapefruit, tomato,
  orange
Lentils, dried
Milk
Molasses

Nuts
  almonds, Brazil,
  cashews, peanuts,
  pecans, walnuts
Parsnips
Peaches, dried
Potatoes
Raisins
Sardines, canned
Spinach, fresh
Whole-grain cereals

Reasons to Use

- Promotes regular heartbeat.
- Promotes normal muscle contraction.
- Regulates transfer of nutrients to cells.
- Maintains water balance in body tissues and cells.
- Preserves or restores normal function of nerve cells, heart cells, skeletal-muscle cells, kidneys, stomach-juice secretion.
- Treats potassium deficiency from illness or taking diuretics (water pills), cortisone drugs or digitalis preparations.

Unproved Speculated Benefits

- Cures alcoholism.
- Cures acne.
- Cures allergies.
- Cures heart disease.
- Helps heal burns.
- Prevents high blood pressure.

Who Needs Additional Amounts?

- People who take diuretics, cortisone drugs or digitalis preparations.
- Anyone with inadequate caloric or nutritional dietary intake or increased nutritional requirements.
- Older people (over 55 years).
- Pregnant or breast-feeding women.

- Women taking oral contraceptives.
- People who abuse alcohol or other drugs.
- Tobacco smokers.
- People with a chronic wasting illness, excess stress for long periods or who have recently undergone surgery.
- Athletes and workers who participate in vigorous physical activities, especially when endurance is an important aspect of the activity.
- Those with part of the gastrointestinal tract surgically removed.
- People with malabsorption illnesses (See Glossary).
- People with recent severe burns or injuries.
- Vegetarians.

Deficiency Symptoms

- Hypokalaemia
- Weakness, paralysis
- Low blood pressure
- Life-threatening, irregular or rapid heartbeat that can lead to cardiac arrest and death

Unproved Speculated Symptoms

- Acne
- Allergies
- High blood pressure

Lab Tests to Detect Deficiency

- Serum-potassium determinations
- Serum creatinine
- Electrocardiograms
- Serum-pH determinations

»→

MINERAL

Dosage and Usage Information

Recommended Dietary Allowance (RDA):
No RDA has been established. Nutritionists recommend a *decrease* in sodium (table salt) intake and an *increase* in foods high in potassium for a total daily intake of 40 to 150 milliequivalents per day.

What this mineral does:
• Potassium is the predominant positive electrolyte in body cells. An enzyme (adenosinetriphosphatase) controls flow of potassium and sodium into and out of cells to maintain normal function of heart, brain, skeletal muscles, normal kidney function, acid-base balance.

Miscellaneous Information:
• Normal potassium content is reduced when foods are canned or frozen.
• Avoid peeling food.
• Avoid cooking food in large amounts of water.
• Keep meat drippings and use as gravies.

Available as:
• Oral solution: Dilute in at least 1/2 glass water or other liquid. Take with meals or 1 to 1-1/2 hours after meals unless otherwise directed by your doctor.
• Special instructions for children.
• Not available by generic name.

Warnings and Precautions

Don't take if you:
• Take potassium-sparing diuretics, such as spironolactone, triamterene or amiloride.
• Are allergic to any potassium supplement.
• Have kidney disease.

Consult your doctor if you have:
• Addison's disease.
• Heart disease.
• Intestinal blockage.
• A stomach ulcer.
• To use diuretics.
• To use heart medicine.
• To use laxatives or if you have chronic diarrhoea.
• To use salt substitutes or low-salt milk.

Over age 55:
• Observe dose regime strictly. Potassium balance is critical. Deviation above or below normal can have serious results.

Pregnancy:
• No problems expected, except with megadoses.

Breast-feeding:
• Studies inconclusive on harm to infant. Consult doctor about supplement.
• Don't take megadoses.

Effect on lab tests:
• ECG and kidney function studies can be affected by too much or too little potassium.
• None expected on blood studies, except serum-potassium levels.

Storage:
• Store in cool, dry area away from direct light, but don't freeze.
• Store safely out of reach of children.
• Don't store in bathroom medicine cabinet. Heat and moisture may change action of the mineral.

Others:
• Take with meals or with food.

Overdose/Toxicity

Signs and symptoms:
Irregular or fast heartbeat, paralysis of arms and legs, blood-pressure drop, convulsions, coma, cardiac arrest.

What to do:
For symptoms of overdosage: Discontinue mineral, and consult doctor. Also see *Adverse Reactions or Side Effects* section below.
For accidental overdosage (such as child taking entire bottle): Dial 999 (emergency). If a person's heart has stopped beating, render CPR until trained help arrives.

➤➤

Potassium Gluconate/Citrate/Ammonium Chloride,

Continued

Adverse Reactions or Side Effects

Reaction or effect	What to do
Black, tarry stool	Seek emergency treatment.
Bloody stool	Seek emergency treatment.
Breathing difficulty	Seek emergency treatment.
Confusion	Discontinue. Call doctor immediately.
Diarrhoea	Discontinue. Call doctor immediately.
Extreme fatigue	Discontinue. Call doctor when convenient.
Heaviness in legs	Discontinue. Call doctor when convenient.
Irregular heartbeat	Seek emergency treatment.
Nausea	Discontinue. Call doctor when convenient.
Numbness in hands or feet	Discontinue. Call doctor when convenient.
Stomach discomfort	Discontinue. Call doctor when convenient.
Tingling in hands and feet	Discontinue. Call doctor when convenient.
Vomiting	Discontinue. Call doctor immediately.
Weakness	Discontinue. Call doctor immediately.

Interaction with Medicine, Vitamins or Minerals

Interacts with	Combined effect
Amiloride	Causes dangerous rise in blood potassium.
Atropine	Increases possibility of intestinal ulcers, which may occur with oral potassium tablets.
Belladonna	Increases possibility of intestinal ulcers, which may occur with oral potassium.
Calcium	Increases possibility of heartbeat irregularities.
Captopril	Increases chance of excessive amounts of potassium.
Cortisone	Decreases effect of potassium.
Digitalis preparations	May cause irregular heartbeat.
Enalapril	Increases chance of excessive amounts of potassium.
Laxatives	May decrease potassium effect.
Spironolactone	Increases blood potassium.
Triamterene	Increases blood potassium.
Vitamin B-12	Extended-release tablets may decrease vitamin B-12 absorption and increase vitamin B-12 requirements.

Interaction with Other Substances

Tobacco decreases absorption. Smokers may require supplementary potassium.

Alcohol intensifies gastrointestinal symptoms.

Cocaine may cause irregular heartbeat.

Marijuana may cause irregular heartbeat.

Beverages
- Salty drinks, such as tomato juice and commercial thirst quenchers, cause increased fluid retention.
- Coffee decreases potassium absorption and intensifies gastrointestinal symptoms.
- Low-salt milk increases fluid retention.

Foods
- Salty foods increase fluid retention.
- Sugar decreases potassium absorption.

MINERAL

Potassium Phosphate

Basic Information

Potassium phosphate is a phosphate supplement. It does not function as a potassium supplement.
Available from natural sources? Yes
Available from synthetic sources? No
Prescription required? Yes, for medical purposes

Natural Sources

Almonds	Peanuts
Beans, dried	Peas
Calves' liver	Poultry
Cheese, cheddar	Pumpkin seeds
Cheese, pasteurized	Red meat
process	Sardines, canned
Eggs	Scallops
Fish	Soya beans
Milk	Sunflower seeds
Milk products	Tuna
	Whole-grain products

Reasons to Use

- Builds strong bones and teeth (with calcium).
- Promotes energy metabolism.
- Promotes growth, maintenance and repair of all body tissues.
- Buffers body fluids for acid-base balance.
- Acidifies urine and reduces possibility of kidney stones.

Unproved Speculated Benefits

- Reduces effects of stress.
- Accelerates growth in children.
- Helps reduce pain of arthritis.

Who Needs Additional Amounts?

- Anyone suffering prolonged vomiting.
- Those with inadequate caloric or dietary intake or increased nutritional requirements.
- Those who take excessive amounts of antacid.
- Older people (over 55 years).
- Those who abuse alcohol or other drugs. Alcoholics probably need phosphate supplementation.
- People with a chronic wasting illness, excess stress for long periods or who have recently undergone surgery.

- Those with liver disease.
- People with hyperparathyroidism.

Deficiency Symptoms

- Bone pain
- Loss of appetite
- Weakness
- Easily broken bones

Unproved Speculated Symptoms

- Rickets

Lab Tests to Detect Deficiency

- Serum phosphorous

Dosage and Usage Information

Recommended Dietary Allowance (RDA):
Estimate of adequate daily intake by the Food and Nutrition Board of the National Research Council, 1980 (See Glossary).

Age	RDA
0–6 months	240mg
6–12 months	360mg
1–10 years	800mg
11–17 years	1200mg
18+ years	800mg
Pregnant	+400mg
Lactating	+400mg

What this mineral does:
- Necessary for utilization of many B-complex vitamins.
- An important constituent of all fats, proteins, carbohydrates and many enzymes.

Available as:
- Tablets: Swallow whole with full glass of liquid. Don't chew or crush. Take with meals or 1 to 1-1/2 hours after meals unless otherwise directed by your doctor.
- Capsules for oral solution: Empty contents into at least 1/2 glass water or other liquid. Don't swallow filled capsule. Take with meals or 1 to 1-1/2 hours after meals unless otherwise directed by your doctor.
- Oral solution: Dilute in at least 1/2 glass water or other liquid. Take with meals or 1 to 1-1/2 hours after meals unless otherwise directed by your doctor. ➤➤

* A constituent of many multivitamin/mineral preparations.

Warnings and Precautions

Don't take if you:
* Have severe kidney disease.
* Have kidney stones and analysis has shown their composition to be magnesium ammonium phosphate.

Consult your doctor if you have:
* Hypoparathyroidism.
* Osteomalacia.
* Acute pancreatitis.
* Chronic kidney disease.
* Rickets.
* Adrenal insufficiency (Addison's disease).
* Dehydration.
* Severe burns.
* Heart disease.

Over age 55:
* No special problems expected.

Pregnancy:
* Take under doctor's supervision only.
* Don't take megadoses.

Breast-feeding:
* Take under doctor's supervision only.
* Don't take megadoses.

Effect on lab tests:
* May show false decrease in bone uptake in technetium-labeled diagnostic-imaging tests.

Storage:
* Store in cool, dry place away from direct light, but don't freeze.
* Store safely out of reach of children.
* Don't store in bathroom medicine cabinet. Heat and moisture may change action of mineral.

Overdose/Toxicity

Signs and symptoms:
Seizures, heartbeat irregularities, shortness of breath.

What to do:
For symptoms of overdosage: Discontinue mineral, and seek emergency treatment. Also see *Adverse Reactions or Side Effects* section below.

For accidental overdosage (such as child taking entire bottle): Dial 999 (emergency).

Adverse Reactions or Side Effects

Reaction or effect	What to do
Abdominal pain	Discontinue. Call doctor immediately.
Bone or joint pain	Discontinue. Call doctor immediately.
Confusion	Discontinue. Call doctor immediately.
Decreased volume of urine in one day	Seek emergency treatment.
Diarrhoea	Discontinue. Call doctor immediately.
Easy fatigue	Discontinue. Call doctor when convenient.
Oedema of feet or legs	Discontinue. Call doctor when convenient.
Headaches	Discontinue. Call doctor immediately.
Muscle cramps	Discontinue. Call doctor when convenient.
Numbness or tingling in hands or feet	Discontinue. Call doctor when convenient.
Unusual thirst	Discontinue. Call doctor when convenient.

≫→

Potassium Phosphate, Continued

Interaction with Medicine, Vitamins or Minerals

Interacts with	Combined effect
Anabolic steroids	Increases risk of edema.
Antacids with aluminium or magnesium	May prevent absorption of phosphates.
Calcium-containing supplements and antacids	Increases risk of depositing calcium in soft tissues. Decreases phosphate absorption.
Captopril	Increases risk of too much potassium (hyperkalaemia).
Cortisone drugs or ACTH	Increases serum sodium.
Digitalis preparations	Increases risk of too much potassium (hyperkalaemia).
Diuretics, potassium-conserving (amiloride, spironelactene, triamterene)	Increases risk of too much potassium (hyperkalaemia).
Emalapril	Increases risk of too much potassium (hyperkalaemia).
Salicylates	May increase plasma concentration of salicylates.
Testosterone	Increases risk of oedema.
Vitamin D	Phosphate absorption enhanced, but may increase chance of too much phosphorous in blood and body cells.

Interaction with Other Substances

Beverages
- Alcoholic beverages decrease available phosphorous for vital body functions.
- Overconsumption of soft drinks may adversely affect absorption of phosphorous and calcium.

Foods
- Overconsumption of rhubarb, spinach and bran may decrease absorption of potassium phosphates.
- Overconsumption of meats and convenience foods may adversely affect absorption of phosphorous and calcium.

Basic Information

Potassium/sodium phosphate is a phosphate supplement. It does not function as a potassium supplement.
Available from natural sources? Yes
Available from synthetic sources? No
Prescription required? Yes for medical purposes

Natural Sources

Almonds	Peanuts
Beans, dried	Peas
Calves' liver	Poultry
Cheese, cheddar	Pumpkin seeds
Cheese, pasteurized	Red meat
process	Sardines, canned
Eggs	Scallops
Fish	Soya beans
Milk	Sunflower seeds
Milk products	Tuna
	Whole-grain products

Reasons to Use

- Builds strong bones and teeth (with calcium).
- Promotes energy metabolism.
- Promotes growth, maintenance and repair of all body tissues.
- Buffers body fluids for acid-base balance.
- Acidifies urine and reduces possibility of kidney stones.

Unproved Speculated Benefits

- Reduces effects of stress.
- Accelerates growth in children.
- Helps reduce pain of arthritis.

Who Needs Additional Amounts?

- People suffering prolonged vomiting.
- Anyone with inadequate caloric or nutritional dietary intake or increased nutritional requirements.
- Those who take excessive amounts of antacids.
- Older people (over 55 years).
- Those who abuse alcohol or other drugs. Alcoholics most probably need phosphate supplementation.

- People with a chronic wasting illness, excess stress for long periods or who have recently undergone surgery.
- Those with liver disease.
- People with hyperparathyroidism.

Deficiency Symptoms

Proven symptoms:
- Bone pain
- Loss of appetite
- Weakness
- Easily broken bones

Unproved Speculated Symptoms

- Rickets

Lab Tests to Detect Deficiency

- Serum phosphorous

Dosage and Usage Information

Recommended Dietary Allowance (RDA):
Estimate of adequate daily intake by the Food and Nutrition Board of the National Research Council, 1980 (See Glossary).

Age	RDA
0–6 months	240mg
6–12 months	360mg
1–10 years	800mg
11–17 years	1200mg
18+ years	800mg
Pregnant	+400mg
Lactating	+400mg

What this mineral does:
- Necessary for utilization of many B-complex vitamins.
- An important constituent of all fats, proteins, carbohydrates and many enzymes.

Available as:
- Tablets: Swallow whole with full glass of liquid. Don't chew or crush. Take with meals or 1 to 1-1/2 hours after meals unless otherwise directed by your doctor.
- Capsules for oral solution: Empty contents into at least 1/2 glass water or other liquid. Don't swallow filled capsule. Take with meals or 1 to 1-1/2 hours after meals unless otherwise directed by your doctor.

⟫➤

MINERAL

Potassium/Sodium Phosphate, Continued

- Oral solution: Dilute in at least 1/2 glass water or other liquid. Take with meals or 1 to 1-1/2 hours after meals unless otherwise directed by your doctor.
- A constituent of many multivitamin/mineral preparations.

Warnings and Precautions

Don't take if you have:
- Severe kidney disease.
- Kidney stones and analysis has shown their composition to be magnesium ammonium phosphate.

Consult your doctor if you have:
- Hypoparathyroidism.
- Osteomalacia.
- Acute pancreatitis.
- Chronic kidney disease.
- Rickets.
- Adrenal insufficiency (Addison's disease).
- Dehydration.
- Severe burns.
- Heart disease.
- Congestive heart failure.
- Liver cirrhosis.
- Oedema.
- Increased sodium in blood.
- High blood pressure.
- Toxaemia of pregnancy.

Over age 55:
- No special problems expected.

Pregnancy:
- Take under doctor's supervision only.
- Don't take megadoses.

Breast-feeding:
- Take under doctor's supervision only.
- Don't take megadoses.

Effect on lab tests:
- May show false decrease in bone uptake in technetium-labeled diagnostic-imaging tests.

Storage:
- Store in cool, dry place away from direct light, but don't freeze.
- Store safely out of reach of children.
- Don't store in bathroom medicine cabinet. Heat and moisture may change action of mineral.

Overdose/Toxicity

Signs and symptoms:
Seizures, heartbeat irregularities, shortness of breath.

What to do:
For symptoms of overdosage: Discontinue mineral, and seek emergency treatment. Also see *Adverse Reactions or Side Effects* section below.
For accidental overdosage (such as child taking entire bottle): Dial 999 (emergency).

Adverse Reactions or Side Effects

Reaction or effect	What to do
Abdominal pain	Discontinue. Call doctor immediately.
Bone or joint pain	Discontinue. Call doctor immediately.
Confusion	Discontinue. Call doctor immediately.
Decreased volume of urine in one day	Seek emergency treatment.
Diarrhoea	Discontinue. Call doctor immediately.
Easy fatigue	Discontinue. Call doctor when convenient.
Oedema of feet or legs	Discontinue. Call doctor when convenient.
Headaches	Discontinue. Call doctor immediately.
Muscle cramps	Discontinue. Call doctor when convenient.
Numbness or tingling in hands or feet	Discontinue. Call doctor when convenient.
Unusual thirst	Discontinue. Call doctor when convenient.

➤➤

Interaction with Medicine, Vitamins or Minerals

Interacts with	Combined effect
Anabolic steroids	Increases risk of oedema.
Antacids with aluminium or magnesium	May prevent absorption of phosphates.
Calcium-containing supplements and antacids	Increases risk of depositing calcium in soft tissues. Decreases phosphate absorption.
Captopril	Increases risk of too much potassium (hyperkalaemia).
Cortisone drugs or ACTH	Increases serum sodium.
Digitalis preparations	Increases risk of too much potassium (hyperkalaemia).
Diuretics, potassium-conserving (amiloride, spironelactene, triamterene)	Increases risk of too much potassium (hyperkalaemia).
Emalapril	Increases risk of too much potassium (hyperkalaemia).
Salicylates	May increase plasma concentration of salicylates.
Testosterone	Increases risk of oedema.
Vitamin D	Phosphate absorption enhanced, but may increase chance of too much phosphorous in blood and body cells.

Interaction with Other Substances

Beverages:
- Alcoholic beverages decrease available phosphorous for vital body functions.
- Overconsumption of soft drinks may adversely affect absorption of phosphorous and calcium.

Foods
- Overconsumption of meats and convenience foods may adversely affect absorption of phosphorous and calcium.
- Overconsumption of rhubarb, spinach and bran may decrease absorption of potassium phosphates.

MINERAL

Selenium

Basic Information
Available from natural sources? Yes
Available from synthetic sources? No
Prescription required? No

Natural Sources

Bran	Liver
Broccoli	Milk
Cabbage	Mushrooms
Celery	Onions
Chicken	Seafood
Cucumbers	Tuna
Egg yolk	Wheat germ
Garlic	Whole-grain products
Kidney	

Note: The selenium content of food varies greatly because of the wide variability of this element in the soil. Accurate levels in food are not available.

Reasons to Use

- Complements vitamin E to act as an efficient anti-oxidant.
- Promotes normal growth and development.
- Functions as anti-oxidant itself.

Unproved Speculated Benefits

- Stimulates immune system.
- Cures cancer.
- Cures arthritis.
- Protects against all hypothesized aging mechanisms.
- Protects against cardiovascular disease, strokes and heart attacks.
- Decreases platelet clumping in bloodstream, and prevents clots at site of blood-vessel damage in heart and brain.
- Increases elasticity and youthfulness of skin.
- Helps control dandruff (selenium sulphide) when applied to scalp. Used this way it exerts anti-fungal and anti-bacterial effects.
- Acts as an aphrodisiac.
- Increases fertility.
- Removes age spots when rubbed on skin.
- Protects against damage caused by tobacco smoking.

Who Needs Additional Amounts?

- Anyone with inadequate caloric or nutritional dietary intake or increased nutritional requirements.
- People who live in areas where soil is selenium-deficient, such as China, New Zealand and central and eastern United States.

Deficiency Symptoms

- Selenium deficiency in the soil and water has resulted in cardiomyopathy and myocardial deaths in humans

Unproved Speculated Symptoms

- Keshan's disease, a fatal heart disease found in children living in certain sections of China
- Cataracts
- Muscular dystrophy
- Retarded growth
- Liver problems
- Infertility
- Some forms of cancer

Lab Tests to Detect Deficiency

- 24-hour urine collection

Dosage and Usage Information

Recommended Dietary Allowance (RDA):
No RDA has been established. Estimated safe intake per day given below:

Age	Estimated Safe Intake
0–6 months	0.01–0.04mg
6–12 months	0.02–0.06mg
1–3 years	0.02–0.08mg
4–6 years	0.03–0.12mg
7–10 years	0.05–0.20mg
11+ years	0.05–0.20mg

What this mineral does:
- Selenium helps defend against damage from oxidation.

Miscellaneous information:
- Should be part of a well-balanced vitamin-mineral regimen.

⟫⟶

- Protection from human degenerative disorders has yet to be proved.
- Experimental studies are trying to prove selenium plays a big part as an "anti-oxidant nutrient" to help protect against damaging "free radicals."
- Organic forms (from foods or brewer's yeast) are less toxic than inorganic sodium selenite.
- No one can be sure of correct amount to be ingested each day. People who eat a balanced diet probably get enough from food.

Available as:
- Tablets or capsules: Swallow whole with full glass of liquid. Don't chew or crush. Take with meals or 1 to 1-1/2 hours after meals unless otherwise directed by your doctor.
- A constituent of many multivitamin/mineral preparations.

Warnings and Precautions

Don't take if you:
- Plan to use it on scalp or skin for seborrhaeic dermatitis or dandruff if you have any inflammation or oozing.

Consult your doctor if you have:
- Plans to take more than the dose recommended by the manufacturer.

Over age 55:
- No problems expected with usual doses.

Pregnancy:
- No problems expected with usual doses.
- Don't take megadoses.

Breast-feeding:
- No problems expected with usual doses.
- Don't take megadoses.

Effect on lab tests:
- May decrease serum vitamin C.

Storage:
- Store in cool, dry place away from direct light, but don't freeze.
- Store safely out of reach of children.
- Don't store in bathroom medicine cabinet. Heat and moisture may change action of mineral.

Others:
- When used on hair, rinse hair carefully to prevent discolouration.
- Workers at industrial sites that manufacture glass, pesticides, rubber, semi-conductors, copper and film are at increased risk of developing toxic symptoms from inhalation, absorption through the skin and ingestion. These may include bronchial pneumonia,

asthma, precipitous drop in blood pressure, red eyes, garlic odour on breath and in urine, headaches, metalic taste, nose and throat irritation, difficulty breathing, vomiting, weakness.

Overdose/Toxicity

Signs and symptoms:
Unlikely to develop if organic selenium is not consumed at a rate greater than dose recommended by the manufacturer.

Possible Consequences of Overdose:
- Individuals in industrial settings have been reported to suffer toxic symptoms of selenium overdoses, including liver disease and cardiomyopathy. Children raised in selenium-rich areas show a higher incidence of decayed, missing and filled teeth.
- Selenium is toxic in megadoses and may cause alopecia, loss of nails, fatigue, nausea, vomiting, sour-milk breath.

What to do:
For symptoms of overdosage: Discontinue mineral, and consult doctor. Also see *Adverse Reactions or Side Effects* section below.

For accidental overdosage (such as child taking entire bottle): Dial 999 (emergency).

_____ ⟩⟩▸

Adverse Reactions or Side Effects

Reaction or effect	What to do
Dizziness and nausea, without other apparent cause	Discontinue. Call doctor immediately.
Fragile or black fingernails	Discontinue. Call doctor when convenient.
Persistent garlic odour on breath and skin	Discontinue. Call doctor when convenient.
Unusual dryness when used on scalp or skin	Discontinue. Call doctor when convenient.
Unusual hair loss or discolouration of hair	Discontinue. Call doctor when convenient.

 ## Interaction with Medicine, Vitamins or Minerals

Interacts with	Combined effect
Vitamin C	May decrease selenium absorption if taken with an inorganic form of selenium.
Vitamin E	Prevents oxidation that might cause breakdown of body chemicals.

 ## Interaction with Other Substances

None known

MINERAL

Basic Information
Available from natural sources? Yes
Available from synthetic sources? No
Prescription required? No

Natural Sources

Bacon	Ham
Beef, dried and fresh	Margarine
Bread	Milk
Butter	Sardines, canned
Clams	Table salt (chief source
Green beans	of sodium)
	Tomatoes, canned

Note: In most commercially tinned vegetables, frozen foods and processed foods, salt is added to improve taste. "Highly processed" foods (also high in sodium) include soups, bouillon, pickles, potato crisps, snack foods, ham.

Reasons to Use

• Helps regulate water balance in body.
• Plays a crucial role in maintaining blood pressure.
• Aids muscle contraction and nerve transmission.
• Regulates body's acid-base balance.

Unproved Speculated Benefits

• Lowers fevers
• Prevents heatstroke

Who Needs Additional Amounts?

• People with a chronic wasting illness, excess stress for long periods or who have recently undergone surgery.
• Anyone who suffers prolonged loss of body fluids from vomiting or diarrhoea.
• Those with Addison's disease.
• People suffering congestive heart failure who take diuretics.
• Those who drink water excessively for prolonged periods. (This is usually a psychiatric condition.)
• People who suffer some types of cancers of the adrenal glands.
• Anyone who suffers infections with high fever.

• Those who have excessive sweating (rare cause).
• People who use diuretics.
• Anyone who cannot eat or drink, such as those with stroke or gastrointestinal upset.
• Those with chronic kidney disease.

Deficiency Symptoms

• Muscle and stomach cramps
• Nausea
• Fatigue
• Mental apathy
• Muscle twitching and cramping (usually in legs)
• Appetite loss

Unproved Speculated Symptoms

• Neuralgia

Lab Tests to Detect Deficiency

• Serum sodium

Dosage and Usage Information

Recommended Dietary Allowance (RDA):
No RDA has been established. Estimated safe intake per day given below.

Age	Estimated Safe Intake
0–6 months	0.115–0.35g
6–12 months	0.25–0.75g
1–3 years	0.325–0.975g
4–6 years	0.45–1.35g
7–10 years	0.60–1.80g
11–17 years	0.90–2.270g
18+ years	1.10–3.30g

What this mineral does:
• As an electrolyte, sodium is present in all body cells. Its most important function is to regulate the balance of water inside and outside cells.

Miscellaneous information:
• We consume most of our sodium as sodium chloride—ordinary table salt.
• The most common problem with sodium in a healthy person is "too-much," rather than "too-little." A typical diet contains 3,000 to 12,000mg of sodium a day. For normal function, we only need 3,000mg.

»→

Sodium, Continued

- Excessive amounts of sodium can be a major factor in development of high blood pressure. Decreasing sodium intake helps control high blood pressure.

Available as:
- Sodium-chloride tablets, but these may cause stomach distress and an overload on the kidneys.

 Warnings and Precautions

Don't take if you have:
- Congestive heart failure.
- Hepatic cirrhosis.
- Hypertension.
- Oedema from any cause.
- A family history of high blood pressure.

Consult your doctor if you have:
- Any heart or blood-vessel disease.
- Bleeding problems.
- Epilepsy.
- Kidney disease.

Over age 55:
- No special problems expected if healthy.

Pregnancy:
- Dietary restriction of sodium in healthy women during pregnancy is not recommended.
- Don't take megadoses.

Breast-feeding:
- Dietary restriction of sodium in healthy women during lactation is not recommended.
- Don't take megadoses.

Effect on lab tests:
- None expected.

Storage:
- Store in cool, dry place away from direct light, but don't freeze.
- Store safely out of reach of children.
- Don't store in bathroom medicine cabinet. Heat and moisture may change action of mineral.

Others:
- Too little sodium occurs almost entirely in people desperately ill with dehydration or those recovering from recent surgery or after excessive sweating from heavy physical activity in a hot environment.
- Proper replacement of sodium deficiencies requires care by your doctor and frequent laboratory studies.

 Overdose/Toxicity

Signs and symptoms:
- Tissue swelling (oedema), stupor, coma.

What to do:
For symptoms of overdosage: Discontinue mineral, and consult doctor. Also see *Adverse Reactions or Side Effects* section below.
For accidental overdosage (such as child taking entire bottle): Dial 999 (emergency).

 Adverse Reactions or Side Effects

Reaction or effect	What to do
With excessive amounts of sodium:	
Anxiety	Discontinue. Call doctor immediately.
Confusion	Discontinue. Call doctor immediately.
Edema	Discontinue. Call doctor immediately.
Nausea	Discontinue. Call doctor immediately.
Restlessness	Discontinue. Call doctor immediately.
Vomiting	Seek emergency treatment.
Weakness	Discontinue. Call doctor immediately.

 Interaction with Medicine, Vitamins or Minerals

None expected

 Interaction with Other Substances

None known

Sulphur

Basic Information

Available from natural sources? Yes
Available from synthetic sources? No
Prescription required? No

Natural Sources

Cabbage	Fish
Clams	Lean beef
Beans, dried	Milk
Eggs	Wheat germ

Reasons to Use

- Plays a role in oxidation-reduction reactions.
- Aids bile secretion in liver.

Unproved Speculated Benefits

- Extends life span.
- Protects against toxic substances.

Who Needs Additional Amounts?

- Supplements probably not needed. No recorded deficiency states.

Deficiency Symptoms

- None

Unproved Speculated Symptoms

- None

Lab Tests to Detect Deficiency

- None available, except for experimental uses.

Dosage and Usage Information

Recommended Dietary Allowance (RDA):
No RDA has been established.

What this mineral does:
- Sulphur is part of the chemical structure of cysteine, methionine, taurine, glutathione.

Available as:
- A constituent of many multivitamin/mineral preparations.

Warnings and Precautions

Don't take if you:
- No known contraindications.

Consult your doctor if you have:
- No known contraindications.

Over age 55:
- No known contraindications.

Pregnancy:
- No known contraindications.
- Don't take megadoses.

Breast-feeding:
- No known contraindications.
- Don't take megadoses.

Effect on lab tests:
- None expected.

Storage:
- Store in cool, dry place away from direct light, but don't freeze.
- Store safely out of reach of children.
- Don't store in bathroom medicine cabinet. Heat and moisture may change action of mineral.

Overdose/Toxicity

Signs and symptoms:
Unlikely to threaten life or cause significant symptoms.

What to do:
For symptoms of overdosage: Discontinue mineral, and consult doctor.
For accidental overdosage (such as child taking entire bottle): Dial 999 (emergency).

Adverse Reactions or Side Effects

None known

Sulphur, Continued

 Interaction with Medicine, Vitamins or Minerals

None known

 Interaction with Other Substances

Tobacco decreases absorption. Smokers may require supplementary sulphur.

Basic Information

Available from natural sources? Yes
Available from synthetic sources? No
Prescription required? No

Natural Sources

Fish

Reasons to Use

• Plays role in metabolism of bones and teeth.

Unproved Speculated Benefits

• Aids in preventing heart attacks.

Who Needs Additional Amounts?

• Supplements probably not needed. No recorded deficiency states.

Deficiency Symptoms

• A vanadium-deficient diet fed to laboratory animals resulted in impaired reproductive ability and increased infant mortality.

Unproved Speculated Symptoms

• None

Lab Tests to Detect Deficiency

• None available, except for experimental purposes.

Dosage and Usage Information

Recommended Dietary Allowance (RDA):
No RDA has been established. Estimated requirements for adults are 0.1 to 0.3mg/day. Dietary intake of vanadium averages 4mg/day.

What this mineral does:
• Unknown in humans, but believed to be essential.

Miscellaneous information:
• Even the most nutritionally inadequate diet contains sufficient quantities to prevent deficiency.

Available as:
• Capsules: Swallow whole with full glass of liquid. Don't chew or crush. Take with meals or 1 to 1-1/2 hours after meals unless otherwise directed by your doctor.
• A constituent of many multivitamin/mineral preparations.

Warnings and Precautions

Don't take if you:
• No known contraindications.

Consult your doctor if you have:
• No known contraindications.

Over age 55:
• No known contraindications.

Pregnancy:
• No known contraindications.
• Don't take megadoses.

Breast-feeding:
• No known contraindications.
• Don't take megadoses.

Effect on lab tests:
• None expected.

Storage:
• Store in cool, dry place away from direct light, but don't freeze.
• Store safely out of reach of children.
• Don't store in bathroom medicine cabinet. Heat and moisture may change action of mineral.

Overdose/Toxicity

Signs and symptoms:
Unlikely to threaten life or cause significant symptoms.

What to do:
For symptoms of overdosage: Discontinue mineral, and consult doctor.
For accidental overdosage (such as child taking entire bottle): Dial 999 (emergency).

MINERAL

Vanadium, Continued

 Adverse Reactions or Side Effects

None expected

 Interaction with Medicine, Vitamins or Minerals

Interacts with	Combined effect
Chromium	Chromium and vanadium may interfere with each other.

 Interaction with Other Substances

Tobacco decreases absorption. Smokers may require supplementary vanadium.

Basic Information
Available from natural sources? Yes
Available from synthetic sources? No
Prescription required? No

Natural Sources

Beef, lean	Pork
Chicken heart	Sesame seeds
Egg yolk	Soya beans
Fish	Sunflower seeds
Herring	Turkey
Lamb	Wheat bran
Maple syrup	Wheat germ
Milk	Whole-grain products
Molasses, black-strap	Yeast
Oysters	

Reasons to Use

- Functions as anti-oxidant.
- Maintains normal taste and smell.
- Promotes normal growth and development.
- Aids wound healing.
- Promotes normal fetal growth.
- Helps synthesize DNA and RNA.
- Promotes cell division, cell repair, cell growth.
- Maintains normal level of vitamin A in blood.

Unproved Speculated Benefits

- Relieves angina.
- Relieves cirrhosis of liver.
- Boosts immunity.
- Prevents cancer.
- Increases male potency and sex drive.
- Enhances other treatments for diabetes mellitus.
- Treats acne.
- Treats arthritis.
- Retards aging.

Who Needs Additional Amounts?

- Anyone with inadequate caloric or nutritional dietary intake or increased nutritional requirements, such as vegetarians.
- Preschool children.
- Older people (over 55 years).
- Pregnant or breast-feeding women.
- Those who abuse alcohol or other drugs.
- People with a chronic wasting illness, excess stress for long periods or those who have recently undergone surgery.
- Those with a portion of the gastrointestinal tract surgically removed.
- People with recent severe burns or injuries.
- Anyone taking diuretics (water pills) for any reason, such as high blood pressure, congestive heart failure, liver disease.
- Women taking oral contraceptives.
- Those who live in areas where soil is deficient in zinc.

Deficiency Symptoms

Moderate deficiency:
- Loss of taste and smell
- Suboptimal growth in children
- Alopecia
- Rashes
- Multiple skin lesions
- Glossitis (See Glossary)
- Stomatitis (See Glossary)
- Blepharitis (See Glossary)
- Paronychia (See Glossary)
- Sterility
- Low sperm count
- Delayed wound healing

Serious deficiency:
- Delayed bone maturation
- Enlarged spleen or liver
- Decreased size of testicles
- Testicular function less than normal
- Decreased growth or dwarfism

Unproved Speculated Symptoms

- Infertility
- Symptoms of immunodeficient diseases, such as recurrent infections, fatigue, diarrhoea, unexplained weight loss, unexplained fever, swollen lymph glands

Lab Tests to Detect Deficiency

- Serum zinc (by atomic absorption spectroscopy)

»»

MINERAL

Dosage and Usage Information

Recommended Dietary Allowance (RDA):
Estimate of adequate daily intake by the Food and Nutrition Board of the National Research Council, 1980 (See Glossary).

Age	RDA
0–6 months	3mg
6–12 months	5mg
1–10 years	10mg
11+ years	15mg
Pregnant	+5mg
Lactating	+10mg

What this mineral does:
• Zinc is a part of the molecular structure of 80 or more known enzymes. These particular enzymes work with red blood cells to move carbon dioxide from tissues to lungs.

Miscellaneous information:
• Zinc toxicity from inhalation is rare but can occur in the following industries and occupations—alloy manufacturing, brass foundry, bronze foundry, electric-fuse manufacturing, gas welding, electroplating, galvanizing, paint manufacturing, metal cutting, metal spraying, rubber manufacturing, roof manufacturing, zinc manufacturing.
• If you take zinc supplements, take with food to decrease gastric irritation.

Available as:
• Tablets: Swallow whole with full glass of liquid. Don't chew or crush. Take with meals or 1 to 1-1/2 hours after meals unless otherwise directed by your doctor.
• A constituent of many multivitamin/mineral preparations.

Warnings and Precautions

Don't take if you have:
• Stomach or duodenal ulcers.

Consult your doctor if you have:
• Plans to take more than the manufacturer's recommended dose.
• To take any calcium supplement or tetracycline drugs. Zinc may interfere with absorption of these medicines.

Over age 55:
• Deficiency more likely.

Pregnancy:
• Many diets are marginally low in zinc and may not supply the zinc estimated to be required during pregnancy. Ask your doctor about supplementation.
• *Overconsumption* is dangerous and can lead to premature labour or stillbirth.
• Don't take megadoses.

Breast-feeding:
• Some diets are marginally low in zinc and may not supply the zinc estimated to be required while breast-feeding. Ask your doctor about supplementation.
• Don't take megadoses.

Effect on lab tests:
• Decreases high-density lipoprotein levels in young males. High-density lipoproteins decrease risk of coronary-artery disease.
• High doses decrease copper in blood.

Storage:
• Store in cool, dry place away from direct light, but don't freeze.
• Store safely out of reach of children.
• Don't store in bathroom medicine cabinet. Heat and moisture may change action of mineral.

Overdose

Signs and symptoms:
Toxicity at RDA doses highly unlikely. Toxic symptoms are extremes of the *Adverse Reactions or Side Effects* listed below. Overdose produces drowsiness, lethargy, lightheadedness, difficulty writing, staggering gait, restlessness, excessive vomiting leading to dehydration.

What to do:
For symptoms of overdosage: Discontinue mineral, and consult doctor. Also see *Adverse Reactions or Side Effects* section below.
For accidental overdosage (such as child taking entire bottle): Dial 999 (emergency).

Adverse Reactions or Side Effects

Reaction or effect	What to do
Abdominal pain	Seek emergency treatment.
Abnormal bleeding	Seek emergency treatment.
Gastric ulceration (burning pain in upper chest relieved by food or antacid)	Discontinue. Call doctor immediately.
Mild diarrhoea	Discontinue. Call doctor when convenient.
Nausea	Discontinue. Call doctor immediately.
Vomiting	Discontinue. Call doctor immediately.

 ## Interaction with Medicine, Vitamins or Minerals

Interacts with	Combined effect
Calcium	Interferes with calcium absorption.
Copper	Decreases absorption of copper. Large doses of zinc must be taken to produce this effect.
Cortisone drugs	May interfere with lab tests measuring zinc.
Diuretics	Increases zinc excretion. Requires taking greater amounts.
Iron	Decreases absorption of iron. Large doses of zinc must be taken to produce this effect.
Oral contraceptives	Lowers zinc blood levels.
Tetracycline	Decreases amount of tetracycline absorbed into bloodstream. Zinc and tetracycline should *not* be mixed. Take at least 2 hours apart.
Vitamin A	Assists in absorption of vitamin A.

 ## Interaction with Other Substances

Alcohol, even in moderate amounts, can increase the excretion of zinc in urine and can impair body's ability to combine zinc into its proper enzyme combinations in the liver.

Beverages
- Coffee should not be consumed at the same time as zinc because it may decrease absorption of zinc.

Amino Acids and Nucleic Acids

Amino acids are the 20 essential amino-acid molecules necessary for the body to synthesize proteins. These chemical molecules participate in building of all living structures.

Recent medical experiments suggest certain amino acids play a vital role in the central nervous system at transmission sites between nerve cells. They are called *neurotransmitters*. In addition, reports suggest some amino acids may protect against cancer and stimulate the immune system. This remains to be proved.

Amino acids listed in this book are available as supplements. Their usefulness as components of our bodies is unquestioned. Their usefulness as supplements remains to be proved.

Nucleic acids are large molecules encoded in the genes and are part of each living cell. They determine what kind of life form a cell will be, such as human, plant or animal. The use of nucleic acids is based on the unproved theory that an extra amount gives added life to "worn-out" cells and tissues.

Nucleic acids taken orally do no good because they are changed or destroyed in the intestinal tract before they can be absorbed. Injecting cells from young animals into our bodies is a dangerous practice. An injection of animal protein into humans may cause anaphylaxis—a serious allergic reaction causing immediate itching, severe drop in blood pressure, loss of consciousness and sometimes death.

Adenosine

Basic Information

Adenosine is a nucleic acid.
Available from natural sources? Yes
Available from synthetic sources? No
Prescription required? No

Natural Sources

All foods

Reasons to Use

- Functions as essential part of every living cell, but supplementary products taken orally are useless.

Unproved Speculated Benefits

Note: These claims are from one researcher, the late Dr. Benjamin Frank. The scientific community does not accept his results because they have never been proved in other studies.
Injectable form:
- Treats congestive heart failure.
- Relieves angina (See Glossary).
- Increases vigour.
- Permits greater exercise endurance.
- Increases life span.
- Improves liver function.
- Enhances memory.
- Relieves problems caused by emphysema.
- Improves skin quality.

Who Needs Additional Amounts?

- No one

Deficiency Symptoms

- None

Unproved Speculated Symptoms

- Aging
- All forms of degenerative diseases

Lab Tests to Detect Deficiency

- None available, except for experimental purposes.

Dosage and Usage Information

Recommended Dietary Allowance (RDA):
No RDA has been established. Oral supplements are destroyed in the intestine and do not get absorbed. Therefore they can exert *no* influence.

What this nucleic acid does:
- Nucleic acids form the substance of DNA (desoxyribonucleic acid) and RNA (ribonucleic acid). "Messages" are transferred because of the actions of the purine and pyrimidine bases of DNA and RNA, which include adenine, guanine, cytosine and thymine. These messages form encoded genetic instructions that guide the development of all living cells.
- Supplements have been advertised for oral use, topical use (as in cosmetics) and injectable use. "Cellular therapy," once popular in Europe, is the practice of injecting preparations of cells from young animals into humans with the false promise of replacing "worn-out" tissues in aging human bodies. These treatments are extremely expensive, dangerous and have been completely discredited.
- No positive effects can be possible with oral forms.

Available as:
- Tablets and capsules: Swallow whole with full glass of liquid. Don't chew or crush. Take with meals or 1 to 1-1/2 hours after meals unless otherwise directed by your doctor. These are normally found in health-food shops.
- Injectable forms are administered by doctor or nurse.

Warnings and Precautions

Don't take if you:
- Have any medical problem listed under *Unproved Speculated Benefits.* There may be safer, more-effective treatments.

Consult your doctor if you have:
- Any medical problems listed under *Unproved Speculated Benefits.* There may be safer, more-effective treatments.

⟫▶

Over age 55:
• There may be safer, more-effective treatments.

Pregnancy:
• There may be safer, more-effective treatments.
• Don't take megadoses.

Breast-feeding:
• There may be safer, more-effective treatments.
• Don't take megadoses.

Effect on lab tests:
• None known.

Storage:
• Store in cool, dry place away from direct light, but don't freeze.
• Store safely out of reach of children.
• Don't store in bathroom medicine cabinet. Heat and moisture may change action of nucleic acid.

Others:
• Injectable forms can cause serious reactions, including anaphylaxis, serum sickness, transfer of disease

 Overdose/Toxicity

Signs and symptoms:
None for oral forms. For injectable forms, see *Adverse Reactions or Side Effects* section below.

What to do:
For symptoms of overdosage: Discontinue nucleic acid, and consult doctor. Also see *Adverse Reactions or Side Effects* section below.
For accidental overdosage (such as child taking entire bottle): Dial 999 (emergency).

 Adverse Reactions or Side Effects

Reaction or effect	What to do
For injectable forms:	
Anaphylaxis—symptoms include immediate severe itching, paleness, low blood pressure, fainting, coma	Yell for help. Don't leave victim. Begin CPR (cardio-pulmonary resuscitation), mouth-to-mouth breathing and external cardiac massage. Have someone call 999 (Emergency). Don't stop CPR until help arrives.
Serum sickness, characterized by fever, oedema of face and ankles, decreased urine output, skin rash	Seek emergency treatment.
Many viral illnesses, such as hepatitis or AIDS, if material is derived from human tissue or injected with contaminated needle	Discontinue. Call doctor immediately.

 Interaction with Medicine, Vitamins or Minerals

None known

 Interaction with Other Substances

None known

NUCLEIC ACID

Arginine

Basic Information

Arginine is an amino acid.
Available from natural sources? Yes
Available from synthetic sources? Yes
Prescription required? No

Natural Sources

Brown rice
Carob
Chocolate
Nuts
Oatmeal
Popcorn

Raisins
Raw cereals
Sesame seeds
Sunflower seeds
Whole-wheat products

Reasons to Use

- Functions as building block of all proteins.
- Stimulates human-growth hormone.

Unproved Speculated Benefits

- Increases metabolism in fat cells to decrease obesity.
- Builds muscle.
- Speeds wound healing.
- Stimulates immune system.
- Inhibits cancer.
- Increases sperm count in males.

Who Needs Additional Amounts?

- Single amino-acid deficiencies are unknown except in people on crash diets consisting of only a few foods.
- Amino-acid deficiencies appear more commonly as a result of total protein deficiency, which is rare in Britain.
- Anyone with inadequate caloric or nutritional dietary intake or increased nutritional requirements.
- Those with inadequate protein dietary intake.
- Children, pregnant or lactating women who are vegan vegetarians.
- People with recent severe burns or injuries.
- Premature infants.

Deficiency Symptoms

- None expected

Unproved Speculated Symptoms

- Male infertility

Lab Tests to Detect Deficiency

- None available, except for experimental purposes.

Dosage and Usage Information

Recommended Dietary Allowance (RDA):
No RDA has been established.

What this amino acid does:
- Provides part of all proteins.

Miscellaneous information:
- Arginine has been reported to increase the activity of some herpes viruses and inhibit others.
- If you take arginine as a supplement, take it on an empty stomach before retiring at night.
- Poorly nourished people have a greater chance of adverse side effects from taking amino-acid supplements, including an amino-acid imbalance.
- The poorer the diet, the greater the chance of an amino-acid supplement creating a harmful combination.

Available as:
- Tablets or capsules: Swallow whole with full glass of liquid. Don't chew or crush. Take with meals or 1 to 1-1/2 hours after meals unless otherwise directed by your doctor.
- Powder for oral solution: Dissolve powder in cold water or juice. Take with meals or 1 to 1-1/2 hours after meals unless otherwise directed by your doctor.

Warnings and Precautions

Don't take if you:
- Are a child or adolescent not fully grown.
- Are allergic to any food protein, such as eggs, milk, wheat.
- Are at risk of poor nutrition for any reason.

⇛➡

Arginine

Consult your doctor if you have:
- Any bone disease.
- Herpes infection (genital or oral).

Over age 55:
- Don't take amino-acid supplements if you are healthy.

Pregnancy:
- Don't take amino-acid supplements if you are healthy and eat an adequate diet.
- Don't take megadoses.

Breast-feeding:
- Don't take amino-acid supplements if you are healthy.
- Don't take megadoses.

Effect on lab tests:
- None known.

Storage:
- Store in cool, dry place away from direct light, but don't freeze.
- Store safely out of reach of children.
- Don't store in bathroom medicine cabinet. Heat and moisture may change action of amino acid.

Others:
- Children and adolescents should *not* take any arginine supplement. It may cause bone deformities.

Overdose/Toxicity

Signs and symptoms:
Unlikely to threaten life or cause significant symptoms.

What to do:
For symptoms of overdosage: Discontinue amino acid, and consult doctor. Also see *Adverse Reactions or Side Effects* section below.
For accidental overdosage (such as child taking entire bottle): Dial 999 (emergency).

Adverse Reactions or Side Effects

Reaction or effect	What to do
Diarrhoea (from large doses)	Decrease dose or discontinue.
Nausea (from large doses)	Decrease dose or discontinue.

Interaction with Medicine, Vitamins or Minerals

None known

Interaction with Other Substances

None known

AMINO ACID

DNA & RNA

Basic Information
DNA and RNA are nucleic acids.
Available from natural sources? Yes
Available from synthetic sources? No
Prescription required? No

Natural Sources

All foods

Reasons to Use

- Functions as essential part of every living cell, but supplementary products taken orally are useless.

Unproved Speculated Benefits

Note: These claims are from one researcher, the late Dr. Benjamin Frank. The scientific community does not accept his results because they have never been proved in other studies.
Injectable form:
- Treats congestive heart failure.
- Relieves angina (See Glossary).
- Increases vigour.
- Permits greater exercise endurance.
- Increases life span.
- Improves liver function.
- Enhances memory.
- Relieves problems caused by emphysema.
- Improves skin quality.

Who Needs Additional Amounts?

- No one

Deficiency Symptoms

- None

Unproved Speculated Symptoms

- Aging
- All forms of degenerative diseases

Lab Tests to Detect Deficiency

- None available, except for experimental purposes.

Dosage and Usage Information

Recommended Dietary Allowance (RDA):
No RDA has been established. Oral supplements are destroyed in the intestine and do not get absorbed. Therefore they can exert *no* influence.

What this nucleic acid does:
- Nucleic acids form the substance of DNA (desoxyribonucleic acid) and RNA (ribonucleic acid). "Messages" are transferred because of the actions of the purine and pyrimidine bases of DNA and RNA, which include adenine, guanine, cytosine and thymine. These messages form encoded genetic instructions that guide the development of all living cells.
- Supplements have been advertised for oral use, topical use (as in cosmetics) and injectable use. "Cellular therapy," once popular in Europe, is the practice of injecting preparations of cells from young animals into humans with the false promise of replacing "worn-out" tissues in aging human bodies. These treatments are extremely expensive, dangerous and have been completely discredited.
- No positive effects can be possible with oral forms.

Available as:
- Tablets and capsules: Swallow whole with full glass of liquid. Don't chew or crush. Take with meals or 1 to 1-1/2 hours after meals unless otherwise directed by your doctor. These are normally found in health-food shops.
- Injectable forms are administered by doctor or nurse.

Warnings and Precautions

Don't take if you:
- Have any medical problem listed under *Unproved Speculated Benefits.* There may be safer, more-effective treatments.

Consult your doctor if you have:
- Any medical problem listed under *Unproved Speculated Benefits.* There may be safer, more-effective treatments.

Over age 55:
• There may be safer, more-effective treatments.

Pregnancy:
• There may be safer, more-effective treatments.
• Don't take megadoses.

Breast-feeding:
• There may be safer, more-effective treatments.
• Don't take megadoses.

Effect on lab tests:
• None known.

Storage:
• Store in cool, dry place away from direct light, but don't freeze.
• Store safely out of reach of children.
• Don't store in bathroom medicine cabinet. Heat and moisture may change action of nucleic acid.

Others:
• Injectable forms can cause serious reactions, including anaphylaxis, serum sickness and transfer of disease.

 ## Overdose/Toxicity

Signs and symptoms:
None for oral forms. For injectable forms, see *Adverse Reactions or Side Effects* section below.

What to do:
For symptoms of overdosage: Discontinue nucleic acid, and consult doctor. Also see *Adverse Reactions or Side Effects* section below.
For accidental overdosage (such as child taking entire bottle): Dial 999 (emergency).

 ## Adverse Reactions or Side Effects

Reaction or effect	What to do
For injectable forms:	
Anaphylaxis— symptoms include immediate severe itching, paleness, low blood pressure, fainting, coma	Yell for help. Don't leave victim. Begin CPR (cardio-pulmonary resuscitation), mouth-to-mouth breathing and external cardiac massage. Have someone call 999 (Emergency). Don't stop CPR until help arrives.
Serum sickness, characterized by fever, oedema of face and ankles, decreased urine output, skin rash	Seek emergency treatment.
Many viral illnesses, such as hepatitis or AIDS, if material is derived from human tissue or injected with contaminated needle	Discontinue. Call doctor immediately.

 ## Interaction with Medicine, Vitamins or Minerals

None known

 ## Interaction with Other Substances

None known

Inosine

Basic Information

Inosine is a nucleic acid.
Available from natural sources? Yes
Available from synthetic sources? No
Prescription required? No

Natural Sources

All foods

Reasons to Use

- Functions as essential part of every living cell, but supplementary products taken orally are useless.

Unproved Speculated Benefits

Note: These claims are from one researcher, the late Dr. Benjamin Frank. The scientific community does not accept his results because they have never been proved in other studies.

Injectable form:
- Treats congestive heart failure.
- Relieves angina (See Glossary).
- Increases vigour.
- Permits greater exercise endurance.
- Increases life span.
- Improves liver function.
- Enhances memory.
- Relieves problems caused by emphysema.
- Improves skin quality.

Who Needs Additional Amounts?

- No one

Deficiency Symptoms

- None

Unproved Speculated Symptoms

- Aging
- All forms of degenerative diseases

Lab Tests to Detect Deficiency

- None available, except for experimental purposes.

Dosage and Usage Information

Recommended Dietary Allowance (RDA):
No RDA has been established. Oral supplements are destroyed in the intestine and do not get absorbed. Therefore they can exert *no* influence.

What this nucleic acid does:
- Nucleic acids form the substance of DNA (desoxyribonucleic acid) and RNA (ribonucleic acid). "Messages" are transferred because of the actions of the purine and pyrimidine bases of DNA and RNA, which include adenine, guanine, cytosine and thymine. These messages form encoded genetic instructions that guide the development of all living cells.
- Supplements have been advertised for oral use, topical use (as in cosmetics) and injectable use. "Cellular therapy," once popular in Europe, is the practice of injecting preparations of cells from young animals into humans with the false promise of replacing "worn-out" tissues in aging human bodies. These treatments are extremely expensive, dangerous and have been completely discredited.
- No positive effects can be possible with oral forms.

Available as:
- Tablets and capsules: Swallow whole with full glass of liquid. Don't chew or crush. Take with meals or 1 to 1-1/2 hours after meals unless otherwise directed by your doctor. These are normally found in health-food shops.
- Injectable forms are administered by doctor or nurse.

Warnings and Precautions

Don't take if you:
- Have any medical problems listed under *Unproved Speculated Benefits.* There may be safer, more-effective treatments.

Consult your doctor if you have:
- Any medical problems listed under *Unproved Speculated Benefits.* There may be safer, more-effective treatments.

»▶

Over age 55:
• There may be safer, more-effective treatments.

Pregnancy:
• There may be safer, more-effective treatments.
• Don't take megadoses.

Breast-feeding:
• There may be safer, more-effective treatments.
• Don't take megadoses.

Effect on lab tests:
• None known.

Storage:
• Store in cool, dry place away from direct light, but don't freeze.
• Store safely out of reach of children.
• Don't store in bathroom medicine cabinet. Heat and moisture may change action of nucleic acid.

Others:
• Injectable forms can cause serious reactions, including anaphylaxis, serum sickness and transfer of disease.

 ## Overdose/Toxicity

Signs and symptoms:
None for oral forms. For injectable forms, see *Adverse Reactions or Side Effects* section below.

What to do:
For symptoms of overdosage: Discontinue nucleic acid, and consult doctor. Also see below.
For accidental overdosage (such as child taking entire bottle): Dial 999 (emergency).

 ## Adverse Reactions or Side Effects

Reaction or effect	What to do
For injectable forms:	
Anaphylaxis—symptoms include immediate severe itching, paleness, low blood pressure, fainting, coma	Yell for help. Don't leave victim. Begin CPR (cardio-pulmonary resuscitation), mouth-to-mouth breathing and external cardiac massage. Have someone call 999 (Emergency). Don't stop CPR until help arrives.
Serum sickness, characterized by fever, oedema of face and ankles, decreased urine output, skin rash	Seek emergency treatment.
Many viral illnesses, such as hepatitis or AIDS, if material is derived from human tissue or injected with contaminated needle	Discontinue. Call doctor immediately.

 ## Interaction with Medicine, Vitamins or Minerals

None known

 ## Interaction with Other Substances

None known

NUCLEIC ACID

L-Cysteine

Basic Information

L-cysteine is an amino acid.
Available from natural sources? Yes
Available from synthetic sources? Yes
Prescription required? No

Natural Sources

Dairy products
Eggs
Meat
Some cereals

Reasons to Use

- Functions as building block of all proteins.
- Eliminates certain toxic chemicals rendering them harmless (anti-oxidant).
- One of the amino acids containing sulphur in a form believed to inactivate free radicals. If so, it protects and preserves cells.

Unproved Speculated Benefits

- Helps build muscle.
- Burns fat.
- Protects against toxins and pollutants, including some found in cigarette smoke and alcohol.
- Combats arthritis.
- May participate in some forms of DNA repair and theoretically extend life span.

Who Needs Additional Amounts?

- Single amino-acid deficiencies are unknown except in people on crash diets consisting of only a few foods.
- Amino-acid deficiencies appear more commonly as a result of total protein deficiency, which is rare in Britain.
- Anyone with inadequate caloric or nutritional dietary intake or increased nutritional requirements.
- Those with inadequate protein dietary intake.
- Children, pregnant or breast-feeding women who are vegan vegetarians.
- People with recent severe burns or injuries.
- Premature infants.

Deficiency Symptoms

In moderate deficiencies:
- Slowed growth in children
- Low levels of essential proteins in blood

In severe deficiencies:
- Apathy
- Depigmentation of hair
- Oedema
- Lethargy
- Liver damage
- Loss of muscle and fat
- Skin lesions
- Weakness

Unproved Speculated Symptoms

- None

Lab Tests to Detect Deficiency

- None available, except for experimental purposes.

Dosage and Usage Information

Recommended Dietary Allowance (RDA):
No RDA has been established.

What this amino acid does:
- Provides part of all proteins.
- Functions in synthesis of glutathione, a substance that may neutralize environmental pollutants including tobacco.

Miscellaneous information:
- Poorly nourished people have a greater chance of adverse side effects from taking amino-acid supplements, including an amino-acid imbalance.
- The poorer the diet, the greater the chance of an amino-acid supplement creating a harmful combination.
- Take L-cysteine supplements with vitamin C. Take 2 to 3 times as much vitamin C as cysteine, milligram to milligram, as a precaution against kidney- and/or bladder-stone formation.

Available as:
- Capsules: Swallow whole with full glass of liquid. Don't chew or crush. Take with meals or 1 to 1-1/2 hours after meals unless otherwise directed by your doctor.

➤➤

Warnings and Precautions

Don't take if you:
- Are allergic to any food protein, such as eggs, milk, wheat.
- Are at risk of poor nutrition for any reason.
- Have diabetes.
- Are self-prescribing without medical supervision.

Consult your doctor if you have:
- Diabetes mellitus.

Over age 55:
- Don't take amino-acid supplements if you are healthy.

Pregnancy:
- Don't take amino-acid supplements if you are healthy.

Breast-feeding:
- Don't take amino-acid supplements if you are healthy.

Effect on lab tests:
- None known.

Storage:
- Store in cool, dry place away from direct light, but don't freeze.
- Store safely out of reach of children.
- Don't store in bathroom medicine cabinet. Heat and moisture may change action of amino acid.

 ## Overdose/Toxicity

Signs and symptoms:
Unlikely to threaten life or cause significant symptoms.

What to do:
For symptoms of overdosage: Discontinue amino acid, and consult doctor.
For accidental overdosage (such as child taking entire bottle): Dial 999 (emergency).

 ## Adverse Reactions or Side Effects

None expected

 ## Interaction with Medicine, Vitamins or Minerals

Interacts with	Combined effect
Monosodium-glutamate	L-cysteine may increase toxicity of monosodium-glutamate in individuals who suffer from the "Chinese-restaurant syndrome." Causes headache, dizziness, disorientation, burning sensations.
Vitamin C	Taken with L-cysteine, vitamin C helps prevent L-cysteine from converting to *cystine*, which may cause bladder and/or kidney stones.

 ## Interaction with Other Substances

None known

AMINO ACID

L-Lysine

Basic Information
L-lysine is an amino acid.
Available from natural sources? Yes
Available from synthetic sources? Yes
Prescription required? No

Natural Sources

Cheese
Eggs
Fish
Lima beans
Milk

Potatoes
Red meat
Soya products
Yeast

Reasons to Use

- Functions as essential building block of all proteins.
- Promotes growth, tissue repair and production of antibodies, hormones, enzymes.

Unproved Speculated Benefits

- Protects against some sexually transmissible herpes viruses.

Who Needs Additional Amounts?

- Single amino-acid deficiencies are unknown except in people on crash diets consisting of only a few foods.
- Amino-acid deficiencies appear more commonly as a result of total protein deficiency, which is rare in Britain.
- Anyone with inadequate caloric or nutritional dietary intake or increased nutritional requirements.
- Those with inadequate protein dietary intake.
- Children, pregnant or breast-feeding women who are vegan vegetarians.
- People with recent severe burns or injuries.
- Premature infants.

Deficiency Symptoms

In moderate deficiencies:
- Slowed growth in children
- Low levels of essential proteins in blood

In severe deficiencies:
- Apathy

- Depigmentation of hair
- Oedema
- Lethargy
- Liver damage
- Loss of muscle and fat
- Skin lesions
- Weakness

Unproved Speculated Symptoms

- None

Lab Tests to Detect Deficiency

- None available, except for experimental purposes.

Dosage and Usage Information

Recommended Dietary Allowance (RDA):
No RDA has been established.

What this amino acid does:
- This is one of eight essential amino acids that the body does not manufacture. All biological amino acids participate in the synthesis of proteins in animal bodies.

Miscellaneous information:
- There is no scientific evidence supplements are needed or helpful.
- Poorly nourished people have a greater chance of adverse side effects from taking amino-acid supplements, including an amino-acid imbalance.
- The poorer the diet, the greater the chance of an amino-acid supplement creating a harmful combination.

Available as:
- Capsules: Swallow whole with full glass of liquid. Don't chew or crush. Take with meals or 1 to 1-1/2 hours after meals unless otherwise directed by your doctor.
- A constituent of many multivitamin/mineral preparations.

Warnings and Precautions

Don't take if you:
- Are allergic to any food protein, such as eggs, milk, wheat.
- Are at risk of poor nutrition for any reason. »➜

- Have diabetes.
- Are self-prescribing without medical supervision.

Consult your doctor if you have:
- Diabetes mellitus.

Over age 55:
- Don't take amino-acid supplements if you are healthy.

Pregnancy:
- Don't take amino-acid supplements if you are healthy.

Breast-feeding:
- Don't take amino-acid supplements if you are healthy.

Effect on lab tests:
- None known.

Storage:
- Store in cool, dry place away from direct light, but don't freeze.
- Store safely out of reach of children.
- Don't store in bathroom medicine cabinet. Heat and moisture may change action of amino acid.

Overdose/Toxicity

Signs and symptoms:
Unlikely to threaten life or cause significant symptoms.

What to do:
For symptoms of overdosage: Discontinue amino acid, and consult doctor.
For accidental overdosage (such as child taking entire bottle): Dial 999 (emergency).

Adverse Reactions or Side Effects

None expected

Interaction with Medicine, Vitamins or Minerals

None expected

Interaction with Other Substances

None known

Methionine

Basic Information

Methionine is an amino acid.
Available from natural sources? Yes
Available from synthetic sources? Yes
Prescription required? No

Natural Sources

Eggs
Fish
Meat
Milk
Note: Not available from plant sources.

Reasons to Use

- Functions as building block of all proteins.
- Cysteine and taurine may rely on methionine for synthesis in the human body.

Unproved Speculated Benefits

- Helps eliminate fatty substances that might obstruct arteries, including those that supply the brain, heart, kidneys.

Who Needs Additional Amounts?

- Single amino-acid deficiencies are unknown except in people on crash diets consisting of only a few foods.
- Amino-acid deficiencies appear more commonly as a result of total protein deficiency, which is rare in Britain.
- Anyone with inadequate caloric or nutritional dietary intake or increased nutritional requirements.
- Those with inadequate protein dietary intake.
- Children, pregnant or breast-feeding women who are vegan vegetarians.
- People with recent severe burns or injuries.
- Premature infants.

Deficiency Symptoms

In moderate deficiencies:
- Slowed growth in children
- Low levels of essential proteins in blood

In severe deficiencies:
- Apathy
- Depigmentation of hair
- Oedema
- Lethargy
- Liver damage
- Loss of muscle and fat
- Skin lesions
- Weakness

Unproved Speculated Symptoms

- None

Lab Tests to Detect Deficiency

- None available, except for experimental purposes.

Dosage and Usage Information

Recommended Dietary Allowance (RDA):
No RDA has been established.

What this amino acid does:
- Provides part of all proteins.

Miscellaneous information:
- This sulphur-containing amino acid (like chlorine and taurine) may help eliminate fatty substances that could cause occlusion of vital arteries.
- Poorly nourished people have a greater chance of adverse side effects from taking amino-acid supplements, including an amino-acid imbalance.
- The poorer the diet, the greater the chance of an amino-acid supplement creating a harmful combination.

Available as:
- Tablets: Swallow whole with full glass of liquid. Don't chew or crush. Take with meals or 1 to 1-1/2 hours after meals unless otherwise directed by your doctor.
- Capsules: Swallow whole with full glass of liquid. Don't chew or crush. Take with or immediately after food to decrease stomach irritation.

➤➤➤

Warnings and Precautions

Don't take if you:
• Are allergic to any food protein, such as eggs, milk, wheat.
• Are at risk of poor nutrition for any reason.

Consult your doctor if you have:
• Self-prescribed methionine without medical supervision.

Over age 55:
• Don't take amino-acid supplements if you are healthy.

Pregnancy:
• Don't take amino-acid supplements if you are healthy.

Breast-feeding:
• Don't take amino-acid supplements if you are healthy.

Effect on lab tests:
• None known.

Storage:
• Store in cool, dry place away from direct light, but don't freeze.
• Store safely out of reach of children.
• Don't store in bathroom medicine cabinet. Heat and moisture may change action of amino acid.

Overdose/Toxicity

Signs and symptoms:
Unlikely to threaten life or cause significant symptoms.

What to do:
For symptoms of overdosage: Discontinue amino acid, and consult doctor.
For accidental overdosage (such as child taking entire bottle): Dial 999 (emergency).

Adverse Reactions or Side Effects

None expected

Interaction with Medicine, Vitamins or Minerals

None known

Interaction with Other Substances

None known

AMINO ACID

213

Orotate

Basic Information
Orotate is an nucleic acid.
Available from natural sources? Yes
Available from synthetic sources? No
Prescription required? No

 Natural Sources

All foods

 Reasons to Use

• Functions as essential part of every living cell, but supplementary products taken orally are useless.

 Unproved Speculated Benefits

Note: These claims are from one researcher, the late Dr. Benjamin Frank. The scientific community does not accept his results because they have never been proved in other studies.
Injectable form:
• Treats congestive heart failure.
• Relieves angina (See Glossary).
• Increases vigour.
• Permits greater exercise endurance.
• Increases life span.
• Improves liver function.
• Enhances memory.
• Improves emphysema.
• Improves skin quality.

 Who Needs Additional Amounts?

• No one

 Deficiency Symptoms

• None

 Unproved Speculated Symptoms

• Aging
• All forms of degenerative diseases

 Lab Tests to Detect Deficiency

• None available, except for experimental purposes.

 Dosage and Usage Information

Recommended Dietary Allowance (RDA):
No RDA has been established. Oral supplements are destroyed in the intestine and do not get absorbed. Therefore they can exert *no* influence.

What this nucleic acid does:
• Nucleic acids form the substance of DNA (desoxyribonucleic acid) and RNA (ribonucleic acid). "Messages" are transferred because of the actions of the purine and pyrimidine bases of DNA and RNA, which include adenine, guanine, cytosine and thymine. These messages form encoded genetic instructions that guide the development of all living cells.
• Supplements have been advertised for oral use, topical use (as in cosmetics) and injectable use. "Cellular therapy," once popular in Europe, is the practice of injecting preparations of cells from young animals into humans with the false promise of replacing "worn-out" tissues in aging human bodies. These treatments are extremely expensive, dangerous and have been completely discredited.
• No positive effects can be possible with oral forms.

Available as:
• Tablets and capsules: Swallow whole with full glass of liquid. Don't chew or crush. Take with meals or 1 to 1-1/2 hours after meals unless otherwise directed by your doctor. These are normally found in health-food shops.
• Injectable forms are administered by doctor or nurse.

 Warnings and Precautions

Don't take if you:
• Have any medical problem listed under *Unproved Speculated Benefits.* There may be safer, more-effective treatments.

Consult your doctor if you have:
• Any medical problem listed under *Unproved Speculated Benefits.* There may be safer, more-effective treatments.

»➤

Over age 55:
• There may be safer, more-effective treatments.

Pregnancy:
• There may be safer, more-effective treatments.
• Don't take megadoses.

Breast-feeding:
• There may be safer, more-effective treatments.
• Don't take megadoses.

Effect on lab tests:
• None known.

Storage:
• Store in cool, dry place away from direct light, but don't freeze.
• Store safely out of reach of children.
• Don't store in bathroom medicine cabinet. Heat and moisture may change action of nucleic acid.

Others:
• Injectable forms can cause serious reactions, including anaphylaxis, serum sickness, transfer of disease.

 Overdose/Toxicity

Signs and symptoms:
None for oral forms. For injectable forms, see *Adverse Reactions or Side Effects* section below.

What to do:
For symptoms of overdosage: Discontinue nucleic acid, and consult doctor. Also see *Adverse Reactions or Side Effects* section below.

For accidental overdosage (such as child taking entire bottle): Dial 999 (emergency).

 Adverse Reactions or Side Effects

Reaction or effect	What to do
For injectable forms:	
Anaphylaxis—symptoms include immediate severe itching, paleness, low blood pressure, fainting, coma	Yell for help. Don't leave victim. Begin CPR (cardio-pulmonary resuscitation), mouth-to-mouth breathing and external cardiac massage. Have someone call 999 (Emergency). Don't stop CPR until help arrives.
Serum sickness, characterized by fever, oedema of face and ankles, decreased urine output, skin rash	Seek emergency treatment.
Many viral illnesses, such as hepatitis or AIDS, if material is derived from human tissue or injected with contaminated needle	Discontinue. Call doctor immediately.

 Interaction with Medicine, Vitamins or Minerals

None known

 Interaction with Other Substances

None known

NUCLEIC ACID

Phenylalanine

Basic Information

Phenylalanine is an amino acid.
Available from natural sources? Yes
Available from synthetic sources? Yes
Prescription required? No

Natural Sources

Almonds	Non-fat dried milk
Avocado	Peanuts
Bananas	Pickled herring
Cheese	Pumpkin seeds
Cottage cheese	Sesame seeds
Lima beans	

Reasons to Use

- Functions as building block of all proteins.
- Can induce significant short-term increases of blood levels of noradrenaline, dopamine and adrenaline. May be harmful at times and helpful at others. Don't take without medical supervision!

Unproved Speculated Benefits

- Treats mental depression.
- Improves memory.
- Diminishes pain.
- Increases mental alertness.
- Promotes sexual interest.
- Releases hormones that suppress appetite.
- Treats Parkinson's disease.

Who Needs Additional Amounts?

- Single amino-acid deficiencies are unknown except in people on crash diets consisting of only a few foods.
- Amino-acid deficiencies appear more commonly as a result of total protein deficiency, which is rare in Britain.
- Anyone with inadequate caloric or nutritional dietary intake or increased nutritional requirements.
- Those with inadequate protein dietary intake.
- Children, pregnant or breast-feeding women who are vegan vegetarians.
- People with recent severe burns or injuries.
- Premature infants.

Deficiency Symptoms

In moderate deficiencies:
- Slowed growth in children
- Low levels of essential proteins in blood

In severe deficiencies:
- Apathy
- Depigmentation of hair
- Oedema
- Lethargy
- Liver damage
- Loss of muscle and fat
- Skin lesions
- Weakness

Unproved Speculated Symptoms

- Lack of sexual interest
- Impotence
- Poor memory
- Obesity

Lab Tests to Detect Deficiency

- None available, except for experimental purposes.

Dosage and Usage Information

Recommended Dietary Allowance (RDA):
No RDA has been established.

What this amino acid does:
- It is involved in production of dopamine and adrenaline, which affect transmission of impulses in the human brain and other parts of the nervous system.

Miscellaneous information:
- Supplements taken by healthy people will not make them healthier.
- Poorly nourished people have a greater chance of adverse side effects from taking amino-acid supplements, including an amino-acid imbalance.
- The poorer the diet, the greater the chance of an amino-acid supplement creating a harmful combination.

»»➤

Phenylalanine

Available as:
- Tablets: Swallow whole with full glass of liquid. Don't chew or crush. Take with meals or 1 to 1-1/2 hours after meals unless otherwise directed by your doctor.

Warnings and Precautions

Don't take if you:
- Are allergic to any food protein, such as eggs, milk, wheat.
- Are at risk of poor nutrition for any reason.
- Suffer from migraine headaches.
- Have phenylketonuria (PKU).
- Have pigmented malignant melanoma, a deadly form of skin cancer.
- Take any monamine oxidase inhibitor as an anti-depressant, including pargyline, isocarboxazid, phenelzine, procarbazine, tranylcypromine.

Consult your doctor if you have:
- High blood pressure.
- Self-medicated with phenylalanine for any reason without medical supervision.

Over age 55:
- Don't take amino-acid supplements if you are healthy.

Pregnancy:
- Don't take amino-acid supplements if you are healthy.

Breast-feeding:
- Don't take amino-acid supplements if you are healthy.

Effect on lab tests:
- None known.

Storage:
- Store in cool, dry place away from direct light, but don't freeze.
- Store safely out of reach of children.
- Don't store in bathroom medicine cabinet. Heat and moisture may change action of amino acid.

Others:
- Phenylalanine may cause high blood pressure to rise even higher.

Overdose/Toxicity

Signs and symptoms:
Unlikely to threaten life or cause significant symptoms.

What to do:
For symptoms of overdosage: Discontinue amino acid, and consult doctor. Also see *Adverse Reactions or Side Effects* section below.

For accidental overdosage (such as child taking entire bottle): Dial 999 (emergency).

Adverse Reactions or Side Effects

Reaction or effect	What to do
Lowers blood pressure	Discontinue. Call doctor immediately.
Raises blood pressure	Discontinue. Call doctor immediately.
Migraine headaches	Discontinue. Call doctor immediately.

Interaction with Medicine, Vitamins or Minerals

Interacts with	Combined effect
Anti-depressant drugs (containing monamine oxidase inhibitors)	Dangerous or life-threatening blood-pressure elevation.
Tyrosine	Additive effect with phenylalanine greatly increases chance of undesirable side effects.

Interaction with Other Substances

None known

AMINO ACID

Taurine

Basic Information

Taurine is an amino acid.
Available from natural sources? Yes
Available from synthetic sources? Yes
Prescription required? No

Natural Sources

Eggs
Fish
Meat
Milk
Note: Not available from plant sources.

Reasons to Use

- May be helpful in treating epilepsy.
- Functions as building block for all proteins.
- Helps regulate nervous system.
- Helps regulate muscle system.

Unproved Speculated Benefits

- May be essential for growth of infants, children, adolescents.

Who Needs Additional Amounts?

- Single amino-acid deficiencies are unknown except in people on crash diets consisting of only a few foods.
- Amino-acid deficiencies appear more commonly as a result of total protein deficiency, which is rare in Britain.
- Anyone with inadequate caloric or nutritional dietary intake or increased nutritional requirements.
- Those with inadequate protein dietary intake.
- Children, pregnant or breast-feeding women who are vegan vegetarians.
- People with recent severe burns or injuries.
- Premature infants.

Deficiency Symptoms

In moderate deficiencies:
- Slowed growth in children
- Low levels of essential proteins in blood

In severe deficiencies:
- Apathy
- Depigmentation of hair
- Oedema
- Lethargy
- Liver damage
- Loss of muscle and fat
- Skin lesions
- Weakness

Unproved Speculated Symptoms

- Vision problems

Lab Tests to Detect Deficiency

- None available, except for experimental purposes.

Dosage and Usage Information

Recommended Dietary Allowance (RDA):
No RDA has been established.

What this amino acid does:
- Provides part of all proteins.

Miscellaneous information:
- Taurine is synthesized from methionine and cystine.
- Supplements are not needed by healthy people who eat well-balanced diets.
- Poorly nourished people have a greater chance of adverse side effects from taking amino-acid supplements, including an amino-acid imbalance.
- The poorer the diet, the greater the chance of an amino-acid supplement creating a harmful combination.

Available as:
- Tablets: Swallow whole with full glass of liquid. Don't chew or crush. Take with meals or 1 to 1-1/2 hours after meals unless otherwise directed by your doctor.
- Capsules: Swallow whole with full glass of liquid. Don't chew or crush. Take with meals or 1 to 1-1/2 hours after meals unless otherwise directed by your doctor.

»»➤

Warnings and Precautions

Don't take if you:
- Are allergic to any food protein such as eggs, milk, wheat.
- Are at risk of poor nutrition for any reason.

Consult your doctor if you have:
- Epilepsy.
- Eye problems.
- Self-prescribed taurine without medical supervision.

Over age 55:
- Don't take amino-acid supplements if you are healthy.

Pregnancy:
- Don't take amino-acid supplements if you are healthy.

Breast-feeding:
- Don't take amino-acid supplements if you are healthy.

Effect on lab tests:
- None known.

Storage:
- Store in cool, dry place away from direct light, but don't freeze.
- Store safely out of reach of children.
- Don't store in bathroom medicine cabinet. Heat and moisture may change action of amino acid.

Overdose/Toxicity

Signs and symptoms:
Unlikely to threaten life or cause significant symptoms.

What to do:
For symptoms of overdosage: Discontinue amino acid, and consult doctor. Also see *Adverse Reactions or Side Effects* section below.
For accidental overdosage (such as child taking entire bottle): Dial 999 (emergency).

Adverse Reactions or Side Effects

Reaction or effect	What to do
Memory deficits	Discontinue. Call doctor when convenient.
May depress normal function of central nervous system	Discontinue. Call doctor immediately.

Interaction with Medicine, Vitamins or Minerals

Interacts with	Combined effect
Anti-convulsants	May decrease frequency of seizures.

Interaction with Other Substances

None known

Tryptophan

Basic Information

Tryptophan is an amino acid.
Available from natural sources? Yes
Available from synthetic sources? Yes
Prescription required? No

Natural Sources

Bananas	Meat
Cottage cheese	Milk
Dried dates	Peanuts
Fish	Turkey

Reasons to Use

• Functions as building block of all proteins.

Unproved Speculated Benefits

• Is an effective sleep aid.
• Acts as an anti-depressant.
• Helps treat cocaine addiction.
• Treats mania and aggressive behaviour.
• Decreases sensitivity to moderate pain.
• Suppresses appetite.

Who Needs Additional Amounts?

• Single amino-acid deficiencies are unknown except in people on crash diets consisting of only a few foods.
• Amino-acid deficiencies appear more commonly as a result of total protein deficiency, which is rare in Britain.
• Anyone with inadequate caloric or nutritional dietary intake or increased nutritional requirements.
• Those with inadequate protein dietary intake.
• Children, pregnant or breast-feeding women who are vegan vegetarians.
• People with recent severe burns or injuries.
• Premature infants.

Deficiency Symptoms

In moderate deficiencies:
• Slowed growth in children
• Low levels of essential proteins in blood

In severe deficiencies:
• Apathy
• Depigmentation of hair
• Oedema
• Lethargy
• Liver damage
• Loss of muscle and fat
• Skin lesions
• Weakness

Unproved Speculated Symptoms

• None

Lab Tests to Detect Deficiency

• None available except for experimental purposes.

Dosage and Usage Information

Recommended Dietary Allowance (RDA):
No RDA has been established.

What this amino acid does:
• Provides part of all proteins.
• Participates in biosynthesis of a neurotransmitter called *serotonin*. Serotonin may be an inducer of certain stages of sleep.

Available as:
• Capsules or tablets: Swallow whole with full glass of liquid. Don't chew or crush. Take with or immediately after food to decrease stomach irritation.

》▶

Warnings and Precautions

Don't take if you:
• Are allergic to any food protein, such as eggs, milk, wheat.
• Are at risk of poor nutrition for any reason.
• Are severely depressed. Other medicines to treat severe depression are more effective.

Consult your doctor if you:
• Take medicines to induce sleep.

Over age 55:
• Don't take amino-acid supplements if you are healthy.

Pregnancy:
• Don't take amino-acid supplements if you are healthy.

Breast-feeding:
• Don't take amino-acid supplements if you are healthy.

Effect on lab tests:
• None known.

Storage:
• Store in cool, dry place away from direct light, but don't freeze.
• Store safely out of reach of children.
• Don't store in bathroom medicine cabinet. Heat and moisture may change action of amino acid.

Others:
• In experimental animal studies of animals with vitamin B-6 deficiency, large doses of tryptophan caused bladder cancer.

 ## Overdose/Toxicity

Signs and symptoms:
Unlikely to threaten life or cause significant symptoms.

What to do:
For symptoms of overdosage: Discontinue amino acid, and consult doctor. Also see *Adverse Reactions or Side Effects* section below.
For accidental overdosage (such as child taking entire bottle): Dial 999 (emergency).

 ## Adverse Reactions or Side Effects

Reaction or effect	What to do
Fatigue	Discontinue. Call doctor when convenient.
Inertia	Discontinue. Call doctor when convenient.
Reduced vigour	Discontinue. Call doctor when convenient.

 ## Interaction with Medicine, Vitamins or Minerals

None known

 ## Interaction with Other Substances

None known

AMINO ACID

Tyrosine

Basic Information

Tyrosine is an amino acid.
Available from natural sources? Yes
Available from synthetic sources? Yes
Prescription required? No

Natural Sources

Almonds	Non-fat dried milk
Avocados	Peanuts
Bananas	Pickled herring
Cheese	Pumpkin seeds
Cottage cheese	Sesame seeds
Lima beans	

Reasons to Use

- Functions as building block of all proteins.
- Can induce significant short-term increases of blood levels of noradrenaline, dopamine and adrenaline. May be harmful at times and helpful at others. Don't take without medical supervision!

Unproved Speculated Benefits

- Treats mental depression.
- Improves memory.
- Diminishes pain.
- Increases mental alertness.
- Promotes sexual interest.
- Releases hormones that suppress appetite.
- Treats Parkinson's disease.

Who Needs Additional Amounts?

- Single amino-acid deficiencies are unknown except in people on crash diets consisting of only a few foods.
- Amino-acid deficiencies appear more commonly as a result of total protein deficiency, which is rare in Britain.
- Anyone with inadequate caloric or nutritional dietary intake or increased nutritional requirements.
- Those with inadequate protein dietary intake.
- Children, pregnant or breast-feeding women who are vegan vegetarians.
- People with recent severe burns or injuries.
- Premature infants.

Deficiency Symptoms

In moderate deficiencies:
- Slowed growth in children
- Low levels of essential proteins in blood

In severe deficiencies:
- Apathy
- Depigmentation of hair
- Oedema
- Lethargy
- Liver damage
- Loss of muscle and fat
- Skin lesions
- Weakness

Unproved Speculated Symptoms

- Lack of sexual interest
- Impotence
- Poor memory
- Obesity

Lab Tests to Detect Deficiency

- None available, except for experimental purposes.

Dosage and Usage Information

Recommended Dietary Allowance (RDA):
No RDA has been established.

What this amino acid does:
- It is involved in production of dopamine and adrenaline, which affect transmission of impulses in the human brain and other parts of the nervous system.

Miscellaneous information:
- Supplements taken by healthy people will not make them healthier.
- Poorly nourished people have a greater chance of adverse side effects from taking amino-acid supplements, including an amino-acid imbalance.
- The poorer the diet, the greater the chance of an amino-acid supplement creating a harmful combination.

Available as:
- Tablets: Swallow whole with full glass of liquid. Don't chew or crush. Take with meals or 1 to 1-1/2 hours after meals unless otherwise directed by your doctor.

Warnings and Precautions

Don't take if you:
- Are allergic to any food protein, such as eggs, milk, wheat.
- Are at risk of poor nutrition for any reason.
- Suffer from migraine headaches.
- Have phenylketonuria (PKU).
- Have pigmented malignant melanoma, a deadly form of skin cancer.
- Take any monamine oxidase inhibitor as an anti-depressant, including pargyline, isocarboxazid, phenelzine, procarbazine, tranylcypromine.

Consult your doctor if you have:
- High blood pressure.
- Self-medicated with tyrosine for any reason without medical supervision.

Over age 55:
- Don't take amino-acid supplements if you are healthy.

Pregnancy:
- Don't take amino-acid supplements if you are healthy.

Breast-feeding:
- Don't take amino-acid supplements if you are healthy.

Effect on lab tests:
- None known.

Storage:
- Store in cool, dry place away from direct light, but don't freeze.
- Store safely out of reach of children.
- Don't store in bathroom medicine cabinet. Heat and moisture may change action of amino acid.

Others:
- Tyrosine may cause high blood pressure to rise even higher at times.

 ## Overdose/Toxicity

Signs and symptoms:
Unlikely to threaten life or cause significant symptoms.

What to do:
For symptoms of overdosage: Discontinue amino acid, and consult doctor. Also see *Adverse Reactions or Side Effects* section below.
For accidental overdosage (such as child taking entire bottle): Dial 999 (emergency).

 ## Adverse Reactions or Side Effects

Reaction or effect	What to do
Lowers blood pressure	Discontinue. Call doctor immediately.
Raises blood pressure	Discontinue. Call doctor immediately.
Migraine headaches	Discontinue. Call doctor immediately.

 ## Interaction with Medicine, Vitamins or Minerals

Interacts with	Combined effect
Anti-depressant drugs (containing monamine oxidase inhibitors)	Dangerous or life-threatening blood-pressure elevation.
Phenylalanine	Additive effect with tyrosine greatly increases chance of undesirable side effects.

 ## Interaction with Other Substances

None known

AMINO ACID

Other Supplements

These substances may play important roles in human health and nutrition, but they are neither vitamins nor minerals. The selected supplements discussed in this book include fats and lipids and miscellaneous supplements.

Fats, along with carbohydrates and proteins, make up our daily food. There has been much publicity regarding the potential dangers of fats in our diet, particularly the dangers of cholesterol, low-density lipoproteins and too much total fat intake. The discussion of all these important items is beyond the scope of this book and is not attempted. I've focussed on a few fatty acids that are making headlines. These include choline, lecithin, gamma-linolenic acid (evening primrose oil), inositol and omega-3 fatty acids (fish oil).

This section also describes what is known and not known about a number of supplements that are widely touted as important to human nutrition. These substances include superoxide dismutase, wheatgrass, barley grass and dietary fibre.

Acidophilus

Basic Information

Acidophilus is a bacterium found in yogurt, kefir and other products.
Chemical this supplements contains:
Enzymes, to aid digestion

Known Effects

- Helps maintain normal bacteria balance in lower intestines.
- Kills monilia, yeast or fungus on contact.

Miscellaneous information:
- Acidophilus is made by fermenting milk using *lactobaccillus acidophilus* and other bacteria.
- It is available as a liquid, in capsules or in milk products, such as yogurt or kefir.

Unproved Speculated Benefits

- Lowers cholesterol.
- Clears up skin problems.
- Helps prevent vaginal yeast infections in women who take antibiotics or who have diabetes.
- Extends life span.
- Helps digestion of milk and milk products in people with lactase deficiency.
- Enhances immunity.

Warnings and Precautions

Don't take if you:
- Have intestinal problems except under a doctor's supervision.

Consult your doctor:
- Before you use acidophilus in vaginal area for yeast infections.
- If you take any medicinal drugs or herbs including aspirin, laxatives, cold and cough remedies, antacids, vitamins, minerals, amino acids, supplements, other prescription or non-prescription drugs.

Pregnancy:
- Problems in pregnant women taking small or usual amounts have not been proved. But the chance of problems does exist. Don't use unless prescribed by your doctor.

Breast-feeding:
- Problems in breast-fed infants of lactating mothers taking small or usual amounts have not been proved. But the chance of problems does exist. Don't use unless prescribed by your doctor.

Infants and children:
- Treating infants and children under 2 with any supplement is hazardous.

Storage:
- Keep cool and dry, but don't freeze. Store safely away from children.

Safe dosage:
- At present no "safe" dosage has been established.

Toxicity

Comparative-toxicity rating not available from standard references.

Adverse Reactions, Side Effects or Overdose Symptoms

None expected

Basic Information

Bee pollen is the microscopic male seed in flowering plants.
Chemicals this supplement contains:
Some vitamins, minerals and amino acids. Bee pollen is expensive and provides inadequate, uncertain quantities of nutrients.

Known Effects

• No beneficial effect in the body has been proved.

Miscellaneous information:
• Available in injectable form and capsules.

Unproved Speculated Benefits

• Acts as anti-aging agent.
• Energizes body.
• Regulates bowels.
• Treats prostate problems.
• Helps weight control.
• Renews skin.
• Reduces risk of heart disease and arthritis.
• Relieves stress.
• Boosts immunity.
• Inhibits cancer.
• Decreases allergy symptoms.

Warnings and Precautions

Don't take if you:
• Are pregnant, think you may be pregnant or plan pregnancy in the near future.

Consult your doctor if you:
• Take this herb for any medical problem that doesn't improve in 2 weeks. There may be safer, more-effective treatments.

Pregnancy:
• Problems in pregnant women taking small or usual amounts have not been proved. But the chance of problems does exist. Don't use unless prescribed by your doctor.

Breast-feeding:
• Problems in breast-fed infants of lactating mothers taking small or usual amounts have not been proved. But the chance of problems does exist. Don't use unless prescribed by your doctor.

Infants and children:
• Treating infants and children under 2 with any supplement is hazardous.

Storage:
• Keep cool and dry, but don't freeze. Store safely away from children.

Safe dosage:
• At present no "safe" dosage has been established.

Toxicity

Comparative-toxicity rating not available from standard references.

For symptoms of toxicity: See *Adverse Reactions, Side Effects or Overdose Symptoms* section below.

Adverse Reactions, Side Effects or Overdose Symptoms

Signs and symptoms	What to do
May cause allergic reactions in those sensitive to pollens. Mild allergic response is characterized by itching, pain at injection site and swelling occurring in 24-48 hours.	Discontinue. Call doctor immediately.
Life-threatening anaphylaxis may follow injection—symptoms include immediate severe itching, paleness, low blood pressure, loss of consciousness, coma	Yell for help. Don't leave victim. Begin CPR (cardiopulmonary resuscitation), mouth to mouth breathing and external cardiac massage. Have someone dial 999 (emergency). Don't stop CPR until help arrives.

SUPPLEMENT

Bioflavinoids (Vitamin P)

Basic Information

Bioflavinoids are a brightly coloured, chemical constituent of pulp and rind of citrus fruits, green pepper, apricots, cherries, grapes, papaya, tomatoes, papaya, broccoli.
Chemicals this supplement contains:
  Hesperidin
  Nobiletin
  Rutin
  Sinensetin
  Tangeretin

Known Effects:

- Treats rare bioflavinoid deficiency characterized by fragile capillaries and unusual bleeding.
- May act as an anti-oxidant, preventing vitamin C and adrenalin from being oxidized by copper-containing enzymes.

Miscellaneous information:

- Bioflavinoids are sold under the brand names Rutin, Hesperiden, CVP, duo-CVP, Hesper capsules, Hesper bitabs and are included in numerous vitamin/mineral supplements.
- Enough bioflavinoids are present in food to make supplements unnecessary in healthy humans.
- Commercial products such as tablets or capsules often contain vitamin C.

Unproved Speculated Benefits

- Increases effectiveness of vitamin C.
- Prevents haemorrhoids.
- Prevents miscarriages.
- Prevents retinal bleeding in people with diabetes and hypertension.
- Prevents capillary fragility.
- Prevents nosebleed.
- Prevents post-partem haemorrhage.
- Prevents menstrual disorders.
- Prevents blood clotting and platelet clumping.
- Prevents easy bruising.

Warnings and Precautions

Don't take if you:

- Have a bleeding problem until studies are done to diagnose the underlying disease.

Consult your doctor if you:

- Self-medicate.
- Take any medicinal drugs or herbs including aspirin, laxatives, cold and cough remedies, antacids, vitamins, minerals, amino acids, supplements, other prescription or non-prescription drugs.

Pregnancy:

- Notify doctor if you take supplements.

Breast-feeding:

- Notify doctor if you take supplements.

Others:

- None expected if you are beyond childhood and under 45, basically healthy and take for only a short time.

Storage:

- Keep cool and dry, but don't freeze. Store safely away from children.

Safe dosage:

- At present no "safe" dosage has been established.

Toxicity

Comparative-toxicity rating not available from standard references.

Adverse Reactions, Side Effects or Overdose Symptoms

None expected

Basic Information

Non-leavening, with a slightly bitter taste. It is an excellent source of B vitamins, protein and minerals.
Chemicals this supplement contains:
  B vitamins
  DNA and RNA
  Trace mineral, chromium

Known Effects

- Supplies B vitamins, protein and minerals.
- Provides bulk to prevent constipation.
- Good source of enzyme-producing vitamins.
- Chromium in brewer's yeast helps regulate sugar metabolism.

Miscellaneous information:
- Out of the can, the bitter taste of brewer's yeast may be unpleasant. Adding it to foods with a strong taste makes it tolerable.
- A good, inexpensive food supplement for aging adults and growing, developing children.
- Can be used in baking, soups, chili and casseroles to increase nutritional content.
- Available in powder, flakes and tablets.

Unproved Speculated Benefits

- Helps treat diabetes.
- Reduces risk of high cholesterol in blood.
- Treats contact dermatitis.

Warnings and Precautions

Don't take if you:
- Have intestinal disease.

Consult your doctor if you:
- Have an acute intestinal upset.
- Take any medicinal drugs or herbs including aspirin, laxatives, cold and cough remedies, antacids, vitamins, minerals, amino acids, supplements, other prescription or non-prescription drugs.

Pregnancy:
- Excellent, inexpensive source of nutrients. Don't overuse.

Breast-feeding:
- Excellent, inexpensive source of nutrients. Don't overuse.

Others:
- Quality and quantity of nutrients vary greatly among commercially available products.
- Brewer's yeast is usually non-toxic if you consume 1 tablespoon or less of the powder or equivalent amounts of tablets or flakes.

Storage:
- Keep cool and dry, but don't freeze. Store safely away from children.

Safe dosage:
- At present no "safe" dosage has been established.

Toxicity

Comparative-toxicity rating not available from standard references.

For symptoms of toxicity: See *Adverse Reactions, Side Effects or Overdose Symptoms* section below.

Adverse Reactions, Side Effects or Overdose Symptoms

Signs and symptoms	What to do
Diarrhoea	Discontinue. Call doctor immediately.
Nausea	Discontinue. Call doctor immediately.

SUPPLEMENT

Choline

Basic Information

Available from natural sources? Yes
Available from synthetic sources? Yes
Prescription required? No

Natural Sources

Cabbage	Green beans
Calves' liver	Lentils
Cauliflower	Rice
Caviar	Soya beans
Eggs	Soy lecithin
Garbanzo beans	Split peas
(chickpeas)	

Found in all animal and plant products.

Reasons to Use

- Protects against damage to cells by oxidation.
- People taking niacin or nicotinic acid for treatment of high-serum cholesterol and triglycerides need lecithin or choline supplements because nicotinic acid and nicotinomide (vitamin B-3) can reduce normal amount of choline and lecithin available for basic body needs.

Unproved Speculated Benefits

- Protects against cardiovascular disease.
- Protects against memory loss.
- Prevents some diseases of the nervous system, such as Alzheimer's disease and tardive dyskinesia (involuntary, abnormal facial movements including grimacing, sticking out tongue and sucking movements).
- Treats Alzheimer's disease.
- Treats liver damage caused by alcoholism.
- Lowers cholesterol level in human serum.

Who Needs Additional Amounts?

- No one.

Deficiency Symptoms

- There are no specific deficiency symptoms in man, although some animals can suffer from lack of choline. Lecithin must be present for choline synthesis in the human body.

Unproved Speculated Symptoms

- Symptoms of heart or blood-vessel disease.
- Decreasing mental alertness.

Lab Tests to Detect Deficiency

- None available, except for experimental purposes.

Dosage and Usage Information

Recommended Dietary Allowance (RDA):
No RDA has been established.

What this supplement does:
- Choline is involved in production of acetylcholine. Acetylcholine must be present in the body for proper function of the nervous system, including mood, behaviour, orientation, personality traits, judgment.

Miscellaneous information:
- Choline's major source is lecithin.
- It is used as a thickener in several foods, including mayonnaise, margarine, ice cream.

Available as:
- Capsules: Swallow whole with full glass of liquid. Don't chew or crush. Take with meals or 1 to 1-1/2 hours after meals unless otherwise directed by your doctor.

➤➤

Warnings and Precautions

Don't take if you:
• Are healthy and eat a well-balanced diet.

Consult your doctor if you have:
• Plans to use choline to treat Alzheimer's disease with lecithin/choline.

Over age 55:
• Don't take if you are healthy.

Pregnancy:
• Don't take if you are healthy. Check with your doctor if you have any questions.

Breast-feeding:
• Don't take if you are healthy. Check with your doctor if you have any questions.

Effect on lab tests:
• May cause inaccurate results in choline/sphingomyelin test as part of examination of amniotic fluid.

Storage:
• Store in cool, dry place away from direct light, but don't freeze.
• Store safely out of reach of children.
• Don't store in bathroom medicine cabinet. Heat and moisture may change action of supplement.

Others:
• Don't take more than 1 gram per day.

Overdose/Toxicity

Signs and symptoms:
Nausea, vomiting, dizziness.

What to do:
For symptoms of overdosage: Discontinue supplement, and consult doctor. Also see *Adverse Reactions or Side Effects* section below.
For accidental overdosage (such as child taking entire bottle): Dial 999 (emergency).

Adverse Reactions or Side Effects

Reaction or effect	What to do
"Fishy" body odour	Discontinue. Call doctor when convenient.

Interaction with Medicine, Vitamins or Minerals

Interacts with	Combined effect
Nicotinic acid (nicotinamide, vitamin B-3)	Decreases choline effectiveness.

Interaction with Other Substances

None known

SUPPLEMENT

Chondroitin Sulphate

Basic Information

This substance is found in cartilages of most mammals.
Chemicals this supplement contains:
Complex protein molecules

Known Effects

• None proved.

Miscellaneous information:
• Available as capsules.

Unproved Speculated Benefits

• Lowers cholesterol levels.
• Lowers triglyceride levels.
• Prolongs clotting time.

Warnings and Precautions

Don't take if you:
• Have bleeding problems.
• Are pregnant, think you may be pregnant or plan pregnancy in the near future.

Consult your doctor if you:
• Take anti-coagulants.
• Take any medicinal drugs or herbs including aspirin, laxatives, cold and cough remedies, antacids, vitamins, minerals, amino acids, supplements, other prescription or non-prescription drugs.

Pregnancy:
• Problems in pregnant women taking small or usual amounts have not been proved. But the chance of problems does exist. Don't use unless prescribed by your doctor.

Breast-feeding:
• Problems in breast-fed infants of lactating mothers taking small or usual amounts have not been proved. But the chance of problems does exist. Don't use unless prescribed by your doctor.

Infants and children:
• Treating infants and children under 2 with any supplement is hazardous.

Others:
• None expected if you are beyond childhood and under 45, basically healthy and take for only a short time.

Storage:
• Keep cool and dry, but don't freeze. Store safely away from children.

Safe dosage:
• At present no "safe" dosage has been established.

Toxicity

Comparative-toxicity rating not available from standard references.

Adverse Reactions, Side Effects or Overdose Symptoms

None expected

Basic Information

Coenzyme Q is part of the mitochondria of cells and is necessary for energy production.
Chemical this supplement contains:
Coenzyme Q10 (a nutrient); found in beef, sardines, spinach, peanuts

Known Effects

• Controls flow of oxygen within individual cells.

Miscellaneous information:
• Oral products are available, but most experts do *not* recommend using them except under medical supervision.

Unproved Speculated Benefits

• Improves heart-muscle metabolism.
• Treats chest pain caused by narrowed coronary arteries (coronary insufficiency).
• Lowers blood pressure.
• Treats congestive heart failure by enhancing pumping action of heart.

Warnings and Precautions

Don't take if you:
• Have heart disease, without consulting doctor.

Consult your doctor if you:
• Take any medicinal drugs or herbs including aspirin, laxatives, cold and cough remedies, antacids, vitamins, minerals, amino acids, supplements, other prescription or non-prescription drugs.

Pregnancy:
• Dangers outweigh any possible benefits. Don't use.

Breast-feeding:
• Dangers outweigh any possible benefits. Don't use.

Infants and children:
• Treating infants and children under 2 with any supplement is hazardous.

Others:
• No contraindications if you are not pregnant and do not take amounts larger than a manufacturer's recommended dosage

Storage:
• Keep cool and dry, but don't freeze. Store safely away from children.

Safe dosage:
• At present no "safe" dosage has been established.

Toxicity

Comparative-toxicity rating not available from standard references.

Adverse Reactions, Side Effects or Overdose Symptoms

None expected

Dessicated Liver

Basic Information

Dessicated liver is a concentrated form of dried liver and is available in tablets or powder.
Chemicals this supplement contains:
  Calcium
  Cholesterol
  Copper
  Iron
  Phosphorus
  Vitamins A, C, D

Known Effects

- Is a good source of vitamins A, C, D and iron, calcium, phosphorus, copper.

Miscellaneous information:
- Healthy people who eat a balanced diet probably do not need this supplement.

Unproved Speculated Benefits

- Acts as an anti-stress agent.
- Cures gum problems.

Warnings and Precautions

Don't take if you:
- Are pregnant, think you may be pregnant or plan pregnancy in the near future.

Consult your doctor if you:
- Take any medicinal drugs or herbs including aspirin, laxatives, cold and cough remedies, antacids, vitamins, minerals, amino acids, supplements, other prescription or non-prescription drugs.

Pregnancy:
- Problems in pregnant women taking small or usual amounts have not been proved. But the chance of problems does exist. Don't use unless prescribed by your doctor.

Breast-feeding:
- Problems in breast-fed infants of lactating mothers taking small or usual amounts have not been proved. But the chance of problems does exist. Don't use unless prescribed by your doctor.

Infants and children:
- Treating infants and children under 2 with any supplement is hazardous.

Others:
- None expected if you are beyond childhood and under 45, basically healthy and take for only a short time.

Storage:
- Keep cool and dry, but don't freeze. Store safely away from children.

Safe dosage:
- At present no "safe" dosage has been established.

Toxicity

Comparative-toxicity rating not available from standard references.

Adverse Reactions, Side Effects or Overdose Symptoms

None expected

Basic Information

Cell walls of plants are made of fibre that give a plant structure and stability. Fibre cannot be broken down by enzymes in the digestive tract, so fibre passes through without being absorbed.

Chemicals this supplement contains: Structured and non-structured substances in plant carbohydrate (starches)

Known Effects

- Absorbs many times its weight in water, causing bulkier stools and lessening chance of constipation.
- Helps control blood-sugar level in people with diabetes.
- Helps reduce cholesterol and triglycerides in blood.

Miscellaneous information:

- Best sources of dietary fibre include fresh fruits, vegetables, nuts, seeds, whole-grain products, potatoes.
- Available commercially in capsules, tablets, chewable tablets, oral suspension and flakes or wafers.

Unproved Speculated Benefits

- Reduces risk of heart disease.
- Reduces risk of cancer of colon and rectum.
- Reduces risk of diverticulitis.

Warnings and Precautions

Don't take if you:
- Have Crohn's disease.

Consult your doctor if you:
- Are pregnant, think you may be pregnant or plan pregnancy in the near future.

Pregnancy:
- Problems in pregnant women taking small or usual amounts have not been proved. But the chance of problems does exist. Don't use unless prescribed by your doctor.

Breast-feeding:
- Problems in breast-fed infants of lactating mothers taking small or usual amounts have not been proved. But the chance of problems does exist. Don't use unless prescribed by your doctor.

Infants and children:
- Treating infants and children under 2 with any supplement is hazardous.

Others:
- Intake of excessive amounts of fiber may decrease absorption of minerals, especially calcium, iron, zinc.

Storage:
- Keep cool and dry, but don't freeze. Store safely away from children.

Safe dosage:
- At present no "safe" dosage has been established. Most experts feel that increasing fiber is healthful, but no one knows for sure the optimal amount.

Toxicity

Comparative-toxicity rating not available from standard references.

For symptoms of toxicity: See *Adverse Reactions, Side Effects or Overdose Symptoms* section below.

Adverse Reactions, Side Effects or Overdose Symptoms

Signs and symptoms	What to do
Bloating of abdomen	Discontinue. Call doctor when convenient.
Excess flatulence	Discontinue. Call doctor when convenient.
Obstruction of large intestine. Rare, but more likely if there is pre-existing inflammatory disease. Symptoms of obstruction are tender, distended abdomen, abdominal pain, fever, no bowel movements.	Discontinue. Call doctor immediately.

SUPPLEMENT

Gamma-Linolenic Acid

Basic Information

Gamma-linolenic acid is found in a supplement called evening primrose oil.
Available from natural sources? Yes
Available from synthetic sources? Yes
Prescription required? No

Natural Sources

Evening primrose (a plant)
Fish
Human mother's milk

Reasons to Use

• Helps inhibit coughing.
• Is an essential nutrient.
• Acts as an astringent.

Unproved Speculated Benefits

• May have an anti-clotting factor, which would make it useful in the prevention of heart attacks caused by thrombosis.
• Helps people suffering from atopic eczema or eczema due to allergy.
• Is used in external preparations to treat skin eruptions, such as psoriasis.
• Helps treat migraines.
• Helps treat asthma.
• Treats arthritis.
• Alleviates symptoms of premenstrual syndrome.
• Treats schizophrenia.
• Is effective against obesity.
• Makes fingernails stronger.
• Treats hangovers.
• General "cure-all" for many other disorders.

Who Needs Additional Amounts?

• Those on greatly restricted fat and oil intake.

Deficiency Symptoms

• None

Unproved Speculated Symptoms

• Eczema-like lesions
• Hair loss
• Reduced immunological response
• Kidney disease
• Inability of wounds to heal properly

Lab Tests to Detect Deficiency

• None available, except for experimental purposes.

Dosage and Usage Information

Recommended Dietary Allowance (RDA):
No RDA has been established.

What this supplement does:
• Functions as one of the sources of essential fatty acids.

Miscellaneous information:
• Evening primrose grows wild. A long spike of yellow flowers opens at night. Oil can be expressed from the tiny seeds of the flower.
• Linolenic acid, working with enzymes, becomes part of some prostaglandins. Prostaglandins sometimes *limit* inflammatory reactions in the body and sometimes *cause* inflammatory reactions. Taking evening primrose oil may cause unpredictable, harmful effects.
• Nutrition authorities do not recommend supplements in healthy people.

Available as:
• Capsules: Swallow whole with full glass of liquid. Don't chew or crush. Take with meals or 1 to 1-1/2 hours after meals unless otherwise directed by your doctor.

⟫➤

Warnings and Precautions

Don't take if you:
• Are healthy and eat a well-balanced diet.

Consult your doctor if you have:
• Any illness.

Over age 55:
• Don't take if you are healthy.

Pregnancy:
• Don't take if you are healthy.

Breast-feeding:
• Don't take if you are healthy.

Effect on lab tests:
• None known.

Storage:
• Store in cool, dry place away from direct light, but don't freeze.
• Store safely out of reach of children.
• Don't store in bathroom medicine cabinet. Heat and moisture may change action of supplement.

Overdose/Toxicity

Signs and symptoms:
Unlikely to threaten life or cause significant symptoms.

What to do:
For symptoms of overdosage: Discontinue supplement, and consult doctor. Also see *Adverse Reactions or Side Effects* section below.
For accidental overdosage (such as child taking entire bottle): Dial 999 (emergency).

Adverse Reactions or Side Effects

Reaction or effect	What to do
Can make symptoms of some problems, such as asthma, migraines, arthritis, worse	Don't take.

Interaction with Medicine, Vitamins or Minerals

None known

Interaction with Other Substances

None known

SUPPLEMENT

Gelatin (Plain)

Basic Information
Gelatin is a tasteless, odourless substance extracted by boiling bones, hoofs and animal tissues.
Chemical this supplement contains:
Proteins

Known Effects

• None except to serve as source of protein.

Miscellaneous information:
• Gelatin is available in capsule or powdered form.

Unproved Speculated Benefits

• Improves condition of broken, splitting, brittle nails.
• Prevents nosebleeds.

Warnings and Precautions

Don't take if you:
• Expect gelatin to cure anything.

Consult your doctor if:
• Conditions you take gelatin for don't improve by themselves.

Pregnancy:
• Problems in pregnant women taking small or usual amounts have not been proved. But the chance of problems does exist. Don't use unless prescribed by your doctor.

Breast-feeding:
• Problems in breast-fed infants of lactating mothers taking small or usual amounts have not been proved. But the chance of problems does exist. Don't use unless prescribed by your doctor.

Infants and children:
• Treating infants and children under 2 with any supplement is hazardous.

Others:
• None expected if you are beyond childhood and under 45, basically healthy and take for only a short time.

Storage:
• Keep cool and dry, but don't freeze. Store safely away from children.

Safe dosage:
• At present no "safe" dosage has been established.

Toxicity

Comparative-toxicity rating not available from standard references.

Adverse Reactions, Side Effects or Overdose Symptoms

None expected

Basic Information

Glandulars are concentrated forms of various animal glands including adrenals, thymus, spleen, intestines.
Chemicals this supplement contains:
Antibiotics
Enzymes
Herbicides
Hormones
Pesticides

Known Effects

- None ever proved or conclusively demonstrated.

Miscellaneous information:
- Glandulars are available as extracts without prescription. They are worthless and may be harmful. Don't use them!

Unproved Speculated Benefits

- Increases sex drive.
- Cures infertility.
- Prevents aging.
- Reverses aging.
- Builds bodies.

Warnings and Precautions

Don't take:
- For any reason.

Consult your doctor if you have:
- Any problem these substances are advertised to help.

Pregnancy:
- Danger outweighs benefits. Don't use.

Breast-feeding:
- Danger outweighs benefits. Don't use.

Infants and children:
- Treating infants and children under 2 with any supplement is hazardous.

Others:
- Don't take these! If toxic symptoms occur, discontinue. Call doctor immediately.

Storage:
- Keep cool and dry, but don't freeze. Store safely away from children.

Safe dosage:
- At present no "safe" dosage has been established.

Toxicity

Comparative-toxicity rating not available from standard references.

For symptoms of toxicity: See *Adverse Reactions, Side Effects or Overdose Symptoms* section below.

Adverse Reactions, Side Effects or Overdose Symptoms

Signs and symptoms	What to do
Intestinal upsets, with nausea, vomiting, diarrhoea	Discontinue. Call doctor immediately.
Numbness	Discontinue. Call doctor when convenient.
Tingling of feet and hands	Discontinue. Call doctor when convenient.

SUPPLEMENT

Inositol

Basic Information

Inositol is also called myo-inositol.
Available from natural sources? Yes
Available from synthetic sources? Yes
Prescription required? No

 Natural Sources

Beans, dried	Nuts
Calves' liver	Oats
Cantaloupe	Pork
Citrus fruit, except	Rice
lemons	Veal
Garbanzo beans	Wheat germ
(chickpeas)	Whole-grain products
Lecithin granules	
Lentils	

 Reasons to Use

- Plays a role similar to choline in helping move fats out of liver.

 Unproved Speculated Benefits

- Protects against cardiovascular disease.
- Protects against peripheral neuritis associated with diabetes. (Some studies have shown promise for this use, but definitive, well-controlled studies have not been done.)
- Protects against hair loss.
- Helps maintain healthy hair.
- Functions as mild anti-anxiety agent.
- Helps control blood-cholesterol level.
- Promotes body's production of lecithin.
- Treats constipation with its stimulating effect on muscular action of alimentary canal.

 Who Needs Additional Amounts?

- Heavy drinkers of coffee, tea, cocoa and other caffeine-containing substances.

 Deficiency Symptoms

- Symptoms develop only in some animals; none are known in humans.

 Unproved Speculated Symptoms

- Eczema
- Constipation
- Abnormalities of the eyes

 Lab Tests to Detect Deficiency

- None available, except for experimental purposes.

 Dosage and Usage Information

Recommended Dietary Allowance (RDA):
No RDA has been established.

What this supplement does:
- Inositol forms an important part of *phospholipids,* which are compounds manufactured in our bodies.

Miscellaneous information:
- Caffeine in large quantities may create an inositol shortage.

Available as:
- Capsules: Swallow whole with full glass of liquid. Don't chew or crush. Take with meals or 1 to 1-1/2 hours after meals unless otherwise directed by your doctor.

➤➤

Inositol

Warnings and Precautions

Don't take if you:
• Are healthy.

Consult your doctor if you have:
• Diabetes with peripheral neuropathy—pain, numbness, tingling, alternating feelings of cold and hot in feet and hands. Medical supervision is necessary.

Over age 55:
• Don't take if you are healthy.

Pregnancy:
• Don't take if you are healthy.

Breast-feeding:
• Don't take if you are healthy.

Effect on lab tests:
• None known.

Storage:
• Store in cool, dry place away from direct light, but don't freeze.
• Store safely out of reach of children.
• Don't store in bathroom medicine cabinet. Heat and moisture may change action of supplement.

Overdose/Toxicity

Signs and symptoms:
Unlikely to threaten life or cause significant symptoms.

What to do:
For symptoms of overdosage: Discontinue supplement, and consult doctor.
For accidental overdosage (such as child taking entire bottle): Dial 999 (emergency).

Adverse Reactions or Side Effects

None expected.

Interaction with Medicine, Vitamins or Minerals

None known

Interaction with Other Substances

Caffeine-containing foods and **beverages** may create inositol shortage in the body.

Jojoba (Coffeeberry, Goatnut)

Basic Information
Biological name is Simmondsia chinensis.
Chemical this supplement contains:
   Amino acids

Known Effects

- Acts as soothing ingredient in many shampoos, pre-electric-shave conditioners, after-shave preparations, skin lotion, makeup remover.

Miscellaneous information:
- Jojoba is unique among plants because its seeds contain a liquid wax oil.
- The plant grows in Arizona and is used as a medicinal herb among Southern Arizona Indians.

Unproved Speculated Benefits

- Suppresses appetite.
- Treats rheumatoid arthritis.
- Treats inflammation.
- Relieves swelling.
- Treats acne.
- Treats warts.
- Treats tuberculosis.

Warnings and Precautions

Don't take if you:
- No contraindications if you are not pregnant and do not take amounts larger than manufacturer's recommended dosage.

Consult your doctor if you:
- Are pregnant, think you may be pregnant or plan pregnancy in the near future.
- Take any medicinal drugs or herbs including aspirin, laxatives, cold and cough remedies, antacids, vitamins, minerals, amino acids, supplements, other prescription or non-prescription drugs.

Pregnancy:
- Problems in pregnant women taking small or usual amounts have not been proved. But the chance of problems does exist. Don't use unless prescribed by your doctor.

Breast-feeding:
- Problems in breast-fed infants of lactating mothers taking small or usual amounts have not been proved. But the chance of problems does exist. Don't use unless prescribed by your doctor.

Infants and children:
- Treating infants and children under 2 with any supplement is hazardous.

Others:
- No beneficial effects when taken by mouth have been proved.

Storage:
- Keep cool and dry, but don't freeze. Store safely away from children.

Safe dosage:
- At present no "safe" dosage has been established.

Toxicity

Comparative-toxicity rating not available from standard references.

Adverse Reactions, Side Effects or Overdose Symptoms

None expected

L-Carnitine

Basic Information

L-carnitine is synthesized in the body from the amino acids lysine and methionine.
Available from natural sources? Yes
Available from synthetic sources? Yes
Prescription required? No

Natural Sources

Avocados
Dairy products
Red meats, especially lamb and beef
Tempeh (fermented soyabean product)

Reasons to Use

• Promotes normal growth and development.

Unproved Speculated Benefits

• Treats and possibly prevents some forms of cardiovascular disease.
• Protects against muscle disease.
• Helps build muscle.
• Protects against liver disease.
• Protects against diabetes.
• Protects against kidney disease.
• Aids in dieting. May make low-calorie diets easier to tolerate by reducing feelings of hunger and weakness.

Who Needs Additional Amounts?

• Anyone with deficient protein or amino acids in their diet because L-carnitine requires essential amino acids to be synthesized by the body.
• Children, pregnant or breast-feeding women who are vegan vegetarians.
• People with recent severe burns or injuries.
• Those on haemodialysis.
• Premature infants.

Deficiency Symptoms

• Muscle fatigue
• Cramps
• Changes in kidney-function chemistry following exercise

Unproved Speculated Symptoms

• Premature aging
• Heartbeat irregularities in someone who has had a heart attack
• Angina (See Glossary)

Lab Tests to Detect Deficiency

• None available, except for experimental purposes.

Dosage and Usage Information

Recommended Dietary Allowance (RDA):
No RDA has been established.

What this supplement does:
• Transports long-chain fatty acids into mitochondria, which are the metabolic furnaces of cells (particularly heart and kidney cells) where they may be oxidized to yield energy.

Miscellaneous information:
• L-carnitine is synthesized in human kidney and liver from the essential amino acids lysine and methionine, plus vitamins B-6, C and iron.

Available as:
• L-carnitine tablets: Swallow whole with full glass of liquid. Don't chew or crush. Take with meals or 1 to 1-1/2 hours after meals unless otherwise directed by your doctor. Avoid DL-carnitine tablets; they may be toxic.

>>➤

SUPPLEMENT

L-Carnitine, Continued

Warnings and Precautions

Don't take if you:
- Are allergic to any food protein, such as eggs, milk, wheat.
- Are at risk of poor nutrition for any reason.
- Are pregnant, think you may be pregnant or plan pregnancy in the near future.

Consult your doctor if you have:
- Any liver or kidney problems.

Over age 55:
- No special problems expected.

Pregnancy:
- Problems in pregnant women taking small or usual amounts have not beem proved. But the chance of problems does exist. Don't use unless prescribed by your doctor.

Breast-feeding:
- Problems in breast-fed infants of lactating mothers taking small or usual amounts have not been proved. But the chance of problems does exist. Don't use unless prescribed by your doctor.

Effect on lab tests:
- None known.

Storage:
- Store in cool, dry place away from direct light, but don't freeze.
- Store safely out of reach of children.
- Don't store in bathroom medicine cabinet. Heat and moisture may change action of supplement.

Overdose/Toxicity

Signs and symptoms:
Muscle weakness.

What to do:
For symptoms of overdosage: Discontinue supplement, and consult doctor. Also see *Adverse Reactions or Side Effects* section below.

For accidental overdosage (such as child taking entire bottle): Dial 999 (emergency).

Adverse Reactions or Side Effects

Reaction or effect	What to do
Symptoms of myasthenia (progressive weakness of certain muscle groups without evidence of atrophy or wasting) have been reported in kidney patients being maintained for prolonged periods on haemodialysis and supplementary DL-carnitine	Don't take supplements without doctor's prescription and supervision.

Interaction with Medicine, Vitamins or Minerals

None expected

Interaction with Other Substances

None known

Basic Information

Available from natural sources? Yes
Available from synthetic sources? Yes
Prescription required? No

Natural Sources

Cabbage
Calves' liver
Cauliflower
Caviar
Eggs
Garbanzo beans
  (chickpeas)

Green beans
Lentils
Rice
Soy lecithin
Soya beans
Split peas

Found in all animal and plant products.

Reasons to Use

- Protects against damage to cells by oxidation.
- Major source of the chemical nutrient choline. Choline's benefits are also lecithin's benefits. See Choline.
- People taking niacin or nicotinic acid for treatment of high-serum cholesterol and triglycerides need lecithin or choline supplements.
- May lower high blood cholesterol or triglycerides in some people.

Unproved Speculated Benefits

- Protects against cardiovascular disease.
- Protects against memory loss.
- Prevents some diseases of the nervous system, such as Alzheimer's disease and tardive dyskinesia (involuntary, abnormal facial movements including grimacing, sticking out tongue and sucking movements).
- Treats Alzheimer's disease.
- Treats liver damage caused by alcoholism.
- Lowers cholesterol level.

Who Needs Additional Amounts?

- No one.

Deficiency Symptoms

- There are no specific deficiency symptoms in man, although some animals can suffer from lack of choline. Lecithin must be present for choline synthesis in the human body.

Unproved Speculated Symptoms

- Symptoms of heart or blood-vessel disease
- Decreasing mental alertness

Lab Tests to Detect Deficiency

- None available, except for experimental purposes.

Dosage and Usage Information

Recommended Dietary Allowance (RDA):
No RDA has been established.

What this supplement does:
- Lecithin is a phospholipid composed of saturated, unsaturated and polyunsaturated fatty acids. It also contains glycerin, phosphorous and choline.
- It is found in chemicals that aid passage of many nutrients from the bloodstream into cells.

Miscellaneous information:
- Is used as a thickener in several foods, including mayonnaise, margarine, ice cream.
- Supplements are not needed by healthy people.

Available as:
- Tablets: Swallow whole with full glass of liquid. Don't chew or crush. Take with meals or 1 to 1-1/2 hours after meals unless otherwise directed by your doctor.
- Liquid: Dilute in at least 1/2 glass of water or other liquid. Take with meals or 1 to 1-1/2 hours after meals unless otherwise directed by your doctor.

⟫▶

SUPPLEMENT

Warnings and Precautions

Don't take if you:
• Are healthy and eat a well-balanced diet.

Consult your doctor if you have:
• Plans to treat Alzheimer's disease with lecithin/choline.

Over age 55:
• No problems expected.

Pregnancy:
• Supplements are not needed.

Breast-feeding:
• Supplements are not needed.

Effect on lab tests:
• May cause inaccurate results in lecithin/sphingomyelin test as part of examination of amniotic fluid.

Storage:
• Store in cool, dry place away from direct light, but don't freeze.
• Store safely out of reach of children.
• Don't store in bathroom medicine cabinet. Heat and moisture may change action of supplement.

Others:
• Don't take more than 1 gram per day.

Overdose/Toxicity

Signs and symptoms:
Nausea, vomiting, dizziness.

What to do:
For symptoms of overdosage: Discontinue supplement, and consult doctor. Also see *Adverse Reactions or Side Effects* section below.
For accidental overdosage (such as child taking entire bottle): Dial 999 (emergency).

Adverse Reactions or Side Effects

Reaction or effect	What to do
"Fishy" body odour	Discontinue. Call doctor when convenient.

Interaction with Medicine, Vitamins or Minerals

Interacts with	Combined effect
Nicotinic acid (nicotinamide, vitamin B-3)	Decreases lecithin effectiveness.

Interaction with Other Substances

None known

Basic Information

This fatty acid is a dietary supplement available in capsules or oil. It is commercially advertised to protect against diseases of the heart and blood vessels.

Chemicals this supplement contains:
Docosahexaenoic acid (DHA)
Eicosapentaenoic acid (EPA)

Known Effects

- Greenland Eskimos who eat foods high in omega-3 fatty acids have very low serum triglycerides and total cholesterol. The cholesterol they do have is mainly high-density-lipoprotein (HDL) cholesterol. These substances are known to protect against deposits of plaque, which can occlude critical blood vessels and cause heart attacks, strokes and other major health problems. Coastal Japanese people have similar diets and similar findings. We *assume* increasing omega-3 in our daily food may give us the same protection.

Miscellaneous information:
- Omega-3 fatty acids come from *cold-water fish*, particularly cod, tuna, salmon, halibut, shark, mackerel. Increasing "oily" fish in the diet may be safer than taking omega-3 fatty-acid supplements.

Unproved Speculated Benefits

- Protects against arthritis.
- Protects against arteriosclerosis.
- Protects against coronary-artery disease.
- Protects against strokes.
- Protects against kidney failure.

Warnings and Precautions

Don't take if you:
- Are pregnant, think you may be pregnant or plan pregnancy in the near future.

Consult your doctor if you:
- Take any medicinal drugs or herbs including aspirin, laxatives, cold and cough remedies, antacids, vitamins, minerals, amino acids, supplements, other prescription or non-prescription drugs.

Pregnancy:
- Problems in pregnant women taking small or usual amounts have not been proved. But the chance of problems does exist. Don't use unless prescribed by your doctor.

Breast-feeding:
- Problems in breast-fed infants of lactating mothers taking small or usual amounts have not been proved. But the chance of problems does exist. Don't use unless prescribed by your doctor.

Infants and children:
- Treating infants and children under 2 with any supplement is hazardous.

Others:
- This fat becomes rancid easily and quickly.
- No one knows how much is beneficial and non-toxic.

Storage:
- Keep cool and dry, but don't freeze. Store safely away from children.

Safe dosage:
- At present no "safe" dosage has been established.

Toxicity

Comparative-toxicity rating not available from standard references.

For symptoms of toxicity: See *Adverse Reactions, Side Effects or Overdose Symptoms* section below.

Adverse Reactions, Side Effects or Overdose Symptoms

Signs and symptoms	What to do
Large amounts may lead to bleeding problems, diminished immunity, predisposition to some malignancies	Discontinue. Call doctor immediately.

Para-Aminobenzoic Acid (PABA)

Basic Information
Available from natural sources? Yes
Available from synthetic sources? Yes
Prescription required? No

Natural Sources

Bran	Molasses
Brown rice	Sunflower seeds
Kidney	Wheat germ
Liver	Whole-grain products
	Yogurt

Reasons to Use

- Shields skin from damage of ultraviolet radiation when used as a topical sunscreen.
- Treats vitiligo, a condition characterized by discolouration or depigmentation of some areas of the skin.

Unproved Speculated Benefits

- Rejuvenates skin.
- Treats arthritis.
- Stops hair loss.
- Restores colour to greying or white hair.
- Treats anaemia.
- Treats constipation.
- Treats headaches.
- Treats skin disorders.

Who Needs Additional Amounts?

- PABA is not an essential nutrient, so no nutritional deficiency has been documented.

Deficiency Symptoms

- None

Unproved Speculated Symptoms

- Eczema

Lab Tests to Detect Deficiency

- None available, except for experimental purposes.

Dosage and Usage Information

Recommended Dietary Allowance (RDA):
No RDA has been established.

What this supplement does:
- Stimulates intestinal bacteria, enabling them to produce folic acid, which aids in production of pantothenic acid.

Miscellaneous information:
- When used topically, PABA helps prevent sunburn.
- *Don't* take oral supplements without doctor's supervision.

Available as:
- A constituent of many multivitamin/mineral preparations.
- A constituent of many topical sunscreen products.

»➤

Para-Aminobenzoic Acid (PABA)

Warnings and Precautions

Don't take if you:
• Take any sulphonamides or antibiotic internally because PABA prevents them from exerting their full effect.

Consult your doctor if you:
• Are pregnant, think you may be pregnant or plan pregnancy in the near future.

Over age 55:
• No problems expected.

Pregnancy:
• Risks outweigh benefits. Don't take internally.
• No problems are expected if you use PABA topically.

Breast-feeding:
• Risks outweigh benefits. Don't take internally.
• No problems are expected if you use PABA topically.

Effect on lab tests:
• None expected.

Storage:
• Store in cool, dry place away from direct light, but don't freeze.
• Store safely out of reach of children.
• Don't store in bathroom medicine cabinet. Heat and moisture may change action of supplement.

Overdose/Toxicity

Signs and symptoms:
Liver disease evidenced by abnormal liver-function tests, jaundice (yellow skin and eyes), vomiting.

Possible consequences of overdose:
PABA is stored in the tissues. In continued high doses, it may prove toxic to the liver. Symptoms of toxicity are nausea and vomiting.

What to do:
For symptoms of overdosage: Discontinue supplement, and consult doctor. Also see *Adverse Reactions or Side Effects* section below.
For accidental overdosage (such as child taking entire bottle): Dial 999 (emergency).

Adverse Reactions or Side Effects

Reaction or effect	What to do
Diarrhoea	Discontinue. Call doctor immediately.
Nausea	Discontinue. Call doctor immediately.
Vomiting	Discontinue. Call doctor immediately.

Interaction with Medicine, Vitamins or Minerals

Interacts with	Combined effect
Antibiotics	Decreases effectiveness of antibiotics.
Folic acid	Increases effectiveness of folic acid.
Sulphonamide ("sulpha drugs")	Decreases effectiveness of sulpha drugs.
Vitamin-B complex	Increases effectiveness of vitamin-B complex.
Vitamin C	Increases effectiveness of vitamin C.

Interaction with Other Substances

None known

Royal Jelly

Basic Information

Royal jelly is a milky-white, gelatinous substance secreted by salivary glands of worker bees to stimulate growth and development of queen bees.

Chemicals this supplement contains:
Pantothenic acid (part of B-complex of vitamins)
10-hydroxydec-2-enoic acid

 ## Known Effects

• None proved or conclusively demonstrated.

Miscellaneous information:
• This substance must be given by injection.

 ## Unproved Speculated Benefits

• Extends life span.
• Treats bone and joint disorders, such as rheumatoid arthritis.
• Protects against leukaemia.
• Contains antibiotic properties.

 ## Warnings and Precautions

Don't take if you:
• Are pregnant, think you may be pregnant or plan pregnancy in the near future.

Consult your doctor if you:
• Take any medicinal drugs or herbs including aspirin, laxatives, cold and cough remedies, antacids, vitamins, minerals, amino acids, supplements, other prescription or non-prescription drugs.

Pregnancy:
• Dangers outweigh any possible benefits. Don't use.

Breast-feeding:
• Dangers outweigh any possible benefits. Don't use.

Infants and children:
• Treating infants and children under 2 with any supplement is hazardous.

Others:
• Dangers outweigh any possible benefits. Don't use.

Storage:
• Keep cool and dry, but don't freeze. Store safely away from children.

Safe dosage:
• At present no "safe" dosage has been established.

 ## Toxicity

Comparative-toxicity rating not available from standard references.

For symptoms of toxicity: See *Adverse Reactions, Side Effects or Overdose Symptoms* section below.

 ## Adverse Reactions, Side Effects or Overdose Symptoms

Signs and symptoms	What to do
Life-threatening anaphylaxis may follow injections—symptoms include immediate severe itching, paleness, low blood pressure, loss of consciousness, coma	Yell for help. Don't leave victim. Begin CPR (cardiopulmonary resuscitation), mouth to mouth breathing and external cardiac massage. Have someone dial 999 (emergency). Don't stop CPR until help arrives.

Basic Information

Biological names of spirulina are Spirulina geitler, Spirulina maxima, Spirulina platenis.
Chemicals this supplement contains:
B-complex vitamins
Beta-carotene
Gamma-linoleic acid (See Glossary)

Known Effects

• None proved or conclusively demonstrated.

Miscellaneous information:
• Spirulina is expensive and tastes terrible.
• It is a blue-green microalgae that grows wild on the surface of brackish, alkaline lakes in the tropics. Spirulina is cultivated commercially in several places, including Mexico, Thailand, Japan and Southern California.
• It is available in powder and tablet forms.

Unproven Speculated Benefits

• Treats obesity.
• Is used as tonic.
• Acts as energy booster.
• Treats diabetes mellitus.

Warnings and Precautions

Don't take if you:
• Are pregnant, think you may be pregnant or plan pregnancy in the near future.

Consult your doctor if you:
• Take any medicinal drugs or herbs including aspirin, laxatives, cold and cough remedies, antacids, vitamins, minerals, amino acids, supplements, other prescription or non-prescription drugs.

Pregnancy:
• Problems in pregnant women taking small or usual amounts have not been proved. But the chance of problems does exist. Don't use unless prescribed by your doctor.

Breast-feeding:
• Problems in breast-fed infants of lactating mothers taking small or usual amounts have not been proved. But the chance of problems does exist. Don't use unless prescribed by your doctor.

Infants and children:
• Treating infants and children under 2 with any supplement is hazardous.

Others:
• No contraindications if you are not pregnant and do not take amounts larger than a reputable manufacturer recommends on the package.

Storage:
• Keep cool and dry, but don't freeze. Store safely away from children.

Safe dosage:
• At present no "safe" dosage has been established.

Toxicity

Comparative-toxicity rating not available from standard references.

For symptoms of toxicity: See *Adverse Reactions, Side Effects or Overdose Symptoms* section below.

Adverse Reactions, Side Effects or Overdose Symptoms

Signs and symptoms	What to do
Diarrhoea	Discontinue. Call doctor immediately.
Nausea	Discontinue. Call doctor immediately.
Vomiting	Discontinue. Call doctor immediately.

Superoxide Dismutase

Basic Information

Superoxide dismutase is an enzyme associated with copper, zinc and manganese.
Chemical this supplement contains:
Enzyme that participates in utilization of copper, zinc and manganese by body cells

Known Effects

- Injectable forms may have anti-oxidant properties.

Miscellaneous information:
- Oral superoxide dismutase is destroyed in the intestines before being absorbed, so oral forms are worthless.
- Available in injectable forms, but these should be used *only* under close medical supervision.

Unproved Speculated Benefits

- Protects against free radicals. (See Glossary.)
- Treats arthritis.
- Treats cancer.
- Treats side effects of radiation.

Warnings and Precautions

Don't take if you:
- Have any medical problems.

Consult your doctor if you:
- Take any medicinal drugs or herbs including aspirin, laxatives, cold and cough remedies, antacids, vitamins, minerals, amino acids, supplements, other prescription or non-prescription drugs.

Pregnancy:
- Don't use without medical supervision.

Breast-feeding:
- Don't use without medical supervision.

Infants and children:
- Treating infants and children under 2 with any supplement is hazardous.

Others:
- Available oral forms are worthless. Injectable forms may cause anaphylaxis.

Storage:
- Keep cool and dry, but don't freeze. Store safely away from children.

Safe dosage:
- At present no "safe" dosage has been established.

Toxicity

Comparative-toxicity rating not available from standard references.

For symptoms of toxicity: See *Adverse Reactions, Side Effects or Overdose Symptoms* section below.

Adverse Reactions, Side Effects or Overdose Symptoms

Signs and symptoms	What to do
Life-threatening anaphylaxis may follow injections— symptoms include immediate severe itching, paleness, low blood pressure, loss of consciousness, coma	Yell for help. Don't leave victim. Begin CPR (cardiopulmonary resuscitation), mouth to mouth breathing and external cardiac massage. Have someone dial 999 (emergency). Don't stop CPR until help arrives.

Basic Information

Wheat germ is the embryo of the wheat grain located at the lower end. It is derived from both root and shoot.
Chemicals this supplement contains:
Calcium
Copper
Manganese
Magnesium
Most B vitamins
Octacosanol
Phosphorus
Vitamin E (one of the richest natural sources)

Known Effects

• Excellent nutritional source of chemicals listed above.

Miscellaneous information:
• Wheat germ is available in food and as flakes to mix with other foods. It is also available as oil, which should be kept tightly covered and refrigerated.

Unproved Speculated Benefits

• Treats muscular dystrophy.
• Improves physical stamina and performance.

Warnings and Precautions

Don't take if you:
• No contraindications if you are not pregnant and do not take amounts larger than manufacturer's recommended dosage.

Consult your doctor if you:
• Are pregnant, think you may be pregnant or plan pregnancy in the near future.
• Take any medicinal drugs or herbs including aspirin, laxatives, cold and cough remedies, antacids, vitamins, minerals, amino acids, supplements, other prescription or non-prescription drugs.

Pregnancy:
• Problems in pregnant women taking small or usual amounts have not been proved. But the chance of problems does exist. Don't use unless prescribed by your doctor.

Breast-feeding:
• Problems in breast-fed infants of lactating mothers taking small or usual amounts have not been proved. But the chance of problems does exist. Don't use unless prescribed by your doctor.

Infants and children:
• Treating infants and children under 2 with any supplement is hazardous.

Others:
• None expected if you are beyond childhood and under 45, basically healthy and take for only a short time.

Storage:
• Keep cool and dry, but don't freeze. Store safely away from children.

Safe dosage:
• At present no "safe" dosage has been established.

Toxicity

Comparative-toxicity rating not available from standard references.

Adverse Reactions, Side Effects or Overdose Symptoms

None expected

SUPPLEMENT

Wheatgrass/Barley Grass, Green Plants (Cabbage, Broccoli, Brussels Sprouts)

Basic Information

These products are derived from roots and leaves.
Chemicals this supplement contains:
Chlorophyll
Superoxide-dismutase

Known Effects

• May function as an anti-oxidant.

Unproved Speculated Benefits

• Protects against pollutants.
• Protects against radiation damage to cells.
• "Detoxifies" body.
• "Purifies" blood.
• Protects against cancer.

Warnings and Precautions

Don't take if you:
• Are pregnant, think you may be pregnant or plan pregnancy in the near future.

Consult your doctor if you:
• Take this herb for any medical problem that doesn't improve in 2 weeks. There may be safer, more-effective treatments.
• Take any medicinal drugs or herbs including aspirin, laxatives, cold and cough remedies, antacids, vitamins, minerals, amino acids, supplements, other prescription or non-prescription drugs.

Pregnancy:
• Problems in pregnant women taking small or usual amounts have not been proved. But the chance of problems does exist. Don't use unless prescribed by your doctor.

Breast-feeding:
• Problems in breast-fed infants of lactating mothers taking small or usual amounts have not been proved. But the chance of problems does exist. Don't use unless prescribed by your doctor.

Infants and children:
• Treating infants and children under 2 with any supplement is hazardous.

Others:
• No contraindications if you are not pregnant and do not take amounts larger than manufacturer's recommended dosage.

Storage:
• Keep cool and dry.

Safe dosage:
• At present no "safe" dosage has been established.

Toxicity

Comparative-toxicity rating not available from standard references.

Adverse Reactions, Side Effects or Overdose Symptoms

None expected

Medicinal Herbs

The following section makes an attempt to provide you with enough knowledge to avoid toxicity if you choose to self-prescribe medicinal herbs. If you collect and use herbal medications, you must be an expert botanist or herbologist. If you buy them, you have the right to know everything about possible side effects, adverse reactions, toxicity and other dangers in using materials that are not subjected to rigid control procedures.

I am not qualified to extol the virtues of herbal medicines. But I feel qualified to point out some of the inherent dangers in using medicinal herbs. That is the main purpose of the following section.

The most important warnings I can give you are:

🍃 Don't use medicinal herbs for infants or children without guidance from an expert and your doctor's approval.

🍃 Don't use medicinal herbs at all unless you know enough to use them safely.

🍃 Don't use medicinal herbs if there is a safer, more effective medicine to use, whatever problem you have.

🍃 If you choose to use medicinal herbs, tell your doctor which ones you use and in what amounts when he or she asks if you take other medications. As you will see in the following charts, these substances could affect various medicines or courses of treatment your doctor may prescribe.

Aconite (Monkshood, Blue Rocket)

Basic Information
Biological name (genus and species):
Aconitum napellus
Parts used for medicinal purposes:
Roots
Leaves
Chemicals this herb contains:
Aconine
Aconitine
Benzoylamine
Neopelline
Picratonitine

Known Effects

• Small amounts stimulate central nervous system and peripheral nerves.
• Large amounts depress central nervous system and peripheral nerves.
• Normalizes heartbeat irregularities.
• A dose as low as 5ml (about 1 teaspoon) of the root can be lethal.

Miscellaneous information:
• Was used for centuries as arrow poison.

Unproved Speculated Benefits

• Decreases fever.
• Treats heartbeat irregularities.
• Increases sweating.
• Decreases blood pressure.
• Treats neuralgias.
• Treats other nerve disorders.

Warnings and Precautions

Don't take if you:
• Are pregnant, think you may be pregnant or plan pregnancy in the near future.
• Have any chronic disease of the gastrointestinal tract, such as stomach or duodenal ulcers, oesophageal reflux (reflux oesophagitis), ulcerative colitis, spastic colitis, diverticulosis, diverticulitis.

Consult your doctor if you:
• Take this herb for any medical problem that doesn't improve in 2 weeks. There may be safer, more effective treatments.
• Take any medicinal drugs or herbs including aspirin, laxatives, cold and cough remedies, antacids, vitamins, minerals, amino acids, supplements, other prescription or non-prescription drugs.

Pregnancy:
• Dangers outweigh any possible benefits. Don't use.

Breast-feeding:
• Dangers outweigh any possible benefits. Don't use.

Infants and children:
• Treating infants and children under 2 with any herbal preparation is hazardous.

Others:
• Dangers outweigh any possible benefits. Don't use.

Storage:
• Keep cool and dry, but don't freeze. Store safely away from children.

Safe dosage:
• At present no "safe" dosage has been established.

Toxicity

Rated dangerous, particularly in children, persons over 55 and those who take larger than appropriate quantities for extended periods of time.

For symptoms of toxicity: See *Adverse Reactions, Side Effects or Overdose Symptoms* section below.

Adverse Reactions, Side Effects or Overdose Symptoms

Signs and symptoms:	What to do:
Burning tongue and lips	Discontinue. Call doctor immediately.
Difficulty swallowing	Discontinue. Call doctor immediately.
Irritability	Discontinue. Call doctor when convenient.
Nausea	Discontinue. Call doctor immediately.
Numbness of tongue and lips	Discontinue. Call doctor immediately.
Restlessness	Discontinue. Call doctor when convenient.
Speech difficulties	Discontinue. Call doctor immediately.
Vision doubled or blurred	Discontinue. Call doctor immediately.
Vomiting	Discontinue. Call doctor immediately.

Basic Information

Biological name (genus and species):
Agave lecheguilla
Parts used for medicinal purposes:
Roots
Leaves
Sap
Chemicals this herb contains:
Diosgenin
Photosensitizing pigment (See Glossary)
Steroidal chemicals (See Glossary)
Vitamin C

Known Effects

- Causes disintegration of red blood cells.
- Irritates skin.
- Irritates lining of gastrointestinal tract.
- Small amounts depress central nervous system.
- Damages cells, dissolves membranes of red blood cells and changes tissue permeability.

Miscellaneous information:
- Is used to make mescal, an alcoholic beverage.
- Fibres are used for rope.
- Sap is used as a syrup.
- Roots and leaves contain active chemicals.

Unproved Speculated Benefits

- Roots and leaves are used to relieve toothache.
- Provides nutrition.
- Is used as hormone replacement.
- Produces immunosuppressive effects on body.
- Causes abortion or miscarriage.
- Treats dysentery.
- Relieves pain of sprains.

Warnings and Precautions

Don't take if you:
- Are pregnant, think you may be pregnant or plan pregnancy in the near future.
- Have symptoms of a disease caused by a hormone deficiency.
- Have any chronic disease of the gastrointestinal tract, such as stomach or duodenal ulcers, oesophageal reflux (reflux oesophagitis), ulcerative colitis, spastic colitis, diverticulosis, diverticulitis.

Consult your doctor if you:
- Have stomach problems.
- Take cortisone, ACTH, testosterone, androgenic steroids.

- Are pregnant, think you may be pregnant or plan pregnancy in the near future.

Pregnancy:
- Problems in pregnant women taking small or usual amounts have not been proved. Don't use unless prescribed by your doctor.

Breast-feeding:
- Problems in breast-fed infants of lactating mothers taking small or usual amounts have not been proved. Don't use unless prescribed by your doctor.

Infants and children:
- Treating infants and children under 2 with any herbal preparation is hazardous.

Others:
- None expected if you are beyond childhood and under 45, basically healthy and take for only a short time.

Storage:
- Keep cool and dry, but don't freeze. Store safely away from children.

Safe dosage:
- At present no "safe" dosage established.

Toxicity

Comparative-toxicity rating not available from standard references.

For symptoms of toxicity: See below.

Adverse Reactions, Side Effects or Overdose Symptoms

Signs and symptoms:	What to do:
Abortion (remote possibility if taken in large amounts)	Seek emergency treatment.
Diarrhoea	Discontinue. Call doctor immediately.
Increased sensitivity to sunlight	Discontinue. Call doctor when convenient.
Jaundice (yellow eyes and skin)	Discontinue. Call doctor immediately.
Nausea	Discontinue. Call doctor immediately.
Skin itching and rash	Discontinue. Call doctor when convenient.
Unusual bleeding	Discontinue. Call doctor immediately.
Vomiting	Discontinue. Call doctor immediately.

Alder, Black (Alder Buckthorn)

Basic Information
Biological name (genus and species):
Rhamnus frangula, Frangula
Parts used for medicinal purposes:
Various parts of the entire plant, frequently
differing by country and/or culture
Chemicals this herb contains:
Anthraquinone glycosides
Emodin
Rhamnose

Known Effects

- Irritates gastrointestinal tract.
- Causes vomiting.

Miscellaneous information:
- Is used in veterinary medicine for its cathartic properties.
- Emetic action (causing vomiting) is less when plant is dried for 1 year or more.

Unproved Speculated Benefits

- Temporarily relieves constipation.

Warnings and Precautions

Don't take if you:
- Are pregnant, think you may be pregnant or plan pregnancy in the near future.
- Have any chronic disease of gastrointestinal tract, such as stomach or duodenal ulcers, oesophageal reflux (reflux oesophagitis), ulcerative colitis, spastic colitis, diverticulosis, diverticulitis.

Consult your doctor if you:
- Take this herb for any medical problem that doesn't improve in 2 weeks. There may be safer, more effective treatments.
- Take any medicinal drugs or herbs including aspirin, laxatives, cold and cough remedies, antacids, vitamins, minerals, amino acids, supplements, other prescription or non-prescription drugs.

Pregnancy:
- Problems in pregnant women taking small or usual amounts have not been proved. But the chance of problems does exist. Don't use unless prescribed by your doctor.

Breast-feeding:
- Problems in breast-fed infants of lactating mothers taking small or usual amounts have not been proved. But the chance of problems does exist. Don't use unless prescribed by your doctor.

Infants and children:
- Treating infants and children under 2 with any herbal preparation is hazardous.

Others:
- None expected if you are beyond childhood and under 45, basically healthy and take for only a short time.

Storage:
- Keep cool and dry, but don't freeze. Store safely away from children.

Safe dosage:
- At present no "safe" dosage has been established.

Toxicity

Rated slightly dangerous, particularly in children, persons over 55 and those who take larger than appropriate quantities for extended periods of time.

For symptoms of toxicity: See *Adverse Reactions, Side Effects or Overdose Symptoms* section below.

Adverse Reactions, Side Effects or Overdose Symptoms

Signs and symptoms:	What to do:
Abdominal cramps, severe	Discontinue. Call doctor immediately.
Abdominal pain	Discontinue. Call doctor when convenient.
Nausea	Discontinue. Call doctor immediately.
Vomiting	Discontinue. Call doctor immediately.

Basic Information

Biological name (genus and species):
Medicago sativa
Parts used for medicinal purposes:
Leaves
Petals/flower
Sprouts
Chemicals this herb contains:
Proteins
Vitamins A, B, D, K

Known Effects

- Provides useful proteins and vitamins for dietary use.
- Stimulates menstruation.
- Stimulates milk production in lactating women.

Miscellaneous information:
- Alfalfa is usually compressed into capsules or brewed as tea.

Unproved Speculated Benefits

- Treats arthritis.
- Treats unusual bleeding.
- Lowers cholesterol.

Warnings and Precautions

Don't take if you:
- Take anti-coagulants, such as warfarin sodium (Coumadin) or heparin.
- Have lupus erythematosus.

Consult your doctor if you:
- Have any bleeding disorder.

Pregnancy:
- Pregnant women should experience no problems taking usual amounts as part of a balanced diet. Other products extracted from this herb have not been proved to cause problems.

Breast-feeding:
- Breast-fed infants of lactating mothers should experience no problems when mother takes usual amounts as part of a balanced diet. Other products extracted from this herb have not been proved to cause problems.

Infants and children:
- Treating infants and children under 2 with any herbal preparation is hazardous.

Others:
- None expected if you are beyond childhood and under 45, basically healthy and take for only a short time.
- Alfalfa sprouts eaten in large amounts may cause one form of anaemia.

Storage:
- Keep cool and dry, but don't freeze. Store safely away from children.

Safe dosage:
- At present no "safe" dosage has been established.

Toxicity

Generally regarded as safe when taken in appropriate quantities for short periods of time.

Adverse Reactions, Side Effects or Overdose Symptoms

None expected

Allspice (Jamaican Pepper, Clove Pepper)

Basic Information

Biological name (genus and species):
Pimenta dioica
Parts used for medicinal purposes:
Berries/fruits
Chemicals this herb contains:
Acid-fixed oil
Eugenol
Resin (See Glossary)
Tannic acid
Volatile oils (See Glossary)

Known Effects

- Irritates mucous membranes including lining of gastrointestinal tract.
- Interferes with absorption of iron and other minerals when taken internally.

Miscellaneous information:

- Active chemicals are in allspice *berries*.
- Provides flavour in toothpaste and other products.
- Is used as an aromatic spice in foods.

Unproved Speculated Benefits

- Aids in expelling gas from intestines to relieve colic or griping.
- Relieves diarrhoea.
- Relieves fatigue.

Warnings and Precautions

Don't take if you:

- Are pregnant, think you may be pregnant or plan pregnancy in the near future.
- Have any chronic disease of the gastrointestinal tract, such as stomach or duodenal ulcers, oesophageal reflux (reflux oesophagitis), ulcerative colitis, spastic colitis, diverticulosis, diverticulitis.

Consult your doctor if you:

- Take any medicinal drugs or herbs, including aspirin, laxatives, cold and cough remedies, antacids, vitamins, minerals, amino acids, supplements, other prescription or non-prescription drugs.

Pregnancy:

- Problems in pregnant women taking small or usual amounts have not been proved. But the chance of problems does exist. Don't use unless prescribed by your doctor.

Breast-feeding:

- Problems in breast-fed infants of lactating mothers taking small or usual amounts have not been proved. But the chance of problems does exist. Don't use unless prescribed by your doctor.

Infants and children:

- Treating infants and children under 2 with any herbal preparation is hazardous.

Others:

- None expected if you are beyond childhood and under 45, basically healthy and take for only a short time.

Storage:

- Keep cool and dry, but don't freeze. Store safely away from children.

Safe dosage:

- At present no "safe" dosage has been established.

Toxicity

Rated relatively safe when taken in appropriate quantities for short periods of time.

For symptoms of toxicity: See *Adverse Reactions, Side Effects or Overdose Symptoms* section below.

Adverse Reactions, Side Effects or Overdose Symptoms

Signs and symptoms:	What to do:
Excess of 5 ml (about 1 teaspoon) of eugenol (a volatile oil found in allspice) may cause convulsions, nausea, vomiting	Discontinue. Call doctor immediately.

Aloe (Mediterranean Aloe, Barbados Aloe, Curacao Aloe, Aloe Vera)

Basic Information

Biological name (genus and species):
Aloe vera, Aloe barbadensis, Aloe officinalis
Parts used for medicinal purposes:
Leaves
Chemicals this herb contains:
Barbaloin (not present in Aloe vera)
Beta-barbaloin (purgative)
Socaloin
Resin (See Glossary)
Tannins (See Glossary)

Known Effects

- Milky exudate (not dried preparations) from leaves helps reduce inflammation and hasten recovery in first- and second-degree burns.
- Acts as cathartic, but whether this is beneficial or dangerous depends on many factors.
- Treats X-ray or radiation burns.
- Interferes with absorption of iron and other minerals when taken internally.

Miscellaneous information:
- Not useful for clearing intestinal tract before surgery because only cleanses small intestine.
- Is used as an ingredient in many over-the-counter laxatives.
- Is used as an ingredient in some cosmetics.

Unproved Speculated Benefits

- Applied to skin, it kills *Pseudomonas aeruginosa,* a bacterium, but probably does not promote healing.
- Taken internally, treats amenorrhoea (lack of menstrual periods).
- Is used as an aphrodisiac.
- Causes breast development to progress more quickly.
- Is applied to head to relieve headache.

Warnings and Precautions

Don't take if you:
- Have ulcers.
- Have small-bowel problems, such as regional enteritis.
- Have ulcerative colitis.
- Have diverticulosis or diverticulitis.
- Have procitis or haemorrhoids

Consult your doctor if you:
- Have any digestive disorder.
- Intend to take internally.

Pregnancy and breast-feeding:
- Problems in pregnant women or in breast-fed infants of lactating mothers taking small or usual amounts have not been proved. But the chance of problems does exist. Don't use unless prescribed by your doctor.

Infants and children:
- Treating infants and children under 2 with any herbal preparation is hazardous.

Others:
- Healing properties of aloe taken internally are still tentative and need more study.

Storage:
- Keep cool and dry, but don't freeze. Store safely away from children.

Safe dosage:
- At present no "safe" dosage has been established.

Toxicity

Generally regarded as safe when taken in appropriate quantities for short periods of time.

For symptoms of toxicity: See below.

Adverse Reactions, Side Effects or Overdose Symptoms

Signs and symptoms:	What to do:
Abdominal cramps	Discontinue. Call doctor when convenient.
Bowel irritation	Discontinue. Call doctor when convenient.
Diarrhoea	Discontinue. Call doctor immediately.
High dose: bloody diarrhoea, shock	Seek emergency treatment.
Minor skin irritation (for external applications)	Cleanse skin with clear water. Do not apply aloe again.
Nausea	Discontinue. Call doctor immediately.
Red urine	Discontinue. Call doctor when convenient.
Urinary frequency, backache, pain on urination with long, continued use	Discontinue. Call doctor immediately.
Vomiting	Discontinue. Call doctor immediately.

Alum Root (American Sanicle)

Basic Information

Biological name (genus and species):
Heuchera
Parts used for medicinal purposes:
Roots
Chemical this herb contains:
Tannins (See Glossary)

Known Effects

• Shrinks tissues.
• Prevents secretion of fluids.

Miscellaneous information:
• Is used externally and internally by some tribes of North-American Indians for many disorders.
• Is used as a douche.

Unproved Speculated Benefits

• Treats heart disease.
• Prevents infection in injured skin.

Warnings and Precautions

Don't take if you:
• Have liver or kidney disease.
• Are pregnant, think you may be pregnant or plan pregnancy in the near future.
• Have any chronic disease of the gastrointestinal tract, such as stomach or duodenal ulcers, oesophageal reflux (reflux oesophagitis), ulcerative colitis, spastic colitis, diverticulosis, diverticulitis.

Consult your doctor if you:
• Take this herb for any medical problem that doesn't improve in 2 weeks. There may be safer, more effective treatments.
• Take any medicinal drugs or herbs including aspirin, laxatives, cold and cough remedies, antacids, vitamins, minerals, amino acids, supplements, other prescription or non-prescription drugs.

Pregnancy:
• Problems in pregnant women taking small or usual amounts have not been proved. But the chance of problems does exist. Don't use unless prescribed by your doctor.

Breast-feeding:
• Problems in breast-fed infants of lactating mothers taking small or usual amounts have not been proved. But the chance of problems does exist. Don't use unless prescribed by your doctor.

Infants and children:
• Treating infants and children under 2 with any herbal preparation is hazardous.

Others:
• Toxic effects greatly outweigh any possible benefits. *Don't take this herb internally!*

Storage:
• Keep cool and dry, but don't freeze. Store safely away from children.

Safe dosage:
• At present no "safe" dosage has been established.

Toxicity

Comparative-toxicity rating not available from standard references. However, it is believed toxic effects greatly outweigh any possible benefits.

For symptoms of toxicity: See *Adverse Reactions, Side Effects or Overdose Symptoms* section below.

Adverse Reactions, Side Effects or Overdose Symptoms

Signs and symptoms:	What to do:
Burning indigestion	Discontinue. Call doctor when convenient.
Oedema (swelling of hands and feet)	Discontinue. Call doctor when convenient.
Jaundice (yellow eyes and skin)	Discontinue. Call doctor immediately.
Nausea	Discontinue. Call doctor immediately.
Vomiting	Discontinue. Call doctor immediately.

American Dogwood (Dogwood, American Boxwood)

Basic Information

Biological name (genus and species):
Cornus florida
Parts used for medicinal purposes:
Bark
Chemicals this herb contains:
Betulic acid
Cornin

Known Effects

- Irritates gastrointestinal tract and acts as a cathartic.
- Causes uterine contractions.

Unproved Speculated Benefits

- Reduces fever.
- Kills bacteria in boils, carbuncles, infected skin rashes, insect bites.

Warnings and Precautions

Don't take if you:
- Are pregnant. It may cause miscarriage.

Consult your doctor if you:
- Take this herb for any medical problem that doesn't improve in 2 weeks. There may be safer, more effective treatments.

Pregnancy:
- Dangers outweigh any possible benefits. Don't use.

Breast-feeding:
- Dangers outweigh any possible benefits. Don't use.

Infants and children:
- Treating infants and children under 2 with any herbal preparation is hazardous.

Storage:
- Keep cool and dry, but don't freeze. Store safely away from children.

Safe dosage:
- At present no "safe" dosage has been established.

Toxicity

Rated relatively safe when taken in appropriate quantities for short periods of time.

For symptoms of toxicity: See *Adverse Reactions, Side Effects or Overdose Symptoms* section below.

Adverse Reactions, Side Effects or Overdose Symptoms

Signs and symptoms:	What to do:
Abortion	Seek emergency treatment.
Dermatitis	Discontinue. Call doctor when convenient.

MEDICINAL HERB

Angelica (Garden Angelica, European Angelica)

Basic Information

Biological name (genus and species):
Angelica archangelica
Parts used for medicinal purposes:
Entire plant
Chemicals this herb contains:
Angelic acid
Resin (See Glossary)
Volatile oils (See Glossary)

Known Effects

Volatile oil gives angelica the following effects:
• Decreases thickness and increases fluidity of mucus from lungs and bronchial tubes.
• Increases perspiration.

Unproved Speculated Benefits

• Seeds and roots are used to reduce odour and volume of intestinal gasses.
• Brings on menstruation.

Warnings and Precautions

Don't take if you:
• Are pregnant, think you may be pregnant or plan pregnancy in the near future.
• Have any chronic disease of the gastrointestinal tract, such as stomach or duodenal ulcers, oesophageal reflux (reflux oesophagitis), ulcerative colitis, spastic colitis, diverticulosis, diverticulitis.

Consult your doctor if you:
• Take this herb for any medical problem that doesn't improve in 2 weeks. There may be safer, more effective treatments.
• Take any medicinal drugs or herbs, including aspirin, laxatives, cold and cough remedies, antacids, vitamins, minerals, amino acids, supplements, other prescription or non-prescription drugs.

Pregnancy:
• Dangers outweigh any possible benefits. Don't use.

Breast-feeding:
• Dangers outweigh any possible benefits. Don't use.

Infants and children:
• Treating infants and children under 2 with any herbal preparation is hazardous.

Others:
• None expected if you are healthy, take it for a short time and do not exceed manufacturer's recommended dosage.

Storage:
• Keep cool and dry, but don't freeze. Store safely away from children.

Safe dosage:
• At present no "safe" dosage has been established.

Toxicity

Rated relatively safe when taken in appropriate quantities for short periods of time.

Adverse Reactions, Side Effects or Overdose Symptoms

None expected

Basic Information

Biological name (genus and species):
Pimpinella anisum
Parts used for medicinal purposes:
Seeds
Chemicals this herb contains:
Anethole
Essential oils (See Glossary)

Known Effects

- Aids in expelling gas from intestinal tract.
- Helps body dispose of excess fluid by increasing amount of urine produced.
- Increases perspiration.
- Decreases thickness and increases fluidity of mucus from lungs and bronchial tubes.
- Causes hallucinations.

Miscellaneous information:
- Anise is also used in perfumes, soaps, beverages, baked goods, liqueur and as a flavouring.

Unproved Speculated Benefits

- Increases sex drive.
- Decreases colic.
- Treats asthma.
- Kills body lice when applied externally.
- Treats bronchitis.

Warnings and Precautions

Don't take if you:
- Are pregnant, think you may be pregnant or plan pregnancy in the near future.
- Have any chronic disease of the gastrointestinal tract, such as stomach or duodenal ulcers, oesophageal reflux (reflux oesophagitis), ulcerative colitis, spastic colitis, diverticulosis, diverticulitis.

Consult your doctor if you:
- Take this herb for any medical problem that doesn't improve in 2 weeks. There may be safer, more effective treatments.
- Take any medicinal drugs or herbs including aspirin, laxatives, cold and cough remedies, antacids, vitamins, minerals, amino acids, supplements, other prescription or non-prescription drugs.

Pregnancy:
- Dangers outweigh any possible benefits. Don't use.

Breast-feeding:
- Dangers outweigh any possible benefits. Don't use.

Storage:
- Keep cool and dry, but don't freeze. Store safely away from children.

Safe dosage:
- At present no "safe" dosage has been established.

Toxicity

Rated relatively safe when taken in appropriate quantities for short periods of time.

For symptoms of toxicity: See *Adverse Reactions, Side Effects or Overdose Symptoms* section below.

Adverse Reactions, Side Effects or Overdose Symptoms

Signs and symptoms:	What to do:
Oil may cause.	
Difficulty breathing	Seek emergency treatment.
Nausea	Discontinue. Call doctor immediately.
Seizures	Seek emergency treatment.
Skin irritation when applied to skin	Discontinue. Call doctor when convenient.
Vomiting	Discontinue. Call doctor immediately.

Asafetida (Devil's Dung)

Basic Information

Biological name (genus and species):
Ferula assafoetida, Ferula foetida
Parts used for medicinal purposes:
Roots
Chemicals this herb contains:
Gum (See Glossary)
Volatile oils (See Glossary)
Resin (See Glossary)

Known Effects

- Irritates lining of gastrointestinal tract and produces laxative effect.

Miscellaneous information:
- Introduced by Arab physicians to European medical practitioners.
- Has garlic-like odour and bitter taste. May have good placebo effect because it is so disagreeable.
- Is used in sack around the neck by some people to repel evil.
- Is used as a condiment.
- Provides flavour as ingredient in Worcestershire sauce.

Unproved Speculated Benefits

- Decreases thickness and increases fluidity of mucus from lungs and bronchial tubes.
- Treats colic (See Glossary).
- Temporarily relieves constipation.
- Treats nerve disorders.

Warnings and Precautions

Don't take if you:
- Are pregnant, think you may be pregnant or plan pregnancy in the near future.
- Have any chronic disease of the gastrointestinal tract, such as stomach or duodenal ulcers, oesophageal reflux (reflux oesophagitis), ulcerative colitis, spastic colitis, diverticulosis, diverticulitis.

Consult your doctor if you:
- Take this herb for any medical problem that doesn't improve in 2 weeks. There may be safer, more effective treatments.
- Take any medicinal drugs or herbs including aspirin, laxatives, cold and cough remedies, antacids, vitamins, minerals, amino acids, supplements, other prescription or non-prescription drugs.

Pregnancy:
- Dangers outweigh any possible benefits. Don't use.

Breast-feeding:
- Dangers outweigh any possible benefits. Don't use.

Infants and children:
- Treating infants and children under 2 with any herbal preparation is hazardous.

Others:
- No contraindications if you are not pregnant and do not exceed manufacturer's recommended dosage.

Storage:
- Keep cool and dry, but don't freeze. Store safely away from children.

Safe dosage:
- At present no "safe" dosage has been established.

Toxicity

Rated relatively safe when taken in appropriate quantities for short periods of time.

For symptoms of toxicity: See *Adverse Reactions, Side Effects or Overdose Symptoms* section below.

Adverse Reactions, Side Effects or Overdose Symptoms

Signs and symptoms:	What to do:
Diarrhoea	Discontinue. Call doctor immediately.

Basic Information

Biological name (genus and species):
Berberis vulgaris
Parts used for medicinal purposes:
Berries/fruits
Rootbark
Chemicals this herb contains:
Berbamine
Berberine
Berberrubine
Columbamine
Hydrastine
Jatrorrhizine
Oxycanthine
Palmatine

Known Effects

- Dilates blood vessels.
- Decreases heart rate.
- Depresses breathing.
- Stimulates intestinal movement.
- Reduces bronchial constriction.
- Kills bacteria on skin.

Miscellaneous information:
- Fruit is made into jelly.
- Roots are used to dye wool.
- Benefits are mainly based in folklore.

Unproved Speculated Benefits

- Treats diarrhoea.
- Treats dyspepsia.
- Treats skin infections.

Warnings and Precautions

Don't take if you:
- Are pregnant, think you may be pregnant or plan pregnancy in the near future.
- Take this herb for any medical problem that doesn't improve in 2 weeks. There may be safer, more effective treatments.

Consult your doctor if you:
- Take any medicinal drugs or herbs including aspirin, laxatives, cold and cough remedies, antacids, vitamins, minerals, amino acids, supplements, other prescription or non-prescription drugs.

Pregnancy:
- Dangers outweigh any possible benefits. Don't use.

Breast-feeding:
- Dangers outweigh any possible benefits. Don't use.

Infants and children:
- Treating infants and children under 2 with any herbal preparation is hazardous.

Others:
- None expected if you are beyond childhood and under 45, not pregnant, basically healthy and take for only a short time.

Storage:
- Keep cool and dry, but don't freeze. Store safely away from children.

Safe dosage:
- At present no "safe" dosage has been established.

Toxicity

Rated slightly dangerous, particularly in children, persons over 55 and those who take larger than appropriate quantities for extended periods of time.

Adverse Reactions, Side Effects or Overdose Symptoms

None expected

MEDICINAL HERB

Barley

Basic Information

Biological name (genus and species):
   Hordeum distichon, Hordeum spp
Parts used for medicinal purposes:
   Various parts of the entire plant, frequently
   differing by country and/or culture
Chemicals this herb contains:
   Ash
   Cellulose
   Hordenine
   Invert sugar
   Lignin
   Malt
   Nitrogen
   Pectin
   Pentosan
   Protein
   Starch
   Sucrose

Known Effects

• Provides nutrition to body.

Miscellaneous information:
• Barley is a grain and primarily contains
  nutrients.

Unproved Speculated Benefits

• Is used as a "restorative" following stomach
  and intestinal irritation.
• Protects scraped tissues.

Warnings and Precautions

Don't take if you:
• Are allergic or sensitive to barley or gluten.

Consult your doctor if you:
• Take this herb for any medical problem that
  doesn't improve in 2 weeks. There may be
  safer, more effective treatments.
• Take any medicinal drugs or herbs including
  aspirin, laxatives, cold and cough remedies,
  antacids, vitamins, minerals, amino acids,
  supplements, other prescription or non-
  prescription drugs.

Pregnancy:
• Problems in pregnant women taking small or
  usual amounts have not been proved. But the
  chance of problems does exist. Don't use
  unless prescribed by your doctor.

Breast-feeding:
• Problems in breast-fed infants of lactating
  mothers taking small or usual amounts have
  not been proved. But the chance of problems
  does exist. Don't use unless prescribed by your
  doctor.

Infants and children:
• Treating infants and children under 2 with any
  herbal preparation is hazardous.

Others:
• Barley infested with fungus can cause
  poisoning in animals.

Storage:
• Keep cool and dry, but don't freeze. Store
  safely away from children.

Safe dosage:
• At present no "safe" dosage has been
  established.

Toxicity

Comparative-toxicity rating not available from
standard references.

Adverse Reactions, Side Effects or Overdose Symptoms

None expected

Basic Information

Biological name (genus and species):
Myrica cerifera
Parts used for medicinal purposes:
Bark
Berries/fruits
Leaves
Chemicals this herb contains:
Gallic acid
Mycricic acid containing palmitin
Myricinic acid, related to saponin
Resin (See Glossary)
Tannic acid

 ## Known Effects

- Shrinks tissues.
- Prevents secretion of fluids.
- Interferes with absorption of iron and other minerals when taken internally.

Miscellaneous information:
- Injections of bark extract have caused cancer in laboratory animals.
- Frequently used as a basic ingredient in cosmetics, pharmaceuticals, candle making.

 ## Unproved Speculated Benefits

Internal use:
- Causes vomiting.
- Treats the common cold.
- Treats diarrhoea.
- Treats jaundice.

External use:
- Heals ulcers.
- Treats gum problems.

 ## Warnings and Precautions

Don't take if you:
- Are pregnant, think you may be pregnant or plan pregnancy in the near future.

Consult your doctor if you:
- Take this herb for any medical problem that doesn't improve in 2 weeks. There may be safer, more effective treatments.
- Take any medicinal drugs or herbs including aspirin, laxatives, cold and cough remedies, antacids, vitamins, minerals, amino acids, supplements, other prescription or non-prescription drugs.

Pregnancy:
- Problems in pregnant women taking small or usual amounts have not been proved. But the chance of problems does exist. Don't use unless prescribed by your doctor.

Breast-feeding:
- Problems in breast-fed infants of lactating mothers taking small or usual amounts have not been proved. But the chance of problems does exist. Don't use unless prescribed by your doctor.

Infants and children:
- Treating infants and children under 2 with any herbal preparation is hazardous.

Others:
- None expected if you are beyond childhood and under 45, basically healthy and take for only a short time.

Storage:
- Keep cool and dry, but don't freeze. Store safely away from children.

Safe dosage:
- At present no "safe" dosage has been established.

 ## Toxicity

Rated relatively safe when taken in appropriate quantities for short periods of time.

 ## Adverse Reactions, Side Effects or Overdose Symptoms

None expected

Bearberry (Uva-ursi)

Basic Information

Biological name (genus and species):
　Arctostaphylos uva-ursi
Parts used for medicinal purposes:
　Leaves
Chemicals this herb contains:
　Arbutin
　Ericolin
　Gallic acid
　Hydroquinolone
　Malic acid
　Quercetin
　Tannins (See Glossary)
　Ursolic acid
　Volatile oils (See Glossary)

 Known Effects

- Shrinks urinary tissues.
- Prevents secretion of fluids.
- Relieves urinary pain.
- Helps body dispose of excess fluid by increasing amount of urine produced.
- Interferes with absorption of iron and other minerals when taken internally.

Miscellaneous information:
- Bearberry turns urine green.

 Unproved Speculated Benefits

Boiled, bruised leaves:
- Act as a sedative.
- Relieve nausea.
- Decrease ringing in ears.
- Treat breathing problems.

 Warnings and Precautions

Don't take if you:
- Are pregnant, think you may be pregnant or plan pregnancy in the near future.

Consult your doctor if you:
- Take this herb for any medical problem that doesn't improve in 2 weeks. There may be safer, more effective treatments.
- Take any medicinal drugs or herbs including aspirin, laxatives, cold and cough remedies, antacids, vitamins, minerals, amino acids, supplements, other prescription or non-prescription drugs.

Pregnancy:
- Problems in pregnant women taking small or usual amounts have not been proved. But the chance of problems does exist. Don't use unless prescribed by your doctor.

Breast-feeding:
- Problems in breast-fed infants of lactating mothers taking small or usual amounts have not been proved. But the chance of problems does exist. Don't use unless prescribed by your doctor.

Infants and children:
- Treating infants and children under 2 with any herbal preparation is hazardous.

Others:
- No contraindications if you are not pregnant and do not take amounts larger than manufacturer's recommended dosage.

Storage:
- Keep cool and dry, but don't freeze. Store safely away from children.

Safe dosage:
- At present no "safe" dosage has been established.

 Toxicity

Rated relatively safe when taken in appropriate quantities for short periods of time.

 Adverse Reactions, Side Effects or Overdose Symptoms

None expected

Basic Information

Biological name (genus and species):
   Betula alba, B. lenta
Parts used for medicinal purposes:
   Bark
   Leaves
Chemicals this herb contains:
   Betulin in bark
   Methyl salicylate (similar to aspirin) in bark
   Resin in shoots and leaves (See Glossary)
   Tar (creosol, phenol, creosote, guaiacol) in
      bark

 ## Known Effects

- Provides counterirritation when applied to skin overlying an inflamed or irritated joint.
- Decreases inflammation in tissues.

Miscellaneous information:
- Leaves have agreeable aromatic odour but bitter taste.

 ## Unproved Speculated Benefits

- Is steeped to extract its medicinal properties for rheumatism and congestive heart failure.
- Treats skin disorders when applied topically.
- Shrinks tissues.
- Treats arthritis.
- Prevents secretion of fluids.

 ## Warnings and Precautions

Don't take if you:
- Are pregnant, think you may be pregnant or plan pregnancy in the near future.

Consult your doctor if you:
- Take this herb for any medical problem that doesn't improve in 2 weeks. There may be safer, more effective treatments.
- Take any medicinal drugs or herbs including aspirin, laxatives, cold and cough remedies, antacids, vitamins, minerals, amino acids, supplements, other prescription or non-prescription drugs.

Pregnancy:
- Problems in pregnant women taking small or usual amounts have not been proved. But the chance of problems does exist. Don't use unless prescribed by your doctor.

Breast-feeding:
- Problems in breast-fed infants of lactating mothers taking small or usual amounts have not been proved. But the chance of problems does exist. Don't use unless prescribed by your doctor.

Infants and children:
- Treating infants and children under 2 with any herbal preparation is hazardous.

Others:
- No contraindications if you are not pregnant and do not take amounts larger than a reputable manufacturer recommends on package.

Storage:
- Keep cool and dry, but don't freeze. Store safely away from children.

Safe dosage:
- At present no "safe" dosage has been established.

 ## Toxicity

Comparative-toxicity rating not available from standard references.

 ## Adverse Reactions, Side Effects or Overdose Symptoms

None expected

Birthroot (Bethroot)

Basic Information

Biological name (genus and species):
Trillium erectum, T. pendulum
Parts used for medicinal purposes:
Various parts of the entire plant, frequently differing by country and/or culture
Chemicals this herb contains:
Resin (See Glossary)
Saponin (See Glossary)
Starch
Tannins (See Glossary)
Volatile oils (See Glossary)

Known Effects

• Irritates mucous membranes.

Miscellaneous information:
• Name *birthroot* resulted from pioneers using this herb to stop bleeding after childbirth.

Unproved Speculated Benefits

• Is used as an aphrodisiac by Indians in southeastern United States.
• Treats gastrointestinal upsets.
• Decreases heartbeat irregularities.
• Controls skin infections.
• Stops excessive bleeding.
• Treats menstrual irregularity or increased menstrual frequency.
• Shrinks tissues.
• Prevents secretion of fluids.
• Decreases thickness and increases fluidity of mucus from lungs and bronchial tubes.
• Is used as an astringent poultice.

Warnings and Precautions

Don't take if you:
• Are pregnant, think you may be pregnant or plan pregnancy in the near future.

Consult your doctor if you:
• Take this herb for any medical problem that doesn't improve in 2 weeks. There may be safer, more effective treatments.
• Take any medicinal drugs or herbs including aspirin, laxatives, cold and cough remedies, antacids, vitamins, minerals, amino acids, supplements, other prescription or non-prescription drugs.

Pregnancy:
• Problems in pregnant women taking small or usual amounts have not been proved. But the chance of problems does exist. Don't use unless prescribed by your doctor.

Breast-feeding:
• Problems in breast-fed infants of lactating mothers taking small or usual amounts have not been proved. But the chance of problems does exist. Don't use unless prescribed by your doctor.

Infants and children:
• Treating infants and children under 2 with any herbal preparation is hazardous.

Others:
• No contraindications if you are not pregnant and do not take amounts larger than manufacturer's recommended dosage.

Storage:
• Keep cool and dry, but don't freeze. Store safely away from children.

Safe dosage:
• At present no "safe" dosage has been established.

Toxicity

Comparative-toxicity rating not available from standard references.

Adverse Reactions, Side Effects or Overdose Symptoms

None expected

Basic Information

Biological name (genus and species):
Polygonum bistorta
Parts used for medicinal purposes:
Various parts of the entire plant, frequently differing by country and/or culture
Chemical this herb contains:
Tannins (See Glossary)

Known Effects

- Precipitates proteins.
- Shrinks tissues.
- Prevents secretion of fluids.
- Interferes with absorption of iron and other minerals.

Unproved Speculated Benefits

Roots:
- Are used for astringent gargle.
- Treat unusual bleeding.
- Cause vomiting.
- Treat cavities in teeth.

Warnings and Precautions

Don't take if you:
- Are pregnant, think you may be pregnant or plan pregnancy in the near future.
- Have any chronic disease of gastrointestinal tract, such as stomach or duodenal ulcers, oesophageal reflux (reflux oesophagitis), ulcerative colitis, spastic colitis, diverticulosis, diverticulitis.

Consult your doctor if you:
- Take this herb for any medical problem that doesn't improve in 2 weeks. There may be safer, more effective treatments.
- Take any medicinal drugs or herbs including aspirin, laxatives, cold and cough remedies, antacids, vitamins, minerals, amino acids, supplements, other prescription or non-prescription drugs.

Pregnancy:
- Dangers outweigh any possible benefits. Don't use.

Breast-feeding:
- Dangers outweigh any possible benefits. Don't use.

Infants and children:
- Treating infants and children under 2 with any herbal preparation is hazardous.

Others:
- No contraindications if you are not pregnant and do not take amounts larger than manufacturer's recommended dosage.

Storage:
- Keep cool and dry, but don't freeze. Store safely away from children.

Safe dosage:
- At present no "safe" dosage has been established.

Toxicity

Comparative-toxicity rating not available from standard references.

For symptoms of toxicity: See *Adverse Reactions, Side Effects or Overdose Symptoms* section below.

Adverse Reactions, Side Effects or Overdose Symptoms

Signs and symptoms:	What to do:
Bleeding from stomach characterized by vomiting bright-red blood or material that looks like coffee grounds	Discontinue. Call doctor immediately.
Kidney damage characterized by blood in urine, decreased urine flow, swelling of hands and feet.	Seek emergency treatment.
Nausea	Discontinue. Call doctor immediately.
Vomiting	Discontinue. Call doctor immediately.

Bitter Lettuce

Basic Information

Biological name (genus and species):
   Lactuca virosa, L. sativa, L. scariola
Parts used for medicinal purposes:
   Latex, which exudes from stem of flower stalks
Chemicals this herb contains:
   Caoutchouc
   Hyoscyamine
   Lactucerol
   Latucic acid
   Lactucin
   Mannite
   Nitrates
   Volatile oils (See Glossary)

 ## Known Effects

• Depresses central nervous system.

 ## Unproved Speculated Benefits

• Acts as a sedative to relieve anxiety or nervous disorders.
• Treats coughs.
• Treats chest pain due to coronary artery disease (angina).
• Causes a "high" when smoked.

 ## Warnings and Precautions

Don't take if you:
• Are pregnant, think you may be pregnant or plan pregnancy in the near future.

Consult your doctor if you:
• Take this herb for any medical problem that doesn't improve in 2 weeks. There may be safer, more effective treatments.
• Take any medicinal drugs or herbs including aspirin, laxatives, cold and cough remedies, antacids, vitamins, minerals, amino acids, supplements, other prescription or non-prescription drugs.

Pregnancy:
• Dangers outweigh any possible benefits. Don't use.

Breast-feeding:
• Dangers outweigh any possible benefits. Don't use.

Infants and children:
• Treating infants and children under 2 with any herbal preparation is hazardous.

Others:
• Dangers outweigh any possible benefits. Don't use.

Storage:
• Keep cool and dry, but don't freeze. Store safely away from children.

Safe dosage:
• At present no "safe" dosage has been established.

 ## Toxicity

Rated relatively safe when taken in appropriate quantities for short periods of time.

For symptoms of toxicity: See *Adverse Reactions, Side Effects or Overdose Symptoms* section below.

 ## Adverse Reactions, Side Effects or Overdose Symptoms

Signs and symptoms:	What to do:
Breathing difficulties	Seek emergency treatment.

Bitter Root (Wild Ipecac, Spreading Dogbane, Rheumatism Weed)

Basic Information

Biological name (genus and species):
Apocynum androsaemifolium
Parts used for medicinal purposes:
Roots, Bark, Petals/flower
Chemicals this herb contains:

Apocynein	Cymarin
Apocynin	Saponin (See Glossary)

Known Effects

- Slows heartbeat.
- Helps body dispose of excess fluid by increasing amount of urine produced.
- Causes vomiting.

Miscellaneous information:
- Bitter root has marked effect on the heart. Prescribed digitalis preparations are far superior in treating heart disorders such as congestive heart failure and heartbeat irregularities.
- Many plants of varying potency and toxicity are called by this name. Be sure you know what you buy and take.
- You will need increased potassium if you take this herb. Take potassium supplement or eat more food high in potassium, such as apricots, citrus fruits, bananas.

Unproved Speculated Benefits

- Treats congestive heart failure.
- Treats palpitations.
- Treats gallstones.
- "Corrects" bile flow.
- Roots and rhizomes are used to make a medicinal preparation to restore normal tone to tissues or to stimulate appetite.

Warnings and Precautions

Don't take if you:
- Are pregnant, think you may be pregnant or plan pregnancy in the near future.
- Have any chronic disease of gastrointestinal tract, such as stomach or duodenal ulcers, oesophageal reflux (reflux oesophagitis), ulcerative colitis, spastic colitis, diverticulosis, diverticulitis.

Consult your doctor if you:
- Take this herb for any medical problem that doesn't improve in 2 weeks. There may be safer, more effective treatments.

- Take any medicinal drugs or herbs including aspirin, laxatives, cold and cough remedies, antacids, vitamins, minerals, amino acids, supplements, other prescription or non-prescription drugs.

Pregnancy:
- Problems in pregnant women taking small or usual amounts have not been proved. But the chance of problems does exist. Don't use unless prescribed by your doctor.

Breast-feeding:
- Problems in breast-fed infants of lactating mothers taking small or usual amounts have not been proved. But the chance of problems does exist. Don't use unless prescribed by your doctor.

Infants and children:
- Treating infants and children under 2 with any herbal preparation is hazardous.

Others:
- Use only under medical supervision.

Storage:
- Keep cool and dry, but don't freeze. Store safely away from children.

Safe dosage:
- At present no "safe" dosage has been established.

Toxicity

Rated slightly dangerous, particularly in children, persons over 55 and those who take larger than appropriate quantities for extended periods of time.

For symptoms of toxicity: See below.

Adverse Reactions, Side Effects or Overdose Symptoms

Signs and symptoms:	What to do:
Precipitous blood-pressure drop—symptoms include, faintness, cold sweat, paleness, rapid pulse.	Seek emergency treatment.
Gastritis	Discontinue. Call doctor when convenient.
Heartbeat irregularities	Seek emergency treatment.
Vomiting	Discontinue. Call doctor immediately.

Bittersweet (European Bittersweet, Bitter Nightshade, Felonwood)

Basic Information
Biological name (genus and species):
Solanum dulcamara
Parts used for medicinal purposes:
Leaves
Roots
Chemicals this herb contains:
Dulcamarin
Saponin (See Glossary)
Solanine
Solanidine

Known Effects

• Depresses central nervous system.

Miscellaneous information:
• Bittersweet is a potentially dangerous herb. Toxic amounts depress nervous system and cause drowsiness. Berries are poisonous.

Unproved Speculated Benefits

• Treats glandular problems of thyroid, pancreas, ovaries.
• Is used as a lymphatic medicine.
• Treats eczema (See Glossary).
• Kills pain.
• Treats arthritis.
• Is used as an aphrodisiac.
• Treats skin diseases.

Warnings and Precautions

Don't take if you:
• Are pregnant, think you may be pregnant or plan pregnancy in the near future.
• Have any chronic disease of the gastrointestinal tract, such as stomach or duodenal ulcers, oesophageal reflux (reflux oesophagitis), ulcerative colitis, spastic colitis, diverticulosis, diverticulitis.

Consult your doctor if you:
• Take this herb for any medical problem that doesn't improve in 2 weeks. There may be safer, more effective treatments.
• Take any medicinal drugs or herbs including aspirin, laxatives, cold and cough remedies, antacids, vitamins, minerals, amino acids, supplements, other prescription or non-prescription drugs.

Pregnancy:
• Dangers outweigh any possible benefits. Don't use.

Breast-feeding:
• Dangers outweigh any possible benefits. Don't use.

Infants and children:
• Treating infants and children under 2 with any herbal preparation is hazardous.

Others:
• Dangers outweigh any possible benefits. Don't use.

Storage:
• Keep cool and dry, but don't freeze. Store safely away from children.

Safe dosage:
• At present no "safe" dosage has been established.

Toxicity

Rated slightly dangerous, particularly in children, persons over 55 and those who take larger than appropriate quantities for extended periods of time.

For symptoms of toxicity: See *Adverse Reactions, Side Effects or Overdose Symptoms* section below.

Adverse Reactions, Side Effects or Overdose Symptoms

Signs and symptoms:	What to do:
Toxins are mostly in unripe fruit, which cause the following symptoms:	
Burning throat	Discontinue. Call doctor when convenient.
Coma	Seek emergency treatment.
Dilated pupils	Discontinue. Call doctor immediately.
Dizziness	Discontinue. Call doctor immediately.
Headache	Discontinue. Call doctor when convenient.
Muscle weakness	Discontinue. Call doctor immediately.
Nausea	Discontinue. Call doctor immediately.
Slow pulse	Seek emergency treatment.
Vomiting	Discontinue. Call doctor immediately.

Basic Information

Biological name (genus and species):
Juglans nigra
Parts used for medicinal purposes:
Husks
Inner bark
Leaves
Chemicals this herb contains:
Ellagic acid
Juglone
Nucin

Known Effects

- Shrinks tissues.
- Prevents secretion of fluids.

Miscellaneous information:
- Nut husks yield brown dye for hair and clothing.

Unproved Speculated Benefits

- Leaves, bark and cut-open ends of nut husks are used to treat fungal infections of skin.

Warnings and Precautions

Don't take if you:
- Are pregnant, think you may be pregnant or plan pregnancy in the near future.
- Have any chronic disease of the gastrointestinal tract, such as stomach or duodenal ulcers, oesophageal reflux (reflux oesophagitis), ulcerative colitis, spastic colitis, diverticulosis, diverticulitis.

Consult your doctor if you:
- Take this herb for any medical problem that doesn't improve in 2 weeks. There may be safer, more effective treatments.
- Take any medicinal drugs or herbs including aspirin, laxatives, cold and cough remedies, antacids, vitamins, minerals, amino acids, supplements, other prescription or non-prescription drugs.

Pregnancy:
- Problems in pregnant women taking small or usual amounts have not been proved. But the chance of problems does exist. Don't use unless prescribed by your doctor.

Breast-feeding:
- Problems in breast-fed infants of lactating mothers taking small or usual amounts have not been proved. But the chance of problems does exist. Don't use unless prescribed by your doctor.

Infants and children:
- Treating infants and children under 2 with any herbal preparation is hazardous.

Others:
- None expected if you are under 45, not pregnant, basically healthy, take it for a short time and do not exceed manufacturer's recommended dosage.

Storage:
- Keep cool and dry, but don't freeze. Store safely away from children.

Safe dosage:
- At present no "safe" dosage has been established.

Toxicity

Comparative-toxicity rating not available from standard references.

For symptoms of toxicity: See *Adverse Reactions, Side Effects or Overdose Symptoms* section below.

Adverse Reactions, Side Effects or Overdose Symptoms

Signs and symptoms:	What to do:
Nausea	Discontinue. Call doctor immediately.
Upper-abdominal pain	Discontinue. Call doctor when convenient.

MEDICINAL HERB

Bladderwrack

Basic Information

Biological name (genus and species):
   Fuycus vesiculosus
Parts used for medicinal purposes:
   Various parts of the entire plant, frequently
   differing by country and/or culture
Chemicals this herb contains:
   Alginic acid
   Bromine iodine
   Fucodin
   Laminarin

Known Effects

• Absorbs water in intestines to form bulk.

Unproved Speculated Benefits

• Treats obesity.
• Increases thyroid activity.
• Kills intestinal parasites.

Warnings and Precautions

Don't take if you:
• Are pregnant, think you may be pregnant or
plan pregnancy in the near future.

Consult your doctor if you:
• Take this herb for any medical problem that
doesn't improve in 2 weeks. There may be
safer, more effective treatments.
• Take any medicinal drugs or herbs including
aspirin, laxatives, cold and cough remedies,
antacids, vitamins, minerals, amino acids,
supplements, other prescription or non-
prescription drugs.

Pregnancy:
• Problems in pregnant women taking small or
usual amounts have not been proved. But the
chance of problems does exist. Don't use
unless prescribed by your doctor.

Breast-feeding:
• Problems in breast-fed infants of lactating
mothers taking small or usual amounts have
not been proved. But the chance of problems
does exist. Don't use unless prescribed by your
doctor.

Infants and children:
• Treating infants and children under 2 with any
herbal preparation is hazardous.

Others:
• None expected if you are under 45, not
pregnant, basically healthy, take it for only a
short time and do not exceed manufacturer's
recommended dosage.

Storage:
• Keep cool and dry, but don't freeze. Store
safely away from children.

Safe dosage:
• At present no "safe" dosage has been
established.

Toxicity

Comparative-toxicity rating not available from
standard references.

Adverse Reactions, Side Effects or Overdose Symptoms

None expected

Basic Information

Biological name (genus and species):
Cincus benedictus
Parts used for medicinal purposes:
Various parts of the entire plant, frequently differing by country and/or culture
Chemicals this herb contains:
Cincin
Volatile oils (See Glossary)

Known Effects

- Stimulates secretions from stomach.
- Irritates mucous membranes.

Miscellaneous information:
- Is applied to skin overlying a joint to cause an irritant to relieve another irritant.
- Effects have not been studied to any great extent.
- Careful handling is necessary to avoid toxic effects on skin.

Unproved Speculated Benefits

- Increases stomach secretions.
- Increases appetite.

Warnings and Precautions

Don't take if you:
- Are pregnant, think you may be pregnant or plan pregnancy in the near future.
- Have any chronic disease of the gastrointestinal tract, such as stomach or duodenal ulcers, oesophageal reflux (reflux oesophagitis), ulcerative colitis, spastic colitis, diverticulosis, diverticulitis.

Consult your doctor if you:
- Take this herb for any medical problem that doesn't improve in 2 weeks. There may be safer, more effective treatments.
- Take any medicinal drugs or herbs including aspirin, laxatives, cold and cough remedies, antacids, vitamins, minerals, amino acids, supplements, other prescription or non-prescription drugs.

Pregnancy:
- Problems in pregnant women taking small or usual amounts have not been proved. But the chance of problems does exist. Don't use unless prescribed by your doctor.

Breast-feeding:
- Problems in breast-fed infants of lactating mothers taking small or usual amounts have not been proved. But the chance of problems does exist. Don't use unless prescribed by your doctor.

Infants and children:
- Treating infants and children under 2 with any herbal preparation is hazardous.

Others:
- None expected if you are beyond childhood and under 45, basically healthy and take for only a short time.

Storage:
- Keep cool and dry, but don't freeze. Store safely away from children.

Safe dosage:
- At present no "safe" dosage has been established.

Toxicity

Comparative-toxicity rating not available from standard references.

For symptoms of toxicity: See *Adverse Reactions, Side Effects or Overdose Symptoms* section below.

Adverse Reactions, Side Effects or Overdose Symptoms

Signs and symptoms:	What to do:
Vomiting	Discontinue. Call doctor immediately.

Blueberry

Basic Information

Biological name (genus and species):
   Vaccinum spp
Parts used for medicinal purposes:
   Leaves
   Stems
Chemicals this herb contains:
   Fatty acids (See Glossary)
   Hydroquinone
   Loeanolic acid
   Neomyrtillin
   Tannins (See Glossary)
   Ursolic acid

Known Effects

- Decreases blood sugar.
- Interferes with absorption of iron and other minerals when taken internally.

Unproved Speculated Benefits

- Treats diarrhoea.
- Treats gastroenteritis.
- Helps body dispose of excess fluid by increasing amount of urine produced.
- Treats and prevents scurvy.

Warnings and Precautions

Don't take if you:
- Are pregnant, think you may be pregnant or plan pregnancy in the near future.

Consult your doctor if you:
- Take this herb for any medical problem that doesn't improve in 2 weeks. There may be safer, more effective treatments.
- Take any medicinal drugs or herbs including aspirin, laxatives, cold and cough remedies, antacids, vitamins, minerals, amino acids, supplements, other prescription or non-prescription drugs.

Pregnancy:
- Problems in pregnant women taking small or usual amounts have not been proved. But the chance of problems does exist. Don't use unless prescribed by your doctor.

Breast-feeding:
- Problems in breast-fed infants of lactating mothers taking small or usual amounts have not been proved. But the chance of problems does exist. Don't use unless prescribed by your doctor.

Infants and children:
- Treating infants and children under 2 with any herbal preparation is hazardous.

Others:
- None expected if you are beyond childhood and under 45, basically healthy and take for only a short time.

Storage:
- Keep cool and dry, but don't freeze. Store safely away from children.

Safe dosage:
- At present no "safe" dosage has been established.

Toxicity

Comparative-toxicity rating not available from standard references.

Adverse Reactions, Side Effects or Overdose Symptoms

None expected

Boneset (Richweed, White Snakeroot, Ague Weed)

Basic Information

Biological name (genus and species):
Eupatorium perfoliatum, E. rugosum
Parts used for medicinal purposes:
Leaves
Petals/flower
Chemicals this herb contains:
Eupatroin
Resin (See Glossary)
Sugar
Tremetrol
Volatile oils (See Glossary)
Wax (See Glossary)

Known Effects

- Irritates gastrointestinal tract.
- Can produce "milk sickness" in humans, an acute disease characterized by trembling, vomiting and severe abdominal pain. It is caused by eating dairy products or beef from cattle poisoned by eating boneset.
- Increases perspiration.
- Causes vomiting.

Miscellaneous information:
- Tremetrol can accumulate slowly in animal bodies and cause toxic symptoms. It may do the same in humans.

Unproved Speculated Benefits

- Decreases blood sugar.
- Treats malaria.
- Treats fever.

Warnings and Precautions

Don't take if you:
- Are pregnant, think you may be pregnant or plan pregnancy in the near future.
- Have any chronic disease of the gastrointestinal tract, such as stomach or duodenal ulcers, oesophageal reflux (reflux oesophagitis), ulcerative colitis, spastic colitis, diverticulosis, diverticulitis.

Consult your doctor if you:
- Take this herb for any medical problem that doesn't improve in 2 weeks. There may be safer, more effective treatments.

- Take any medicinal drugs or herbs including aspirin, laxatives, cold and cough remedies, antacids, vitamins, minerals, amino acids, supplements, other prescription or non-prescription drugs.

Pregnancy:
- Dangers outweigh any possible benefits. Don't use.

Breast-feeding:
- Dangers outweigh any possible benefits. Don't use.

Infants and children:
- Treating infants and children under 2 with any herbal preparation is hazardous.

Others:
- Dangers outweigh any possible benefits. Don't use.

Storage:
- Keep cool and dry, but don't freeze. Store safely away from children.

Safe dosage:
- At present no "safe" dosage has been established.

Toxicity

Comparative-toxicity rating not available from standard references.

For symptoms of toxicity: See below.

Adverse Reactions, Side Effects or Overdose Symptoms

Signs and symptoms:	What to do:
Breathing difficulties	Seek emergency treatment.
Coma	Seek emergency treatment.
Drooling	Discontinue. Call doctor when convenient.
Muscle trembling	Discontinue. Call doctor immediately.
Nausea	Discontinue. Call doctor immediately.
Stiffness	Discontinue. Call doctor when convenient.
Vomiting	Discontinue. Call doctor immediately.
Weakness	Discontinue. Call doctor when convenient.

Buchu (Honey Buchu, Short-Leaf Mountain Buchu)

Basic Information

Biological name (genus and species):
Barosma betulina
Parts used for medicinal purposes:
Leaves
Chemicals this herb contains:
Diasmin
Hesperidin
I-enthone
Mucilage (See Glossary)
Resin (See Glossary)
Volatile oils (See Glossary)

Known Effects

- Helps body dispose of excess fluid by increasing amount of urine produced.
- Works as a urinary antiseptic.
- Aids in expelling gas from intestinal tract.

Miscellaneous information:
- Has peppermint-like odour.
- This herb is no longer used by medical profession.

Unproved Speculated Benefits

- Treats kidney stones.
- Treats chronic prostatitis.
- Treats bladder irritation.
- Treats urethral irritation.
- Stimulates central nervous system.
- Increases perspiration.

Warnings and Precautions

Don't take if you:
- Are pregnant, think you may be pregnant or plan pregnancy in the near future.
- Have any chronic disease of the gastrointestinal tract, such as stomach or duodenal ulcers, oesophageal reflux (reflux oesophagitis), ulcerative colitis, spastic colitis, diverticulosis, diverticulitis.

Consult your doctor if you:
- Take this herb for any medical problem that doesn't improve in 2 weeks. There may be safer, more effective treatments.
- Take any medicinal drugs or herbs including aspirin, laxatives, cold and cough remedies, antacids, vitamins, minerals, amino acids, supplements, other prescription or non-prescription drugs.

Pregnancy:
- Dangers outweigh any possible benefits. Don't use.

Breast-feeding:
- Dangers outweigh any possible benefits. Don't use.

Infants and children:
- Treating infants and children under 2 with any herbal preparation is hazardous.

Others:
- None expected if you are under 45, not pregnant, basically healthy, take it for only a short time and do not exceed small doses.

Storage:
- Keep cool and dry, but don't freeze. Store safely away from children.

Safe dosage:
- At present no "safe" dosage has been established.

Toxicity

Rated relatively safe when taken in appropriate quantities for short periods of time.

For symptoms of toxicity: See *Adverse Reactions, Side Effects or Overdose Symptoms* section below.

Adverse Reactions, Side Effects or Overdose Symptoms

Signs and symptoms:	What to do:
Nausea	Discontinue. Call doctor immediately.
Vomiting	Discontinue. Call doctor immediately.

Buckthorn

Basic Information

Biological name (genus and species):
Rhamnus cathartica
Parts used for medicinal purposes:
Bark
Berries/fruits
Chemicals this herb contains:
Anthra-quinone
Emodin

Known Effects

* Irritates gastrointestinal tract and causes watery, explosive bowel movements.

Miscellaneous information:
* Several dyes are made from juice of berries. Children can have toxic symptoms after eating as few as 20 berries.
* Syrup of buckthorn is made from berries

Unproved Speculated Benefits

* Is used as laxative.

Warnings and Precautions

Don't take if you:
* Are pregnant, think you may be pregnant or plan pregnancy in the near future.
* Have any chronic disease of the gastrointestinal tract, such as stomach or duodenal ulcers, oesophageal reflux (reflux oesophagitis), ulcerative colitis, spastic colitis, diverticulosis, diverticulitis.

Consult your doctor if you:
* Take this herb for any medical problem that doesn't improve in 2 weeks. There may be safer, more effective treatments.
* Take any medicinal drugs or herbs including aspirin, laxatives, cold and cough remedies, antacids, vitamins, minerals, amino acids, supplements, other prescription or non-prescription drugs.

Pregnancy:
* Dangers outweigh any possible benefits. Don't use.

Breast-feeding:
* Dangers outweigh any possible benefits. Don't use.

Infants and children:
* Treating infants and children under 2 with any herbal preparation is hazardous.

Others:
* None expected if you are under 45, not pregnant, basically healthy, take it for only a short time and do not exceed manufacturer's recommended dosage.

Storage:
* Keep cool and dry, but don't freeze. Store safely away from children.

Safe dosage:
* At present no "safe" dosage has been established.

Toxicity

Comparative-toxicity rating not available from standard references.

For symptoms of toxicity: See *Adverse Reactions, Side Effects or Overdose Symptoms* section below.

Adverse Reactions, Side Effects or Overdose Symptoms

Signs and symptoms:	What to do:
Diarrhoea, severe and watery	Discontinue. Call doctor immediately.
Kidney damage with large amounts over long period of time; characterized by blood in urine, decreased urine flow, swelling of hands and feet	Seek emergency treatment.
Nausea	Discontinue. Call doctor immediately.
Vomiting	Discontinue. Call doctor immediately.

MEDICINAL HERB

Burdock (Edible Burdock, Lappa, Great Burdock)

Basic Information

Biological name (genus and species):
    Arctium lappa
Parts used for medicinal purposes:
    Roots
    Seeds
Chemicals this herb contains:
    Arctiin
    Inulin
    Tannins (See Glossary)
    Volatile oils (See Glossary)

Known Effects

- Burdock contains no pharmacologically active chemicals, but it may be contaminated by atropine-like chemicals that can be poisonous.
- Interferes with absorption of iron and other minerals when taken internally.

Unproved Speculated Benefits

- Treats skin disorders.
- Treats gout.
- Stimulates body's defenses against disease.

Warnings and Precautions

Don't take if you:
- Are pregnant, think you may be pregnant or plan pregnancy in the near future.

Consult your doctor if you:
- Take this herb for any medical problem that doesn't improve in 2 weeks. There may be safer, more effective treatments.
- Take any medicinal drugs or herbs including aspirin, laxatives, cold and cough remedies, antacids, vitamins, minerals, amino acids, supplements, other prescription or non-prescription drugs.

Pregnancy:
- Dangers outweigh any possible benefits. Don't use.

Breast-feeding:
- Dangers outweigh any possible benefits. Don't use.

Infants and children:
- Treating infants and children under 2 with any herbal preparation is hazardous.

Storage:
- Keep cool and dry, but don't freeze. Store safely away from children.

Safe dosage:
- At present no "safe" dosage has been established.

Toxicity

Rated relatively safe when taken in appropriate quantities for short periods of time.

For symptoms of toxicity: See *Adverse Reactions, Side Effects or Overdose Symptoms* section below.

Adverse Reactions, Side Effects or Overdose Symptoms

Signs and symptoms:	What to do:
Dilated pupils	Discontinue. Call doctor immediately.
Dry mouth	Discontinue. Call doctor when convenient.
Hallucinations	Seek emergency treatment.

Calamus Root (Sweet Root, Acore, Rat Root, Sweet Flag, Sweet Myrtle, Sweet Cane, Sweet Sedge, Flagroot, Calamus)

Basic Information

Biological name (genus and species):
Acorus calamus
Parts used for medicinal purposes:
Roots
Chemicals this herb contains:
Asarone
Beta-asarone
Camphene
Caryophyllene
Eugenol
Pinene
Volatile oils (See Glossary)

Known Effects

- Aids in expelling gas from the intestinal tract.
- Depresses central nervous system.
- Causes hallucinations.

Miscellaneous information:
- Used primarily in India for many illnesses.
- Essential oil extracted from the root causes cancer in rats.

Unproved Speculated Benefits

- Treats asthma.
- Treats coughs.
- Treats dyspepsia.
- Treats convulsions.
- Treats epilepsy.
- Treats hysteria.
- Treats insanity.
- Treats intestinal parasites.
- Is used as an aphrodisiac.
- Reduces fever.

Warnings and Precautions

Don't take if you:
- Are pregnant, think you may be pregnant or plan pregnancy in the near future.

Consult your doctor if you:
- Take this herb for any medical problem that doesn't improve in 2 weeks. There may be safer, more effective treatments.
- Take any medicinal drugs or herbs including aspirin, laxatives, cold and cough remedies, antacids, vitamins, minerals, amino acids, supplements, other prescription or non-prescription drugs.

Pregnancy:
- Problems in pregnant women taking small or usual amounts have not been proved. But the chance of problems does exist. Don't use unless prescribed by your doctor.

Breast-feeding:
- Problems in breast-fed infants of lactating mothers taking small or usual amounts have not been proved. But the chance of problems does exist. Don't use unless prescribed by your doctor.

Infants and children:
- Treating infants and children under 2 with any herbal preparation is hazardous.

Others:
- None expected if you are under 45, not pregnant, basically healthy, take it for only a short time and do not exceed manufacturer's recommended dosage.

Storage:
- Keep cool and dry, but don't freeze. Store safely away from children.

Safe dosage:
- At present no "safe" dosage has been established.

Toxicity

Rated dangerous, particularly in children, persons over 55 and those who take larger than appropriate quantities for extended periods of time.

For symptoms of toxicity: See *Adverse Reactions, Side Effects or Overdose Symptoms* section below.

Adverse Reactions, Side Effects or Overdose Symptoms

Signs and symptoms:	What to do:
Drowsiness	Discontinue. Call doctor when convenient.
Hallucinations	Seek emergency treatment.

California Poppy

Basic Information

Biological name (genus and species):
Eschoscholtzia californica
Parts used for medicinal purposes:
Entire plant, except roots
Chemicals this herb contains:
Coptisine
Sanguinarine

 Known Effects

- Feeble narcotic action.
- Increases perspiration.
- Depresses central nervous system.

Miscellaneous information:
- Does not contain any narcotic derivatives, such as morphine or codeine. The poppy plant that has narcotic properties is different from this one.

 Unproved Speculated Benefits

- Is used by drug abusers for sedative or mind-altering effects.

 Warnings and Precautions

Don't take if you:
- Are pregnant, think you may be pregnant or plan pregnancy in the near future.

Consult your doctor if you:
- Take this herb for any medical problem that doesn't improve in 2 weeks. There may be safer, more effective treatments.
- Take any medicinal drugs or herbs including aspirin, laxatives, cold and cough remedies, antacids, vitamins, minerals, amino acids, supplements, other prescription or non-prescription drugs.

Pregnancy:
- Problems in pregnant women taking small or usual amounts have not been proved. But the chance of problems does exist. Don't use unless prescribed by your doctor.

Breast-feeding:
- Problems in breast-fed infants of lactating mothers taking small or usual amounts have not been proved. But the chance of problems does exist. Don't use unless prescribed by your doctor.

Infants and children:
- Treating infants and children under 2 with any herbal preparation is hazardous.

Others:
- None expected if you are beyond childhood and under 45, basically healthy and take for only a short time.

Storage:
- Keep cool and dry, but don't freeze. Store safely away from children.

Safe dosage:
- At present no "safe" dosage has been established.

 Toxicity

Rated slightly dangerous, particularly in children, persons over 55 and those who take larger than appropriate quantities for extended periods of time.

 Adverse Reactions, Side Effects or Overdose Symptoms

None expected

Capsicum (Red-Hot Pepper, Hot Pepper, Cayenne, Chili Pepper, Africa Pepper, American Pepper, Red Pepper, Spanish Pepper)

Basic Information

Biological name (genus and species):
Capsicum frutescens, Capsicum annum
Parts used for medicinal purposes:
Berries/fruits
Chemicals this herb contains:
Apsaicine
Capsacutin
Capsico
Capsaicin

Known Effects

- Provides counterirritation when applied to skin overlying an inflamed or irritated joint.
- No effects are expected on the body, either good or bad, when herb is used in very small amounts to enhance the flavour of food.

Miscellaneous information:
- Available in powder form.
- Available as fresh food.
- Is used in small amounts as a condiment.

Unproved Speculated Benefits

- Reduces incidence of clotting in blood vessels (thromboembolism).
- Relieves toothache.
- Wards off infections.
- Settles "upset stomach."
- Treats intestinal disorders.
- Is used as external rub or poultice.

Warnings and Precautions

Don't take if you:
- Are pregnant, think you may be pregnant or plan pregnancy in the near future.
- Have a bleeding problem.
- Have any chronic disease of the gastrointestinal tract, such as stomach or duodenal ulcers, oesophageal reflux (reflux oesophagitis), ulcerative colitis, spastic colitis, diverticulosis, diverticulitis.

Consult your doctor if you:
- Take this herb for any medical problem that doesn't improve in 2 weeks. There may be safer, more effective treatments.
- Take any medicinal drugs or herbs including aspirin, laxatives, cold and cough remedies, antacids, vitamins, minerals, amino acids, supplements, other prescription or non-prescription drugs.

Pregnancy:
- Problems in pregnant women taking small or usual amounts have not been proved. But the chance of problems does exist. Don't use unless prescribed by your doctor.

Breast-feeding:
- Problems in breast-fed infants of lactating mothers taking small or usual amounts have not been proved. But the chance of problems does exist. Don't use unless prescribed by your doctor.

Infants and children:
- Treating infants and children under 2 with any herbal preparation is hazardous.

Storage:
- Keep cool and dry, but don't freeze. Store safely away from children.

Safe dosage:
- At present no "safe" dosage has been established.

Toxicity

Rated relatively safe when taken in appropriate quantities for short periods of time.

For symptoms of toxicity: See *Adverse Reactions, Side Effects or Overdose Symptoms* section below.

Adverse Reactions, Side Effects or Overdose Symptoms

Signs and symptoms:	What to do:
Diarrhoea, regular or bloody	Discontinue. Call doctor immediately.
Nausea	Discontinue. Call doctor immediately.
Vomiting	Discontinue. Call doctor immediately.
Vomiting blood	Seek emergency treatment.

Caraway

Basic Information
Biological name (genus and species):
   Carum carvi
Parts used for medicinal purposes:
   Leaves
   Seeds
Chemicals this herb contains:
   Calcium oxalate
   Carveo
   Carvone, as volatile oils (See Glossary)
   Dihydrocarvone
   Fatty acids (See Glossary)
   Proteins

Known Effects

- Acts as an aromatic (See Glossary).
- Aids in expelling gas from intestinal tract.
- No effects are expected on the body, either good or bad, when herb is used in very small amounts to enhance the flavour of food.

Miscellaneous information:
- Is used as a flavouring agent in baking.
- Oil is used in making ice cream.

Unproved Speculated Benefits

- Reduces flatulence in infants.
- Treats abdominal cramping.
- Treats nausea.
- Treats scabies.

Warnings and Precautions

Don't take if you:
- Are pregnant, think you may be pregnant or plan pregnancy in the near future.
- Have any chronic disease of the gastrointestinal tract, such as stomach or duodenal ulcers, oesophageal reflux (reflux oesophagitis), ulcerative colitis, spastic colitis, diverticulosis, diverticulitis.

Consult your doctor if you:
- Take this herb for any medical problem that doesn't improve in 2 weeks. There may be safer, more effective treatments.
- Take any medicinal drugs or herbs including aspirin, laxatives, cold and cough remedies, antacids, vitamins, minerals, amino acids, supplements, other prescription or non-prescription drugs.

Pregnancy:
- Problems in pregnant women taking small or usual amounts have not been proved. But the chance of problems does exist. Don't use unless prescribed by your doctor.

Breast-feeding:
- Problems in breast-fed infants of lactating mothers taking small or usual amounts have not been proved. But the chance of problems does exist. Don't use unless prescribed by your doctor.

Infants and children:
- Treating infants and children under 2 with any herbal preparation is hazardous.

Others:
- None expected if you are under 45, not pregnant, basically healthy, take it for only a short time and do not exceed manufacturer's recommended dosage.

Storage:
- Keep cool and dry, but don't freeze. Store safely away from children.

Safe dosage:
- At present no "safe" dosage has been established.

Toxicity

Comparative-toxicity rating not available from standard references.

For symptoms of toxicity: See *Adverse Reactions, Side Effects or Overdose Symptoms* section below.

Adverse Reactions, Side Effects or Overdose Symptoms

Signs and symptoms:	What to do:
In very large amounts only:	
Central-nervous-system depression	Seek emergency treatment.
Nausea	Discontinue. Call doctor immediately.
Vomiting	Discontinue. Call doctor immediately.

Basic Information

Biological name (genus and species):
Ellettaria cardamonum, Amonum
cardamonum

Parts used for medicinal purposes:
Seeds

Chemicals this herb contains:
Dipentene
Fixed oil (See Glossary)
Gum (See Glossary)
Limonene
Terpene alcohol
Terpinene
Starch
Volatile oils (See Glossary)
Yellow coloring

Known Effects

• Aids in expelling gas from intestinal tract.
• No effects are expected on the body, either
good or bad, when herb is used in very small
amounts to enhance the flavour of food.

Miscellaneous information:
• Provides flavour.

Unproved Speculated Benefits

• Acts as vigorous laxative.
• Causes explosive, watery diarrhoea.

Warnings and Precautions

Don't take if you:
• Are pregnant, think you may be pregnant or
plan pregnancy in the near future.
• Have any chronic disease of the
gastrointestinal tract, such as stomach or
duodenal ulcers, oesophageal reflux (reflux
oesophagitis), ulcerative colitis, spastic
colitis, diverticulosis, diverticulitis.

Consult your doctor if you:
• Take this herb for any medical problem that
doesn't improve in 2 weeks. There may be
safer, more effective treatments.
• Take any medicinal drugs or herbs including
aspirin, laxatives, cold and cough remedies,
antacids, vitamins, minerals, amino acids,
supplements, other prescription or non-
prescription drugs.

Pregnancy:
• Problems in pregnant women taking small or
usual amounts have not been proved. But the
chance of problems does exist. Don't use
unless prescribed by your doctor.

Breast-feeding:
• Problems in breast-fed infants of lactating
mothers taking small or usual amounts have
not been proved. But the chance of problems
does exist. Don't use unless prescribed by your
doctor.

Infants and children:
• Treating infants and children under 2 with any
herbal preparation is hazardous.

Others:
• None expected if you are beyond childhood
and under 45, basically healthy and take for
only a short time.

Storage:
• Keep cool and dry, but don't freeze. Store
safely away from children.

Safe dosage:
• At present no "safe" dosage has been
established.

Toxicity

Comparative-toxicity rating not available from
standard references.

For symptoms of toxicity: See *Adverse
Reactions, Side Effects or Overdose Symptoms*
section below.

Adverse Reactions, Side Effects or Overdose Symptoms

Signs and symptoms:	What to do:
Diarrhoea	Discontinue. Call doctor immediately.
Nausea	Discontinue. Call doctor immediately.
Vomiting	Discontinue. Call doctor immediately.

MEDICINAL HERB

Cascara Sagrada (Cascara Buckthorn)

Basic Information

Biological name (genus and species):
Rhamnus purshiana
Parts used for medicinal purposes:
Bark
Chemicals this herb contains:
Anthraquinone
Cascarosides

Known Effects

• Causes irritation to gastrointestinal tract and can cause watery, explosive diarrhoea.

Miscellaneous information:
• Not recommended for prolonged use.
• This is a standard medicinal product.

Unproved Speculated Benefits

• Treats chronic constipation.

Warnings and Precautions

Don't take if you:
• Are pregnant, think you may be pregnant or plan pregnancy in the near future.
• Have any chronic disease of the gastrointestinal tract, such as stomach or duodenal ulcers, oesophageal reflux (reflux oesophagitis), ulcerative colitis, spastic colitis, diverticulosis, diverticulitis.

Consult your doctor if you:
• Take this herb for any medical problem that doesn't improve in 2 weeks. There may be safer, more effective treatments.
• Take any medicinal drugs or herbs including aspirin, laxatives, cold and cough remedies, antacids, vitamins, minerals, amino acids, supplements, other prescription or non-prescription drugs.

Pregnancy:
• Dangers outweigh any possible benefits. Don't use.

Breast-feeding:
• Dangers outweigh any possible benefits. Don't use.

Infants and children:
• Treating infants and children under 2 with any herbal preparation is hazardous.

Others:
• None expected if you are under 45, not pregnant, basically healthy, take it for only a short time and do not exceed small doses.

Storage:
• Keep cool and dry, but don't freeze. Store safely away from children.

Safe dosage:
• At present no "safe" dosage has been established.

Toxicity

Rated slightly dangerous, particularly in children, persons over 55 and those who take larger than appropriate quantities for extended periods of time.

For symptoms of toxicity: See *Adverse Reactions, Side Effects or Overdose Symptoms* section below.

Adverse Reactions, Side Effects or Overdose Symptoms

Signs and symptoms:	What to do:
With excessive dosage:	
Diarrhoea, violent and watery	Discontinue. Call doctor immediately.
Nausea	Discontinue. Call doctor immediately.
Vomiting	Discontinue. Call doctor immediately.

Basic Information

Biological name (genus and species):
Catalpa bignonioides
Parts used for medicinal purposes:
Various parts of the entire plant, frequently differing by country and/or culture
Chemicals this herb contains:
Catalpin
Catalposide

Known Effects

• Irritates gastrointestinal tract.

Unproved Speculated Benefits

• Treats asthma.

Warnings and Precautions

Don't take if you:
• Are pregnant, think you may be pregnant or plan pregnancy in the near future.
• Have any chronic disease of the gastrointestinal tract, such as stomach or duodenal ulcers, oesophageal reflux (reflux oesophagitis), ulcerative colitis, spastic colitis, diverticulosis, diverticulitis.

Consult your doctor if you:
• Take this herb for any medical problem that doesn't improve in 2 weeks. There may be safer, more effective treatments.
• Take any medicinal drugs or herbs including aspirin, laxatives, cold and cough remedies, antacids, vitamins, minerals, amino acids, supplements, other prescription or non-prescription drugs.

Pregnancy:
• Dangers outweigh any possible benefits. Don't use.

Breast-feeding:
• Dangers outweigh any possible benefits. Don't use.

Infants and children:
• Treating infants and children under 2 with any herbal preparation is hazardous.

Others:
• Dangers outweigh any possible benefits. Don't use.

Storage:
• Keep cool and dry, but don't freeze. Store safely away from children.

Safe dosage:
• At present no "safe" dosage has been established.

Toxicity

Comparative-toxicity rating not available from standard references.

For symptoms of toxicity: See *Adverse Reactions, Side Effects or Overdose Symptoms* section below.

Adverse Reactions, Side Effects or Overdose Symptoms

Signs and symptoms:	What to do:
Precipitous blood-pressure drop— symptoms include, faintness, cold sweat, paleness, rapid pulse	Seek emergency treatment.
Cold, clammy skin	Discontinue. Call doctor when convenient.
Diarrhoea	Discontinue. Call doctor immediately.
Nausea	Discontinue. Call doctor immediately.
Rapid, weak pulse	Seek emergency treatment.
Vomiting	Discontinue. Call doctor immediately.

MEDICINAL HERB

Catechu, Black

Basic Information

Biological name (genus and species):
   Acacia catechu
Parts used for medicinal purposes:
   Various parts of the entire plant, frequently
   differing by country and/or culture
Chemical this herb contains:
   Tannins (See Glossary)

Known Effects

- Shrinks tissues.
- Prevents secretion of fluids.
- Interferes with absorption of iron and other
  minerals when taken internally.

Unproved Speculated Benefits

- Decreases unusual bleeding.
- Treats chronic diarrhoea.
- Is used as gargle for sore throat.

Warnings and Precautions

Don't take if you:
- Are pregnant, think you may be pregnant or
  plan pregnancy in the near future.
- Have any chronic disease of the
  gastrointestinal tract, such as stomach or
  duodenal ulcers, oesophageal reflux (reflux
  oesophagitis), ulcerative colitis, spastic
  colitis, diverticulosis, diverticulitis.

Consult your doctor if you:
- Take this herb for any medical problem that
  doesn't improve in 2 weeks. There may be
  safer, more effective treatments.
- Take any medicinal drugs or herbs including
  aspirin, laxatives, cold and cough remedies,
  antacids, vitamins, minerals, amino acids,
  supplements, other prescription or non-
  prescription drugs.

Pregnancy:
- Dangers outweigh any possible benefits. Don't
  use.

Breast-feeding:
- Dangers outweigh any possible benefits. Don't
  use.

Infants and children:
- Treating infants and children under 2 with any
  herbal preparation is hazardous.

Others:
- None expected if you are under 45, not
  pregnant, basically healthy, take it for only a
  short time and do not exceed manufacturer's
  recommended dosage.

Storage:
- Keep cool and dry, but don't freeze. Store
  safely away from children.

Safe dosage:
- At present no "safe" dosage has been
  established.

Toxicity

Comparative-toxicity rating not available from
standard references.

For symptoms of toxicity: See *Adverse
Reactions, Side Effects or Overdose Symptoms*
section below.

Adverse Reactions, Side Effects or Overdose Symptoms

Signs and symptoms:	What to do:
Diarrhoea	Discontinue. Call doctor immediately.
Kidney damage characterized by blood in urine, decreased urine flow, swelling of hands and feet	Seek emergency treatment.
Vomiting	Discontinue. Call doctor immediately.

Basic Information

Biological name (genus and species):
Catha edulis
Parts used for medicinal purposes:
Leaves
Chemicals this herb contains:
Cathidine
Cathine (a form of ephedrine)
Celastrin
Choline
Ratine
Tannins (See Glossary)

Known Effects

- Stimulates brain and spinal cord through synapses.
- Interferes with absorption of iron and other minerals when taken internally.

Miscellaneous information:
- Can be habit forming. Addicts become talkative then depressed and apathetic.

Unproved Speculated Benefits

- Leaves chewed or steeped to make tea to treat fatigue.
- Suppresses appetite.

Warnings and Precautions

Don't take if you:
- Are pregnant, think you may be pregnant or plan pregnancy in the near future.
- Have heart trouble.
- Have high blood pressure.

Consult your doctor if you:
- Take this herb for any medical problem that doesn't improve in 2 weeks. There may be safer, more effective treatments.
- Take any medicinal drugs or herbs including aspirin, laxatives, cold and cough remedies, antacids, vitamins, minerals, amino acids, supplements, other prescription or non-prescription drugs.

Pregnancy:
- Dangers outweigh any possible benefits. Don't use.

Breast-feeding:
- Dangers outweigh any possible benefits. Don't use.

Infants and children:
- Treating infants and children under 2 with any herbal preparation is hazardous.

Storage:
- Keep cool and dry, but don't freeze. Store safely away from children.

Safe dosage:
- At present no "safe" dosage has been established.

Toxicity

Rated slightly dangerous, particularly in children, persons over 55 and those who take larger than appropriate quantities for extended periods of time.

For symptoms of toxicity: See *Adverse Reactions, Side Effects or Overdose Symptoms* section below.

Adverse Reactions, Side Effects or Overdose Symptoms

Signs and symptoms:	What to do:
Large amounts:	
Breathing difficulties	Seek emergency treatment.
Depression	Discontinue. Call doctor when convenient.
Euphoria	Discontinue. Call doctor when convenient.
Increased blood pressure	Discontinue. Call doctor immediately.
Increased heart rate	Seek emergency treatment.
Paralysis	Seek emergency treatment.
Stomach irritation, with bleeding	Discontinue. Call doctor immediately.

MEDICINAL HERB

Catnip (Catnep, Catmint)

Basic Information

Biological name (genus and species):
   Nepeta cataria
Parts used for medicinal purposes:
   Leaves
Chemicals this herb contains:
   Acetic acid
   Buteric acid
   Citral
   Dipentene
   Lifronella
   Limonene
   Nepetalic acid
   Tannins (See Glossary)
   Terpene
   Valeric acid
   Volatile oils (See Glossary)

Known Effects

- Stimulates central nervous system.
- Relieves spasm in skeletal or smooth muscle.
- Interferes with absorption of iron and other minerals when taken internally.

Miscellaneous information:
- Catnip is not a psychedelic or euphoria-producing drug, despite several reports to the contrary.

Unproved Speculated Benefits

- Steeped leaves produce increased sweating for reducing fevers.
- Leaves used as snuff to treat colic. (See Glossary.)
- Treats insomnia.

Warnings and Precautions

Don't take if you:
- Are pregnant, think you may be pregnant or plan pregnancy in the near future.

Consult your doctor if you:
- Take this herb for any medical problem that doesn't improve in 2 weeks. There may be safer, more effective treatments.
- Take any medicinal drugs or herbs including aspirin, laxatives, cold and cough remedies, antacids, vitamins, minerals, amino acids, supplements, other prescription or non-prescription drugs.

Pregnancy:
- Problems in pregnant women taking small or usual amounts have not been proved. But the chance of problems does exist. Don't use unless prescribed by your doctor.

Breast-feeding:
- Problems in breast-fed infants of lactating mothers taking small or usual amounts have not been proved. But the chance of problems does exist. Don't use unless prescribed by your doctor.

Infants and children:
- Treating infants and children under 2 with any herbal preparation is hazardous.

Others:
- None expected if you are beyond childhood and under 45, basically healthy and take for only a short time.

Storage:
- Keep cool and dry, but don't freeze. Store safely away from children.

Safe dosage:
- At present no "safe" dosage has been established.

Toxicity

Generally regarded as safe when taken in appropriate quantities for short periods of time.

Adverse Reactions, Side Effects or Overdose Symptoms

None expected

Basic Information

Biological name (genus and species):
Apium graveolens
Parts used for medicinal purposes:
Juice
Roots
Seeds
Chemicals this herb contains:
D-limonene
Nitrates
Resin (See Glossary)
Sedanoloid
Sedanonic anhydrides
Volatile oils (See Glossary)

Known Effects

- Relieves spasm in skeletal or smooth muscle.
- Causes uterine contractions, whether pregnant or not.
- Celery juice reduces blood pressure.
- Reduces gas in gastrointestinal tract.

Miscellaneous information:
- No effects are expected on the body, either good or bad, when herb is used in very small amounts to enhance the flavour of food.
- When eaten as a common food, no problems are expected for anyone.
- Workers in celery fields may develop skin rashes.

Unproved Speculated Benefits

- Seeds act as anti-oxidant.
- Acts as a sedative.
- Treats dysmenorrhoea (menstrual cramps).
- Treats arthritis.
- Roots act as aphrodisiac.

Warnings and Precautions

Don't take if you:
- Are in your third trimester of a pregnancy.

Consult your doctor if you:
- Take this herb for any medical problem that doesn't improve in 2 weeks. There may be safer, more effective treatments.
- Take any medicinal drugs or herbs including aspirin, laxatives, cold and cough remedies, antacids, vitamins, minerals, amino acids, supplements, other prescription or non-prescription drugs.

Pregnancy:
- Pregnant women should experience no problems taking usual amounts as part of a balanced diet. Don't drink large quantities of celery juice.

Breast-feeding:
- Breast-fed infants of lactating mothers should experience no problems when mother takes usual amounts as part of a balanced diet. Other products extracted from this herb have not been proved to cause problems.

Infants and children:
- Treating infants and children under 2 with any herbal preparation is hazardous.

Others:
- None expected if you are beyond childhood and under 45, not pregnant, basically healthy and take for only a short time.

Storage:
- Keep cool and dry, but don't freeze. Store safely away from children.

Safe dosage:
- At present no "safe" dosage has been established.

Toxicity

Rated relatively safe when taken in appropriate quantities for short periods of time.

For symptoms of toxicity: See *Adverse Reactions, Side Effects or Overdose Symptoms* section below.

Adverse Reactions, Side Effects or Overdose Symptoms

Signs and symptoms:	What to do:
Deep sedation with large amounts	Seek emergency treatment.
Premature labour	Seek emergency treatment.

Centuary (Minor Centuary)

Basic Information

Biological name (genus and species):
Centaurium erythraea, C. umbellatum
Parts used for medicinal purposes:
Petals/flower
Chemicals this herb contains:
Amarogentin
Erytaurin
Erythrocentaurin
Gentiopicrin
Gentisin

Known Effects

• Increases stomach secretions.

Unproved Speculated Benefits

• Treats malaria.
• Reduces fever.

Warnings and Precautions

Don't take if you:
• Are pregnant, think you may be pregnant or plan pregnancy in the near future.
• Have any chronic disease of the gastrointestinal tract, such as stomach or duodenal ulcers, oesophageal reflux (reflux oesophagitis), ulcerative colitis, spastic colitis, diverticulosis, diverticulitis.

Consult your doctor if you:
• Take this herb for any medical problem that doesn't improve in 2 weeks. There may be safer, more effective treatments.
• Take any medicinal drugs or herbs including aspirin, laxatives, cold and cough remedies, antacids, vitamins, minerals, amino acids, supplements, other prescription or non-prescription drugs.

Pregnancy:
• Problems in pregnant women taking small or usual amounts have not been proved. But the chance of problems does exist. Don't use unless prescribed by your doctor.

Breast-feeding:
• Problems in breast-fed infants of lactating mothers taking small or usual amounts have not been proved. But the chance of problems does exist. Don't use unless prescribed by your doctor.

Infants and children:
• Treating infants and children under 2 with any herbal preparation is hazardous.

Others:
• None expected if you are beyond childhood and under 45, basically healthy and take for only a short time.

Storage:
• Keep cool and dry, but don't freeze. Store safely away from children.

Safe dosage:
• At present no "safe" dosage has been established.

Toxicity

Comparative-toxicity rating not available from standard references.

For symptoms of toxicity: See *Adverse Reactions, Side Effects or Overdose Symptoms* section below.

Adverse Reactions, Side Effects or Overdose Symptoms

Signs and symptoms:	What to do:
Only with very large amounts or accidental overdose:	
Nausea	Discontinue. Call doctor immediately.
Vomiting	Discontinue. Call doctor immediately.

Basic Information

Biological name (genus and species):
Anthemis flores, A. nobilis
Parts used for medicinal purposes:
Various parts of the entire plant, frequently differing by country and/or culture
Chemicals this herb contains:

Antheme	Resin (See Glossary)
Anthemic acid	Tannic acid
Anthesterol	Tiglic acid
Apigenin	Volatile oils (See Glossary)
Chamazulene	

Known Effects

- Used as an aromatic. (See Glossary.)
- Irritates mucous membranes.
- Decreases spasm of smooth or skeletal muscle.
- Reduces inflammation.
- Interferes with absorption of iron and other minerals when taken internally.
- Kills bacteria on skin.

Miscellaneous information:
- Flowers are used to make extract and herbal tea.

Unproved Speculated Benefits

Internal use:
- Treats minor infections.
- Treats diarrhoea.
- Treats indigestion.
- Relieves cramps.
- Decreases intestinal gas.

External use:
- Is used as a poultice. (See Glossary.) It is occasionally used as a way to apply medication to skin abscesses.

Warnings and Precautions

Don't take if you:
- Are pregnant, think you may be pregnant or plan pregnancy in the near future.
- Have any chronic disease of the gastrointestinal tract, such as stomach or duodenal ulcers, oesophageal reflux (reflux oesophagitis), ulcerative colitis, spastic colitis, diverticulosis, diverticulitis.

Consult your doctor if you:
- Take this herb for any medical problem that doesn't improve in 2 weeks. There may be safer, more effective treatments.

- Take any medicinal drugs or herbs including aspirin, laxatives, cold and cough remedies, antacids, vitamins, minerals, amino acids, supplements, other prescription or non-prescription drugs.

Pregnancy:
- Dangers outweigh any benefits. Don't use.

Breast-feeding:
- Dangers outweigh any benefits. Don't use.

Infants and children:
- Treating infants and children under 2 with any herbal preparation is hazardous.

Others:
- Dangers outweigh any possible benefits. Don't use.

Storage:
- Keep cool and dry, but don't freeze. Store safely away from children.

Safe dosage:
- At present no "safe" dosage has been established.

Toxicity

Comparative-toxicity rating not available from standard references.

For symptoms of toxicity: See below.

Adverse Reactions, Side Effects or Overdose Symptoms

Signs and symptoms:	What to do:
Allergic reactions in individuals who are sensitized to ragweed pollens (rare)	Discontinue. Call doctor immediately.
Life-threatening anaphylaxis may follow injections—symptoms include: immediate, severe itching, paleness, low blood pressure, loss of consciousness, coma	Yell for help. Don't leave victim. Begin CPR (cardiopulmonary resuscitation), mouth to mouth breathing and external cardiac massage. Have someone dial 999 (emergency). Don't stop CPR until help arrives.
Skin irritation	Discontinue. Call doctor when convenient.
Vomiting	Discontinue. Call doctor immediately.

Chickweed

Basic Information

Biological name (genus and species):
Stellaria media
Parts used for medicinal purposes:
Various parts of the entire plant, frequently differing by country and/or culture
Chemicals this herb contains:
Ascorbic acid (vitamin C)
Potash salts
Rutin

Known Effects

- Reduces thickness of mucus in lungs.
- Increases urine production.

Miscellaneous information:
- Chickweed has been proved ineffective for medicinal purposes.

Unproved Speculated Benefits

Internal use:
- Treats asthma
- Protects scraped tissues.
- Treats gastrointestinal disorders.
- Is used as a vitamin-C supplement.
- Relieves constipation

External use:
- Is used as an ointment for rashes and sores.

Warnings and Precautions

Don't take if you:
- Are pregnant, think you may be pregnant or plan pregnancy in the near future.

Consult your doctor if you:
- Take this herb for any medical problem that doesn't improve in 2 weeks. There may be safer, more effective treatments.
- Take any medicinal drugs or herbs including aspirin, laxatives, cold and cough remedies, antacids, vitamins, minerals, amino acids, supplements, other prescription or non-prescription drugs.

Pregnancy:
- Problems in pregnant women taking small or usual amounts have not been proved. But the chance of problems does exist. Don't use unless prescribed by your doctor.

Breast-feeding:
- Problems in breast-fed infants of lactating mothers taking small or usual amounts have not been proved. But the chance of problems does exist. Don't use unless prescribed by your doctor.

Infants and children:
- Treating infants and children under 2 with any herbal preparation is hazardous.

Others:
- None expected if you are beyond childhood and under 45, basically healthy and take for only a short time.

Storage:
- Keep cool and dry, but don't freeze. Store safely away from children.

Safe dosage:
- At present no "safe" dosage has been established.

Toxicity

Rated relatively safe when taken in appropriate quantities for short periods of time.

For symptoms of toxicity: See *Adverse Reactions, Side Effects or Overdose Symptoms* section below.

Adverse Reactions, Side Effects or Overdose Symptoms

Signs and symptoms:	What to do:
Temporary paralysis (large amounts only)	Seek emergency treatment.

Basic Information

Biological name (genus and species):
Cichorium intybus
Parts used for medicinal purposes:
Roots
Chemicals this herb contains:
Ascorbic acid (vitamin C)
Inulin
Vitamin A

 ## Known Effects

- Reduces kidney inflammation.
- Helps body dispose of excess fluid by increasing amount of urine produced.

 ## Unproved Speculated Benefits

- Treats dyspepsia.

 ## Warnings and Precautions

Don't take if you:
- Are pregnant, think you may be pregnant or plan pregnancy in the near future.

Consult your doctor if you:
- Take this herb for any medical problem that doesn't improve in 2 weeks. There may be safer, more effective treatments.
- Take any medicinal drugs or herbs including aspirin, laxatives, cold and cough remedies, antacids, vitamins, minerals, amino acids, supplements, other prescription or non-prescription drugs.

Pregnancy:
- Problems in pregnant women taking small or usual amounts have not been proved. But the chance of problems does exist. Don't use unless prescribed by your doctor.

Breast-feeding:
- Problems in breast-fed infants of lactating mothers taking small or usual amounts have not been proved. But the chance of problems does exist. Don't use unless prescribed by your doctor.

Infants and children:
- Treating infants and children under 2 with any herbal preparation is hazardous.

Storage:
- Keep cool and dry, but don't freeze. Store safely away from children.

Safe dosage:
- At present no "safe" dosage has been established.

 ## Toxicity

Comparative-toxicity rating not available from standard references.

 ## Adverse Reactions, Side Effects or Overdose Symptoms

None expected

MEDICINAL HERB

Chinese Rhubarb (Canton Rhubarb, Shensi Rhubarb)

Basic Information

Biological name (genus and species):
Rheum officinalis, R. palmatum
Parts used for medicinal purposes:
Roots
Chemicals this herb contains:
Aloe-emodin
Anthraquinone
Chrysophanol
Emodin
Tannins (See Glossary)

Known Effects

- Shrinks tissues.
- Prevents secretion of fluids.
- Irritates mucous membranes of intestinal tract.
- Interferes with absorption of iron and other minerals when taken internally.

Miscellaneous information:
- This is *not* the garden variety of rhubarb.

Unproved Speculated Benefits

- Relieves diarrhoea (in small amounts).

Warnings and Precautions

Don't take if you:
- Are pregnant, think you may be pregnant or plan pregnancy in the near future.
- Have any chronic disease of the gastrointestinal tract, such as stomach or duodenal ulcers, oesophageal reflux (reflux oesophagitis), ulcerative colitis, spastic colitis, diverticulosis, diverticulitis.

Consult your doctor if you:
- Take this herb for any medical problem that doesn't improve in 2 weeks. There may be safer, more effective treatments.
- Take any medicinal drugs or herbs including aspirin, laxatives, cold and cough remedies, antacids, vitamins, minerals, amino acids, supplements, other prescription or non-prescription drugs.

Pregnancy:
- Avoid overeating this herb.

Breast-feeding:
- Avoid overeating this herb.

Infants and children:
- Treating infants and children under 2 with any herbal preparation is hazardous.

Others:
- None expected if you are under 45, not pregnant, basically healthy, take it for only a short time and do not exceed manufacturer's recommended dosage.

Storage:
- Keep cool and dry, but don't freeze. Store safely away from children.

Safe dosage:
- At present no "safe" dosage has been established.

Toxicity

Rated relatively safe when taken in appropriate quantities for short periods of time.

For symptoms of toxicity: See *Adverse Reactions, Side Effects or Overdose Symptoms* section below.

Adverse Reactions, Side Effects or Overdose Symptoms

Signs and symptoms:	What to do:
Cramping, abdominal pain	Discontinue. Call doctor immediately.
Explosive, watery diarrhoea	Discontinue. Call doctor immediately.

Cinnamon (Camphor, Hon-Sho)

Basic Information

Biological name (genus and species):
Cinnamonum camphora
Parts used for medicinal purposes:
Leaves
Roots
Chemicals this herb contains:

Camphor oil	Limonene
Cineol	Mannitol
Cinnamaldehyde	Safrole
Fatty acids	Tannins (See Glossary)
Gum (See Glossary)	Oils

Known Effects

- Aids in expelling gas from intestinal tract.
- Shrinks tissues.
- Prevents secretion of fluids.
- Provides flavour.
- Safrole is a possible carcinogen.
- Interferes with absorption of iron and other minerals when taken internally.

Miscellaneous information:
- Sometimes cinnamon is mixed with marijuana then smoked.
- Used as placticizer to make celluloid, explosives and other chemicals.

Unproved Speculated Benefits

- None

Warnings and Precautions

Don't take if you:
- Are pregnant, think you may be pregnant or plan pregnancy in the near future.
- Have any chronic disease of the gastrointestinal tract, such as stomach or duodenal ulcers, oesophageal reflux (reflux oesophagitis), ulcerative colitis, spastic colitis, diverticulosis, diverticulitis.

Consult your doctor if you:
- Take this herb for any medical problem that doesn't improve in 2 weeks. There may be safer, more effective treatments.
- Take any medicinal drugs or herbs including aspirin, laxatives, cold and cough remedies, antacids, vitamins, minerals, amino acids, supplements, other prescription or non-prescription drugs.

Pregnancy:
- Dangers outweigh any possible benefits. Don't use.

Breast-feeding:
- Dangers outweight any possible benefits. Don't use.

Infants and children:
- Treating infants and children under 2 with any herbal preparation is hazardous.

Others:
- None expected if you are beyond childhood and under 45, not pregnant, basically healthy and take for only a short time.

Storage:
- Keep cool and dry, but don't freeze. Store safely away from children.

Safe dosage:
- At present no "safe" dosage has been established.

Toxicity

Rated dangerous, particularly in children, persons over 55 and those who take larger than appropriate quantities for extended periods of time.

For symptoms of toxicity: See below.

Adverse Reactions, Side Effects or Overdose Symptoms

Signs and symptoms:	What to do:
Convulsions	Seek emergency treatment.
Dizziness	Discontinue. Call doctor immediately.
Hallucinations	Seek emergency treatment.
Large overdose (0.5ml/kg body weight) can cause coma or kidney damage	Seek emergency treatment.
Nausea	Discontinue. Call doctor immediately.
Skin contact with oil can cause redness and burning sensation	Discontinue. Call doctor when convenient.
Vomiting	Discontinue. Call doctor immediately.

Coconut

Basic Information

Biological name (genus and species):
  Cocus nucifera
Parts used for medicinal purposes:
  Oil from seeds
Chemicals this herb contains:
  Fixed oil (See Glossary)
  Tannins (See Glossary)
  Trilaurin
  Trimyristin
  Triolein
  Tripalmatic acid
  Tripalmatin
  Tristearin

Known Effects

- Shrinks tissues.
- Prevents secretion of fluids.
- Interferes with absorption of iron and other minerals when taken internally.

Miscellaneous information:

- Is used in making soaps, scalp applications, hand creams, some foodstuffs.
- Coconut-oil-based soaps are useful for marine purposes because they are not easily precipitated by saltwater or salty solutions.

Unproved Speculated Benefits

- Kills intestinal parasites.
- Relieves toothache.

Warnings and Precautions

Don't take if you:

- Have any chronic disease of the gastrointestinal tract, such as stomach or duodenal ulcers, oesophageal reflux (reflux oesophagitis), ulcerative colitis, spastic colitis, diverticulosis, diverticulitis.

Consult your doctor if you:

- Take this herb for any medical problem that doesn't improve in 2 weeks. There may be safer, more effective treatments.
- Take any medicinal drugs or herbs including aspirin, laxatives, cold and cough remedies, antacids, vitamins, minerals, amino acids, supplements, other prescription or non-prescription drugs.

Pregnancy:

- Pregnant women should experience no problems taking usual amounts as part of a balanced diet. Other products extracted from this herb have not been proved to cause problems.

Breast-feeding:

- Breast-fed infants of lactating mothers should experience no problems when mother takes usual amounts as part of a balanced diet. Other products extracted from this herb have not been proved to cause problems.

Infants and children:

- Treating infants and children under 2 with any herbal preparation is hazardous.

Others:

- None expected if you are beyond childhood and under 45, basically healthy and take for only a short time.

Storage:

- Keep cool and dry, but don't freeze. Store safely away from children.

Safe dosage:

- At present no "safe" dosage has been established.

Toxicity

Comparative-toxicity rating not available from standard references.

For symptoms of toxicity: See *Adverse Reactions, Side Effects or Overdose Symptoms* section below.

Adverse Reactions, Side Effects or Overdose Symptoms

Signs and symptoms:	What to do:
Diarrhoea	Discontinue. Call doctor immediately.

Cohosh, Black (Black Snakeroot, Squaw Root, Rattle Root)

Basic Information

Biological name (genus and species):
   Cimicifuga spp
Parts used for medicinal purposes:
   Rhizomes
   Roots
Chemicals this herb contains:
   Cimicifugin
   Isoferulic acid
   Oleic acid
   Palmitic acid
   Tannins (See Glossary)

Known Effects

* Irritates gastrointestinal system.
* Roots and rhizomes impair digestive function and cause an uncomfortable feeling of indigestion.
* Interferes with absorption of iron and other minerals when taken internally.

Unproved Speculated Benefits

* Treats arthritis.
* Treats diarrhoea.
* Treats coughs.
* Is used as an antidote for rattlesnake poison.

Warnings and Precautions

Don't take if you:
* Are pregnant, think you may be pregnant or plan pregnancy in the near future.
* Have any chronic disease of the gastrointestinal tract, such as stomach or duodenal ulcers, oesophageal reflux (reflux oesophagitis), ulcerative colitis, spastic colitis, diverticulosis, diverticulitis.

Consult your doctor if you:
* Take this herb for any medical problem that doesn't improve in 2 weeks. There may be safer, more effective treatments.
* Take any medicinal drugs or herbs including aspirin, laxatives, cold and cough remedies, antacids, vitamins, minerals, amino acids, supplements, other prescription or non-prescription drugs.

Pregnancy:
* Problems in pregnant women taking small or usual amounts have not been proved. But the chance of problems does exist. Don't use unless prescribed by your doctor.

Breast-feeding:
* Problems in breast-fed infants of lactating mothers taking small or usual amounts have not been proved. But the chance of problems does exist. Don't use unless prescribed by your doctor.

Infants and children:
* Treating infants and children under 2 with any herbal preparation is hazardous.

Others:
* Dangers outweigh any possible benefits. Don't use.

Storage:
* Keep cool and dry, but don't freeze. Store safely away from children.

Safe dosage:
* At present no "safe" dosage has been established.

Toxicity

Rated slightly dangerous, particularly in children, persons over 55 and those who take larger than appropriate quantities for extended periods of time.

For symptoms of toxicity: See *Adverse Reactions, Side Effects or Overdose Symptoms* section below.

Adverse Reactions, Side Effects or Overdose Symptoms

Signs and symptoms:	What to do:
Gastroenteritis, characterized by stomach pain, nausea, diarrhoea	Discontinue. Call doctor immediately.
Nausea	Discontinue. Call doctor immediately.
Vomiting	Discontinue. Call doctor immediately.

Cohosh, Blue (Papoose Root, Squaw Root)

Basic Information
Biological name (genus and species):
   Caulophyllum thalictroides
Parts used for medicinal purposes:
   Roots
Chemicals this herb contains:
   Leontin (a saponin)
   Methylcystine
   Coulosaponin

Known Effects

- Stimulates contraction of smooth muscle (blood vessels including small muscles surrounding certain arteries and muscle fibres in the uterus).
- Raises blood pressure.

Unproved Speculated Benefits

- Treats menstrual problems.
- Stimulates uterine contractions during labour.
- Elevates blood pressure.

Warnings and Precautions

Don't take if you:
- Are pregnant, think you may be pregnant or plan pregnancy in the near future.
- Have any chronic disease of the gastrointestinal tract, such as stomach or duodenal ulcers, oesophageal reflux (reflux oesophagitis), ulcerative colitis, spastic colitis, diverticulosis, diverticulitis.

Consult your doctor if you:
- Take this herb for any medical problem that doesn't improve in 2 weeks. There may be safer, more effective treatments.
- Take any medicinal drugs or herbs including aspirin, laxatives, cold and cough remedies, antacids, vitamins, minerals, amino acids, supplements, other prescription or non-prescription drugs.

Pregnancy:
- Dangers outweigh any possible benefits. Don't use.

Breast-feeding:
- Dangers outweigh any possible benefits. Don't use.

Infants and children
- Treating infants and children under 2 with any herbal preparation is hazardous.

Others:
- Don't self-medicate for *any* purpose. May cause toxic symptoms.

Storage:
- Keep cool and dry, but don't freeze. Store safely away from children.

Safe dosage:
- At present no "safe" dosage has been established.

Toxicity

Rated slightly dangerous, particularly in children, persons over 55 and those who take larger than appropriate quantities for extended periods of time.

For symptoms of toxicity: See *Adverse Reactions, Side Effects or Overdose Symptoms* section below.

Adverse Reactions, Side Effects or Overdose Symptoms

Signs and symptoms:	What to do:
Chest pain	Seek emergency treatment.
Convulsions	Seek emergency treatment.
Dilated pupils	Discontinue. Call doctor immediately.
Headache	Discontinue. Call doctor immediately.
Nausea	Discontinue. Call doctor immediately.
Stomach irritation, with possible bleeding	Discontinue. Call doctor immediately.
Thirst	Discontinue. Call doctor when convenient.
Vomiting	Discontinue. Call doctor immediately.
Weakness	Discontinue. Call doctor immediately.

Basic Information

Biological name (genus and species):
   Actaea alba, A. arguta
Parts used for medicinal purposes:
   Various parts of the entire plant, frequently
   differing by country and/or culture
Chemicals this herb contains:
   Glycosides (See Glossary)
   Protoanemonin
   Volatile oils (See Glossary)

Known Effects

- Irritates mucous membranes.

Unproved Speculated Benefits

- Acts as mild sedative to relieve anxiety.
- Helps bring on menstruation.

Warnings and Precautions

Don't take if you:
- Are pregnant, think you may be pregnant or plan pregnancy in the near future.
- Have any chronic disease of the gastrointestinal tract, such as stomach or duodenal ulcers, oesophageal reflux (reflux oesophagitis), ulcerative colitis, spastic colitis, diverticulosis, diverticulitis.

Consult your doctor if you:
- Take this herb for any medical problem that doesn't improve in 2 weeks. There may be safer, more effective treatments.
- Take any medicinal drugs or herbs including aspirin, laxatives, cold and cough remedies, antacids, vitamins, minerals, amino acids, supplements, other prescription or non-prescription drugs.

Pregnancy:
- Dangers outweigh any possible benefits. Don't use.

Breast-feeding:
- Dangers outweigh any possible benefits. Don't use.

Infants and children:
- Treating infants and children under 2 with any herbal preparation is hazardous.

Others:
- This product will *not* help you and may cause toxic symptoms.

Storage:
- Keep cool and dry, but don't freeze. Store safely away from children.

Safe dosage:
- At present no "safe" dosage has been established.

Toxicity

Comparative-toxicity rating not available from standard references.

For symptoms of toxicity: See *Adverse Reactions, Side Effects or Overdose Symptoms* section below.

Adverse Reactions, Side Effects or Overdose Symptoms

Signs and symptoms:	What to do:
Diarrhoea (sometimes bloody)	Discontinue. Call doctor immediately.
Hallucinations	Seek emergency treatment.
Nausea	Discontinue. Call doctor immediately.
Skin rashes or eye irritation, if used on skin or in eye	Discontinue. Call doctor immediately.
Vomiting	Discontinue. Call doctor immediately.

MEDICINAL HERB

Coltsfoot (Coughwort, Horse-Hoof)

Basic Information

Biological name (genus and species):
Tussilago farfara
Parts used for medicinal purposes:
Berries/fruits
Leaves
Chemicals this herb contains:
Caoutchouc
Pectin
Resin (See Glossary)
Tannins (See Glossary)
Volatile oils (See Glossary)

Known Effects

- Shrinks tissues.
- Prevents secretion of fluids.
- Interferes with absorption of iron and other minerals when taken internally.

Miscellaneous information:
- Has been found to have carginogenic properties.

Unproved Speculated Benefits

Internal use:
- Treats persistent cough.
External use:
- Soothes various skin disorders.

Warnings and Precautions

Don't take if you:
- Are pregnant, think you may be pregnant or plan pregnancy in the near future.

Consult your doctor if you:
- Take this herb for any medical problem that doesn't improve in 2 weeks. There may be safer, more effective treatments.
- Take any medicinal drugs or herbs including aspirin, laxatives, cold and cough remedies, antacids, vitamins, minerals, amino acids, supplements, other prescription or non-prescription drugs.

Pregnancy:
- Problems in pregnant women taking small or usual amounts have not been proved. But the chance of problems does exist. Don't use unless prescribed by your doctor.

Breast-feeding:
- Problems in breast-fed infants of lactating mothers taking small or usual amounts have not been proved. But the chance of problems does exist. Don't use unless prescribed by your doctor.

Infants and children:
- Treating infants and children under 2 with any herbal preparation is hazardous.

Others:
- None expected if you are under 45, not pregnant, basically healthy, take it for only a short time and do not exceed manufacturer's recommended dosage.

Storage:
- Keep cool and dry, but don't freeze. Store safely away from children.

Safe dosage:
- At present no "safe" dosage has been established.

Toxicity

Rated relatively safe when taken in small quantities for short periods of time. However, cumulative effects may produce malignant growths.

Adverse Reactions, Side Effects or Overdose Symptoms

None expected

Comfrey (Knitbone)

Basic Information

Biological name (genus and species):
Symphytum officinale
Parts used for medicinal purposes:
Leaves
Roots
Chemicals this herb contains:
Allantoin
Consolidine
Mucilage (See Glossary)
Phosphorous
Potassium
Pyrrolizidine
Starch
Symphytocynglossine
Tannins (See Glossary)
Vitamins A and C

Known Effects

- Shrinks tissues.
- Prevents secretion of fluids.
- Interferes with absorption of iron and other minerals when taken internally.

Unproved Speculated Benefits

- Roots and leaves are used in poultices to heal wounds and ulcers. (See Glossary.)
- Protects scraped tissues.
- Is used as a laxative by providing bulk.
- Helps body dispose of excess fluid by increasing the amount of urine produced.

Warnings and Precautions

Don't take if you:
- Are pregnant, think you may be pregnant or plan pregnancy in the near future.
- Need to restrict potassium in your diet.

Consult your doctor if you:
- Take this herb for any medical problem that doesn't improve in 2 weeks. There may be safer, more effective treatments.
- Take any medicinal drugs or herbs including aspirin, laxatives, cold and cough remedies, antacids, vitamins, minerals, amino acids, supplements, other prescription or non-prescription drugs.

Pregnancy:
- Problems in pregnant women taking small or usual amounts have not been proved. But the chance of problems does exist. Don't use unless prescribed by your doctor.

Breast-feeding:
- Problems in breast-fed infants of lactating mothers taking small or usual amounts have not been proved. But the chance of problems does exist. Don't use unless prescribed by your doctor.

Infants and children:
- Treating infants and children under 2 with any herbal preparation is hazardous.

Others:
- None expected if you are beyond childhood and under 45, basically healthy and take for only a short time.

Storage:
- Keep cool and dry, but don't freeze. Store safely away from children.

Safe dosage:
- At present no "safe" dosage has been established.

Toxicity

Rated relatively safe when taken in appropriate quantities for short periods of time.

For symptoms of toxicity: See *Adverse Reactions, Side Effects or Overdose Symptoms* section below.

Adverse Reactions, Side Effects or Overdose Symptoms

Signs and symptoms:	What to do:
Coma	Seek emergency treatment.
Drowsiness	Discontinue. Call doctor immediately.
Lethargy	Discontinue. Call doctor immediately.

MEDICINAL HERB

Cottonwood (Balm of Gilead)

Basic Information

Biological name (genus and species):
Populus deltoides, P. candicans, P. spp
Parts used for medicinal purposes:
Roots
Chemicals this herb contains:
Salacin

Known Effects

- Acts as an anti-inflammatory.
- Reduces pain.
- Reduces fever.

Miscellaneous information:
- Used extensively by North-American Indians for many disorders.

Unproved Speculated Benefits

- Relieves toothache.
- Treats arthritis.
- Treats heart diseases.
- Treats any illness accompanied by fever, pain or inflammation.

Warnings and Precautions

Don't take if you:
- Are pregnant, think you may be pregnant or plan pregnancy in the near future.

Consult your doctor if you:
- Take this herb for any medical problem that doesn't improve in 2 weeks. There may be safer, more effective treatments.
- Take any medicinal drugs or herbs including aspirin, laxatives, cold and cough remedies, antacids, vitamins, minerals, amino acids, supplements, other prescription or non-prescription drugs.

Pregnancy:
- Problems in pregnant women taking small or usual amounts have not been proved. But the chance of problems does exist. Don't use unless prescribed by your doctor.

Breast-feeding:
- Problems in breast-fed infants of lactating mothers taking small or usual amounts have not been proved. But the chance of problems does exist. Don't use unless prescribed by your doctor.

Infants and children:
- Treating infants and children under 2 with any herbal preparation is hazardous.

Others:
- None expected if you are beyond childhood and under 45, basically healthy and take for only a short time.

Storage:
- Keep cool and dry, but don't freeze. Store safely away from children.

Safe dosage:
- At present no "safe" dosage has been established.

Toxicity

Comparative-toxicity rating not available from standard references.

For symptoms of toxicity: See *Adverse Reactions, Side Effects or Overdose Symptoms* section below.

Adverse Reactions, Side Effects or Overdose Symptoms

Signs and symptoms:	What to do:
Coma	Seek emergency treatment.
Confusion	Discontinue. Call doctor immediately.
Convulsions	Seek emergency treatment.

Basic Information

Biological name (genus and species):
Agropyrum repens
Parts used for medicinal purposes:
Roots
Chemicals this herb contains:
Dextrose (simple sugar) Levulose (simple sugar)
Gum (See Glossary)   Mannite
Inosite   Silica
Lactic acid   Vannilin

Known Effects

- Helps body dispose of excess fluid by increasing amount of urine produced.
- If contaminated with ergot, causes constriction of blood vessels and muscular spasm of uterus.

Miscellaneous information:
- Frequently contaminated with a poisonous fungus containing ergot. Discard *any* grass that has a black coating.

Unproved Speculated Benefits

- Protects scraped tissues.
- Is used as a nutrient.
- Treats bladder infections.
- Treats arthritis.

Warnings and Precautions

Don't take if you:
- Are pregnant, think you may be pregnant or plan pregnancy in the near future.
- Have liver disease.
- Have any chronic disease of the gastrointestinal tract, such as stomach or duodenal ulcers, oesophageal reflux (reflux oesophagitis), ulcerative colitis, spastic colitis, diverticulosis, diverticulitis.

Consult your doctor if you:
- Take this herb for any medical problem that doesn't improve in 2 weeks. There may be safer, more effective treatments.
- Take any medicinal drugs or herbs including aspirin, laxatives, cold and cough remedies, antacids, vitamins, minerals, amino acids, supplements, other prescription or non-prescription drugs.

Pregnancy:
- Dangers outweigh any possible benefits. Don't use.

Breast-feeding:
- Dangers outweigh any possible benefits. Don't use.

Infants and children:
- Treating infants and children under 2 with any herbal preparation is hazardous.

Others:
- None expected if you are beyond childhood and under 45, basically healthy take it for only a short time and do not exceed manufacturer's recommended dosage.

Storage:
- Keep cool and dry, but don't freeze. Store safely away from children.

Safe dosage:
- At present no "safe" dosage has been established.

Toxicity

Comparative-toxicity rating not available from standard references.

For symptoms of toxicity: See *Adverse Reactions, Side Effects or Overdose Symptoms* section below.

Adverse Reactions, Side Effects or Overdose Symptoms

Signs and symptoms:	What to do:
Only if contaminated with ergot:	
Coma	Seek emergency treatment.
Diarrhoea	Discontinue. Call doctor when convenient.
Rapid, weak pulse	Seek emergency treatment.
Tingling, itching	Discontinue. Call doctor when convenient.
Unquenchable thirst	Discontinue. Call doctor immediately.
Vomiting	Discontinue. Call doctor immediately.

Cow Parsnip (Hogweed, Keck)

Basic Information
Biological name (genus and species):
   Heracleum lanatum
Parts used for medicinal purposes:
   Fruit
   Leaves
   Roots
   Seeds
Chemicals this herb contains:
   Volatile oils (See Glossary)

Known Effects

- Decreases thickness and increases fluidity of mucus from lungs and bronchial tubes.
- Depresses central nervous system.
- Decreases spasm of smooth muscle or skeletal muscle.

Miscellaneous information:
- Young plants may look like hemlock, which is poisonous.

Unproved Speculated Benefits

- Fruits and leaves are used as a sedative.

Warnings and Precautions

Don't take if you:
- Are pregnant, think you may be pregnant or plan pregnancy in the near future.

Consult your doctor if you:
- Take this herb for any medical problem that doesn't improve in 2 weeks. There may be safer, more effective treatments.
- Take any medicinal drugs or herbs including aspirin, laxatives, cold and cough remedies, antacids, vitamins, minerals, amino acids, supplements, other prescription or non-prescription drugs.

Pregnancy:
- Dangers outweigh any possible benefits. Don't use.

Breast-feeding:
- Dangers outweigh any possible benefits. Don't use.

Infants and children:
- Treating infants and children under 2 with any herbal preparation is hazardous.

Others:
- None expected if you are beyond childhood and under 45, basically healthy and take for only a short time.

Storage:
- Keep cool and dry, but don't freeze. Store safely away from children.

Safe dosage:
- At present no "safe" dosage has been established.

Toxicity

Comparative-toxicity rating not available from standard references.

Adverse Reactions, Side Effects or Overdose Symptoms

None reported

Basic Information

Biological name (genus and species):
   Geranium maculatum
Parts used for medicinal purposes:
   Roots
   Leaves
Chemicals this herb contains:
   Colouring materials

Gallic acid	Starch
Gum (See Glossary)	Sugar
Pectin	Tannins (See Glossary)

Known Effects

- Produces puckering.
- Shrinks tissues.
- Prevents secretion of fluids.
- May increase blood clotting.
- Interferes with absorption of iron and other minerals when taken internally.

Miscellaneous information:
- Is used as a mouthwash.
- Is used as a gargle for sore throat.
- Used in traps to kill Japanese beetles which are attracted to it. They die when they eat cranesbill leaves.

Unproved Speculated Benefits

- Acts as an astringent.
- Decreases nosebleeds.
- Treats bleeding from stomach, mouth, intestines.
- Treats diarrhoea.
- Is used as a poultice. (See Glossary.) Occasionally used as a means of applying medications.

Warnings and Precautions

Don't take if you:
- Are pregnant, think you may be pregnant or plan pregnancy in the near future.
- Have any chronic disease of the gastrointestinal tract, such as stomach or duodenal ulcers, oesophageal reflux (reflux oesophagitis), ulcerative colitis, spastic colitis, diverticulosis, diverticulitis.

Consult your doctor if you:
- Take this herb for any medical problem that doesn't improve in 2 weeks. There may be safer, more effective treatments.

- Take any medicinal drugs or herbs including aspirin, laxatives, cold and cough remedies, antacids, vitamins, minerals, amino acids, supplements, other prescription or non-prescription drugs.

Pregnancy:
- Problems in pregnant women taking small or usual amounts have not been proved. But the chance of problems does exist. Don't use unless prescribed by your doctor.

Breast-feeding:
- Problems in breast-fed infants of lactating mothers taking small or usual amounts have not been proved. But the chance of problems does exist. Don't use unless prescribed by your doctor.

Infants and children:
- Treating infants and children under 2 with any herbal preparation is hazardous.

Others:
- None expected if you are beyond childhood and under 45, basically healthy and take for only a short time.

Storage:
- Keep cool and dry, but don't freeze. Store safely away from children.

Safe dosage:
- At present no "safe" dosage has been established.

Toxicity

Comparative-toxicity rating not available from standard references.

For symptoms of toxicity: See below.

Adverse Reactions, Side Effects or Overdose Symptoms

Signs and symptoms:	What to do:
Diarrhoea	Discontinue. Call doctor immediately.
Kidney damage characterized by blood in urine, decreased urine flow, swelling of hands and feet	Seek emergency treatment.
Nausea	Discontinue. Call doctor immediately.
Vomiting	Discontinue. Call doctor immediately.

Cubeb (Tailed Pepper, Java Pepper)

Basic Information

Biological name (genus and species):
Piper cubeba
Parts used for medicinal purposes:
Berries/fruits
Chemicals this herb contains:
Cubebic acid
Cubebin
Fixed oil (See Glossary)
Gum (See Glossary)
Resin (See Glossary)
Sesquiterpene alcohol (cubeb camphor)
Terpenes
Volatile oils (See Glossary)

Known Effects

• Cubebic acid irritates the ureter, bladder and urethra.

Miscellaneous information:
• Active chemicals are in fully grown, *unripe* fruit.

Unproved Speculated Benefits

• Helps body dispose of excess fluid by increasing amount of urine produced.
• Is used as urinary antiseptic.
• Decreases thickness and increases fluidity of mucus from lungs and bronchial tubes.
• Aids in expelling gas from intestinal tract.

Warnings and Precautions

Don't take if you:
• Are pregnant, think you may be pregnant or plan pregnancy in the near future.
• Have any chronic disease of the gastrointestinal tract, such as stomach or duodenal ulcers, oesophageal reflux (reflux oesophagitis), ulcerative colitis, spastic colitis, diverticulosis, diverticulitis.

Consult your doctor if you:
• Take this herb for any medical problem that doesn't improve in 2 weeks. There may be safer, more effective treatments.
• Have chronic intestinal disease. Cubeb may make it worse.

Pregnancy:
• Problems in pregnant women taking small or usual amounts have not been proved. But the chance of problems does exist. Don't use unless prescribed by your doctor.

Breast-feeding:
• Problems in breast-fed infants of lactating mothers taking small or usual amounts have not been proved. But the chance of problems does exist. Don't use unless prescribed by your doctor.

Infants and children:
• Treating infants and children under 2 with any herbal preparation is hazardous.

Others:
• None expected if you are under 45, not pregnant, basically healthy, take it for only a short time and do not exceed manufacturer's recommded dosage.

Storage:
• Keep cool and dry, but don't freeze. Store safely away from children.

Safe dosage:
• At present no "safe" dosage has been established.

Toxicity

Comparative-toxicity rating not available from standard references.

For symptoms of toxicity: See *Adverse Reactions, Side Effects or Overdose Symptoms* section below.

Adverse Reactions, Side Effects or Overdose Symptoms

Signs and symptoms:	What to do:
Nausea	Discontinue. Call doctor immediately.
Vomiting	Discontinue. Call doctor immediately.

Basic Information

Biological name (genus and species):
Turnera diffusa
Parts used for medicinal purposes:
Leaves
Chemicals this herb contains:
Arbutin
Chlorophyll
Damianian
Resin (See Glossary)
Starch
Sugar
Tannins (See Glossary)
Volatile oils (See Glossary)

Known Effects

- Stimulates muscular contractions of intestinal tract.
- Interferes with absorption of iron and other minerals when taken internally.

Miscellaneous Information:
- Tastes very bitter.

Unproved Speculated Benefits

- Acts as a purgative.
- Is used as an aphrodisiac.
- Is used as a headache remedy.
- Decreases or cures bedwetting.

Warnings and Precautions

Don't take if you:
- Are pregnant, think you may be pregnant or plan pregnancy in the near future.
- Have any chronic disease of the gastrointestinal tract, such as stomach or duodenal ulcers, oesophageal reflux (reflux oesophagitis), ulcerative colitis, spastic colitis, diverticulosis, diverticulitis.
- Have kidney or urinary-tract disease.

Consult your doctor if you:
- Take this herb for any medical problem that doesn't improve in 2 weeks. There may be safer, more effective treatments.
- Take any medicinal drugs or herbs including aspirin, laxatives, cold and cough remedies, antacids, vitamins, minerals, amino acids, supplements, other prescription or non-prescription drugs.

Pregnancy:
- Dangers outweigh any possible benefits. Don't use.

Breast-feeding:
- Dangers outweigh any possible benefits. Don't use.

Infants and children:
- Treating infants and children under 2 with any herbal preparation is hazardous.

Others:
- None expected if you are under 45, not pregnant, basically healthy, take it for only a short time and do not exceed manufacturer's recommended dosage.

Storage:
- Keep cool and dry, but don't freeze. Store safely away from children.

Safe dosage:
- At present no "safe" dosage has been established.

Toxicity

Rated relatively safe when taken in appropriate quantities for short periods of time.

For symptoms of toxicity: See *Adverse Reactions, Side Effects or Overdose Symptoms* section below.

Adverse Reactions, Side Effects or Overdose Symptoms

Signs and symptoms:	What to do:
No documented cases reported. Theoretically:	
Diarrhoea	Discontinue. Call doctor immediately.
Nausea	Discontinue. Call doctor immediately.
Urinary frequency	Discontinue. Call doctor when convenient.
Vomiting	Discontinue. Call doctor immediately.

Dandelion

Basic Information

Biological name (genus and species):
Taraxacum officinale
Parts used for medicinal purposes:
Leaves
Roots
Young tops
Chemicals this herb contains:
Bitters (See Glossary)
Fats
Gluten
Gum (See Glossary)
Inulin
Iron
Niacin
Potash
Proteins
Resin (See Glossary)
Teraxacerin
Vitamins A and C

Known Effects

- Helps body dispose of excess fluid by increasing amount of urine produced.
- Stimulates stomach secretions.

Miscellaneous information:
- Is a source of vitamins A and C.

Unproved Speculated Benefits

- Treats dyspepsia.
- Treats constipation.

Warnings and Precautions

Don't take if you:
- Are pregnant, think you may be pregnant or plan pregnancy in the near future.

Consult your doctor if you:
- Take this herb for any medical problem that doesn't improve in 2 weeks. There may be safer, more effective treatments.
- Take any medicinal drugs or herbs including aspirin, laxatives, cold and cough remedies, antacids, vitamins, minerals, amino acids, supplements, other prescription or non-prescription drugs.

Pregnancy:
- Problems in pregnant women taking small or usual amounts have not been proved. But the chance of problems does exist. Don't use unless prescribed by your doctor.

Breast-feeding:
- Problems in breast-fed infants of lactating mothers taking small or usual amounts have not been proved. But the chance of problems does exist. Don't use unless prescribed by your doctor.

Infants and children:
- Treating infants and children under 2 with any herbal preparation is hazardous.

Others:
- None expected if you are beyond childhood and under 45, basically healthy and take for only a short time.

Storage:
- Keep cool and dry, but don't freeze. Store safely away from children.

Safe dosage:
- At present no "safe" dosage has been established.

Toxicity

Generally regarded as safe when taken in appropriate quantities for short periods of time.

Adverse Reactions, Side Effects or Overdose Symptoms

None expected

Basic Information

Biological name (genus and species):
Sambucus canadensis
Parts used for medicinal purposes:
Bark
Berries/fruits
Inner bark
Leaves
Chemicals this herb contains:

Albumin	Tannic acid
Cyanide	Tyrosin
Itydrocyanic aid	Viburnic acid
Resin (See Glossary)	Vitamin C
Rutin	Volatile oils (See Glossary)
Sambucine	Wax (See Glossary)

Sambunigrin—found in stem; breaks down
   to cyanide

Known Effects

- Bark, berries and leaves irritate the gastrointestinal tract and act as a laxative and purgative.
- Causes vomiting (sometimes).
- Helps body dispose of excess fluid by increasing amount of urine produced.
- Increases perspiration.

Miscellaneous information:
- Stems contain cyanide and can be *extremely* toxic.

Unproved Speculated Benefits

- Treats headache.
- Treats arthritis.
- Treats gout.
- Treats the common cold.
- Treats fevers.
- Treats sore throat.
- Treats abdominal pain.
- Aids discomfort of menstrual cramps.
- Poultices promote healing of bruises and sprains. (See Glossary.)

Warnings and Precautions

Don't take if you:
- Are pregnant, think you may be pregnant or plan pregnancy in the near future.
- Have any chronic disease of the gastrointestinal tract, such as stomach or duodenal ulcers, oesophageal reflux (reflux oesophagitis), ulcerative colitis, spastic colitis, diverticulosis, diverticulitis.

Consult your doctor if you:
- Take this herb for any medical problem that doesn't improve in 2 weeks. There may be safer, more effective treatments.
- Take any medicinal drugs or herbs including aspirin, laxatives, cold and cough remedies, antacids, vitamins, minerals, amino acids, supplements, other prescription or non-prescription drugs.

Pregnancy:
- Dangers outweigh any possible benefits. Don't use.

Breast-feeding:
- Dangers outweigh any possible benefits. Don't use.

Infants and children:
- Treating infants and children under 2 with any herbal preparation is hazardous.

Others:
- Ripe berries are probably non-toxic.
- Beware of stems. Enough cyanide from them could cause death.

Storage:
- Keep cool and dry, but don't freeze. Store safely away from children.

Safe dosage:
- At present no "safe" dosage has been established.

Toxicity

Rated slightly dangerous, particularly in children, persons over 55 and those who take larger than appropriate quantities for extended periods of time.

For symptoms of toxicity: See *Adverse Reactions, Side Effects or Overdose Symptoms* section below.

Adverse Reactions, Side Effects or Overdose Symptoms

Signs and symptoms:	What to do:
Abdominal pain	Discontinue. Call doctor immediately.
Diarrhoea	Discontinue. Call doctor immediately.
Nausea	Discontinue. Call doctor immediately.
Vomiting	Discontinue. Call doctor immediately.

Eyebright

Basic Information

Biological name (genus and species):
   Euphrasia officinalis
Parts used for medicinal purposes:
   Entire plant, except roots
Chemicals this herb contains:
   Bitters (See Glossary)
   Tannins (See Glossary)
   Volatile oils (See Glossary)

Known Effects

- Shrinks tissues.
- Prevents secretion of fluids.
- Interferes with absorption of iron and other minerals when taken internally.

Miscellaneous information:
- No proved benefits.

Unproved Speculated Benefits

- Is used as an eyewash to relieve discomfort caused from eyestrain or minor irritation.
- Is used internally for many alleged benefits.

Warnings and Precautions

Don't take if you:
- Are pregnant, think you may be pregnant or plan pregnancy in the near future.

Consult your doctor if you:
- Take this herb for any medical problem that doesn't improve in 2 weeks. There may be safer, more effective treatments.
- Take any medicinal drugs or herbs including aspirin, laxatives, cold and cough remedies, antacids, vitamins, minerals, amino acids, supplements, other prescription or non-prescription drugs.

Pregnancy:
- Problems in pregnant women taking small or usual amounts have not been proved. But the chance of problems does exist. Don't use unless prescribed by your doctor.

Breast-feeding:
- Problems in breast-fed infants of lactating mothers taking small or usual amounts have not been proved. But the chance of problems does exist. Don't use unless prescribed by your doctor.

Infants and children:
- Treating infants and children under 2 with any herbal preparation is hazardous.

Others:
- None expected if you are under 45, not pregnant, basically healthy, take it for only a short time and do not exceed manufacturer's recommended dosage.

Storage:
- Keep cool and dry, but don't freeze. Store safely away from children.

Safe dosage:
- At present no "safe" dosage has been established.

Toxicity

Rated relatively safe when taken in appropriate quantities for short periods of time.

Adverse Reactions, Side Effects or Overdose Symptoms

None expected

Basic Information

Biological name (genus and species):
Foeniculum vulgare
Parts used for medicinal purposes:
Berries/fruits
Roots
Stems
Chemicals this herb contains:
Anethole
Fixed oil (See Glossary)
Volatile oils (See Glossary)

Known Effects

- Aids in expelling gas from intestinal tract.
- Stimulates respiration.
- Increases stomach acidity.

Miscellaneous information:
- Provides flavour.

Unproved Speculated Benefits

- Treats dyspepsia.
- Is used for common colds.
- Is used for coughs.

Warnings and Precautions

Don't take if you:
- Are pregnant, think you may be pregnant or plan pregnancy in the near future.
- Have any chronic disease of the gastrointestinal tract, such as stomach or duodenal ulcers, oesophageal reflux (reflux oesophagitis), ulcerative colitis, spastic colitis, diverticulosis, diverticulitis.

Consult your doctor if you:
- Take this herb for any medical problem that doesn't improve in 2 weeks. There may be safer, more effective treatments.
- Take any medicinal drugs or herbs including aspirin, laxatives, cold and cough remedies, antacids, vitamins, minerals, amino acids, supplements, other prescription or non-prescription drugs.

Pregnancy:
- Dangers outweigh any possible benefits. Don't use.

Breast-feeding:
- Dangers outweigh any possible benefits. Don't use.

Infants and children:
- Treating infants and children under 2 with any herbal preparation is hazardous.

Others:
- If you stay away from the oil extract, none expected if you are beyond childhood and under 45, basically healthy and take for only a short time.

Storage:
- Keep cool and dry, but don't freeze. Store safely away from children.

Safe dosage:
- At present no "safe" dosage has been established.

Toxicity

Generally regarded as safe when taken in appropriate quantities for short periods of time.

For symptoms of toxicity: See *Adverse Reactions, Side Effects or Overdose Symptoms* section below.

Adverse Reactions, Side Effects or Overdose Symptoms

Signs and symptoms:	What to do:
Oil extracted from fennel may cause:	
Congestive heart failure	Seek emergency treatment.
Nausea	Discontinue. Call doctor immediately.
Seizures	Seek emergency treatment.
Vomiting	Discontinue. Call doctor immediately.

Fenugreek

Basic Information
Biological name (genus and species):
  Trigonella foenum-graecum
Parts used for medicinal purposes:
  Seeds
Chemicals this herb contains:
  Choline
  Fixed oil (See Glossary)
  Iron
  Lecithin
  Mucilage (See Glossary)
  Phosphates (See Glossary)
  Protein
  Trigonelline
  Trimethylamine
  Volatile oils (See Glossary)

Known Effects

- Increases stomach acidity.

Miscellaneous information:
- Fenugreek has a disagreeable odour and bitter taste.
- Prescribed frequently by vets, particularly for horses.

Unproved Speculated Benefits

- Seeds act as a bulk laxative.
- Protects scraped tissues.

Warnings and Precautions

Don't take if you:
- Are pregnant, think you may be pregnant or plan pregnancy in the near future.

Consult your doctor if you:
- Take this herb for any medical problem that doesn't improve in 2 weeks. There may be safer, more effective treatments.
- Take any medicinal drugs or herbs including aspirin, laxatives, cold and cough remedies, antacids, vitamins, minerals, amino acids, supplements, other prescription or non-prescription drugs.

Pregnancy:
- Problems in pregnant women taking small or usual amounts have not been proved. But the chance of problems does exist. Don't use unless prescribed by your doctor.

Breast-feeding:
- Problems in breast-fed infants of lactating mothers taking small or usual amounts have not been proved. But the chance of problems does exist. Don't use unless prescribed by your doctor.

Infants and children:
- Treating infants and children under 2 with any herbal preparation is hazardous.

Storage:
- Keep cool and dry, but don't freeze. Store safely away from children.

Safe dosage:
- At present no "safe" dosage has been established.

Toxicity

Rated relatively safe when taken in appropriate quantities for short periods of time.

Adverse Reactions, Side Effects or Overdose Symptoms

None expected

Basic Information

Biological name (genus and species):
    Chrysanthemum parthenium
Parts used for medicinal purposes:
    Bark
    Dried flowers
    Leaves
Chemicals this herb contains:
    Parthenolide
    Pyrethrins
    Santamarin

Known Effects

- Kills insects.
- Decreases thickness and increases fluidity of mucus from lungs and bronchial tubes.
- Stimulates uterine contractions.

Unproved Speculated Benefits

Leaves:
- Treat menstrual disorders.
- Treat common cold.
- Treat indigestion and diarrhea.
- Stimulate appetite.
- Decreases oedema.
- Make childbirth easier.

Dried flowers:
- Treat intestinal parasites (worms).
- Start menstrual flow.
- Cause abortion.
- Stimulate appetite.
- Aid in expelling gas from intestinal tract.

Warnings and Precautions

Don't take if you:
- Are allergic to pyrethrins.
- Are pregnant, think you may be pregnant or plan pregnancy in the near future.

Consult your doctor if you:
- Take this herb for any medical problem that doesn't improve in 2 weeks. There may be safer, more effective treatments.
- Take any medicinal drugs or herbs including aspirin, laxatives, cold and cough remedies, antacids, vitamins, minerals, amino acids, supplements, other prescription or non-prescription drugs.

Pregnancy:
- Dangers outweigh any possible benefits. Don't use.

Breast-feeding:
- Dangers outweigh any possible benefits. Don't use.

Infants and children:
- Treating infants and children under 2 with any herbal preparation is hazardous.

Others:
- Feverfew has no proven usefulness. It may be dangerous.

Storage:
- Keep cool and dry, but don't freeze. Store safely away from children.

Safe dosage:
- At present no "safe" dosage has been established.

Toxicity

Generally regarded as safe when taken in very small quantities for short periods of time.

For symptoms of toxicity: See *Adverse Reactions, Side Effects or Overdose Symptoms* section below.

Adverse Reactions, Side Effects or Overdose Symptoms

Signs and symptoms:	What to do:
Life-threatening anaphylaxis may follow injections—symptoms include immediate severe itching, paleness, low blood pressure, loss of consciousness, coma	Yell for help. Don't leave victim. Begin CPR (cardiopulmonary resuscitation), mouth to mouth breathing and external cardiac massage. Have someone dial 999 (emergency). Don't stop CPR until help arrives.

Flaxseed (Linseed)

Basic Information

Biological name (genus and species):
Linum usitatissimum
Parts used for medicinal purposes:
Seeds
Chemicals this herb contains:
Gum (See Glossary)
Fixed oil (See Glossary)
Linamarin
Mucilage (See Glossary)
Protein
Tannins (See Glossary)
Wax (See Glossary)

Known Effects

- Protects scraped tissues.
- Forms bulk in intestinal tract.
- Interferes with absorption of iron and other minerals when taken internally.

Miscellaneous information:
- All parts of flax can contain toxic chemicals, but immature seeds grown in warm climates may have higher toxic concentrations.
- Linamarin may be converted to cyanide in the body.

Unproved Speculated Benefits

- Soothes coughs.
- Oil softens or smoothes skin.
- Is used as a bulk-forming laxative.
- Is used for poultices to apply to chest for colds and coughs. (See Glossary.)

Warnings and Precautions

Don't take if you:
- Are pregnant, think you may be pregnant or plan pregnancy in the near future.

Consult your doctor if you:
- Take this herb for any medical problem that doesn't improve in 2 weeks. There may be safer, more effective treatments.
- Take any medicinal drugs or herbs including aspirin, laxatives, cold and cough remedies, antacids, vitamins, minerals, amino acids, supplements, other prescription or non-prescription drugs.

Pregnancy:
- Dangers outweigh any possible benefits. Don't use.

Breast-feeding:
- Dangers outweigh any possible benefits. Don't use.

Infants and children:
- Treating infants and children under 2 with any herbal preparation is hazardous.

Others:
- None expected if you are beyond childhood and under 45, basically healthy and take for only a short time.

Storage:
- Keep cool and dry, but don't freeze. Store safely away from children.

Safe dosage:
- At present no "safe" dosage has been established.

Toxicity

Comparative-toxicity rating not available from standard references.

For symptoms of toxicity: See *Adverse Reactions, Side Effects or Overdose Symptoms* section below.

Adverse Reactions, Side Effects or Overdose Symptoms

Signs and symptoms:	What to do:
Convulsions	Seek emergency treatment.
Fast breathing	Discontinue. Call doctor immediately.
Paralysis	Seek emergency treatment.
Unusual excitement	Discontinue. Call doctor immediately.
Weakness	Discontinue. Call doctor immediately.

Basic Information

Biological name (genus and species):
Fritillia vericillia, F. meleagris
Parts used for medicinal purposes:
Roots
Chemicals this herb contains:
Frimitime
Fritilline
Peimine
Peiminine
Verticine
Verticilline
(Peimine and peiminine may resemble steroid hormones.)

Known Effects

- Peimine and peiminine may affect the electrical system of the heart.
- Decreases blood pressure.
- Increases blood sugar.

Miscellaneous information:
- Only roots have medicinal properties.

Unproved Speculated Benefits

- Reduces fevers.
- Decreases thickness and increases fluidity of mucus from lungs and bronchial tubes.
- Increases flow of breast milk in lactating women.

Warnings and Precautions

Don't take if you:
- Are pregnant, think you may be pregnant or plan pregnancy in the near future.
- Have heart disease.

Consult your doctor if you:
- Take this herb for any medical problem that doesn't improve in 2 weeks. There may be safer, more effective treatments.
- Take any medicinal drugs or herbs including aspirin, laxatives, cold and cough remedies, antacids, vitamins, minerals, amino acids, supplements, other prescription or non-prescription drugs.

Pregnancy:
- Dangers outweigh any possible benefits. Don't use.

Breast-feeding:
- Dangers outweigh any possible benefits. Don't use.

Infants and children:
- Treating infants and children under 2 with any herbal preparation is hazardous.

Others:
- None expected if you are beyond childhood and under 45, not pregnant, basically healthy and take for only a short time.

Storage:
- Keep cool and dry, but don't freeze. Store safely away from children.

Safe dosage:
- At present no "safe" dosage has been established.

Toxicity

Comparative-toxicity rating not available from standard references.

For symptoms of toxicity: See *Adverse Reactions, Side Effects or Overdose Symptoms* section below.

Adverse Reactions, Side Effects or Overdose Symptoms

Signs and symptoms:	What to do:
Heart block characterized by slow heart rate (below 50)	Seek emergency treatment.
Heartbeat irregularity	Discontinue. Call doctor immediately.

Galanga Major & Minor (India Root, Chinese Ginger)

Basic Information

Biological name (genus and species)
Alpinia galanga, Alpinia officinarum
Parts used for medicinal purposes:
Various parts of the entire plant, frequently differing by country and/or culture
Chemicals this herb contains:
Cineloe
Galangin
Galangol
Kaempferid
Resin (See Glossary)
Volatile oils (See Glossary)

Known Effects

- Anti-bacterial effect acts against bacterial germs, such as streptococci, staphylococci and coliform bacteria.

Miscellaneous information:
- Related botanically and pharmacologically to ginger.
- Known and used by ancient Greeks and Arabs.

Unproved Speculated Benefits

- Aids in expelling gas from intestinal tract.
- Treats impotence.
- Reduces excess phlegm caused by allergies.
- Treats painful teeth and gums.
- Stimulates respiration.

Warnings and Precautions

Don't take if you:
- Are pregnant, think you may be pregnant or plan pregnancy in the near future.
- Have any chronic disease of the gastrointestinal tract, such as stomach or duodenal ulcers, oesophageal reflux (reflux oesophagitis), ulcerative colitis, spastic colitis, diverticulosis, diverticulitis.

Consult your doctor if you:
- Take this herb for any medical problem that doesn't improve in 2 weeks. There may be safer, more effective treatments.
- Take any medicinal drugs or herbs including aspirin, laxatives, cold and cough remedies, antacids, vitamins, minerals, amino acids, supplements, other prescription or non-prescription drugs.

Pregnancy:
- Problems in pregnant women taking small or usual amounts have not been proved. But the chance of problems does exist. Don't use unless prescribed by your doctor.

Breast-feeding:
- Problems in breast-fed infants of lactating mothers taking small or usual amounts have not been proved. But the chance of problems does exist. Don't use unless prescribed by your doctor.

Infants and children:
- Treating infants and children under 2 with any herbal preparation is hazardous.

Others:
- None expected if you are under 45, not pregnant, basically healthy, take it for only a short time and do not exceed manufacturer's recommended dosage.

Storage:
- Keep cool and dry, but don't freeze. Store safely away from children.

Safe dosage:
- At present no "safe" dosage has been established.

Toxicity

Comparative-toxicity rating not available from standard references.

For symptoms of toxicity: See *Adverse Reactions, Side Effects or Overdose Symptoms* section below.

Adverse Reactions, Side Effects or Overdose Symptoms

Signs and symptoms:	What to do:
Diarrhoea	Discontinue. Call doctor immediately.
Nausea	Discontinue. Call doctor immediately.
Vomiting	Discontinue. Call doctor immediately.

Basic Information

Biological name (genus and species):
Galega officinalis
Parts used for medicinal purposes:
*Various parts of the entire plant, frequently
differing by country and/or culture*
Chemicals this herb contains:
Bitters (See Glossary)
Galegine
Tannins (See Glossary)

 ## Known Effects

- Reduces blood sugar.
- Interferes with absorption of iron and other minerals when taken internally.

Miscellaneous information:
- Plant smells bad when it is bruised.

 ## Unproved Speculated Benefits

- Treats diabetes.
- Increases flow of breast milk in lactating women.

 ## Warnings and Precautions

Don't take if you:
- Are pregnant, think you may be pregnant or plan pregnancy in the near future.

Consult your doctor if you:
- Take this herb for any medical problem that doesn't improve in 2 weeks. There may be safer, more effective treatments.
- Take any medicinal drugs or herbs including aspirin, laxatives, cold and cough remedies, antacids, vitamins, minerals, amino acids, supplements, other prescription or non-prescription drugs.

Pregnancy:
- Problems in pregnant women taking small or usual amounts have not been proved. But the chance of problems does exist. Don't use unless prescribed by your doctor.

Breast-feeding:
- Problems in breast-fed infants of lactating mothers taking small or usual amounts have not been proved. But the chance of problems does exist. Don't use unless prescribed by your doctor.

Infants and children:
- Treating infants and children under 2 with any herbal preparation is hazardous.

Others:
- None expected if you are under 45, not pregnant, basically healthy, take it for only a short time and do not exceed manufacturer's recommended dosage.

Storage:
- Keep cool and dry, but don't freeze. Store safely away from children.

Safe dosage:
- At present no "safe" dosage has been established.

 ## Toxicity

Comparative-toxicity rating not available from standard references.

For symptoms of toxicity: See *Adverse Reactions, Side Effects or Overdose Symptoms* section below.

 ## Adverse Reactions, Side Effects or Overdose Symptoms

Signs and symptoms:	What to do:
Headache	Discontinue. Call doctor when convenient.
Jitteriness	Discontinue. Call doctor when convenient.
Weakness	Discontinue. Call doctor immediately.

Gambier (Pale Catechu, Gambir)

Basic Information

Biological name (genus and species):
  Uncaria gambier
Parts used for medicinal purposes:
  Leaves
  Twigs
Chemicals this herb contains:
  Catechin
  Catechutannic acid
  Tannins (See Glossary)

Known Effects

- Shrinks tissues.
- Prevents secretion of fluids.
- Interferes with absorption of iron and other minerals when taken internally.

Unproved Speculated Benefits

- Decreases unusual bleeding.
- Treats chronic diarrhoea.
- Is used as gargle for sore throats.

Warnings and Precautions

Don't take if you:
- Have any chronic disease of the gastrointestinal tract, such as stomach or duodenal ulcers, oesophageal reflux (reflux oesophagitis), ulcerative colitis, spastic colitis, diverticulosis, diverticulitis.

Consult your doctor if you:
- Take this herb for any medical problem that doesn't improve in 2 weeks. There may be safer, more effective treatments.
- Take any medicinal drugs or herbs including aspirin, laxatives, cold and cough remedies, antacids, vitamins, minerals, amino acids, supplements, other prescription or non-prescription drugs.

Pregnancy:
- Dangers outweigh any possible benefits. Don't use.

Breast-feeding:
- Dangers outweigh any possible benefits. Don't use.

Infants and children:
- Treating infants and children under 2 with any herbal preparation is hazardous.

Storage:
- Keep cool and dry, but don't freeze. Store safely away from children.

Safe dosage:
- At present no "safe" dosage has been established.

Toxicity

Rated relatively safe when taken in appropriate quantities for short periods of time.

For symptoms of toxicity: See *Adverse Reactions, Side Effects or Overdose Symptoms* section below.

Adverse Reactions, Side Effects or Overdose Symptoms

Signs and symptoms:	What to do:
Diarrhoea	Discontinue. Call doctor immediately.
Kidney damage characterized by blood in urine, decreased urine flow, swelling of hands and feet	Seek emergency treatment.
Vomiting	Discontinue. Call doctor immediately.

Basic Information

Biological name (genus and species):
Allium sativum
Parts used for medicinal purposes:
Bulb
Chemicals this herb contains:
Allicin
Allyl disulphides
Phytoncides
Unsaturated aldehydes
Volatile oils (See Glossary)

 ## Known Effects

- Kills larvae.
- Stops germs from reproducing.
- Decreases thickness and increases fluidity of mucus from lungs and bronchial tubes.
- Stimulates perspiration.
- Helps body dispose of excess fluid by increasing amount of urine produced.
- No effects are expected on the body, either good or bad, when herb is used in very small amounts to enhance the flavour of food.

Miscellaneous information:
- Is used as a condiment.
- Avoid using garlic as a medicinal herb in *any amount* with children! It is acceptable to use garlic as a flavouring in children's food.

 ## Unproved Speculated Benefits

- Treats hypertension.
- Treats cramping abdominal pain in adults.
- Lowers high blood fats (hyperlipidaemia hypercholesterolaemia).
- Reddens skin by increasing blood flow to it.

 ## Warnings and Precautions

Don't take if you:
- Have any medical problem that your doctor is treating you for. Consult him or her first.

Consult your doctor if you:
- Take this herb for any medical problem that doesn't improve in 2 weeks. There may be safer, more effective treatments.
- Take any medicinal drugs or herbs including aspirin, laxatives, cold and cough remedies, antacids, vitamins, minerals, amino acids, supplements, other prescription or non-prescription drugs.

Pregnancy:
- Problems in pregnant women taking small or usual amounts have not been proved. Don't take unless prescribed by your doctor.

Breast-feeding:
- Problems in breast-fed infants of lactating mothers taking small or usual amounts have not been proved. Don't take unless prescribed by your doctor

Infants and children:
- Treating infants and children under 2 with any herbal preparation is hazardous.

Others:
- None expected if you are beyond childhood and under 45, basically healthy and take small amounts for only a short time.

Storage:
- Keep cool and dry, but don't freeze. Store safely away from children.

Safe dosage:
- At present no "safe" dosage has been established.

 ## Toxicity

Comparative-toxicity rating not available from standard references.

For symptoms of toxicity: See *Adverse Reactions, Side Effects or Overdose Symptoms* section below.

 ## Adverse Reactions, Side Effects or Overdose Symptoms

Signs and symptoms:	What to do:
Precipitous blood-pressure drop— symptoms include, faintness, cold sweat, paleness, rapid pulse	Seek emergency treatment.
Increased number of circulating white blood cells as determined by laboratory studies	Discontinue. Call doctor immediately.
Skin eruptions	Discontinue. Call doctor when convenient.

Gentian (Yellow Gentian)

Basic Information

Biological name (genus and species):
Gentiana lutea
Parts used for medicinal purposes:
Roots
Chemicals this herb contains:
Gentiamarin
Gentiin
Gentiopicrin
Gentisin
Mesogentioigenin
Protogentiogenin
Sugar
Xanthone pigment

Known Effects

- Irritates mucous membranes.
- Kills plasmodium, which causes malaria.

Miscellaneous information:
- Has been known and used since ancient times in Greece.

Unproved Speculated Benefits

- Increase contractions of stomach muscles.
- Stimulates gastric secretions.
- Is used as a tonic to stimulate appetite.
- Aids digestion.

Warnings and Precautions

Don't take if you:
- Are pregnant, think you may be pregnant or plan pregnancy in the near future.
- Have any chronic disease of the gastrointestinal tract, such as stomach or duodenal ulcers, oesophageal reflux (reflux oesophagitis), ulcerative colitis, spastic colitis, diverticulosis, diverticulitis.

Consult your doctor if you:
- Take this herb for any medical problem that doesn't improve in 2 weeks. There may be safer, more effective treatments.
- Take any medicinal drugs or herbs including aspirin, laxatives, cold and cough remedies, antacids, vitamins, minerals, amino acids, supplements, other prescription or non-prescription drugs.

Pregnancy:
- Problems in pregnant women taking small or usual amounts have not been proved. But the chance of problems does exist. Don't use unless prescribed by your doctor.

Breast-feeding:
- Problems in breast-fed infants of lactating mothers taking small or usual amounts have not been proved. But the chance of problems does exist. Don't use unless prescribed by your doctor.

Infants and children:
- Treating infants and children under 2 with any herbal preparation is hazardous.

Others:
- None expected if you are under 45, not pregnant, basically healthy, take it for only a short time and do not exceed manufacturer's recommended dosage.

Storage:
- Keep cool and dry, but don't freeze. Store safely away from children.

Safe dosage:
- At present no "safe" dosage has been established.

Toxicity

Rated relatively safe when taken in appropriate quantities for short periods of time.

For symptoms of toxicity: See *Adverse Reactions, Side Effects or Overdose Symptoms* section below.

Adverse Reactions, Side Effects or Overdose Symptoms

Signs and symptoms:	What to do:
Nausea	Discontinue. Call doctor immediately.
Vomiting	Discontinue. Call doctor immediately.

German Chamomile (Mazanilla, Matricaria, Hungarian Chamomile)

Basic Information
Biological name (genus and species):
  Matricaria chamomilla
Parts used for medicinal purposes:
  Petals/flower
Chemicals this herb contains:
  Alphabisabolol
  Azulene
  Fatty acid
  Furfural
  Paraffin hydrocarbons
  Sesquiterpene
  Sesquiterpene alcohol
  Tannins (See Glossary)

Known Effects

- Acts as an anti-inflammatory.
- Weakens muscles.
- Interferes with absorption of iron and other minerals when taken internally.

Miscellaneous information:
- Ice cream, sweet and liqueur manufacturers use small, non-toxic amounts for flavouring.

Unproved Speculated Benefits

- Relieves spasms in skeletal or smooth muscle.
- Is used as a tonic.
- Is used as a sedative.
- Aids in expelling gas from intestinal tract.

Warnings and Precautions

Don't take if you:
- Are pregnant, think you may be pregnant or plan pregnancy in the near future.
- Have any chronic disease of the gastrointestinal tract, such as stomach or duodenal ulcers, oesophageal reflux (reflux oesophagitis), ulcerative colitis, spastic colitis, diverticulosis, diverticulitis.

Consult your doctor if you:
- Take this herb for any medical problem that doesn't improve in 2 weeks. There may be safer, more effective treatments.
- Take any medicinal drugs or herbs including aspirin, laxatives, cold and cough remedies, antacids, vitamins, minerals, amino acids, supplements, other prescription or non-prescription drugs.

Pregnancy:
- Problems in pregnant women taking small or usual amounts have not been proved. But the chance of problems does exist. Don't use unless prescribed by your doctor.

Breast-feeding:
- Problems in breast-fed infants of lactating mothers taking small or usual amounts have not been proved. But the chance of problems does exist. Don't use unless prescribed by your doctor.

Infants and children:
- Treating infants and children under 2 with any herbal preparation is hazardous.

Others:
- None expected if you are beyond childhood and under 45, basically healthy and take for only a short time.

Storage:
- Keep cool and dry, but don't freeze. Store safely away from children.

Safe dosage:
- At present no "safe" dosage has been established.

Toxicity

Generally regarded as safe when taken in appropriate quantities for short periods of time.

For symptoms of toxicity: See *Adverse Reactions, Side Effects or Overdose Symptoms* section below.

Adverse Reactions, Side Effects or Overdose Symptoms

Signs and symptoms:	What to do:
Diarrhoea	Discontinue. Call doctor immediately.
Excess sedation	Discontinue. Call doctor immediately.
Nausea	Discontinue. Call doctor immediately.
Skin eruptions	Discontinue. Call doctor when convenient.
Vomiting	Discontinue. Call doctor immediately.

MEDICINAL HERB

Ginger

Basic Information

Biological name (genus and species):
   Zingiber
Parts used for medicinal purposes:
   Roots
Chemicals this herb contains:
   Bisabolene
   Borneal
   Cineole
   Citral
   Sequiterpene
   Volatile oils (See Glossary)
   Zingerone
   Zingiberene

Known Effects

- Aids in expelling gas from intestinal tract.
- Provides counterirritation when applied to skin overlying an inflamed or irritated joint.
- No effects are expected on the body, either good or bad, when herb is used in very small amounts to enhance the flavour of food.

Miscellaneous information:
- Is used as a flavouring agent.

Unproved Speculated Benefits

- Treats indigestion.
- Treats abdominal discomfort.

Warnings and Precautions

Don't take if you:
- Are pregnant, think you may be pregnant or plan pregnancy in the near future.
- Have any chronic disease of the gastrointestinal tract, such as stomach or duodenal ulcers, oesophageal reflux (reflux oesophagitis), ulcerative colitis, spastic colitis, diverticulosis, diverticulitis.

Consult your doctor if you:
- Take this herb for any medical problem that doesn't improve in 2 weeks. There may be safer, more effective treatments.
- Take any medicinal drugs or herbs including aspirin, laxatives, cold and cough remedies, antacids, vitamins, minerals, amino acids, supplements, other prescription or non-prescription drugs.
- Have stomach or intestinal diseases.

Pregnancy:
- Problems in pregnant women taking small or usual amounts have not been proved. But the chance of problems does exist. Don't use unless prescribed by your doctor.

Breast-feeding:
- Problems in breast-fed infants of lactating mothers taking small or usual amounts have not been proved. But the chance of problems does exist. Don't use unless prescribed by your doctor.

Infants and children:
- Treating infants and children under 2 with any herbal preparation is hazardous.

Others:
- None expected if you are under 45, not pregnant, basically healthy, take it for only a short time and do not exceed manufacturer's recommended dosage.

Storage:
- Keep cool and dry, but don't freeze. Store safely away from children.

Safe dosage:
- At present no "safe" dosage has been established.

Toxicity

Comparative-toxicity rating not available from standard references.

For symptoms of toxicity: See *Adverse Reactions, Side Effects or Overdose Symptoms* section below.

Adverse Reactions, Side Effects or Overdose Symptoms

Signs and symptoms:	What to do:
Diarrhoea	Discontinue. Call doctor immediately.
Nausea	Discontinue. Call doctor immediately.
Vomiting	Discontinue. Call doctor immediately.

Basic Information

Biological name (genus and species):
Panax quinquefolium
Parts used for medicinal purposes:
Roots
Chemicals this herb contains:

Arabinose	Mucilage (See Glossary)
Camphor	Panaxosides
Gineosides	Resin (See Glossary)
	Saponin (See Glossary)
	Starch

Known Effects

- Stimulates brain, heart, blood vessels.
- Decreases blood sugar.
- Increases secretion of histamine.
- Decreases eosinophils in blood.
- Increases corticosteroid content of blood.

Miscellaneous information:
- A favorite Chinese remedy used for almost everything.
- A native plant in the state of Georgia, USA.

Unproved Speculated Benefits

- Treats biological "stress."
- Is used as an aphrodisiac.
- Increases mental and physical efficiency.
- Treats impotence.
- Treats anaemia.
- Treats hardening of the arteries.
- Reduces depression.
- Treats diabetes.
- Treats ulcers.
- Treats oedema.

Warnings and Precautions

Don't take if you:
- Are pregnant, think you may be pregnant or plan pregnancy in the near future.
- Have any chronic disease of the gastrointestinal tract, such as stomach or duodenal ulcers, oesophageal reflux (reflux oesophagitis), ulcerative colitis, spastic colitis, diverticulosis, diverticulitis.

Consult your doctor if you:
- Take this herb for any medical problem that doesn't improve in 2 weeks. There may be safer, more effective treatments.
- Take any medicinal drugs or herbs including aspirin, laxatives, cold and cough remedies, antacids, vitamins, minerals, amino acids, supplements, other prescription or non-prescription drugs.

Pregnancy:
- Problems in pregnant women taking small or usual amounts have not been proved. But the chance of problems does exist. Don't use unless prescribed by your doctor.

Breast-feeding:
- Problems in breast-fed infants of lactating mothers taking small or usual amounts have not been proved. But the chance of problems does exist. Don't use unless prescribed by your doctor.

Infants and children:
- Treating infants and children under 2 with any herbal preparation is hazardous.

Others:
- None expected if you are under 45, not pregnant, basically healthy, take it for only a short time and do not exceed manufacturer's recommended dosage.

Storage:
- Keep cool and dry, but don't freeze. Store safely away from children.

Safe dosage:
- At present no "safe" dosage has been established.

Toxicity

Generally regarded as safe when taken in appropriate quantities for short periods of time.

For symptoms of toxicity: See *Adverse Reactions, Side Effects or Overdose Symptoms* section below.

Adverse Reactions, Side Effects or Overdose Symptoms

Signs and symptoms:	What to do:
Diarrhoea	Discontinue. Call doctor immediately.
Insomnia	Discontinue. Call doctor when convenient.
Nervousness	Discontinue. Call doctor when convenient.
Nausea	Discontinue. Call doctor immediately.
Vomiting	Discontinue. Call doctor immediately.

Goldenseal

Basic Information

Biological name (genus and species):
Hydrastis canadensis
Parts used for medicinal purposes:
Rhizomes
Roots
Chemicals this herb contains:

Albumin	Lignin
Berberine	Resin (See Glossary)
Candine	Starch
Fats	Sugar
Hydrastine	Volatile oils (See Glossary)

Known Effects

- Decreases uterine bleeding.
- Large amounts stimulate central nervous system.
- Large amounts given intravenously can reduce blood pressure.
- Depresses muscle tone of small blood vessels.

Miscellaneous information:
- Has a very bitter taste.

Unproved Speculated Benefits

- Treats dyspepsia.
- Increases appetite.

Warnings and Precautions

Don't take if you:
- Are pregnant, think you may be pregnant or plan pregnancy in the near future.
- Have any chronic disease of the gastrointestinal tract, such as stomach or duodenal ulcers, oesophageal reflux (reflux oesophagitis), ulcerative colitis, spastic colitis, diverticulosis, diverticulitis.

Consult your doctor if you:
- Take this herb for any medical problem that doesn't improve in 2 weeks. There may be safer, more effective treatments.
- Take any medicinal drugs or herbs including aspirin, laxatives, cold and cough remedies, antacids, vitamins, minerals, amino acids, supplements, other prescription or non-prescription drugs.

Pregnancy:
- Dangers outweigh any possible benefits. Don't use.

Breast-feeding:
- Dangers outweigh any possible benefits. Don't use.

Infants and children:
- Treating infants and children under 2 with any herbal preparation is hazardous.

Others:
- None expected if you are under 45, not pregnant, basically healthy, take it for only a short time and do not exceed manufacturer's recommended dosage.

Storage:
- Keep cool and dry, but don't freeze. Store safely away from children.

Safe dosage:
- At present no "safe" dosage has been established.

Toxicity

Rated slightly dangerous, particularly in children, persons over 55 and those who take larger than appropriate quantities for extended periods of time.

For symptoms of toxicity: See *Adverse Reactions, Side Effects or Overdose Symptoms* section below.

Adverse Reactions, Side Effects or Overdose Symptoms

Signs and symptoms:	What to do:
Breathing difficulties	Seek emergency treatment.
Diarrhoea	Discontinue. Call doctor immediately.
Mouth and throat irritation	Discontinue. Call doctor immediately.
Nausea	Discontinue. Call doctor immediately.
Numbness of hands and feet	Discontinue. Call doctor immediately.
Vomiting	Discontinue. Call doctor immediately.
Weakness leading to paralysis of muscles	Seek emergency treatment.

Gotu Cola (Kola, Gbanja Kola)

Basic Information

Biological name (genus and species):
   Cola nitida
Parts used for medicinal purposes:
   Seeds/nuts
Chemicals this herb contains:
   Caffeine
   Catechol
   Epicatechol
   Theobromine

 ## Known Effects

- Stimulates central nervous system.
- Helps body dispose of excess fluid by increasing amount of urine produced.
- Acts as an astringent.
- Shrinks tissues.
- Prevents secretion of fluids.
- No effects are expected on the body, either good or bad, when herb is used in very small amounts to enhance the flavour of food.

 ## Unproved Speculated Benefits

- Decreases fatigue.
- Increases sex drive.
- Treats high blood pressure and congestive heart failure.

 ## Warnings and Precautions

Don't take if you:
- Are pregnant, think you may be pregnant or plan pregnancy in the near future.
- Have any chronic disease of the gastrointestinal tract, such as stomach or duodenal ulcers, oesophageal reflux (reflux oesophagitis), ulcerative colitis, spastic colitis, diverticulosis, diverticulitis.

Consult your doctor if you:
- Take this herb for any medical problem that doesn't improve in 2 weeks. There may be safer, more effective treatments.
- Take any medicinal drugs or herbs including aspirin, laxatives, cold and cough remedies, antacids, vitamins, minerals, amino acids, supplements, other prescription or non-prescription drugs.

Pregnancy:
- Dangers outweigh any possible benefits. Don't use.

Breast-feeding:
- Dangers outweigh any possible benefits. Don't use.

Infants and children:
- Treating infants and children under 2 with any herbal preparation is hazardous.

Others:
- None expected if you are under 45, not pregnant, basically healthy, take it for only a short time and do not exceed manufacturer's recommended dosage.

Storage:
- Keep cool and dry, but don't freeze. Store safely away from children.

Safe dosage:
- At present no "safe" dosage has been established.

 ## Toxicity

Rated relatively safe when taken in appropriate quantities for short periods of time.

For symptoms of toxicity: See *Adverse Reactions, Side Effects or Overdose Symptoms* section below.

 ## Adverse Reactions, Side Effects or Overdose Symptoms

Signs and symptoms:	What to do:
Aggravates peptic ulcers in stomach, duodenum or oesophagus	Discontinue. Call doctor immediately.
Inability to sleep	Discontinue. Call doctor when convenient.
Nervousness	Discontinue. Call doctor when convenient.

Grape Hyacinth

Basic Information

Biological name (genus and species):
Muscari racemonsum, M. comosum
Parts used for medicinal purposes:
Bulb
Chemicals this herb contains:
Cosmisic acid
Saponin (See Glossary)

 ## Known Effects

• Irritates gastrointestinal tract.

 ## Unproved Speculated Benefits

• Treats constipation.
• Stimulates central nervous system.
• Helps body dispose of excess fluid by increasing amount of urine produced.

 ## Warnings and Precautions

Don't take if you:
• Are pregnant, think you may be pregnant or plan pregnancy in the near future.
• Have any chronic disease of the gastrointestinal tract, such as stomach or duodenal ulcers, oesophageal reflux (reflux oesophagitis), ulcerative colitis, spastic colitis, diverticulosis, diverticulitis.

Consult your doctor if you:
• Take this herb for any medical problem that doesn't improve in 2 weeks. There may be safer, more effective treatments.
• Take any medicinal drugs or herbs including aspirin, laxatives, cold and cough remedies, antacids, vitamins, minerals, amino acids, supplements, other prescription or non-prescription drugs.

Pregnancy:
• Dangers outweigh any possible benefits. Don't use.

Breast-feeding:
• Dangers outweigh any possible benefits. Don't use.

Infants and children:
• Treating infants and children under 2 with any herbal preparation is hazardous.

Others:
• No evidence of any useful therapeutic effect. Don't use.

Storage:
• Keep cool and dry, but don't freeze. Store safely away from children.

Safe dosage:
• At present no "safe" dosage has been established.

 ## Toxicity

Comparative-toxicity rating not available from standard references.

For symptoms of toxicity: See *Adverse Reactions, Side Effects or Overdose Symptoms* section below.

 ## Adverse Reactions, Side Effects or Overdose Symptoms

Signs and symptoms:	What to do:
Diarrhoea	Discontinue. Call doctor immediately.
Nausea	Discontinue. Call doctor immediately.
Vomiting	Discontinue. Call doctor immediately.

Grindelia (Gumweed, Rosinweed)

Basic Information

Biological name (genus and species):
Grindelia camporum, G. humilus, G. squarrosa
Parts used for medicinal purposes:
Leaves
Chemicals this herb contains:
Balsamic resin
Grindelol
Robustic acid
Saponins (See Glossary)
Tannins (See Glossary)
Volatile oils (See Glossary)

Known Effects

- Depresses central nervous system in high amounts.
- Dilates pupils of eyes.
- Decreases heart rate.
- Increases blood pressure.
- Interferes with absorption of iron and other minerals when taken internally.

Unproved Speculated Benefits

- Decreases thickness and increases fluidity of mucus from lungs and bronchial tubes.
- Acts as a sedative.
- Treats asthma.
- Treats bronchitis.
- Soothes and heals burns when applied topically.
- Treats vaginitis.
- Is used in poultices as a means of applying medications (See Glossary.)

Warnings and Precautions

Don't take if you:
- Are pregnant, think you may be pregnant or plan pregnancy in the near future.

Consult your doctor if you:
- Take this herb for any medical problem that doesn't improve in 2 weeks. There may be safer, more effective treatments.
- Take any medicinal drugs or herbs including aspirin, laxatives, cold and cough remedies, antacids, vitamins, minerals, amino acids, supplements, other prescription or non-prescription drugs.

Pregnancy:
- Dangers outweigh any possible benefits. Don't use.

Breast-feeding:
- Dangers outweigh any possible benefits. Don't use.

Infants and children:
- Treating infants and children under 2 with any herbal preparation is hazardous.

Storage:
- Keep cool and dry, but don't freeze. Store safely away from children.

Safe dosage:
- At present no "safe" dosage has been established.

Toxicity

Rated slightly dangerous, particularly in children, persons over 55 and those who take larger than appropriate quantities for extended periods of time.

For symptoms of toxicity: See *Adverse Reactions, Side Effects or Overdose Symptoms* section below.

Adverse Reactions, Side Effects or Overdose Symptoms

Signs and symptoms:	What to do:
Kidney damage characterized by blood in urine, decreased urine flow, swelling of hands and feet	Seek emergency treatment.

Guaiac

Basic Information

Biological name (genus and species):
Guaiacum officinale, G. sanctum
Parts used for medicinal purposes:
Stems
Chemicals this herb contains:
Guaiaconic acid
Guaiaretic acid
Resin (See Glossary)
Saponin (See Glossary)
Vanillin

Known Effects

- Irritates gastrointestinal tract.
- Increases perspiration.
- Tests for oxidizing enzymes to detect blood in stool or urine.

Miscellaneous information:

- When added to a stool specimen, hydrogen peroxide and guaiac establish the presence or absence of blood. This test is a useful screening procedure to detect malignant and non-malignant disorders of the intestinal tract.

Unproved Speculated Benefits

- Treats arthritis.
- Treats scrofula.
- Treats constipation.
- Reduces oedema

Warnings and Precautions

Don't take if you:

- Are pregnant, think you may be pregnant or plan pregnancy in the near future.
- Have any chronic disease of the gastrointestinal tract, such as stomach or duodenal ulcers, oesophageal reflux (reflux oesophagitis), ulcerative colitis, spastic colitis, diverticulosis, diverticulitis.

Consult your doctor if you:

- Take this herb for any medical problem that doesn't improve in 2 weeks. There may be safer, more effective treatments.
- Take any medicinal drugs or herbs including aspirin, laxatives, cold and cough remedies, antacids, vitamins, minerals, amino acids, supplements, other prescription or non-prescription drugs.

Pregnancy:

- Dangers outweigh any possible benefits. Don't use.

Breast-feeding:

- Dangers outweigh any possible benefits. Don't use.

Infants and children:

- Treating infants and children under 2 with any herbal preparation is hazardous.

Others:

- None expected if you are under 45, not pregnant, basically healthy, take it for only a short time and do not exceed manufacturer's recommended dosage.

Storage:

- Keep cool and dry, but don't freeze. Store safely away from children.

Safe dosage:

- At present no "safe" dosage has been established.

Toxicity

Comparative-toxicity rating not available from standard references.

For symptoms of toxicity: See *Adverse Reactions, Side Effects or Overdose Symptoms* section below.

Adverse Reactions, Side Effects or Overdose Symptoms

Signs and symptoms:	What to do:
Nausea	Discontinue. Call doctor immediately.
Vomiting	Discontinue. Call doctor immediately.

Harmel (Wild Rue, African Rue, Syrian Rue)

Basic Information

Biological name (genus and species):
Peganum harmala
Parts used for medicinal purposes:
Various parts of the entire plant, frequently
differing by country and/or culture
Chemicals this herb contains:
Harmaline
Harmalol
Harmine
Peganine

Known Effects

- Causes hallucinations.
- Destroys bacteria (germs) or suppresses their growth or reproduction.

Miscellaneous information:
- Wild rue is often abused where it grows in Arizona, New Mexico and Texas.

Unproved Speculated Benefits

- Destroys intestinal worms.
- Decreases pain.

Warnings and Precautions

Don't take if you:
- Are pregnant, think you may be pregnant or plan pregnancy in the near future.

Consult your doctor if you:
- Take this herb for any medical problem that doesn't improve in 2 weeks. There may be safer, more effective treatments.
- Take any medicinal drugs or herbs including aspirin, laxatives, cold and cough remedies, antacids, vitamins, minerals, amino acids, supplements, other prescription or non-prescription drugs.

Pregnancy:
- Dangers outweigh any possible benefits. Don't use.

Breast-feeding:
- Dangers outweigh any possible benefits. Don't use.

Infants and children:
- Treating infants and children under 2 with any herbal preparation is hazardous.

Others:
- Dangers outweigh any possible benefits. Don't use.

Storage:
- Keep cool and dry, but don't freeze. Store safely away from children.

Safe dosage:
- At present no "safe" dosage has been established.

Toxicity

Rated slightly dangerous, particularly in children, persons over 55 and those who take larger than appropriate quantities for extended periods of time.

For symptoms of toxicity: See *Adverse Reactions, Side Effects or Overdose Symptoms* section below.

Adverse Reactions, Side Effects or Overdose Symptoms

Signs and symptoms:	What to do:
Hallucinations	Seek emergency treatment.
Muscle weakness	Discontinue. Call doctor immediately.

MEDICINAL HERB

Hawthorn

Basic Information

Biological name (genus and species):
Crataegus oxyacantha
Parts used for medicinal purposes:
Berries/fruits
Leaves
Chemicals this herb contains:
Anthocyanin-type pigments
Cratagolic acid
Flavinonoid
Glycosides (See Glossary)
Purines
Saponins (See Glossary)

Known Effects

- Depresses respiration.
- Depresses heart rate.
- Causes irregular heartbeats.
- Causes congestive heart failure.
- Relaxes smooth muscle of uterus and intestines.
- Constricts bronchial tubes.

Unproved Speculated Benefits

- Treats high blood pressure.
- May have value in other cardiovascular disorders, but studies need to be completed before doses, efficacy and safety can be established. Do *not* self-medicate!

Warnings and Precautions

Don't take if you:
- Are pregnant, think you may be pregnant or plan pregnancy in the near future.
- Have heart disease.

Consult your doctor if you:
- Take this herb for any medical problem that doesn't improve in 2 weeks. There may be safer, more effective treatments.
- Take any medicinal drugs or herbs including aspirin, laxatives, cold and cough remedies, antacids, vitamins, minerals, amino acids, supplements, other prescription or non-prescription drugs.

Pregnancy:
- Dangers outweigh any possible benefits. Don't use.

Breast-feeding:
- Dangers outweigh any possible benefits. Don't use.

Infants and children:
- Treating infants and children under 2 with any herbal preparation is hazardous.

Others:
- Any possible beneficial uses have been supplanted by other chemicals that are safer, more-effective and easier to control.

Storage:
- Keep cool and dry, but don't freeze. Store safely away from children.

Safe dosage:
- At present no "safe" dosage has been established.

Toxicity

Comparative-toxicity rating not available from standard references.

For symptoms of toxicity: See *Adverse Reactions, Side Effects or Overdose Symptoms* section below.

Adverse Reactions, Side Effects or Overdose Symptoms

Signs and symptoms:	What to do:
Breathing difficulties	Seek emergency treatment.
Heartbeat irregularities	Seek emergency treatment.

Basic Information

Biological name (genus and species):
    Heliotropium europaem
Parts used for medicinal purposes:
    Juice
    Leaves
    Seeds
Chemicals this herb contains:
    Heliotrine
    Lassiocarpine

Known Effects

• Kills liver cells.
• Stimulates production of bile.

Miscellaneous information:
• Heliotrope is a common weed.

Unproved Speculated Benefits

• Leaves and juice are used to treat ulcers, warts polyps and tumours

Warnings and Precautions

Don't take if you:
• Are pregnant, think you may be pregnant or plan pregnancy in the near future.

Consult your doctor if you:
• Take this herb for any medical problem that doesn't improve in 2 weeks. There may be safer, more effective treatments.
• Take any medicinal drugs or herbs including aspirin, laxatives, cold and cough remedies, antacids, vitamins, minerals, amino acids, supplements, other prescription or non-prescription drugs.

Pregnancy:
• Dangers outweigh any possible benefits. Don't use.

Breast-feeding:
• Dangers outweigh any possible benefits. Don't use.

Infants and children:
• Treating infants and children under 2 with any herbal preparation is hazardous.

Storage:
• Keep cool and dry, but don't freeze. Store safely away from children.

Safe dosage:
• At present no "safe" dosage has been established.

Toxicity

Rated slightly dangerous, particularly in children, persons over 55 and those who take larger than appropriate quantities for extended periods of time.

For symptoms of toxicity: See *Adverse Reactions, Side Effects or Overdose Symptoms* section below.

Adverse Reactions, Side Effects or Overdose Symptoms

Signs and symptoms:	What to do:
Jaundice (yellow eyes and skin)	Discontinue. Call doctor immediately.

MEDICINAL HERB

Hellebore (American Hellebore, Green Hellebore, Liliaceae)

Basic Information

Biological name (genus and species):
  Veratrum viride
Parts used for medicinal purposes:
  Rhizome
  Root
Chemicals this herb contains:
  Germidine
  Germitrine
  Jervine
  Pseudojervine
  Rubijervine
  Veratrum alkaloids

Known Effects

- Decreases blood pressure.
- Decreases heart rate.
- Depresses central nervous system.

Unproved Speculated Benefits

- Treats hypertension.
- Treats toxaemia of pregnancy.
- Irritates gastrointestinal system.

Warnings and Precautions

Don't take if you:
- Are pregnant, think you may be pregnant or plan pregnancy in the near future.
- Have any chronic disease of the gastrointestinal tract, such as stomach or duodenal ulcers, oesophageal reflux (reflux oesophagitis), ulcerative colitis, spastic colitis, diverticulosis, diverticulitis.

Consult your doctor if you:
- Take this herb for any medical problem that doesn't improve in 2 weeks. There may be safer, more effective treatments.
- Take any medicinal drugs or herbs including aspirin, laxatives, cold and cough remedies, antacids, vitamins, minerals, amino acids, supplements, other prescription or non-prescription drugs.

Pregnancy:
- Dangers outweigh any possible benefits. Don't use.

Breast-feeding:
- Dangers outweigh any possible benefits. Don't use.

Infants and children:
- Treating infants and children under 2 with any herbal preparation is hazardous.

Others:
- *All* parts of the plant may be toxic.

Storage:
- Keep cool and dry, but don't freeze. Store safely away from children.

Safe dosage:
- At present no "safe" dosage has been established.

Toxicity

Rated dangerous, particularly in children, persons over 55 and those who take larger than appropriate quantities for extended periods of time.

For symptoms of toxicity: See *Adverse Reactions, Side Effects or Overdose Symptoms* section below.

Adverse Reactions, Side Effects or Overdose Symptoms

Signs and symptoms:	What to do:
Abdominal pain	Discontinue. Call doctor immediately.
Burning sensation in mouth	Discontinue. Call doctor when convenient.
Diarrhoea	Discontinue. Call doctor immediately.
Headache	Discontinue. Call doctor when convenient.
Nausea	Discontinue. Call doctor immediately.
Precipitous blood-pressure drop— symptoms include, faintness, cold sweat, paleness, rapid pulse	Seek emergency treatment.
Vomiting	Discontinue. Call doctor immediately.

Helonias (False Unicorn Root, Fairy Wand)

Basic Information

Biological name (genus and species):
Chamaelirium luteum
Parts used for medicinal purposes:
Roots
Chemicals this herb contains:
Chamaelirin
Saponin (See Glossary)

Known Effects

- Irritates gastrointestinal system.
- Helps body dispose of excess fluid by increasing amount of urine produced.
- Produces puckering.

Unproved Speculated Benefits

- Prevents miscarriage.
- Treats menopause symptoms.
- Increases appetite.
- Acts as a vigorous laxative.

Warnings and Precautions

Don't take if you:
- Are pregnant, think you may be pregnant or plan pregnancy in the near future.
- Have any chronic disease of the gastrointestinal tract, such as stomach or duodenal ulcers, oesophageal reflux (reflux oesophagitis), ulcerative colitis, spastic colitis, diverticulosis, diverticulitis.

Consult your doctor if you:
- Take this herb for any medical problem that doesn't improve in 2 weeks. There may be safer, more effective treatments.
- Take any medicinal drugs or herbs including aspirin, laxatives, cold and cough remedies, antacids, vitamins, minerals, amino acids, supplements, other prescription or non-prescription drugs.

Pregnancy:
- Dangers outweigh any possible benefits. Don't use.

Breast-feeding:
- Dangers outweigh any possible benefits. Don't use.

Infants and children:
- Treating infants and children under 2 with any herbal preparation is hazardous.

Others:
- None expected if you are beyond childhood and under 45, basically healthy and take for only a short time.

Storage:
- Keep cool and dry, but don't freeze. Store safely away from children.

Safe dosage:
- At present no "safe" dosage has been established.

Toxicity

Comparative-toxicity rating not available from standard references.

For symptoms of toxicity: See *Adverse Reactions, Side Effects or Overdose Symptoms* section below.

Adverse Reactions, Side Effects or Overdose Symptoms

Signs and symptoms:	What to do:
Diarrhoea	Discontinue. Call doctor immediately.
Nausea	Discontinue. Call doctor immediately.

Henbane (Hyoscyamus)

Basic Information
Biological name (genus and species):
Hyoscyamus niger
Parts used for medicinal purposes:
Berries/fruits
Leaves
Roots
Chemicals this herb contains:
Hyoscyamine
Scopolamine

Known Effects

- Blocks effects of parasympathetic nervous system causing increased heart rate, dilated pupils, dry mouth, hallucinations, urinary retention, reduced contractions of gastrointestinal tract.

Miscellaneous information:
- Henbane is poisonous, especially to children!

Unproved Speculated Benefits

- Treats whooping cough.
- Treats asthma.
- Is used as a mouthwash.
- Acts as a sedative.
- Is used as a pain killer.

Warnings and Precautions

Don't take if you:
- Are pregnant, think you may be pregnant or plan pregnancy in the near future.

Consult your doctor if you:
- Take this herb for any medical problem that doesn't improve in 2 weeks. There may be safer, more effective treatments.
- Take any medicinal drugs or herbs including aspirin, laxatives, cold and cough remedies, antacids, vitamins, minerals, amino acids, supplements, other prescription or non-prescription drugs.

Pregnancy:
- Dangers outweigh any possible benefits. Don't use.

Breast-feeding:
- Dangers outweigh any possible benefits. Don't use.

Infants and children:
- Treating infants and children under 2 with any herbal preparation is hazardous.

Others:
- Must be obtained from a reliable source. Unpredictable concentrations can be dangerous.

Storage:
- Keep cool and dry, but don't freeze. Store safely away from children.

Safe dosage:
- At present no "safe" dosage has been established.

Toxicity

Rated dangerous, particularly in children, persons over 55 and those who take larger than appropriate quantities for extended periods of time.

For symptoms of toxicity: See *Adverse Reactions, Side Effects or Overdose Symptoms* section below.

Adverse Reactions, Side Effects or Overdose Symptoms

Signs and symptoms:	What to do:
Delirium	Seek emergency treatment.
Hallucinations	Seek emergency treatment.
Rapid heartbeat	Seek emergency treatment.

Basic Information

Biological name (genus and species):
Humulus lupulus
Parts used for medicinal purposes:
Berries/fruits
Chemicals this herb contains:
Humulene
Lupulinic acid
Lupulon

Known Effects

- Inhibits growth and development of germs.
- Depresses central nervous system.

Miscellaneous information:
- If fruit is not fresh, it smells bad.
- Hops are used extensively in brewing industry.
- Produces odours because it evaporates at room temperature.

Unproved Speculated Benefits

- Is used as a tonic.
- Treats dyspepsia.
- Helps body dispose of excess fluid by increasing amount of urine produced.
- Treats insomnia.
- Causes hallucinations.

Warnings and Precautions

Don't take if you:
- Are pregnant, think you may be pregnant or plan pregnancy in the near future.

Consult your doctor if you:
- Take this herb for any medical problem that doesn't improve in 2 weeks. There may be safer, more effective treatments.
- Take any medicinal drugs or herbs including aspirin, laxatives, cold and cough remedies, antacids, vitamins, minerals, amino acids, supplements, other prescription or non-prescription drugs.

Pregnancy:
- Problems in pregnant women taking small or usual amounts have not been proved. But the chance of problems does exist. Don't use unless prescribed by your doctor.

Breast-feeding:
- Problems in breast-fed infants of lactating mothers taking small or usual amounts have not been proved. But the chance of problems does exist. Don't use unless prescribed by your doctor.

Infants and children:
- Treating infants and children under 2 with any herbal preparation is hazardous.

Others:
- None expected if you are beyond childhood and under 45, basically healthy and take for only a short time.

Storage:
- Keep cool and dry, but don't freeze. Store safely away from children.

Safe dosage:
- At present no "safe" dosage has been established.

Toxicity

Rated relatively safe when taken in appropriate quantities for short periods of time.

Adverse Reactions, Side Effects or Overdose Symptoms

None expected

MEDICINAL HERB

Horehound

Basic Information

Biological name (genus and species):
   Marrubium vulgare
Parts used for medicinal purposes:
   Flowers
   Leaves
Chemicals this herb contains:
   Marrubiin
   Resin (See Glossary)
   Tannins (See Glossary)
   Volatile oils (See Glossary)

Known Effects

- Aids in expelling gas from intestinal tract.
- Decreases thickness and increases fluidity of mucus from lungs and bronchial tubes.
- Increases stomach secretions.
- Interferes with absorption of iron and other minerals when taken internally.

Miscellaneous information:
- Leaves and flowers are used to make tincture.

Unproved Speculated Benefits

- Is used as a cough and cold remedy.
- Relieves various symptoms.
- Increases perspiration.

Warnings and Precautions

Don't take if you:
- Are pregnant, think you may be pregnant or plan pregnancy in the near future.
- Have any chronic disease of the gastrointestinal tract, such as stomach or duodenal ulcers, oesophageal reflux (reflux oesophagitis), ulcerative colitis, spastic colitis, diverticulosis, diverticulitis.

Consult your doctor if you:
- Take this herb for any medical problem that doesn't improve in 2 weeks. There may be safer, more effective treatments.
- Take any medicinal drugs or herbs including aspirin, laxatives, cold and cough remedies, antacids, vitamins, minerals, amino acids, supplements, other prescription or non-prescription drugs.

Pregnancy:
- Problems in pregnant women taking small or usual amounts have not been proved. But the chance of problems does exist. Don't use unless prescribed by your doctor.

Breast-feeding:
- Problems in breast-fed infants of lactating mothers taking small or usual amounts have not been proved. But the chance of problems does exist. Don't use unless prescribed by your doctor.

Infants and children:
- Treating infants and children under 2 with any herbal preparation is hazardous.

Others:
- None expected if you are beyond childhood and under 45, basically healthy and take for only a short time.

Storage:
- Keep cool and dry, but don't freeze. Store safely away from children.

Safe dosage:
- At present no "safe" dosage has been established.

Toxicity

Comparative-toxicity rating not available from standard references.

For symptoms of toxicity: See *Adverse Reactions, Side Effects or Overdose Symptoms* section below.

Adverse Reactions, Side Effects or Overdose Symptoms

Signs and symptoms:	What to do:
Diarrhoea	Discontinue. Call doctor immediately.
Nausea	Discontinue. Call doctor immediately.
Vomiting	Discontinue. Call doctor immediately.

Basic Information

Biological name (genus and species):
   Aesculus hippocastanum
Parts used for medicinal purposes:
   Bark
   Leaves
   Seeds/nuts
Chemicals this herb contains:
   Aesculin
   Argyroscin
   Capsuloescinic acid
   Escin

Known Effects

- Increases bleeding time (a laboratory test for blood clotting).
- Irritates mucous membrane.

Miscellaneous information:
- There are more reliable, safer anti-coagulants
- Eating even a few nuts can cause toxic symptoms.

Unproved Speculated Benefits

- Is used as anti-coagulant.
- 4% solution is used as sunscreen.

Warnings and Precautions

Don't take if you:
- Are pregnant, think you may be pregnant or plan pregnancy in the near future.
- Have any chronic disease of the gastrointestinal tract, such as stomach or duodenal ulcers, oesophageal reflux (reflux oesophagitis), ulcerative colitis, spastic colitis, diverticulosis, diverticulitis.

Consult your doctor if you:
- Take this herb for any medical problem that doesn't improve in 2 weeks. There may be safer, more effective treatments.
- Take any medicinal drugs or herbs including aspirin, laxatives, cold and cough remedies, antacids, vitamins, minerals, amino acids, supplements, other prescription or non-prescription drugs.

Pregnancy:
- Dangers outweigh any possible benefits. Don't use.

Breast-feeding:
- Dangers outweigh any possible benefits. Don't use.

Infants and children:
- Treating infants and children under 2 with any herbal preparation is hazardous.

Storage:
- Keep cool and dry, but don't freeze. Store safely away from children.

Safe dosage:
- At present no "safe" dosage has been established.

Toxicity

Rated slightly dangerous, particularly in children, persons over 55 and those who take larger than appropriate quantities for extended periods of time.

For symptoms of toxicity: See *Adverse Reactions, Side Effects or Overdose Symptoms* section below.

Adverse Reactions, Side Effects or Overdose Symptoms

Signs and symptoms:	What to do:
Lack of coordination	Discontinue. Call doctor immediately.
Nausea	Discontinue. Call doctor immediately.
Unusual bleeding	Discontinue. Call doctor immediately.
Vomiting	Discontinue. Call doctor immediately.

MEDICINAL HERB

Horsemint

Basic Information

Biological name (genus and species):
   Monarda punctata
Parts used for medicinal purposes:
   Leaves
   Stems
Chemicals this herb contains:
   Carvacrol
   Cyemene
   d-limonene
   Hydrothymoquinone
   Linalool
   Monarda oil
   Thymol

Known Effects

- Irritates tissues and mucous membranes.
- Kills germs when used on the skin for external infections.

Unproved Speculated Benefits

Internal use:
- Kills intestinal parasites.
- Aids in expelling gas from intestinal tract.
- Treats abdominal cramps.
- Treats nausea.

External use:
- Kills fungus infections on skin.
- Kills bacterial infections on skin.

Warnings and Precautions

Don't take if you:
- Are pregnant, think you may be pregnant or plan pregnancy in the near future.
- Have any chronic disease of the gastrointestinal tract, such as stomach or duodenal ulcers, oesophageal reflux (reflux oesophagitis), ulcerative colitis, spastic colitis, diverticulosis, diverticulitis.

Consult your doctor if you:
- Take this herb for any medical problem that doesn't improve in 2 weeks. There may be safer, more effective treatments.
- Take any medicinal drugs or herbs including aspirin, laxatives, cold and cough remedies, antacids, vitamins, minerals, amino acids, supplements, other prescription or non-prescription drugs.

Pregnancy:
- Problems in pregnant women taking small or usual amounts have not been proved. But the chance of problems does exist. Don't use unless prescribed by your doctor.

Breast-feeding:
- Problems in breast-fed infants of lactating mothers taking small or usual amounts have not been proved. But the chance of problems does exist. Don't use unless prescribed by your doctor.

Infants and children:
- Treating infants and children under 2 with any herbal preparation is hazardous.

Others:
- None expected if you are under 45, not pregnant, basically healthy, take it for only a short time and do not exceed manufacturer's recommended dosage.

Storage:
- Keep cool and dry, but don't freeze. Store safely away from children.

Safe dosage:
- At present no "safe" dosage has been established.

Toxicity

Comparative-toxicity rating not available from standard references.

For symptoms of toxicity: See *Adverse Reactions, Side Effects or Overdose Symptoms* section below.

Adverse Reactions, Side Effects or Overdose Symptoms

Signs and symptoms:	What to do:
Diarrhoea	Discontinue. Call doctor immediately.
Nausea	Discontinue. Call doctor immediately.
Skin rash when used on skin	Discontinue. Call doctor when convenient.
Vomiting	Discontinue. Call doctor immediately.

Basic Information

Biological name (genus and species):
Armoraciae radix, Cochlearia armoracia
Parts used for medicinal purposes:
Roots
Chemicals this herb contains:
Allyl isothiocyanate
Sinigriu

Known Effects

External:
• Irritates skin.
• Blisters skin.
Internal:
• Irritates gastrointestinal tract.
Miscellaneous information:
• Eating large amounts of raw root can be toxic.
• Horseradish is used to add flavour to foods.
• No effects are expected on the body, either good or bad, when herb is used in very small amounts to enhance the flavour of food.

Unproved Speculated Benefits

• Stimulates appetite.

Warnings and Precautions

Don't take if you:
• Are pregnant, think you may be pregnant or plan pregnancy in the near future.
• Have any chronic disease of the gastrointestinal tract, such as stomach or duodenal ulcers, oesophageal reflux (reflux oesophagitis), ulcerative colitis, spastic colitis, diverticulosis, diverticulitis.

Consult your doctor if you:
• Take this herb for any medical problem that doesn't improve in 2 weeks. There may be safer, more effective treatments.
• Take any medicinal drugs or herbs including aspirin, laxatives, cold and cough remedies, antacids, vitamins, minerals, amino acids, supplements, other prescription or non-prescription drugs.

Pregnancy:
• Problems in pregnant women taking small or usual amounts have not been proved. But the chance of problems does exist. Don't use unless prescribed by your doctor.

Breast-feeding:
• Problems in breast-fed infants of lactating mothers taking small or usual amounts have not been proved. But the chance of problems does exist. Don't use unless prescribed by your doctor.

Infants and children:
• Treating infants and children under 2 with any herbal preparation is hazardous.

Others:
• None expected if you are beyond childhood and under 45, basically healthy and take for only a short time.
• Eating large amounts of raw root can be toxic.

Storage:
• Keep cool and dry, but don't freeze. Store safely away from children.

Safe dosage:
• At present no "safe" dosage has been established.

Toxicity

Comparative-toxicity rating not available from standard references.

For symptoms of toxicity: See *Adverse Reactions, Side Effects or Overdose Symptoms* section below.

Adverse Reactions, Side Effects or Overdose Symptoms

Signs and symptoms:	What to do:
Diarrhoea, with blood	Discontinue. Call doctor immediately.
Nausea	Discontinue. Call doctor immediately.
Vomiting	Discontinue. Call doctor immediately.
Vomiting, with blood	Seek emergency treatment.

MEDICINAL HERB

Horsetails (Shave Grass, Bottle Brush, Field Horsetail)

Basic Information

Biological name (genus and species):
Equisetum arvense
Parts used for medicinal purposes:
Stems
Chemicals this herb contains:
Aconitic acid
Equisitine
Fatty acids
Nicotine
Silica
Starch

Known Effects

- Shrinks tissues.
- Prevents secretion of fluids.

Unproved Speculated Benefits

- Treats diarrhoea.
- Treats dyspepsia.
- Helps body dispose of excess fluid by increasing amount of urine produced.
- Helps heal sores on skin.

Warnings and Precautions

Don't take if you:
- Are pregnant, think you may be pregnant or plan pregnancy in the near future.
- Have heart disease.

Consult your doctor if you:
- Take this herb for any medical problem that doesn't improve in 2 weeks. There may be safer, more effective treatments.
- Take any medicinal drugs or herbs including aspirin, laxatives, cold and cough remedies, antacids, vitamins, minerals, amino acids, supplements, other prescription or non-prescription drugs.

Pregnancy:
- Dangers outweigh any possible benefits. Don't use.

Breast-feeding:
- Dangers outweigh any possible benefits. Don't use.

Infants and children:
- Treating infants and children under 2 with any herbal preparation is hazardous.

Others:
- None expected if you are beyond childhood and under 45, basically healthy and take for only a short time.

Storage:
- Keep cool and dry, but don't freeze. Store safely away from children.

Safe dosage:
- At present no "safe" dosage has been established.

Toxicity

Rated slightly dangerous, particularly in children, persons over 55 and those who take larger than appropriate quantities for extended periods of time.

For symptoms of toxicity: See *Adverse Reactions, Side Effects or Overdose Symptoms* section below.

Adverse Reactions, Side Effects or Overdose Symptoms

Signs and symptoms:	What to do:
Cold hands and feet	Discontinue. Call doctor when convenient.
Fever	Discontinue. Call doctor immediately.
Gait disturbances	Discontinue. Call doctor immediately.
Heartbeat irregularities	Seek emergency treatment.
Muscle weakness	Discontinue. Call doctor immediately.
Weight loss	Discontinue. Call doctor when convenient.

Houseleek (Jupiter's Eye, Thor's Beard)

Basic Information

Biological name (genus and species):
Sempervivum tectorum, Sempervivum
Parts used for medicinal purposes:
Leaves
Chemical this herb contains:
Malic acid

Known Effects

• Shrinks tissues.
• Prevents secretion of fluids.

Unproved Speculated Benefits

• Helps body dispose of excess fluid by increasing amount of urine produced.
• As a poultice is used to treat insect bites, burns, bruises, skin disease. (See Glossary)

Warnings and Precautions

Don't take if you:
• Are pregnant, think you may be pregnant or plan pregnancy in the near future.
• Have any chronic disease of the gastrointestinal tract, such as stomach or duodenal ulcers, oesophageal reflux (reflux oesophagitis), ulcerative colitis, spastic colitis, diverticulosis, diverticulitis.

Consult your doctor if you:
• Take this herb for any medical problem that doesn't improve in 2 weeks. There may be safer, more effective treatments.
• Take any medicinal drugs or herbs including aspirin, laxatives, cold and cough remedies, antacids, vitamins, minerals, amino acids, supplements, other prescription or non-prescription drugs.

Pregnancy:
• Problems in pregnant women taking small or usual amounts have not been proved. But the chance of problems does exist. Don't use unless prescribed by your doctor.

Breast-feeding:
• Problems in breast-fed infants of lactating mothers taking small or usual amounts have not been proved. But the chance of problems does exist. Don't use unless prescribed by your doctor.

Infants and children:
• Treating infants and children under 2 with any herbal preparation is hazardous.

Others:
• None expected if you are beyond childhood and under 45, basically healthy and take for only a short time.

Storage:
• Keep cool and dry, but don't freeze. Store safely away from children.

Safe dosage:
• At present no "safe" dosage has been established.

Toxicity

Comparative-toxicity rating not available from standard references.

For symptoms of toxicity: See *Adverse Reactions, Side Effects or Overdose Symptoms* section below.

Adverse Reactions, Side Effects or Overdose Symptoms

Signs and symptoms:	What to do:
Vomiting	Discontinue. Call doctor immediately.
Watery, explosive diarrhoea	Discontinue. Call doctor immediately.

Huckleberry

Basic Information

Biological name (genus and species):
Vaccinum myrtillus
Parts used for medicinal purposes:
Entire plant
Chemicals this herb contains:
Fatty acids
Hydroquinone
Loeanolic acid
Neomyrtillin
Tannins (See Glossary)
Ursolic acid

Known Effects

- Decreases blood sugar.
- Helps body dispose of excess fluid by increasing amount of urine produced.
- Interferes with absorption of iron and other minerals when taken internally.

Unproved Speculated Benefits

- Treats diarrhoea.
- Treats gastroenteritis.
- Treats and prevents scurvy.

Warnings and Precautions

Don't take if you:
- Are allergic to blueberries or huckleberries.

Consult your doctor if you:
- Take this herb for any medical problem that doesn't improve in 2 weeks. There may be safer, more effective treatments.
- Take any medicinal drugs or herbs including aspirin, laxatives, cold and cough remedies, antacids, vitamins, minerals, amino acids, supplements, other prescription or non-prescription drugs.

Pregnancy:
- Pregnant women should experience no problems taking usual amounts as part of a balanced diet. Other products extracted from this herb have not been proved to cause problems.

Breast-feeding:
- Breast-fed infants of lactating mothers should experience no problems when mother takes usual amounts as part of a balanced diet. Other products extracted from this herb have not been proved to cause problems.

Infants and children:
- Treating infants and children under 2 with any herbal preparation is hazardous.

Others:
- None expected if you are beyond childhood and under 45, basically healthy and take for only a short time.

Storage:
- Keep cool and dry, but don't freeze. Store safely away from children.

Safe dosage:
- At present no "safe" dosage has been established.

Toxicity

Generally regarded as safe when taken in appropriate quantities for short periods of time.

Adverse Reactions, Side Effects or Overdose Symptoms

None expected

Hydrangea (Seven Barks, Peegee)

Basic Information

Biological name (genus and species):
   Hydrangea paniculata
Parts used for medicinal purposes:
   Roots
Chemicals this herb contains:
   Hydrangin (can change to cyanide)
   Resin (See Glossary)
   Saponin (See Glossary)
   Volatile oils (See Glossary)

Known Effects

- Aids in expelling gas from intestinal tract.
- Shrinks tissues.
- Prevents secretion of fluids.

Miscellaneous information:
- Leaves contain cyanide. Smoking can cause mind-altering effects and toxicity.

Unproved Speculated Benefits

- Treats cystitis.
- Treats bladder stones.
- Treats dyspepsia.

Warnings and Precautions

Don't take if you:
- Are pregnant, think you may be pregnant or plan pregnancy in the near future.
- Have any chronic disease of the gastrointestinal tract, such as stomach or duodenal ulcers, oesophageal reflux (reflux oesophagitis), ulcerative colitis, spastic colitis, diverticulosis, diverticulitis.

Consult your doctor if you:
- Take this herb for any medical problem that doesn't improve in 2 weeks. There may be safer, more effective treatments.
- Take any medicinal drugs or herbs including aspirin, laxatives, cold and cough remedies, antacids, vitamins, minerals, amino acids, supplements, other prescription or non-prescription drugs.

Pregnancy:
- Dangers outweigh any possible benefits. Don't use.

Breast-feeding:
- Dangers outweigh any possible benefits. Don't use.

Infants and children:
- Treating infants and children under 2 with any herbal preparation is hazardous.

Storage:
- Keep cool and dry, but don't freeze. Store safely away from children.

Safe dosage:
- At present no "safe" dosage has been established.

Toxicity

Rated relatively safe when taken in appropriate quantities for short periods of time.

For symptoms of toxicity: See *Adverse Reactions, Side Effects or Overdose Symptoms* section below.

Adverse Reactions, Side Effects or Overdose Symptoms

Signs and symptoms:	What to do:
Dizziness	Discontinue. Call doctor immediately.
Heavy feeling in chest	Discontinue. Call doctor immediately.
Nausea	Discontinue. Call doctor immediately.
Vomiting	Discontinue. Call doctor immediately.

Indian Nettle (Kuppi, Mercury Weed, Indian Acalypha, Hierba de Cancer)

Basic Information

Biological name (genus and species):
Acalypha indica, A. virginica
Parts used for medicinal purposes:
Leaves
Chemicals this herb contains:
Acalyphine
Cyanogenic glycoside (See Glossary)
Inositol methylether
Resin (See Glossary)
Triacetomamine
Volatile oils (See Glossary)

Known Effects

- Irritates stomach lining.
- Decreases thickness and increases fluidity of mucus from lungs and bronchial tubes.
- Causes vomiting.

Miscellaneous information:
- Basic ingredients are similar to ipecac.

Unproved Speculated Benefits

- Stimulates bowel movements.
- Is used as a poultice. (See Glossary)
- Is used as a mouthwash.

Warnings and Precautions

Don't take if you:
- Are pregnant, think you may be pregnant or plan pregnancy in the near future.

Consult your doctor if you:
- Take this herb for any medical problem that doesn't improve in 2 weeks. There may be safer, more effective treatments.
- Take any medicinal drugs or herbs including aspirin, laxatives, cold and cough remedies, antacids, vitamins, minerals, amino acids, supplements, other prescription or non-prescription drugs.

Pregnancy:
- Dangers outweigh any possible benefits. Don't use.

Breast-feeding:
- Dangers outweigh any possible benefits. Don't use.

Infants and children:
- Treating infants and children under 2 with any herbal preparation is hazardous.

Others:
- None expected if you are under 45, not pregnant, basically healthy, take it for only a short time and do not exceed manufacturer's recommended dosage.

Storage:
- Keep cool and dry, but don't freeze. Store safely away from children.

Safe dosage:
- At present no "safe" dosage has been established.

Toxicity

Rated relatively safe when taken in appropriate quantities for short periods of time.

For symptoms of toxicity: See *Adverse Reactions, Side Effects or Overdose Symptoms* section below.

Adverse Reactions, Side Effects or Overdose Symptoms

Signs and symptoms:	What to do:
Diarrhoea	Discontinue. Call doctor immediately.
Nausea	Discontinue. Call doctor immediately.
Vomiting	Discontinue. Call doctor immediately.

Indian Tobacco (Lobelia, Asthma Weed)

Basic Information

Biological name (genus and species):
   Lobelia inflata
Parts used for medicinal purposes:
   Leaves
   Seeds
Chemicals this herb contains:
   Isolobenine
   Lobelanine
   Lobelidine
   Lobeline
   Nor-lobelaine

Known Effects

- Large amounts stimulate central nervous system.
- Small amounts depress central nervous system as blood level drops.
- Activates vomiting centre in people not accustomed to lobelia.

Miscellaneous information:
- Sometimes advertised as "legal grass." Do not be misled! Toxic effects can be dangerous.

Unproved Speculated Benefits

- Treats asthma.
- Decreases thickness and increases fluidity of mucus from lungs and bronchial tubes.
- Promotes weight loss.

Warnings and Precautions

Don't take if you:
- Are pregnant, think you may be pregnant or plan pregnancy in the near future.
- Have any chronic disease of the gastrointestinal tract, such as stomach or duodenal ulcers, oesophageal reflux (reflux oesophagitis), ulcerative colitis, spastic colitis, diverticulosis, diverticulitis.

Consult your doctor if you:
- Take this herb for any medical problem that doesn't improve in 2 weeks. There may be safer, more effective treatments.
- Take any medicinal drugs or herbs including aspirin, laxatives, cold and cough remedies, antacids, vitamins, minerals, amino acids, supplements, other prescription or non-prescription drugs.

Pregnancy:
- Dangers outweigh any possible benefits. Don't use.

Breast-feeding:
- Dangers outweigh any possible benefits. Don't use.

Infants and children:
- Treating infants and children under 2 with any herbal preparation is hazardous.

Others:
- Dangers outweigh any possible benefits. Don't use.

Storage:
- Keep cool and dry, but don't freeze. Store safely away from children.

Safe dosage:
- At present no "safe" dosage has been established.

Toxicity

Rated slightly dangerous, particularly in children, persons over 55 and those who take larger than appropriate quantities for extended periods of time.

For symptoms of toxicity: See *Adverse Reactions, Side Effects or Overdose Symptoms* section below.

Adverse Reactions, Side Effects or Overdose Symptoms

Signs and symptoms:	What to do:
Coma	Seek emergency treatment.
Diarrhoea	Discontinue. Call doctor immediately.
Excess salivation	Discontinue. Call doctor when convenient.
Excess tear formation	Discontinue. Call doctor when convenient.
Giddiness	Discontinue. Call doctor when convenient.
Headache	Discontinue. Call doctor when convenient.
Nausea	Discontinue. Call doctor immediately.
Stupor	Seek emergency treatment.
Tremors	Discontinue. Call doctor immediately.
Vomiting	Discontinue. Call doctor immediately.

Indigo, Wild

Basic Information

Biological name (genus and species):
Baptisia tinctoria
Parts used for medicinal purposes:
Roots
Chemicals this herb contains:
Baptisin
Baptisine
Bapitoxine
Cystisine
Quinolizidine

Known Effects

- Irritates gastrointestinal-lining membrane.
- Causes watery, explosive bowel movements.
- Causes vomiting.

Miscellaneous information:
- Blue dye in wild indigo is inferior to domestically grown indigo.

Unproved Speculated Benefits

- Treats typhoid fever.
- Treats amoebiasis

Warnings and Precautions

Don't take if you:
- Are pregnant, think you may be pregnant or plan pregnancy in the near future.
- Have any chronic disease of the gastrointestinal tract, such as stomach or duodenal ulcers, oesophageal reflux (reflux oesophagitis), ulcerative colitis, spastic colitis, diverticulosis, diverticulitis.

Consult your doctor if you:
- Take this herb for any medical problem that doesn't improve in 2 weeks. There may be safer, more effective treatments.
- Take any medicinal drugs or herbs including aspirin, laxatives, cold and cough remedies, antacids, vitamins, minerals, amino acids, supplements; other prescription or non-prescription drugs.

Pregnancy:
- Dangers outweigh any possible benefits. Don't use.

Breast-feeding:
- Dangers outweigh any possible benefits. Don't use.

Infants and children:
- Treating infants and children under 2 with any herbal preparation is hazardous.

Others:
- None expected if you are under 45, not pregnant, basically healthy, take it for only a short time and do not exceed manufacturer's recommended dosage.

Storage:
- Keep cool and dry, but don't freeze. Store safely away from children.

Safe dosage:
- At present no "safe" dosage has been established.

Toxicity

Comparative-toxicity rating not available from standard references.

For symptoms of toxicity: See *Adverse Reactions, Side Effects or Overdose Symptoms* section below.

Adverse Reactions, Side Effects or Overdose Symptoms

Signs and symptoms:	What to do:
Diarrhoea	Discontinue. Call doctor immediately.
Nausea	Discontinue. Call doctor immediately.
Vomiting	Discontinue. Call doctor immediately.

Basic Information

Biological name (genus and species):
Chondrus crispus, Gigartina mamillosa
Parts used for medicinal purposes:
Entire plant
Chemicals this herb contains:
Bromine
Calcium
Carrageenan
Chlorine
Protein
Sodium

Known Effects

- Protects scraped tissues.
- Interferes with blood-clotting mechanism.

Miscellaneous information:
- Used for hand lotions and as substitute for gelatin in jellies.
- Chemically similar to agar, a substance used in laboratories as a base for growing germ cultures.

Unproved Speculated Benefits

- Forms bulky stools.
- Treats coughs.
- Treats diarrhoea.

Warnings and Precautions

Don't take if you:
- Are pregnant, think you may be pregnant or plan pregnancy in the near future.
- Have any chronic disease of the gastrointestinal tract, such as stomach or duodenal ulcers, oesophageal reflux (reflux oesophagitis), ulcerative colitis, spastic colitis, diverticulosis, diverticulitis.
- Take anti-coagulants.

Consult your doctor if you:
- Take this herb for any medical problem that doesn't improve in 2 weeks. There may be safer, more effective treatments.
- Take any medicinal drugs or herbs including aspirin, laxatives, cold and cough remedies, antacids, vitamins, minerals, amino acids, supplements, other prescription or non-prescription drugs.

Pregnancy:
- Problems in pregnant women taking small or usual amounts have not been proved. But the chance of problems does exist. Don't use unless prescribed by your doctor.

Breast-feeding:
- Problems in breast-fed infants of lactating mothers taking small or usual amounts have not been proved. But the chance of problems does exist. Don't use unless prescribed by your doctor.

Infants and children:
- Treating infants and children under 2 with any herbal preparation is hazardous.

Others:
- None expected if you are under 45, not pregnant, basically healthy, take it for only a short time and do not exceed manufacturer's recommended dosage.

Storage:
- Keep cool and dry, but don't freeze. Store safely away from children.

Safe dosage:
- At present no "safe" dosage has been established.

Toxicity

Comparative-toxicity rating not available from standard references.

For symptoms of toxicity: See *Adverse Reactions, Side Effects or Overdose Symptoms* section below.

Adverse Reactions, Side Effects or Overdose Symptoms

Signs and symptoms:	What to do:
May interact with other anti-coagulants to increase anti-coagulant effect	Discontinue. Call doctor immediately.
Nausea	Discontinue. Call doctor immediately.

Jalap Root (Conqueror Root, High John Root, Ipomea, Turpeth)

Basic Information

Biological name (genus and species):
Exagonium purga
Parts used for medicinal purposes:
Roots
Chemicals this herb contains:
Convolvulin
Gum (See Glossary)
Jalapin
Jalapinolic acid
Starch
Sugar
Volatile oils (See Glossary)

Known Effects

• Irritates the gastrointestinal system.

Unproved Speculated Benefits

• Treats constipation.

Warnings and Precautions

Don't take if you:
• Are pregnant, think you may be pregnant or plan pregnancy in the near future.
• Have any chronic disease of the gastrointestinal tract, such as stomach or duodenal ulcers, oesophageal reflux (reflux oesophagitis), ulcerative colitis, spastic colitis, diverticulosis, diverticulitis.

Consult your doctor if you:
• Take this herb for any medical problem that doesn't improve in 2 weeks. There may be safer, more effective treatments.
• Take any medicinal drugs or herbs including aspirin, laxatives, cold and cough remedies, antacids, vitamins, minerals, amino acids, supplements, other prescription or non-prescription drugs.

Pregnancy:
• Dangers outweigh any possible benefits. Don't use.

Breast-feeding:
• Dangers outweigh any possible benefits. Don't use.

Infants and children:
• Treating infants and children under 2 with any herbal preparation is hazardous.

Others:
• None expected if you are under 45, not pregnant, basically healthy, take it for only a short time and do not exceed manufacturer's recommended dosage.

Storage:
• Keep cool and dry, but don't freeze. Store safely away from children.

Safe dosage:
• At present no "safe" dosage has been established.

Toxicity

Comparative-toxicity rating not available from standard references.

For symptoms of toxicity: See *Adverse Reactions, Side Effects or Overdose Symptoms* section below.

Adverse Reactions, Side Effects or Overdose Symptoms

Signs and symptoms:	What to do:
Explosive, watery diarrhoea, with possible fluid and electrolyte depletion leading to weakness and possible heartbeat irregularities	Discontinue. Call doctor immediately.

Jamaican Dogwood (Fish-Poison Tree)

Basic Information

Biological name (genus and species):
Piscidia piscipula
Parts used for medicinal purposes:
Bark
Chemicals this herb contains:
Piscidin
Rotenone

Known Effects

- Causes hallucinations.
- Treats painful conditions.
- Depresses uterine contractions.

Miscellaneous information:
- Poisonous to fish.
- Active chemicals in bark have odour similar to opium.

Unproved Speculated Benefits

- Produces euphoria.
- Treats dysmenorrhoea (painful menstruation).

Warnings and Precautions

Don't take if you:
- Are pregnant, think you may be pregnant or plan pregnancy in the near future.

Consult your doctor if you:
- Take this herb for any medical problem that doesn't improve in 2 weeks. There may be safer, more effective treatments.
- Take any medicinal drugs or herbs including aspirin, laxatives, cold and cough remedies, antacids, vitamins, minerals, amino acids, supplements, other prescription or non-prescription drugs.

Pregnancy:
- Problems in pregnant women taking small or usual amounts have not been proved. But the chance of problems does exist. Don't use unless prescribed by your doctor.

Breast-feeding:
- Problems in breast-fed infants of lactating mothers taking small or usual amounts have not been proved. But the chance of problems does exist. Don't use unless prescribed by your doctor.

Infants and children:
- Treating infants and children under 2 with any herbal preparation is hazardous.

Others:
- None expected if you are beyond childhood and under 45, basically healthy and take for only a short time.

Storage:
- Keep cool and dry, but don't freeze. Store safely away from children.

Safe dosage:
- At present no "safe" dosage has been established.

Toxicity

Rated slightly dangerous, particularly in children, persons over 55 and those who take larger than appropriate quantities for extended periods of time.

For symptoms of toxicity: See *Adverse Reactions, Side Effects or Overdose Symptoms* section below.

Adverse Reactions, Side Effects or Overdose Symptoms

Signs and symptoms:	What to do:
Hallucinations	Seek emergency treatment.

Jequirity Bean (Crab's Eyes, Indian Licorice, Rosary Pea)

Basic Information

Biological name (genus and species):
Abrus precatorius
Parts used for medicinal purposes:
Seeds/beans
Chemicals this herb contains:
Abric acid
Abrive
Glycyrrhizin
Hemoglutin
N-methyltryptophan
Toxalbumin abrin

Known Effects

• Toxalbumin in seed causes cell destruction.

Miscellaneous information:
• No longer used therapeutically.
• Causes toxic reactions with ingestion.
• Common weed in Florida, Central America and South America.

Unproved Speculated Benefits

• Is used as drops for eye problems.

Warnings and Precautions

Don't take if you:
• Are pregnant, think you may be pregnant or plan pregnancy in the near future.
• Have any chronic disease of the gastrointestinal tract, such as stomach or duodenal ulcers, oesophageal reflux (reflux oesophagitis), ulcerative colitis, spastic colitis, diverticulosis, diverticulitis.

Consult your doctor if you:
• Take this herb for any medical problem that doesn't improve in 2 weeks. There may be safer, more effective treatments.
• Take any medicinal drugs or herbs including aspirin, laxatives, cold and cough remedies, antacids, vitamins, minerals, amino acids, supplements, other prescription or non-prescription drugs.

Pregnancy:
• Dangers outweigh any possible benefits. Don't use.

Breast-feeding:
• Dangers outweigh any possible benefits. Don't use.

Infants and children:
• Treating infants and children under 2 with any herbal preparation is hazardous.

Others:
• Dangers outweigh any possible benefits for *anyone.* Don't use. Swallowing even one bean can cause toxic symptoms hours or even days after eating.

Storage:
• Keep cool and dry, but don't freeze. Store safely away from children.

Safe dosage:
• At present no "safe" dosage has been established.

Toxicity

Rated dangerous, particularly in children, persons over 55 and those who take larger than appropriate quantities for extended periods of time.

For symptoms of toxicity: See *Adverse Reactions, Side Effects or Overdose Symptoms* section below.

Adverse Reactions, Side Effects or Overdose Symptoms

Signs and symptoms:	What to do:
Convulsions	Seek emergency treatment.
Diarrhoea	Discontinue. Call doctor immediately.
Increased heart rate	Discontinue. Call doctor immediately.
Kidney damage characterized by blood in urine, decreased urine flow, swelling of hands and feet	Seek emergency treatment.
Nausea	Discontinue. Call doctor immediately.
Vomiting	Discontinue. Call doctor immediately.

Basic Information

Biological name (genus and species):
  Ceanothus americanus
Parts used for medicinal purposes:
  Roots
Chemicals this herb contains:
  Ceanothic acid
  Malonic acid
  Orthophosphoric acid
  Oxalic acid
  Pyrophosphoric acid
  Resin (See Glossary)
  Succinic acid
  Tannins (See Glossary)

Known Effects

- Shrinks tissues.
- Prevents secretion of fluids.
- Increases blood clotting.
- Interferes with absorption of iron and other minerals when taken internally.

Unproved Speculated Benefits

- Treats syphilis (archaic).
- Is used as a "spleen" remedy.
- Stops mild bleeding from broken capillaries in skin.
- Decreases thickness and increases fluidity of mucus from lungs and bronchial tubes.
- Acts as a sedative.
- Relieves spasm in skeletal muscle or smooth muscle.
- Treats depression.

Warnings and Precautions

Don't take if you:
- Are pregnant, think you may be pregnant or plan pregnancy in the near future.

Consult your doctor if you:
- Take this herb for any medical problem that doesn't improve in 2 weeks. There may be safer, more effective treatments.
- Take any medicinal drugs or herbs including aspirin, laxatives, cold and cough remedies, antacids, vitamins, minerals, amino acids, supplements, other prescription or non-prescription drugs.

Pregnancy:
- Problems in pregnant women taking small or usual amounts have not been proved. But the chance of problems does exist. Don't use unless prescribed by your doctor.

Breast-feeding:
- Problems in breast-fed infants of lactating mothers taking small or usual amounts have not been proved. But the chance of problems does exist. Don't use unless prescribed by your doctor.

Infants and children:
- Treating infants and children under 2 with any herbal preparation is hazardous.

Others:
- None expected if you are under 45, not pregnant, basically healthy, take it for only a short time and do not exceed manufacturer's recommended dosage.

Storage:
- Keep cool and dry, but don't freeze. Store safely away from children.

Safe dosage:
- At present no "safe" dosage has been established.

Toxicity

Comparative-toxicity rating not available from standard references.

For symptoms of toxicity: See *Adverse Reactions, Side Effects or Overdose Symptoms* section below.

Adverse Reactions, Side Effects or Overdose Symptoms

Signs and symptoms:	What to do:
Prolonged minor bleeding	Discontinue. Call doctor immediately.

Jimson Weed (Sacred Datura, Thorn Apple, Stramonium)

Basic Information

Biological name (genus and species):
   Datura stramonium
Parts used for medicinal purposes:
   Leaves
   Seeds
Chemicals this herb contains:
   Atropine
   Hyoscyamine
   Scopolamine

Known Effects

- Negates normal activity of acetylcholine, an important chemical at the synapses (connection between nerve cells) of heart, brain, smooth muscles and glands.

Miscellaneous information:
- There are more-refined, predictable sources for active chemicals.
- Highest concentration of toxins are in seeds but may be in all parts of the plant.

Unproved Speculated Benefits

- Treats asthma.
- Treats gastrointestinal problems.
- Produces hallucinations.
- Acts as a sedative.

Warnings and Precautions

Don't take if you:
- Are pregnant, think you may be pregnant or plan pregnancy in the near future.
- Have heart disease.

Consult your doctor if you:
- Take this herb for any medical problem that doesn't improve in 2 weeks. There may be safer, more effective treatments.
- Take any medicinal drugs or herbs including aspirin, laxatives, cold and cough remedies, antacids, vitamins, minerals, amino acids, supplements, other prescription or non-prescription drugs.

Pregnancy:
- Dangers outweigh any possible benefits. Don't use.

Breast-feeding:
- Dangers outweigh any possible benefits. Don't use.

Infants and children:
- Treating infants and children under 2 with any herbal preparation is hazardous.

Others:
- Dangers outweigh any possible benefits. Don't use.

Storage:
- Keep cool and dry, but don't freeze. Store safely away from children.

Safe dosage:
- At present no "safe" dosage has been established.

Toxicity

Rated dangerous, particularly in children, persons over 55 and those who take larger than appropriate quantities for extended periods of time.

For symptoms of toxicity: See *Adverse Reactions, Side Effects or Overdose Symptoms* section below.

Adverse Reactions, Side Effects or Overdose Symptoms

Signs and symptoms:	What to do:
Convulsions	Seek emergency treatment.
Dilated pupils	Discontinue. Call doctor immediately.
Dry mouth	Discontinue. Call doctor when convenient.
Extremely fast heart rate	Seek emergency treatment.
Flushing	Discontinue. Call doctor when convenient.
Hallucinations	Seek emergency treatment.
Increased blood pressure	Discontinue. Call doctor immediately.
Unconsciousness	Seek emergency treatment.

Basic Information

Biological name (genus and species):
Juniperus communis or J. depressa
Parts used for medicinal purposes:
Berries/fruits
Chemicals this herb contains:

Alcohols	Sabinal
Alpha-pinene	Sugar
Cadinene	Tannins (See Glossary)
Camphene	Terpinene
Flavone	Volatile oils (See Glossary)
Resin (See Glossary)	

Known Effects

- Irritates kidneys.
- May cause hallucinations.
- Interferes with absorption of iron and other minerals when taken internally.

Miscellaneous information:
- Provides flavour in gin.

Unproved Speculated Benefits

- Treats chronic kidney disorders.
- Aids in expelling gas from intestinal tract.
- Causes abortions (miscarriages).
- Treats colic.
- Treats flatulence.
- Helps body dispose of excess fluid by increasing amount of urine produced.

Warnings and Precautions

Don't take if you:
- Are pregnant, think you may be pregnant or plan pregnancy in the near future.
- Have kidney disease.
- Have any chronic disease of the gastrointestinal tract, such as stomach or duodenal ulcers, oesophageal reflux (reflux oesophagitis), ulcerative colitis, spastic colitis, diverticulosis, diverticulitis.

Consult your doctor if you:
- Take this herb for any medical problem that doesn't improve in 2 weeks. There may be safer, more effective treatments.
- Take any medicinal drugs or herbs including aspirin, laxatives, cold and cough remedies, antacids, vitamins, minerals, amino acids, supplements, other prescription or non-prescription drugs.

Pregnancy:
- Dangers outweigh any possible benefits. Don't use.

Breast-feeding:
- Dangers outweigh any possible benefits. Don't use.

Infants and children:
- Treating infants and children under 2 with any herbal preparation is hazardous.

Others:
- None expected if you are under 45, not pregnant, basically healthy, take it for only a short time and do not exceed manufacturer's recommended dosage.

Storage:
- Keep cool and dry, but don't freeze. Store safely away from children.

Safe dosage:
- At present no "safe" dosage has been established.

Toxicity

Rated slightly dangerous, particularly in children, persons over 55 and those who take larger than appropriate quantities for extended periods of time.

For symptoms of toxicity: See *Adverse Reactions, Side Effects or Overdose Symptoms* section below.

Adverse Reactions, Side Effects or Overdose Symptoms

Signs and symptoms:	What to do:
Single dose:	
Diarrhoea, watery, explosive	Discontinue. Call doctor immediately.
Small, repeated doses:	
Convulsions	Seek emergency treatment.
Hallucinations	Seek emergency treatment.
Kidney damage	Discontinue. Call doctor immediately.
Personality changes	Discontinue. Call doctor immediately.

Kava-Kava

Basic Information

Biological name (genus and species):
Piper methysticum
Parts used for medicinal purposes:
Roots
Chemicals this herb contains:
Demethoxyyangonin
Dihydrokawin
Dihydromethysticin
Flavorawin A
Kawain
Methysticin
Starch
Yangonin

Known Effects

- Depresses the central nervous system.
- Produces skin pigmentation.

Miscellaneous information:
- Is used to make a fermented liquor.
- Sedative effect is very mild.

Unproved Speculated Benefits

- Is used as a sedative for anxiety disorders.
- Induces restful sleep.
- Treats fatigue.
- Helps body dispose of excess fluid by increasing amount of urine produced.
- Is used as a genito-urinary antiseptic.
- Treats coughs.
- Is used as a douche.

Warnings and Precautions

Don't take if you:
- Are pregnant, think you may be pregnant or plan pregnancy in the near future.

Consult your doctor if you:
- Take this herb for any medical problem that doesn't improve in 2 weeks. There may be safer, more effective treatments.
- Take any medicinal drugs or herbs including aspirin, laxatives, cold and cough remedies, antacids, vitamins, minerals, amino acids, supplements, other prescription or non-prescription drugs.

Pregnancy:
- Problems in pregnant women taking small or usual amounts have not been proved. But the chance of problems does exist. Don't use unless prescribed by your doctor.

Breast-feeding:
- Problems in breast-fed infants of lactating mothers taking small or usual amounts have not been proved. But the chance of problems does exist. Don't use unless prescribed by your doctor.

Infants and children:
- Treating infants and children under 2 with any herbal preparation is hazardous.

Others:
- None expected if you are beyond childhood and under 45, basically healthy and take for only a short time.

Storage:
- Keep cool and dry, but don't freeze. Store safely away from children.

Safe dosage:
- At present no "safe" dosage has been established.

Toxicity

Rated slightly dangerous, particularly in children, persons over 55 and those who take larger than appropriate quantities for extended periods of time.

For symptoms of toxicity: See *Adverse Reactions, Side Effects or Overdose Symptoms* section below.

Adverse Reactions, Side Effects or Overdose Symptoms

Signs and symptoms:	What to do:
Oversedation	Discontinue. Call doctor immediately.
Repeated small amounts may lead to undesirable skin colouring, inflammation of the body and eyes	Discontinue. Call doctor immediately.

Basic Information

Biological name (genus and species):
Laminaria, Fucus, Sargassum
Parts used for medicinal purposes:
Leaves
Chemicals this herb contains:
Alginic acid
Bromine
Iodine
Potassium
Sodium

Known Effects

• Provides bulk for bowel movements.

Miscellaneous information:
• Iodine can interfere with normal thyroid function.

Unproved Speculated Benefits

• Treats chronic constipation without catharsis.
• Softens stools.
• Treats ulcers.
• Controls obesity.

Warnings and Precautions

Don't take if you:
• Are pregnant, think you may be pregnant or plan pregnancy in the near future.
• Are allergic to iodine in any form, particularly if you have had an allergic reaction to injected dye used for X-ray studies of the kidney or other organs.

Consult your doctor if you:
• Take this herb for any medical problem that doesn't improve in 2 weeks. There may be safer, more effective treatments.
• Take any medicinal drugs or herbs including aspirin, laxatives, cold and cough remedies, antacids, vitamins, minerals, amino acids, supplements, other prescription or non-prescription drugs.

Pregnancy:
• Problems in pregnant women taking small or usual amounts have not been proved. But the chance of problems does exist. Don't use unless prescribed by your doctor.

Breast-feeding:
• Problems in breast-fed infants of lactating mothers taking small or usual amounts have not been proved. But the chance of problems does exist. Don't use unless prescribed by your doctor.

Infants and children:
• Treating infants and children under 2 with any herbal preparation is hazardous.

Others:
• None expected if you are under 45, not pregnant, basically healthy, take it for only a short time and do not exceed manufacturer's recommended dosage.

Storage:
• Keep cool and dry, but don't freeze. Store safely away from children.

Safe dosage:
• At present no "safe" dosage has been established.

Toxicity

Comparative-toxicity rating not available from standard references.

Adverse Reactions, Side Effects or Overdose Symptoms

None expected

MEDICINAL HERB

Lemongrass

Basic Information

Biological name (genus and species):
Cymbopogon citracus
Parts used for medicinal purposes:
Various parts of the entire plant, frequently
differing by country and/or culture
Chemicals this herb contains:
Citronellal
Methylneptenone
Terpene
Terpene alcohol

Known Effects

- In insecticides kills insects, but less efficiently
than malathion or parathione.

Miscellaneous information:
- Is used in perfumes.
- Sometimes used as an insect repellent.

Unproved Speculated Benefits

- Treats constipation.

Warnings and Precautions

Don't take if you:
- Are pregnant, think you may be pregnant or
plan pregnancy in the near future.
- Have any chronic disease of the
gastrointestinal tract, such as stomach or
duodenal ulcers, oesophageal reflux (reflux
oesophagitis), ulcerative colitis, spastic
colitis, diverticulosis, diverticulitis.

Consult your doctor if you:
- Take this herb for any medical problem that
doesn't improve in 2 weeks. There may be
safer, more effective treatments.
- Take any medicinal drugs or herbs including
aspirin, laxatives, cold and cough remedies,
antacids, vitamins, minerals, amino acids,
supplements, other prescription or non-
prescription drugs.

Pregnancy:
- Problems in pregnant women taking small or
usual amounts have not been proved. But the
chance of problems does exist. Don't use
unless prescribed by your doctor.

Breast-feeding:
- Problems in breast-fed infants of lactating
mothers taking small or usual amounts have
not been proved. But the chance of problems
does exist. Don't use unless prescribed by your
doctor.

Infants and children:
- Treating infants and children under 2 with any
herbal preparation is hazardous.

Others:
- None expected if you are beyond childhood
and under 45, basically healthy and take for
only a short time.

Storage:
- Keep cool and dry, but don't freeze. Store
safely away from children.

Safe dosage:
- At present no "safe" dosage has been
established.

Toxicity

Comparative-toxicity rating not available from
standard references.

For symptoms of toxicity: See *Adverse
Reactions, Side Effects or Overdose Symptoms*
section below.

Adverse Reactions, Side Effects or Overdose Symptoms

Signs and symptoms:	What to do:
Diarrhoea	Discontinue. Call doctor immediately.
Nausea	Discontinue. Call doctor immediately.
Vomiting	Discontinue. Call doctor immediately.

Licorice, Common (Licorice Root, Spanish Licorice Root)

Basic Information

Biological name (genus and species):
Glycyrrhiza glabra
Parts used for medicinal purposes:
Roots
Chemicals this herb contains:
Asparagine
Fat
Glycyrrhizin
Gum (See Glossary)
Pentacyclic terpenes
Protein
Sugar
Yellow dye

 ## Known Effects

- Decreases inflammation.
- Provides oestrogen-like hormone effects.
- Decreases spasm of smooth muscle or skeletal muscle.
- Decreases thickness and increases fluidity of mucus from lungs and bronchial tubes.

Miscellaneous information;
- *Warning:* Consuming large amounts of licorice may lead to high blood pressure.

 ## Unproved Speculated Benefits

- Protects scraped tissues.
- Softens or soothes skin.
- Treats coughs.

 ## Warnings and Precautions

Don't take if you:
- Are pregnant, think you may be pregnant or plan pregnancy in the near future.
- Have heart disease.
- Take diuretics.

Consult your doctor if you:
- Take this herb for any medical problem that doesn't improve in 2 weeks. There may be safer, more effective treatments.
- Take any medicinal drugs or herbs including aspirin, laxatives, cold and cough remedies, antacids, vitamins, minerals, amino acids, supplements, other prescription or non-prescription drugs.

Pregnancy:
- Dangers outweigh any possible benefits. Don't use.

Breast-feeding:
- Dangers outweigh any possible benefits. Don't use.

Infants and children:
- Treating infants and children under 2 with any herbal preparation is hazardous.

Others:
- None expected if you are under 45, not pregnant, basically healthy, take it for only a short time and do not exceed manufacturer's recommended dosage.

Storage:
- Keep cool and dry, but don't freeze. Store safely away from children.

Safe dosage:
- At present no "safe" dosage has been established.

 ## Toxicity

Rated slightly dangerous, particularly in children, persons over 55 and those who take larger than appropriate quantities for extended periods of time.

For symptoms of toxicity: See *Adverse Reactions, Side Effects or Overdose Symptoms* section below.

 ## Adverse Reactions, Side Effects or Overdose Symptoms

Signs and symptoms:	What to do:
Causes sodium retention in blood, which may lead to oedema, lung congestion	Discontinue. Call doctor immediately.
Depletes sodium from cells; may cause weakness, nausea, heartbeat irregularities	Discontinue. Call doctor immediately.
High blood pressure	Discontinue. Call doctor immediately.

MEDICINAL HERB

363

Liferoot (Golden Groundsel, Squaw Weed)

Basic Information

Biological name (genus and species):
Senecio vulgaris, S. aureus
Parts used for medicinal purposes:
Roots
Chemicals this herb contains:
Pyrrolizidine (has high potential for causing liver disorders, including cancer)

Known Effects

• Increases blood pressure.
• Stimulates uterine contractions.

Unproved Speculated Benefits

• Treats menstrual irregularities.
• Treats dysmenorrhoea (painful menstruation).
• Treats excessive menstrual bleeding (menorrhagia).
• Helps relieve vaginal discharge.
• Causes overdue labour to begin.

Warnings and Precautions

Don't take if you:
• Are pregnant, think you may be pregnant or plan pregnancy in the near future.

Consult your doctor if you:
• Take this herb for any medical problem that doesn't improve in 2 weeks. There may be safer, more effective treatments.
• Take any medicinal drugs or herbs including aspirin, laxatives, cold and cough remedies, antacids, vitamins, minerals, amino acids, supplements, other prescription or non-prescription drugs.

Pregnancy:
• Dangers outweigh any possible benefits. Don't use.

Breast-feeding:
• Dangers outweigh any possible benefits. Don't use.

Infants and children:
• Treating infants and children under 2 with any herbal preparation is hazardous.

Others:
• None expected if you are beyond childhood and under 45, basically healthy and take for only a short time.

Storage:

• Keep cool and dry, but don't freeze. Store safely away from children.

Safe dosage:

• At present no "safe" dosage has been established.

Toxicity

Rated slightly dangerous, particularly in children, persons over 55 and those who take larger than appropriate quantities for extended periods of time.

For symptoms of toxicity: See *Adverse Reactions, Side Effects or Overdose Symptoms* section below.

Adverse Reactions, Side Effects or Overdose Symptoms

Signs and symptoms:	What to do:
Abnormal liver function tests	Discontinue. Call doctor immediately.
Jaundice (yellow eyes and skin)	Discontinue. Call doctor immediately.

Basic Information

Biological name (genus and species):
Convallaria majalis
Parts used for medicinal purposes:
Berries/fruits
Petals/flower
Roots
Chemicals this herb contains:
Convallamarin
Convallarin
Convallatoxin (highly toxic)

Known Effects

- Increases efficiency of heart-muscle contraction.
- Helps body dispose of excess fluid by increasing amount of urine produced.

Miscellaneous information:
- Although lily-of-the-valley has similar action to digitalis, there are safer, less-expensive, more-reliable products to use.

Unproved Speculated Benefits

- Treats congestive heart failure.
- Treats heartbeat irregularities.
- Improves circulation.

Warnings and Precautions

Don't take if you:
- Are pregnant, think you may be pregnant or plan pregnancy in the near future.
- Have any chronic disease of the gastrointestinal tract, such as stomach or duodenal ulcers, oesophageal reflux (reflux oesophagitis), ulcerative colitis, spastic colitis, diverticulosis, diverticulitis.
- Have heart disease.

Consult your doctor if you:
- Take this herb for any medical problem that doesn't improve in 2 weeks. There may be safer, more effective treatments.
- Take any medicinal drugs or herbs including aspirin, laxatives, cold and cough remedies, antacids, vitamins, minerals, amino acids, supplements, other prescription or non-prescription drugs.

Pregnancy:
- Dangers outweigh any possible benefits. Don't use.

Breast-feeding:
- Dangers outweigh any possible benefits. Don't use.

Infants and children:
- Treating infants and children under 2 with any herbal preparation is hazardous.

Others:
- Dangers outweigh any possible benefits. Don't use.

Storage:
- Keep cool and dry, but don't freeze. Store safely away from children.

Safe dosage:
- At present no "safe" dosage has been established.

Toxicity

Rated dangerous, particularly in children, persons over 55 and those who take larger than appropriate quantities for extended periods of time.

For symptoms of toxicity: See *Adverse Reactions, Side Effects or Overdose Symptoms* section below.

Adverse Reactions, Side Effects or Overdose Symptoms

Signs and symptoms:	What to do:
Heartbeat irregularities	Seek emergency treatment.
Nausea	Discontinue. Call doctor immediately.
Vomiting	Discontinue. Call doctor immediately.

Linden Tree (American, Lime Tree in Europe)

Basic Information

Biological name (genus and species):
Tilia europea
Parts used for medicinal purposes:
Petals/flower
Chemicals this herb contains:
Tannins (See Glossary)
Volatile oils (See Glossary)

Known Effects

- Decreases spasm of smooth or skeletal muscle.
- Shrinks tissues.
- Prevents secretion of fluids.
- Increases perspiration.
- Interferes with absorption of iron and other minerals when taken internally.

Unproved Speculated Benefits

- Treats coughs.
- Decreases thickness and increases fluidity of mucus from lungs and bronchial tubes.
- Reduces fever.

Warnings and Precautions

Don't take if you:
- Are pregnant, think you may be pregnant or plan pregnancy in the near future.

Consult your doctor if you:
- Take this herb for any medical problem that doesn't improve in 2 weeks. There may be safer, more effective treatments.
- Take any medicinal drugs or herbs including aspirin, laxatives, cold and cough remedies, antacids, vitamins, minerals, amino acids, supplements, other prescription or non-prescription drugs.

Pregnancy:
- Problems in pregnant women taking small or usual amounts have not been proved. But the chance of problems does exist. Don't use unless prescribed by your doctor.

Breast-feeding:
- Problems in breast-fed infants of lactating mothers taking small or usual amounts have not been proved. But the chance of problems does exist. Don't use unless prescribed by your doctor.

Infants and children:
- Treating infants and children under 2 with any herbal preparation is hazardous.

Others:
- None expected if you are under 45, not pregnant, basically healthy, take it for only a short time and do not exceed manufacturer's recommended dosage.

Storage:
- Keep cool and dry, but don't freeze. Store safely away from children.

Safe dosage:
- At present no "safe" dosage has been established.

Toxicity

Rated relatively safe when taken in appropriate quantities for short periods of time.

For symptoms of toxicity: See *Adverse Reactions, Side Effects* or *Overdose Symptoms* section below.

Adverse Reactions, Side Effects or Overdose Symptoms

Signs and symptoms:	What to do:
Drowsiness	Discontinue. Call doctor when convenient.

Mace (Nutmeg)

Basic Information

Biological name (genus and species):
Myristica fragrans
Parts used for medicinal purposes:
Fibrous covering,
Seeds
Chemicals this herb contains:

Elemicin	Methyleugenol
Eugenol	Methylisoeugenol
Fixed oil (See Glossary)	Myristicin
Isoeugenol	Protein
Methoxyeugenol	Starch

Known Effects

- Stimulates muscular movement of intestinal tract.
- Stimulates central nervous system.

Miscellaneous information:

- May produce hallucinations.
- No effects are expected on the body, either good or bad, when herb is used in very small amounts to enhance the flavour of food.
- Nutmeg is the seed. Mace is the fibrous covering.

Unproved Speculated Benefits

- Alters mood.
- Treats digestive disorders.
- Treats cholera.
- Causes abortion.
- Triggers menstruation to begin.
- Arouses or enhances instinctive sexual desire.

Warnings and Precautions

Don't take if you:

- Are pregnant, think you may be pregnant or plan pregnancy in the near future.
- Have any chronic disease of the gastrointestinal tract, such as stomach or duodenal ulcers, oesophageal reflux (reflux oesophagitis), ulcerative colitis, spastic colitis, diverticulosis, diverticulitis.

Consult your doctor if you:

- Take this herb for any medical problem that doesn't improve in 2 weeks. There may be safer, more effective treatments.
- Take any medicinal drugs or herbs including aspirin, laxatives, cold and cough remedies, antacids, vitamins, minerals, amino acids, supplements, other prescription or non-prescription drugs.

Pregnancy:

- Dangers outweigh any possible benefits. Don't use.

Breast-feeding:

- Dangers outweigh any possible benefits. Don't use.

Infants and children:

- Treating infants and children under 2 with any herbal preparation is hazardous.

Others:

- Mind-altering and hallucinogenic effects are unpleasant. Do not use nutmeg for these purposes.

Storage:

- Keep cool and dry, but don't freeze. Store safely away from children.

Safe dosage:

- At present no "safe" dosage has been established.

Toxicity

Rated slightly dangerous, particularly in children, persons over 55 and those who take larger than appropriate quantities for extended periods of time.

For symptoms of toxicity: See *Adverse Reactions, Side Effects or Overdose Symptoms* section below.

Adverse Reactions, Side Effects or Overdose Symptoms

Signs and symptoms:	What to do:
Diarrhoea	Discontinue. Call doctor immediately.
Drowsiness	Discontinue. Call doctor when convenient.
Hallucinations	Seek emergency treatment.
Nausea	Discontinue. Call doctor immediately.
Reduced body temperature	Discontinue. Call doctor immediately.
Vomiting	Discontinue. Call doctor immediately.
Weak, thready, rapid pulse	Seek emergency treatment.

MEDICINAL HERB

367

Malabar Nut (Adotodai, Parettia, Vasaka)

Basic Information

Biological name (genus and species):
Adhatoda vasica
Parts used for medicinal purposes:
Leaves
Chemicals this herb contains:
Adhatodic acid
Peganine
Vasicine

Known Effects

- Dilates bronchial tubes.
- Decreases thickness and increases fluidity of mucus from lungs and bronchial tubes.

Unproved Speculated Benefits

- Treats coughs and colds.
- Treats bronchitis.
- Treats asthma.

Warnings and Precautions

Don't take if you:
- Are pregnant, think you may be pregnant or plan pregnancy in the near future.
- Have any chronic disease of the gastrointestinal tract, such as stomach or duodenal ulcers, oesophageal reflux (reflux oesophagitis), ulcerative colitis, spastic colitis, diverticulosis, diverticulitis.

Consult your doctor if you:
- Take this herb for any medical problem that doesn't improve in 2 weeks. There may be safer, more effective treatments.
- Take any medicinal drugs or herbs including aspirin, laxatives, cold and cough remedies, antacids, vitamins, minerals, amino acids, supplements, other prescription or non-prescription drugs.

Pregnancy:
- Problems in pregnant women taking small or usual amounts have not been proved. But the chance of problems does exist. Don't use unless prescribed by your doctor.

Breast-feeding:
- Problems in breast-fed infants of lactating mothers taking small or usual amounts have not been proved. But the chance of problems does exist. Don't use unless prescribed by your doctor.

Infants and children:
- Treating infants and children under 2 with any herbal preparation is hazardous.

Others:
- None expected if you are under 45, not pregnant, basically healthy, take it for only a short time and do not exceed manufacturer's recommended dosage.

Storage:
- Keep cool and dry, but don't freeze. Store safely away from children.

Safe dosage:
- At present no "safe" dosage has been established.

Toxicity

Rated slightly dangerous, particularly in children, persons over 55 and those who take larger than appropriate quantities for extended periods of time.

For symptoms of toxicity: See *Adverse Reactions, Side Effects or Overdose Symptoms* section below.

Adverse Reactions, Side Effects or Overdose Symptoms

Signs and symptoms:	What to do:
Diarrhoea	Discontinue. Call doctor immediately.
Nausea	Discontinue. Call doctor immediately.
Vomiting	Discontinue. Call doctor immediately.

Male Fern (Aspidium)

Basic Information

Biological name (genus and species):
Dryopteris filix-mass, Dryopteris
Parts used for medicinal purposes:
Leaves, Roots
Chemicals this herb contains:

Albaspadin	Resin (See Glossary)
Aspidin	Starch
Aspidinol	Sugar
Filicic acid	Tannins (See Glossary)
Filmaron acid	Volatile oils (See Glossary)
Flavaspininic acid	Wax

Known Effects

- Destroys intestinal worms.
- Decreases normal muscle function.
- Interferes with absorption of iron and other minerals when taken internally.

Unproved Speculated Benefits

- None

Warnings and Precautions

Don't take if you:
- Are pregnant, think you may be pregnant or plan pregnancy in the near future.
- Have any chronic disease of the gastrointestinal tract, such as stomach or duodenal ulcers, oesophageal reflux (reflux oesophagitis), ulcerative colitis, spastic colitis, diverticulosis, diverticulitis.
- Are over age 55.
- Have heart disease.
- Have kidney disease.

Consult your doctor if you:
- Take this herb for any medical problem that doesn't improve in 2 weeks. There may be safer, more effective treatments.
- Take any medicinal drugs or herbs including aspirin, laxatives, cold and cough remedies, antacids, vitamins, minerals, amino acids, supplements, other prescription or non-prescription drugs.

Pregnancy:
- Dangers outweigh any possible benefits. Don't use.

Breast-feeding:
- Dangers outweigh any possible benefits. Don't use.

Infants and children:
- Treating infants and children under 2 with any herbal preparation is hazardous.

Others:
- Dangers outweigh any possible benefits. Don't use.

Storage:
- Keep cool and dry, but don't freeze. Store safely away from children.

Safe dosage:
- At present no "safe" dosage has been established.

Toxicity

Rated dangerous, particularly in children, persons over 55 and those who take larger than appropriate quantities for extended periods of time.

For symptoms of toxicity: See *Adverse Reactions, Side Effects or Overdose Symptoms* section below.

Adverse Reactions, Side Effects or Overdose Symptoms

Signs and symptoms:	What to do:
Abdominal cramping	Discontinue. Call doctor when convenient.
Breathing difficulty	Seek emergency treatment.
Coma	Seek emergency treatment.
Convulsions	Seek emergency treatment.
Diarrhoea	Discontinue. Call doctor immediately.
Headache	Discontinue. Call doctor when convenient.
Heartbeat irregularities	Seek emergency treatment.
Impaired vision	Discontinue. Call doctor when convenient.
Nausea	Discontinue. Call doctor immediately.
Vomiting	Discontinue. Call doctor immediately.

Mandrake (Love Apple, Satan's Apple)

Basic Information

Biological name (genus and species):
Mandragora officanarum
Parts used for medicinal purposes:
Roots
Chemicals this herb contains:
Hyoscyamine
Mandragorin
Scopolamine

Known Effects

- Increases heart rate.
- Dilates pupils.
- Causes dry mouth.
- Causes urinary retention.
- Causes hallucinations.
- Reduces muscular movements of intestinal tract.

Unproved Speculated Benefits

- Relieves pain.
- Acts as a sedative.
- Is used as an aphrodisiac.
- Treats ulcers.
- Treats skin diseases.
- Treats haemorrhoids.
- Destroys or repels demons.
- Causes explosive, watery diarrhoea.
- Is used as an anaesthetic.

Warnings and Precautions

Don't take if you:
- Are pregnant, think you may be pregnant or plan pregnancy in the near future.
- Have heart disease.

Consult your doctor if you:
- Take this herb for any medical problem that doesn't improve in 2 weeks. There may be safer, more effective treatments.
- Take any medicinal drugs or herbs including aspirin, laxatives, cold and cough remedies, antacids, vitamins, minerals, amino acids, supplements, other prescription or non-prescription drugs.

Pregnancy:
- Dangers outweigh any possible benefits. Don't use.

Breast-feeding:
- Dangers outweigh any possible benefits. Don't use.

Infants and children:
- Treating infants and children under 2 with any herbal preparation is hazardous.

Others:
- None expected if you are beyond childhood and under 45, basically healthy and take for only a short time.

Storage:
- Keep cool and dry, but don't freeze. Store safely away from children.

Safe dosage:
- At present no "safe" dosage has been established.

Toxicity

Rated dangerous, particularly in children, persons over 55 and those who take larger than appropriate quantities for extended periods of time.

For symptoms of toxicity: See *Adverse Reactions, Side Effects or Overdose Symptoms* section below.

Adverse Reactions, Side Effects or Overdose Symptoms

Signs and symptoms:	What to do:
Coma	Seek emergency treatment.
Confusion	Discontinue. Call doctor immediately.
Irregular heartbeat	Seek emergency treatment.

Basic Information

Biological name (genus and species):
Althea officinalis
Parts used for medicinal purposes:
Leaves
Roots
Chemicals this herb contains:
Asparagine
Fat
Mucilage (See Glossary)
Pectin
Starch
Sugar

Known Effects

- Softens or soothes skin.

Miscellaneous information:
- Marshmallow plant is used as a "filler" in a variety of pills.

Unproved Speculated Benefits

- Protects injured or scraped skin or mucous membranes.
- Used as a poultice for applying medications. (See Glossary.)

Warnings and Precautions

Don't take if you:
- Are pregnant, think you may be pregnant or plan pregnancy in the near future.
- Have any chronic disease of the gastrointestinal tract, such as stomach or duodenal ulcers, oesophageal reflux (reflux oesophagitis), ulcerative colitis, spastic colitis, diverticulosis, diverticulitis.

Consult your doctor if you:
- Take this herb for any medical problem that doesn't improve in 2 weeks. There may be safer, more effective treatments.
- Take any medicinal drugs or herbs including aspirin, laxatives, cold and cough remedies, antacids, vitamins, minerals, amino acids, supplements, other prescription or non-prescription drugs.

Pregnancy:
- Problems in pregnant women taking small or usual amounts have not been proved. But the chance of problems does exist. Don't use unless prescribed by your doctor.

Breast-feeding:
- Problems in breast-fed infants of lactating mothers taking small or usual amounts have not been proved. But the chance of problems does exist. Don't use unless prescribed by your doctor.

Infants and children:
- Treating infants and children under 2 with any herbal preparation is hazardous.

Others:
- None expected if you are beyond childhood and under 45, basically healthy and take for only a short time.

Storage:
- Keep cool and dry, but don't freeze. Store safely away from children.

Safe dosage:
- At present no "safe" dosage has been established.

Toxicity

Comparative-toxicity rating not available from standard references.

Adverse Reactions, Side Effects or Overdose Symptoms

None expected

MEDICINAL HERB

Mayapple (American Mandrake)

Basic Information
Biological name (genus and species):
　Podophyllum peltatum
Parts used for medicinal purposes:
　Roots
Chemicals this herb contains:
　Alpha-peltatin
　Beta-peltatin
　Podophyllotoxin

Known Effects

- Inhibits or prevents cell division.
- Stimulates gastrointestinal tract.

Unproved Speculated Benefits

- Treats constipation.
- Treats recurrent faecal impactions.
- Is used as topical application for virus infections of skin around genitals.

Warnings and Precautions

Don't take if you:
- Are pregnant, think you may be pregnant or plan pregnancy in the near future.
- Have any chronic disease of the gastrointestinal tract, such as stomach or duodenal ulcers, oesophageal reflux (reflux oesophagitis), ulcerative colitis, spastic colitis, diverticulosis, diverticulitis.

Consult your doctor if you:
- Take this herb for any medical problem that doesn't improve in 2 weeks. There may be safer, more effective treatments.
- Take any medicinal drugs or herbs including aspirin, laxatives, cold and cough remedies, antacids, vitamins, minerals, amino acids, supplements, other prescription or non-prescription drugs.

Pregnancy:
- Problems in pregnant women taking small or usual amounts have not been proved. But the chance of problems does exist. Don't use unless prescribed by your doctor.

Breast-feeding:
- Problems in breast-fed infants of lactating mothers taking small or usual amounts have not been proved. But the chance of problems does exist. Don't use unless prescribed by your doctor.

Infants and children:
- Treating infants and children under 2 with any herbal preparation is hazardous.

Others:
- None expected if you are beyond childhood and under 45, basically healthy and take for only a short time.

Storage:
- Keep cool and dry, but don't freeze. Store safely away from children.

Safe dosage:
- At present no "safe" dosage has been established.

Toxicity

Rated slightly dangerous, particularly in children, persons over 55 and those who take larger than appropriate quantities for extended periods of time.

For symptoms of toxicity: See *Adverse Reactions, Side Effects or Overdose Symptoms* section below.

Adverse Reactions, Side Effects or Overdose Symptoms

Signs and symptoms:	What to do:
Diarrhoea	Discontinue. Call doctor immediately.
Drowsiness	Discontinue. Call doctor when convenient.
Lethargy	Discontinue. Call doctor when convenient.
Nausea	Discontinue. Call doctor immediately.
Unconsciousness	Seek emergency treatment.
Vomiting	Discontinue. Call doctor immediately.

Meadowsweet (Spirea, Queen-of-the-Meadow)

Basic Information

Biological name (genus and species):
   Filipendula ulmaria
Parts used for medicinal purposes:
   Petals/flower
   Roots
Chemicals this herb contains:
   Gallic acid
   Methyl salicylate
   Salicylic acid
   Salicylic aldehyde
   Tannic acid
   Volatile oils (See Glossary)

Known Effects

- Shrinks tissues.
- Prevents secretion of fluids.

Unproved Speculated Benefits

- Helps body dispose of excess fluid by increasing amount of urine produced.
- Treats diarrhoea
- Reduces pain.

Warnings and Precautions

Don't take if you:
- Are pregnant, think you may be pregnant or plan pregnancy in the near future.
- Have chronic kidney problems.

Consult your doctor if you:
- Take this herb for any medical problem that doesn't improve in 2 weeks. There may be safer, more effective treatments.
- Take any medicinal drugs or herbs including aspirin, laxatives, cold and cough remedies, antacids, vitamins, minerals, amino acids, supplements, other prescription or non-prescription drugs.

Pregnancy:
- Problems in pregnant women taking small or usual amounts have not been proved. But the chance of problems does exist. Don't use unless prescribed by your doctor.

Breast-feeding:
- Problems in breast-fed infants of lactating mothers taking small or usual amounts have not been proved. But the chance of problems does exist. Don't use unless prescribed by your doctor.

Infants and children:
- Treating infants and children under 2 with any herbal preparation is hazardous.

Others:
- None expected if you are under 45, not pregnant, basically healthy, take it for only a short time and do not exceed manufacturer's recommended dosage.

Storage:
- Keep cool and dry, but don't freeze. Store safely away from children.

Safe dosage:
- At present no "safe" dosage has been established.

Toxicity

Generally regarded as safe when taken in appropriate quantities for short periods of time.

For symptoms of toxicity: See *Adverse Reactions, Side Effects or Overdose Symptoms* section below.

Adverse Reactions, Side Effects or Overdose Symptoms

Signs and symptoms:	What to do:
Coma	Seek emergency treatment.
Kidney damage characterized by blood in urine, decreased urine flow, swelling of hands and feet	Seek emergency treatment.
Lethargy	Discontinue. Call doctor when convenient.
Unconsciousness	Seek emergency treatment.

Mexican Sarsaparilla

Basic Information

Biological name (genus and species):
Smilax aristolochiaefolia, S. regelii,
S. febrifuga, S. ornata
Parts used for medicinal purposes:
Bark
Berries
Roots
Chemicals this herb contains:
Resin (See Glossary)
Sarsasapogenin
Smilagenin
Starch
Stigmasterol
Volatile oils (See Glossary)

Known Effects

- Depresses central nervous system.
- Irritates mucous membranes.
- Irritates gastrointestinal tract.
- Helps body dispose of excess fluid by increasing amount of urine produced.

Miscellaneous information:
- Berries are edible.
- Berries, bark and other parts of plant are used to make the soft drink of the same name.

Unproved Speculated Benefits

- Relieves toothache.
- Increases sexual potency.
- Treats psoriasis.
- Temporarily relieves constipation.

Warnings and Precautions

Don't take if you:
- Are pregnant, think you may be pregnant or plan pregnancy in the near future.

Consult your doctor if you:
- Take this herb for any medical problem that doesn't improve in 2 weeks. There may be safer, more effective treatments.
- Take any medicinal drugs or herbs including aspirin, laxatives, cold and cough remedies, antacids, vitamins, minerals, amino acids, supplements, other prescription or non-prescription drugs.

Pregnancy:
- Problems in pregnant women taking small or usual amounts have not been proved. But the chance of problems does exist. Don't use unless prescribed by your doctor.

Breast-feeding:
- Problems in breast-fed infants of lactating mothers taking small or usual amounts have not been proved. But the chance of problems does exist. Don't use unless prescribed by your doctor.

Infants and children:
- Treating infants and children under 2 with any herbal preparation is hazardous.

Others:
- None expected if you are under 45, not pregnant, basically healthy, take it for only a short time and do not exceed manufacturer's recommended dosage.

Storage:
- Keep cool and dry, but don't freeze. Store safely away from children.

Safe dosage:
- At present no "safe" dosage has been established.

Toxicity

Rated relatively safe when taken in appropriate quantities for short periods of time.

Adverse Reactions, Side Effects or Overdose Symptoms

None expected

Milkweed, Common (Blood-flower)

Basic Information

Biological name (genus and species):
Asclepias syriaca
Parts used for medicinal purposes:
Roots
Chemicals this herb contains:
Asclepiadin   Galitoxin
Asclepion (a bitter)

Known Effects

- Irritates and stimulates gastrointestinal tract.
- Decreases thickness and increases fluidity of mucus from lungs and bronchial tubes.
- Increases perspiration.

Miscellaneous information:
- *All parts* of milkweed plant may be toxic.

Unproved Speculated Benefits

- Treats bronchitis.
- Treats arthritis.

Warnings and Precautions

Don't take if you:
- Are pregnant, think you may be pregnant or plan pregnancy in the near future.
- Have any chronic disease of the gastrointestinal tract, such as stomach or duodenal ulcers, oesophageal reflux (reflux oesophagitis), ulcerative colitis, spastic colitis, diverticulosis, diverticulitis.

Consult your doctor if you:
- Take this herb for any medical problem that doesn't improve in 2 weeks. There may be safer, more effective treatments.
- Take any medicinal drugs or herbs including aspirin, laxatives, cold and cough remedies, antacids, vitamins, minerals, amino acids, supplements, other prescription or non-prescription drugs.

Pregnancy:
- Dangers outweigh any possible benefits. Don't use.

Breast-feeding:
- Dangers outweigh any possible benefits. Don't use.

Infants and children:
- Treating infants and children under 2 with any herbal preparation is hazardous.

Others:
- Dangers outweigh any possible benefits. Don't use.

Storage:
- Keep cool and dry, but don't freeze. Store safely away from children.

Safe dosage:
- At present no "safe" dosage has been established.

Toxicity

Rated slightly dangerous, particularly in children, persons over 55 and those who take larger than appropriate quantities for extended periods of time.

For symptoms of toxicity: See *Adverse Reactions, Side Effects or Overdose Symptoms* section below.

Adverse Reactions, Side Effects or Overdose Symptoms

Signs and symptoms:	What to do:
Coma	Seek emergency treatment.
Diarrhoea	Discontinue. Call doctor immediately.
Drowsiness	Discontinue. Call doctor when convenient.
Jaundice (yellow skin and eyes)	Discontinue. Call doctor immediately.
Kidney damage characterized by blood in urine, decreased urine flow, swelling of hands and feet	Seek emergency treatment.
Lethargy	Discontinue. Call doctor when convenient.
Loss of appetite	Discontinue. Call doctor when convenient.
Nausea	Discontinue. Call doctor immediately.
Seizures	Seek emergency treatment.
Unsteady gait	Discontinue. Call doctor immediately.
Vomiting	Discontinue. Call doctor immediately.

Milkwort

Basic Information

Biological name (genus and species):
  Polygala vulgaris, P. senega
Parts used for medicinal purposes:
  Roots
Chemical this herb contains:
  Saponins (See Glossary)

Known Effects

- Causes increased secretions from bronchial tubes.
- Irritates intestinal tract.
- Decreases thickness and increases fluidity of mucus from lungs and bronchial tubes.
- Helps body dispose of excess fluid by increasing amount of urine produced.
- Increases perspiration.

Unproved Speculated Benefits

- Treats croup.
- Treats arthritis.
- Treats hives.
- Treats gout.
- Treats pleurisy.
- Treats constipation.
- Increases milk production in lactating women.

Warnings and Precautions

Don't take if you:
- Are pregnant, think you may be pregnant or plan pregnancy in the near future.
- Have any chronic disease of the gastrointestinal tract, such as stomach or duodenal ulcers, oesophageal reflux (reflux oesophagitis), ulcerative colitis, spastic colitis, diverticulosis, diverticulitis.

Consult your doctor if you:
- Take this herb for any medical problem that doesn't improve in 2 weeks. There may be safer, more effective treatments.
- Take any medicinal drugs or herbs including aspirin, laxatives, cold and cough remedies, antacids, vitamins, minerals, amino acids, supplements, other prescription or non-prescription drugs.

Pregnancy:
- Dangers outweigh any possible benefits. Don't use.

Breast-feeding:
- Dangers outweigh any possible benefits. Don't use.

Infants and children:
- Treating infants and children under 2 with any herbal preparation is hazardous.

Others:
- None expected if you are under 45, not pregnant, basically healthy, take it for only a short time and do not exceed manufacturer's recommended dosage.

Storage:
- Keep cool and dry, but don't freeze. Store safely away from children.

Safe dosage:
- At present no "safe" dosage has been established.

Toxicity

Comparative-toxicity rating not available from standard references.

For symptoms of toxicity: See *Adverse Reactions, Side Effects or Overdose Symptoms* section below.

Adverse Reactions, Side Effects or Overdose Symptoms

Signs and symptoms:	What to do:
Coma	Seek emergency treatment.
Diarrhoea	Discontinue. Call doctor immediately.
Drowsiness	Discontinue. Call doctor when convenient.
Lethargy	Discontinue. Call doctor when convenient.
Nausea, violent	Discontinue. Call doctor immediately.
Vomiting	Discontinue. Call doctor immediately.

Basic Information

Biological name (genus and species):
Phoradendron serotinum
Parts used for medicinal purposes:
Berries/fruits
Leaves
Stems
Chemicals this herb contains:
Beta phenylethylamine
Tyramine

Known Effects

- Stimulates central nervous system.
- Increases blood pressure.
- Causes contraction of smooth muscle in intestines or uterus.

Miscellaneous information:
- Mistletoe is particularly dangerous for people taking monamine-oxidase medications to treat high blood pressure.

Unproved Speculated Benefits

- Controls excessive bleeding after childbirth.
- Treats cholera.
- Calms nervousness.

Warnings and Precautions

Don't take if you:
- Are pregnant, think you may be pregnant or plan pregnancy in the near future.
- Have any chronic disease of the gastrointestinal tract, such as stomach or duodenal ulcers, oesophageal reflux (reflux oesophagitis), ulcerative colitis, spastic colitis, diverticulosis, diverticulitis.

Consult your doctor if you:
- Take this herb for any medical problem that doesn't improve in 2 weeks. There may be safer, more effective treatments.
- Take any medicinal drugs or herbs including aspirin, laxatives, cold and cough remedies, antacids, vitamins, minerals, amino acids, supplements, other prescription or non-prescription drugs.

Pregnancy:
- Dangers outweigh any possible benefits. Don't use.

Breast-feeding:
- Dangers outweigh any possible benefits. Don't use.

Infants and children:
- Treating infants and children under 2 with any herbal preparation is hazardous.

Others:
- Do not allow children to eat berries of this popular Christmas plant. As few as one or two berries may cause toxic symptoms.

Storage:
- Keep cool and dry, but don't freeze. Store safely away from children.

Safe dosage:
- At present no "safe" dosage has been established.

Toxicity

Rated slightly dangerous, particularly in children, persons over 55 and those who take larger than appropriate quantities for extended periods of time.

For symptoms of toxicity: See *Adverse Reactions, Side Effects or Overdose Symptoms* section below.

Adverse Reactions, Side Effects or Overdose Symptoms

Signs and symptoms:	What to do:
Convulsions	Seek emergency treatment.
Diarrhoea	Discontinue. Call doctor immediately.
Hallucinations	Seek emergency treatment.
Increased blood pressure	Discontinue. Call doctor immediately.
Nausea	Discontinue. Call doctor immediately.
Slow heartbeat	Seek emergency treatment.
Vomiting	Discontinue. Call doctor immediately.

Mormon Tea (Nevada Jointfir)

Basic Information

Biological name (genus and species):
  Ephedra nevadensis, E. trifurca
Parts used for medicinal purposes:
  Stems
Chemical this herb contains:
  Ephedrine

Known Effects

- Stimulates central nervous system.
- Increases blood pressure.
- Increases heart rate.
- Helps body dispose of excess fluid by increasing amount of urine produced.

Unproved Speculated Benefits

- Elevates mood.
- Treats congestive heart failure, kidney failure, liver failure.
- Decreases appetite.
- Stimulates energy.
- Treats fatigue.

Warnings and Precautions

Don't take if you:
- Are pregnant, think you may be pregnant or plan pregnancy in the near future.
- Have diabetes mellitus. It may make control with diet or insulin more difficult.
- Have heart disease.

Consult your doctor if you:
- Take this herb for any medical problem that doesn't improve in 2 weeks. There may be safer, more effective treatments.
- Take any medicinal drugs or herbs including aspirin, laxatives, cold and cough remedies, antacids, vitamins, minerals, amino acids, supplements, other prescription or non-prescription drugs.

Pregnancy:
- Dangers outweigh any possible benefits. Don't use.

Breast-feeding:
- Dangers outweigh any possible benefits. Don't use.

Infants and children:
- Treating infants and children under 2 with any herbal preparation is hazardous.

Others:
- None expected if you are beyond childhood and under 45, not pregnant, basically healthy and take for only a short time.

Storage:
- Keep cool and dry, but don't freeze. Store safely away from children.

Safe dosage:
- At present no "safe" dosage has been established.

Toxicity

Rated slightly dangerous, particularly in children, persons over 55 and those who take larger than appropriate quantities for extended periods of time.

For symptoms of toxicity: See *Adverse Reactions, Side Effects or Overdose Symptoms* section below.

Adverse Reactions, Side Effects or Overdose Symptoms

Signs and symptoms:	What to do:
Excessively high blood pressure	Seek emergency treatment.
Irregular heartbeat	Seek emergency treatment.
Rapid heartbeat	Discontinue. Call doctor immediately.

Basic Information

Biological name (genus and species):
Ipomoea purpurea
Parts used for medicinal purposes:
Seeds
Chemicals this herb contains:
Cetyl alcohol
Dihydroxycinnamic acid
Lysergic acid
Scopoletin

Known Effects

- Stimulates central nervous system.
- Stimulates gastrointestinal tract.

Miscellaneous information.
- May cause hallucinations.

Unproved Speculated Benefits

- Is used as purgative for constipation.
- Elevates mood.

Warnings and Precautions

Don't take if you:
- Are pregnant, think you may be pregnant or plan pregnancy in the near future.
- Have any chronic disease of the gastrointestinal tract, such as stomach or duodenal ulcers, oesophageal reflux (reflux oesophagitis), ulcerative colitis, spastic colitis, diverticulosis, diverticulitis.

Consult your doctor if you:
- Take this herb for any medical problem that doesn't improve in 2 weeks. There may be safer, more effective treatments.
- Take any medicinal drugs or herbs including aspirin, laxatives, cold and cough remedies, antacids, vitamins, minerals, amino acids, supplements, other prescription or non-prescription drugs.

Pregnancy:
- Problems in pregnant women taking small or usual amounts have not been proved. But the chance of problems does exist. Don't use unless prescribed by your doctor.

Breast-feeding:
- Problems in breast-fed infants of lactating mothers taking small or usual amounts have not been proved. But the chance of problems does exist. Don't use unless prescribed by your doctor.

Infants and children:
- Treating infants and children under 2 with any herbal preparation is hazardous.

Others:
- None expected if you are beyond childhood and under 45, basically healthy and take for only a short time.

Storage:
- Keep cool and dry, but don't freeze. Store safely away from children.

Safe dosage:
- At present no "safe" dosage has been established.

Toxicity

Rated slightly dangerous, particularly in children, persons over 55 and those who take larger than appropriate quantities for extended periods of time.

For symptoms of toxicity: See *Adverse Reactions, Side Effects or Overdose Symptoms* section below.

Adverse Reactions, Side Effects or Overdose Symptoms

Signs and symptoms:	What to do:
Confusion	Discontinue. Call doctor immediately.
Diarrhoea, explosive and watery	Discontinue. Call doctor immediately.
Disturbed vision	Discontinue. Call doctor immediately.
Hallucinations	Seek emergency treatment.
Nausea	Discontinue. Call doctor immediately.
Vomiting	Discontinue. Call doctor immediately.

Mountain Ash (Rowan Tree)

Basic Information

Biological name (genus and species):
Sorbus aucuparia
Parts used for medicinal purposes:
Berries/fruits
Seeds
Chemicals this herb contains:
Fixed oil (See Glossary)
Malic acid
Sorbic acid
Sorbitol
Sorbose

Known Effects

- Irritates and stimulates gastrointestinal tract.
- Helps body dispose of excess fluid by increasing amount of urine produced.

Miscellaneous information:
- Is used as a sweetener.

Unproved Speculated Benefits

- Prevents scurvy.
- Treats haemorrhoids.
- Treats stomach and duodenal ulcers.

Warnings and Precautions

Don't take if you:
- Are pregnant, think you may be pregnant or plan pregnancy in the near future.

Consult your doctor if you:
- Take this herb for any medical problem that doesn't improve in 2 weeks. There may be safer, more effective treatments.
- Take any medicinal drugs or herbs including aspirin, laxatives, cold and cough remedies, antacids, vitamins, minerals, amino acids, supplements, other prescription or non-prescription drugs.

Pregnancy:
- Problems in pregnant women taking small or usual amounts have not been proved. But the chance of problems does exist. Don't use unless prescribed by your doctor.

Breast-feeding:
- Problems in breast-fed infants of lactating mothers taking small or usual amounts have not been proved. But the chance of problems does exist. Don't use unless prescribed by your doctor.

Infants and children:
- Treating infants and children under 2 with any herbal preparation is hazardous.

Others:
- None expected if you are beyond childhood and under 45, basically healthy and take for only a short time.

Storage:
- Keep cool and dry, but don't freeze. Store safely away from children.

Safe dosage:
- At present no "safe" dosage has been established.

Toxicity

Comparative-toxicity rating not available from standard references.

For symptoms of toxicity: See *Adverse Reactions, Side Effects or Overdose Symptoms* section below.

Adverse Reactions, Side Effects or Overdose Symptoms

Signs and symptoms:	What to do:
Diarrhoea	Discontinue. Call doctor immediately.

Mountain Tobacco (Leopard's Bane, Wolf's Bane)

Basic Information

Biological name (genus and species):
Arnica montana
Parts used for medicinal purposes:
Petals/flower
Chemicals this herb contains:
Angelic acid
Arnidendiol (also found in dandelion flowers).
Choline
Fatty acids
Formic acid
Thymohydroquinone

Known Effects

- Provides counterirritation when applied to skin overlying an inflamed or irritated joint.
- Depresses central nervous system.
- Irritates gastrointestinal tract.

Unproved Speculated Benefits

- Relieves discomfort of sprains, strains, bruises when applied to skin over injury.

Warnings and Precautions

Don't take if you:
- Are pregnant, think you may be pregnant or plan pregnancy in the near future.
- Have any chronic disease of the gastrointestinal tract, such as stomach or duodenal ulcers, oesophageal reflux (reflux oesophagitis), ulcerative colitis, spastic colitis, diverticulosis, diverticulitis.

Consult your doctor if you:
- Take this herb for any medical problem that doesn't improve in 2 weeks. There may be safer, more effective treatments.
- Take any medicinal drugs or herbs including aspirin, laxatives, cold and cough remedies, antacids, vitamins, minerals, amino acids, supplements, other prescription or non-prescription drugs.

Pregnancy:
- Dangers outweigh any possible benefits. Don't use.

Breast-feeding:
- Dangers outweigh any possible benefits. Don't use.

Infants and children:
- Treating infants and children under 2 with any herbal preparation is hazardous.

Others:
- Don't take internally. Probably safe for application to skin.

Storage:
- Keep cool and dry, but don't freeze. Store safely away from children.

Safe dosage:
- At present no "safe" dosage has been established.

Toxicity

Rated slightly dangerous, particularly in children, persons over 55 and those who take larger than appropriate quantities for extended periods of time.

For symptoms of toxicity: See *Adverse Reactions, Side Effects or Overdose Symptoms* section below.

Adverse Reactions, Side Effects or Overdose Symptoms

Signs and symptoms:	What to do:
Explosive, watery diarrhoea	Discontinue. Call doctor immediately.
Heartbeat irregularities	Seek emergency treatment.
Muscle weakness	Discontinue. Call doctor immediately.
Nausea	Discontinue. Call doctor immediately.
Precipitous blood-pressure drop—symptoms include, faintness, cold sweat, paleness, rapid pulse	Seek emergency treatment.
Vomiting	Discontinue. Call doctor immediately.

Mulberry

Basic Information

Biological name (genus and species):
Morus rubra
Parts used for medicinal purposes:
Bark
Berries/fruits
Chemicals this herb contains:
Unidentified

 Known Effects

- Stimulates gastrointestinal tract.
- Depresses central nervous system.

 Unproved Speculated Benefits

- Reduces fever.
- Induces drowsiness.
- Acts as a mild laxative.

 Warnings and Precautions

Don't take if you:
- Are pregnant, think you may be pregnant or plan pregnancy in the near future.
- Have any chronic disease of the gastrointestinal tract, such as stomach or duodenal ulcers, oesophageal reflux (reflux oesophagitis), ulcerative colitis, spastic colitis, diverticulosis, diverticulitis.

Consult your doctor if you:
- Take this herb for any medical problem that doesn't improve in 2 weeks. There may be safer, more effective treatments.
- Take any medicinal drugs or herbs including aspirin, laxatives, cold and cough remedies, antacids, vitamins, minerals, amino acids, supplements, other prescription or non-prescription drugs.

Pregnancy:
- Dangers outweigh any possible benefits. Don't use.

Breast-feeding:
- Dangers outweigh any possible benefits. Don't use.

Infants and children:
- Treating infants and children under 2 with any herbal preparation is hazardous.

Others:
- This product will not help you and may cause toxic symptoms.

Storage:
- Keep cool and dry, but don't freeze. Store safely away from children.

Safe dosage:
- At present no "safe" dosage has been established.

 Toxicity

Comparative-toxicity rating not available from standard references.

For symptoms of toxicity: See *Adverse Reactions, Side Effects or Overdose Symptoms* section below.

 Adverse Reactions, Side Effects or Overdose Symptoms

Signs and symptoms:	What to do:
Diarrhoea	Discontinue. Call doctor immediately.
Hallucinations	Seek emergency treatment.
Nausea	Discontinue. Call doctor immediately.
Vomiting	Discontinue. Call doctor immediately.

Basic Information

Biological name (genus and species):
Verbascum thapsiforme, V. phlomoides,
V. thapsus
Parts used for medicinal purposes:
Leaves
Chemical this herb contains:
Saponins (See Glossary)

Known Effects

- Covers and protects scraped tissues.
- Softens and soothes irritated skin.
- Shrinks tissues.
- Prevents secretion of fluids.

Miscellaneous information:
- Action of mullein when taken orally is probably too weak to be effective.

Unproved Speculated Benefits

- Smoking mullein relieves bronchial irritation.
- Topical applications treat sunburn, haemorrhoids, injured skin and mucous membranes.

Warnings and Precautions

Don't take if you:
- Are pregnant, think you may be pregnant or plan pregnancy in the near future.

Consult your doctor if you:
- Take this herb for any medical problem that doesn't improve in 2 weeks. There may be safer, more effective treatments.
- Take any medicinal drugs or herbs including aspirin, laxatives, cold and cough remedies, antacids, vitamins, minerals, amino acids, supplements, other prescription or non-prescription drugs.

Pregnancy:
- Problems in pregnant women taking small or usual amounts have not been proved. But the chance of problems does exist. Don't use unless prescribed by your doctor.

Breast-feeding:
- Problems in breast-fed infants of lactating mothers taking small or usual amounts have not been proved. But the chance of problems does exist. Don't use unless prescribed by your doctor.

Infants and children:
- Treating infants and children under 2 with any herbal preparation is hazardous.

Others:
- None expected if you are beyond childhood and under 45, basically healthy and take for only a short time.

Storage:
- Keep cool and dry, but don't freeze. Store safely away from children.

Safe dosage:
- At present no "safe" dosage has been established.

Toxicity

Comparative-toxicity rating not available from standard references.

Adverse Reactions, Side Effects or Overdose Symptoms

None expected

Myrrh

Basic Information

Biological name (genus and species):
   Commiphora molmol
Parts used for medicinal purposes:
   Leaves
   Resin from stems
Chemicals this herb contains:
   Acetic acid
   Formic acid
   Myrrholic acids
   Resin (See Glossary)
   Volatile oils (See Glossary)

Known Effects

- Stimulates muscular movements of intestines.
- Shrinks tissues.
- Prevents secretion of fluids to mucous membranes.
- Stimulates gastrointestinal tract.
- Aids in expelling gas from intestinal tract.

Miscellaneous information:
- Primary use of myrrh is in perfumes and incense.

Unproved Speculated Benefits

- Causes watery, explosive bowel movements.
- Treats dyspepsia.
- Is used as mouthwash.

Warnings and Precautions

Don't take if you:
- Are pregnant, think you may be pregnant or plan pregnancy in the near future.

Consult your doctor if you:
- Take this herb for any medical problem that doesn't improve in 2 weeks. There may be safer, more effective treatments.
- Take any medicinal drugs or herbs including aspirin, laxatives, cold and cough remedies, antacids, vitamins, minerals, amino acids, supplements, other prescription or non-prescription drugs.

Pregnancy:
- Problems in pregnant women taking small or usual amounts have not been proved. But the chance of problems does exist. Don't use unless prescribed by your doctor.

Breast-feeding:
- Problems in breast-fed infants of lactating mothers taking small or usual amounts have not been proved. But the chance of problems does exist. Don't use unless prescribed by your doctor.

Infants and children:
- Treating infants and children under 2 with any herbal preparation is hazardous.

Others:
- None expected if you are under 45, not pregnant, basically healthy, take it for only a short time and do not exceed manufacturer's recommended dosage.

Storage:
- Keep cool and dry, but don't freeze. Store safely away from children.

Safe dosage:
- At present no "safe" dosage has been established.

Toxicity

Comparative-toxicity rating not available from standard references.

For symptoms of toxicity: See *Adverse Reactions, Side Effects or Overdose Symptoms* section below.

Adverse Reactions, Side Effects or Overdose Symptoms

Signs and symptoms:	What to do:
Convulsions	Seek emergency treatment.
Drowsiness	Discontinue. Call doctor when convenient.
Lethargy	Discontinue. Call doctor when convenient.

Basic Information

Biological name (genus and species):
Myrtus communis
Parts used for medicinal purposes:
Leaves
Chemicals this herb contains:
d-pinene
Eucalyptol
Myrol

Known Effects

- Irritates mucous membranes.
- Large amounts may depress central nervous system.

Miscellaneous Information:
- Myrtle is used as a condiment, flavouring and perfume essence.

Unproved Speculated Benefits

- Is used as gargle.
- Treats stomach irritations.
- Treats bronchitis.
- Treats cystitis.

Warnings and Precautions

Don't take if you:
- Are pregnant, think you may be pregnant or plan pregnancy in the near future.
- Have chronic kidney disease.

Consult your doctor if you:
- Take this herb for any medical problem that doesn't improve in 2 weeks. There may be safer, more effective treatments.
- Take any medicinal drugs or herbs including aspirin, laxatives, cold and cough remedies, antacids, vitamins, minerals, amino acids, supplements, other prescription or non-prescription drugs.

Pregnancy:
- Problems in pregnant women taking small or usual amounts have not been proved. But the chance of problems does exist. Don't use unless prescribed by your doctor.

Breast-feeding:
- Problems in breast-fed infants of lactating mothers taking small or usual amounts have not been proved. But the chance of problems does exist. Don't use unless prescribed by your doctor.

Infants and children:
- Treating infants and children under 2 with any herbal preparation is hazardous.

Others:
- None expected if you are beyond childhood and under 45, basically healthy and take for only a short time.

Storage:
- Keep cool and dry, but don't freeze. Store safely away from children.

Safe dosage:
- At present no "safe" dosage has been established.

Toxicity

Comparative-toxicity rating not available from standard references.

For symptoms of toxicity: See *Adverse Reactions, Side Effects or Overdose Symptoms* section below.

Adverse Reactions, Side Effects or Overdose Symptoms

Signs and symptoms:	What to do:
Coma	Seek emergency treatment.
Convulsions	Seek emergency treatment.
Kidney damage characterized by blood in urine, decreased urine flow, swelling of hands and feet	Seek emergency treatment.

Oak Bark

Basic Information

Biological name (genus and species):
Quercus
Parts used for medicinal purposes:
Bark
Seeds
Chemical this herb contains:
Quercitannic acid

Known Effects

- Shrinks tissues.
- Prevents secretion of fluids.
- Causes protein molecules to clump together.

Unproved Speculated Benefits

- Treats haemorrhoids.
- Treats diarrhoea.
- Is used as gargle for sore throats.

Warnings and Precautions

Don't take if you:
- Are pregnant, think you may be pregnant or plan pregnancy in the near future.
- Have any chronic disease of the gastrointestinal tract, such as stomach or duodenal ulcers, oesophageal reflux (reflux oesophagitis), ulcerative colitis, spastic colitis, diverticulosis, diverticulitis.

Consult your doctor if you:
- Take this herb for any medical problem that doesn't improve in 2 weeks. There may be safer, more effective treatments.
- Take any medicinal drugs or herbs including aspirin, laxatives, cold and cough remedies, antacids, vitamins, minerals, amino acids, supplements, other prescription or non-prescription drugs.

Pregnancy:
- Dangers outweigh any possible benefits. Don't use.

Breast-feeding:
- Dangers outweigh any possible benefits. Don't use.

Infants and children:
- Treating infants and children under 2 with any herbal preparation is hazardous.

Others:
- None expected if you are beyond childhood and under 45, basically healthy and take for only a short time.

Storage:
- Keep cool and dry, but don't freeze. Store safely away from children.

Safe dosage:
- At present no "safe" dosage has been established.

Toxicity

Comparative-toxicity rating not available from standard references.

For symptoms of toxicity: See *Adverse Reactions, Side Effects or Overdose Symptoms* section below.

Adverse Reactions, Side Effects or Overdose Symptoms

Signs and symptoms:	What to do:
Constipation	Discontinue. Call doctor when convenient.
Dry mouth	Discontinue. Call doctor when convenient.
Increased urination	Discontinue. Call doctor when convenient.
Jaundice (yellow skin and eyes)	Discontinue. Call doctor immediately.
Kidney damage characterized by blood in urine, decreased urine flow, swelling of hands and feet	Seek emergency treatment.
Skin eruptions	Discontinue. Call doctor when convenient.
Thirst	Discontinue. Call doctor when convenient.

Basic Information

Biological name (genus and species):
Avena sativa
Parts used for medicinal purposes:
Seeds
Chemicals this herb contains:
Albumin
Gluten
Gum oil
Protein compound
Salts
Saponin (See Glossary)
Starch
Sugar

Known Effects

- Stimulates muscular contractions.
- Coats and protects scraped tissues.
- Stimulates central nervous system.

Miscellaneous information:
- "Feeling his oats" refers to the stimulant effect of this herb on some animals, particularly horses.

Unproved Speculated Benefits

- Is a satisfactory food source.
- Is used as a tonic.
- Decreases depression.
- Decreases dependence on nicotine and narcotics.

Warnings and Precautions

Don't take if you:
- No absolute contraindications.

Consult your doctor if you:
- Take this herb for any medical problem that doesn't improve in 2 weeks. There may be safer, more effective treatments.
- Take any medicinal drugs or herbs including aspirin, laxatives, cold and cough remedies, antacids, vitamins, minerals, amino acids, supplements, other prescription or non-prescription drugs.

Pregnancy:
- Pregnant women should experience no problems taking usual amounts as part of a balanced diet. Other products extracted from this substance have not been proved to cause problems.

Breast-feeding:
- Breast-fed infants of lactating mothers should experience no problems when mother takes usual amounts as part of a balanced diet. Other products extracted from this substance have not been proved to cause problems.

Infants and children:
- Treating infants and children under 2 with any herbal preparation is hazardous.

Others:
- None expected if you are beyond childhood and under 45, basically healthy and take for only a short time.

Storage:
- Keep cool and dry, but don't freeze. Store safely away from children.

Safe dosage:
- At present no "safe" dosage has been established.

Toxicity

Comparative-toxicity rating not available from standard references.

Adverse Reactions, Side Effects or Overdose Symptoms

None expected

MEDICINAL HERB

Orris Root (Black Flag)

Basic Information

Biological name (genus and species):
Iris versicolor, Iris spp
Parts used for medicinal purposes:
Roots
Chemicals this herb contains:
Gum (See Glossary)
Oleoresin (See Glossary)
Tannins (See Glossary)

Known Effects

- Depresses central nervous system.
- Causes vomiting.
- Interferes with absorption of iron and other minerals when taken internally.

Unproved Speculated Benefits

- Treats skin disorders.
- Treats arthritis.
- Treats tumours.

Warnings and Precautions

Don't take if you:
- Are pregnant, think you may be pregnant or plan pregnancy in the near future.
- Have any chronic disease of the gastrointestinal tract, such as stomach or duodenal ulcers, oesophageal reflux (reflux oesophagitis), ulcerative colitis, spastic colitis, diverticulosis, diverticulitis.

Consult your doctor if you:
- Take this herb for any medical problem that doesn't improve in 2 weeks. There may be safer, more effective treatments.
- Take any medicinal drugs or herbs including aspirin, laxatives, cold and cough remedies, antacids, vitamins, minerals, amino acids, supplements, other prescription or non-prescription drugs.

Pregnancy:
- Problems in pregnant women taking small or usual doses have not been proved. But the chance of problems does exist. Don't use unless prescribed by your doctor.

Breast-feeding:
- Problems in breast-fed infants of lactating mothers taking small or usual doses have not been proved. But the chance of problems does exist. Don't use unless prescribed by your doctor.

Infants and children:
- Treating infants and children under 2 with any herbal preparation is hazardous.

Others:
- Don't use. This product will not help you and may cause toxic symptoms.

Storage:
- Keep cool and dry, but don't freeze. Store safely away from children.

Safe dosage:
- At present no "safe" dosage has been established.

Toxicity

Rated relatively safe when taken in appropriate quantities for short periods of time.

For symptoms of toxicity: See *Adverse Reactions, Side Effects or Overdose Symptoms* section below.

Adverse Reactions, Side Effects or Overdose Symptoms

Signs and symptoms:	What to do:
Burning sensation in throat and mouth	Discontinue. Call doctor when convenient.
Cramping abdominal pain	Discontinue. Call doctor when convenient.
Nausea	Discontinue. Call doctor immediately.
Vomiting	Discontinue. Call doctor immediately.
Watery diarrhoea	Discontinue. Call doctor immediately.

Basic Information

Biological name (genus and species):
  Carica papaya
Parts used for medicinal purposes:
  Berries/fruits
  Inner bark
  Stems
Chemicals this herb contains:
  Amlylolytic enzyme
  Caricin
  Myrosin
  Peptidase
  Vitamins C and E

Known Effects

- Stimulates stomach to increase secretions.
- Releases histamine from body tissues.
- Depresses central nervous system.
- Kills some intestinal parasites.

Miscellaneous information:
- When eaten as a common food, no problems are expected.
- Is used as a meat tenderizer

Unproved Speculated Benefits

- Aids digestion.
- Liquifies excessive mucus in mouth and stomach.
- Inner bark treats sore teeth.

Warnings and Precautions

Don't take if you:
- Are pregnant, think you may be pregnant or plan pregnancy in the near future.
- Have any chronic disease of the gastrointestinal tract, such as stomach or duodenal ulcers, oesophageal reflux (reflux oesophagitis), ulcerative colitis, spastic colitis, diverticulosis, diverticulitis.

Consult your doctor if you:
- Take this herb for any medical problem that doesn't improve in 2 weeks. There may be safer, more effective treatments.
- Take any medicinal drugs or herbs including aspirin, laxatives, cold and cough remedies, antacids, vitamins, minerals, amino acids, supplements, other prescription or non-prescription drugs.

Pregnancy:
- Pregnant women should experience no problems taking usual amounts as part of a balanced diet. Other products extracted from this herb have not been proved to cause problems.

Breast-feeding:
- Breast-fed infants of lactating mothers should experience no problems when mother takes usual amounts as part of a balanced diet. Other products extracted from this herb have not been proved to cause problems.

Infants and children:
- Treating infants and children under 2 with any herbal preparation is hazardous.

Others:
- None expected if you are beyond childhood and under 45, basically healthy and take for only a short time.

Storage:
- Keep cool and dry, but don't freeze. Store safely away from children.

Safe dosage:
- At present no "safe" dosage has been established.

Toxicity

Generally regarded as safe when taken in appropriate quantities for short periods of time.

For symptoms of toxicity: See *Adverse Reactions, Side Effects or Overdose Symptoms* section below.

Adverse Reactions, Side Effects or Overdose Symptoms

Signs and symptoms:	What to do:
Heartburn caused by irritation of lower part of oesophagus	Discontinue. Call doctor when convenient.

Parsley

Basic Information

Biological name (genus and species):
  Petroselinum sativum
Parts used for medicinal purposes:
  Berries/fruits
  Leaves
  Roots
  Stems
Chemicals this herb contains:
  Apiin (Also called parsley camphor)
  Apiol
  Pinene
  Volatile oils (See Glossary)

Known Effects

- Decreases blood pressure.
- Decreases pulse rate.
- Aids digestion.
- Helps body dispose of excess fluid by increasing amounts of urine produced.

Miscellaneous information:
- When fresh sprigs are eaten, no problems are expected.

Unproved Speculated Benefits

- Treats painful menstruation.
- Causes abortions.
- Treats dyspepsia.

Warnings and Precautions

Don't take if you:
- Are pregnant, think you may be pregnant or plan pregnancy in the near future.
- Have any chronic disease of the gastrointestinal tract, such as stomach or duodenal ulcers, oesophageal reflux (reflux oesophagitis), ulcerative colitis, spastic colitis, diverticulosis, diverticulitis.

Consult your doctor if you:
- Take this herb for any medical problem that doesn't improve in 2 weeks. There may be safer, more effective treatments.
- Take any medicinal drugs or herbs including aspirin, laxatives, cold and cough remedies, antacids, vitamins, minerals, amino acids, supplements, other prescription or non-prescription drugs.

Pregnancy:
- Dangers outweigh any possible benefits. Avoid taking *any* herbal medication made from parsley. It is all right to eat fresh parsley as a condiment.

Breast-feeding:
- Dangers outweigh any possible benefits. Avoid taking *any* herbal medication made from parsley. It is all right to eat fresh parsley as a condiment.

Infants and children:
- Treating infants and children under 2 with any herbal preparation is hazardous.

Others:
- None expected if you are beyond childhood and under 45, not pregnant, basically healthy and take for only a short time.

Storage:
- Keep cool and dry, but don't freeze. Store safely away from children.

Safe dosage:
- At present no "safe" dosage has been established.

Toxicity

Rated relatively safe when taken in appropriate quantities for short periods of time.

For symptoms of toxicity: See *Adverse Reactions, Side Effects or Overdose Symptoms* section below.

Adverse Reactions, Side Effects or Overdose Symptoms

Signs and symptoms:	What to do:
Dizziness	Discontinue. Call doctor immediately.
Jaundice (yellow skin and eyes)	Discontinue. Call doctor immediately.
Nausea	Discontinue. Call doctor immediately.
Vomiting	Discontinue. Call doctor immediately.

Basic Information

Biological name (genus and species):
Mitchella repens
Parts used for medicinal purposes:
Stems
Chemicals this herb contains:
Dextrin
Mucilage (See Glossary)
Saponins (See Glossary)
Wax (See Glossary)

Known Effects

• Helps body dispose of excess fluid by increasing amount of urine produced.
• Shrinks tissues.
• Prevents secretion of fluids.

Unproved Speculated Benefits

• Makes labour less difficult.
• Helps flow of milk in lactating women.
• Treats insomnia.
• Decreases diarrhoea.
• Treats congestive heart failure, kidney failure, liver failure.

Warnings and Precautions

Don't take if you:
• Are pregnant, think you may be pregnant or plan pregnancy in the near future.

Consult your doctor if you:
• Take this herb for any medical problem that doesn't improve in 2 weeks. There may be safer, more effective treatments.
• Take any medicinal drugs or herbs including aspirin, laxatives, cold and cough remedies, antacids, vitamins, minerals, amino acids, supplements, other prescription or non-prescription drugs.

Pregnancy:
• Problems in pregnant women taking small or usual amounts have not been proved. But the chance of problems does exist. Don't use unless prescribed by your doctor.

Breast-feeding:
• Problems in breast-fed infants of lactating mothers taking small or usual amounts have not been proved. But the chance of problems does exist. Don't use unless prescribed by your doctor.

Infants and children:
• Treating infants and children under 2 with any herbal preparation is hazardous.

Others:
• None expected if you are beyond childhood and under 45, basically healthy and take for only a short time.

Storage:
• Keep cool and dry, but don't freeze. Store safely away from children.

Safe dosage:
• At present no "safe" dosage has been established.

Toxicity

Rated relatively safe when taken in appropriate quantities for short periods of time.

Adverse Reactions, Side Effects or Overdose Symptoms

None expected

Pasque Flower (May Flower, Pulsatilla)

Basic Information

Biological name (genus and species):
  Anemone pulsatilla
Parts used for medicinal purposes:
  Petals/flower
  Roots
Chemicals this herb contains:
  Anemone camphor
  Ranunculin
  Tannins (See Glossary)
  Volatile oils (See Glossary)

Known Effects

- Irritates mucous membranes.
- Shrinks tissues.
- Prevents secretion of fluids.
- Decreases thickness and increases fluidity of mucus from lungs and bronchial tubes.
- Interferes with absorption of iron and other minerals when taken internally.

Unproved Speculated Benefits

- Treats menstrual disorders.
- Depresses sexual excitement.
- Increases sexual strength.

Warnings and Precautions

Don't take if you:
- Are pregnant, think you may be pregnant or plan pregnancy in the near future.
- Have any chronic disease of the gastrointestinal tract, such as stomach or duodenal ulcers, oesophageal reflux (reflux oesophagitis), ulcerative colitis, spastic colitis, diverticulosis, diverticulitis.

Consult your doctor if you:
- Take this herb for any medical problem that doesn't improve in 2 weeks. There may be safer, more effective treatments.
- Take any medicinal drugs or herbs including aspirin, laxatives, cold and cough remedies, antacids, vitamins, minerals, amino acids, supplements, other prescription or non-prescription drugs.

Pregnancy:
- Dangers outweigh any possible benefits. Don't use.

Breast-feeding:
- Dangers outweigh any possible benefits. Don't use.

Infants and children:
- Treating infants and children under 2 with any herbal preparation is hazardous.

Others:
- None expected if you are beyond childhood and under 45, basically healthy and take for only a short time.

Storage:
- Keep cool and dry, but don't freeze. Store safely away from children.

Safe dosage:
- At present no "safe" dosage has been established.

Toxicity

Rated slightly dangerous, particularly in children, persons over 55 and those who take larger than appropriate quantities for extended periods of time.

For symptoms of toxicity: See *Adverse Reactions, Side Effects or Overdose Symptoms* section below.

Adverse Reactions, Side Effects or Overdose Symptoms

Signs and symptoms:	What to do:
Abdominal pain	Discontinue. Call doctor when convenient.
Diarrhoea	Discontinue. Call doctor immediately.
Kidney damage characterized by blood in urine, decreased urine flow, swelling of hands and feet	Seek emergency treatment.
Nausea	Discontinue. Call doctor immediately.
Vomiting	Discontinue. Call doctor immediately.

Basic Information

Biological name (genus and species):
Passiflora incarnata
Parts used for medicinal purposes:
Flowers
Fruit
Chemicals this herb contains:
Cyanogenic glycosides (See Glossary)
Harmaline
Harman
Harmine
Harmol

Known Effects

- Depresses nerve transfer in spinal cord and brain.
- Increases respiratory rate.
- Slightly depresses central nervous system.
- Causes hallucinations.

Miscellaneous information:
- Smoking passion flower reportedly causes mental changes similar to marijuana.

Unproved Speculated Benefits

- Reduces headaches.
- Treats epilepsy.
- Treats convulsions.
- Treats insomnia.
- Is used as "nerve tonic."
- Acts as a tranquilizer.

Warnings and Precautions

Don't take if you:
- Are pregnant, think you may be pregnant or plan pregnancy in the near future.

Consult your doctor if you:
- Take this herb for any medical problem that doesn't improve in 2 weeks. There may be safer, more effective treatments.
- Take any medicinal drugs or herbs including aspirin, laxatives, cold and cough remedies, antacids, vitamins, minerals, amino acids, supplements, other prescription or non-prescription drugs.

Pregnancy:
- Dangers outweigh any possible benefits. Don't use.

Breast-feeding:
- Dangers outweigh any possible benefits. Don't use.

Infants and children:
- Treating infants and children under 2 with any herbal preparation is hazardous.

Others:
- This product will not help you. It may cause toxic symptoms.

Storage:
- Keep cool and dry, but don't freeze. Store safely away from children.

Safe dosage:
- At present no "safe" dosage has been established.

Toxicity

Rated relatively safe when taken in appropriate quantities for short periods of time.

For symptoms of toxicity: See *Adverse Reactions, Side Effects or Overdose Symptoms* section below.

Adverse Reactions, Side Effects or Overdose Symptoms

Signs and symptoms:	What to do:
Convulsions	Seek emergency treatment.
Decreased body temperature	Discontinue. Call doctor immediately.
Hallucinations	Seek emergency treatment.
Muscle paralysis, including muscles used in breathing	Seek emergency treatment.

Peach

Basic Information

Biological name (genus and species):
   Prunus persica or other Prunus species
Parts used for medicinal purposes:
   Bark
   Leaves
   Roots
   Seeds
Chemicals this herb contains:
   Cyanide, especially in kernels
   Phloretin
   Volatile oils *(See Glossary)*

Known Effects

- Irritates and stimulates gastrointestinal tract.

Miscellaneous information:
- North-American Indians made tea from bark.
- Fruit, except for peach pit, is safe.

Unproved Speculated Benefits

- Treats constipation (leaves).
- Treats systemic infections (bark and roots).

Warnings and Precautions

Don't take if you:
- Are pregnant, think you may be pregnant or plan pregnancy in the near future.
- Have any chronic disease of the gastrointestinal tract, such as stomach or duodenal ulcers, oesophageal reflux (reflux oesophagitis), ulcerative colitis, spastic colitis, diverticulosis, diverticulitis.

Consult your doctor if you:
- Take this herb for any medical problem that doesn't improve in 2 weeks. There may be safer, more effective treatments.
- Take any medicinal drugs or herbs including aspirin, laxatives, cold and cough remedies, antacids, vitamins, minerals, amino acids, supplements, other prescription or non-prescription drugs.

Pregnancy:
- Dangers of taking this as a medicinal herb outweigh any possible benefits. Avoid pits! There should be no problems with fruit.

Breast-feeding:
- Dangers of taking this as a medicinal herb outweigh any possible benefits. Avoid pits! There should be no problems with fruit.

Infants and children:
- Treating infants and children under 2 with any herbal preparation is hazardous.

Others:
- Pits will not help you. They may cause toxic symptoms.

Storage:
- Keep cool and dry, but don't freeze. Store safely away from children.

Safe dosage:
- At present no "safe" dosage has been established.

Toxicity

Comparative-toxicity rating not available from standard references.

For symptoms of toxicity: See *Adverse Reactions, Side Effects or Overdose Symptoms* section below.

Adverse Reactions, Side Effects or Overdose Symptoms

Signs and symptoms:	What to do:
Diarrhoea	Discontinue. Call doctor immediately.
Nausea	Discontinue. Call doctor immediately.
Vomiting	Discontinue. Call doctor immediately.

Basic Information

Biological name (genus and species):
   Anacyclus pyrethrum
Parts used for medicinal purposes:
   Various parts of the entire plant, frequently
   differing by country and/or culture
Chemical this herb contains:
   Pellitorine

Known Effects

• Kills insects.

Miscellaneous information:
• Tastes bitter.

Unproved Speculated Benefits

• Relieves pain from toothache or gum infections.
• Relieves facial pain.
• Increases saliva flow.

Warnings and Precautions

Don't take if you:
• Are pregnant, think you may be pregnant or plan pregnancy in the near future.
• Have any chronic disease of the gastrointestinal tract, such as stomach or duodenal ulcers, oesophageal reflux (reflux oesophagitis), ulcerative colitis, spastic colitis, diverticulosis, diverticulitis.

Consult your doctor if you:
• Take this herb for any medical problem that doesn't improve in 2 weeks. There may be safer, more effective treatments.
• Take any medicinal drugs or herbs including aspirin, laxatives, cold and cough remedies, antacids, vitamins, minerals, amino acids, supplements, other prescription or non-prescription drugs.

Pregnancy:
• Problems in pregnant women taking small or usual amounts have not been proved. But the chance of problems does exist. Don't use unless prescribed by your doctor.

Breast-feeding:
• Problems in breast-fed infants of lactating mothers taking small or usual amounts have not been proved. But the chance of problems does exist. Don't use unless prescribed by your doctor.

Infants and children:
• Treating infants and children under 2 with any herbal preparation is hazardous.

Others:
• None expected if you are beyond childhood and under 45, basically healthy and take for only a short time.

Storage:
• Keep cool and dry, but don't freeze. Store safely away from children.

Safe dosage:
• At present no "safe" dosage has been established.

Toxicity

Comparative-toxicity rating not available from standard references.

For symptoms of toxicity: See *Adverse Reactions, Side Effects or Overdose Symptoms* section below.

Adverse Reactions, Side Effects or Overdose Symptoms

Signs and symptoms:	What to do:
Diarrhoea	Discontinue. Call doctor immediately.
Nausea	Discontinue. Call doctor immediately.
Vomiting	Discontinue. Call doctor immediately.

MEDICINAL HERB

Pennyroyal

Basic Information

Biological name (genus and species):
Mentha pulegium, Hedeoma pulegioides
Parts used for medicinal purposes:
Entire plant
Chemical this herb contains:
Puligone (yellow or green-yellow oil)

Known Effects

- Stimulates uterine contractions.
- Depresses central nervous system.
- Irritates mucous membranes.
- Reddens skin by increasing blood supply to it.
- Increases salivation.
- Can cause severe liver and kidney damage.

Miscellaneous information:
- Pennyroyal is used as a flavouring agent.
- As little as 2 ounces of the essential oil can cause severe liver and kidney damage.

Unproved Speculated Benefits

- Causes abortions.
- Decreases intestinal cramps and flatulence.
- "Purifies" blood.
- Treats colds.
- Regulates menstruation.
- Increases perspiration.

Warnings and Precautions

Don't take if you:
- Are pregnant, think you may be pregnant or plan pregnancy in the near future.

Consult your doctor if you:
- Take this herb for any medical problem that doesn't improve in 2 weeks. There may be safer, more effective treatments.
- Take any medicinal drugs or herbs including aspirin, laxatives, cold and cough remedies, antacids, vitamins, minerals, amino acids, supplements, other prescription or non-prescription drugs.

Pregnancy:
- Dangers outweigh any possible benefits. Don't use.

Breast-feeding:
- Dangers outweigh any possible benefits. Don't use.

Infants and children:
- Treating infants and children under 2 with any herbal preparation is hazardous.

Others:
- Don't use in an attempt to induce abortion. Pennyroyal can be deadly.

Storage:
- Keep cool and dry, but don't freeze. Store safely away from children.

Safe dosage:
- At present no "safe" dosage has been established.

Toxicity

Rated relatively safe when taken in appropriate quantities for short periods of time.

For symptoms of toxicity: See *Adverse Reactions, Side Effects or Overdose Symptoms* section below.

Adverse Reactions, Side Effects or Overdose Symptoms

Signs and symptoms:	What to do:
Bleeding from gastrointestinal tract	Seek emergency treatment.
Blood in urine	Seek emergency treatment.
Jaundice (yellow skin and eyes)	Discontinue. Call doctor immediately.
Seizures	Seek emergency treatment.
Unusual vaginal bleeding	Seek emergency treatment.

Basic Information

Biological name (genus and species):
    Mentha piperita
Parts used for medicinal purposes:
    Flowering tops
    Leaves
Chemicals this herb contains:
    Menthol
    Menthone
    Methyl acetate
    Tannic acid
    Terpenes (See Glossary)
    Volatile oils (See Glossary)

Known Effects

- Increases stomach acidity.
- Irritates and stimulates gastrointestinal tract.
- Irritates mucous membranes.
- Interferes with absorption of iron and other minerals when taken internally.

Miscellaneous information:
- Peppermint is used to add flavour to medical and non-medical preparations.
- No effects are expected on the body, either good or bad, when herb is used in very small amounts to enhance the flavour of food.

Unproved Speculated Benefits

- Treats colic.
- Treats abdominal cramps.
- Aids in expelling gas from intestinal tract.

Warnings and Precautions

Don't take if you:
- Are pregnant, think you may be pregnant or plan pregnancy in the near future.
- Have any chronic disease of the gastrointestinal tract, such as stomach or duodenal ulcers, oesophageal reflux (reflux oesophagitis), ulcerative colitis, spastic colitis, diverticulosis, diverticulitis.

Consult your doctor if you:
- Take this herb for any medical problem that doesn't improve in 2 weeks. There may be safer, more effective treatments.
- Take any medicinal drugs or herbs including aspirin, laxatives, cold and cough remedies, antacids, vitamins, minerals, amino acids, supplements, other prescription or non-prescription drugs.

Pregnancy:
- Problems in pregnant women taking small or usual amounts have not been proved. But the chance of problems does exist. Don't use unless prescribed by your doctor.

Breast-feeding:
- Problems in breast-fed infants of lactating mothers taking small or usual amounts have not been proved. But the chance of problems does exist. Don't use unless prescribed by your doctor.

Infants and children:
- Treating infants and children under 2 with any herbal preparation is hazardous.

Others:
- None expected if you are under 45, not pregnant, basically healthy, take it for only a short time and do not exceed manufacturer's recommended dosage.

Storage:
- Keep cool and dry, but don't freeze. Store safely away from children.

Safe dosage:
- At present no "safe" dosage has been established.

Toxicity

Comparative-toxicity rating not available from standard references.

For symptoms of toxicity: See *Adverse Reactions, Side Effects or Overdose Symptoms* section below.

Adverse Reactions, Side Effects or Overdose Symptoms

Signs and symptoms:	What to do:
Drowsiness	Discontinue. Call doctor when convenient.
Vomiting	Discontinue. Call doctor immediately.

Periwinkle (Madagascar or Cape Periwinkle, Old Maid)

Basic Information

Biological name (genus and species):
   Catharanthus roseus, Vinca rosea
Parts used for medicinal purposes:
   Leaves
Chemicals this herb contains:
   Vinblastine
   Vincristine
   Vinleurosine
   Vinrosidine

Known Effects

- Inhibits growth and development of germs.
- Depresses bone-marrow production, damaging body's blood-cell-manufacturing processes.
- Effective in treatment of several different types of malignant tumours.
- Reduces granulocytes—white blood cells—in body.

Miscellaneous information:
- When purified, derivatives of Vinca (vincristine sulphate, vinblastine sulphate), are used to treat cancer under rigidly controlled supervision.

Unproved Speculated Benefits

- Ointment decreases inflammation.
- Treats sore throats and inflamed tonsils.
- Treats diabetes mellitus.
- Causes hallucinations when smoked.

Warnings and Precautions

Don't take if you:
- Are pregnant, think you may be pregnant or plan pregnancy in the near future.
- Have any chronic disease of the gastrointestinal tract, such as stomach or duodenal ulcers, oesophageal reflux (reflux oesophagitis), ulcerative colitis, spastic colitis, diverticulosis, diverticulitis.

Consult your doctor if you:
- Take this herb for any medical problem that doesn't improve in 2 weeks. There may be safer, more effective treatments.
- Take any medicinal drugs or herbs including aspirin, laxatives, cold and cough remedies, antacids, vitamins, minerals, amino acids, supplements, other prescription or non-prescription drugs.

Pregnancy:
- Dangers outweigh any possible benefits. Don't use.

Breast-feeding:
- Dangers outweigh any possible benefits. Don't use.

Infants and children:
- Treating infants and children under 2 with any herbal preparation is hazardous.

Others:
- This product will not help you. It may cause toxic symptoms.

Storage:
- Keep cool and dry, but don't freeze. Store safely away from children.

Safe dosage:
- At present no "safe" dosage has been established.

Toxicity

Rated slightly dangerous, particularly in children, persons over 55 and those who take larger than appropriate quantities for extended periods of time.

For symptoms of toxicity: See *Adverse Reactions, Side Effects or Overdose Symptoms* section below.

Adverse Reactions, Side Effects or Overdose Symptoms

Signs and symptoms:	What to do:
Drowsiness	Discontinue. Call doctor when convenient.
Hair loss	Discontinue. Call doctor when convenient.
Nausea	Discontinue. Call doctor immediately.
Seizures	Seek emergency treatment.
Yellow eyes, dark urine and yellow skin resulting from destruction of some liver cells	Seek emergency treatment.

Basic Information

Biological name (genus and species):
Chimaphila
Parts used for medicinal purposes:
Leaves
Chemicals this herb contains:
Arbutin
Chimaphilin
Chlorophyll
Ericolin
Minerals
Pectic acid
Tannins (See Glossary)
Urson

 ## Known Effects

- Helps body dispose of excess fluid by increasing amount of urine produced.
- Interferes with absorption of iron and other minerals when taken internally.

 ## Unproved Speculated Benefits

- Treats indigestion or mild stomach upsets.
- Treats irritations of urinary tract (kidney, bladder, urethra).

 ## Warnings and Precautions

Don't take if you:
- Are pregnant, think you may be pregnant or plan pregnancy in the near future.
- Have any chronic disease of the gastrointestinal tract, such as stomach or duodenal ulcers, oesophageal reflux (reflux oesophagitis), ulcerative colitis, spastic colitis, diverticulosis, diverticulitis.

Consult your doctor if you:
- Take this herb for any medical problem that doesn't improve in 2 weeks. There may be safer, more effective treatments.
- Take any medicinal drugs or herbs including aspirin, laxatives, cold and cough remedies, antacids, vitamins, minerals, amino acids, supplements, other prescription or non-prescription drugs.

Pregnancy:
- Dangers outweigh any possible benefits. Don't use.

Breast-feeding:
- Dangers outweigh any possible benefits. Don't use.

Infants and children:
- Treating infants and children under 2 with any herbal preparation is hazardous.

Others:
- None expected if you are under 45, not pregnant, basically healthy, take it for only a short time and do not exceed manufacturer's recommended dosage.

Storage:
- Keep cool and dry, but don't freeze. Store safely away from children.

Safe dosage:
- At present no "safe" dosage has been established.

 ## Toxicity

Comparative-toxicity rating not available from standard references.

For symptoms of toxicity: See *Adverse Reactions, Side Effects or Overdose Symptoms* section below.

 ## Adverse Reactions, Side Effects or Overdose Symptoms

Signs and symptoms:	What to do:
Diarrhoea	Discontinue. Call doctor immediately.
Nausea	Discontinue. Call doctor immediately.
Skin eruptions	Discontinue. Call doctor when convenient.
Vomiting	Discontinue. Call doctor immediately.

MEDICINAL HERB

Pitcher Plant

Basic Information
Biological name (genus and species):
   Sarracenia
Parts used for medicinal purposes:
   Roots
Chemicals this herb contains:
   Resin (See Glossary)
   Yellow dye

Known Effects

- Irritates gastrointestinal tract.
- Has diuretic properties.

Unproved Speculated Benefits

- Treats constipation.
- Treats indigestion.
- Increases amount of urine kidneys produce.

Warnings and Precautions

Don't take if you:
- Are pregnant, think you may be pregnant or plan pregnancy in the near future.

Consult your doctor if you:
- Take this herb for any medical problem that doesn't improve in 2 weeks. There may be safer, more-effective treatments.
- Take any medicinal drugs or herbs including aspirin, laxatives, cold and cough remedies, antacids, vitamins, minerals, amino acids, supplements, other prescription or non-prescription drugs.

Pregnancy:
- Problems in pregnant women taking small or usual amounts have not been proved. But the chance of problems does exist. Don't use unless prescribed by your doctor.

Breast-feeding:
- Problems in breast-fed infants of lactating mothers taking small or usual amounts have not been proved. But the chance of problems does exist. Don't use unless prescribed by your doctor.

Infants and children:
- Treating infants and children under 2 with any herbal preparation is hazardous.

Others:
- None expected if you are under 45, not pregnant, basically healthy, take it for only a short time and do not exceed manufacturer's recommended dosage.

Storage:
- Keep cool and dry, but don't freeze. Store safely away from children.

Safe dosage:
- At present no "safe" dosage has been established.

Toxicity

Comparative-toxicity rating not available from standard references.

Adverse Reactions, Side Effects or Overdose Symptoms

None expected

Pleurisy Root (Butterfly Weed)

Basic Information

Biological name (genus and species):
Asclepias tuberosa
Parts used for medicinal purposes:
Roots
Chemicals this herb contains:
Asclepiadin
Asclepion
Galitoxin
Volatile oils (See Glossary)

 ## Known Effects

- Decreases thickness and increases fluidity of mucus from lungs and bronchial tubes.
- Irritates mucous membranes.
- Stimulates and irritates gastrointestinal tract.

 ## Unproved Speculated Benefits

- Acts as a strong laxative to cause watery, explosive bowel movements.
- Increases perspiration.

 ## Warnings and Precautions

Don't take if you:
- Are pregnant, think you may be pregnant or plan pregnancy in the near future.
- Have any chronic disease of the gastrointestinal tract, such as stomach or duodenal ulcers, oesophageal reflux (reflux oesophagitis), ulcerative colitis, spastic colitis, diverticulosis, diverticulitis.

Consult your doctor if you:
- Take this herb for any medical problem that doesn't improve in 2 weeks. There may be safer, more effective treatments.
- Take any medicinal drugs or herbs including aspirin, laxatives, cold and cough remedies, antacids, vitamins, minerals, amino acids, supplements, other prescription or non-prescription drugs.

Pregnancy:
- Dangers outweigh any possible benefits. Don't use.

Breast-feeding:
- Dangers outweigh any possible benefits. Don't use.

Infants and children:
- Treating infants and children under 2 with any herbal preparation is hazardous.

Others:
- Dangers outweigh any possible benefits. Don't use.

Storage:
- Keep cool and dry, but don't freeze. Store safely away from children.

Safe dosage:
- At present no "safe" dosage has been established.

 ## Toxicity

Comparative-toxicity rating not available from standard references.

For symptoms of toxicity: See *Adverse Reactions, Side Effects or Overdose Symptoms* section below.

 ## Adverse Reactions, Side Effects or Overdose Symptoms

Signs and symptoms:	What to do:
Appetite loss	Discontinue. Call doctor when convenient.
Coma	Seek emergency treatment.
Diarrhoea	Discontinue. Call doctor immediately.
Lethargy	Discontinue. Call doctor when convenient.
Muscle weakness	Discontinue. Call doctor immediately.
Nausea	Discontinue. Call doctor immediately.
Vomiting	Discontinue. Call doctor immediately.

Poke (Pokeweed, Scoke)

Basic Information

Biological name (genus and species):
   Phytolacca americana
Parts used for medicinal purposes:
   Leaves
   Roots
   Seeds
Chemicals this herb contains:
   Asparagine
   Mitogen
   Phytolaccigenin
   Resin (See Glossary)
   Saponins (See Glossary)

Known Effects

• Stimulates and irritates gastrointestinal tract.

Miscellaneous information:
• All parts of native plants are poisonous. Don't take it. Children are especially vulnerable to toxic effects.
• Leaves are boiled and eaten as flavouring in some areas, particularly the southern United States. Used this way, pokeberry may be toxic. Don't use!

Unproved Speculated Benefits

• Treats chronic arthritis.
• Treats constipation.

Warnings and Precautions

Don't take if you:
• Are pregnant, think you may be pregnant or plan pregnancy in the near future.
• Have any chronic disease of the gastrointestinal tract, such as stomach or duodenal ulcers, oesophageal reflux (reflux oesophagitis), ulcerative colitis, spastic colitis, diverticulosis, diverticulitis.

Consult your doctor if you:
• Take this herb for any medical problem that doesn't improve in 2 weeks. There may be safer, more effective treatments.
• Take any medicinal drugs or herbs including aspirin, laxatives, cold and cough remedies, antacids, vitamins, minerals, amino acids, supplements, other prescription or non-prescription drugs.

Pregnancy:
• Dangers outweigh any possible benefits. Don't use.

Breast-feeding:
• Dangers outweigh any possible benefits. Don't use.

Infants and children:
• Treating infants and children under 2 with any herbal preparation is hazardous.

Others:
• Handling roots may cause skin abrasions.

Storage:
• Keep cool and dry, but don't freeze. Store safely away from children.

Safe dosage:
• At present no "safe" dosage has been established.

Toxicity

Comparative-toxicity rating not available from standard references.

For symptoms of toxicity: See *Adverse Reactions, Side Effects or Overdose Symptoms* section below.

Adverse Reactions, Side Effects or Overdose Symptoms

Signs and symptoms:	What to do:
Decreased heart rate	Seek emergency treatment.
Diarrhoea	Discontinue. Call doctor immediately.
Nausea	Discontinue. Call doctor immediately.
Skin eruptions	Discontinue. Call doctor when convenient.
Vomiting	Discontinue. Call doctor immediately.

Basic Information

Biological name (genus and species):
Punica granatum
Parts used for medicinal purposes:
Bark
Berries/fruits, including rind
Chemicals this herb contains:
Isopelletierine
Methylisopelletierine
Pelletierine
Pseudopelletierine
Tannins (See Glossary)

Known Effects

Rind and bark:
• Shrinks tissues.
• Prevents secretion of fluids.
• Destroys intestinal worms.
• Interferes with absorption of iron and other minerals when taken internally.

Miscellaneous information:
• Fruits are edible and non-toxic. Bark and rind contain herbal-medicinal properties.

Unproved Speculated Benefits

• Treats stasis ulcers and "bed sores."

Warnings and Precautions

Don't take if you:
• Are pregnant, think you may be pregnant or plan pregnancy in the near future.
• Have any chronic disease of the gastrointestinal tract, such as stomach or duodenal ulcers, oesophageal reflux (reflux oesophagitis), ulcerative colitis, spastic colitis, diverticulosis, diverticulitis.

Consult your doctor if you:
• Take this herb for any medical problem that doesn't improve in 2 weeks. There may be safer, more effective treatments.
• Take any medicinal drugs or herbs including aspirin, laxatives, cold and cough remedies, antacids, vitamins, minerals, amino acids, supplements, other prescription or non-prescription drugs.

Pregnancy:
• Taken internally as a medicinal herb, dangers outweigh any possible benefits. Don't use. Eating fruit as part of the diet will not cause problems.

Breast-feeding:
• Taken internally as a medicinal herb, dangers outweigh any possible benefits. Don't use. Eating fruit as part of the diet will not cause problems.

Infants and children:
• Treating infants and children under 2 with any herbal preparation is hazardous.

Others:
• Taken internally, dangers outweigh any possible benefits. Don't use.

Storage:
• Keep cool and dry, but don't freeze. Store safely away from children.

Safe dosage:
• At present no "safe" dosage has been established.

Toxicity

Comparative-toxicity rating not available from standard references.

For symptoms of toxicity: See *Adverse Reactions, Side Effects or Overdose Symptoms* section below.

Adverse Reactions, Side Effects or Overdose Symptoms

Signs and symptoms:	What to do:
Diarrhoea	Discontinue. Call doctor immediately.
Dilated pupils	Seek emergency treatment.
Dizziness	Discontinue. Call doctor immediately.
Double vision	Seek emergency treatment.
Nausea	Discontinue. Call doctor immediately.
Vomiting	Discontinue. Call doctor immediately.
Weakness	Discontinue. Call doctor immediately.

Poplar Bud

Basic Information

Biological name (genus and species):
    Populus candicans
Parts used for medicinal purposes:
    Leaf bud
Chemicals this herb contains:
    Chrysin
    Gallic acid
    Humulene
    Malic acid
    Mannite
    Populin
    Resin (See Glossary)
    Salicin
    Tectochrysin

Known Effects

* Blocks pain impulses to brain.
* Changes fever-conrol "thermostat" in brain.

Miscellaneous information:
* Anti-oxidant effect helps prevent rancidity in ointments.
* Poplar bud is used as an additive in several pharmaceutical preparations.

Unproved Speculated Benefits

* Reduces pain of sprains and bruises when applied to skin.
* Treats coughs and colds when taken internally.
* Reduces fever.

Warnings and Precautions

Don't take if you:
* Are pregnant, think you may be pregnant or plan pregnancy in the near future.
* Have any chronic disease of the gastrointestinal tract, such as stomach or duodenal ulcers, oesophageal reflux (reflux oesophagitis), ulcerative colitis, spastic colitis, diverticulosis, diverticulitis.

Consult your doctor if you:
* Take this herb for any medical problem that doesn't improve in 2 weeks. There may be safer, more effective treatments.
* Take any medicinal drugs or herbs including aspirin, laxatives, cold and cough remedies, antacids, vitamins, minerals, amino acids, supplements, other prescription or non-prescription drugs.

Pregnancy:
* Problems in pregnant women taking small or usual amounts have not been proved. But the chance of problems does exist. Don't use unless prescribed by your doctor.

Breast-feeding:
* Problems in breast-fed infants of lactating mothers taking small or usual amounts have not been proved. But the chance of problems does exist. Don't use unless prescribed by your doctor.

Infants and children:
* Treating infants and children under 2 with any herbal preparation is hazardous.

Others:
* None expected if you are beyond childhood and under 45, basically healthy and take for only a short time.

Storage:
* Keep cool and dry, but don't freeze. Store safely away from children.

Safe dosage:
* At present no "safe" dosage has been established.

Toxicity

Comparative-toxicity rating not available from standard references.

For symptoms of toxicity: See *Adverse Reactions, Side Effects or Overdose Symptoms* section below.

Adverse Reactions, Side Effects or Overdose Symptoms

Signs and symptoms:	What to do:
Itching and redness of skin	Apply hydrocortisone ointment, available without prescription.
Skin rash	Apply hydrocortisone ointment, available without prescription.

Basic Information

Biological name (genus and species):
Xanthoxylum americanum *(northern)*
Xanthoxylum clava-herculus *(southern)*
Parts used for medicinal purposes:
Bark
Berries/fruits
Chemicals this herb contains:
Acid amide
Asarinin
Berberine
Herculin
Xanthoxyletin
Xanthyletin

Known Effects

- Stimulates and irritates gastrointestinal tract.
- Increases perspiration.

Unproved Speculated Benefits

- Stimulates appetite.
- Treats arthritis.
- Decreases flatulence.

Warnings and Precautions

Don't take if you:
- Are pregnant, think you may be pregnant or plan pregnancy in the near future.
- Have any chronic disease of the gastrointestinal tract, such as stomach or duodenal ulcers, oesophageal reflux (reflux oesophagitis), ulcerative colitis, spastic colitis, diverticulosis, diverticulitis.

Consult your doctor if you:
- Take this herb for any medical problem that doesn't improve in 2 weeks. There may be safer, more effective treatments.
- Take any medicinal drugs or herbs including aspirin, laxatives, cold and cough remedies, antacids, vitamins, minerals, amino acids, supplements, other prescription or non-prescription drugs.

Pregnancy:
- Problems in pregnant women taking small or usual amounts have not been proved. But the chance of problems does exist. Don't use unless prescribed by your doctor.

Breast-feeding:
- Problems in breast-fed infants of lactating mothers taking small or usual amounts have not been proved. But the chance of problems does exist. Don't use unless prescribed by your doctor.

Infants and children:
- Treating infants and children under 2 with any herbal preparation is hazardous.

Others:
- None expected if you are beyond childhood and under 45, basically healthy and take for only a short time.

Storage:
- Keep cool and dry, but don't freeze. Store safely away from children.

Safe dosage:
- At present no "safe" dosage has been established.

Toxicity

Comparative-toxicity rating not available from standard references.

For symptoms of toxicity: See *Adverse Reactions, Side Effects or Overdose Symptoms* section below.

Adverse Reactions, Side Effects or Overdose Symptoms

Signs and symptoms:	What to do:
Diarrhoea	Discontinue. Call doctor immediately.
Nausea	Discontinue. Call doctor immediately.
Vomiting	Discontinue. Call doctor immediately.

MEDICINAL HERB

Prickly Poppy (Thistle Poppy, Mexican Poppy)

Basic Information

Biological name (genus and species):
   Argemone mexicana
Parts used for medicinal purposes:
   Seeds
Chemicals this herb contains:
   Berberine
   Dihydrosanquinarine
   Protopine
   Sanquinarine

Known Effects

• Depresses central nervous system very mildly.

Miscellaneous information:
• This poppy is not the origin of morphine, codeine or other narcotics.

Unproved Speculated Benefits

• Smoking prickly poppy produces euphoria.
• Reduces pain.

Warnings and Precautions

Don't take if you:
• Are pregnant, think you may be pregnant or plan pregnancy in the near future.
• Have any chronic disease of the gastrointestinal tract, such as stomach or duodenal ulcers, oesophageal reflux (reflux oesophagitis), ulcerative colitis, spastic colitis, diverticulosis, diverticulitis.

Consult your doctor if you:
• Take this herb for any medical problem that doesn't improve in 2 weeks. There may be safer, more effective treatments.
• Take any medicinal drugs or herbs including aspirin, laxatives, cold and cough remedies, antacids, vitamins, minerals, amino acids, supplements, other prescription or non-prescription drugs.

Pregnancy:
• Dangers outweigh any possible benefits. Don't use.

Breast-feeding:
• Dangers outweigh any possible benefits. Don't use.

Infants and children:
• Treating infants and children under 2 with any herbal preparation is hazardous.

Others:
• Dangers outweigh any possible benefits. Don't use.

Storage:
• Keep cool and dry, but don't freeze. Store safely away from children.

Safe dosage:
• At present no "safe" dosage has been established.

Toxicity

Rated slightly dangerous, particularly in children, persons over 55 and those who take larger than appropriate quantities for extended periods of time.

For symptoms of toxicity: See *Adverse Reactions, Side Effects or Overdose Symptoms* section below.

Adverse Reactions, Side Effects or Overdose Symptoms

Signs and symptoms:	What to do:
Diarrhoea	Discontinue. Call doctor immediately.
Dizziness	Discontinue. Call doctor immediately.
Fluid retention	Discontinue. Call doctor when convenient.
Loss of consciousness	Seek emergency treatment.
Nausea	Discontinue. Call doctor immediately.
Swollen abdomen	Discontinue. Call doctor when convenient.
Vision disturbances	Discontinue. Call doctor immediately.
Vomiting	Discontinue. Call doctor immediately.

Prostrate Knotweed (Pigweed)

Basic Information

Biological name (genus and species):
   Polygonum aviculare
Parts used for medicinal purposes:
   *Various parts of the entire plant, frequently
   differing by country and/or culture*
Chemicals this herb contains:
   Avicularin
   Emodin
   Quercetin 3-arabinoside

Known Effects

- Reduces capillary fragility.
- Reduces capillary permeability.
- Retards destruction of adrenaline.

Unproved Speculated Benefits

- Causes watery, explosive bowel movements.
- Treats kidney and bladder stones.

Warnings and Precautions

Don't take if you:
- Are pregnant, think you may be pregnant or plan pregnancy in the near future.
- Have any chronic disease of the gastrointestinal tract, such as stomach or duodenal ulcers, oesophageal reflux (reflux oesophagitis), ulcerative colitis, spastic colitis, diverticulosis, diverticulitis.

Consult your doctor if you:
- Take this herb for any medical problem that doesn't improve in 2 weeks. There may be safer, more effective treatments.
- Take any medicinal drugs or herbs including aspirin, laxatives, cold and cough remedies, antacids, vitamins, minerals, amino acids, supplements, other prescription or non-prescription drugs.

Pregnancy:
- Problems in pregnant women taking small or usual amounts have not been proved. But the chance of problems does exist. Don't use unless prescribed by your doctor.

Breast-feeding:
- Problems in breast-fed infants of lactating mothers taking small or usual amounts have not been proved. But the chance of problems does exist. Don't use unless prescribed by your doctor.

Infants and children:
- Treating infants and children under 2 with any herbal preparation is hazardous.

Others:
- None expected if you are under 45, not pregnant, basically healthy, take it for only a short time and do not exceed manufacturer's recommended dosage.

Storage:
- Keep cool and dry, but don't freeze. Store safely away from children.

Safe dosage:
- At present no "safe" dosage has been established.

Toxicity

Rated relatively safe when taken in appropriate quantities for short periods of time.

For symptoms of toxicity: See *Adverse Reactions, Side Effects or Overdose Symptoms* section below.

Adverse Reactions, Side Effects or Overdose Symptoms

Signs and symptoms:	What to do:
Abdominal pain	Discontinue. Call doctor when convenient.
Diarrhoea	Discontinue. Call doctor immediately.
Nausea	Discontinue. Call doctor immediately.
Skin eruptions	Discontinue. Call doctor when convenient.
Vomiting	Discontinue. Call doctor immediately.

Psyllium

Basic Information

Biological name (genus and species):
    Plantago psyllium
Parts used for medicinal purposes:
    Seeds
Chemicals this herb contains:
    Glycosides (See Glossary)
    Mucilage (See Glossary)

Known Effects

- Produces bulky bowel movements (1 gram swells 8-14 times its size when placed in water).
- Softens stools.

Miscellaneous information:
- Psyllium is a popular product and available over-the-counter without prescription.

Unproved Speculated Benefits

- Treats constipation.
- Protects scraped tissues.

Warnings and Precautions

Don't take if you:
- Are pregnant, think you may be pregnant or plan pregnancy in the near future.

Consult your doctor if you:
- Take this herb for any medical problem that doesn't improve in 2 weeks. There may be safer, more effective treatments.
- Take any medicinal drugs or herbs including aspirin, laxatives, cold and cough remedies, antacids, vitamins, minerals, amino acids, supplements, other prescription or non-prescription drugs.

Pregnancy:
- Problems in pregnant women taking small or usual amounts have not been proved. But the chance of problems does exist. Don't use unless prescribed by your doctor.

Breast-feeding:
- Problems in breast-fed infants of lactating mothers taking small or usual amounts have not been proved. But the chance of problems does exist. Don't use unless prescribed by your doctor.

Infants and children:
- Treating infants and children under 2 with any herbal preparation is hazardous.

Others:
- None expected if you are beyond childhood and under 45, basically healthy and take for only a short time.

Storage:
- Keep cool and dry, but don't freeze. Store safely away from children.

Safe dosage:
- At present no "safe" dosage has been established.

Toxicity

Comparative-toxicity rating not available from standard references.

Adverse Reactions, Side Effects or Overdose Symptoms

None expected

Basic Information

Biological name (genus and species):
Echinacea angustifolia, E. pallida
Parts used for medicinal purposes:
Various parts of the entire plant, frequently differing by country and/or culture
Chemicals this herb contains:
Betaine
Echinacin
Echinoside
Fatty acids
Inulin
Resin (See Glossary)
Sucrose

 ## Known Effects

- Kills insects, especially houseflies.
- Possible anti-tumour activity.

Miscellaneous information:
- Another herb, *Rudbeckia laciniata,* is also called *coneflower* and has been reported to be toxic. If you take *any* coneflower, be sure it is *Echinacea angustifolia.*

 ## Unproved Speculated Benefits

- Acts as natural anti-toxin for internal and external infections.
- "Blood purifier."
- Helps heal wounds.

 ## Warnings and Precautions

Don't take if you:
- Are pregnant, think you may be pregnant or plan pregnancy in the near future.

Consult your doctor if you:
- Take this herb for any medical problem that doesn't improve in 2 weeks. There may be safer, more effective treatments.
- Take any medicinal drugs or herbs including aspirin, laxatives, cold and cough remedies, antacids, vitamins, minerals, amino acids, supplements, other prescription or non-prescription drugs.

Pregnancy:
- Problems in pregnant women taking small or usual amounts have not been proved. But the chance of problems does exist. Don't use unless prescribed by your doctor.

Breast-feeding:
- Problems in breast-fed infants of lactating mothers taking small or usual amounts have not been proved. But the chance of problems does exist. Don't use unless prescribed by your doctor.

Infants and children:
- Treating infants and children under 2 with any herbal preparation is hazardous.

Others:
- None expected if you are beyond childhood and under 45, basically healthy and take for only a short time.

Storage:
- Keep cool and dry, but don't freeze. Store safely away from children.

Safe dosage:
- At present no "safe" dosage has been established.

 ## Toxicity

Comparative-toxicity rating not available from standard references.

 ## Adverse Reactions, Side Effects or Overdose Symptoms

None reported

MEDICINAL HERB

Rauwolfia (Snakeroot, Chandra, Sarpaganda)

Basic Information

Biological name (genus and species):
Rauwolfia serpentina
Parts used for medicinal purposes:
Roots
Chemicals this herb contains:

Arnajaline	Serpentine
Deserpidine	Serpentinine
Reserpine	Yohimbine
Rescinnamine	

Known Effects

- Reduces blood pressure.
- Depresses activity of central nervous system.
- Acts as a hypnotic.

Miscellaneous information:
- Snakeroot depletes catecholamines and serotonin from nerves in central nervous system.
- Refined snakeroot has been used extensively in recent years to treat hypertension.
- Animal studies suggest snakeroot may *produce* cancers.

Unproved Speculated Benefits

- Decreases anxiety.
- Decreases fever.
- Kills intestinal parasites.
- In India, it is used as antidote for snakebites.

Warnings and Precautions

Don't take if you:
- Are pregnant, think you may be pregnant or plan pregnancy in the near future.
- Have any chronic disease of the gastrointestinal tract, such as stomach or duodenal ulcers, oesophageal reflux (reflux oesophagitis), ulcerative colitis, spastic colitis, diverticulosis, diverticulitis.

Consult your doctor if you have:
- Take this herb for any medical problem that doesn't improve in 2 weeks. There may be safer, more effective treatments.
- Take any medicinal drugs or herbs including aspirin, laxatives, cold and cough remedies, antacids, vitamins, minerals, amino acids, supplements, other prescription or non-prescription drugs.

Pregnancy and breast-feeding:
- Dangers outweigh any benefits. Don't use.

Infants and children:
- Treating infants and children under 2 with any herbal preparation is hazardous.

Others:
- Dangers outweigh any benefits. Don't use.

Storage:
- Keep cool and dry, but don't freeze. Store safely away from children.

Safe dosage:
- At present no "safe" dosage established.

Toxicity

Rated slightly dangerous, particularly in children, persons over 55 and those who take larger than appropriate quantities for extended periods of time.

For symptoms of toxicity: See *Adverse Reactions, Side Effects or Overdose Symptoms* section below.

Adverse Reactions, Side Effects or Overdose Symptoms

Signs and symptoms:	What to do:
Bizarre dreams	Discontinue. Call doctor when convenient.
Decreased libido and sexual performance	Discontinue. Call doctor when convenient.
Diarrhoea	Discontinue. Call doctor immediately.
Drowsiness	Discontinue. Call doctor when convenient.
Nasal congestion	Discontinue. Call doctor when convenient.
Precipitous blood-pressure drop— symptoms include faintness, cold sweat, paleness, rapid pulse	Seek emergency treatment.
Slow heartbeat	Seek emergency treatment.
Stupor	Seek emergency treatment.
Upper-abdominal pain	Discontinue. Call doctor when convenient.

Red Clover (Pavine Clover, Cowgrass)

Basic Information

Biological name (genus and species):
Trifolium pratense
Parts used for medicinal purposes:
Flowers
Chemical this herb contains:
Glycosides (See Glossary)

Known Effects

- Decreases irritation and muscular movement (peristalsis) of gastrointestinal tract.
- Decreases activity of central nervous system.

Unproved Speculated Benefits

- Reduces upper-abdominal cramps.
- Treats indigestion.
- Loosens secretions in bronchial tubes due to infections or chronic lung disease.
- Suppresses appetite.
- Treats cancers. (Controlled studies show no evidence of benefit. Using red clover for this purpose delays obtaining proper medical care.)

Warnings and Precautions

Don't take if you:
- Are pregnant, think you may be pregnant or plan pregnancy in the near future.

Consult your doctor if you:
- Take this herb for any medical problem that doesn't improve in 2 weeks. There may be safer, more effective treatments.
- Take any medicinal drugs or herbs including aspirin, laxatives, cold and cough remedies, antacids, vitamins, minerals, amino acids, supplements, other prescription or non-prescription drugs.

Pregnancy:
- Problems in pregnant women taking small or usual amounts have not been proved. But the chance of problems does exist. Don't use unless prescribed by your doctor.

Breast-feeding:
- Problems in breast-fed infants of lactating mothers taking small or usual amounts have not been proved. But the chance of problems does exist. Don't use unless prescribed by your doctor.

Infants and children:
- Treating infants and children under 2 with any herbal preparation is hazardous.

Others:
- None expected if you are beyond childhood and under 45, basically healthy and take for only a short time.

Storage:
- Keep cool and dry, but don't freeze. Store safely away from children.

Safe dosage:
- At present no "safe" dosage has been established.

Toxicity

Generally regarded as safe when taken in appropriate quantities for short periods of time.

Adverse Reactions, Side Effects or Overdose Symptoms

None expected

Red Raspberry

Basic Information

Biological name (genus and species):
  Rubus strigosus, R. idaeus
Parts used for medicinal purposes:
  Bark
  Leaves
  Roots
Chemicals this herb contains:
  Citric acid
  Tannins (See Glossary)

Known Effects

- Relaxes uterine spasms.
- Relaxes intestinal spasms.
- Interferes with absorption of iron and other minerals when taken internally.

Miscellaneous information:
- Berries are delicious, nutritious and non-toxic.
- When eaten as a common food, no problems are expected for anyone.

Unproved Speculated Benefits

- Regulates labour pains.
- Decreases excessive menstrual bleeding.
- Is used as gargle for sore throats.

Warnings and Precautions

Don't take if you:
- Are pregnant, think you may be pregnant or plan pregnancy in the near future.

Consult your doctor if you:
- Take this herb for any medical problem that doesn't improve in 2 weeks. There may be safer, more effective treatments.
- Take any medicinal drugs or herbs including aspirin, laxatives, cold and cough remedies, antacids, vitamins, minerals, amino acids, supplements, other prescription or non-prescription drugs.

Pregnancy:
- Problems in pregnant women taking small or usual amounts have not been proved. But the chance of problems does exist. Don't use unless prescribed by your doctor.

Breast-feeding:
- Problems in breast-fed infants of lactating mothers taking small or usual amounts have not been proved. But the chance of problems does exist. Don't use unless prescribed by your doctor.

Infants and children:
- Treating infants and children under 2 with any herbal preparation is hazardous.

Others:
- None expected if you are beyond childhood and under 45, basically healthy and take for only a short time.

Storage:
- Keep cool and dry, but don't freeze. Store safely away from children.

Safe dosage:
- At present no "safe" dosage has been established.

Toxicity

Comparative-toxicity rating not available from standard references.

Adverse Reactions, Side Effects or Overdose Symptoms

None expected

Basic Information

Biological name (genus and species):
   Krameria triandra
Parts used for medicinal purposes:
   Various parts of the entire plant, frequently
   differing by country and/or culture
Chemicals this herb contains:
   Calcium oxalate
   Gum (See Glossary)
   Lignin
   N-Methyltyrosine
   Saccharine
   Starch
   Tannins (See Glossary)

Known Effects

- Shrinks tissues.
- Prevents secretion of fluids.
- Causes protein molecules to clump together.
- Interferes with absorption of iron and other minerals when taken internally.

Unproved Speculated Benefits

- Treats sore throat.
- Treats haemorrhoids.
- Treats chronic bowel inflammations.
- Treats diarrhoea.

Warnings and Precautions

Don't take if you:
- Are pregnant, think you may be pregnant or plan pregnancy in the near future.
- Have any chronic disease of the gastrointestinal tract, such as stomach or duodenal ulcers, oesophageal reflux (reflux oesophagitis), ulcerative colitis, spastic colitis, diverticulosis, diverticulitis.

Consult your doctor if you:
- Take this herb for any medical problem that doesn't improve in 2 weeks. There may be safer, more effective treatments.
- Take any medicinal drugs or herbs including aspirin, laxatives, cold and cough remedies, antacids, vitamins, minerals, amino acids, supplements, other prescription or non-prescription drugs.

Pregnancy:
- Dangers outweigh any possible benefits. Don't use.

Breast-feeding:
- Dangers outweigh any possible benefits. Don't use.

Infants and children:
- Treating infants and children under 2 with any herbal preparation is hazardous.

Others:
- None expected if you are beyond childhood and under 45, basically healthy and take for only a short time.

Storage:
- Keep cool and dry, but don't freeze. Store safely away from children.

Safe dosage:
- At present no "safe" dosage has been established.

Toxicity

Comparative-toxicity rating not available from standard references.

For symptoms of toxicity: See *Adverse Reactions, Side Effects or Overdose Symptoms* section below.

Adverse Reactions, Side Effects or Overdose Symptoms

Signs and symptoms:	What to do:
Diarrhoea	Discontinue. Call doctor immediately.
Kidney damage characterized by blood in urine, decreased urine flow, swelling of hands and feet	Seek emergency treatment.
Nausea	Discontinue. Call doctor immediately.
Vomiting	Discontinue. Call doctor immediately.

Rheumatism Root (Wild-Yam Root)

Basic Information

Biological name (genus and species):
Dioscarea villosa
Parts used for medicinal purposes:
Roots
Chemicals this herb contains:
Dioscin
Diosgenin
Resin (See Glossary)

Known Effects

- Breaks membranous covering, destroying red blood cells (toxic to fish and amoeba).
- Decreases thickness and increases fluidity of mucus from lungs and bronchial tubes.
- Helps body dispose of excess fluid by increasing amount of urine produced.

Miscellaneous information:
- Diosgenin is a steroid base used to synthesize cortisone and progesterone (hormones).

Unproved Speculated Benefits

- Treats arthritis by allegedly removing accumulated waste in joints.

Warnings and Precautions

Don't take if you:
- Are pregnant, think you may be pregnant or plan pregnancy in the near future.
- Have any chronic disease of the gastrointestinal tract, such as stomach or duodenal ulcers, oesophageal reflux (reflux oesophagitis), ulcerative colitis, spastic colitis, diverticulosis, diverticulitis.

Consult your doctor if you:
- Take this herb for any medical problem that doesn't improve in 2 weeks. There may be safer, more effective treatments.
- Take any medicinal drugs or herbs including aspirin, laxatives, cold and cough remedies, antacids, vitamins, minerals, amino acids, supplements, other prescription or non-prescription drugs.

Pregnancy:
- Dangers outweigh any possible benefits. Don't use.

Breast-feeding:
- Dangers outweigh any possible benefits. Don't use.

Infants and children:
- Treating infants and children under 2 with any herbal preparation is hazardous.

Others:
- None expected if you are beyond childhood and under 45, basically healthy and take for only a short time.

Storage:
- Keep cool and dry, but don't freeze. Store safely away from children.

Safe dosage:
- At present no "safe" dosage has been established.

Toxicity

Generally regarded as safe when taken in appropriate quantities for short periods of time.

For symptoms of toxicity: See *Adverse Reactions or Side Effects* section below.

Adverse Reactions or Side Effects

Signs and symptoms:	What to do:
Diarrhoea	Discontinue. Call doctor immediately.
Nausea	Discontinue. Call doctor immediately.
Vomiting	Discontinue. Call doctor immediately.

Basic Information

Biological name (genus and species):
Rosa
Parts used for medicinal purposes:
Berries/fruits
Petals/flower
Chemicals this herb contains:
Ascorbic acid
Cyanogenic glycoside (See Glossary)
Quercitrin
Tannins (See Glossary)
Vitamins A and C
Volatile oils (See Glossary)

Known Effects

- Shrinks tissues.
- Prevents secretion of fluids.
- Interferes with absorption of iron and other minerals when taken internally.

Miscellaneous information:
- North-American Indians formerly used fruit as a food source. Leaves are used to make tea or salad and smoked like tobacco.
- Rose hips are used in vitamin-C supplements.
- Adds flavour to foods during cooking.

Unproved Speculated Benefits

- None

Warnings and Precautions

Don't take if you:
- Are pregnant, think you may be pregnant or plan pregnancy in the near future.

Consult your doctor if you:
- No contraindications if you are not pregnant and do not take amounts larger than manufacturer's recommended dosage.

Pregnancy:
- Problems in pregnant women taking small or usual amounts have not been proved. But the chance of problems does exist. Don't use unless prescribed by your doctor.

Breast-feeding:
- Problems in breast-fed infants of lactating mothers taking small or usual amounts have not been proved. But the chance of problems does exist. Don't use unless prescribed by your doctor.

Infants and children:
- Treating infants and children under 2 with any herbal preparation is hazardous.

Others:
- None expected if you are beyond childhood and under 45, basically healthy and take for only a short time.

Storage:
- Keep cool and dry, but don't freeze. Store safely away from children.

Safe dosage:
- At present no "safe" dosage has been established.

Toxicity

Comparative-toxicity rating not available from standard references.

Adverse Reactions, Side Effects or Overdose Symptoms

None expected

MEDICINAL HERB

Rosemary

Basic Information

Biological name (genus and species):
   Rosmarinus officinalis
Parts used for medicinal purposes:
   Berries/fruits
   Leaves
Chemicals this herb contains:
   Bitters (See Glossary)
   Borneol   Pinene
   Camphene   Resin (See Glossary)
   Camphor   Tannins (See Glossary)
   Cineole   Volatile oils (See Glossary)

Known Effects

- Volatile oils irritate tissue and kill bacteria.
- Acts as an astringent.
- Increases perspiration.
- Increases stomach acidity.

Miscellaneous information:
- Non-medical uses of rosemary include as an ingredient in perfumes, hair lotions and soaps.
- No effects are expected on the body, either good or bad, when herb is used in very small amounts to enhance the flavour of food.

Unproved Speculated Benefits

- Aids in expelling gas from intestinal tract.
- Triggers onset of menstrual period.
- Reddens skin by increasing blood supply to it.
- Stimulates appetite.

Warnings and Precautions

Don't take if you:
- Are pregnant, think you may be pregnant or plan pregnancy in the near future.
- Have any chronic disease of the gastrointestinal tract, such as stomach or duodenal ulcers, oesophageal reflux (reflux oesophagitis), ulcerative colitis, spastic colitis, diverticulosis, diverticulitis.

Consult your doctor if you:
- Take this herb for any medical problem that doesn't improve in 2 weeks. There may be safer, more effective treatments.
- Take any medicinal drugs or herbs including aspirin, laxatives, cold and cough remedies, antacids, vitamins, minerals, amino acids, supplements, other prescription or non-prescription drugs.

Pregnancy:
- Problems in pregnant women taking small or usual amounts have not been proved. But the chance of problems does exist. Don't use unless prescribed by your doctor.

Breast-feeding:
- Problems in breast-fed infants of lactating mothers taking small or usual amounts have not been proved. But the chance of problems does exist. Don't use unless prescribed by your doctor.

Infants and children:
- Treating infants and children under 2 with any herbal preparation is hazardous.

Others:
- None expected if you are beyond childhood and under 45, basically healthy and take for only a short time.

Storage:
- Keep cool and dry, but don't freeze. Store safely away from children.

Safe dosage:
- At present no "safe" dosage has been established.

Toxicity

Rated relatively safe when taken in appropriate quantities for short periods of time.

For symptoms of toxicity: See *Adverse Reactions, Side Effects or Overdose Symptoms* section below.

Adverse Reactions, Side Effects or Overdose Symptoms

Signs and symptoms:	What to do:
Diarrhoea	Discontinue. Call doctor immediately.
Nausea	Discontinue. Call doctor immediately.
Skin eruptions	Discontinue. Call doctor when convenient.
Vomiting	Discontinue. Call doctor immediately.

Basic Information

Biological name (genus and species):
Ruta graveolens
Parts used for medicinal purposes:
Entire plant
Chemicals this herb contains:
Esters
Methyl-nonylketone
Phenols
Rutin
Tannins (See Glossary)
Volatile oils (See Glossary)

Known Effects

- Stimulates uterine contractions.
- Prolongs action of adrenaline.
- Relieves spasm in skeletal or smooth muscle.
- Decreases capillary fragility.
- Interferes with absorption of iron and other minerals when taken internally.

Unproved Speculated Benefits

- Causes onset of menstruation.
- May cause abortion.
- Treats hysteria.
- Treats intestinal parasites (worms).
- Treats colic.
- Controls bleeding after delivering a baby.

Warnings and Precautions

Don't take if you:
- Are pregnant, think you may be pregnant or plan pregnancy in the near future.
- Have any chronic disease of the gastrointestinal tract, such as stomach or duodenal ulcers, oesophageal reflux (reflux oesophagitis), ulcerative colitis, spastic colitis, diverticulosis, diverticulitis.

Consult your doctor if you:
- Take this herb for any medical problem that doesn't improve in 2 weeks. There may be safer, more effective treatments.
- Take any medicinal drugs or herbs including aspirin, laxatives, cold and cough remedies, antacids, vitamins, minerals, amino acids, supplements, other prescription or non-prescription drugs.

Pregnancy:
- Dangers outweigh any possible benefits. Don't use.

Breast-feeding:
- Dangers outweigh any possible benefits. Don't use.

Infants and children:
- Treating infants and children under 2 with any herbal preparation is hazardous.

Others:
- None expected if you are beyond childhood and under 45, not pregnant, basically healthy and take for only a short time.

Storage:
- Keep cool and dry, but don't freeze. Store safely away from children.

Safe dosage:
- At present no "safe" dosage has been established.

Toxicity

Rated relatively safe when taken in appropriate quantities for short periods of time.

For symptoms of toxicity: See *Adverse Reactions, Side Effects or Overdose Symptoms* section below.

Adverse Reactions, Side Effects or Overdose Symptoms

Signs and symptoms:	What to do:
Abdominal pain	Discontinue. Call doctor when convenient.
Abortion	Seek emergency treatment.
Confusion	Discontinue. Call doctor immediately.
Diarrhoea	Discontinue. Call doctor immediately.
Jaundice (yellow skin and eyes)	Discontinue. Call doctor immediately.
Nausea	Discontinue. Call doctor immediately.
Skin rashes	Discontinue. Call doctor when convenient.
Vomiting	Discontinue. Call doctor immediately.

Saffron (Saffron Crocus)

Basic Information

Biological name (genus and species):
Crocus sativus
Parts used for medicinal purposes:
Berries/fruits
Chemicals this herb contains:
Glycosides (See Glossary)
Volatile oils (See Glossary)

Known Effects

- Reduces irritation of gastrointestinal tract.
- Increases perspiration.
- Increases fluidity of bronchial secretions.

Miscellaneous information:
- No effects are expected on the body, either good or bad, when herb is used in very small amounts to enhance the flavour of food.

Unproved Speculated Benefits

- Stimulates respiration in asthma, whooping cough.
- Causes abortions.
- Arouses or enhances instinctive sexual desire.

Warnings and Precautions

Don't take if you:
- Are pregnant, think you may be pregnant or plan pregnancy in the near future.
- Have any chronic disease of the gastrointestinal tract, such as stomach or duodenal ulcers, oesophageal reflux (reflux oesophagitis), ulcerative colitis, spastic colitis, diverticulosis, diverticulitis.

Consult your doctor if you:
- Take this herb for any medical problem that doesn't improve in 2 weeks. There may be safer, more effective treatments.
- Take any medicinal drugs or herbs including aspirin, laxatives, cold and cough remedies, antacids, vitamins, minerals, amino acids, supplements, other prescription or non-prescription drugs.

Pregnancy:
- Dangers outweigh any possible benefits. Don't use.

Breast-feeding:
- Dangers outweigh any possible benefits. Don't use.

Infants and children:
- Treating infants and children under 2 with any herbal preparation is hazardous.

Others:
- None expected if you are under 45, not pregnant, basically healthy, take it for only a short time and do not exceed manufacturer's recommended dosage.

Storage:
- Keep cool and dry, but don't freeze. Store safely away from children.

Safe dosage:
- At present no "safe" dosage has been established.

Toxicity

Rated relatively safe when taken in appropriate quantities for short periods of time.

For symptoms of toxicity: See *Adverse Reactions, Side Effects or Overdose Symptoms* section below.

Adverse Reactions, Side Effects or Overdose Symptoms

Signs and symptoms:	What to do:
Diarrhoea	Discontinue. Call doctor immediately.
Dizziness	Discontinue. Call doctor immediately.
Nosebleeds	Discontinue. Call doctor when convenient.
Slow heart rate	Seek emergency treatment.
Stupor	Seek emergency treatment.
Vomiting	Discontinue. Call doctor immediately.

Basic Information

Biological name (genus and species):
Salvia officinalis
Parts used for medicinal purposes:
Leaves
Chemicals this herb contains:
Terpene
Thujone
Camphor
Resin (See Glossary)
Salvene
Tannins (See Glossary)
Volatile oils (See Glossary)

 ## Known Effects

- Depresses fever-control center in brain.
- Relieves spasm in skeletal or smooth muscle.
- Stimulates gastrointestinal tract.
- Stimulates central nervous system.
- Interferes with absorption of iron and other minerals when taken internally.

Miscellaneous information:
- Sage is used as a flavouring agent and in perfume.
- Salvia is *not* the brush sage of the desert or red sage.
- No effects are expected on the body, either good or bad, when herb is used in very small amounts to enhance the flavour of food. However, prolonged use of large amounts can cause seizures and unconsciousness.

 ## Unproved Speculated Benefits

- Aids in expelling gas from intestinal tract.
- Repels insects.
- Decreases salivation.
- Treats coughs and colds.

 ## Warnings and Precautions

Don't take if you:
- Are pregnant, think you may be pregnant or plan pregnancy in the near future.

Consult your doctor if you:
- Take this herb for any medical problem that doesn't improve in 2 weeks. There may be safer, more effective treatments.
- Take any medicinal drugs or herbs including aspirin, laxatives, cold and cough remedies, antacids, vitamins, minerals, amino acids, supplements, other prescription or non-prescription drugs.

Pregnancy:
- Problems in pregnant women taking small or usual amounts have not been proved. But the chance of problems does exist. Don't use unless prescribed by your doctor.

Breast-feeding:
- May reduce milk flow. Don't use.

Infants and children:
- Treating infants and children under 2 with any herbal preparation is hazardous.

Others:
- None expected if you are beyond childhood and under 45, basically healthy and take for only a short time.

Storage:
- Keep cool and dry, but don't freeze. Store safely away from children.

Safe dosage:
- At present no "safe" dosage has been established.

 ## Toxicity

Generally regarded as safe when taken in appropriate quantities for short periods of time.

For symptoms of toxicity: See *Adverse Reactions, Side Effects or Overdose Symptoms* section below.

 ## Adverse Reactions, Side Effects or Overdose Symptoms

Signs and symptoms:	What to do:
Dry mouth	Discontinue. Call doctor when convenient.

St. John's Wort (Klamath Weed)

Basic Information
Biological name (genus and species):
    Hypericum perforatum
Parts used for medicinal purposes:
    Petals/flower
Chemicals this herb contains:
    Hypericin
    Resin (See Glossary)
    Tannins (See Glossary)
    Volatile oils (See Glossary)

Known Effects

- Causes photosensitization.
- Interferes with absorption of iron and other minerals when taken internally.
- Slightly depresses central nervous system.

Unproved Speculated Benefits

- Acts as an anti-depressant.
- Repels or destroys "demons."
- Relieves anxiety.

Warnings and Precautions

Don't take if you:
- Are pregnant, think you may be pregnant or plan pregnancy in the near future.

Consult your doctor if you:
- Take this herb for any medical problem that doesn't improve in 2 weeks. There may be safer, more effective treatments.
- Take any medicinal drugs or herbs including aspirin, laxatives, cold and cough remedies, antacids, vitamins, minerals, amino acids, supplements, other prescription or non-prescription drugs.

Pregnancy:
- Problems in pregnant women taking small or usual amounts have not been proved. But the chance of problems does exist. Don't use unless prescribed by your doctor.

Breast-feeding:
- Problems in breast-fed infants of lactating mothers taking small or usual amounts have not been proved. But the chance of problems does exist. Don't use unless prescribed by your doctor.

Infants and children:
- Treating infants and children under 2 with any herbal preparation is hazardous.

Others:
- None expected if you are beyond childhood and under 45, basically healthy and take for only a short time.

Storage:
- Keep cool and dry, but don't freeze. Store safely away from children.

Safe dosage:
- At present no "safe" dosage has been established.

Toxicity

Rated slightly dangerous, particularly in children, persons over 55 and those who take larger than appropriate quantities for extended periods of time.

For symptoms of toxicity: See *Adverse Reactions, Side Effects or Overdose Symptoms* section below.

Adverse Reactions, Side Effects or Overdose Symptoms

Signs and symptoms:	What to do:
Abnormal skin colouring	Discontinue. Call doctor when convenient.

Basic Information

Biological name (genus and species):
  Sassafrass albidum
Parts used for medicinal purposes
  Bark
  Roots
Chemicals this herb contains:
  Cadinene
  Camphor
  Eugenol
  Phennandrene
  Pinene
  Safrol

Known Effects

• Depresses central nervous system.
• Irritates mucous membranes.

Miscellaneous information:
• Banned in United states as a flavouring agent because of proved carcinogenic potential.

Unproved Speculated Benefits

• Is used as spring "tonic" and "stimulant."
• Is used as "blood thinner."
• Treats common cold.

Warnings and Precautions

Don't take if you:
• Are pregnant, think you may be pregnant or plan pregnancy in the near future.
• Have any chronic disease of the gastrointestinal tract, such as stomach or duodenal ulcers, oesophageal reflux (reflux oesophagitis), ulcerative colitis, spastic colitis, diverticulosis, diverticulitis.

Consult your doctor if you:
• Take this herb for any medical problem that doesn't improve in 2 weeks. There may be safer, more effective treatments.
• Take any medicinal drugs or herbs including aspirin, laxatives, cold and cough remedies, antacids, vitamins, minerals, amino acids, supplements, other prescription or non-prescription drugs.

Pregnancy:
• Risk outweighs potential benefits. Don't take.

Breast-feeding:
• Risk outweighs potential benefits. Don't take.

Infants and children:
• Treating infants and children under 2 with any herbal preparation is hazardous.

Others:
• None expected if you are beyond childhood and under 45, basically healthy and take for only a short time.

Storage:
• Keep cool and dry, but don't freeze. Store safely away from children.

Safe dosage:
• At present no "safe" dosage has been established.

Toxicity

Has carcinogenic potential. Don't use.

For symptoms of toxicity: See *Adverse Reactions, Side Effects or Overdose Symptoms* section below.

Adverse Reactions, Side Effects or Overdose Symptoms

Signs and symptoms:	What to do:
Breathing difficulties	Seek emergency treatment.
Coma	Seek emergency treatment.
Dilated pupils	Discontinue. Call doctor immediately.
Fainting	Discontinue. Call doctor immediately.
Frequent nosebleeds	Discontinue. Call doctor when convenient.
Heart, liver, kidney damage characterized by swelling of extremities, shortness of breath, jaundice (yellow skin and eyes), blood in urine	Seek emergency treatment.
Nausea	Discontinue. Call doctor immediately.
Vomiting	Discontinue. Call doctor immediately.

Saw Palmetto (Sabal)

Basic Information

Biological name (genus and species):
Serenoa repens
Parts used for medicinal purposes:
Seeds
Chemicals this herb contains:
Capric
Caproic
Caprylic
Lauric
Oleic
Palmitic
Resin (See Glossary)

Known Effects

- Irritates mucous membranes.
- Helps body dispose of excess fluid by increasing amount of urine produced.

Miscellaneous information:

- Berries are edible but don't taste good.
- Reported to enlarge female breasts and to treat benign prostatic hypertrophy. Studies have conclusively shown this herb will *not* accomplish either.

Unproved Speculated Benefits

- Treats chronic cystitis.
- Treats urethritis and other inflammations of male genito-urinary tract, including prostatitis.
- Reduces accumulated fluid in the body resulting from heart, kidney or liver diseases.

Warnings and Precautions

Don't take if you:

- Are pregnant, think you may be pregnant or plan pregnancy in the near future.
- Have any chronic disease of the gastrointestinal tract, such as stomach or duodenal ulcers, oesophageal reflux (reflux oesophagitis), ulcerative colitis, spastic colitis, diverticulosis, diverticulitis.

Consult your doctor if you:

- Take this herb for any medical problem that doesn't improve in 2 weeks. There may be safer, more effective treatments.
- Take any medicinal drugs or herbs including aspirin, laxatives, cold and cough remedies, antacids, vitamins, minerals, amino acids, supplements, other prescription or non-prescription drugs.

Pregnancy:

- Problems in pregnant women taking small or usual amounts have not been proved. But the chance of problems does exist. Don't use unless prescribed by your doctor.

Breast-feeding:

- Problems in breast-fed infants of lactating mothers taking small or usual amounts have not been proved. But the chance of problems does exist. Don't use unless prescribed by your doctor.

Infants and children:

- Treating infants and children under 2 with any herbal preparation is hazardous.

Others:

- None expected if you are under 45, not pregnant, basically healthy, take it for only a short time and do not exceed manufacturer's recommended dosage.

Storage:

- Keep cool and dry, but don't freeze. Store safely away from children.

Safe dosage:

- At present no "safe" dosage has been established.

Toxicity

Rated relatively safe when taken in appropriate quantities for short periods of time.

For symptoms of toxicity: See *Adverse Reactions, Side Effects or Overdose Symptoms* section below.

Adverse Reactions, Side Effects or Overdose Symptoms

Signs and symptoms:	What to do:
Diarrhoea	Discontinue. Call doctor immediately.
Nausea	Discontinue. Call doctor immediately.
Vomiting	Discontinue. Call doctor immediately.

Basic Information

Biological name (genus and species):
Cytisus scoparius
Parts used for medicinal purposes:
Leaves
Chemicals this herb contains:
Cytisine
Genisteine
Hydroxytyramine
Sarothamnine
Scaparin
Sparteine

Known Effects

- Stimulates uterine contractions.
- Helps body dispose of excess fluid by increasing amount of urine produced.
- Sometimes causes sharp rise in blood pressure.

Unproved Speculated Benefits

- Treats congestive heart failure.
- Produces sedative-hypnotic effect when smoked.

Warnings and Precautions

Don't take if you:
- Are pregnant, think you may be pregnant or plan pregnancy in the near future.
- Have any chronic disease of the gastrointestinal tract, such as stomach or duodenal ulcers, oesophageal reflux (reflux oesophagitis), ulcerative colitis, spastic colitis, diverticulosis, diverticulitis.

Consult your doctor if you:
- Take this herb for any medical problem that doesn't improve in 2 weeks. There may be safer, more effective treatments.
- Take any medicinal drugs or herbs including aspirin, laxatives, cold and cough remedies, antacids, vitamins, minerals, amino acids, supplements, other prescription or non-prescription drugs.

Pregnancy:
- Problems in pregnant women taking small or usual amounts have not been proved. But the chance of problems does exist. Don't use unless prescribed by your doctor.

Breast-feeding:
- Problems in breast-fed infants of lactating mothers taking small or usual amounts have not been proved. But the chance of problems does exist. Don't use unless prescribed by your doctor.

Infants and children:
- Treating infants and children under 2 with any herbal preparation is hazardous.

Others:
- None expected if you are beyond childhood and under 45, basically healthy and take for only a short time.

Storage:
- Keep cool and dry, but don't freeze. Store safely away from children.

Safe dosage:
- At present no "safe" dosage has been established.

Toxicity

Rated slightly dangerous, particularly in children, persons over 55 and those who take larger than appropriate quantities for extended periods of time.

For symptoms of toxicity: See *Adverse Reactions, Side Effects or Overdose Symptoms* section below.

Adverse Reactions, Side Effects or Overdose Symptoms

Signs and symptoms:	What to do:
Diarrhoea	Discontinue. Call doctor immediately.
Nausea	Discontinue. Call doctor immediately.
Vomiting	Discontinue. Call doctor immediately.

Silverwood (Goose-tansy)

Basic Information
Biological name (genus and species):
   Potentilla answerina
Parts used for medicinal purposes:
   Entire plant
Chemicals this herb contains:
   Ellagic acid
   Kinovic acid
   Tannins (See Glossary)

Known Effects

- Shrinks tissues.
- Prevents secretion of fluids.
- Causes protein molecules to clump together.
- Stimulates uterine contractions.
- Interferes with absorption of iron and other minerals when taken internally.

Unproved Speculated Benefits

- Treats dysmenorrhoea (painful menstruation).
- When used with lobelia, treats tetanus in absence of medical help.

Warnings and Precautions

Don't take if you:
- Are pregnant, think you may be pregnant or plan pregnancy in the near future.
- Have any chronic disease of the gastrointestinal tract, such as stomach or duodenal ulcers, oesophageal reflux (reflux oesophagitis), ulcerative colitis, spastic colitis, diverticulosis, diverticulitis.

Consult your doctor if you:
- Take this herb for any medical problem that doesn't improve in 2 weeks. There may be safer, more effective treatments.
- Take any medicinal drugs or herbs including aspirin, laxatives, cold and cough remedies, antacids, vitamins, minerals, amino acids, supplements, other prescription or non-prescription drugs.

Pregnancy:
- Dangers outweigh any possible benefits. Don't use.

Breast-feeding:
- Dangers outweigh any possible benefits. Don't use.

Infants and children:
- Treating infants and children under 2 with any herbal preparation is hazardous.

Others:
- None expected if you are under 45, not pregnant, basically healthy, take it for only a short time and do not exceed manufacturer's recommended dosage.

Storage:
- Keep cool and dry, but don't freeze. Store safely away from children.

Safe dosage:
- At present no "safe" dosage has been established.

Toxicity

Comparative-toxicity rating not available from standard references.

For symptoms of toxicity: See *Adverse Reactions, Side Effects or Overdose Symptoms* section below.

Adverse Reactions, Side Effects or Overdose Symptoms

Signs and symptoms:	What to do:
Diarrhoea	Discontinue. Call doctor immediately.
Nausea	Discontinue. Call doctor immediately.
Painful urination	Discontinue. Call doctor when convenient.
Vomiting	Discontinue. Call doctor immediately.

Basic Information

Biological name (genus and species):
Ulmus fulva
Parts used for medicinal purposes:
Inner bark
Chemicals this herb contains:
Calcium
Calcium oxalate
Mucilage (See Glossary)
Polysaccharide
Starch
Tannins (See Glossary)

Known Effects

- Decreases thickness and increases fluidity of mucus from lungs and bronchial tubes.
- Protects scraped tissues.
- Interferes with absorption of iron and other minerals when taken internally.

Unproved Speculated Benefits

- Decreases discomfort of cough.

Warnings and Precautions

Don't take if you:
- Are pregnant, think you may be pregnant or plan pregnancy in the near future.

Consult your doctor if you:
- Take this herb for any medical problem that doesn't improve in 2 weeks. There may be safer, more effective treatments.
- Take any medicinal drugs or herbs including aspirin, laxatives, cold and cough remedies, antacids, vitamins, minerals, amino acids, supplements, other prescription or non-prescription drugs.

Pregnancy:
- Dangers outweigh any possible benefits. Don't use.

Breast-feeding:
- Dangers outweigh any possible benefits. Don't use.

Infants and children:
- Treating infants and children under 2 with any herbal preparation is hazardous.

Others:
- None expected if you are beyond childhood and under 45, basically healthy and take for only a short time.

Storage:
- Keep cool and dry, but don't freeze. Store safely away from children.

Safe dosage:
- At present no "safe" dosage has been established.

Toxicity

Rated relatively safe when taken in appropriate quantities for short periods of time.

For symptoms of toxicity: See *Adverse Reactions, Side Effects or Overdose Symptoms* section below.

Adverse Reactions, Side Effects or Overdose Symptoms

Signs and symptoms:	What to do:
Skin rash	Discontinue. Call doctor when convenient.

Snakeplant

Basic Information

Biological name (genus and species):
  Rivea corymbosa
Parts used for medicinal purposes:
  Seeds
Chemicals this herb contains:
  Five related LSD-like alkaloids:
    Chanoclavine
    D-isolysergic acid amide
    D-lysergic acid amide
    Elymoclavine
    Lysergol

Known Effects

• Depresses central nervous system.

Miscellaneous information:
• Snakeplant is used primarily by Mexican Indians in religious ceremonies. They call it *badah.*

Unproved Speculated Benefits

• Changes mood.
• Causes hallucinations.

Warnings and Precautions

Don't take if you:
• Are pregnant, think you may be pregnant or plan pregnancy in the near future.
• Have any chronic disease of the gastrointestinal tract, such as stomach or duodenal ulcers, oesophageal reflux (reflux oesophagitis), ulcerative colitis, spastic colitis, diverticulosis, diverticulitis.

Consult your doctor if you:
• Take this herb for any medical problem that doesn't improve in 2 weeks. There may be safer, more effective treatments.
• Take any medicinal drugs or herbs including aspirin, laxatives, cold and cough remedies, antacids, vitamins, minerals, amino acids, supplements, other prescription or non-prescription drugs.

Pregnancy:
• Dangers outweigh any possible benefits. Don't use.

Breast-feeding:
• Dangers outweigh any possible benefits. Don't use.

Infants and children:
• Treating infants and children under 2 with any herbal preparation is hazardous.

Others:
• Dangers outweigh any possible benefits. Don't use.

Storage:
• Keep cool and dry, but don't freeze. Store safely away from children.

Safe dosage:
• At present no "safe" dosage has been established.

Toxicity

Rated slightly dangerous, particularly in children, persons over 55 and those who take larger than appropriate quantities for extended periods of time.

For symptoms of toxicity: See *Adverse Reactions, Side Effects or Overdose Symptoms* section below.

Adverse Reactions, Side Effects or Overdose Symptoms

Signs and symptoms:	What to do:
Blurred vision	Discontinue. Call doctor immediately.
Coma	Seek emergency treatment.
Confusion	Discontinue. Call doctor immediately.
Hallucinations	Seek emergency treatment.
Nausea	Discontinue. Call doctor immediately.
Stupor	Discontinue. Call doctor immediately.
Vomiting	Discontinue. Call doctor immediately.

Snakeroot (Virginia Snakeroot, Serpentaria)

Basic Information

Biological name (genus and species):
Aristolochia serpentaria
Parts used for medicinal purposes:
Roots
Chemicals this herb contains:
Borneol
Serpentaria
Terpene
Volatile oils (See Glossary)

Known Effects

- Stimulates stomach secretions.
- Stimulates smooth-muscle contractions of gastrointestinal tract and heart.

Unproved Speculated Benefits

- Increases circulation.
- Stimulates heart action.
- Treats dyspepsia.
- Reduces fever.
- Treats sores on skin.

Warnings and Precautions

Don't take if you:
- Are pregnant, think you may be pregnant or plan pregnancy in the near future.
- Have any chronic disease of the gastrointestinal tract, such as stomach or duodenal ulcers, oesophageal reflux (reflux oesophagitis), ulcerative colitis, spastic colitis, diverticulosis, diverticulitis.

Consult your doctor if you:
- Take this herb for any medical problem that doesn't improve in 2 weeks. There may be safer, more effective treatments.
- Take any medicinal drugs or herbs including aspirin, laxatives, cold and cough remedies, antacids, vitamins, minerals, amino acids, supplements, other prescription or non-prescription drugs.

Pregnancy:
- Dangers outweigh any possible benefits. Don't use.

Breast-feeding:
- Dangers outweigh any possible benefits. Don't use.

Infants and children:
- Treating infants and children under 2 with any herbal preparation is hazardous.

Others:
- None expected if you are under 45, not pregnant, basically healthy, take it for only a short time and do not exceed manufacturer's recommended dosage.

Storage:
- Keep cool and dry, but don't freeze. Store safely away from children.

Safe dosage:
- At present no "safe" dosage has been established.

Toxicity

Rated relatively safe when taken in appropriate quantities for short periods of time.

For symptoms of toxicity: See *Adverse Reactions, Side Effects or Overdose Symptoms* section below.

Adverse Reactions, Side Effects or Overdose Symptoms

Signs and symptoms:	What to do:
Diarrhoea	Discontinue. Call doctor immediately.
Nausea	Discontinue. Call doctor immediately.
Tenesmus (spasm of rectal sphincter)	Discontinue. Call doctor when convenient.
Vomiting	Discontinue. Call doctor immediately.

Spanish Broom

Basic Information

Biological name (genus and species):
   Spartium junceum
Parts used for medicinal purposes:
   Petals/flower
Chemicals this herb contains:
   Anagyrine
   Cytisine
   Methylcystinine

Known Effects

- Stimulates uterine contractions.
- Helps body dispose of excess fluid by increasing amount of urine produced.
- Stimulates gastrointestinal tract.
- Causes vomiting.

Unproved Speculated Benefits

- Induces labour.
- Causes watery, explosive bowel movements.

Warnings and Precautions

Don't take if you:
- Are pregnant, think you may be pregnant or plan pregnancy in the near future.
- Have any chronic disease of the gastrointestinal tract, such as stomach or duodenal ulcers, oesophageal reflux (reflux oesophagitis), ulcerative colitis, spastic colitis, diverticulosis, diverticulitis.

Consult your doctor if you:
- Take this herb for any medical problem that doesn't improve in 2 weeks. There may be safer, more effective treatments.
- Take any medicinal drugs or herbs including aspirin, laxatives, cold and cough remedies, antacids, vitamins, minerals, amino acids, supplements, other prescription or non-prescription drugs.

Pregnancy:
- Dangers outweigh any possible benefits. Don't use.

Breast-feeding:
- Dangers outweigh any possible benefits. Don't use.

Infants and children:
- Treating infants and children under 2 with any herbal preparation is hazardous.

Others:
- None expected if you are under 45, not pregnant, basically healthy, take it for only a short time and do not exceed manufacturer's recommended dosage.

Storage:
- Keep cool and dry, but don't freeze. Store safely away from children.

Safe dosage:
- At present no "safe" dosage has been established.

Toxicity

Comparative-toxicity rating not available from standard references.

For symptoms of toxicity: See *Adverse Reactions, Side Effects or Overdose Symptoms* section below.

Adverse Reactions, Side Effects or Overdose Symptoms

Signs and symptoms:	What to do:
Diarrhoea	Discontinue. Call doctor immediately.
Kidney damage characterized by blood in urine, decreased urine flow, swelling of hands and feet	Seek emergency treatment.
Muscle weakness	Discontinue. Call doctor immediately.
Nausea	Discontinue. Call doctor immediately.
Vomiting	Discontinue. Call doctor immediately.

Basic Information

Biological name (genus and species):
Mentha spicata
Parts used for medicinal purposes:
Leaves
Petals/flower
Chemicals this herb contains:
Carvone
Resin (See Glossary)
Volatile oils (See Glossary)

Known Effects

• Stimulates muscular action of gastrointestinal tract.

Miscellaneous information:
• Spearmint is used as a flavouring agent in many foods.

Unproved Speculated Benefits

• Aids in expelling gas from intestinal tract.

Warnings and Precautions

Don't take if you:
• Are pregnant, think you may be pregnant or plan pregnancy in the near future.
• Have any chronic disease of the gastrointestinal tract, such as stomach or duodenal ulcers, oesophageal reflux (reflux oesophagitis), ulcerative colitis, spastic colitis, diverticulosis, diverticulitis.

Consult your doctor if you:
• Take this herb for any medical problem that doesn't improve in 2 weeks. There may be safer, more effective treatments.
• Take any medicinal drugs or herbs including aspirin, laxatives, cold and cough remedies, antacids, vitamins, minerals, amino acids, supplements, other prescription or non-prescription drugs.

Pregnancy:
• Problems in pregnant women taking small or usual amounts have not been proved. But the chance of problems does exist. Don't use unless prescribed by your doctor.

Breast-feeding:
• Problems in breast-fed infants of lactating mothers taking small or usual amounts have not been proved. But the chance of problems does exist. Don't use unless prescribed by your doctor.

Infants and children:
• Treating infants and children under 2 with any herbal preparation is hazardous.

Others:
• None expected if you are under 45, not pregnant, basically healthy, take it for only a short time and do not exceed manufacturer's recommended dosage.

Storage:
• Keep cool and dry, but don't freeze. Store safely away from children.

Safe dosage:
• At present no "safe" dosage has been established.

Toxicity

Comparative-toxicity rating not available from standard references.

For symptoms of toxicity: See *Adverse Reactions, Side Effects or Overdose Symptoms* section below.

Adverse Reactions, Side Effects or Overdose Symptoms

Signs and symptoms:	What to do:
Convulsions and coma in children	Seek emergency treatment.
Diarrhoea	Discontinue. Call doctor immediately.
Nausea	Discontinue. Call doctor immediately.
Vomiting	Discontinue. Call doctor immediately.

Strawberry (Earth Mulberry)

Basic Information

Biological name (genus and species):
Fragaria vesa, F. americana
Parts used for medicinal purposes:
Berries
Leaves
Roots
Chemicals this herb contains:
Catechins
Leucoanthocyanin
Minerals
Vitamin C

Known Effects

- Shrinks tissues.
- Prevents secretion of fluids.
- Prevents scurvy.
- Inhibits production of histamines.
- Precipitates proteins.

Miscellaneous information:
- Wild strawberry is a member of the rose family.

Unproved Speculated Benefits

- Increases effectiveness of antihistamines.
- Berries treat kidney stones.
- Roots and leaves treat eczema, diarrhoea, toothache, skin ulcers.

Warnings and Precautions

Don't take if you:
- Are allergic to strawberries.

Consult your doctor if you:
- Take this herb for any medical problem that doesn't improve in 2 weeks. There may be safer, more effective treatments.
- Take any medicinal drugs or herbs including aspirin, laxatives, cold and cough remedies, antacids, vitamins, minerals, amino acids, supplements, other prescription or non-prescription drugs.

Pregnancy:
- Pregnant women should experience no problems taking usual amounts as part of a balanced diet. Other products extracted from this herb have not been proved to cause problems.

Breast-feeding:
- Breast-fed infants of lactating mothers should experience no problems when mother takes usual amounts as part of a balanced diet. Other products extracted from this herb have not been proved to cause problems.

Infants and children:
- Treating infants and children under 2 with any herbal preparation is hazardous.

Others:
- None expected if you are beyond childhood and under 45, basically healthy and take for only a short time.

Storage:
- Keep cool and dry, but don't freeze. Store safely away from children.

Safe dosage:
- At present no "safe" dosage has been established.

Toxicity

Generally regarded as safe when taken in appropriate quantities for short periods of time.

Adverse Reactions, Side Effects or Overdose Symptoms

None expected

Basic Information

Biological name (genus and species):
Rhus glabra, R. blabrum
Parts used for medicinal purposes:
Bark
Berries
Leaves
Chemicals this herb contains:
Albumin
Malic acid
Resin (See Glossary)
Tannins (See Glossary)
Volatile oils (See Glossary)

 Known Effects

Bark:
• Shrinks tissues.
• Prevents secretion of fluids.
• Inhibits growth and development of germs.
Berries:
• Help body dispose of excess fluid by increasing amount of urine produced.
• Interfere with absorption of iron and other minerals when taken internally.

Miscellaneous information:
• In same plant family as poison ivy and poison oak.

 Unproved Speculated Benefits

• Treats diarrhoea.
• Treats rectal bleeding.
• Treats asthma when leaves are smoked.

Warnings and Precautions

Don't take if you:
• Are pregnant, think you may be pregnant or plan pregnancy in the near future.

Consult your doctor if you:
• Take this herb for any medical problem that doesn't improve in 2 weeks. There may be safer, more effective treatments.
• Take any medicinal drugs or herbs including aspirin, laxatives, cold and cough remedies, antacids, vitamins, minerals, amino acids, supplements, other prescription or non-prescription drugs.

Pregnancy:
• Problems in pregnant women taking small or usual amounts have not been proved. But the chance of problems does exist. Don't use unless prescribed by your doctor.

Breast-feeding:
• Problems in breast-fed infants of lactating mothers taking small or usual amounts have not been proved. But the chance of problems does exist. Don't use unless prescribed by your doctor.

Infants and children:
• Treating infants and children under 2 with any herbal preparation is hazardous.

Others:
• None expected if you are beyond childhood and under 45, basically healthy and take for only a short time.

Storage:
• Keep cool and dry, but don't freeze. Store safely away from children.

Safe dosage:
• At present no "safe" dosage has been established.

 Toxicity

Comparative-toxicity rating not available from standard references.

 Adverse Reactions, Side Effects or Overdose Symptoms

None expected

Sundew

Basic Information

Biological name (genus and species):
  Drosea rotundifolia
Parts used for medicinal purposes:
  Various parts of the entire plant, frequently
  differing by country and/or culture
Chemicals this herb contains:
  Citric acid
  Droserone
  Malic acid
  Resin (See Glossary)
  Tannins (See Glossary)

Known Effects

- Interferes with absorption of iron and other minerals when taken internally.
- Loosens bronchial secretions.

Unproved Speculated Benefits

- Treats whooping cough.
- Treats laryngitis.
- Treats smoker's cough.

Warnings and Precautions

Don't take if you:
- Are pregnant, think you may be pregnant or plan pregnancy in the near future.

Consult your doctor if you:
- Take this herb for any medical problem that doesn't improve in 2 weeks. There may be safer, more effective treatments.
- Take any medicinal drugs or herbs including aspirin, laxatives, cold and cough remedies, antacids, vitamins, minerals, amino acids, supplements, other prescription or non-prescription drugs.

Pregnancy:
- Problems in pregnant women taking small or usual amounts have not been proved. But the chance of problems does exist. Don't use unless prescribed by your doctor.

Breast-feeding:
- Problems in breast-fed infants of lactating mothers taking small or usual amounts have not been proved. But the chance of problems does exist. Don't use unless prescribed by your doctor.

Infants and children:
- Treating infants and children under 2 with any herbal preparation is hazardous.

Others:
- None expected if you are beyond childhood and under 45, basically healthy and take for only a short time.

Storage:
- Keep cool and dry, but don't freeze. Store safely away from children.

Safe dosage:
- At present no "safe" dosage has been established.

Toxicity

Comparative-toxicity rating not available from standard references.

Adverse Reactions, Side Effects or Overdose Symptoms

None expected

Basic Information

Biological name (genus and species):
Helianthus annuus
Parts used for medicinal purposes:
Leaves
Petals/flower
Seeds
Chemicals this herb contains:
Arachidic acid
Behenic acid
Linoleic acid
Linolenic acid
Oleic acid
Palmitic acid
Stearic acid
Vitamin E

Known Effects

- Reduces blood sugar.
- Decreases inflammation in bronchi.

Miscellaneous information:
- Sunflower is a food source.

Unproved Speculated Benefits

- Treats vitamin-E deficiency.
- Treats bronchial irritation and common colds.
- Reduces fevers.
- Relieves pain of arthritis.
- Increases urine flow.
- Increases perspiration.

Warnings and Precautions

Don't take if you:
- No contraindications if you are not pregnant and do not take amounts larger than manufacturer's recommended dosage.

Consult your doctor if you:
- Take this herb for any medical problem that doesn't improve in 2 weeks. There may be safer, more effective treatments.
- Take any medicinal drugs or herbs including aspirin, laxatives, cold and cough remedies, antacids, vitamins, minerals, amino acids, supplements, other prescription or non-prescription drugs.

Pregnancy:
- Problems in pregnant women taking small or usual amounts have not been proved. But the chance of problems does exist. Don't use unless prescribed by your doctor.

Breast-feeding:
- Problems in breast-fed infants of lactating mothers taking small or usual amounts have not been proved. But the chance of problems does exist. Don't use unless prescribed by your doctor.

Infants and children:
- Treating infants and children under 2 with any herbal preparation is hazardous.

Others:
- None expected if you are beyond childhood and under 45, basically healthy and take for only a short time.

Storage:
- Keep cool and dry, but don't freeze. Store safely away from children.

Safe dosage:
- At present no "safe" dosage has been established.

Toxicity

Comparative-toxicity rating not available from standard references.

Adverse Reactions, Side Effects or Overdose Symptoms

None expected

Sweet Violet

Basic Information

Biological name (genus and species):
Viola odorata, V. pedapa
Parts used for medicinal purposes:
Leaves
Seeds
Chemicals this herb contains:
Glycosides (See Glossary)
Myrosin

Known Effects

- Irritates mucous membranes.
- Stimulates gastrointestinal tract.

Miscellaneous information:
- Sweet violet was used to treat cancer as early as 500 B.C., but evidence of real benefit is lacking.

Unproved Speculated Benefits

- Is used as poultice to treat cancer. (See Glossary.)
- Treats skin disease.
- Is used as a mild laxative.
- Causes vomiting.
- Decreases thickness and increases fluidity of mucus from lungs and bronchial tubes.
- Treats coughs.

Warnings and Precautions

Don't take if you:
- Are pregnant, think you may be pregnant or plan pregnancy in the near future.
- Have any chronic disease of the gastrointestinal tract, such as stomach or duodenal ulcers, oesophageal reflux (reflux oesophagitis), ulcerative colitis, spastic colitis, diverticulosis, diverticulitis.

Consult your doctor if you:
- Take this herb for any medical problem that doesn't improve in 2 weeks. There may be safer, more effective treatments.
- Take any medicinal drugs or herbs including aspirin, laxatives, cold and cough remedies, antacids, vitamins, minerals, amino acids, supplements, other prescription or non-prescription drugs.

Pregnancy:
- Problems in pregnant women taking small or usual amounts have not been proved. But the chance of problems does exist. Don't use unless prescribed by your doctor.

Breast-feeding:
- Problems in breast-fed infants of lactating mothers taking small or usual amounts have not been proved. But the chance of problems does exist. Don't use unless prescribed by your doctor.

Infants and children:
- Treating infants and children under 2 with any herbal preparation is hazardous.

Others:
- None expected if you are beyond childhood and under 45, basically healthy and take for only a short time.

Storage:
- Keep cool and dry, but don't freeze. Store safely away from children.

Safe dosage:
- At present no "safe" dosage has been established.

Toxicity

Comparative-toxicity rating not available from standard references.

For symptoms of toxicity: See *Adverse Reactions, Side Effects or Overdose Symptoms* section below.

Adverse Reactions, Side Effects or Overdose Symptoms

Signs and symptoms:	What to do:
Seeds:	
Diarrhoea	Discontinue. Call doctor immediately.
Nausea	Discontinue. Call doctor immediately.
Vomiting	Discontinue. Call doctor immediately.

Basic Information

Biological name (genus and species):
Tanacetum vulgare
Parts used for medicinal purposes:
Entire plant
Chemicals this herb contains:
Bitters (See Glossary)
Borneol
Camphor
Resin (See Glossary)
Tanacetone
Thujone

Known Effects

- Stimulates uterine contractions.
- Stimulates appetite.
- Kills intestinal parasites.

Miscellaneous information:
- Tansy is a powerful herb that should be avoided or used *only* under strict medical supervision.

Unproved Speculated Benefits

- Treats pain.
- Causes euphoria.
- Treats roundworms and pinworms.
- Treats menstrual difficulties.

Warnings and Precautions

Don't take if you:
- Are pregnant, think you may be pregnant or plan pregnancy in the near future.
- Have any chronic disease of the gastrointestinal tract, such as stomach or duodenal ulcers, oesophageal reflux (reflux oesophagitis), ulcerative colitis, spastic colitis, diverticulosis, diverticulitis.

Consult your doctor if you:
- Take this herb for any medical problem that doesn't improve in 2 weeks. There may be safer, more effective treatments.
- Take any medicinal drugs or herbs including aspirin, laxatives, cold and cough remedies, antacids, vitamins, minerals, amino acids, supplements, other prescription or non-prescription drugs.

Pregnancy:
- Dangers outweigh any possible benefits. Don't use.

Breast-feeding:
- Dangers outweigh any possible benefits. Don't use.

Infants and children:
- Treating infants and children under 2 with any herbal preparation is hazardous.

Others:
- Dangers outweigh any possible benefits. Don't use.

Storage:
- Keep cool and dry, but don't freeze. Store safely away from children.

Safe dosage:
- At present no "safe" dosage has been established.

Toxicity

Rated dangerous, particularly in children, persons over 55 and those who take larger than appropriate quantities for extended periods of time.

For symptoms of toxicity: See *Adverse Reactions, Side Effects or Overdose Symptoms* section below.

Adverse Reactions, Side Effects or Overdose Symptoms

Signs and symptoms:	What to do:
Coma	Seek emergency treatment.
Convulsions	Seek emergency treatment.
Diarrhoea	Discontinue. Call doctor immediately.
Dilated pupils	Seek emergency treatment.
Nausea	Discontinue. Call doctor immediately.
Vomiting	Discontinue. Call doctor immediately.
Weak, rapid pulse	Seek emergency treatment.

Thyme, Common

Basic Information

Biological name (genus and species):
    Thymus vulgaris
Parts used for medicinal purposes:
    Berries/fruits
    Leaves
Chemicals this herb contains:
    Gum (See Glossary)
    Tannins (See Glossary)
    Thyme oil

Known Effects

- Inhibits growth and development of germs.
- Stimulates gastrointestinal tract.
- Decreases thickness of bronchial secretions.
- Interferes with absorption of iron and other minerals when taken internally.

Unproved Speculated Benefits

- Reduces flatulence.
- Treats coughs.
- Treats bronchitis.
- Treats hookworm.
- Treats bacterial infections.

Warnings and Precautions

Don't take if you:
- Are pregnant, think you may be pregnant or plan pregnancy in the near future.

Consult your doctor if you:
- Take this herb for any medical problem that doesn't improve in 2 weeks. There may be safer, more effective treatments.
- Take any medicinal drugs or herbs including aspirin, laxatives, cold and cough remedies, antacids, vitamins, minerals, amino acids, supplements, other prescription or non-prescription drugs.

Pregnancy:
- Problems in pregnant women taking small or usual amounts have not been proved. But the chance of problems does exist. Don't use unless prescribed by your doctor.

Breast-feeding:
- Problems in breast-fed infants of lactating mothers taking small or usual amounts have not been proved. But the chance of problems does exist. Don't use unless prescribed by your doctor.

Infants and children:
- Treating infants and children under 2 with any herbal preparation is hazardous.

Others:
- None expected if you are beyond childhood and under 45, basically healthy and take for only a short time.

Storage:
- Keep cool and dry, but don't freeze. Store safely away from children.

Safe dosage:
- At present no "safe" dosage has been established.

Toxicity

Rated relatively safe when taken in appropriate quantities for short periods of time.

For symptoms of toxicity: See *Adverse Reactions, Side Effects or Overdose Symptoms* section below.

Adverse Reactions, Side Effects or Overdose Symptoms

Signs and symptoms:	What to do:
Diarrhoea	Discontinue. Call doctor immediately.
Nausea	Discontinue. Call doctor immediately.
Vomiting	Discontinue. Call doctor immediately.

Basic Information

Biological name (genus and species):
Coumarouna odorata, Dipteryx odorta
Parts used for medicinal purposes:
Seeds
Chemicals this herb contains:
Coumarin
Gum (See Glossary)
Sitosterin
Starch
Stigmasterin
Sugar

Known Effects

• Delays or stops blood clotting.
• Acts as anti-coagulant. Coumarin interferes with synthesis of vitamin K in the human intestines. The absence of adequate vitamin K prevents blood clotting.

Miscellaneous information:
• The tonka bean was once a common adulterant of vanilla extracts.
• Is used as flavouring in tobacco.

Unproved Speculated Benefits

• Prevents clotting in deep veins.
• Prevents blood clots from breaking away from blood vessels and lodging in vital organs, such as lung or brain. Its use must be monitored carefully with frequent laboratory studies (prothrombin time).

Warnings and Precautions

Don't take if you:
• Are pregnant, think you may be pregnant or plan pregnancy in the near future.

Consult your doctor if you:
• Take this herb for any medical problem that doesn't improve in 2 weeks. There may be safer, more effective treatments.
• Take any medicinal drugs or herbs including aspirin, laxatives, cold and cough remedies, antacids, vitamins, minerals, amino acids, supplements, other prescription or non-prescription drugs.

Pregnancy:
• Dangers outweigh any possible benefits. Don't use.

Breast-feeding:
• Dangers outweigh any possible benefits. Don't use.

Infants and children:
• Treating infants and children under 2 with any herbal preparation is hazardous.

Others:
• Dangers outweigh any possible benefits. Don't use.

Storage:
• Keep cool and dry, but don't freeze. Store safely away from children.

Safe dosage:
• At present no "safe" dosage has been established.

Toxicity

Comparative-toxicity rating not available from standard references.

For symptoms of toxicity: See *Adverse Reactions, Side Effects or Overdose Symptoms* section below.

Adverse Reactions, Side Effects or Overdose Symptoms

Signs and symptoms:	What to do:
Atrophy of testicles	Discontinue. Call doctor when convenient.
Jaundice (yellow skin and eyes)	Discontinue. Call doctor when convenient.
Retards growth	Discontinue. Call doctor when convenient.
Uncontrollable internal bleeding	Seek emergency treatment.

Tormentil

Basic Information

Biological name (genus and species):
Potentill erecta, P. tormentil
Parts used for medicinal purposes:
Roots
Chemicals this herb contains:
Ellagic acid
Kinovic
Tannins (See Glossary)

Known Effects

- Shrinks tissues.
- Prevents secretion of fluids.
- Interferes with absorption of iron and other minerals when taken internally.

Unproved Speculated Benefits

- Treats diarrhoea.
- Treats sore throat.
- Is used as poultice for wounds. (See Glossary.)

Warnings and Precautions

Don't take if you:
- Are pregnant, think you may be pregnant or plan pregnancy in the near future.
- Have any chronic disease of the gastrointestinal tract, such as stomach or duodenal ulcers, oesophageal reflux (reflux oesophagitis), ulcerative colitis, spastic colitis, diverticulosis, diverticulitis.

Consult your doctor if you:
- Take this herb for any medical problem that doesn't improve in 2 weeks. There may be safer, more effective treatments.
- Take any medicinal drugs or herbs including aspirin, laxatives, cold and cough remedies, antacids, vitamins, minerals, amino acids, supplements, other prescription or non-prescription drugs.

Pregnancy:
- Problems in pregnant women taking small or usual amounts have not been proved. But the chance of problems does exist. Don't use unless prescribed by your doctor.

Breast-feeding:
- Problems in breast-fed infants of lactating mothers taking small or usual amounts have not been proved. But the chance of problems does exist. Don't use unless prescribed by your doctor.

Infants and children:
- Treating infants and children under 2 with any herbal preparation is hazardous.

Others:
- None expected if you are beyond childhood and under 45, basically healthy and take for only a short time.

Storage:
- Keep cool and dry, but don't freeze. Store safely away from children.

Safe dosage:
- At present no "safe" dosage has been established.

Toxicity

Comparative-toxicity rating not available from standard references.

For symptoms of toxicity: See *Adverse Reactions, Side Effects or Overdose Symptoms* section below.

Adverse Reactions, Side Effects or Overdose Symptoms

Signs and symptoms:	What to do:
Diarrhoea	Discontinue. Call doctor immediately.
Kidney damage characterized by blood in urine, decreased urine flow, swelling of hands and feet	See emergency treatment.
Nausea	Discontinue. Call doctor immediately.
Vomiting	Discontinue. Call doctor immediately.

Unicorn Root (Star Grass, Colic Root)

Basic Information

Biological name (genus and species):
Aletris farinosa
Parts used for medicinal purposes:
Leaves
Roots
Chemicals this herb contains:
Diosgenin
Resin (See Glossary)
Saponins (See Glossary)
Volatile oils (See Glossary)

Known Effects

• Reduces smooth-muscle spasms.

Miscellaneous information:
• Serves as base substance to produce synthetic progesterone (a female hormone).

Unproved Speculated Benefits

• Treats painful menstruation.
• Decreases chances of miscarriage.
• Soothes sore breasts.
• Relieves flatulence.
• Relieves arthritis.

Warnings and Precautions

Don't take if you:
• Are pregnant, think you may be pregnant or plan pregnancy in the near future.
• Have any chronic disease of the gastrointestinal tract, such as stomach or duodenal ulcers, oesophageal reflux (reflux oesophagitis), ulcerative colitis, spastic colitis, diverticulosis, diverticulitis.

Consult your doctor if you:
• Take this herb for any medical problem that doesn't improve in 2 weeks. There may be safer, more effective treatments.
• Take any medicinal drugs or herbs including aspirin, laxatives, cold and cough remedies, antacids, vitamins, minerals, amino acids, supplements, other prescription or non-prescription drugs.

Pregnancy:
• Problems in pregnant women taking small or usual doses have not been proved. But the chance of problems does exist. Don't use unless prescribed by your doctor.

Breast-feeding:
• Problems in breast-fed infants of lactating mothers taking small or usual doses have not been proved. But the chance of problems does exist. Don't use unless prescribed by your doctor.

Infants and children:
• Treating infants and children under 2 with any herbal preparation is hazardous.

Others:
• None expected if you are under 45, not pregnant, basically healthy, take it for only a short time and do not exceed manufacturer's recommended dosage.

Storage:
• Keep cool and dry, but don't freeze. Store safely away from children.

Safe dosage:
• At present no "safe" dosage has been established.

Toxicity

Rated slightly dangerous, particularly in children, persons over 55 and those who take larger than appropriate quantities for extended periods of time.

For symptoms of toxicity: See *Adverse Reactions, Side Effects or Overdose Symptoms* section below.

Adverse Reactions, Side Effects or Overdose Symptoms

Signs and symptoms:	What to do:
Diarrhoea	Discontinue. Call doctor immediately.
Lethargy	Discontinue. Call doctor when convenient.
Vomiting	Discontinue. Call doctor immediately.

Valerian (Garden Heliotrope, Tobacco Root)

Basic Information

Biological name (genus and species):
Valeriana edulis, V. officinalis
Parts used for medicinal purposes:
Rhizomes
Roots
Chemicals this herb contains:
Acetic acid
Butyric acid
Camphene
Chatinine
Formic acid
Glycosides (See Glossary)
Pinene
Resin (See Glossary)
Valeric acid
Valerine
Volatile oils (See Glossary)

Known Effects

• Depresses central nervous system.

Miscellaneous information:
• Cats are attracted to this herb.

Unproved Speculated Benefits

• Treats anxiety.
• Treats insomnia.
• Treats convulsions.
• Causes sedation.

Warnings and Precautions

Don't take if you:
• Are pregnant, think you may be pregnant or plan pregnancy in the near future.

Consult your doctor if you:
• Take this herb for any medical problem that doesn't improve in 2 weeks. There may be safer, more effective treatments.
• Take any medicinal drugs or herbs including aspirin, laxatives, cold and cough remedies, antacids, vitamins, minerals, amino acids, supplements, other prescription or non-prescription drugs.

Pregnancy:
• Problems in pregnant women taking small or usual amounts have not been proved. But the chance of problems does exist. Don't use unless prescribed by your doctor.

Breast-feeding:
• Problems in breast-fed infants of lactating mothers taking small or usual amounts have not been proved. But the chance of problems does exist. Don't use unless prescribed by your doctor.

Infants and children:
• Treating infants and children under 2 with any herbal preparation is hazardous.

Others:
• None expected if you are beyond childhood and under 45, basically healthy and take for only a short time.

Storage:
• Use fresh material only. Dried valerian loses potency.

Safe dosage:
• At present no "safe" dosage has been established.

Toxicity

Rated relatively safe when taken in appropriate quantities for short periods of time.

For symptoms of toxicity: See *Adverse Reactions, Side Effects or Overdose Symptoms* section below.

Adverse Reactions, Side Effects or Overdose Symptoms

Signs and symptoms:	What to do:
Diarrhoea	Discontinue. Call doctor immediately.
Nausea	Discontinue. Call doctor immediately.
Vomiting	Discontinue. Call doctor immediately.

Vervain (European Vervaine, Verbena)

Basic Information

Biological name (genus and species):
Verbena officinalis
Parts used for medicinal purposes:
Roots
Chemical this herb contains:
Verbenaline

Known Effects

- Stimulates gastrointestinal tract.
- Stimulates parasympathetic branch of autonomic nervous system.

Unproved Speculated Benefits

- Treats coughs.
- Treats upper-abdominal pain.
- Induces vomiting.

Warnings and Precautions

Don't take if you:
- Are pregnant, think you may be pregnant or plan pregnancy in the near future.
- Have any chronic disease of the gastrointestinal tract, such as stomach or duodenal ulcers, oesophageal reflux (reflux oesophagitis), ulcerative colitis, spastic colitis, diverticulosis, diverticulitis.

Consult your doctor if you:
- Take this herb for any medical problem that doesn't improve in 2 weeks. There may be safer, more effective treatments.
- Take any medicinal drugs or herbs including aspirin, laxatives, cold and cough remedies, antacids, vitamins, minerals, amino acids, supplements, other prescription or non-prescription drugs.

Pregnancy:
- Problems in pregnant women taking small or usual amounts have not been proved. But the chance of problems does exist. Don't use unless prescribed by your doctor.

Breast-feeding:
- Problems in breast-fed infants of lactating mothers taking small or usual amounts have not been proved. But the chance of problems does exist. Don't use unless prescribed by your doctor.

Infants and children:
- Treating infants and children under 2 with any herbal preparation is hazardous.

Others:
- None expected if you are under 45, not pregnant, basically healthy, take it for only a short time and do not exceed manufacturer's recommended dosage.

Storage:
- Keep cool and dry, but don't freeze. Store safely away from children.

Safe dosage:
- At present no "safe" dosage has been established.

Toxicity

Generally regarded as safe when taken in appropriate quantities for short periods of time.

For symptoms of toxicity: See *Adverse Reactions, Side Effects or Overdose Symptoms* section below.

Adverse Reactions, Side Effects or Overdose Symptoms

Signs and symptoms:	What to do:
Diarrhoea	Discontinue. Call doctor immediately.
Nausea	Discontinue. Call doctor immediately.
Vomiting	Discontinue. Call doctor immediately.

Virginian Skullcap

Basic Information

Biological name (genus and species):
Scutellaria lateriflora
Parts used for medicinal purposes:
Entire plant
Chemicals this herb contains:
Cellulose
Fat
Scutellarin
Sugar
Tannins (See Glossary)

Known Effects

- Increases stomach acidity.
- Irritates mucous membranes.
- Relieves spasm in skeletal or smooth muscle.
- Interferes with absorption of iron and other minerals when taken internally.

Unproved Speculated Benefits

- Stimulates appetite.
- Relieves intestinal cramps.

Warnings and Precautions

Don't take if you:
- Are pregnant, think you may be pregnant or plan pregnancy in the near future.

Consult your doctor if you:
- Take this herb for any medical problem that doesn't improve in 2 weeks. There may be safer, more effective treatments.
- Take any medicinal drugs or herbs including aspirin, laxatives, cold and cough remedies, antacids, vitamins, minerals, amino acids, supplements, other prescription or non-prescription drugs.

Pregnancy:
- Problems in pregnant women taking small or usual amounts have not been proved. But the chance of problems does exist. Don't use unless prescribed by your doctor.

Breast-feeding:
- Problems in breast-fed infants of lactating mothers taking small or usual amounts have not been proved. But the chance of problems does exist. Don't use unless prescribed by your doctor.

Infants and children:
- Treating infants and children under 2 with any herbal preparation is hazardous.

Others:
- None expected if you are under 45, not pregnant, basically healthy, take it for only a short time and do not exceed manufacturer's recommended dosage.

Storage:
- Keep cool and dry, but don't freeze. Store safely away from children.

Safe dosage:
- At present no "safe" dosage has been established.

Toxicity

Rated relatively safe when taken in appropriate quantities for short periods of time.

For symptoms of toxicity: See *Adverse Reactions, Side Effects or Overdose Symptoms* section below.

Adverse Reactions, Side Effects or Overdose Symptoms

Signs and symptoms:	What to do:
Confusion	Discontinue. Call doctor immediately.
Giddiness	Discontinue. Call doctor when convenient.
Irregular heartbeat	Seek emergency treatment.
Stupor	Seek emergency treatment.

Basic Information

Biological name (genus and species):
Nasturtium officinale
Parts used for medicinal purposes:
Various parts of the entire plant, frequently differing by country and/or culture
Chemicals this herb contains:
Several trace element minerals, such as vanadium and cobalt
Vitamins A, C, B-1 and B-2

Known Effects

- Provides a good source of vitamins and minerals to treat or prevent various deficiencies.

Miscellaneous information:
- Watercress is a nutritious food source. Toxicity is unlikely.

Unproved Speculated Benefits

- Treats kidney infections.
- Treats urinary bladder stones.
- Increases urine flow.
- Treats heart disease.
- Diminishes pain during childbirth.

Warnings and Precautions

Don't take if you:
- No contraindications if you are not pregnant and do not take amounts larger than a reputable manufacturer recommends on the package.

Consult your doctor if you:
- Take this herb for any medical problem that doesn't improve in 2 weeks. There may be safer, more effective treatments.
- Take any medicinal drugs or herbs including aspirin, laxatives, cold and cough remedies, antacids, vitamins, minerals, amino acids, supplements, other prescription or non-prescription drugs.

Pregnancy:
- Problems in pregnant women taking small or usual amounts have not been proved. But the chance of problems does exist. Don't use unless prescribed by your doctor.

Breast-feeding:
- Problems in breast-fed infants of lactating mothers taking small or usual amounts have not been proved. But the chance of problems does exist. Don't use unless prescribed by your doctor.

Infants and children:
- Treating infants and children under 2 with any herbal preparation is hazardous.

Others:
- None expected if you are beyond childhood and under 45, basically healthy and take for only a short time.

Storage:
- Keep cool and dry, but don't freeze. Store safely away from children.

Safe dosage:
- At present no "safe" dosage has been established.

Toxicity

Comparative-toxicity rating not available from standard references.

Adverse Reactions, Side Effects or Overdose Symptoms

None expected

White Pine

Basic Information

Biological name (genus and species):
  Pinus strobus, P. alba
Parts used for medicinal purposes:
  Inner bark
Chemicals this herb contains:
  Coniferin
  Coniferyl alcohol
  Mucilage (See Glossary)
  Oleoresin
  Tannic acid
  Vanillin
  Volatile oils (See Glossary)

Known Effects

• Decreases thickness and increases fluidity of mucus from lungs and bronchial tubes.

Unproved Speculated Benefits

• Treats coughs when mixed with other expectorants.

Warnings and Precautions

Don't take if you:
• Are pregnant, think you may be pregnant or plan pregnancy in the near future.

Consult your doctor if you:
• Take this herb for any medical problem that doesn't improve in 2 weeks. There may be safer, more effective treatments.
• Take any medicinal drugs or herbs including aspirin, laxatives, cold and cough remedies, antacids, vitamins, minerals, amino acids, supplements, other prescription or non-prescription drugs.

Pregnancy:
• Problems in pregnant women taking small or usual amounts have not been proved. But the chance of problems does exist. Don't use unless prescribed by your doctor.

Breast-feeding:
• Problems in breast-fed infants of lactating mothers taking small or usual amounts have not been proved. But the chance of problems does exist. Don't use unless prescribed by your doctor.

Infants and children:
• Treating infants and children under 2 with any herbal preparation is hazardous.

Others:
• None expected if you are beyond childhood and under 45, basically healthy and take for only a short time.

Storage:
• Keep cool and dry, but don't freeze. Store safely away from children.

Safe dosage:
• At present no "safe" dosage has been established.

Toxicity

Rated slightly dangerous, particularly in children, persons over 55 and those who take larger than appropriate quantities for extended periods of time.

Adverse Reactions, Side Effects or Overdose Symptoms

None expected

Willow (Black Willow, Pussy Willow, Yellow Willow)

Basic Information

Biological name (genus and species):
Salix nigra
Parts used for medicinal purposes:
Bark
Chemicals this herb contains:
Salicin
Salinigrin
Tannins (See Glossary)

Known Effects

- Causes protein molecules to clump together.
- Produces puckering.
- Interferes with absorption of iron and other minerals when taken internally.

Miscellaneous information:
- Tannins may help heal *open* wounds.

Unproved Speculated Benefits

- Shrinks tissues.
- Prevents secretion of fluids.
- Acts as an antiseptic for ulcerated surfaces on skin.
- Treats arthritis.

Warnings and Precautions

Don't take if you:
- Are pregnant, think you may be pregnant or plan pregnancy in the near future.

Consult your doctor if you:
- Take this herb for any medical problem that doesn't improve in 2 weeks. There may be safer, more effective treatments.
- Take any medicinal drugs or herbs including aspirin, laxatives, cold and cough remedies, antacids, vitamins, minerals, amino acids, supplements, other prescription or non-prescription drugs.

Pregnancy:
- Problems in pregnant women taking small or usual doses have not been proved. But the chance of problems does exist. Don't use unless prescribed by your doctor.

Breast-feeding:
- Problems in breast-fed infants of lactating mothers taking small or usual doses have not been proved. But the chance of problems does exist. Don't use unless prescribed by your doctor.

Infants and children:
- Treating infants and children under 2 with any herbal preparation is hazardous.

Others:
- None expected if you are under 45, not pregnant, basically healthy, take it for only a short time and do not exceed manufacturer's recommended dosage.
- Salicylate poisoning is possible. Symptoms include dizziness, vomiting, ringing in ears.

Storage:
- Keep cool and dry, but don't freeze. Store safely away from children.

Safe dosage:
- At present no "safe" dosage has been established.

Toxicity

Comparative-toxicity rating not available from standard references.

For symptoms of toxicity: See *Adverse Reactions, Side Effects or Overdose Symptoms* section below.

Adverse Reactions, Side Effects or Overdose Symptoms

Signs and symptoms:	What to do:
Dizziness	Discontinue. Call doctor immediately.
Ringing in ears	Discontinue. Call doctor when convenient.
Vomiting	Discontinue. Call doctor immediately.

MEDICINAL HERB

445

Wintergreen (Boxberry, Teaberry)

Basic Information

Biological name (genus and species):
   Gaultheria procumbens
Parts used for medicinal purposes:
   Leaves
   Roots
   Stems
Chemicals this herb contains:
   Methyl salicylate
   Monotropitoside

Known Effects

- Blocks impulses to pain centre in brain.
- Irritates stomach.

Miscellaneous information:
- Toxicity is unlikely unless you consume very large amounts of the entire plant.

Unproved Speculated Benefits

- Relieves headache.
- Treats toothache.
- Treats pain of sprains and bruises.

Warnings and Precautions

Don't take if you:
- Are pregnant, think you may be pregnant or plan pregnancy in the near future.

Consult your doctor if you:
- Take this herb for any medical problem that doesn't improve in 2 weeks. There may be safer, more effective treatments.
- Take any medicinal drugs or herbs including aspirin, laxatives, cold and cough remedies, antacids, vitamins, minerals, amino acids, supplements, other prescription or non-prescription drugs.

Pregnancy:
- Dangers outweigh any possible benefits. Don't use.

Breast-feeding:
- Dangers outweigh any possible benefits. Don't use.

Infants and children:
- Treating infants and children under 2 with any herbal preparation is hazardous.

Others:
- None expected if you are beyond childhood and under 45, not pregnant, basically healthy and take for only a short time.

Storage:
- Keep cool and dry, but don't freeze. Store safely away from children.

Safe dosage:
- At present no "safe" dosage has been established.

Toxicity

Rated slightly dangerous, particularly in children, persons over 55 and those who take larger than appropriate quantities for extended periods of time.

Adverse Reactions, Side Effects or Overdose Symptoms

None expected

Basic Information

Biological name (genus and species):
Hamamelis virginiana
Parts used for medicinal purposes:
Bark
Leaves
Twigs
Chemicals this herb contains:
Bitters (See Glossary)
Calcium oxalate
Gallic acid
Hamamelitannin
Hexose sugar
Tannins (See Glossary)
Volatile oils (See Glossary)

Known Effects

- Shrinks tissues (ointments, solutions, suppositories).
- Interferes with absorption of iron and other minerals when taken internally.

Unproved Speculated Benefits

- Acts as a sedative.
- Treats diarrhoea.
- Soothes irritated skin or haemorrhoids.
- Prevents secretion of fluids.

Warnings and Precautions

Don't take if you:
- Are pregnant, think you may be pregnant or plan pregnancy in the near future.
- Have any chronic disease of the gastrointestinal tract, such as stomach or duodenal ulcers, oesophageal reflux (reflux oesophagitis), ulcerative colitis, spastic colitis, diverticulosis, diverticulitis.

Consult your doctor if you:
- Take this herb for any medical problem that doesn't improve in 2 weeks. There may be safer, more effective treatments.
- Take any medicinal drugs or herbs including aspirin, laxatives, cold and cough remedies, antacids, vitamins, minerals, amino acids, supplements, other prescription or non-prescription drugs.

Pregnancy:
- Dangers outweigh any possible benefits. Don't use.

Breast-feeding:
- Dangers outweigh any possible benefits. Don't use.

Infants and children:
- Treating infants and children under 2 with any herbal preparation is hazardous.

Others:
- When used externally, no toxicity is expected.
- When used internally, no toxicity expected if you are beyond childhood and under 45, not pregnant, basically healthy and take for only a short time.

Storage:
- Keep cool and dry, but don't freeze. Store safely away from children.

Safe dosage:
- At present no "safe" dosage has been established.

Toxicity

Rated relatively safe when taken in appropriate quantities for short periods of time.

For symptoms of toxicity: See *Adverse Reactions, Side Effects or Overdose Symptoms* section below.

Adverse Reactions, Side Effects or Overdose Symptoms

Signs and symptoms:	What to do:
Constipation	Discontinue. Call doctor when convenient.
Jaundice (yellow skin and eyes)	Discontinue. Call doctor immediately.
Nausea	Discontinue. Call doctor immediately.
Vomiting	Discontinue. Call doctor immediately.

Woodruff (Woodward Herb)

Basic Information

Biological name (genus and species):
Asperula odorata, Galium odoratum
Parts used for medicinal purposes:
Entire plant
Chemicals this herb contains:
Asperuloside
Bitters (See Glossary)
Coumarin
Oil
Tannins (See Glossary)

Known Effects

- Stimulates gastrointestinal tract.
- Decreases thickness and increases fluidity of mucus from lungs and bronchial tubes.
- Interferes with absorption of iron and other minerals when taken internally.

Miscellaneous information:
- Woodruff is used as a flavouring agent in May wine.
- It is used in sachets for its pleasant odour.

Unproved Speculated Benefits

- Treats coughs.
- Aids in expelling gas from intestinal tract.

Warnings and Precautions

Don't take if you:
- Are pregnant, think you may be pregnant or plan pregnancy in the near future.

Consult your doctor if you:
- Take this herb for any medical problem that doesn't improve in 2 weeks. There may be safer, more effective treatments.
- Take any medicinal drugs or herbs including aspirin, laxatives, cold and cough remedies, antacids, vitamins, minerals, amino acids, supplements, other prescription or non-prescription drugs.

Pregnancy:
- Problems in pregnant women taking small or usual amounts have not been proved. But the chance of problems does exist. Don't use unless prescribed by your doctor.

Breast-feeding:
- Problems in breast-fed infants of lactating mothers taking small or usual amounts have not been proved. But the chance of problems does exist. Don't use unless prescribed by your doctor.

Infants and children:
- Treating infants and children under 2 with any herbal preparation is hazardous.

Others:
- None expected if you are beyond childhood and under 45, basically healthy and take for only a short time.

Storage:
- Keep cool and dry, but don't freeze. Store safely away from children.

Safe dosage:
- At present no "safe" dosage has been established.

Toxicity

Comparative-toxicity rating not available from standard references.

Adverse Reactions, Side Effects or Overdose Symptoms

None expected

Basic Information

Biological name (genus and species):
Chenopodium ambrosioides
Parts used for medicinal purposes:
Roots
Berries/fruits
Chemicals this herb contains:

Ascaridol	Saponin (See Glossary)
Calcium	Terpene (See Glossary)
Cymene	Vitamins A and C
d-camphor	Volatile oils (See Glossary)
l-limonene	

Known Effects

- Inhibits growth and development of germs.
- Decreases blood pressure.
- Decreases heart rate.
- Depresses central nervous system.
- Decreases stomach contractions.

Unproved Speculated Benefits

- Is used externally as a poultice. (See Glossary)
- Treats arthritis.
- Kills intestinal parasites.

Warnings and Precautions

Don't take if you:
- Are pregnant, think you may be pregnant or plan pregnancy in the near future.
- Have any chronic disease of the gastrointestinal tract, such as stomach or duodenal ulcers, oesophageal reflux (reflux oesophagitis), ulcerative colitis, spastic colitis, diverticulosis, diverticulitis.

Consult your doctor if you:
- Take this herb for any medical problem that doesn't improve in 2 weeks. There may be safer, more effective treatments.
- Take any medicinal drugs or herbs including aspirin, laxatives, cold and cough remedies, antacids, vitamins, minerals, amino acids, supplements, other prescription or non-prescription drugs.

Pregnancy:
- Dangers outweigh any possible benefits. Don't use.

Breast-feeding:
- Dangers outweigh any possible benefits. Don't use.

Infants and children:
- Treating infants and children under 2 with any herbal preparation is hazardous.

Others:
- None expected if you are under 45, not pregnant, basically healthy, take it for only a short time and do not exceed manufacturer's recommended dosage.

Storage:
- Keep cool and dry, but don't freeze. Store safely away from children.

Safe dosage:
- At present no "safe" dosage has been established.

Toxicity

Rated slightly dangerous, particularly in children, persons over 55 and those who take larger than appropriate quantities for extended periods of time.

For symptoms of toxicity: See *Adverse Reactions, Side Effects or Overdose Symptoms* section below.

Adverse Reactions, Side Effects or Overdose Symptoms

Signs and symptoms:	What to do:
Breathing difficulties	Seek emergency treatment.
Drowsiness	Discontinue. Call doctor when convenient.
Headache	Discontinue. Call doctor when convenient.
Hearing problems	Discontinue. Call doctor immediately.
Nausea	Discontinue, Call doctor immediately.
Ringing in ears	Discontinue. Call doctor when convenient.
Slow heartbeat	Seek emergency treatment.
Stomach ulcers	Discontinue. Call doctor immediately.
Vision problems	Discontinue. Call doctor immediately.
Vomiting	Discontinue. Call doctor immediately.

Wormwood (Absinthium, Ajerjo)

Basic Information

Biological name (genus and species):
　Artemisia absinthium
Parts used for medicinal purposes:
　Berries/fruits
　Leaves
Chemicals this herb contains:
　Absinthol
　Thujone
　Volatile oils (See Glossary)

Others:
• This product will *not* help you and may cause toxic symptoms.

Storage:
• Keep cool and dry, but don't freeze. Store safely away from children.

Safe dosage:
• At present no "safe" dosage has been established.

Known Effects

• Depresses central nervous system.
• Thujone causes mind-altering changes and may lead to psychosis.
• Increases stomach acidity.

Miscellaneous information:
• Wormwood can be habit-forming, like ethyl alcohol.

Toxicity

Rated slightly dangerous, particularly in children, persons over 55 and those who take larger than appropriate quantities for extended periods of time.

For symptoms of toxicity: See *Adverse Reactions, Side Effects or Overdose Symptoms* section below.

Unproved Speculated Benefits

• Treats anxiety.
• Acts as a mild sedative.
• Stimulates appetite.

Adverse Reactions, Side Effects or Overdose Symptoms

Signs and symptoms:	What to do:
Convulsions	Seek emergency treatment.
Stupor	Seek emergency treatment.
Trembling	Discontinue. Call doctor when convenient.

Warnings and Precautions

Don't take if you:
• Are pregnant, think you may be pregnant or plan pregnancy in the near future.

Consult your doctor if you:
• Take this herb for any medical problem that doesn't improve in 2 weeks. There may be safer, more effective treatments.
• Take any medicinal drugs or herbs including aspirin, laxatives, cold and cough remedies, antacids, vitamins, minerals, amino acids, supplements, other prescription or non-prescription drugs.

Pregnancy:
• Dangers outweigh any possible benefits. Don't use.

Breast-feeding:
• Dangers outweigh any possible benefits. Don't use.

Infants and children:
• Treating infants and children under 2 with any herbal preparation is hazardous.

Basic Information

Biological name (genus and species):
Achillea millefolium
Parts used for medicinal purposes:
Berries/fruits
Leaves
Chemicals this herb contains:
Achilleic acid
Achilleine
Bitters (See Glossary)
Caledivain
Tannins (See Glossary)
Volatile oils (See Glossary)

Known Effects

- Reduces blood-clotting time.
- Interferes with absorption of iron and other minerals when taken internally.

Unproved Speculated Benefits

- Acts as a mild sedative to cause drowsiness.
- Treats amenorrhoea. (See Glossary.)

Warnings and Precautions

Don't take if you:
- Are pregnant, think you may be pregnant or plan pregnancy in the near future.

Consult your doctor if you:
- Take this herb for any medical problem that doesn't improve in 2 weeks. There may be safer, more effective treatments.
- Take any medicinal drugs or herbs including aspirin, laxatives, cold and cough remedies, antacids, vitamins, minerals, amino acids, supplements, other prescription or non-prescription drugs.

Pregnancy:
- Problems in pregnant women taking small or usual amounts have not been proved. But the chance of problems does exist. Don't use unless prescribed by your doctor.

Breast-feeding:
- Problems in breast-fed infants of lactating mothers taking small or usual amounts have not been proved. But the chance of problems does exist. Don't use unless prescribed by your doctor.

Infants and children:
- Treating infants and children under 2 with any herbal preparation is hazardous.

Others:
- None expected if you are under 45, not pregnant, basically healthy, take it for only a short time and do not exceed manufacturer's recommended dosage.

Storage:
- Keep cool and dry, but don't freeze. Store safety away from children.

Safe dosage:
- At present no "safe" dosage has been established.

Toxicity

Generally regarded as safe when taken in appropriate quantities for short periods of time.

Adverse Reactions, Side Effects or Overdose Symptoms

None expected

Yellow Cedar (Arbor Vitae)

Basic Information

Biological name (genus and species):
Thuja occidentalis
Parts used for medicinal purposes:
Leaves
Chemicals this herb contains:
Fenchone
Pinipirin
Tannins (See Glossary)
Thujetic acid
Thujone
Volatile oils (See Glossary)

Known Effects

- Stimulates central nervous system.
- Stimulates heart muscle to contract more efficiently.
- Destroys intestinal worms.
- Causes uterine contractions.
- Interferes with absorption of iron and other minerals when taken internally.

Miscellaneous information:
- Yellow cedar has caused deaths when it was misused to cause abortions.

Unproved Speculated Benefits

- Relieves muscular aches and pains.
- Treats warts.
- Causes abortions (miscarriages).

Warnings and Precautions

Don't take if you:
- Are pregnant, think you may be pregnant or plan pregnancy in the near future.

Consult your doctor if you:
- Take this herb for any medical problem that doesn't improve in 2 weeks. There may be safer, more effective treatments.
- Take any medicinal drugs or herbs including aspirin, laxatives, cold and cough remedies, antacids, vitamins, minerals, amino acids, supplements, other prescription or non-prescription drugs.

Pregnancy:
- Dangers outweigh any possible benefits. Don't use.

Breast-feeding:
- Dangers outweigh any possible benefits. Don't use.

Infants and children:
- Treating infants and children under 2 with any herbal preparation is hazardous.

Others:
- Dangers outweigh any possible benefits. Don't use.

Storage:
- Keep cool and dry, but don't freeze. Store safely away from children.

Safe dosage:
- At present no "safe" dosage has been established.

Toxicity

Comparative-toxicity rating not available from standard references.

For symptoms of toxicity: See *Adverse Reactions, Side Effects or Overdose Symptoms* section below.

Adverse Reactions, Side Effects or Overdose Symptoms

Signs and symptoms:	What to do:
Abortion	Seek emergency treatment.
Coma	Seek emergency treatment.
Convulsions	Seek emergency treatment.
Precipitous blood-pressure drop— symptoms include, faintness, cold sweat, paleness, rapid pulse	Seek emergency treatment.

Basic Information

Biological name (genus and species):
Rumex crispus
Parts used for medicinal purposes:
Leaves
Roots
Chemical this herb contains:
Potassium oxalate

Known Effects

- Irritates skin when handled.
- Stimulates gastrointestinal tract.

Miscellaneous information:
- Is used as food in salads.

Unproved Speculated Benefits

- Temporarily relieves constipation.

Warnings and Precautions

Don't take if you:
- Are pregnant, think you may be pregnant or plan pregnancy in the near future.
- Have any chronic disease of the gastrointestinal tract, such as stomach or duodenal ulcers, oesophageal reflux (reflux oesophagitis), ulcerative colitis, spastic colitis, diverticulosis, diverticulitis.

Consult your doctor if you:
- Take this herb for any medical problem that doesn't improve in 2 weeks. There may be safer, more effective treatments.
- Take any medicinal drugs or herbs including aspirin, laxatives, cold and cough remedies, antacids, vitamins, minerals, amino acids, supplements, other prescription or non-prescription drugs.

Pregnancy:
- Dangers outweigh any possible benefits. Don't use.

Breast-feeding:
- Dangers outweigh any possible benefits. Don't use.

Infants and children:
- Treating infants and children under 2 with any herbal preparation is hazardous.

Others:
- Dangers outweigh any possible benefits. Don't use.

Storage:
- Keep cool and dry, but don't freeze. Store safely away from children.

Safe dosage:
- At present no "safe" dosage has been established.

Toxicity

Rated slightly dangerous, particularly in children, persons over 55 and those who take larger than appropriate quantities for extended periods of time.

For symptoms of toxicity: See *Adverse Reactions, Side Effects or Overdose Symptoms* section below.

Adverse Reactions, Side Effects or Overdose Symptoms

Signs and symptoms:	What to do:
Diarrhoea	Discontinue. Call doctor immediately.
Kidney damage characterized by blood in urine, decreased urine flow, swelling of hands and feet	Seek emergency treatment.
Nausea	Discontinue. Call doctor immediately.
Skin eruptions	Discontinue. Call doctor when convenient.
Vomiting	Discontinue. Call doctor immediately.

MEDICINAL HERB

Yellow Lady's Slipper

Basic Information

Biological name (genus and species):
  Cypripedium pubescens
Parts used for medicinal purposes:
  Roots
Chemicals this herb contains:
  Resin (See Glossary)
  Tannins (See Glossary)
  Volatile acid
  Volatile oils (See Glossary)

Known Effects

- Irritates mucous membranes.
- Stimulates gastrointestinal tract.
- Increases perspiration.

Miscellaneous information:
- Hairs on stems and leaves irritate body when touched. May produce skin eruption similar to poison ivy.

Unproved Speculated Benefits

- Acts as a sedative to treat anxiety or restlessness.
- Increases perspiration.
- Aids in expelling gas from intestinal tract.
- Relieves spasm in skeletal smooth or smooth muscle.

Warnings and Precautions

Don't take if you:
- Are pregnant, think you may be pregnant or plan pregnancy in the near future.
- Have any chronic disease of the gastrointestinal tract, such as stomach or duodenal ulcers, oesophageal reflux (reflux oesophagitis), ulcerative colitis, spastic colitis, diverticulosis, diverticulitis.

Consult your doctor if you:
- Take this herb for any medical problem that doesn't improve in 2 weeks. There may be safer, more effective treatments.
- Take any medicinal drugs or herbs including aspirin, laxatives, cold and cough remedies, antacids, vitamins, minerals, amino acids, supplements, other prescription or non-prescription drugs.

Pregnancy:
- Problems in pregnant women taking small or usual amounts have not been proved. But the chance of problems does exist. Don't use unless prescribed by your doctor.

Breast-feeding:
- Problems in breast-fed infants of lactating mothers taking small or usual amounts have not been proved. But the chance of problems does exist. Don't use unless prescribed by your doctor.

Infants and children:
- Treating infants and children under 2 with any herbal preparation is hazardous.

Others:
- None expected if you are beyond childhood and under 45, basically healthy and take for only a short time.

Storage:
- Keep cool and dry, but don't freeze. Store safely away from children.

Safe dosage:
- At present no "safe" dosage has been established.

Toxicity

Rated relatively safe when taken in appropriate quantities for short periods of time.

For symptoms of toxicity: See *Adverse Reactions, Side Effects or Overdose Symptoms* section below.

Adverse Reactions, Side Effects or Overdose Symptoms

Signs and symptoms:	What to do:
Drowsiness	Discontinue. Call doctor when convenient.
Nausea	Discontinue. Call doctor immediately.
Vomiting	Discontinue. Call doctor immediately.

Yerba Mate (Paraguay Tea, South American Holly)

Basic Information

Biological name (genus and species):
   Ilex paraguariensis St. Hill
Parts used for medicinal purposes:
   Leaves
Chemical this herb contains:
   Caffeine

Known Effects

- Stimulates central nervous system.
- Helps body dispose of excess fluid by increasing amount of urine produced.
- Causes hallucinations.

Unproved Speculated Benefits

- Is used as a laxative.
- Increases perspiration.

Warnings and Precautions

Don't take if you:
- Are pregnant, think you may be pregnant or plan pregnancy in the near future.
- Have any chronic disease of the gastrointestinal tract, such as stomach or duodenal ulcers, oesophageal reflux (reflux oesophagitis), ulcerative colitis, spastic colitis, diverticulosis, diverticulitis.

Consult your doctor if you:
- Take this herb for any medical problem that doesn't improve in 2 weeks. There may be safer, more effective treatments.
- Take any medicinal drugs or herbs including aspirin, laxatives, cold and cough remedies, antacids, vitamins, minerals, amino acids, supplements, other prescription or non-prescription drugs.

Pregnancy:
- Dangers outweigh any possible benefits. Don't use.

Breast-feeding:
- Dangers outweigh any possible benefits. Don't use.

Infants and children:
- Treating infants and children under 2 with any herbal preparation is hazardous.

Others:
- None expected if you are beyond childhood and under 45, not pregnant, basically healthy and take for only a short time.

Storage:
- Keep cool and dry, but don't freeze. Store safely away from children.

Safe dosage:
- At present no "safe" dosage has been established.

Toxicity

Rated relatively safe when taken in appropriate quantities for short periods of time.

For symptoms of toxicity: See *Adverse Reactions, Side Effects or Overdose Symptoms* section below.

Adverse Reactions, Side Effects or Overdose Symptoms

Signs and symptoms:	What to do:
Confusion	Seek emergency treatment.
Excessive urination	Discontinue. Call doctor when convenient.
Hallucinations	Seek emergency treatment.
Heartburn	Discontinue. Call doctor when convenient.
Insomnia	Discontinue. Call doctor when convenient.
Irritability	Discontinue. Call doctor when convenient.
Nausea	Discontinue. Call doctor immediately.
Nervousness	Discontinue. Call doctor when convenient.
Rapid heartbeat	Seek emergency treatment.

Yerba Santa (Bear's Weed)

Basic Information

Biological name (genus and species):
Eriodictyon californicum

Parts used for medicinal purposes:
Leaves

Chemicals this herb contains:
Formic acid
Pentatriacontane eriodicytyol
Resin (See Glossary)
Tannic acid
Tannins (See Glossary)

Known Effects

- Masks taste of bitter medicines.
- Decreases thickness and increases fluidity of mucus from lungs and bronchial tubes.
- Interferes with absorption of iron and other minerals when taken internally.

Unproved Speculated Benefits

- Treats hay fever and other nasal allergies.
- Treats haemorrhoids.

Warnings and Precautions

Don't take if you:
- Are pregnant, think you may be pregnant or plan pregnancy in the near future.
- Have any chronic disease of the gastrointestinal tract, such as stomach or duodenal ulcers, oesophageal reflux (reflux oesophagitis), ulcerative colitis, spastic colitis, diverticulosis, diverticulitis.

Consult your doctor if you:
- Take this herb for any medical problem that doesn't improve in 2 weeks. There may be safer, more effective treatments.
- Take any medicinal drugs or herbs including aspirin, laxatives, cold and cough remedies, antacids, vitamins, minerals, amino acids, supplements, other prescription or non-prescription drugs.

Pregnancy:
- Dangers outweigh any possible benefits. Don't use.

Breast-feeding:
- Dangers outweigh any possible benefits. Don't use.

Infants and children:
- Treating infants and children under 2 with any herbal preparation is hazardous.

Others:
- None expected if you are beyond childhood and under 45, not pregnant, basically healthy and take for only a short time.

Storage:
- Keep cool and dry, but don't freeze. Store safely away from children.

Safe dosage:
- At present no "safe" dosage has been established.

Toxicity

Comparative-toxicity rating not available from standard references.

For symptoms of toxicity: See *Adverse Reactions, Side Effects or Overdose Symptoms* section below.

Adverse Reactions, Side Effects or Overdose Symptoms

Signs and symptoms:	What to do:
Diarrhoea	Discontinue. Call doctor immediately.
Nausea	Discontinue. Call doctor immediately.
Vomiting	Discontinue. Call doctor immediately.

Basic Information

Biological name (genus and species):
Corynanthe yohimbe
Parts used for medicinal purposes:
Bark
Chemical this herb contains:
Yohimbine, also called quebrachine, aphrodine or corynine

Known Effects

- Blocks responses of parts of autonomic nervous system.
- Increases blood pressure.
- Acts as a local anaesthetic.
- Inhibits monamine oxidase and may cause alarming blood-pressure rise—even strokes—when taken with cheese, red wine or other foods or supplements containing tyromines.
- Causes hallucinations.

Miscellaneous information:
- Yohimbe can produce severe anxiety when given intravenously.

Unproved Speculated Benefits

- Arouses or enhances sexual desire.
- Treats impotency.
- Treats painful menstrual cramps.
- Treats chest pain due to coronary artery disease (angina).
- Treats arteriosclerosis.

Warnings and Precautions

Don't take if you:
- Are pregnant, think you may be pregnant or plan pregnancy in the near future.
- Have kidney or liver disease.

Consult your doctor if you:
- Take this herb for any medical problem that doesn't improve in 2 weeks. There may be safer, more effective treatments.
- Take any medicinal drugs or herbs including aspirin, laxatives, cold and cough remedies, antacids, vitamins, minerals, amino acids, supplements, other prescription or non-prescription drugs.

Pregnancy:
- Dangers outweigh any possible benefits. Don't use.

Breast-feeding:
- Dangers outweigh any possible benefits. Don't use.

Infants and children:
- Treating infants and children under 2 with any herbal preparation is hazardous.

Others:
- This product will *not* help you and may cause toxic symptoms.

Storage:
- Keep cool and dry, but don't freeze. Store safely away from children.

Safe dosage:
- At present no "safe" dosage has been established.

Toxicity

Rated dangerous, particularly in children, persons over 55 and those who take larger than appropriate quantities for extended periods of time.

For symptoms of toxicity: See *Adverse Reactions, Side Effects or Overdose Symptoms* section below.

Adverse Reactions, Side Effects or Overdose Symptoms

Signs and symptoms:	What to do:
Abdominal pain	Discontinue. Call doctor when convenient.
Fatigue	Discontinue. Call doctor when convenient.
Hallucinations	Seek emergency treatment.
High blood pressure	Discontinue. Call doctor immediately.
Muscle paralysis	Seek emergency treatment.
Weakness	Discontinue. Call doctor immediately.

Toxicity Ratings for Herbs

The following list has been compiled from several sources. The toxicity rating is an average of ratings previously published by other experts. The list is included here for your consideration before you take a medicinal herb or suggest it for someone else.

Achuma   *Trichocereus pachanoi*
Rated slightly dangerous, particularly for children, people over 55 and those who take larger-than-appropriate quantities for extended periods of time.

Agrimony   *Agrimonia eupatoria*
Rated relatively safe when taken in appropriate quantities for short periods of time.

Akee   *Blighia sapida*
Rated dangerous, particularly for children, people over 55 and those who take larger than appropriate quantities for extended periods.

Alder   *Alnus glutinosa*
Rated relatively safe when taken in appropriate quantities for short periods of time.

Alexandrian senna   *Cassia senna*
Rated slightly dangerous, particularly for children, people over 55 and those who take larger-than-appropriate quantities for extended periods of time.

Alfalfa   *Medicago sativa*
Generally regarded as safe when taken in appropriate quantities for short periods of time.

Allspice   *Pimenta dioica*
Rated relatively safe when taken in appropriate quantities for short periods of time.

Aloe   *Aloe barbadensis*
Generally regarded as safe when taken in appropriate quantities for short periods of time.

American ginseng
Panax quinquefolius
Generally regarded as safe when taken in appropriate quantities for short periods of time.

American hellebore
Veratrum viride
Rated dangerous, particularly for children, people over 55 and those who take larger-than-appropriate quantities for extended periods of time.

American mistletoe
Phoradendron serotinum
Rated slightly dangerous, particularly for children, people over 55 and those who take larger-than-appropriate quantities for extended periods of time.

Angelica   *Angelica archangelica*
Rated relatively safe when taken in appropriate quantities for short periods of time.

Anise   *Pimpinella anisum*
Rated relatively safe when taken in appropriate quantities for short periods of time.

Annual mercury
Mercurialis annua
Rated dangerous, particularly for children, people over 55 and those who take larger-than-appropriate quantities for extended periods of time.

Apple   *Malus sylvestris*
Generally regarded as safe when taken in appropriate quantities for short periods of time.

Apricot   *Prunus armeniaca*
Rated slightly dangerous, particularly for children, people over 55 and those who take larger-than-appropriate quantities for extended periods of time.

Arrowpoison tree
Acokanthera schimperi
Rated dangerous, particularly for children, people over 55 and those who take larger-than-appropriate quantities for extended periods of time.

Arrowroot   *Maranta arundinacea*
Generally regarded as safe when taken in appropriate quantities for short periods of time.

Asafetida   *Ferula assa-foetida*
Rated relatively safe when taken in appropriate quantities for short periods of time.

Ashwagandha
Withania somniferum
Rated dangerous, particularly for children, people over 55 and those who take larger-than-appropriate quantities for extended periods of time.

Autumn crocus
Colchicum autumnale
Rated dangerous, particularly for children, people over 55 and those who take larger-than-appropriate quantities for extended periods of time.

Aveloz   *Euphorbia tirucalli*
Rated dangerous, particularly for children, people over 55 and those who take larger-than-appropriate quantities for extended periods of time.

Aztec tobacco   *Nicotiana rustica*
Rated dangerous, particularly for children, people over 55 and those who take larger-than-appropriate quantities for extended periods of time.

Balsam of Peru
Myroxylon balsamum var.
Rated slightly dangerous, particularly for children, people over 55 and those who take larger-than-appropriate quantities for extended periods of time.

Balsam pear   *Momordica charantia*
Rated slightly dangerous, particularly for children, people over 55 and those who take larger-than-appropriate quantities for extended periods of time.

Baneberry   *Actaea pachypoda*
Rated slightly dangerous, particularly for children, people over 55 and those who take larger-than-appropriate quantities for extended periods of time.

Barbasco   *Dioscorea composita*
Rated slightly dangerous, particularly for children, people over 55 and those who take larger-than-appropriate quantities for extended periods of time.

Barberry   *Berberis vulgaris*
Rated slightly dangerous, particularly for children, people over 55 and those who take larger-than-appropriate quantities for extended periods of time.

Basil   *Ocimum basilicum*
Rated relatively safe when taken in appropriate quantities for short periods of time.

Bay   *Laurus nobilis*
Rated relatively safe when taken in appropriate quantities for short periods of time.

Bayberry *Myrica cerifera*
Rated relatively safe when taken in appropriate quantities for short periods of time.

Bayrum tree *Pimenta racemosa*
Rated relatively safe when taken in appropriate quantities for short periods of time.

Bean *Phaseolus vulgaris*
Generally regarded as safe when taken in appropriate quantities for short periods of time.

Bearberry *Arctostaphylos uva-ursi*
Rated relatively safe when taken in appropriate quantities for short periods of time.

Belladonna *Atropa bella-donna*
Rated dangerous, particularly for children, people over 55 and those who take larger-than-appropriate quantities for extended periods of time.

Benzoin *Styrax benzoin*
Rated slightly dangerous, particularly for children, people over 55 and those who take larger-than-appropriate quantities for extended periods of time.

Betel pepper *Piper betel*
Rated slightly dangerous, particularly for children, people over 55 and those who take larger-than-appropriate quantities for extended periods of time.

Betel-nut *Areca catechu*
Rated relatively safe when taken in appropriate quantities for short periods of time.

Betony *Stachys officinalis*
Rated relatively safe when taken in appropriate quantities for short periods of time.

Bitter root
Apocynum androsaemifolium
Rated slightly dangerous, particularly for children, people over 55 and those who take larger-than-appropriate quantities for extended periods of time.

Bittersweet *Solanum dulcamara*
Rated slightly dangerous, particularly for children, people over 55 and those who take larger-than-appropriate quantities for extended periods of time.

Black cohosh *Cimicifuga racemosa*
Rated slightly dangerous, particularly for children, people over 55 and those who take larger-than-appropriate quantities for extended periods of time.

Black locust *Robinia pseudoacacia*
Rated slightly dangerous, particularly for children, people over 55 and those who take larger-than-appropriate quantities for extended periods of time.

Black pepper *Piper nigrum*
Rated slightly dangerous, particularly for children, people over 55 and those who take larger-than-appropriate quantities for extended periods of time.

Bloodroot *Sanguinaria canadensis*
Rated slightly dangerous, particularly for children, people over 55 and those who take larger-than-appropriate quantities for extended periods of time.

Blue cohosh
Caulophyllum thalictroides
Rated slightly dangerous, particularly for children, people over 55 and those who take larger-than-appropriate quantities for extended periods of time.

Blue flag *Iris versicolor*
Rated relatively safe when taken in appropriate quantities for short periods of time.

Boldo *Peumus boldus*
Rated dangerous, particularly for children, people over 55 and those who take larger-than-appropriate quantities for extended periods of time.

Bolek hena *Justicia pectoralis*
Rated slightly dangerous, particularly for children, people over 55 and those who take larger-than-appropriate quantities for extended periods of time.

Boneset *Eupatorium perfoliatum*
Rated relatively safe when taken in appropriate quantities for short periods of time.

Borage   *Borago officinalis*
Generally regarded as safe when taken in appropriate quantities for short periods of time.

Borrachero   *Datura candida*
Rated dangerous, particularly for children, people over 55 and those who take larger-than-appropriate quantities for extended periods of time.

Boxwood   *Buxus sempervirens*
Rated slightly dangerous, particularly for children, people over 55 and those who take larger-than-appropriate quantities for extended periods of time.

Brazilian peppertree
Schinus terebinthifolius
Rated slightly dangerous, particularly for children, people over 55 and those who take larger-than-appropriate quantities for extended periods of time.

Buchu   *Barosma betulina*
Rated relatively safe when taken in appropriate quantities for short periods of time.

Buckthorn   *Frangula alnus*
Rated slightly dangerous, particularly for children, people over 55 and those who take larger-than-appropriate quantities for extended periods of time.

Bugleweed   *Ajuga reptans*
Rated relatively safe when taken in appropriate quantities for short periods of time.

Bulbous buttercup
Ranunculus bulbosus
Rated relatively safe when taken in appropriate quantities for short periods of time.

Burdock   *Arctium lappa*
Rated relatively safe when taken in appropriate quantities for short periods of time.

Caapi   *Banisteriopsis caapi*
Rated slightly dangerous, particularly for children, people over 55 and those who take larger-than-appropriate quantities for extended periods of time.

Cabbagebark   *Andira inermis*
Rated slightly dangerous, particularly for children, people over 55 and those who take larger-than-appropriate quantities for extended periods of time.

Cabeza de angel
Calliandra anomala
Rated slightly dangerous, particularly for children, people over 55 and those who take larger-than-appropriate quantities for extended periods of time.

Cajeput   *Melaleuca leucadendron*
Rated relatively safe when taken in appropriate quantities for short periods of time.

California bay
Umbellularia californica
Rated slightly dangerous, particularly for children, people over 55 and those who take larger-than-appropriate quantities for extended periods of time.

California poppy
Eschscholzia californica
Rated slightly dangerous, particularly for children, people over 55 and those who take larger-than-appropriate quantities for extended periods of time.

Camphor   *Cinnamomum camphora*
Rated relatively safe when taken in appropriate quantities for short periods of time.

Canaigre   *Rumex hymenosepalus*
Rated slightly dangerous, particularly for children, people over 55 and those who take larger-than-appropriate quantities for extended periods of time.

Cananga   *Cananga odorata*
Rated slightly dangerous, particularly for children, people over 55 and those who take larger-than-appropriate quantities for extended periods of time.

Candlenut   *Aleurites moluccana*
Rated slightly dangerous, particularly for children, people over 55 and those who take larger-than-appropriate quantities for extended periods of time.

Carrot *Daucus carota*
Rated relatively safe when taken in appropriate quantities for short periods of time.

Cascara sagrada
Rhamnus purshianus
Rated slightly dangerous, particularly for children, people over 55 and those who take larger-than-appropriate quantities for extended periods of time.

Cascarilla *Croton eleuteria*
Rated slightly dangerous, particularly for children, people over 55 and those who take larger-than-appropriate quantities for extended periods of time.

Cassava *Manihot esculenta*
Rated slightly dangerous, particularly for children, people over 55 and those who take larger-than-appropriate quantities for extended periods of time.

Cassie *Acacia farnesiana*
Generally regarded as safe when taken in appropriate quantities for short periods of time.

Castor *Ricinus communis*
Rated dangerous, particularly for children, people over 55 and those who take larger-than-appropriate quantities for extended periods of time.

Cat powder *Actinidia polygama*
Rated slightly dangerous, particularly for children, people over 55 and those who take larger-than-appropriate quantities for extended periods of time.

Catnip *Nepeta cataria*
Generally regarded as safe when taken in appropriate quantities for short periods of time.

Celandine *Chelidonium majus*
Rated slightly dangerous, particularly for children, people over 55 and those who take larger-than-appropriate quantities for extended periods of time.

Celery *Apium graveolens*
Rated relatively safe when taken in appropriate quantities for short periods of time.

Cherry-laurel *Prunus laurocerasus*
Rated slightly dangerous, particularly for children, people over 55 and those who take larger-than-appropriate quantities for extended periods of time.

Chickweed *Stellaria media*
Rated relatively safe when taken in appropriate quantities for short periods of time.

Chili *Capsicum annuum*
Rated relatively safe when taken in appropriate quantities for short periods of time.

Chinaberry *Melia azedarach*
Rated dangerous, particularly for children, people over 55 and those who take larger-than-appropriate quantities for extended periods of time.

Chinese rhubarb *Rheum officinale*
Rated relatively safe when taken in appropriate quantities for short periods of time.

Christmas rose *Helleborus niger*
Rated dangerous, particularly for children, people over 55 and those who take larger-than-appropriate quantities for extended periods of time.

Christthorn *Ziziphus spina-christi*
Rated relatively safe when taken in appropriate quantities for short periods of time.

Cinnamon *Cinnamomum verum*
Rated relatively safe when taken in appropriate quantities for short periods of time.

Clary sage *Salvia sclarea*
Rated relatively safe when taken in appropriate quantities for short periods of time.

Climbing onion *Bowiea volubilis*
Rated dangerous, particularly for children, people over 55 and those who take larger-than-appropriate quantities for extended periods of time.

Clove *Syzygium aromaticum*
Rated relatively safe when taken in appropriate quantities for short periods of time.

Coca *Erythroxylum coca*
Rated slightly dangerous, particularly for children, people over 55 and those who take larger-than-appropriate quantities for extended periods of time.

Cocoa *Theobroma cacao*
Rated relatively safe when taken in appropriate quantities for short periods of time.

Coffee *Coffea arabica*
Rated relatively safe when taken in appropriate quantities for short periods of time.

Colocynth *Citrullus colocynthis*
Rated dangerous, particularly for children, people over 55 and those who take larger-than-appropriate quantities for extended periods of time.

Coltsfoot *Tussilago farfara*
Rated relatively safe when taken in appropriate quantities for short periods of time.

Columbine *Aquilegia vulgaris*
Rated slightly dangerous, particularly for children, people over 55 and those who take larger-than-appropriate quantities for extended periods of time.

Comfrey *Symphytum peregrinum*
Rated relatively safe when taken in appropriate quantities for short periods of time.

Common milkweed
Asclepias syriaca
Rated slightly dangerous, particularly for children, people over 55 and those who take larger-than-appropriate quantities for extended periods of time.

Condurango
Marsdenia reichenbachii
Rated slightly dangerous, particularly for children, people over 55 and those who take larger-than-appropriate quantities for extended periods of time.

Coral bean *Erythrina fusca*
Rated slightly dangerous, particularly for children, people over 55 and those who take larger-than-appropriate quantities for extended periods of time.

Corkwood *Duboisia myoporoides*
Rated dangerous, particularly for children, people over 55 and those who take larger-than-appropriate quantities for extended periods of time.

Corncockle *Agrostemma githago*
Rated slightly dangerous, particularly for children, people over 55 and those who take larger-than-appropriate quantities for extended periods of time.

Cranesbill *Geranium maculatum*
Rated relatively safe when taken in appropriate quantities for short periods of time.

Creosotebush *Larrea tridentata*
Rated relatively safe when taken in appropriate quantities for short periods of time.

Culebra *Methystichodendron amesia*
Rated dangerous, particularly for children, people over 55 and those who take larger-than-appropriate quantities for extended periods of time.

Daffodil *Narcissus tazetta*
Rated dangerous, particularly for children, people over 55 and those who take larger-than-appropriate quantities for extended periods of time.

Dagga *Leonotis leonurus*
Rated slightly dangerous, particularly for children, people over 55 and those who take larger-than-appropriate quantities for extended periods of time.

Damiana *Turnera diffusa*
Rated relatively safe when taken in appropriate quantities for short periods of time.

Dandelion *Taraxacum officinale*
Generally regarded as safe when taken in appropriate quantities for short periods of time.

Darnel *Lolium temulentum*
Rated dangerous, particularly for children, people over 55 and those who take larger-than-appropriate quantities for extended periods of time.

Deer's tongue   *Trilisa odoratissima*
Rated relatively safe when taken in
appropriate quantities for short periods
of time.

Devil's claw
Harpagophytum procumbens
Rated relatively safe when taken in
appropriate quantities for short periods
of time.

Devil's shoestring
Tephrosia virginiana
Rated slightly dangerous, particularly
for children, people over 55 and those
who take larger-than-appropriate
quantities for extended periods of time.

Digitalis   *Digitalis purpurea*
Rated dangerous, particularly for
children, people over 55 and those who
take larger-than-appropriate quantities
for extended periods of time.

Dill   *Anethum graveolens*
Generally regarded as safe when taken
in appropriate quantities for short
periods of time.

Dinque pinque
Rauvolfia tetraphylla
Rated slightly dangerous, particularly
for children, people over 55 and those
who take larger-than-appropriate
quantities for extended periods of time.

Dodo   *Elaeophorbia drupifera*
Rated slightly dangerous, particularly
for children, people over 55 and those
who take larger-than-appropriate
quantities for extended periods of time.

Dogwood   *Cornus florida*
Rated relatively safe when taken in
appropriate quantities for short periods
of time.

Dong quai   *Angelica polymorpha*
Rated slightly dangerous, particularly
for children, people over 55 and those
who take larger-than-appropriate
quantities for extended periods of time.

Dove's dung
Ornithogalum umbellatum
Rated slightly dangerous, particularly
for children, people over 55 and those
who take larger-than-appropriate
quantities for extended periods of time.

Dragon's blood
Daemonorops draco
Rated slightly dangerous, particularly
for children, people over 55 and those
who take larger-than-appropriate periods of time.

Dumbcane   *Dieffenbachia seguine*
Rated slightly dangerous, particularly
for children, people over 55 and those
who take larger-than-appropriate
quantities for extended periods of time.

Dwarf mallow   *Malva rotundifolia*
Generally regarded as safe when taken
in appropriate quantities for short
periods of time.

Dyer's broom   *Genista tinctoria*
Rated dangerous, particularly for
children, people over 55 and those who
take larger-than-appropriate quantities
for extended periods of time.

Elderberry   *Sambucus canadensis*
Rated slightly dangerous, particularly
for children, people over 55 and those
who take larger-than-appropriate
quantities for extended periods of time.

Epena   *Virola calophylla*
Rated slightly dangerous, particularly
for children, people over 55 and those
who take larger-than-appropriate
quantities for extended periods of time.

Eucalyptus   *Eucalyptus spp.*
Rated relatively safe when taken in
appropriate quantities for short periods
of time.

European goldenrod
Solidago virgaurea
Generally regarded as safe when taken
in appropriate quantities for short
periods of time.

European mistletoe   *Viscum album*
Rated slightly dangerous, particularly
for children, people over 55 and those
who take larger-than-appropriate
quantities for extended periods of time.

Eyebright   *Euphrasis officinalis*
Rated relatively safe when taken in

appropriate quantities for short periods of time.

Fennel   *Foeniculum vulgare*
Generally regarded as safe when taken in appropriate quantities for short periods of time.

Fenugreek
Trigonella foenum-graecum
Rated relatively safe when taken in appropriate quantities for short periods of time.

Feverfew
Chrysanthemum parthenium
Generally regarded as safe when taken in appropriate quantities for short periods of time.

Field horsetail   *Equisetum arvense*
Rated slightly dangerous, particularly for children, people over 55 and those who take larger-than-appropriate quantities for extended periods of time.

Fo-ti   *Polygonum multiflorum*
Rated relatively safe when taken in appropriate quantities for short periods of time.

Fool's parsley   *Aesthusa cynapium*
Rated dangerous, particularly for children, people over 55 and those who take larger-than-appropriate quantities for extended periods of time.

Fringe tree   *Chionanthus virginica*
Rated slightly dangerous, particularly for children, people over 55 and those who take larger-than-appropriate quantities for extended periods of time.

Gambir   *Uncaria gambir*
Rated relatively safe when taken in appropriate quantities for short periods of time.

Gentian   *Gentiana lutea*
Rated relatively safe when taken in appropriate quantities for short periods of time.

German chamomile
Matricaria chamomilla
Generally regarded as safe when taken in appropriate quantities for short periods of time.

Giant milkweed   *Calotropis procera*
Rated slightly dangerous, particularly for children, people over 55 and those who take larger-than-appropriate quantities for extended periods of time.

Glory lily   *Gloriosa superba*
Rated dangerous, particularly for children, people over 55 and those who take larger-than-appropriate quantities for extended periods of time.

Goa   *Andira araroba*
Rated slightly dangerous, particularly for children, people over 55 and those who take larger-than-appropriate quantities for extended periods of time.

Golden chain
Laburnum anagyroides
Rated dangerous, particularly for children, people over 55 and those who take larger-than-appropriate quantities for extended periods of time.

Golden dewdrop   *Duranta repens*
Rated slightly dangerous, particularly for children, people over 55 and those who take larger-than-appropriate quantities for extended periods of time.

Goldenseal   *Hydrastis canadensis*
Rated slightly dangerous, particularly for children, people over 55 and those who take larger-than-appropriate quantities for extended periods of time.

Gotu kola   *Centella asiatica*
Rated slightly dangerous, particularly for children, people over 55 and those who take larger-than-appropriate quantities for extended periods of time.

Granadilla
Passiflora quadrangularis
Rated relatively safe when taken in appropriate quantities for short periods of time.

Ground ivy   *Glechoma hederacea*
Rated relatively safe when taken in appropriate quantities for short periods of time.

Guarana *Paullina cupana*
Rated relatively safe when taken in appropriate quantities for short periods of time.

Gum arabic *Acacia senegal*
Generally regarded as safe when taken in appropriate quantities for short periods of time.

Harmel *Peganum harmala*
Rated slightly dangerous, particularly for children, people over 55 and those who take larger-than-appropriate quantities for extended periods of time.

Hawthorn *Crataegus oxyacantha*
Rated slightly dangerous, particularly for children, people over 55 and those who take larger-than-appropriate quantities for extended periods of time.

Heart-of-Jesus *Caladium bicolor*
Rated slightly dangerous, particularly for children, people over 55 and those who take larger-than-appropriate quantities for extended periods of time.

Heliotrope
Heliotropium europaeum
Rated slightly dangerous, particularly for children, people over 55 and those who take larger-than-appropriate quantities for extended periods of time.

Henbane *Hyoscyamus niger*
Rated dangerous, particularly for children, people over 55 and those who take larger-than-appropriate quantities for extended periods of time.

Henna *Lawsonia inermis*
Rated relatively safe when taken in appropriate quantities for short periods of time.

Herb paris *Paris quadrifolia*
Rated slightly dangerous, particularly for children, people over 55 and those who take larger-than-appropriate quantities for extended periods of time.

Holly *Ilex opaca*
Rated relatively safe when taken in appropriate quantities for short periods of time.

Holy sage *Salvia divinorum*
Rated relatively safe when taken in appropriate quantities for short periods of time.

Homalomena *Homalomena sp.*
Rated slightly dangerous, particularly for children, people over 55 and those who take larger-than-appropriate quantities for extended periods of time.

Honey locust *Gleditsia triacanthos*
Rated relatively safe when taken in appropriate quantities for short periods of time.

Hops *Humulus lupulus*
Rated relatively safe when taken in appropriate quantities for short periods of time.

Horse chestnut
Aesculus hippocastanum
Rated slightly dangerous, particularly for children, people over 55 and those who take larger-than-appropriate quantities for extended periods of time.

Iboga *Tabernanthe iboga*
Rated dangerous, particularly for children, people over 55 and those who take larger-than-appropriate quantities for extended periods of time.

Indian acalypha *Acalypha indica*
Rated relatively safe when taken in appropriate quantities for short periods of time.

Indian hemp
Apocynum cannabinum
Rated slightly dangerous, particularly for children, people over 55 and those who take larger-than-appropriate quantities for extended periods of time.

Indian senna *Cassia angustifolia*
Rated slightly dangerous, particularly for children, people over 55 and those who take larger-than-appropriate quantities for extended periods of time.

Indian tobacco *Lobelia inflata*
Rated slightly dangerous, particularly for children, people over 55 and those who take larger-than-appropriate quantities for extended periods of time.

Indigo   *Indigofera tinctoria*
Rated relatively safe when taken in
appropriate quantities for short periods
of time.

Intoxicating mint
Lagochilus inebrians
Rated slightly dangerous, particularly
for children, people over 55 and those
who take larger-than-appropriate
quantities for extended periods of time.

Ivy   *Hedera helix*
Rated slightly dangerous, particularly
for children, people over 55 and those
who take larger-than-appropriate
quantities for extended periods of time.

Jaborandi   *Pilocarpus spp.*
Rated slightly dangerous, particularly
for children, people over 55 and those
who take larger-than-appropriate
quantities for extended periods of time.

Jack-in-the-pulpit
Arisaema triphyllum
Rated slightly dangerous, particularly
for children, people over 55 and those
who take larger-than-appropriate
quantities for extended periods of time.

Jalap root   *Ipomoea purga*
Rated slightly dangerous, particularly
for children, people over 55 and those
who take larger-than-appropriate
quantities for extended periods of time.

Jamaica dogwood   *Piscidia piscipula*
Rated slightly dangerous, particularly
for children, people over 55 and those
who take larger-than-appropriate
quantities for extended periods of time.

Jamaican quassia   *Picrasma excelsa*
Rated dangerous, particularly for
children, people over 55 and those who
take larger-than-appropriate quantities
for extended periods of time.

Jequerity   *Abrus precatorius*
Rated dangerous, particularly for
children, people over 55 and those who
take larger-than-appropriate quantities
for extended periods of time.

Jimsonweed   *Datura stramonium*
Rated dangerous, particularly for
children, people over 55 and those who
take larger-than-appropriate quantities
for extended periods of time.

Jojoba   *Simmondsia chinensis*
Rated relatively safe when taken in
appropriate quantities for short periods
of time.

Juniper   *Juniperus communis*
Rated slightly dangerous, particularly
for children, people over 55 and those
who take larger-than-appropriate
quantities for extended periods of time.

Jurema   *Mimosa hostilis*
Rated slightly dangerous, particularly
for children, people over 55 and those
who take larger-than-appropriate
quantities for extended periods of time.

Kamyuye   *Hoslundia opposita*
Rated dangerous, particularly for
children, people over 55 and those who
take larger-than-appropriate quantities
for extended periods of time.

Katum   *Mitragyna speciosa*
Rated slightly dangerous, particularly
for children, people over 55 and those
who take larger-than-appropriate
quantities for extended periods of time.

Kava-kava   *Piper methysticum*
Rated slightly dangerous, particularly
for children, people over 55 and those
who take larger-than-appropriate
quantities for extended periods of time.

Khat   *Catha edulis*
Rated slightly dangerous, particularly
for children, people over 55 and those
who take larger-than-appropriate
quantities for extended periods of time.

Knotweed   *Polygonum aviculare*
Rated relatively safe when taken in
appropriate quantities for short periods
of time.

Kola nuts   *Cola acuminata*
Rated relatively safe when taken in
appropriate quantities for short periods
of time.

Kola *Cola nitida*
Rated relatively safe when taken in appropriate quantities for short periods of time.

Kwashi *Pancratium trianthum*
Rated dangerous, particularly for children, people over 55 and those who take larger-than-appropriate quantities for extended periods of time.

Lance-leaf periwinkle
Catharanthus lanceus
Rated slightly dangerous, particularly for children, people over 55 and those who take larger-than-appropriate quantities for extended periods of time.

Lantana *Lantana camara*
Rated slightly dangerous, particularly for children, people over 55 and those who take larger-than-appropriate quantities for extended periods of time.

Larkspur *Consolida ambigua*
Rated dangerous, particularly for children, people over 55 and those who take larger-than-appropriate quantities for extended periods of time.

Latua *Latua pubiflora*
Rated dangerous, particularly for children, people over 55 and those who take larger-than-appropriate quantities for extended periods of time.

Lavender *Lavandula angustifolia*
Rated relatively safe when taken in appropriate quantities for short periods of time.

Lavender-cotton
Santolina chamaecyparissus
Rated slightly dangerous, particularly for children, people over 55 and those who take larger-than-appropriate quantities for extended periods of time.

Lemon verbena *Aloysia triphylla*
Rated relatively safe when taken in appropriate quantities for short periods of time.

Lettuce *Lactuca virosa*
Rated relatively safe when taken in appropriate quantities for short periods of time.

Licorice *Glycyrrhiza glabra*
Rated slightly dangerous, particularly for children, people over 55 and those who take larger-than-appropriate quantities for extended periods of time.

Life root *Senecio aureus*
Rated slightly dangerous, particularly for children, people over 55 and those who take larger-than-appropriate quantities for extended periods of time.

Lily-of-the-valley
Convallaria majalis
Rated slightly dangerous, particularly for children, people over 55 and those who take larger-than-appropriate quantities for extended periods of time.

Lima bean *Phaseolus lunatus*
Rated relatively safe when taken in appropriate quantities for short periods of time.

Linden *Tilia europaea*
Rated relatively safe when taken in appropriate quantities for short periods of time.

Luckynut *Thevetia peruviana*
Rated dangerous, particularly for children, people over 55 and those who take larger-than-appropriate quantities for extended periods of time.

Madagascar periwinkle
Catharanthus roseus
Rated slightly dangerous, particularly for children, people over 55 and those who take larger-than-appropriate quantities for extended periods of time.

Malabar nut *Adhatoda vasica*
Rated slightly dangerous, particularly for children, people over 55 and those who take larger-than-appropriate quantities for extended periods of time.

Male fern *Dryopteris filix-mas*
Rated relatively safe when taken in appropriate quantities for short periods of time.

Manaca *Brunfelsia uniflorus*
Rated dangerous, particularly for children, people over 55 and those who

take larger-than-appropriate quantities for extended periods of time.

Manchineel   *Hippomane mancinella*
Rated dangerous, particularly for children, people over 55 and those who take larger-than-appropriate quantities for extended periods of time.

Mandrake   *Mandragora officinarum*
Rated dangerous, particularly for children, people over 55 and those who take larger-than-appropriate quantities for extended periods of time.

Mangosteen   *Garcinia hanburyi*
Rated slightly dangerous, particularly for children, people over 55 and those who take larger-than-appropriate quantities for extended periods of time.

Maraba   *Kaempferia galanga*
Rated relatively safe when taken in appropriate quantities for short periods of time.

Marigold   *Calendula officinalis*
Generally regarded as safe when taken in appropriate quantities for short periods of time.

Marijuana   *Cannabis sativa*
Rated relatively safe when taken in appropriate quantities for short periods of time.

Marsh tea   *Ledum palustre*
Rated slightly dangerous, particularly for children, people over 55 and those who take larger-than-appropriate quantities for extended periods of time.

Marula   *Sclerocarya caffra*
Rated slightly dangerous, particularly for children, people over 55 and those who take larger-than-appropriate quantities for extended periods of time.

Mastic   *Pistacia lentiscus*
Rated relatively safe when taken in appropriate quantities for short periods of time.

Mate   *Ilex paraguariensis*
Rated relatively safe when taken in appropriate quantities for short periods of time.

Mayapple   *Podophyllum peltatum*
Rated slightly dangerous, particularly for children, people over 55 and those who take larger-than-appropriate quantities for extended periods of time.

Meadowsweet   *Filipendula ulmaria*
Generally regarded as safe when taken in appropriate quantities for short periods of time.

Mescal   *Agave sisalana*
Generally regarded as safe when taken in appropriate quantities for short periods of time.

Mescal bean   *Sophora secundiflora*
Rated slightly dangerous, particularly for children, people over 55 and those who take larger-than-appropriate quantities for extended periods of time.

Mesquite   *Prosopis juliflora*
Rated relatively safe when taken in appropriate quantities for short periods of time.

Mexican calea   *Calea zacathechichi*
Rated slightly dangerous, particularly for children, people over 55 and those who take larger-than-appropriate quantities for extended periods of time.

Mezereon   *Daphne mezereum*
Rated dangerous, particularly for children, people over 55 and those who take larger-than-appropriate quantities for extended periods of time.

Mohodu   *Cineraria aspera*
Rated slightly dangerous, particularly for children, people over 55 and those who take larger-than-appropriate quantities for extended periods of time.

Mole plant   *Euphorbia lathyris*
Rated dangerous, particularly for children, people over 55 and those who take larger-than-appropriate quantities for extended periods of time.

Monkshood   *Aconitum napellus*
Rated dangerous, particularly for children, people over 55 and those who take larger-than-appropriate quantities for extended periods of time.

Moonseed *Menispermum canadense*
Rated slightly dangerous, particularly for children, people over 55 and those who take larger-than-appropriate quantities for extended periods of time.

Mormon tea *Ephedra nevadensis*
Rated slightly dangerous, particularly for children, people over 55 and those who take larger-than-appropriate quantities for extended periods of time.

Morning Glory *Ipomoea violacea*
Rated slightly dangerous, particularly for children, people over 55 and those who take larger-than-appropriate quantities for extended periods of time.

Motherwort *Leonurus cardiaca*
Rated relatively safe when taken in appropriate quantities for short periods of time.

Mountain laurel *Kalmia latifolia*
Rated dangerous, particularly for children, people over 55 and those who take larger-than-appropriate quantities for extended periods of time.

Mountain tobacco *Arnica montana*
Rated slightly dangerous, particularly for children, people over 55 and those who take larger-than-appropriate quantities for extended periods of time.

Mugwort *Artemisia vulgaris*
Rated slightly dangerous, particularly for children, people over 55 and those who take larger-than-appropriate quantities for extended periods of time.

Muira puama
Ptychopetalum olacoides
Rated slightly dangerous, particularly for children, people over 55 and those who take larger-than-appropriate quantities for extended periods of time.

Musk okra *Abelmoschus moschatus*
Generally regarded as safe when taken in appropriate quantities for short periods of time.

Nene *Coleus blumei*
Rated slightly dangerous, particularly for children, people over 55 and those who take larger-than-appropriate quantities for extended periods of time.

Niando *Alchornea floribunda*
Rated dangerous, particularly for children, people over 55 and those who take larger-than-appropriate quantities for extended periods of time.

Night-blooming cereus
Selenicereus grandiflorus
Rated relatively safe when taken in appropriate quantities for short periods of time.

Nightshade *Solanum nigrum*
Rated slightly dangerous, particularly for children, people over 55 and those who take larger-than-appropriate quantities for extended periods of time.

Niopo *Anadenathera peregrina*
Rated slightly dangerous, particularly for children, people over 55 and those who take larger-than-appropriate quantities for extended periods of time.

Nutmeg *Myristica fragrans*
Rated slightly dangerous, particularly for children, people over 55 and those who take larger-than-appropriate quantities for extended periods of time.

Nux-vomica *Strychnos nux-vomica*
Rated dangerous, particularly for children, people over 55 and those who take larger-than-appropriate quantities for extended periods of time.

Oleander *Nerium oleander*
Rated dangerous, particularly for children, people over 55 and those who take larger-than-appropriate quantities for extended periods of time.

Opium poppy *Papaver somniferum*
Rated slightly dangerous, particularly for children, people over 55 and those who take larger-than-appropriate quantities for extended periods of time.

Ordeal bean
Physostigma venenosum
Rated dangerous, particularly for children, people over 55 and those who take larger-than-appropriate quantities for extended periods of time.

Oregon grape   *Mahonia aquifolia*
Rated slightly dangerous, particularly
for children, people over 55 and those
who take larger-than-appropriate
quantities for extended periods of time.

Oriental ginseng   *Panax ginseng*
Generally regarded as safe when taken
in appropriate quantities for short
periods of time.

Pakistani ephedra
Ephedra geraridiana
Rated slightly dangerous, particularly
for children, people over 55 and those
who take larger-than-appropriate
quantities for extended periods of time.

Pao d'arco   *Tabebuia sp.*
Rated slightly dangerous, particularly
for children, people over 55 and those
who take larger-than-appropriate
quantities for extended periods of time.

Papaya   *Carica papaya*
Generally regarded as safe when taken
in appropriate quantities for short
periods of time.

Parsley   *Petroselinum crispum*
Rated relatively safe when taken in
appropriate quantities for short periods
of time.

Partridgeberry   *Mitchella repens*
Rated relatively safe when taken in
appropriate quantities for short periods
of time.

Pasque flower   *Anemone pulsatilla*
Rated slightly dangerous, particularly
for children, people over 55 and those
who take larger-than-appropriate
quantities for extended periods of time.

Passionflower   *Passiflora incarnata*
Rated relatively safe when taken in
appropriate quantities for short periods
of time.

Pearly everlasting
Anaphalis margaritacea
Generally regarded as safe when taken
in appropriate quantities for short
periods of time.

Peegee   *Hydrangea paniculata*
Rated relatively safe when taken in
appropriate quantities for short periods
of time.

Pennyroyal   *Hedeoma pulegioides*
Rated relatively safe when taken in
appropriate quantities for short periods
of time.

Peony   *Paeonia officinalis*
Rated dangerous, particularly for
children, people over 55 and those who
take larger-than-appropriate quantities
for extended periods of time.

Perilla   *Perilla frutescens*
Rated relatively safe when taken in
appropriate quantities for short periods
of time.

Periwinkle   *Vinca minor*
Rated dangerous, particularly for
children, people over 55 and those who
take larger-than-appropriate quantities
for extended periods of time.

Peruvian peppertree   *Schinus molle*
Rated slightly dangerous, particularly
for children, people over 55 and those
who take larger-than-appropriate
quantities for extended periods of time.

Peyote   *Lophophora williamsii*
Rated relatively safe when taken in
appropriate quantities for short periods
of time.

Physic nut   *Jatropha curcas*
Rated dangerous, particularly for
children, people over 55 and those who
take larger-than-appropriate quantities
for extended periods of time.

Pineapple   *Ananas comosus*
Rated relatively safe when taken in
appropriate quantities for short periods
of time.

Pink clover   *Trifolium pratense*
Generally regarded as safe when taken
in appropriate quantities for short
periods of time.

HERB TOXICITY

471

Pinkroot   *Spigelia marilandica*
Rated dangerous, particularly for
children, people over 55 and those who
take larger-than-appropriate quantities
for extended periods of time.

Piule   *Rhynchosia pyramidalis*
Rated slightly dangerous, particularly
for children, people over 55 and those
who take larger-than-appropriate
quantities for extended periods of time.

Plantain   *Plantago major*
Generally regarded as safe when taken
in appropriate quantities for short
periods of time.

Poinsettia   *Euphorbia pulcherrima*
Rated dangerous, particularly for
children, people over 55 and those who
take larger-than-appropriate quantities
for extended periods of time.

Poison hemlock
Conium maculatum
Rated dangerous, particularly for
children, people over 55 and those who
take larger-than-appropriate quantities
for extended periods of time.

Poison ivy   *Rhus toxicodendron*
Rated slightly dangerous, particularly
for children, people over 55 and those
who take larger-than-appropriate
quantities for extended periods of time.

Pokeweed   *Phytolacca americana*
Rated dangerous, particularly for
children, people over 55 and those who
take larger-than-appropriate quantities
for extended periods of time.

Potato   *Solanum tuberosum*
Rated relatively safe when taken in
appropriate quantities for short periods
of time.

Prickly poppy   *Argemone mexicana*
Rated slightly dangerous, particularly
for children, people over 55 and those
who take larger-than-appropriate
quantities for extended periods of time.

Privet   *Ligustrum vulgare*
Rated slightly dangerous, particularly
for children, people over 55 and those

who take larger-than-appropriate
quantities for extended periods of time.

Pyrethrum
Chrysanthemum cinerariifolium
Rated relatively safe when taken in
appropriate quantities for short periods
of time.

Queen's delight   *Stillingia sylvatica*
Rated dangerous, particularly for
children, people over 55 and those who
take larger-than-appropriate quantities
for extended periods of time.

Quinine   *Cinchona sp.*
Rated relatively safe when taken in
appropriate quantities for short periods
of time.

Redroot   *Lachnanthes tinctoria*
Rated slightly dangerous, particularly
for children, people over 55 and those
who take larger-than-appropriate
quantities for extended periods of time.

Roman chamomile
Chamaemelum nobile
Generally regarded as safe when taken
in appropriate quantities for short
periods of time.

Roselle   *Hibiscus sabdarriffa*
Generally regarded as safe when taken
in appropriate quantities for short
periods of time.

Rosemary   *Rosmarinus officinalis*
Rated relatively safe when taken in
appropriate quantities for short periods
of time.

Rosinweed   *Grindelia spp.*
Rated slightly dangerous, particularly
for children, people over 55 and those
who take larger-than-appropriate
quantities for extended periods of time.

Rubber vine
Cryptostegia grandifolia
Rated dangerous, particularly for
children, people over 55 and those who
take larger-than-appropriate quantities
for extended periods of time.

Rue   *Ruta graveolens*
Rated relatively safe when taken in

appropriate quantities for short periods of time.

Sabadilla   *Schoenocaulon officinale*
Rated dangerous, particularly for children, people over 55 and those who take larger-than-appropriate quantities for extended periods of time.

Sabine   *Juniperus sabina*
Rated slightly dangerous, particularly for children, people over 55 and those who take larger-than-appropriate quantities for extended periods of time.

Saffron   *Crocus sativus*
Rated relatively safe when taken in appropriate quantities for short periods of time.

Sage   *Salvia officinalis*
Generally regarded as safe when taken in appropriate quantities for short periods of time.

Sago cycas   *Cycas revoluta*
Rated dangerous, particularly for children, people over 55 and those who take larger-than-appropriate quantities for extended periods of time.

Sanchi ginseng   *Panax notoginseng*
Generally regarded as safe when taken in appropriate quantities for short periods of time.

Sandalwood   *Santalum album*
Rated relatively safe when taken in appropriate quantities for short periods of time.

Sandbox tree   *Hura crepitans*
Rated dangerous, particularly for children, people over 55 and those who take larger-than-appropriate quantities for extended periods of time.

Sarpaganda   *Rauwolfia serpentina*
Rated slightly dangerous, particularly for children, people over 55 and those who take larger-than-appropriate quantities for extended periods of time.

Sarsaparilla   *Smilax aristolochiifolia*
Rated relatively safe when taken in appropriate quantities for short periods of time.

Sassafras   *Sassafras albidum*
Rated relatively safe when taken in appropriate quantities for short periods of time.

Sassybark
Erythrophleum suaveolens
Rated dangerous, particularly for children, people over 55 and those who take larger-than-appropriate quantities for extended periods of time.

Saw palmetto   *Serenoa repens*
Rated relatively safe when taken in appropriate quantities for short periods of time.

Scarlet poppy   *Papaver bracteatum*
Rated slightly dangerous, particularly for children, people over 55 and those who take larger-than-appropriate quantities for extended periods of time.

Scopolia   *Scopolia carniolica*
Rated dangerous, particularly for children, people over 55 and those who take larger-than-appropriate quantities for extended periods of time.

Scotch broom   *Cytisus scoparius*
Rated slightly dangerous, particularly for children, people over 55 and those who take larger-than-appropriate quantities for extended periods of time.

Sea Island cotton
Gossypium barbadense
Rated slightly dangerous, particularly for children, people over 55 and those who take larger-than-appropriate quantities for extended periods of time.

Sea onion   *Urginea maritima*
Rated dangerous, particularly for children, people over 55 and those who take larger-than-appropriate quantities for extended periods of time.

Seven barks   *Hydrangea arborescens*
Rated relatively safe when taken in appropriate quantities for short periods of time.

Shanshi   *Coriaria thymifolia*
Rated dangerous, particularly for children, people over 55 and those who take larger-than-appropriate quantities for extended periods of time.

Shavegrass   *Equisetum hyemale*
Rated slightly dangerous, particularly for children, people over 55 and those who take larger-than-appropriate quantities for extended periods of time.

Sinicuichi   *Heimia salicifolia*
Rated slightly dangerous, particularly for children, people over 55 and those who take larger-than-appropriate quantities for extended periods of time.

Skunk cabbage
Symplocarpus foetidus
Rated slightly dangerous, particularly for children, people over 55 and those who take larger-than-appropriate quantities for extended periods of time.

Slash pine   *Pinus elliottii*
Rated slightly dangerous, particularly for children, people over 55 and those who take larger-than-appropriate quantities for extended periods of time.

Slippery elm   *Ulmus rubra*
Rated relatively safe when taken in appropriate quantities for short periods of time.

Snakeplant   *Rivea corymbosa*
Rated slightly dangerous, particularly for children, people over 55 and those who take larger-than-appropriate quantities for extended periods of time.

Snakeroot   *Aristolochia serpentaria*
Rated relatively safe when taken in appropriate quantities for short periods of time.

Soaptree   *Quillaja saponaria*
Rated relatively safe when taken in appropriate quantities for short periods of time.

Soksi   *Mirabilis multiflora*
Rated slightly dangerous, particularly for children, people over 55 and those who take larger-than-appropriate quantities for extended periods of time.

Soma   *Sarcostemma acidum*
Rated slightly dangerous, particularly for children, people over 55 and those who take larger-than-appropriate quantities for extended periods of time.

Southernwood
Artemisia abrotanum
Rated slightly dangerous, particularly for children, people over 55 and those who take larger-than-appropriate quantities for extended periods of time.

Spiny ginseng
Eleutherococcus senticosus
Generally regarded as safe when taken in appropriate quantities for short periods of time.

Spurge   *Chamaesyee hypericifolia*
Rated dangerous, particularly for children, people over 55 and those who take larger-than-appropriate quantities for extended periods of time.

St. John's wort
Hypericum perforatum
Rated slightly dangerous, particularly for children, people over 55 and those who take larger-than-appropriate quantities for extended periods of time.

Star anise   *Illicium verum*
Rated slightly dangerous, particularly for children, people over 55 and those who take larger-than-appropriate quantities for extended periods of time.

Stinging nettle   *Urtica dioica*
Generally regarded as safe when taken in appropriate quantities for short periods of time.

Strawberry tree   *Arbutus unedo*
Rated slightly dangerous, particularly for children, people over 55 and those who take larger-than-appropriate quantities for extended periods of time.

Sumbul   *Ferula sumbul*
Rated relatively safe when taken in appropriate quantities for short periods of time.

Surinam quassia   *Quassia amara*
Rated dangerous, particularly for

children, people over 55 and those who take larger-than-appropriate quantities for extended periods of time.

Sweet flag *Acorus calamus*
Rated slightly dangerous, particularly for children, people over 55 and those who take larger-than-appropriate quantities for extended periods of time.

Sweetclover *Melilotus officinalis*
Rated relatively safe when taken in appropriate quantities for short periods of time.

Tansy *Tanacetum vulgare*
Rated relatively safe when taken in appropriate quantities for short periods of time.

Tarragon *Artemisia dracunculus*
Rated relatively safe when taken in appropriate quantities for short periods of time.

Tea *Camellia sinensis*
Rated relatively safe when taken in appropriate quantities for short periods of time.

Thornapple *Datura innoxia*
Rated dangerous, particularly for children, people over 55 and those who take larger-than-appropriate quantities for extended periods of time.

Thyme *Thymus vulgaris*
Rated relatively safe when taken in appropriate quantities for short periods of time.

Tobacco *Nicotiana tabacum*
Rated dangerous, particularly for children, people over 55 and those who take larger-than-appropriate quantities for extended periods of time.

Tomato *Lycopersicon esculentum*
Rated relatively safe when taken in appropriate quantities for short periods of time.

Tonka bean *Dipteryx odorata*
Rated relatively safe when taken in appropriate quantities for short periods of time.

Traveler's joy *Clematis vitalba*
Rated slightly dangerous, particularly for children, people over 55 and those who take larger-than-appropriate quantities for extended periods of time.

Tree tobacco *Nicotiana glauca*
Rated dangerous, particularly for children, people over 55 and those who take larger-than-appropriate quantities for extended periods of time.

Tua-tua *Jatropha gossypiifolia*
Rated dangerous, particularly for children, people over 55 and those who take larger-than-appropriate quantities for extended periods of time.

Tupa *Lobelia tupa*
Rated slightly dangerous, particularly for children, people over 55 and those who take larger-than-appropriate quantities for extended periods of time.

Unicorn root *Aletris farinosa*
Rated slightly dangerous, particularly for children, people over 55 and those who take larger-than-appropriate quantities for extended periods of time.

Unmatal *Datura metel*
Rated dangerous, particularly for children, people over 55 and those who take larger-than-appropriate quantities for extended periods of time.

Upland cotton *Gossypium hirsutum*
Rated slightly dangerous, particularly for children, people over 55 and those who take larger-than-appropriate quantities for extended periods of time.

Valerian *Valeriana officinalis*
Rated relatively safe when taken in appropriate quantities for short periods of time.

Vanilla *Vanilla planifolia*
Rated relatively safe when taken in appropriate quantities for short periods of time.

Verbena *Verbena officinalis*
Generally regarded as safe when taken in appropriate quantities for short periods of time.

Vilca *Anadenathera colubrina*
Rated slightly dangerous, particularly for children, people over 55 and those who take larger-than-appropriate quantities for extended periods of time.

Virginian scullcap
Scutellaria lateriflora
Rated relatively safe when taken in appropriate quantities for short periods of time.

Wahoo *Euonymus atropurpureas*
Rated slightly dangerous, particularly for children, people over 55 and those who take larger-than-appropriate quantities for extended periods of time.

Water fennel
Onenanthe phellandrium
Rated dangerous, particularly for children, people over 55 and those who take larger-than-appropriate quantities for extended periods of time.

Water hemlock *Cicuta maculata*
Rated dangerous, particularly for children, people over 55 and those who take larger-than-appropriate quantities for extended periods of time.

Winter savory *Satureja montana*
Rated relatively safe when taken in appropriate quantities for short periods of time.

Wintergreen
Gaultheria procumbens
Rated slightly dangerous, particularly for children, people over 55 and those who take larger-than-appropriate quantities for extended periods of time.

Witch-hazel *Hamamelis virginiana*
Rated relatively safe when taken in appropriate quantities for short periods of time.

Woodrose *Argyreia nervosa*
Rated slightly dangerous, particularly for children, people over 55 and those who take larger-than-appropriate quantities for extended periods of time.

Woodruff *Galium odoratum*
Generally regarded as safe when taken in appropriate quantities for short periods of time.

Wormseed
Chenopodium ambrosioides
Rated slightly dangerous, particularly for children, people over 55 and those who take larger-than-appropriate quantities for extended periods of time.

Wormwood *Artemisia absinthium*
Rated slightly dangerous, particularly for children, people over 55 and those who take larger-than-appropriate quantities for extended periods of time.

Yarrow *Achillea millefolium*
Generally regarded as safe when taken in appropriate quantities for short periods of time.

Yellow dock *Rumex crispus*
Rated slightly dangerous, particularly for children, people over 55 and those who take larger-than-appropriate quantities for extended periods of time.

Yellow jessamine
Gelsemium sempervirens
Rated dangerous, particularly for children, people over 55 and those who take larger-than-appropriate quantities for extended periods of time.

Yellow ladyslipper
Cypripedium calceolus
Rated relatively safe when taken in appropriate quantities for short periods of time.

Yohimbe *Pausinystalia johimbe*
Rated slightly dangerous, particularly for children, people over 55 and those who take larger-than-appropriate quantities for extended periods of time.

Yoko *Paullinia yoko*
Rated relatively safe when taken in appropriate quantities for short periods of time.

Glossary

Abortifacient—Induces abortions (miscarriages).

Absorption—Process by which nutrients are absorbed through the lining of the intestinal tract into capillaries and into the bloodstream. Nutrients must be absorbed to affect the body.

Acids—Compounds often found in plant tissues, especially fruits, that shrink tissues and prevent secretion of fluids. They taste sour or tart.

Active principle—Chemical component of a plant or compound that has a therapeutic effect.

Acute—Short, relatively severe. Usually referred to in connection with an illness. Opposite of acute is *chronic*.

Addiction—Psychological or physiological dependence on a drug. With true addictions, severe symptoms appear when the addicted person stops taking the drug on which he is dependent.

Adrenal gland—Gland located immediately adjacent to the kidney that produces adrenaline and several steroid hormones, including cortisone and hydrocortisone.

Adulterant—Substance that makes another substance impure when the two are mixed together.

Allergen—Capable of producing an allergic response.

Allergy—Excessive sensitivity to a substance.

Alumina—Another term for aluminium oxide or hydrated aluminium oxide.

Amenorrhoea—Absence of menstruation.

Amino acid—Chemical building blocks that help produce proteins in the body.

Anabolic—Building up of tissues in the body. It is a destructive metabolism.

Anaemia—Too few healthy red blood cells in the bloodstream or too little haemoglobin in the red blood cells. Anaemia is usually caused by excessive blood loss, such as excessive bleeding or menstruation, increased blood destruction, such as haemolytic anaemia or leukaemia, or decreased blood production, such as iron-deficiency anaemia.

Anaemia, pernicious—Anaemia caused by vitamin B-12 deficiency. Symptoms include easy fatigue, weakness, lemon-coloured skin, numbness and tingling of hands and feet, and symptoms of degeneration of the central nervous system, such as irritability, emotional problems, personality changes and paralysis of extremities.

Anaesthetic—Used to abolish pain.

Anaphylaxis—Severe allergic response to a substance. Symptoms include wheezing, itching, nasal congestion, hives, immediate intense burning of hands and feet, collapse with severe drop in blood pressure, loss of consciousness and cardiac arrest. Symptoms of anaphylaxis appear within a few seconds or minutes after exposure to substance causing reaction—this can be medication or herbs taken by injection, by mouth, vaginally, rectally, through a breathing apparatus or applied to skin. Anaphylaxis is an uncommon occurrence, but when it occurs, it is a *severe medical emergency*! Without appropriate immediate treatment, it can cause death. Yell for help. Don't leave victim. Begin CPR (cardiopulmonary resuscitation), mouth-to-mouth breathing and external cardiac massage. Have someone dial 999. Don't stop CPR until help arrives.

Angina (angina pectoris)—Chest pain, with sensation of impending death. Pain may radiate into jaw, ear lobes, between shoulder blades or down shoulder and arm on either side, most frequently the left side. Pain is caused by a temporary reduction in the amount of oxygen to the heart muscle through narrowed, diseased coronary arteries.

Antacid—Neutralizes acid. In medical terms, the neutralized acid is located in the stomach, oesophagus or first part of the duodenum.

Anti-bacterial—Destroys bacteria (germs) or suppresses their growth or reproduction.

Antibiotic—Inhibits growth of germs or kills germs. When it inhibits growth, it is called *bacteriostatic*. When it kills germs, it is called *bacteriocidal*.

Anti-cholinergic—Reduces nerve impulses through the part of the autonomic nervous system called *parasympathetic*.

Anti-coagulant—Delays or stops blood clotting.

Anti-emetic—Prevents or stops nausea and vomiting.

Anti-helmintic—Destroys intestinal worms.

Antihistamine—Prevents histamine, the chemical in body tissues that dilates smallest blood vessels, constricts smooth muscle surrounding bronchial tubes and stimulates stomach secretions, from acting on tissues of the body.

Anti-hypertensive—Reduces blood pressure.

Anti-mitotic—Inhibits or prevents cell division.

Anti-neoplastic—Inhibits or prevents growth of neoplasms (cancers).

Anti-oxidant—Prevents oxidation (combining with oxygen). Anti-oxidant substances include superoxide dismutase, selenium, vitamins C and E, and zinc.

Anti-pyretic—Reduces fevers.

Antiseptic—Prevents or retards growth of germs.

Anti-spasmodic—Relieves spasm in skeletal or smooth muscle.

Aperitive—Stimulates the appetite.

Aphrodisiac—Arouses or enhances instinctive sexual desire.

Aromatic—Chemical with a spicy fragrance and stimulant characteristics used to relieve various symptoms.

Artery—Blood vessel that carries blood away from the heart.

Asthma—Disease with recurrent attacks of breathing difficulty characterized by wheezing. It is caused by spasms of the bronchial tubes, which can be caused by many factors including adverse reactions to drugs, vitamins, minerals or medicinal herbs.

Astringent—Shrinks tissues and prevents secretion of fluids.

Bacteria—Microscopic germs. Some bacteria contribute to health; others cause disease.

Bitters—Medicine with a bitter taste. Used as a tonic or appetizer.

Blepharitis—Inflammation of eyelid.

Blood sugar (blood glucose)—Necessary element in blood to sustain life. The blood level of glucose is determined by insulin, a hormone secreted by the pancreas. When the pancreas no longer satisfies this function, the disease *diabetes mellitus* results.

Bronchitis—Inflammation of the breathing tubes.

Bulb—Modified plant bulb with scaly leaves that grows beneath the soil.

Carcinogen—Chemical or substance that can cause cancer.

Cardiac arrhythmias—Abnormal heart rate or rhythm.

Cardiac—Pertaining to the heart.

Carminative—Aids in expelling gas from the intestinal tract.

Cathartic—Very strong laxative that produces explosive, watery bowel movements.

Cell—Unit of protoplasm, the essential living matter of all plants and animals.

Central nervous system—Brain and spinal cord and their nerve endings.

Central-nervous-system depressant—Causes changes in the body, including changes in consciousness, lethargy, loss of judgment or coma.

Chronic—Disease of long standing. Opposite of *acute*.

Co-enzyme—Heat-stable molecule that must be loosely associated with an enzyme for the enzyme to perform its function.

Colic—Abdominal pain that recurs in a pattern every few seconds or minutes.

Collagen—Gelatinous protein used to make body tissues.

Congestive—Excess accumulation of blood. In congestive heart failure, blood congregates in lungs, liver, kidney and other parts to cause shortness of breath, swelling of ankles, sleep disturbances, rapid heartbeat and easy fatigue.

Conjunctivitis—Inflammation of the outer membrane of the eye.

Constriction—Tightness or pressure.

Contraceptive—Prevents pregnancy.

Contraindication—Inadvisability of using a substance that may cause harm under specific circumstances. For example, high-caloric intake in someone who is overweight is contraindicated.

Convulsion—Violent, uncontrollable contraction of the voluntary muscles.

Corticosteroid (adrenocorticosteroid)—Hormones produced by the body or manufactured synthetically.

Counterirritant—Process of applying an irritating substance to the skin to produce increased blood circulation to the area. Classic example (now considered an outdated treatment) is mustard plaster applied to the chest to relieve bronchial congestion or cough.

Cyanogenic glycoside(s)—Sugars that have the capacity to be used in the production of cyanide.

Cystitis—Inflammation of the urinary bladder.

DNA (desoxyribonucleic acid)—Complex protein chemical in genes that determines the type of life form into which a cell will develop.

Decoction—Extract of a crude drug obtained by boiling the substance in water.

Dehiscent—Fruit that splits open when ripe.

Delirium—Temporary mental disturbance accompanied by hallucinations, agitation, incoherence.

Demonic—Destroys or repels demons.

Demulcent—Mucilagenous or oily substance capable of protecting scraped tissues.

Dermatitis—Skin inflammation or irritation.

Diaphoretic—Increases perspiration.

Diuretic—Increases urine flow. Most diuretics force kidneys to excrete more than the usual amount of sodium. Sodium forces more water and urine to be excreted.

Dosage—The amount of medicine to be taken for a specific problem. Dosages may be listed as liquids (ml or millilitres, cc or cubic centimetres, teaspoons, tablespoons), dry weight (kg or kilograms, mg or milligrams, g or grams) or by biological assay (Retinol Units, International Units).

Drupe—Fleshy fruit with a hard stone, such as an apricot or peach.

Duodenum—First 12 inches of small intestine.

Dysentery—Disorder with inflammation of the intestines, especially the colon, accompanied by pain, a feeling of urgent need to have bowel movements and frequent stools containing blood or mucus.

Dysmenorrhoea—Painful or difficult menstruation.

Dyspepsia—Digestion impairment causing uncomfortable feeling of indigestion.

Eczema—Non-contagious disease of skin characterized by redness, itching, scaling and lesions with discharge. Frequently becomes encrusted. Eczema primarily affects young children. The underlying cause is usually an allergy to many things, including foods, wool, skin lotions. The disorder may begin in month-old babies. It usually subsides by age 3 but may flare again at age 10 to 12 and last through puberty.

Electrolyte—Chemical substance with an available electron in its atomic structure that can transmit electrical impulses when dissolved in fluids.

Emetic—Causes vomiting.

Emmenagogue—Triggers onset of menstrual period.

Emollient—Softens or soothes.

Emphysema—Lung disease characterized by loss of elasticity of muscles surrounding air sacs. Lungs cannot supply adequate oxygen to body cells for normal function.

Endometriosis—Medical condition in which uterine tissue is found outside the uterus. Symptoms include pain, abnormal menstruation, infertility.

Enzyme—Protein chemical that accelerates a chemical reaction in the body without being consumed in the process.

Epilepsy—Symptom or disease characterized by episodes of brain disturbance that cause convulsions and loss of consciousness.

Essential oils—Same as *volatile oils*. Oils evaporate at room temperature.

Eupeptic—Promotes optimum digestion.

Expectorant—Decreases thickness and increases fluidity of mucus from the lungs and bronchial tubes.

Extract—Solution prepared by soaking plant in solvent, then allowing solution to evaporate.

Extremity—Arm, hand, leg, foot.

Fat-soluble—Dissolves in fat.

Fatty acids—Nutritional substances found in nature that are fats or lipids. These include triglycerides, cholesterol, fatty acids and prostaglandins. *Fatty acids* include stearic, palmitic, linoleic, linolenic, eicosapentaenoic (EPA), decosahexanoic acid. Other lipids of nutritional importance include lecithin, choline, gamma-linoleic acid and inositol.

Fixed oil(s)—Lipids, fats or waxes often made from seeds of plants.

Flatulence—Distention of the stomach or other parts of the intestinal tract with air or other gases.

Fluid extract—Alcoholic solution of a chemical or drug of plant origin. Fluid extracts usually contain 1g of dry drug in each milliliter.

Free radicals—Highly reactive molecules with an unpaired free electron that combines with any other molecule that accepts it. Free radicals are usually toxic oxygen molecules that damage cell membranes and fat molecules. To protect against possible damage from free radicals, the body has several defenses. The most important appears at present to be anti-oxidant substances, such as superoxide dismutase, selenium, vitamin C, vitamin E, zinc and others.

G6PD—Deficiency of glucose 6-phosphate, a chemical necessary for glucose metabolism. Some people have inherited deficiencies of this substance and have added risks when taking some drugs.

Gastritis—Inflammation of the lining of the stomach.

Gastroenteritis—Inflammation of stomach and intestines characterized by pain, nausea and diarrhea.

Gastrointestinal—Pertaining to stomach, small intestine, large intestine, colon, rectum and sometimes the liver, pancreas and gallbladder.

Generic—Relating to or descriptive of an entire group or class.

Gingivitis—Inflammation of the gums surrounding teeth.

Gland—Cells that manufacture and excrete materials not required for their own metabolic needs.

Glossitis—Inflammation of the tongue.

Gluten—Mixture of plant proteins occurring in grains, chiefly corn and wheat. People who are sensitive to gluten develop gastrointestinal symptoms that can be controlled only by eating a gluten-free diet.

Glycoside(s)—Plant substance that produces a sugar and other substances when combined with oxygen and hydrogen.

Griping—Intestinal cramps.

Gums—Translucent substances without form. Usually a decomposition product of cellulose. Gums dissolve in water.

Haematuria—Blood in the urine.

Haemoglobin—Pigment necessary for red cells to transport oxygen. Iron is a necessary component of haemoglobin.

Haemolysis—Breaking a membranous covering or destroying red blood cells.

Haemorrhage—Extensive bleeding.

Haemostatic—Prevents bleeding and promotes clotting of blood.

Hallucinogen—Produces hallucinations—apparent sights, sounds or other sensual experiences that do not actually exist or do not exist for other people.

Heart block—An electrical disturbance in the controlling system of the heartbeat. Heart block can cause unconsciousness and in its worst form can lead to cardiac arrest.

Hepatitis—Inflammation of liver cells, usually accompanied by *jaundice*.

Herb—Plant or plant part valued for its medicinal qualities, pleasant aroma or pleasing taste.

Histamine—Chemical in the body tissues that constricts the smooth muscle surrounding bronchial tubes, dilates small blood vessels, allows leakage of fluid to form itching skin and hives and increases secretion of acid in stomach.

Hives—Elevated patches on skin usually caused by an allergic reaction accompanied by a release of histamine into the body tissues. Patches are redder or paler than the surrounding skin and itch intensely.

Homeopathy—Practice of using extremely small doses of medicines and herbs to cause the same symptoms the disease causes. Homeopaths (practitioners of homeopathy) acknowledge no diseases, only symptoms.

Hormone—Chemical substance produced by endocrine glands—thymus, pituitary, thyroid, parathyroid, adrenal, ovaries, testicles, pancreas—that regulates many body functions to maintain homeostasis (a steady state).

Humectant—Moistens or dilutes.

Hypercalcaemia—Abnormally high level of calcium in the blood.

Hypertension—High blood pressure.

Hypocalcaemia—Abnormally low level of calcium in the blood.

Hypoglycaemia—Abnormally low blood sugar.

Impotence—Inability of a male to achieve and maintain an erection of the penis to allow satisfying sexual intercourse.

Indehiscent—Fruit that remains closed upon reaching maturity.

Inflorescence—Flowerhead of a plant.

Infusion—Product that results when a drug or herb is steeped to extract its medicinal properties.

Insomnia—Inability to sleep.

Interaction—Change in body's response to one substance when another is taken. Interactions may increase the response, decrease the response, cause toxicity or completely change the response expected from either substance. Interactions may occur between drugs and drugs, drugs and vitamins, drugs and herbs, drugs and foods, vitamins and vitamins, minerals and minerals, vitamins and foods, minerals and foods, vitamins and herbs, herbs and herbs.

International units—Measurement of biological activity. In the case of vitamin E, 1 International Unit (IU) equals 1 milligram (mg) (1IU = 1mg).

I.U. or IU—International units.

Jaundice—Symptom of liver damage, bile obstruction or excessive red-blood-cell destruction. Jaundice is characterized by yellowing of the whites of the eyes, yellow skin, dark urine and light stool.

Kidney stones—Small, solid stones made from calcium, cysteine, cholesterol and other chemicals in the bloodstream. They are produced in the kidneys.

Lactagogue—Increases the flow of breast milk in a woman.

Lactase—Enzyme that helps body convert lactose to glucose and galactose.

Lactase deficiency—Lack of adequate supply of enzyme *lactase*. People with lactase deficiency have difficulty digesting milk and milk products.

Larvacide—Kills larvae.

Latex—Milky juice produced by plants.

Laxative—Stimulates bowel movements.

LDH—Abbreviation for lactic dehydrogenase, a blood test to measure liver function and to detect damage to the heart muscle.

Libido—Sex drive.

Lipid—Fat or fatty substance.

Lymph glands—Glands located in the lymph vessels of the body that trap foreign material, including infectious material, and protect the bloodstream from becoming infected.

Maceration—Softening of a plant by soaking.

Magnesia—Another term for magnesium hydroxide.

Malabsorption—Poor absorption of nutrients from the intestinal tract into the bloodstream.

Mcg—Abbreviation for microgram, which is 1/1,000,000th (1/1-millionth) of a gram or 1/1,000th of a milligram.

Megadose—Very large dose. In terms of *recommended dietary allowance (RDA)*, anything 10 or more times the RDA is considered megadose. Nutritionists urge no one take megadoses of *any* substance because these doses may be toxic, cause an imbalance of other nutrients, cause damage to an unborn child and do not provide benefits beyond rational doses.

Menopause—End of menstruation in the female caused by decreased production of female hormones. Symptoms include hot flushes, irritability, vaginal dryness, changes in the skin and bones.

Metabolism—Chemical and physical processes in the maintenance of life.

Mg—Abbreviation for milligram, which is 1/1,000th of a gram.

Migraine—Periodic headaches caused by constriction of arteries in the skull. Symptoms include visual disturbances, nausea, vomiting, light sensitivity and severe pain.

Milk sickness—Intolerance to milk and milk products due to a deficiency of an enzyme called *lactase*.

Mitogen—Causes nucleus of cell to divide; leads to a new cell.

Mucilage—Gelatinous substance that contains proteins and polysaccharides.

Narcotic—Depresses the central nervous system, reduces pain and causes drowsiness and euphoria. Narcotics are addicting substances.

Naturopathy—Medical practice that uses herbs and various methods to return body to healthy state by stimulating innate defenses—never supplanting them—with drugs. In early years, many naturopathic doctors were ill-prepared to practice a healing profession. Many received mail-order degrees and had little training. However by the 1950s, some degree of academic acceptability returned.

Neuropathy—Group of symptoms caused by abnormalities in sensory or motor nerves. Symptoms include tingling and numbness in hands or feet, followed by gradually progressive muscular weakness.

Oestrogens—Female sex hormones that must be present for secondary sexual characteristics of the female to develop. Oestrogens serve many functions in the body, including preparation of the uterus to receive a fertilized egg.

Oleoresin—*Resins* and *volatile oils* in a homogenous mixture.

Osteoporosis—Softening of bones.

Oxidation—Combining a substance with oxygen.

Parasympathetic—Division of the autonomic (also called *automatic*) nervous system. Parasympathetic nerves control functions of digestion, heart and lung activity, constriction of eye pupils and many other normal functions of the body.

Parkinson's disease—Disease of the central nervous system characterized by a fixed, emotionless expression of the face, slower-than-normal muscle movements, tremor (particularly when attempting to reach or hold objects), weakness, changed gait and a forward-leaning posture.

Paronychia—Infection around a fingernail bed.

Peduncle—Stalk attached to a flower.

Pellagra—Disease caused by a deficiency of thiamine (vitamin B-1). Symptoms include diarrhoea, skin inflammation and dementia (brain disturbance).

Peristalsis—Wave of contractions of the intestinal tract.

Pernicious anaemia—See *Anaemia, pernicious*.

Pharyngitis—Inflammation of the throat.

Phenylketonuria—Inherited disease caused by lack of an enzyme necessary for converting phenylalanine into a form the body can use. Accumulation of too much phenylalanine can cause poor mental and physical development in a newborn. In Britain a test is carried out at birth to detect the disease. When detected early and treated, phenylketonuria symptoms can be prevented by dietary control.

Phosphates—Salts of phosphoric acid. Important part of the body system that controls acid-base balance. Other chemicals involved in acid-base balance include sodium, potassium, bicarbonate and proteins.

Photosensitization—Process by which a substance or organism becomes sensitive to light.

Photosensitizing pigment—Pigment that makes a substance sensitive to light.

Potassium—Important element found in body tissue that plays a critical role in electrolyte and fluid balance in the body.

Poultice—Applied to a body surface to provide heat and moisture. Material is held between layers of muslin or other cloth. Poultices contain an active substance and a base. They are placed on any part of the body and changed when cool. Purpose is to relieve pain and reduce congestion or inflammation.

Prostate—Gland in the male that surrounds the neck of the bladder and urethra. In older men, it may become infected (prostatitis) or obstructed (prostatic hypertrophy), cause urinary difficulties or become cancerous.

Psoriasis—Chronic, recurrent skin disease characterized by patches of flaking skin with discolouration.

Psychosis—Mental disorder characterized by deranged personality, loss of contact with reality, delusions and hallucinations.

Purgative—Powerful laxative usually leading to explosive, watery diarrhoea.

Purine foods—Foods metabolized into uric acid; these include anchovies, brains, liver, sweetbreads, sardines, meat extracts, oysters, lobster and other shellfish.

RDA—See *Recommended dietary allowance*.

Recommended dietary allowance—Recommendations based on data derived from different population groups and ages. The quoted RDA figures represent the *average* amount of a particular nutrient needed per day to maintain good health in the average healthy person. Data for these recommendations have been collected and analyzed by the US Food and Nutritional Board of the National Research Council. These figures serve as a reference point for comparison. The latest revised amounts were published in 1980, with a new revision promised soon. It is only within the framework of statistical probability that RDA can be used legitimately and meaningfully.

RNA (ribonucleic acid)—Complex protein chemical in genes that determines the type of life form into which a cell will develop.

Renal—Pertaining to the kidneys.

Resin—Complex chemicals, usually hard, transparent or translucent, that frequently cause adverse effects in the body.

Retina—Inner covering of the eyeball on which images form to be perceived in the brain via the optic nerve.

Rhizome—Root-like, horizontal-growing stem growing just below the surface of the soil.

Rickets—Bone disease caused by vitamin-D deficiency. Bones become bent and distorted during infancy or childhood if there is insufficient vitamin D for normal growth and development.

Rubefacient—Reddens skin by increasing blood supply to it.

Saponin(s)—Chemicals from plants, frequently associated with adverse or toxic reactions. They uniformly produce soapy lathers.

Sedative—Reduces excitement or anxiety.

SGOT—Abbreviation for serum glutamic oxaloacetic transaminase, a blood test to measure liver function or detect damage to the heart muscle.

Spasmolytic—Decreases spasm of smooth muscle or skeletal (striated) muscle.

Steroidal chemicals—Group of chemicals with same properties as steroids. Steroids are fat-soluble compounds with carbon and acid components. They are found in nature in the form of hormones and bile acids, and in plants as naturally occurring drugs, such as digitalis.

Stimulant—Stimulates (temporarily arouses or accelerates) physiological activity of an organ or organ system.

Stomachic—Promotes increased contraction of stomach muscles.

Stomatitis—Inflammation of the mouth.

Stroke—Sudden, severe attack that results in brain damage. Usually sudden paralysis or speech difficulty results from injury to the brain or spinal cord by a blood clot, haemorrhage or occlusion of blood supply to the brain from a narrowed or blocked artery.

Tannins—Complex acidic mixtures of chemicals.

Tenesmus—Urgent feeling of having to have a bowel movement or to urinate.

Terpenes—Complex hydrocarbons ($C_{10}H_{16}$). Most volatile oils are mostly terpenes.

Thrombophlebitis—Inflammation of a vein, usually caused by a blood clot. If the clot becomes detached and travels to the lung, the condition is called *thromboembolism*.

Tincture—Solution of chemicals in a highly alcoholic solvent made by simple solution.

Tonic—Medicinal preparations used to restore normal tone to tissues or to stimulate the appetite.

Toxicity—Poisonous reaction that impairs body functions or damages cells.

Toxin—Poison in dead or live organism.

Tranquilizer—Calms a person without clouding mental function.

Tremor—Involuntary trembling.

Tyramine—Chemical component of the body. In normal quantities, without interference from other chemicals, tyramine helps sustain normal blood pressure. In the presence of some drugs—monamine-oxidase inhibitors and some rauwolfia compounds—tyramine levels can rise and cause toxic or fatal levels in the blood.

Urethra—Hollow tube through which urine (and semen in men) is transported from the bladder to outside the body.

Uterus—Hollow, muscular organ in the female in which an embryo develops into a fetus. Menstruation occurs when the lining sloughs periodically.

Vein—Blood vessel that returns blood to the heart.

Virus—Infectious organism that reproduces in the cells of an infected host.

Volatile oils—Chemicals that evaporate at room temperature.

Water-soluble—Dissolves in water.

Wax—High-molecular-weight hydrocarbons; they are insoluble in water.

Yeast—Single-cell organism that can cause infection of the skin, mouth, vagina, rectum and other parts of the gastrointestinal system. The terms *yeast*, *fungus* and *monilia* are used interchangeably.

Metric Chart

The following units of measurement and weight are commonly used in establishing doses of vitamins, minerals, supplements and medicinal herbs.

Unit	Abbreviation	Volume	Approximate British Equivalent
Cubic centimetre	cc	0.000001 cubic metres	0.061 cubic inch
Litre	l	1 litre	1.76 pints
Decilitre	dl	0.10 litre	3.38 fluid ounces
Centilitre	cl	0.01 litre	0.338 fluid ounce
Mililitre	ml	0.001 litre	0.27 fluid dram
Kilogram	kg	1,000 grams	2.2046 pounds
Gram	g or gr	1 gram	0.035 ounce
Milligram	mg	0.001 gram	0.015 grain
Microgram	mcg	0.000001 gram	0.00015 grain

Index

INDEX

487

C

Caapi 461
Cabbage 254
Cabbagebark 461
Cabeza de angel 461
Cadmium 121
Cajeput 461
Caladium bicolor 466
Calamus root 285
Calcifidiol 33, 34, 35, 38, 43, 46
Calcitonin 35, 38, 43, 46
Calcitrol 35, 36, 37, 38, 43, 46
Calcium 1, 3, 27, 34, 35, 37, 38, 43,
    46, 76, 78, 80, 82, 84, 87, 89, 91,
    95, 98, 101, 103, 106, 107, 108, 110,
    122, 123, 126, 129, 132, 133, 134,
    140, 143, 144, 147, 152, 155, 158,
    161, 164, 167, 170, 173, 176, 179,
    180, 182, 183, 196, 197, 234, 235
Calcium carbonate 86, 87, 88
Calcium carbonate/magnesia 89,
    90
Calcium carbonate/magnesia/
    simethicone 91, 92
Calcium citrate 93, 94, 95
Calcium glubionate 96, 97, 98
Calcium gluconate 99, 100, 101
Calcium lactate 102, 103, 104
Calcium/magnesium carbonate
    105, 106
Calcium/magnesium carbonate/
    magnesium oxide 107, 108
Calcium phosphate 109, 110, 111
Calea zacatechichi 469
Calendula officinalis 469
California bay 461
California poppy 286, 461
Calliandra anomala 461
Calotropis procera 465
Camellia sinensis 475
Camphor 301, 461
Canaigre 461
Cananga 461
Cananga odorata 461
Cancer 217, 221, 223, 269, 285, 398,
    410, 434
Candlenut 461
Cannabis sativa 469
Canton rhubarb 300
Cape periwinkle 398
Capillary fragility 417
Capillary permeability 407
Capsicum 287
Capsicum annum 287, 462
Capsicum frutescens 287
Captopril 152, 155, 158, 161, 164, 167,
    170, 173, 176, 179, 182, 185
Caraway 288
Carbidopa-levodopa 63
Carbuncles 22
Carcinogen 301, 421

Cardamom seed 289
Cardiac arrest 86, 93, 150, 153, 156,
    159, 162, 165, 168, 171, 174, 177
Cardi-Omega 3
Cardiomyopathy 186
Carica papaya 389, 471
Caries, dental 39, 133
Carrot 462
Carum carvi 288
Cascara buckthorn 290
Cascara sagrada 290, 462
Cascarilla 462
Cassava 462
Cassia angustifolia 466
Cassia senna 458
Cassie 462
Castor 462
Cat powder 462
Catalpa 291
Catalpa bignonioides 291
Catecholamines 410
Catechu, black 292
Catha 293
Catha edulis 293, 467
Catharanthus lanceus 468
Catharanthus roseus 398, 468
Catmint 294
Catnep 294
Catnip 294, 462
Caulophyllum thalictroides 304,
    460
Caustic alkalis poisoning 112
Cayenne 287
Ceantholus americanus 357
Cecon 479
Celandine 462
Celery 295, 462
Celery fruit 295
Cell destruction 356
Cellular therapy 200, 204, 206, 214
Cellulose sodium phosphate 77,
    79, 81, 83, 85, 90, 92, 109, 111,145
Centella asiatica 465
Centurium erythracea 296
Centurium umbellatun 296
Chamaelirium luteum 339
Chamaemelum nobile 472
Chamaesyee hypericifolia 474
Chamomile 297
Chandra 410
Charcoal, activated 112, 113
Chelidonium majus 462
Chenodiol 58, 61
Chenopodium ambrosioides 449,
    476
Cherry-laurel 462
Chickweed 298, 462
Chicory 299
Chili 287, 462
Chimaphila 399
Chinaberry 462
Chinese ginger 322

Chinese rhubarb 300, 462
Chinese-restaurant syndrome 209
Chionanthus virginica 465
Chlorambucil 69
Chloramphenicol 30, 52, 68, 69
Chloride 3, 114, 115
Chlorine 114, 115
Cholesterol 146, 235, 245, 247
Cholestyramine 24, 30, 35, 38, 43,
    46, 49, 55, 66, 126, 129, 132, 140,
    143
Choline 230, 231, 240, 245
Chrondroitin sulphate 232
Chondrus crispus 353
Christmas rose 462
Christthorn 462
Chromium 3, 116, 117, 194, 229
Chromosome abnormalities 56
Chronic constipation 77, 79, 83, 85,
    87, 90, 94, 97, 100, 103, 106, 109,
    111, 123, 145
Chrysanthemum cinerariifolium
    472
Chrysanthemum parthenium 319,
    465
Cichorium intybus 299
Cicuta maculata 476
Cimicifuga racemosa 460
Cimicifuga species 303
Cinchona sp. 472
Cincus benedictus 279
Cineraria aspera 469
Cinnamomum camphora 301, 461
Cinnamomum verum 462
Cinnamon 301, 462
Cirrhosis 56, 72, 120, 184, 190
Citrullus colocynthis 463
Clary sage 462
Clematis vitalba 475
Climbing onion 462
Clove 462
Clove pepper 260
Cobalt 118, 119, 121, 443
Cobalt-stabilized beer 119
Coca 463
Cochlearia armoracia 345
Cocoa 463
Coconut 302
Cocus nucifera 302
Codeine 286, 406
Coenzyme Q 4, 233
Coffee 463
Coffea arabica 463
Coffeeberry 242
Cohosh, black 303
Cohosh, blue 304
Cohosh, white 305
Cola acuminata 467
Cola nitida 331, 468
Colchicine 30, 119
Colchicum autumnale 459
Colestipol 24, 35, 38, 43, 46, 49, 55, 66

INDEX

489

INDEX

491

216, 218, 220, 222, 244, 262, 309, 396

Liver disease 23, 34, 37, 42, 48, 54, 56, 57, 60, 68, 72, 73, 117, 120, 147, 180, 183

Liver-function tests 364

Lobelia 351

Lobelia inflata 351, 466

Lobelia tupa 475

Lolium temulentum 463

Lophophora williamsii 471

Love apple 370

Low-salt milk 151, 154, 157, 160, 163, 166, 169, 172, 175, 178

Luckynut 468

Lycopersicon esculentum 475

Lysine 243

Lysyl 120

M

Mace 367

Madagascar periwinkle 398, 468

Mag-Ox 400

Magnesium 3, 76, 77, 78, 79, 80, 81, 82, 83, 84, 85, 86, 88, 89, 90, 91, 92, 93, 95, 96, 98, 99, 101, 102, 103, 105, 107, 108, 109, 110, 111, 122, 144, 145, 147, 182, 185

Magnesium ammonium phosphate 181, 184

Magnesium poisoning 86, 93, 96, 99, 102, 105

Mahonia aquifolia 471

Malabar nut 368, 468

Malabsorption illnesses 10, 150, 153, 156, 159, 162, 165, 168, 171, 174, 177

Malaria 326

Malathion 362

Male fern 369, 468

Malus sylvestris 459

Malva rotundifolia 464

Manaca 468

Manchineel 469

Mandragora officanarum 370, 469

Mandrake 370, 469

Manganese 3, 118, 146, 147, 252

Mangosteen 469

Manihot esculenta 462

Maraba 469

Maranta arundinacea 459

Marigold 469

Marrubium vulgare 342

Marsdenia reichenbachii 463

Marsh tea 469

Marshmallow plant 371

Marula 469

Mastic 469

Mate 469

Matricaria 327

Matricaria chamomilla 327, 465

May flower 392

May wine 448

Mayapple 372, 469

Maypop 393

Mazantila 327

Meadowsweet 373, 469

Mecamylamine 58, 61, 77, 79, 81, 83, 85, 90, 92, 109, 111, 145

Medicago saliva 259

Medicago sativa 458

Medicinal herbs 5, 14, 235-457

Mediterranean aloe 261

Megadoses 1, 2

Megaloblastic anaemia 50

Melaleuca leucadendron 461

Melia azedarach 462

Melilotus officinalis 475

Menadiol 53, 54, 55, 481

Menadiol sodium diphosphate 53, 4

Menispermum canadense 470

Menstrual bleeding 1

Mentha piperita 397

Mentha pulegium 396, 471

Mentha spicata 429

Mercaptopurine 69

Mercurialis annua 459

Mercury weed 350

Mescal 469

Mesquite 469

Metabolic alkalosis 114

Methionine 4, 191, 212, 213, 218, 243, 243

Methotrexate 52

Methyl alcohol poisoning 112

Methystichodendron amesia 463

Mexican calea 469

Mexican poppy 406

Mexican sarsaparilla 374

Mezereon 469

Migraine headaches 217, 223, 237

Milk, low-salt 151, 154, 157, 160, 163, 166, 169, 172, 175, 178

Milk sickness 281

Milkweed, common 375

Milkwort 376

Mimosa hostilis 467

Mineral charts 175-197

Mineral oil 24, 27, 35, 38, 43, 46, 49, 55, 66

Minor centuary 296

Mintox 478

Mirabilis multiflora 474

Miscarriage 263, 417, 452

Mistletoe 377

Mitchella repens 391, 471

Mitragyna speciosa 467

Mohodu 469

Mole plant 469

Molybdenum 3, 121, 148, 149

Momordica charantia 459

Monamine oxidase 217, 223, 377, 457

Monarda punctata 344

Monilia 226

Monkshood 256, 469

Monosodium-glutamate 209

Moonseed 470

Mormon tea 378, 470

Morning glory 379

Morphine 286, 406

Morus rubra 382

Motherwort 470

Mountain ash 380

Mountain laurel 470

Mountain tobacco 381, 470

Mugwort 470

Muira puama 470

Mulberry 382

Mullein 383

Multivitamin with fluoride 39, 40

Multivitamin/mineral preparations 3, 4, 9, 10

Muropolysaccharides 146

Muscari comosum 332

Muscari racemonsum 332

Musk okra 470

Myasthenia 244

Myo-inositol 240

Myocardial infarction 120, 186

Myoglobin 125, 128, 131, 139, 142

Myopathies 33, 36, 41, 44

Myotonia congenita 136

Myrica cerifera 269, 460

Myristica fragrans 367, 470

Myroxylon balsamum var. 459

Myrrh 384

Myrtle 385

Myrtus communis 385

N

Narcissus tazetta 463

Nasturtium officinale 443

National Academy of Sciences 11

National Council Against Health Fraud 1

Nene 470

Neomycin 24, 30, 119

Neonatal hypocalcaemia 86, 93, 96, 99, 102, 105

Nepeta cataria 294, 462

Nephrosis 121

Nerium oleander 470

Nervous system parasympathetic 340

Neuropathy, sensory 68

Neutralca-S 478

Nevada jointfir 378

Niacin 56, 57, 58, 59, 68, 230, 245

Niacinamide 56, 59, 60, 61

INDEX